HEART OF EUROPE
A Short History of Poland

HEART OF EUROPE

A Short History of Poland

NORMAN DAVIES

Oxford   New York

OXFORD UNIVERSITY PRESS

Oxford University Press, Great Clarendon Street, Oxford OX2 6DP

Oxford New York
Athens Auckland Bangkok Bogota Bombay
Buenos Aires Calcutta Cape Town Dar es Salaam
Delhi Florence Hong Kong Istanbul Karachi
Kuala Lumpur Madras Madrid Melbourne
Mexico City Nairobi Paris Singapore
Taipei Tokyo Toronto Warsaw
and associated companies in
Berlin Ibadan

Oxford is a registered trade mark of Oxford University Press

First published 1984
First issued, with corrections, as an Oxford University Press paperback 1986

British Library Cataloguing in Publication Data
Data available

Library of Congress Cataloging in Publication Data
Davies, Norman.
Heart of Europe.
Includes bibliographical references and index.
1. Poland—History. I. Title.
DK4140.D385 1986 943.8 85-21592
ISBN 0-19-285152-7 (pbk.)

15 17 19 20 18 16 14

Printed in Great Britain by
Cox & Wyman Ltd,
Reading, Berkshire

For
MYSZKA
who roared

Martwe znasz prawdy, nieznane dla ludu;
Widzisz świat w proszku, w każdej gwiazd iskierce;
Nie znasz prawd żywych, nie obaczysz cudu!
Miej serce i patrzaj w serce!

You understand dead truths beyond the wit
                              of common folk;
You can see the world in a grain of powder,
                    in every spark of the heavens.
But living truths escape you; you do not
                              see the miracle.
So take courage, and look into people's hearts!

PREFACE
TO THE HARDBACK EDITION

No history book which sets out to relate the Past to the Present
is ever written at the right moment. By the time that the
author's observations are published, the Present will always
have moved on; and the reader's perspective will have
changed. In this respect, the work of the contemporary
historian is more akin to the shifting assignments of the leader
writer than to that of the dispassionate analyst of completed
histories. Yet March 1983 may not be the worst moment to
review the roots of the present Polish crisis, since events in
Poland seem to have reached stalemate. It might not be quite
so untimely as, say, November 1981, when various observers
were forecasting an imminent resolution of the crisis, either by
the victory of the SOLIDARITY movement or by some sort of
Soviet *démarche*. Now at least there seems to be a lull in storm,
a truce of exhaustion in the war between the Government and
the people. But none of the basic issues have been resolved.
One can be sure that 1983, 1984, and 1985 will bring new
surprises, and new twists of fortune, before Poland emerges
from the conflict either crushed for a season, or confidently
launched on a new course.

Yet some attempt to put current developments into their
historical context is long overdue. As always happens in a
major international event, the Polish Crisis has produced its
crop of instant experts who previously paid no attention to
Poland's affairs, and whose awareness of events before 1980
(or at the most 1970 or 1968) leaves much to be desired.
Political scientists who analyse 'Soviet-style systems' without
reference to the fourth dimension are strong on the defects of
official policy, but weak on the specific characteristics of
Polish society. Economists, who correctly recognized the

vii

portents of Poland's distress, have frequently attributed the
political explosion of the 1980s to the mistaken economic
policies of the 1970s, not realizing that economic failure was
itself but the outward manifestation of political conflicts of
much greater duration. Many sympathetic reporters who
witnessed the stirring scenes in the Lenin Shipyards in 1980,
or who watched the triumph of the ZOMO in 1981–2, could
vaguely perceive the Poles' own acute sense of History in
action, without being able to recognize the echoes and the
symbols. After a two-year barrage of media coverage, Western
opinion was indeed made aware that there was more at stake
in Poland than the price of meat or the mistakes of a corrupt,
totalitarian regime. But few people in the outside world had
the means to look beneath the surface, and to glimpse the
depth and antiquity of the issues involved.

At which point, in December 1981, Oxford University Press
had the good luck and good judgement to publish *God's
Playground: A History of Poland,* a work conceived in obscurity
years before with no great hope of topicality. Not surprisingly,
since two volumes to span a millennium were judged by some
to be excessive, demands were made for a shorter, more
condensed version. Not surprisingly, since an academic work
has to assume the proportions required by its scope and
contents, the author declined. *God's Playground* is still available,
unbowed and unabridged, for those who dare to read.[1] By
way of compromise, however, the present volume was
designed to treat the same subject but with different aims in
mind.

Heart of Europe: A Short History of Poland makes no pretence of
presenting a full and balanced survey of Polish affairs over
the last thousand years. Although each chapter contains a
brief chronological narrative, the emphasis has been firmly
placed on those elements of Poland's Past which have
had the greatest impact on present attitudes. For this
reason, many topics which feature prominently in *God's
Playground*—the Polish Reformation, the Baltic Trade, Polish
Jewry, the Emancipation of the Serfs, the politics of the
Prussians or the Ottomans, or whatever—here receive only the
barest of mentions. Other elements—notably the purely
Polish, national, element, the Church, Polish Literature, the

Intelligentsia, Russian relations, and the last two centuries in general—have been given special attention.

For similar reasons, the main chapters have been written in reverse chronological order. Chapter I deals with the contemporary period; Chapter II with the Second World War: Chapter III with the pre-war era,...and so on. Eventually, after bouncing back off the bedrock of the Middle Ages and Prehistory, the text comes full circle and Chapter VI deals with 'The Past in the Polish Present'. In this way, the narrative leads from the more familiar to the less familiar. Having first examined the outlines of today's Poland, and having then descended into the past layer by layer, it attempts to relate each of the main themes of earlier Polish History to later developments. The approach may perhaps be compared to that of the archaeologist who delves into his subject from the most modern level on the surface, through a descending order of the more ancient levels underneath. For most readers it will be a journey from the known into the unknown and back again. Its weaknesses, from the viewpoint of the historical purist, are that by implication it might confuse precedent and 'post-cedent' with cause and effect, and that it distorts the relevant weight of particular factors, important today, which may have been less important in the past. Its strength, hopefully, is that it highlights the topics of special relevance for understanding the foundations of the Present. Like the geographer who knows that every projection of the three-dimensional earth on to a two-dimensional map involves some sort of distortion, so the historian is unable to reconstruct the Past in any perfect or exact manner. One can only trust to one's judgement that this particular Projection is properly suited to the particular purpose in mind.

A series of small tabular appendices encompass a body of factual and ancillary material which would otherwise have clogged the text with superfluous debris.

Inevitably, although *Heart of Europe* is quite different from *God's Playground,* a fair amount of textual piracy, both deliberate and accidental, has been committed. For once, the plagiarist need not apologize. Indeed, readers are heartily encouraged to seek out the source of such plagiarisms and thereby to extend their reading on points of special interest.

In the intervening period, the opinions which took shape during the writing of *God's Playground* have not radically changed. The notion that People's Poland was heading for disaster was not terribly original; but it proved to be correct, and so did the prediction that the opposition would be ruthlessly crushed, 'attacked by a wave of police and military repression'.[2] In general, an attachment to the Romantic view of Polish History has been strengthened, together with an awareness of the persistence of long-standing Polish political divisions. On balance, recent events have confirmed the conviction that the Polish Romantics had a more profound understanding than their Positivist rivals of their own and their country's nature, and that, in the last analysis, they are more realistic than the self-professed 'realists'. Hence the quotation from Mickiewicz's poem Romantyczność (Romanticism) which appears alongside the book's dedication.[3] Polish readers will know what is meant.

The title, *Heart of Europe,* suggested itself during the writing of the final sections of the book, when the depth of the Polish tragedy and the mortal dangers of the present crisis made themselves felt with mounting urgency. The image of Poland as one of our continent's most vital organs, traditionally the home of our most intimate feelings and emotions, seemed particularly appropriate. What is more, it coincided most happily with the Catholic symbol of the Sacred Heart of Jesus, which is widely revered in Poland, and whose official recognition by the Vatican in 1765 was granted largely in response to the petitions of Polish religious orders. On investigation, the title also matched Poland's geographical location in the dead centre of Europe (even if, as my unimaginative publisher had to remark, the human heart is actually located somewhat off-centre in the human body). Of course, it turned out the idea was anything but original. As long ago as 1836, Juliusz Słowacki had elaborated the metaphor in a much more elegant and ironic fashion:

> Jeśli Europa jest nimfą—Neapol
> Jest nimfy okiem błękitnem—*Warszawa*
> *Sercem*—cierniami w nodze: Sewastopol,
> Azow, Odessa, Petersburg, Mitawa—

Paryż jej głową—a Londyn kołnierzem
Nakrochmalonym—a zaś Rzym . . . szkaplerzem.[4]

If Europe is a Nymph, then Naples is the nymph's bright-blue eye—Warsaw is her heart, whilst Sevastopol, Azov, Odessa, Petersburg, and Mitau are the sharp points of her feet. Paris is her head—London her starched collar—and Rome her boney shoulder.

Obviously, in the bitter aftermath of the November Rising, when Słowacki had taken refuge in southern Italy and when the Vatican had turned its back on Poland's troubles together with the Western powers, the poet resented the aloofness of Poland's faint-hearted friends almost as keenly as the heavy-footed oppression of the Russians. That thought is not original either.

Thanks and acknowledgements are due to a number of benefactors and helpers. *Heart of Europe* was written during a Visiting Fellowship at the Slavic Research Center of the University of Hokkaido In Japan, and I gratefully acknowledge the support afforded me by the Director, Professor Takayuki Ito, and his amiable staff. A word of personal appreciation must be extended to my closest colleagues at Hokkaido, Professor Jesse Zeldin and Dr Yutaka Akino, whose encouragement and practical assistance greatly helped to keep my pen in motion. Another special debt is owed to several academic correspondents, to one at the Institute of Literary Research in Warsaw, to another at the Australian National University in Canberra, and in particular to a member of the Philological Department of the Jagiellonian University in Cracow, whose detailed answers to questions on various Romantic and cultural matters grew into a veritable correspondence course on Polish Literature. The early reviewers of *God's Playground*[5] produced an immense supply both of comfort and of corrections, which have been utilized wherever possible. The typescript was prepared by Miss Shiori Takakura, and Danuta Garton Ash corrected the Polish text. The index was compiled with the assistance of Mr Andrzej Suchcitz. A grant was received from the De Brzezie Lanckoroński Foundation.

Norman Davies
1 March 1983

PREFACE
TO THE PAPERBACK EDITION

In the two years since the text of *Heart of Europe* was first completed, little has happened to shake its conclusions. Poland remains in a state of suspended animation. General Jaruzelski remains in power. The Party apparatus remains sullen and moribund. The Opposition, though less inclined to open forms of protest, remains defiant. Although Martial Law was rescinded, the regime found new instruments of repression. The security forces continue their daily task of harassment and control. Although Lech Wałęsa is still nominally a free citizen, many of his colleagues from the SOLIDARITY leadership, including Michnik, Lis, Frasyniuk, and (according to official sources) 196 others, are back in prison. The Church Hierarchy under Cardinal Glemp continues to prevaricate. The economy continues to stagnate, with few signs of fundamental recovery. The people, weary and increasingly apathetic, continue to bear their cross. There has been no serious attempt either to 'normalize' the country on the Soviet or Czechoslovak model or to initiate a genuine national Dialogue. The stalemate is staler than ever.

The social effects of the protracted crisis have best been described as Poland's 'pauperization'. A rich country has been beggared; and it is the ordinary people who suffer the consequences. The standard of living sinks, while prices rise together with all the other indices of social distress. In 1985, an estimated one-third of the population lives below the subsistence level, on incomes under 6,000 zlotys per month. The waiting time for apartments varies between 15 years in Warsaw and 26 years in Wrocław. With an average consumption of over 10 litres per head of pure alcohol (1982), alcoholism is rife, even among the young. Drug addiction has made its appearance. One of the worst records of environmental pollution in Europe, especially in the industrial South-West, has produced an alarming rise in infant mortality, in environment-related diseases, and in the overall death-rate. Life expectancy is falling. A Health Service stretched beyond endurance, which survived for years on medical aid from the West and has seen surgical wards closed down for want of elementary equipment, has also to watch while a Polish Ambassador announces the 'fraternal gift' of medical supplies to Nicaragua. Meanwhile, according to the Institute of Strategic Studies in London, expenditure on armaments in Poland in 1980–2 rose by 30 per cent. The priorities of the regime are clear.

One long-running sensation was provided by the Popiełuszko Trial—or rather by the trial of four policemen accused of murdering a pro-SOLIDARITY priest. In October 1984, Father Jerzy Popiełuszko, who acted as the chaplain of the 'Huta Warszawa' steelmill in Warsaw and whose monthly masses 'for the Fatherland' had made him famous even beyond Poland, was kidnapped, beaten, tortured, and killed in a clandestine operation organized by the Ministry of the Interior. In a communist country, the silencing of a persistent opponent may have been routine; but the murder of a priest was rare, and the public prosecution and sentencing of communist functionaries for a crime committed in the course of duty was unique. Some observers felt that the policemen were simply being punished for their incompetence, and government apologists both in court and outside repeatedly implied that the turbulent priest had himself provoked a well-deserved fate. Yet the main puzzle was to explain why the open trial was allowed to proceed at all in the full blaze of publicity. With the General under attack, not only from the advocates of dialogue but also from the Moscow-backed Party *beton*, who believed his handling of the opposition to be altogether too lenient, it can be argued that he was laying down for all to see the limits which repression would not be permitted to exceed. Once again, the *Terrore alla polacca* was shown, by the standards of the Soviet Block, to be hopelessly half-hearted and ambiguous.

Be that as it may, the major clue to the protracted
immobility of the Polish scene obviously lay in the continuing
saga of the Soviet succession. With no firm lead from Moscow,
Warsaw was bound to hesitate. As it proved, Brezhnev's death
in November 1982 had not resolved the leadership struggle.
No sooner had the ailing Andropov begun to establish his
authority than he, too, was struck down, only to be replaced
by yet another terminal invalid. Konstantin Chernyenko
lasted a mere thirteen months. These three deaths in the
Kremlin, which preceded the long overdue emergence of an
apparently healthy and self-confident Leader in the person of
Michail Gorbachev on 11 March 1985, concluded the decade
of gerontocracy. These were *'les trois coups'* which heralded the
lifting of the curtain on the Moscow stage after the longest
interval of inaction in Soviet history.

In this light, remarks in the final chapter of *Heart of Europe*
originally addressed to the prospects and options of Andropov's reign (see pp. 454 ff.) can reasonably be applied to the
onset of the Gorbachev era. For, if Chernyenko was the last of
Brezhnev's coterie, Gorbachev has undoubtedly assumed the
mantle of Andropov, with the promise of energetic, autocratic
innovation. A quiescent Poland may not be at the top of the
new Leader's urgent priorities, but sooner or later it will
present him with some of his most fateful decisions. One
simply does not know what was said when Gorbachev met
Jaruzelski in the Polish capital after the meeting on 25 June to
renew the Warsaw Pact for another twenty years; but it can be
fairly surmised that orders were given to hold the communist
fort in Poland until long-term plans can be imposed. When
the new policy comes, as come it must, the long years of Soviet
indecision will end, and the Polish Crisis which began in
August 1980 can be expected to enter its decisive phase.

I am truly grateful to those readers of the First Edition who
sent in letters of appreciation, sometimes with lists of textual
corrections. All too often, many of the proposed amendments
were even more inaccurate than the original mistakes.
However, most of the known errors—amongst them, the
unforgivable confusion between Thucydides and Xenophon
(p. 87), and the curious posting of the 'Polish Cavalry' to the

ramparts of Bar, i.e. a 'Polish Calvary' (p. 222)—have now
been corrected, both in this text as in the French and Polish
editions at present in preparation.

Norman Davies
14 July 1985

CONTENTS

MAPS AND DIAGRAMS

ILLUSTRATIONS

xxi

Acknowledgements: The author and publishers are grateful to the following for permission to reproduce illustrations in this volume: A. Krauze (Plates 1, 8); Associated Press (Plate 2); Sikorski Institute (Plates 3, 4b, 7b); Polish Library, London (Plate 4a); Muzeum Narodowe, Warsaw (Plates 5, 6, 7a).

A NOTE ON POLISH SPELLING

Hard experience has shown that the mere sight of Polish names is sufficient to deter many people who would otherwise take a closer interest in Polish affairs. Anglo-Saxon readers need to be assured at the outset that Polish pronunciation is far easier than it looks, and that a few minutes of study will suffice to obtain a working knowledge of the necessary sounds. There is no need to flounder in the steps of 'the inarticulate in pursuit of the unpronounceable'. Despite appearances, all Polish spelling is consistent and phonetic; all the main vowels are simple, as in Italian; and the characteristic stress on the penultimate syllable of each word is very regular. English-speaking readers face an infinitely easier task in trying to master Polish pronunciation than Polish-speakers faced with English. In order to do the job properly, one should consult the introductory chapter on pronunciation in any one of the many Polish grammars, such as *Colloquial Polish,* by B. Mazur (Routledge and Keagan Paul, London, 1982). Otherwise the following notes may serve as a useful guide:

(1) *Vowels.* All Polish vowels are simple and of even length. Many short words are pronounced almost as they would be in English:

a ——	*sam*	(alone)	as 'Sam'
e ——	*ten*	(this)	as 'ten'
i ——	*lis*	(fox)	as 'lease'
o ——	*lot*	(flight)	as 'lot'
{ ó ——	*lód*	(ice)	as 'loot' }
{ u ——	*huk*	(roar)	as 'hook' }
y ——	*byt*	(existence)	as 'bit'

There are two nasal vowels, ą and ę, which approximate to the French *on* and *ein,* but which may be recognizably pronounced as *om* and *en*:

dąb (oak) as 'domp'; *pęk* (bundle) as 'penk'

(2) *Consonants.* Polish consonants mainly cause confusion because of their unfamiliar visual appearance, not because of their complicated sounds. It is unfortunate that the Polish language was first transcribed into the Latin alphabet by medieval clerks who chose to adopt a variation of Czech spelling which was already far removed from the original Latin. The result is an excess of consonantal clusters where one or two simple sounds have to be represented by three, four, or even five letters. In this respect, the Cyrillic alphabet used in Russian, where one symbol represents one sound, causes much less despair for beginners.

(i) *f, h, k, l, m, n, p, r, s,* and *t,* are similar in Polish to their English equivalents.

(ii) *b, d, g,* and *z,* are the same voiced consonants as in English, except in the terminal position where they are unvoiced and become, as in German, *p, t, k,* and *s* respectively.

(iii) There are several Polish consonants, and consonantal combinations, whose sounds are written in a totally different way from the English equivalents:

———*c*	= 'ts', as in *car* (Tsar)
———*ć, ci, cz*	= 'ch' in different variations as in 'hatch', 'cheese', or 'chapel'
———*ch*	= guttural 'ch', as in Scots 'loch'
———*j*	= consonantal 'y' as in *jak* (how) like 'yak'
———*ł*	= 'w' as in *piła* (saw) like 'w' in 'peewit'
———*ń*	= soft ñ, like the Spanish 'mañana'
———*rz*	= French 'ge' as in général, e.g. *rząd* (Government), in combinations becomes 'sh', e.g. *przez* (through) as 'pshess'
———*ś, si, sz*	= 'sh' in different variations, as in 'hash', 'sheep', or 'sham'

——*w*   = 'v' as in *waza* (vase)
——*ż, ź, zi*   = *French* 'j' as in *żurnal* (journal, Fr)
——*dzi, dź, dż* = English 'j' as in *dżinsy* (jeans), *dżem* (jam) etc.
——*szcz*   = 'shch' together, as in 'fish-chips'

(3) *Stress.* The stress in Polish words virtually always falls on the penultimate syllable:

     teléfon (telephone)   *Kráków* (Cracow)
     telefóny (telephones)   *Krakówski* (Cracovian)
     telefonísta (telephonist)   *Krakowiánka* (Cracovian girl)

A very few nouns of foreign origin, especially with Latin or Greek endings, may have the stress on the ante-penultimate syllable:

     História (history); *múzyka* (music): *biblióteka* (Library)

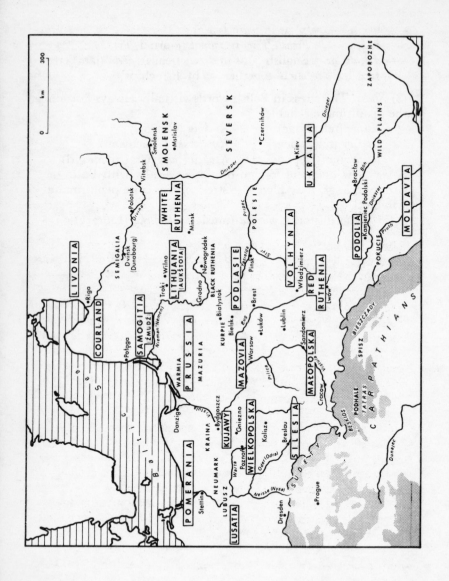

CHAPTER I

THE LEGACY OF HUMILIATION

Poland since the Second World War

There can be few countries in the world where the system of government is held in greater public disrepute than it is in Poland. Whatever one may think about the events of 1980-1, no reasonable observer could deny that the emergence of the free SOLIDARITY movement proved conclusively that the Polish communist regime had lost the confidence of everyone except its own élite. Indeed, the declaration of a State of War on 13 December 1981 must be regarded as a tacit admission that the communists could only keep control through the exercise of brute force. Some critics would argue that the regime had been gradually losing credit over the previous ten or fifteen years. Others would assert that it never enjoyed any viable measure of public support from the start. Certainly from the standpoint of classical liberalism, which holds that governments should rule with the consent of the governed, the Polish People's Republic was not merely a political cadaver; it should never have been born in the first place.

Poland, of course, is far from having the only dictatorship in the world, and, for all its tribulations, can hardly be reckoned a particularly violent country. The members of the United Nations Organization include rather more dictatorships than democracies; and by standards current amongst them, the communist regime in Poland has consistently refrained from the more extreme forms of political violence. Poland cannot be charged with crimes of the same order that have befallen the unhappy *disparidos* of Argentina or the victims of the

1

fanatical Pol Pot in Cambodia, or of the lunatic Field-Marshal Idi Amin 'Dada' in Uganda. Most pertinently perhaps, communist Poland has refused to follow the example of its patron and mentor, the Soviet Union, where the tally of political victims has run into tens of millions well within the span of living memory. Political oppression in Poland, though ugly enough at close quarters, and extremely uncomfortable for the thousands detained in internment camps, has offended less by its physical cruelty than by its moral corruption and its intellectual absurdity. For in terms of the dominant trends and aspirations of Polish society, it has no compelling reason to exist.

After all, most dictatorships came into being through clearly defined domestic circumstances. Some, especially in Africa, can be justified by the need to separate warring tribes or irreconcilable communities living within the same state. Many, as in Spain in the 1930s, emerge as the result of civil war. Some, as in the case of the communist revolutions in China or Cuba, are accepted because of the intolerable social oppression which preceded them. Others, as in the case of Nazi Germany, were democratically elected by a majority of citizens willing to surrender their individual rights in the cause of national defence or national aggrandizement. Some, again, especially in the traditionalist monarchies of the Third World like Saudi Arabia, exist because the people have never known anything different. A few, like the Vatican State or the Tibet of the late Dalai Lama, have existed by virtue of the ruler's infallible religious status. Even in the most deplorable instances of European or Japanese imperialism, it has been argued that India, or Angola, or Mexico, or Korea was bound to undergo a phase of colonial exploitation in order to benefit in due course from contact with its more developed oppressors. Dictatorships, in other words, are sometimes an unavoidable evil and are not necessarily inimical to all forms of progress.

But in Poland no such domestic rationale pertained. Poland, if left to itself at the end of the Second World War, might have produced its own form of democracy, as in 1921, or possibly its own variety of dictatorship, as in 1926. Given their established traditions and allegiances, the Poles could not conceivably have spawned a communist regime of their own accord. There were hardly enough native Polish communists to run a factory, let alone a country of some thirty million people. In the economic sphere, Poland had everything to gain by association with the advanced economies of Western Europe and North America, but little from dependence on the backward and war-torn economy of the USSR.

What actually happened in 1944–8 was that the Soviet Union forcibly imposed a Soviet-style communist system on Poland, regardless of the people's wishes or the country's independent interests. (See below, p. 100 ff.) In the words of the great Stalin himself, introducing Communism into Poland was 'like fitting a cow with a saddle'. It is this grotesque disharmony between the outlook of the ruling communist establishment and the traditions of the nation as a whole which has underlain each of the recurrent crises in Poland since the War. It is the experience of this alien tyranny, so familiar to Poles in earlier periods of their history, which has moulded the attitudes of the post-war generation.

．　＊　＊　＊　＊　＊

Five Phases

Despite the visions of harmony and prosperity to which all communists are thought to aspire, nowhere in the world have they actually showed signs of putting their ideals into practice. The initial stage of 'building socialism', not to mention the final stage of true communism, has taken a long time to realize. In Poland in particular, the ideal has obstinately remained far removed from the reality. Indeed, since the communists' own theory calls for the eventual withering of the state and the Party, one can well understand their reluctance to move forward too fast. As the Polish riddle asks: 'What is the best road to Socialism?' The answer, from everyone's point of view it would seem, is 'the longest one'.

Forty years ago, when the Polish communists could first dream about taking power, they set no timetable for achieving their goals; but it is clear that they hoped to establish a stable basis for building a classless and prosperous society within decades rather than centuries. Instead, between the beginnings of communist rule during the Soviet Liberation in 1944–5 and the Military Coup of 1981, they have led their country in five uneasy stages from the ruins of War to the ruins of the communist peace.

1 *The Communist Take-over: from the Soviet Liberation to the One-Party State, July 1944 to December 1948*

Once the Soviet Army had occupied the territory which the Soviets had reserved for the post-war Polish Republic, a lengthy process of political reconstruction lay before the Soviet political engineers. Indeed, it is unlikely at the outset that they knew what they were aiming to construct. The Liberation itself took almost a year, with the retreating German Army fighting every inch of the way. (See p. 73 ff.) Stettin (the future Szczecin) held out until 26 April 1945: Breslau (the future Wrocław) until 6 May; and Hirschberg (the future Jelenia Góra) until 2 May 1945—the date of the fall of Berlin. After that, several immense civilian operations had to be put in motion. Almost every Polish city—except for the fortunate Cracow—had to be rebuilt from the wartime rubble; corpses had to be buried; streets repaved; power stations reconnected; transport restarted. Some five million Germans and a lesser number of Ukrainians had to be screened, collected, and expelled from the country in accordance with the Potsdam agreement. Similar numbers of refugees, repatriates, and internal migrants—including a quarter of a million Polish Jews on their way to Palestine—crowded the roads and railway stations. The Western Territories, newly annexed from Germany, had to be provided with a skeleton administration, and completely repopulated largely by Poles from the provinces annexed by the Soviet Union. All the country's industries had to be reorganized in accordance with the nationalization Law of January 1946. Over one million peasants had to be installed in new farms, in accordance with the Decree of Agrarian Reform of 6 September 1946. And to cap it all, a bitter civil war, lasting over two years, had to be fought to suppress the remnants of the wartime resistance. (See p. 80 ff.) It is not surprising that political events moved slowly.

During this initial period, the Soviet authorities placed little trust in the Polish communists. They relied first and foremost on their own security services, who were busily purging every Polish town and village of its active 'antisocialist elements'. They made great use of those few noncommunist Poles, who could be persuaded to collaborate and to act as figure-heads for the new governmental bodies. After all, in 1945, it was only seven years since Stalin had ordered the total liquidation of the Polish Communist Party (KPP) and the execution of some 5,000 of its activists; and it was only three years since the KPP's replacement, the Polish Workers' Party (PPR), had been formed. Even if the Polish communists had been willing to take power at that stage, there were far too few of them to do so.[1]

The Governments of the immediate post-war years succeeded each other thick and fast. The original Polish Committee of National Liberation (PKWN) was a Soviet creature flown into Poland in July 1944 to take charge of the liberated territories under the protection of the Soviet Army. On 31 December 1944, it changed its name to that of Provisional Government of the Polish Republic (RTRP), but was only recognized as such by the USSR. The Provisional Government of National Unity (TRJN) resulted from the merger of the existing Soviet-sponsored body with a group associated with the leader of the Peasant Movement, Stanisław Mikołajczyk, the only representative of the legal Polish Government-in-Exile in London who agreed to return home. It lasted from 28 June 1945 to January 1947. The first elected Government assumed office on 6 February 1947 in circumstances which Britain, France, and the USA denounced as failing to meet the requirements of the Potsdam Agreement for 'free and unfettered elections'. It was headed by a candidate of the Soviet-managed Democratic Bloc, the socialist and ex-inmate of Auschwitz, Józef Cyrankiewicz. In due course, Cyrankiewicz presided over the transformation of his pseudo-democratic government into the fully-fledged, Soviet-style, one party state, and was rewarded with a career lasting twenty-five years. Mikołajczyk was lucky. Having been crudely slandered in the Parliament as a foreign spy, he fled for his life in October 1947 back to London.

By this time, the Kremlin was preparing to upstage the Polish communists. With the onset of the Cold War, and the beginning of the Berlin Blockade, Stalin was growing more impatient of provisional arrangements. In March 1948, Cyrankiewicz travelled to Moscow and received his instructions for forming a new ruling Party from the amalgamation of his own rump Socialist Party (PPS), with the communist PPR. The pro-communist Peasant fraction (ZSL), and the so-called Democratic Movement (SD) were to maintain their separate existence under the Party's patronage. At this same juncture, Tito's defiance of the Soviet Union in Yugoslavia was making Stalin especially nervous of disobedient communists; and Władysław Gomułka, the established secretary of the PPR since 1943, was certainly a man with his own mind. So Gomułka had to go. In September 1948, he was forced into a humiliating public recantation of his miserable errors, and eventually into prison. This meant that the founding Congress of the Polish United Workers' Party (PZPR) in December 1948 turned into a triumph for Gomułka's rival, Bolesław Bierut, a former official of Comintern, who to this point had been masquerading as a 'non-party' figure. Bierut, who already held the post of President of the Republic, emerged from the Congress with the much more important office of First Secretary. The imitation Soviet Poland had received its imitation Stalin. The new Poland had created its New Order.

2 *Polish Stalinism, December 1948 to October 1956*

Just as the Stalinist Revolution of 1929 initiated the formative period in the creation of the modern Soviet Union, so Poland's specially close association with the USSR in the final years of the Stalin Era left lasting marks on the Polish People's Republic. And just as the Soviet Union, whilst condemning a careful selection of Stalin's crimes against the Party, has never attempted to reform or replace the main institutions of Stalin's Russia, so the greatest part of the Stalinist innovations in Poland have remained intact to this day. The adoption of Marxism-Leninism as the sole ideology; the establishment of an extravagantly large conscript army; the Command Economy based on central planning; the mania for heavy industry; the Constitution of 1952; and, above all, the monopoly power of the Polish United Workers Party have never been successfully challenged. Communist Poland, like the rest of the Camp to which it belongs, is essentially a Stalinist creation. To all intents and purposes, the Stalinist period coincided with the reign in Warsaw of Konstanty Rokossowski, a Soviet Marshal of Polish origin—who served as Deputy Premier, Minister of Defence, member of the Politburo, and President Bierut's watch-dog.

The Constitution of the People's Republic was inaugurated on 22 July 1952, on the eighth anniversary of Soviet rule in Poland. For the most part, it appeared to introduce a model democracy, with guaranteed civil liberties, universal suffrage, parliamentary government consisting of the President's Council of State, an elected *Sejm* or Assembly of deputies, and a Council of Ministers answerable to the Assembly. In practice, this 'People's Democracy' was a legal fiction. The 'working people of town and countryside', whom the Constitution named as the recipients of political power, were its helpless victims. They had no right to put up their own candidates for central and local government, and no voice in the workings of the Party, which had arrogated to itself the right to manage the state on their behalf. All effective power lay in the hands of the Party's Political Bureau, in its First Secretary, and in the privileged élite of the *nomenklatura* whom he appointed. (See p. 49–50.) Reality lay in the dictatorship of the Party over the people.

The motor of Stalinist policy was fuelled by the paranoia emanating from the highest circles in Moscow, and born of a belief that the Soviet Bloc was about to be attacked by the rampant forces of American imperialism armed with the H-bomb. The result was a frenzy of re-armament, and of gigantic construction projects. The Polish Army was expanded by conscription to a standing force of 400,000 men. The officer corps was politicized through the Army Political Academy (WAP), founded in 1951. In due course, in 1955, Poland took its place as a founding member of the Warsaw Pact, the Soviet Bloc's answer to NATO. On the economic front, the Council of Mutual Economic Assistance (CMEA or Comecon), the answer to the Common Market, was founded in 1949 to

facilitate joint planning. Absolute priority was given to heavy
industry—especially coal, iron, and steel, and to the arms
industry. New towns and new suburbs were thrown together
to house the influx of workers from the countryside. In order to
assure food supplies, agriculture was turned over to compulsory collectivization. The Peasantry was evicted from its plots,
and handed over to the 'Polish Agricultural Enterprises'
(PGR), which were Russian *kolkhozy* in all but name. To break
the people's traditional attachment to religion, the Roman
Catholic Church was openly attacked. In 1950, all Church
property was confiscated. Priests were arrested in droves. In
1952, the Cardinal-Primate, Archbishop Stefan Wyszyński,
was deported to a remote monastery.

To the outside observer, it is the mental attitudes of
Stalinism which seem most remarkable. Xenophobia was the
official fashion. Any contact with the outside world was
instantly denounced, creating a social atmosphere where
political trials looked normal and innocent men and women
could be arbitrarily sentenced as foreign spies. People were
encouraged to live communally, and to think collectively.
They no longer belonged to themselves as individuals, or to
their families, but to their work-force, their shock-brigades, or
their regiment. The Russian system of informers was introduced in factories and schools. Stakhanovites, the heroes of
labour, were glorified for the emulation of the masses.
Conformism in dress and thought was encouraged. A specific
form of megalomania took hold. All the public works of the
day had to be colossal. Bigger was thought to mean better.
Quantitative production was the ultimate good. Statistics
acquired a magical value. Workers were enslaved by their
ever-increasing work norms. In art, Socialist Realism gained
exclusive approval, with novels about tractor drivers, and
paintings about concrete factories. However miserable and
downtrodden the writers actually felt, they were ordered to
exude Optimism. In public architecture, a taste developed for
marble, for soaring façades with heavy columns and vulgar
pinnacles. The symbols of the age were provided by the Palace
of Culture and Sciences in Warsaw, an unsolicited gift from
the USSR, and the new town of Nowa Huta near Cracow,
which boasted the largest steelworks in Poland together with

soulless acres of primitive workers' housing and no church.

Adulation of the USSR was *de rigueur*. Statues of Stalin proliferated. Katowice was renamed 'Stalinogród'. An attempt was made to modify the Polish language by introducing the Russian habit of speaking in the second person plural, per *Wy* in place of the standard Polish third person singular, per *Pan* or *Pani*. (This habit still obtains in Party circles.)

Even so, Stalinism never gained the same pitch of ferocity in Poland that reigned in neighbouring countries. The political trials did not develop into show trials or wholesale purges. The middle class and the intellectuals, though harassed, were not liquidated. The Church was not suppressed. The peasants were not deported, nor driven to famine. Collectivization was slow and incomplete.

Indeed, Poland so dragged its feet, that by the time the Great Leader died in 1953, the Stalinist frenzy was beginning to subside. In December 1954, the hated Ministry of Security (though not, of course, the Security Office) was abolished. In 1955 also, the censorship relaxed sufficiently to permit the first veiled hints of criticism. Gomułka was surreptitiously released from detention. Collectivization was quietly abandoned. When Krushchev launched his attack on Stalin at the Twentieth Congress of the CPSU in February 1956, the Thaw in Poland was already swelling into a flood. It was the Polish comrades who leaked the 'secret speech'. To cap it all, it was announced in Moscow that Bierut had died of heart failure.

The Polish reaction to Krushchev's tack in Moscow was to try to follow suit. The Polish Party wanted to regain control of its affairs from the stranglehold of the military and the security services, for it knew that popular resentment could not be long contained. In June 1956, seventy-four workers and militiamen died in the city of Poznań following riots over 'Bread and Freedom'. The obvious move was to appoint a Party leader with a greater measure of public confidence and a more pragmatic approach to national problems. The obvious man was Gomułka, the victim of 1948. Unfortunately, Krushchev could not see the point. Fraternal parties were not supposed to take independent initiatives, even if they were only trying to imitate Krushchev. In October, when the eighth Plenum of the PZPR was summoned to elect the new

Secretary, Krushchev flew into Warsaw airport unannounced in an apoplectic rage. The Soviet Army marched out of its barracks, and the Soviet Fleet appeared off Gdańsk. It was rumoured that Marshal Rokossowski was plotting a 'coup' and had prepared his proscription list. In the end, the matter was settled peacefully. Both Krushchev and Gomułka were down-to-earth communists, and both knew that the grosser absurdities of Stalinism had to cease. Once Krushchev was convinced of Gomułka's basic loyalty, he did not argue. Rokossowski and his advisers were to return home. The PZPR was to take direct charge of the People's Republic. In this way, the 'Polish Spring bloomed in October'; and the Stalinist nightmare passed.

3 *National Communism: the Heyday of the PZPR, October 1956 to August 1980*

Gomułka's defiance of the Soviet Union in October 1956 created a head of steam which was to turn the wheels of Poland's political life for the next twenty-five years. Gomułka proved that the Polish communists could manage their own affairs without direct supervision by Russian advisers—and still remain loyal to the Soviet Union. In line with the trend elsewhere in the communist world, Gomułka was a proponent of the views that there were 'many roads to Socialism'. He rejected any slavish imitation of the Soviet model, and believed strongly that Poland's specific traditions demanded a specifically national brand of Communism. At the same time, having witnessed the fate of his Hungarian comrade, Imre Nagy, who paid with his life for taking the same ideas to their logical conclusion: and having been treated to a personal viewing of a Soviet nuclear test, he well understood his limits. Furthermore, despite the initial wave of popularity, he was too old a campaigner to think that the Polish people really loved their communists. A native 'Red' might be preferable to a Russian commissar; but in the last resort everyone knew that the communist regime in Poland rested on Soviet power. Hence the deal was struck—an autonomous, national brand of Communism in return for continuing subservience to the

USSR. The Polish People's Republic ceased to be a puppet state, and became a client state.

As a result of his understanding with the Soviets—sealed during his visit to Moscow in November 1956—Gomułka was empowered to make a series of strategic concessions to popular demands and to permit the three specific features of the Polish order—an independent Catholic Church, a free peasantry, and a curious brand of bogus political pluralism. In retrospect, one can see that these concessions were intended as provisional measures which were to be withdrawn as soon as the PZPR felt strong enough to progress towards the more orthodox model of socialist society. No committed communist would have admitted that the ultimate vision was to leave Poland as a Catholic country with free peasants and an open political arena. What actually happened, of course, was that the PZPR never gained the strength or the confidence to advance beyond the compromises. On the contrary, as the Party floundered amidst crises of ever more frequent recurrence, the Church, the peasants, and the political dissidents went from strength to strength. In the end, after twenty-five years of the strategy, it was the Party, and not its opponents, which collapsed.

The position of the Roman Catholic Church in Poland after the Second World War was stronger than at any previous period of its thousand-year mission. Its strength can be explained in part by the suffering of the war years, which turned people's minds to the solace of religion: in part by the law of human cussedness, which increased people's loyalties to the Church just because their government forbade it: but largely by the ethnic and cultural remodelling of Polish society during and after the War. In 1773, at the First Partition, Polish Catholics formed barely 50 per cent of the total population; in 1921, in the frontiers of the inter-war Republic, they formed 66 per cent; in 1946, in consequence of the murder of the Polish Jews by the Nazis and the expulsion of the Germans and Ukrainians, they formed no less than 96 per cent. For the first time in history, Poland was a truly Catholic country: and it was this supercharged catholic society which was given an atheist, communist Government. What a recipe! Add to that a series of formidable personalities at the head of Church affairs,—including two long-serving Primates, Cardinal August Hlond, (1926–48) and Cardinal Stefan Wyszyński (1948–81), and two extraordinary Cardinal Archbishops of Cracow, Prince Adam Stefan Sapieha (1911–51) and Karol Wojtyła, (1965–78)—and it is not hard to see that in the battle for minds of the Poles the Party was hopelessly outmatched both in the quality of its generals and the quantity of its troops. So the Party took the path of discretion, and proposed a compromise. In essence, the Party undertook to refrain from attacking the Church, if the Church undertook to refrain from undermining the State. The Church was excluded from the schools and from the media, but was to enjoy free contact with the Vatican, full control over ecclesiastical appointments, property, and finance, and absolute freedom of worship. It has kept its seminaries, its own social and intellectual clubs, and its own University—the Catholic University of Lublin (KUL). It is the sole, truly independent Church in the whole Soviet Bloc. The critical agreement of December 1956 was confirmed in detail by the apostolic constitution of 26 June 1972. Evidently, in striking this bargain, the communists felt that time was on their side. Sociologists had predicted that rapid industrialization and urbanization would break the cultural patterns of traditional society, and the bond of the people with their Church. They were mistaken. The new industrial proletariat turned out to be as devotedly Catholic as the old peasantry. Poland has not followed the path of religious indifference so common in Western Europe. The tireless, twenty-year struggle of the inhabitants of Nowa Huta to build their own church, in a model industrial suburb which was officially designed without one, symbolizes the triumph of the Church in modern Polish society as a whole. In 1978, the election of Cardinal Wojtyła as Pope John Paul II conferred the ultimate accolade of the Polish Church triumphant.

The survival of the Polish peasantry has also defied earlier predictions. In calling off the collectivization campaign of the Stalinist period, Gomułka was guided by his own experiences as a young trainee in the Ukraine twenty years before when he had witnessed the mass murders and mass hunger at first hand. He had no wish for such terrible disasters in Poland.

Collective farms were only retained in those few districts where they made good sense—as on the large former German estates of the Recovered Territories. Rather more than 80 per cent of cultivated land reverted to the private plots of individual peasant families. Again, as in the case of their religious policy, the communists felt that time was on their side. They have no love for peasants, whom they regard as a social anachronism with 'antisocial' tendencies. But again the experts believed that over a generation or so, the independent peasantry would simply wither away. There was no point in crushing them by force *à la russe,* if their position could be gradually eroded by the state's monopoly hold on farm prices, agricultural machinery, and fertilizer sales, by bureaucratic chicanery over land deeds; and by massive investment in the public sector. As things turned out, this policy proved a catastrophe. It persecuted the class which fed the nation. It deprived the private sector of the means to adopt modern agricultural methods, whilst failing to raise the abysmal productivity of the state farms. After forty years of progress, Poland is on the verge of starvation. A country with some of the most broad and fertile farming land of Europe, which ought to be flowing with milk and honey, is plagued with food shortages. Bread riots have sparked off repeated political crises. Food rationing, and food queues, have become a way of life. But the private peasantry survives.

In political affairs, Poland's much vaunted pluralist form of Socialism, though essentially bogus, has given considerable scope for variety and experiment. Every visitor from the West was urged to admire the multi-party system, the collaboration of 'progressive Catholics' with the communist authorities and the presence in parliament of 'non-party deputies'. The visitors were never told that all the minor parties and political associations were rigidly controlled by obligatory adherence to the Party-run Front of National Unity (FJN): that the senior trend in the progressive Catholic movement, the PAX Organization, was proscribed by the Roman Catholi͏   ͏-
chy: or that all non-party candidates had to be vet͏
Party's electoral commission before being invited ͏
takes no great expertise to realize that no i͏
political bodies have been permitted to function͏

On the other hand, it must be admitted, within the limits dictated by the Party, that many shades of opinion were openly expressed, that numerous factions and pressure groups were allowed to flourish both within and without the Party, and that the resulting political debate in Poland was far more sophisticated than in most other communist countries. In launching this strategy, Gomułka undoubtedly felt that a wayward nation had to be granted considerable rein in order to be ridden successfully. A façade of political freedom would reduce the likelihood of active opposition, whilst the Party consolidated its own standing. As a loyal Leninist, Gomułka would never surrender the Party's monopoly of power; but as a convinced Marxist, he would have believed that the success of the Party's social and economic policies would in time foster the legitimacy which the regime so desperately lacked. It was a fair gamble, which at first appeared to be paying off. Many Poles were prepared to give Gomułka the benefit of the doubt, and welcomed the undoubted benefits—freer discussion, a lively press, possibilities for foreign travel. Only after a long period of cumulative disillusionment did Gomułka and his successor, Edward Gierek, convince their subjects that the communist regime was only playing with political liberalization, and had no serious intention of granting lasting concessions. Active opposition first surfaced in March 1968, and erupted again in 1970, 1976, and decisively in 1980, when the emergence of SOLIDARITY heralded the imminent collapse of the established system.

Over the twenty-four years following Gomułka's establishment of the national communist regime, the fortunes of the ruling PZPR rose and fell in two great waves—the first associated with the rule of Gomułka himself to December 1970; the second with that of Edward Gierek, from December 1970 to September 1980. The rhythm of both leaders' careers was remarkably similar. Each man enjoyed an initial 'honeymoon period', in which he appeared to have honourably saved the nation from the fate worse than death. (A Soviet invasion.) Gomułka's honeymoon lasted for three or four years, Gierek's for perhaps two. Each man then moved into a period when hopes for a new economic strategy offset disappointments on the political front. Gomułka achieved his 'Little Stabilization' between 1960 and 1967; Gierek launched his bold plan for modernization in 1972 amidst signs of increasing prosperity. Each man survived a violent challenge to his authority—Gomułka in the events of 1968, and Gierek in those of June 1976. Each man lingered on for a season amidst the ruins of his policies until another violent shock relieved him of his misery. Gomułka was dispatched by the Baltic Riots of December 1970; Gierek by the strikes of 1980. Both men had tried to square the Polish circle, and failed.

Gierek's failure is particularly instructive, since it exposed the fatal inability of a communist regime to learn from its mistakes. Although the young Gierek had passed his early years as an *émigré* miner in two of the most doctrinaire Stalinist parties in Europe (the Communist Parties of France and Belgium), and had made his reputation in Silesia as the tough Party boss of a tough mining community, he entered the stage in the crisis of 1970-1 as the tribune of the people. He visited the shipyards of the Baltic ports, where blood had been shed, and the textile factories of Łódź, where the strikes had been led by women, and was shown talking to the workers and sympathizing with their angry complaints. He promised inquiries, reforms, and punishment of the guilty. Instead of political concessions, however, he placed all his faith in a new economic strategy, which, significantly enough, was to be based not on the long overdue structural reforms of industry and agriculture, but on foreign trade and foreign credit. The communist regime turned its back on the workers and peasants, and tried to earn its salvation from capitalist entrepreneurs in the decadent West. Extravagant loans were raised from bankers bloated with Arab petro-dollars; and expensive modern technology was ordered to revitalize the next generation of Polish industry. Interest on the loans was to be repaid by selling the products of the new industry on the world market. Alas! By 1976, it was clear that a depressed world market did not need substandard Polish exports, and that Polish industry was too inefficient to produce them in any case. What is more, having created a phoney prosperity by raising wages and freezing food prices on the strength of extravagent state subsidies, Gierek found he could no longer meet his obligations on the home front. As a result, he was driven into the same mistake as Gomułka before him—an arbitrary proposal to increase food prices overnight, followed by a popular outburst of rioting, notably at the Ursus tractor factory in Warsaw and in the armaments works at Radom. He beat a hasty retreat. The proposals were rescinded. But the only way for the Polish economy to survive was for still more loans to be raised, to pay both for interest due on earlier borrowing and for the spiralling subsidies. With the Polish foreign debt accelerating beyond the twenty-billion dollar mark—a figure equivalent to the entire foreign debt of the USSR—collapse was just a matter of time. Gierek was on the gambler's rush, with no real hope of a winning number. It was surprising that the regime lingered as long as it did. In July 1980, when another pathetic attempt was made to raise food prices without consultation or preparation, it was faced not with sporadic riots but with the determined opposition of a united people. Blind to the need for political change, the communist regime had staked its future on an economic palliative, and had reaped its deserts. SOLIDARITY was about to be born.

4 *The Interval of SOLIDARITY, August 1980 to December 1981*

For thirty-six years, Polish politics had taken little account of the people in whose name the Party reigned. Thirty-six million people were the passive object of politics. In 1980, they rose up determined to become one of its active subjects. The SOLIDARITY Movement was the incarnation of that determination. The ruling Party suffered a stroke from which it is unlikely to recover.

The growth of a consolidated and organized Opposition— as distinct from the informal, unorganized opposition of the nation, which has always existed—had taken place gradually over a dozen years. The events of 1968 with their nasty anti-Semitic overtones produced a crop of dissident intellectuals, several of whom, like Adam Michnik or Jacek Kuroń, had a left-wing or Marxist past. The Baltic Riots of 1970 produced a generation of angry and disillusioned workers, especially in Gdańsk and Szczecin. The Party's machinations over the amendments to the Constitution in 1975–76, which formalized Poland's dependence on the USSR, spawned a group of nationalist dissidents, later known as the Committee for an Independent Poland (KPN). The events of June 1976, where ordinary workers were punished for their part in protests at Radom and at the Ursus tractor factory in Warsaw, brought the first sign of coalescence. The Committee for Workers' Defence (KOR) was set up by Lipiński, Kuroń, and others and openly acted as an information and liaison centre. The Pope's election in 1978, and even more his triumphal visit to his homeland in June 1979, created a psychological uplift which broke the chains of fear and anxiety preventing ordinary Poles from being themselves. The Pope made no overt comments on the political scene: but the blatant contrast between the authentic, spontaneous authority of the Church, and the artificial authority of the Party was exposed to the full view of the television cameras. After that, the die was cast. The crack in the crust of the Polish communists' world had been opened. Only one small disturbance was needed to release a pent-up eruption of popular resentment.

The final trigger was provided by the Party's latest food-price hike. At first, in July, a rash of local strikes seemed to be heading in the same direction as their predecessors in 1970 and 1976. Protests over food shortages fuelled a plethora of minor grievances directed against all manner of hardships and abuses. One might have expected the Party to respond with a matching set of promises and wage rises, a cosmetic change of government, an attempt to raise further foreign loans, a new reformist strategy at the most. But on this occasion it soon became clear that the workers would not be fobbed off. In mid-August, the strike committee in the vast Lenin Shipyards of Gdańsk rejected a favourable settlement of their own local claim, on the grounds that to do so would betray their fellow strikers elsewhere. It was the moment of truth. The realization dawned that the Party's monopoly of power was being challenged by the concerted action of workers up and down the country—under the ironic slogan of 'WORKERS OF ALL ENTERPRISES—UNITE'. On 31 August in the Gdańsk Agreement and later in a separate agreement signed with the miners' representatives at Jastrzębie in Silesia, government negotiators were obliged to meet the most important of the

strikers' demands. In return for confirmation of the Party's
leading political role, they formally accepted a long list of
concessions including the workers' right to strike, their right to
organize themselves into free trade unions, their right to
construct a monument to colleagues killed in 1970, and a
relaxation of the censorship. In direct consequence of these
agreements, delegates of strike committees from every province of Poland joined together as the National Co-ordinating
Committee of a new Independent Self-governing Trades
Union (NSZZ). They called their new organization SOLI-
DARNOŚĆ (Solidarity); and they elected as their Chairman
the thirty-seven-year-old unemployed electrician, who had
climbed over the wall of the Lenin Shipyards to lead the
crucial strike in Gdańsk—Lech Wałęsa.

   The fifteen months of SOLIDARITY's legal activity were
crowded with projects of reform, disputes, conflicts, arguments, agreements, scares, and alarums which followed each
other in dizzy succession. Political life was alive and spontaneous for the first time in a generation. In November, there was
an agony of suspense while the Warsaw District Court
dithered over the Union's legal registration. In December,
with the Soviet Army on manœuvres, came the first, open
threat of a Soviet invasion. In the Spring, there was a
protracted struggle over the recognition of SOLIDARNOŚĆ
WIEJSKA (Rural Solidarity), the peasants' Union, accompanied by the uproar when in March Solidarity activists were
assaulted by the Militia in Bydgoszcz. Only Wałęsa's superhu-
man efforts prevented a General Strike. Throughout the
summer months, feverish preparations led the way to Solidarity's First National Congress, held in Gdańsk in two sessions in
September 1981, and the passing of the movement's statutes
and resolutions. In the autumn, all Poland's universities and
colleges joined an academic strike over academic reform.
Finally, frustration born of the failure to extract any
substantial commitment from the authorities on numerous
projects of reform under discussion led to an angry meeting of
the Executive on 3 December 1981 where calls were made for
free elections and a referendum on Poland's alliance with the
Soviet Union. Secret microphones planted by the authorities
recorded Wałęsa's agitated voice proclaiming the hopelessness

of trying to reach agreement with an incalcitrant Party. The day of reckoning was at hand.

Much may be said—and much is being written—about the complex make-up of the SOLIDARITY Movement, with its worker activists, its intellectual advisers, its Catholics, its students, peasants, old-age pensioners, and hangers-on of all shapes and sizes. Much may be said of Wałęsa's daily battle to hold the balance of the radicals and the counsellors of restraint. Much remains to be studied about SOLIDARITY's colossal intellectual output—its press, its broadsheets, its debates, its sponsorship of historical enquiries, its ideas on economic and social reform.[2] But two facts require no comment. Firstly, with close on ten million members, SOLI-DARITY represented almost every single family in the land, and thereby expressed the will of the overwhelming majority of the Polish nation. Secondly, SOLIDARITY remained true to its non-violent ideals. No steps were taken to provide it with the means of self-defence. When on 13 December 1981 it was attacked by the communist security forces with tanks, guns, and batons, it had no arms, no independent communication network, and no plan of campaign. From this, flowed its lasting moral victory.

No one can deny that SOLIDARITY became a mighty political force. Equally, it has to be admitted that SOLIDAR-ITY was extremely reluctant to flex its political muscles. Although individual members may sometimes have voiced inflammatory opinions, although many local branches may have demanded immediate action to end abuses, there was never any concerted attempt to overthrow the Party or to launch an insurrection. The weapon of a General Strike, which could have been used at any juncture, was never actually invoked. Despite criticisms emanating from Party circles and echoed by the more thoughtless sections of the Western Press, SOLIDARITY desperately worked for a political compromise. The particular solution, emerging from the discussions of 1981, was some form of council of national reconciliation in which each of the three main forces of the political arena—the Church, the Party, and SOLIDAR-ITY—could all be represented. What is more, the SOLIDAR-ITY leaders had good reason to believe that such a com-

promise would be both attainable and viable. Their expectations were encouraged both by the Primate, Cardinal Wyszyński, and his successor in June 1981 Archbishop Józef Glemp,
and by the official Party line of these months which had
adopted the reassuring slogan of *Odnowa* (Renewal). In
looking for the causes of the failure of the hoped-for
compromise, one must look less into the motives of SOLI-
DARITY, and more into those of the Party.

For the outstanding development of 1980–1 was the rapid
paralysis and eventual collapse of the ruling PZPR. Of course,
in one sense it was the rise of SOLIDARITY which was
responsible for the Party's demise. But that was just the final
blow. The Party collapsed at the culmination of a long process
of decay, which had been sapping respect for its corrupt
leaders, its failed policies, and its irrelevant ideology for years.
After all, if the Party had either been worthy of respect or
strong enough to enforce its customary dictatorship, SOLI-
DARITY could not have arisen in the first place. Now, when
the challenge came, a Party which insisted on the preservation
of its 'leading role' at every turn, proved incapable of
leadership. It is no accident, after Gierek's inevitable removal
on 5 September, that his successor, Stanisław Kania was a
proponent of compromise and caution. As the long-term head
of the Party's Administrative Department, responsible for
military, security, and internal political affairs, he was in the
best position to know the true extent of the Party's weakness.
With one-third of the Party's three million members joining
SOLIDARITY, largely from the lower ranks of the *actif,* the
tentacles of the Party machine were no longer responding to
the centre. The Party's nervous system was broken. Party
directives, instead of being instantly obeyed, were being
ignored, or, still worse, openly debated. In due course, the
comrades of Toruń caught the mood of the day by calling for
a 'horizontal movement' linking all the Party's grass-roots
organizations in defiance of the traditional system of vertical
discipline. The Extraordinary Party Congress convened in
July 1981 turned out to be truly extraordinary in that the
elections for the Central Committee were democratically
organized on the basis of an open list of candidates in place of
the usual closed list selected in advanced by the higher organs.

As a result, 90 per cent of the old Committee failed to be re-elected—an unheard-of departure. The policy resolutions of the Congress proved less surprising, with most of the burning issues left conveniently vague for future decision.

At this point, the inner core of the communist establishment must have been close to despair. On the one hand they lived under intense pressure from the Soviet comrades, whose marines were practising amphibious landings on the Baltic shore in yet another delicate demonstration of Moscow's resolve. On the other hand, they had lost the certainty that the Party machine could respond coherently to any plan of action. The loud-mouthed hard-liners of the new Political Bureau, like Albin Siwak, would obviously oppose any scheme for a compromise with SOLIDARITY or for a Council of National Reconciliation. The new soft-liners, like the professor of sociology from Cracow, Hieronim Kubiak, would probably dislike any scheme for SOLIDARITY's forcible suppression. The Party's rank and file would be hopelessly split, whichever course were chosen. So it was time to act without them. The Army Command and the security forces had been held in quarantine from the democratic virus; but a demand for setting up a trade union branch within the Militia showed that the disease was spreading fast into the vital organs of the body politick. The Party had lost the capacity of curing itself. Those few elements which still possessed the will to act were being driven to save themselves, and if possible, to salvage whatever remained of the old order.

In the absence of documentary evidence, the genesis and timing of the December Coup are bound to be the object of intense speculation. But the main lines were clear. There was no way that a vast operation involving the deployment and logistical support of hundreds of thousands of troops, and the co-ordination of several services, could have been planned in a few days, or even a few weeks. No doubt, skeleton contingency plans were drawn up well in advance by silent departments whose duty is to have plans for every eventuality. But detailed local information needed to bring outlines up to date must have taken time to collect. Most importantly, the moves whereby the authors of the Coup could manœuvre themselves into a position for launching the operation in secret must have been made deliberately and with the utmost stealth. It is probable that the threatened Soviet invasion of December 1980 was only called off in consequence of an undertaking that the Polish Army would do the Soviets' work for them. The first move was made in February 1981, when General Wojciech Jaruzelski, the Minister of Defence, was promoted to the post of Prime Minister. The second move came in September with the removal of Kania, the living reflection of the Party's paralysis, and the further promotion of Jaruzelski to the supreme position of Party Secretary. The third came in October when Jaruzelski attended a meeting with Wałęsa and the Primate to create the illusion that compromise was still being sought. The fourth, also in October, sent thousands of small military patrols into the towns and villages, ostensibly to help with the distribution of food, but also to collect information and to spread the image of the Army as the people's friend. The fifth was to discredit the leaders of SOLIDARITY—a task undertaken with relish by the daily Television News (DTV) throughout the autumn—and if possible to goad them into ever more extreme pronouncements. Thereafter, it was only a matter of waiting until the squads were trained and the troops were ready. Ideally, SOLIDARITY should have been pushed into some open act of rebellion; but the edited tapes of Wałęsa's outburst at Radom served perfectly well. The Coup was launched, in the night, nine days later.

Which only leaves the intriguing question of who exactly the authors of the Coup were. What precisely is meant by 'the core of the communist establishment', which apparently could act independently of the main Party apparatus, and if necessary, overthrow it, or arrogate its functions? The answer lay not just with General Jaruzelski and his immediate associates like General Siwicki or General Kiszczak—who moved quietly into the Political Bureau and the Ministry of the Interior in September. It was all those people, in uniform or out, who held key positions in all the sensitive areas of government and industry, but especially in the military, security, and intelligence services, who owe their first allegiance to the Soviet agencies that gave them those positions in the first place. It should have been no revelation. When the

Church had been ignored; when SOLIDARITY had been suppressed and suspended; when the Party itself had been overruled, and pushed into a secondary role, the reality was laid bare. The core of the communist Establishment in Poland consisted of the servile agents of the Soviet Union.

5 *The Military Dictatorship, from December 1981*

General Jaruzelski's Coup of 13 December 1981 took almost everyone by surprise. It surprised the Western experts, who, with very few exceptions had argued how the structure of the Soviet system precluded a take-over by the Military. It surprised the members of the Council of State who were given only a couple of hours' notice to legalize the 'state of war'. It certainly surprised the leaders of SOLIDARITY, most of whom were arrested in their beds during the first night. Most Poles awoke on the morning of the 13th, to find tanks on the streets, army check-points at every crossroads, and the Proclamation of Martial Law (printed earlier in the Soviet Union) posted on every corner. In the course of the next week, most of the spontaneous protest strikes in mines, shipyards, and factories up and down the country were broken by mobile squads of the ZOMO police,* operating behind army cordons. At some points, there were repeated occupations and reoccupations. At two mines in Silesia, 'Wujek' and 'Piast', there were protracted underground sit-ins; at the Wujek mine, seven men were killed for resisting. But, in general, resistance was swiftly crushed. The element of surprise was very effective. By the end of the year, the armed forces were incontestably in control of the country.

Throughout 1982, Poland was officially ruled by a Military Council of National Salvation (WRON)—popularly known as *wrona* or 'The Crow'. (See p. 377–8.) General Jaruzelski presided over a group made up exclusively, according to its own pronouncements, of serving Polish officers. Tens of

---

*ZOMO—*Zmotoryzowane Oddziały Milicji Obywatelskiej* (Motorized Detachments of the Citizens' Militia)—an élite of paramilitary riot squads, some 10,000 strong. Heavily armed, and supported by armoured transports and air ferries, they have no equivalent in Britain or America, and do not undertake normal, civilian police duties: reminiscent possibly of the CRS in France.

thousands of innocent citizens were arrested without charge. Some 10,000 were detained in forty-nine internment camps. There were reports of beatings and deaths. Countless people were coerced into signing 'pledges of loyalty', (that is, pledges of disloyalty to SOLIDARITY) on pain of their livelihood or their liberty. All official institutions, from the Ministries to the railway stations or public libraries, were subject to the orders of a military commissar, and were purged of unreliable elements. The principal industrial enterprises were militarized. The work-force answered to army discipline. The rules of Martial Law permitted the authorities to impose a night-time curfew, to curtail all transport and travel, to record all telephone conversations, to ban all social gatherings, and to punish the least sign of dissent by on-the-spot fines or instant arrest. By the implicit admissions of the WRON's own pronouncements, it had declared war on Polish society. On whom else? All pretence of legality was cast aside. For weeks, official spokesmen denied that Wałęsa, the leader of SOLIDARITY, had been either arrested or interned. He was 'helping the authorities', but happened to be unavailable for comment. He was eventually served with a pre-dated internment order, when an international outcry forced clarification of his position. Whenever the courts were rash enough to acquit persons charged with alleged offences against Martial Law, the defendants could be declared 'a threat to public order' and incarcerated in a psychiatric ward. The Ministry of Justice saw no shame in such lawless proceedings, which it openly reported presumably to intimidate an already frightened populace.

Despite repeated attempts, the remnants of SOLIDARITY were unable to challenge the iron grip of the Military. The year 1982 began with a slogan, widely chalked on walls by SOLIDARITY sympathizers: *Zima wasza, wiosna nasza*—'the winter is yours, the Spring will be ours'. But Spring never came. Minor demonstrations and token strikes, usually on the 13th of each month, were contained. Major disturbances on 31 August, the second anniversary of the Gdańsk agreement, and on 10 November, the anniversary of SOLIDARITY's legal registration, did not present the ZOMO with any insuperable problem. In several provincial cities—at Nowa Huta, at Lubin

in Silesia, and particularly at Wrocław—outbreaks of determined resistance persisted well into the autumn. But all the
logistics of repression, treachery, and misinformation stood on
the side of the Crow. On 8 October the authorities felt strong
enough to announce that SOLIDARITY, and all other free
unions, had been abolished, not merely 'suspended', and in
November to release a powerless Wałęsa. In December, most
internees, though not political prisoners, were released. By this
time Government spokesmen had begun to talk disparagingly
of SOLIDARITY members as 'criminals', and to brag that
'the Spring, too, will be ours'.

Step by step, as the communists took stock of their
miraculous escape, they tried to re-establish control over the
organizations which had earlier repudiated them. Their main
target, to begin with, was the intelligentsia, that incurable
source, from their point of view, of festering dissent. The
Journalists' Association (SDP) was abolished in March; the
Film Makers' Union and the Actors' Union (ZASP), which
had bravely boycotted the official media, were dissolved in
December. Even PAX, the Party's pet association of 'progressive Catholics' had to be purged. Perhaps the WRON thought
it was attacking the roots of the crisis; but it was only
scratching the surface. No important sector of Polish society
was won over to the communists' cause.

All Jaruzelski's attempts at constructive politics fell flat.
Despite the Primate's initial desire to compromise, the
General did not re-establish any real dialogue with the
Church. His fine-sounding Patriotic Movement for National
Rebirth (PRON) was packed with his own dependants talking
exclusively to themselves. His new, official Trade Unions were
shunned by everyone who could not be pressured into joining.
The declaration of the 'suspension' of the State of War at the
end of December, was greeted as an empty gesture.

Economic performance continued to deteriorate. Contrary
to the claims of official propaganda, which had blamed
everything on SOLIDARITY, the suppression of SOLIDAR-
ITY did not produce any overall improvement. Despite a
modest increase in one or two sectors, such as coal production,
industrial productivity actually decreased. For the fourth year
running, Poland's GNP suffered a further catastrophic drop,

of over 15 per cent. The mounting Foreign Debt headed towards thirty billion dollars; even current interest payments had to be rescheduled. The demand for food was eased by the draconian and long overdue price rises of up to 300 per cent, introduced in February; but most Poles continued to survive on the breadline. Queuing remained a way of life. The Government expressed its hope for self-sufficiency in food by 1990. The standard of living plummeted. The vast gap between the purchasing power of the average family and the goods available for sale continued to widen, even though real incomes fell by over 25 per cent. Government finance, with the budget deficit accelerating through the hundreds of milliards of zlotys, was running out of control. The imbalance of Foreign Trade could only be regulated by the summary cancellation of imports, on which the revival of industry would depend. Poland, which is a rich country blessed with great natural resources, sank into a state of abject poverty unparalleled in Europe.

As a result of the December Coup, Poland's standing on the international scene lost all semblance of respectability. The military regime was widely seen as a surrogate of the Soviet Union, and was treated as such. The USA pointedly introduced economic sanctions against the USSR as well as against Poland, demanding that the State of War be rescinded, that the internees be released, and that genuine Dialogue be initiated. Although American policy caused friction among America's Western allies, who were scrambling at that very time to close a series of deals with Moscow over the Siberian pipeline project, it left no room for doubt concerning the ultimate responsibility for Poland's distress. The overthrow of Poland's Soviet-controlled civilian dictatorship by a Soviet-controlled military dictatorship could hardly be regarded as a major shift in the balance of international power; but it provided a suitable occasion for giving the world a lesson in East European realities. Those well-intentioned pundits, who had revived their delusions about the supposed 'convergence' of the Soviet and the Western worlds, received a rude set-back. Two Polish Ambassadors, in Washington and Tokyo, defected; and by their pathetic reversal of roles, from staunch Communist loyalist to eager democrat overnight, exposed the wretched morale on which the communist élite is founded. Candles, which were lighted on Christmas Eve in the windows of The White House and the Vatican alike, symbolized the lengthy vigil expected by Poland's foreign friends. The Polish Government reacted angrily when its measures of limited relaxation did not bring the expected withdrawal of Western sanctions. As always on such occasions, it was assumed that the comfortable leaders of the Western democracies, having made their token gesture, would soon forget their love for Poland.

It must be said, however, that many harsh words were fired at the military regime in Poland without due attention to the precise target. Indeed, it is quite clear that the Polish authorities took great pains to conceal what was really afoot, and may well have welcomed the deafening barrage of inaccurate foreign criticism. For, in spite of everything, the conduct of policy in Poland lacked many of the characteristics ingredients not only of military take-overs elsewhere in the world but also of the usual Soviet-style programmes of 'normalization'. The repression was highly selective, and strangely half-hearted. It lacked the gratuitous violence of Afghanistan or El Salvador, with which it was competing for headline space in the world's newspapers. It lacked the wholesale social terror which reigned in Kadar's Hungary after 1956, or the systematic purges of Husak's 'normalization' in Czechoslovakia after 1968. It did not resort to mass deportations, which would have been a sure sign of Soviet initiative; and it lacked any note of urgency to restore the rule of the Party. Above all, it lacked any direct involvement by Soviet personnel. For some reason, which had not become entirely clear by the end of the State of War, the Military Regime did not feel inclined to exploit its new-found powers to the full. It was curiously inhibited, and by Soviet standards, unbelievably restrained. Its immobility remained an unsolved riddle. Much may be attributed to the paralysis of the Party machine which had suffered the political equivalent of a nervous breakdown, and which was incapable of reassuming power even if ordered to do so. But that was not the whole story. There were tell-tale hints that Jaruzelski's fight behind the scenes against his comrades and his would-be allies was

even more crucial than his public confrontation with SOLI-
DARITY. One had to wonder what was happening in the
silent wrangle between the various factions of the Polish
communist camp. One had to wonder why the Western press
was allowed to remain in Warsaw in force, despite occasional
molestations, unless, perhaps, it was reporting the wrong
things. It was hard to imagine, if the presence of Western
pressmen and television crews did not serve someone's interest,
why an all-powerful police state could not have them all
unceremoniously expelled. Most interestingly, one had to
wonder about Jaruzlski's role in the run-up to Brezhnev's
succession in Moscow. Jaruzelski was certainly engaged in a
holding operation, and playing the waiting game. But, to the
outside world at least, it was not immediately evident for
whom or for what he was waiting.

For Jaruzelski was not merely Moscow's man in Poland. He
was the servant of the military interest within the Soviet
apparatus, the batman of the Soviet marshals. By taking over
the People's Republic himself, he had saved the Soviet Army
from a very unpleasant task. At the same time, by deploying
the Polish armed forces, he had raised the stakes against an
eventual Soviet invasion of Poland. He was the first Polish
leader since the war who put Poland in a position capable of
defending itself. His *démarche* cut both ways. He crushed the
hopes of SOLIDARITY; but he equally forestalled the
prospect of a vendetta against Poland by the more doctrinaire
comrades in Moscow and Warsaw. No one was to know which
of the two opposite dangers he judged the more menacing,
and to what extent, if any, Marshal Kulikov disagreed. All one
can say is that he had been schooled by the Soviet Military for
the eventuality of political intervention in Poland ever since
Rokossowski's expulsion in 1956. He had taken over the duties
of the last remaining Soviet general officers in Poland—in
1960 as the head of the Army's Political Department, and in
1965 as the Chief of the General Staff. As Minister of Defence,
he had served *ex officio* as a deputy commander of the Warsaw
Pact joint forces for some fifteen years, in the closest possible
association with the Soviet top brass. In 1981–2, when he
added the posts of Prime Minister, First Secretary, and
Chairman of the WRON to his collection, he had ensured, for

the time being at least, that no one else could muscle his way on to the Polish political stage. At which point, Yuri I. Andropov appeared at the controls of the Soviet Bloc, but with no indication whether his elevation was connected with the ambitions of the marshals, or not. Twelve months after the December Coup, the fate of People's Poland was back where it had started nearly forty years before—in the hands of the Soviet Military, and of their Polish military aides; but there was no clue as to where it would end up. Nor could there be. The formulation of Soviet policy after Brezhnev's death, like the progress of the Polish Revolution, was still in a state of suspense.

Spiders' Webs and Galley-slaves

In a world dominated by the international systems of the two nuclear superpowers, many countries have willingly accepted constraints on their national sovereignty. In the interests of common defence and of mutual economic assistance, the members both of NATO and the Warsaw Pact, of the European Common Market and of Comecon, are obliged to honour agreements which limit their absolute freedom of action. Even the Non-aligned Nations think fit to form an association of their own to protect their status, and to formulate a common front. Full independence is virtually extinct. Limited sovereignty is the norm. In the Western liberal view, however, the essence of limited sovereignty lies in its voluntary nature, and hence in its revocability. In this, it must be clearly distinguished from other forms of *in*voluntary association which can more properly be likened to the old-fashioned relationship between man and dog.

As one might expect, the two rival superpowers make every effort to denigrate the characteristics of their opponent's system and to inflate the virtues of their own. Official terminology supports these natural prejudices. One's 'potential adversary' is invariably found to be in dubious possession of 'satellites', 'secret police', 'armies of occupation', 'propaganda', and 'spies'; whilst one's own side is uniquely blessed with 'allies', 'security agencies', 'defence forces', 'information services' and 'intelligence-gathering personnel'. If one were to

Map 2.   The Polish People's Republic (1983)

believe every word of 'Radio Free Europe', the Soviet Bloc is made up exclusively of Moscow's 'captive nations'. If one were to believe Radio Moscow or Radio Warsaw, both NATO and the Common Market are mere dependencies of the expansionist forces of world Capitalism, and hence of 'American Imperialism'.

In trying to define the status and position of the Polish People's Republic, therefore, it is essential to cut through the verbiage of the subject and to examine in some detail the nature of the links between Poland the Soviet Union. Official spokesmen in Warsaw, whilst emphasizing that 'the Soviet Alliance' is the mainstay of Poland's position in the world, always take pains to stress that the alliance is indeed a voluntary association of free and equal partners. In their eyes, the term 'Soviet satellite' is both inaccurate and insulting. They also use the concept of limited sovereignty to suggest that Poland's relationship to the Warsaw Pact and to COMECON is essentially the same as that of Britain or West Germany to NATO or to the Common Market. In response to remarks about the presence of the Soviet Army in Poland, they point out quite correctly that there are more American bases in Britain or West Germany than Soviet bases in Poland. Such arrangements between allies, it seems, are perfectly normal. If the question of economic exploitation arises, they say quite correctly that the Soviet Union has been providing Poland with considerable financial and commercial aid in recent years. Certainly, the more naïve sort of Western tourist who imagines that there must be Russian tanks on every street corner in Warsaw, will be bitterly disappointed. At the same time, just because Soviet forces keep a low profile, one should not assume that the Soviet Union has no effective means of controlling its allies. In actual fact, the levers of Soviet control are far more varied and elaborate than meets the casual eye.

Right from the start, the geopolitical framework of post-war Europe was constructed to tie Poland permanently to Soviet tutelage. Poland's new frontiers deprived it of all direct contact with non-communist countries, and with its only two sympathetic pre-war neighbours—Romania and Hungary. A country enclosed on three sides by Soviet might was unlikely

to feel adventurous. Furthermore, the Russians' insistence
that Poland be awarded former German territories far beyond
anything that Poles had previously considered Polish, ensured
a lengthy term of dependence. For Poland's possession of the
Western Territories, constituting no less than 32.4 per cent of
the whole, was bound to raise the spectre of post-war German
revanchism, and hence the long-term need for Soviet protection against Germany. This factor alone explains why many
Poles, though hostile to the Soviet Union, were obliged to
reconcile themselves to Soviet supremacy. It did not diminish
until the Polish–West German Treaty of 7 December 1970,
and the Federal Republic of Germany's *de facto* recognition of
Poland's western frontier on the Oder–Niesse Line. As a result,
the Soviet occupation forces have been much smaller than
would otherwise have been required.

However, the function of the Soviet military garrison in
Poland is rather more serious than its modest numbers might
suggest. On the one hand, it is perfectly true that Soviet troops
have been stationed in Poland ever since 1945 on the basis of
an Allied agreement authorizing the USSR to protect its lines
of communication with occupied Germany. It is also true that
the two divisions based at the Soviet base HQ at Legnica in
Silesia,* and the smaller units based on the Baltic coast near
Szczecin and in the port of Świnoujście, pose no immediate
threat. On the other hand, it must be realized that the present
diminutive garrison is the remnant of the colossal Soviet Army
of occupation which inflicted fearful repressions on Poland in
the early post-war years, and that it can act at a moment's
notice as the advance guard of an invasion force drawn from
Soviet divisions permanently stationed near by in East
Germany, in Czechoslovakia, and in the Soviet military
districts of Kaliningrad, Byelorussia, and Ukraine. Most
telling, perhaps, is the Soviet's proven record. On several
occasions at moments of political crisis in Poland—in October
1956, for instance, or in December 1980—the Soviet Government has not shrunk from deploying its forces, including the
Baltic Fleet, in demonstrations of political intent. The fate of

---

*Legnica also serves as the HQ of the Warsaw Pact's Northern Group of
Forces—one of three such command centres in Eastern Europe.

Hungary in 1956 and of Czechoslovakia in 1968 shows that those intentions are serious. The Soviet Union's allies can have few illusions, if they dare to exercise their limited sovereignty in ways displeasing to the Kremlin, that they run the risk of crushing military punishment. Indeed, the Soviet leadership makes no secret of its position. It was no accident that in November 1968 Leonid Brezhnev chose Warsaw as his platform for launching the Doctrine which bears his name, and which asserts the duty of all fraternal parties to intervene by force in defence of 'the gains of Socialism'. Given this background, there can be no doubt that the Soviet military presence in Poland is designed in the first instance as an earnest of Poland's good behaviour, and if need be, as a reminder of much greater instruments of coercion held in reserve.

What is more, Poland's own military establishment is directly dependent on the Soviet Union. Fifteen Army divisions, fifty-five air force squadrons, a navy of 158 warships, and a pool of over one million trained men constitutes a force to be reckoned with by any standards. But its scope for independent action is extremely small. The armed forces of the People's Republic, first formed in 1943 inside the Soviet Union, are created in the image of their Soviet masters. The main strategic reserve is allocated to the Warsaw Pact under Soviet command. Almost all the officer corps belongs to the communist party, and all the senior officers are trained in Soviet academies. Until 1981, the General Staff functioned as a subordinate department of the Party Secretariat. The military-political agencies owe absolute allegiance to the Soviet Union, and eager young conscripts are weaned on the notion that Polish patriotism and admiration of the Soviet Union are one and the same thing. All military equipment conforms to Soviet standards, and most of it, together with the main fuel reserves, communications networks, and ammunition dumps, is supplied and controlled by Soviet agencies. Key items, such as warheads for missiles or transporters for the parachute brigades, are normally withheld. As was amply proved in the events of December 1981, the Polish Army can be used very efficiently in defence of Soviet interests; but it has been deprived since birth of the will and the means for defending Poland against the Soviet Union. (See Chapter VI, section 2.)

Behind the regular military screen, the communist state possesses specialized security organs whose size and resources far exceed those of any Western country. In Poland, there is the élite Internal Security Corps (WOW), formerly the KBW, with some 65,000 men; the Military Frontier Defence Force (WOP) with some 20,000; the heavily armed Motorized Detachments of the Citizens' Militia (ZOMO), which provide the spearhead units of a unified state police force, 350,000 strong, backed up in turn by the still larger Volunteer Reserve (ORMO) and the National Defence League (LOK). Behind them, stands the Internal Military Service (WSW), the Party's private guard for controlling the Army; together with the military intelligence and counter-intelligence services and the all-pervasive Security Service (the SB), formerly the UB, the local Polish underling of the Soviet KGB. All these formations, both in uniform and in plain clothes, were established after the War by the Soviet Union, and for their first few years were largely staffed by Russian personnel specially imported for the purpose. Since 1956, they have been freed from their Russian advisers, at least at the lower levels. During the Polish October of that year, there were signs that the KBW, which appeared in Warsaw in full combat kit, might have resisted Soviet intervention. Since then, there has been no evidence of waywardness. When the time came in December 1981 to suppress the SOLIDARITY Movement, to break the strikes, and to crush the internal opposition, the security forces were more than equal to their task. Indeed, the military elements of the security apparatus were not called on to act in anything more than a supervisory role.

Of course, armies and security forces are only sent into action in exceptional circumstances. In this, they may be likened to the English umbrella which is carried at all times, but in the hope that the clouds overhead will not actually burst. In between the periodic cloudbursts, the security umbrella of the Soviet-style state is kept folded. Indeed, since the communist leadership also possesses a formidable arsenal of civilian and organizational controls, it can usually count on creating the appearance of political stability and of social quiescence. Through the characteristic combination of both coercive and organizational controls, it can graduate its response to any internal challenge with great precision, and can escape many of the overt displays of terror and brutality, which typify less sophisticated dictatorships relying exclusively on crude coercive methods.

The essence of good policing lies in prevention rather than punishment, and the same could be said of bureaucratic controls in general. The ordinary citizens of a communist state are so enmeshed by petty rules and regulations, that meekness and subservience towards the authorities is the only way to ensure a quiet life. Permits, licences, and official stamps are required for most of the operations of everyday living. Passbooks, identity cards, and written permissions proliferate. Although People's Poland does not operate an internal passport system like the USSR, a system of residence permits effectively empowers the Militia to oversee people's movements. Passports for foreign travel are not issued by right, but only for approved purposes. The individual is forced to limit his habits and aspirations to the narrow parameters laid down by the ruling Establishment.

In defining the official parameters, personnel policy has great importance. It is an axiom of Soviet practice that every position of authority in every sphere of public life must be held by persons dependent on the grace and favour of the ruling Party. All state and Party officials are subject to rigorous hierarchical discipline, akin to that of an army. Their higher ranks form a closed élite enjoying monopoly power together with sole access to the fixed list of the most influential and remunerative appointments—the *nomenklatura* (see p. 49–50). State and party organs at regional, city, and district level follow the same procedures as their seniors in central government. To establish this monopoly in the first place required considerable ruthlessness and blood-letting. In Poland, the task was undertaken by the Soviet security services in 1944–7, when any official showing the least lack of subservience was instantly dismissed, demoted, or deported. Thereafter, the machine could be kept running with a minimum of overt violence. All posts are filled by the Party's nominees, trained in the Party's own academies, and kept in check by the security services and by the threat of periodic purges. It involves a network of political patronage on a scale unthinkable in pluralist societies. In theory at least, no one capable of making a decision which might be hostile to the communist Establishment can ever reach a position to make it.

The whole governmental system is structured to prevent all forms of independent initiative. Lenin's principles of Democratic Centralism have been applied in Poland with only minor variations from the Soviet model. Firstly, on the principle of 'dual power', all offices of state are 'shadowed' by parallel offices within the apparatus of the Party. Hence the Council of State and the Council of Ministers are subordinated to the Party's Political Bureau; the President of the Republic and the Prime Minister take their orders from the First Secretary; the Minister of Foreign Affairs answers to the head of the Party's Department of Foreign Affairs; and the village mayor to the secretary of the Party's village committee. The 'Socialist state' is nothing more than the administrative branch of the ruling communist Party. Secondly, individual members of the *nomenklatura* are encouraged to hold positions simultaneously in both State and Party. It is more than likely, therefore, that the leading ministers are also party secretaries or members of the Party's Central Committee. Party organs habitually nominate comrades from their own number to run the state offices dependent on them. Thirdly, every rung of the Party ladder is formally required to execute the orders of the rungs above. Every party member must obey the instructions of his superiors. As a result, the situation is achieved where the Party dictates to the state; the Political Bureau dictates to the Party as a whole; and the First Secretary, once established, dictates to the Political Bureau. Democratic Centralism involves an arrangement where centralization is pushed to extremes, and where democracy runs in reverse.[3]

From the point of view of the Soviet Union, the system offers maximum control for minimum effort. So long as the First Secretary of the fraternal party is kept loyal to the Soviet interest, the whole of the State-and-Party pyramid beneath him can be assumed to be in line. (It is rather reminiscent of the good old days of monarchical rule, where, by placing one's candidate on the throne of a client state, one was assured of a dependent ally.) Yet even here, it seems that little is left to chance. There are a hundred and one reasons why the secretaries of fraternal parties, conditioned by long years of service in an atmosphere of adulation for all things Soviet, should refrain from biting the hand that feeds them. But there have been some grave lapses. Moscow can not have forgotten Tito, Imre Nagy, Mao, or Dubček. Just in case, therefore, it would make good sense, if the fraternal Secretaries were included in the secret personnel policy of the Communist Party of the Soviet Union itself. The existence of an integrated *nomenklatura* for the whole Soviet Bloc can only be surmised; but it would run true to form and would match similar interlocking devices which can be observed in other areas of the Soviet polity.

Ideology is not always thought of as an instrument of control, rather as a justification for controls; but it does serve a very practical purpose. Ideology is a weapon for disarming potential opposition. If enough people in society can be convinced that history is governed by scientific laws: that Soviet-style Socialism is the inevitable product of historical progress: and that the Soviet Union embodies all the finest socialist ideals of peace, equality, and justice, then rational people should be incapable of defying the rule of the Soviet government and its chosen allies. In Poland, as in other countries of the Soviet Bloc, it is these vulgar political propositions, rather than the finer points of Marxism-Leninism, or of Marxism which receive official backing in the elaborate propaganda machines in education, the media, and the armed forces.

Of course, to be effective, propaganda must be supported by a rigorous Censorship—an institution which in the communist canon far exceeds the practice common enough all over the world, for ruling establishments to suppress harmful or embarrassing information. Working under Soviet guidance, the Polish censors not only excise 'negative data'; they systematically manufacture the 'positive data', which pre-empts the possibility of rational criticism. Hence the term—*cenzura prewencyjna* (pre-emptive Censorship). The Censors' top priority is to defend the prestige and security of USSR. It would be understandable, though deplorable, if they merely strove to suppress attacks on Soviet policy, curiosity about Soviet military affairs, or knowledge of Soviet disasters, war crimes, and environmental pollution. But they go much further. They rework statistics and rewrite history to the point where reliable information no longer exists for sensible discussion, let alone criticism. Ever since the publication in London in 1977 of a defecting Polish censor's set of detailed instructions, these matters are known in great detail.[4] But it seems that they may have backfired. Deprived of credible information about Soviet policy, the average Pole in the street believes every rumour he hears, and curses the Russians for everything. Would-be reformers have no firm knowledge on which to base proposals for reform.

Poland's economic system is highly dependent. A command economy, organized in the Soviet image on the basis of Central Planning, it was designed to keep all enterprises of production, distribution, and supply strictly under the Party's monopolistic control. Furthermore, since the Planning Commissions of Comecon's member states are now obliged to follow the guidelines of Comecon's own Planning, and since Comecon has adopted a strategic policy of allocating specialized economic tasks, no member state except the Soviet Union can aspire to self-sufficiency. (Romania made a bid to resist full integration into Comecon in the 1960s, but has gradually been forced to relent.) Oddly enough, Poland's economic crisis may well succeed in disrupting the integrated economies of the whole Soviet Bloc. Shortfalls in Polish production and supplies are found to have a knock-on effect. Equally, with two-thirds of Poland's foreign trade lying in the Comecon sphere, and with 80 per cent of her oil and iron ore coming from the USSR, it is inconceivable that she could long pursue any divergent economic policy without the Soviets' support and prior approval.

Legal constraints are all-embracing. The Polish Constitution of 1952 was exceptional in Eastern Europe for not putting the 'leading role' of the ruling Party and the alliance with the Soviet Union into the category of cardinal law. But these omissions were rectified in the controversial constitutional amendments of February 1976, which probably mark the moment when the Soviet comrades began to grow uneasy about Polish developments. The implications are stark. Any attempt to shake off the monopoly of the Soviet Union's communist allies in Poland, or any move to withdraw from the institutions of the Soviet Bloc, can be denounced as unconstitutional and illegal. The Soviet Union is fully entitled to, intervene in Poland and to defend the status quo, in accordance with the declarations not just of Soviet interest but of Polish law. It is on this point that the Polish regime's unquestioned legality must be contrasted with its undoubted illegitimacy.

Diplomatic constraints, too, are often underrated. The curious conduct of the Soviet Ambassador in Warsaw, who enjoys direct access to the Party Secretary, has long been the subject of comment; but it is not always clear by what right he can justify his unique privileges over the rest of the diplomatic corps. The answer lies, among other things, in the Polish-Soviet Treaty of Friendship, Mutual Aid, and Co-operation signed on 21 April 1945, and renewed in 1965 for a further twenty years. This treaty, signed not by a recognized Polish Government but merely by the Moscow-led Provisional Government of the Polish Republic (RTRP), committed Poland to the Soviet view of Polish frontiers: to a Soviet guarantee of Poland's internal security: and to Soviet tutelage in foreign affairs. (See p. 73–80.) Henceforth, any Polish initiative which the Kremlin may judge to be 'unfriendly' can be construed as an infringement of the Treaty, and as the occasion for an invocation of the relevant articles of the Polish Constitution or of the Brezhnev Doctrine. It is the Soviet Ambassador's duty to remind the Polish First Secretary of this reality on all possible occasions.

Above all, there is a psychological factor at work—the factor of fear. Almost every Polish family guards memories of friends or relatives who were deported to Siberia in 1939–40; killed in Soviet captivity during the War; assaulted during the Liberation; or arrested by the Soviet security forces for belonging to the wartime Resistance or, in the 1950s, for being a 'foreign spy and *provocateur*'. Although the horrors of the German Occupation were even more severe, it is the memories of Soviet crimes which persist, simply because the Soviet

threat has not diminished. No Pole who knows his country's
history, strewn with wars and insurrections against Russia,
can doubt what the penalties for rebellion will be. (See
Chapters IV and V.) It is a paralysing fear which inhibits the
very thought of independence and freedom. In a characteristic
euphemism of Party jargon, it is described as 'a necessary
awareness of objective reality'.

The climate of fear, and the accompanying conspiracies, of
silence, mendacity, and flattery, are perpetuated by the
absence of the rule of law. For lawlessness is the corner-stone
of Leninism. Lenin's concept of *Partiinost* (Party supremacy)
puts the Party bosses above the law, and exposes everyone and
everything to the mercy of the Party's whim. It overrides all
sense of constitutionality, all freedoms, all title to property,
even 'social property'. It paralyses all thoughts of independent
justice, of equality before the Law, even of Socialism, since the
means of production, like the judiciary, are held at the disposal
not of society as a whole but of the Party bosses. Of course,
constitutions, legal codes, and legal systems exist; and on
paper they can look very enlightened. Indeed, if the Party so
decrees, they can be made to operate in a mild and humane
fashion; and society can enjoy a season of 'socialist legality'.
But nothing fundamental can change. Since, in the last resort,
the Law is the servant of the Party, the Law can protect no
man on the evil day from the Party's displeasure. By the same
token, the constitution and formal treaties of the People's
Republic are unable to protect Poland from the Soviet Union.
For the leaders of the fraternal parties stand in the same state
of lawless vulnerability to the Soviet Party in which their own
subjects stand in relation to them. They all stand exposed to
the fickle command of their superiors. They have no
guarantee of their position, no title to their status or territory,
no protection from harassment, no court of appeal, no hope of
self-defence through legal means, no feeling of confidence that
their rulers, too, must answer to some higher authority. Under
Leninism, there is no authority higher than the Party
leadership. In the Soviet Bloc, there is no higher authority
than the Kremlin. There is no rule of Law above the dictator
of the day. Obviously, Krushchev could decree that Stalin's
reign of terror be suspended, just as some future Soviet leader

could order its reactivation. A Brezhnev or an Androprov may dictate that a greater or a lesser degree of control be exercised according to his private judgement of the consequences. Gomułka could dictate that Bierut's brand of Stalinism be dismantled, just as Gierek or Jaruzelski has dictated that the Party's control be exercised through different combinations of consumerism, toleration, and repression. But there is no concept and no institution within the Soviet system, short of the arbitrary succession of a new dictator, which can call the Party's actions to book. Unlike the Tsars, or Louis XIV, the Party boss does not even have a confessor. He is not merely the autocrat, or the absolute 'Sun King' by divine right; he is a despot devoid of all moral restraint, the modern successor to Nebuchadnezzar or Genghis Khan. He is the one free man in the whole system—free to be as cunning as Lenin, as paranoid as Stalin, as quirkish as Krushchev, as dull as Brezhnev. What is more, in relation to the mortals beneath him, his particular mode of the 'dictatorship of the proletariat', can be imitated by all the descending hierarchy of petty despots right down the endless links of the political chain. From the supreme web of the Soviet *nomenklatura* with the Grand Spider at its centre, web upon tangled web radiates out from the Kremlin into the farthest reaches of the Soviet empire—the webs of central committees, of republican committees, of provincial committees, of city committees, of rural committees; the webs of the fraternal Parties, and of the fraternal Party's committees; the webs of party cells from Cuba to Kamchatka, from Archangel to Angola, from Lübeck Bay to Yuzhno Sakhalinsk. Every web has its 'spider'; and the spiders, even the benevolent ones, recognize no Law higher than their own.

Such a state of official lawlessness is so alien to Americans and to West Europeans, (not to mention the Japanese) that most serious attempts to describe it are instinctively dismissed as flights of fancy. Not surprisingly, Western opinion is most receptive to analysts who try to explain the workings of communist regimes through the dead conventions of political science or through social or economic concepts based on Western experience. The 'one-party state' or the Party's 'proletarian power-base' or 'interest groups in communist society' are intelligible; although their relevance to the

Leninist system is limited. Any approach which has to rely on metaphors and comparisons can be ignored as 'poetical' and 'unscientific'. Yet Western commentators looking at the Soviet world face walls of incomprehension in front and behind. They find it difficult to imagine a system where official lawlessness is the norm, not the exception, and still more to convince a sceptical Western audience conditioned for centuries by the opposite assumptions. They can well understand the state of lawlessness which Hobbes judged to have preceded the formation of governments, but not a Government which operates without the Hobbesian fiction of a social contract between the governors and the governed. After all, they would argue, Hobbes invented the social contract in order to justify absolutist, not democratic rule (—as if anyone in Russia had ever paid attention to Hobbes). They jib at the very idea of a polity whose guardians can change the rules of their own ideology from day to day for their own convenience, and to everyone else's stupefaction. They see the rigid structures of transmission, but not the infinite flexibility at the centre. It may be that they simply do not possess the language to describe what they see. (Just as the removal of an American president, and the prospect of an impeachment in good Cromwellian style, caught Russian commentators literally without the words to describe it.)

As a matter of fact, however, Western analysts do have a suitable vocabulary to hand. Lawlessness, as distinct from common law-breaking, is not unknown in Western societies. It may be foreign to Western political theory, to Western (Roman) ideas about Law, and to Western democratic practice; but it was certainly the basis of the social order on the old American 'Frontier', and it has become an all too familiar phenomenon in the sleasier neighbourhoods of the larger Western cities. The criminal underworld, with its godfathers and cousins, its syndicates and alliances, its rackets and kickbacks, its mobsters and hit men, answers to a political culture where lawlessness is a way of life, and where honest people protest at their peril. For the *mafioso*, as for the Leninist, the power of *Cosa Nostra* is the supreme Good, to which all other principles must be subordinated. Curiously enough, in a year when Andropov has launched a campaign against crime in the Soviet Union, which Brezhnev claimed did not exist; the Polish regime, which last year legally registered SOLI-DARITY, now refers to its leaders as 'criminals'. But for people in the West, brought up to treat all Law and legal authority with respect, any talk of a 'lawless Government' sounds like a contradiction in terms; and a comparison between the political culture of the world's largest empire and that of Gangland is as odd as the talk about spiders.

Of course, there are many other aspects of the Soviet polity—and the Marxist elements in particular—which have nothing in common with the Mafia; and Leninism is not alone in maintaining that the Governors of an ideal society are entitled to stand above the Law. The point has been proposed and debated by political philosophers ever since Socrates and Plato. All that is necessary, if one wants to apply it to contemporary polities, is to keep in mind the essential contrast in concepts of Law between communist and Western, liberal systems. To assume that the standing of the Law under a Soviet-style regime is the same as in the constitutional democracies of the West is to argue from the start from a false premiss.

In any brief review of the links between Poland and the Soviet Union, there can be no intention of drawing up a balance sheet of damage and benefit. The aim is simply to indicate the main facts on which any estimate of the nature of the relationship can be based. Nor is there any point in quibbling over labels. If the Soviets and the Polish commu-nists insist on calling each other 'allies', it is their privilege to do so. But it is not what most people would understand by an alliance.

Another traditional metaphor is that of the ship of state, ploughing hostile seas across the uncharted ocean of the future. On this line of thought, People's Poland must be seen as a war galley of the great Fleet of Communism commanded above decks by a corps of overseers, propelled below by a press-ganged crew shackled to the bench; and rowed to the tap of a martial drum. It sails due astern of the great Soviet flagship to which it is fastened by a heavy, spidery chain. Unfortunately, most of the Polish overseers are half-hearted in their job; the crew consists of former freemen, who still long for their liberty and who are sons of Themistocles, not Xerxes; and no one wants to listen to the drum. As a result, the Polish galley is slewing from side to side. The decks are already awash. If she capsizes, she threatens to drag her neighbours with her to the bottom. So urgent action is needed. Either the overseers drive the convicts to row in unison, or the flagship will send a boarding party to help them. Better still, they could hand over the galley to the crew, and let them row as volunteers. Best of all, if the Soviet admiral would only agree to cut his losses, he could axe the chain, and set the 'Poland' free.

For Poland is indeed a society divided against itself. The overseers and the galley-slaves, the bureaucrats and the common people, may live on the same boat; but they pull in opposite directions. So long as they stay divided, their ship will never sail smoothly.

Two Nations

It is curious to note that Karl Marx's basic idea (of social conflict arising from the division of society into two opposed elements, the oppressors and the oppressed) was first popularized in the novel *Coningsby,* published in 1844 by Benjamin Disraeli. Disraeli called the phenomenon 'the two nations'. Twenty years later, as Conservative Prime Minister of Great Britain at the time when Marx was still working on *Das Kapital* in the Reading Room of the British Museum, Disraeli attacked the class-ridden society of his day by launching universal male suffrage and the beginnings of modern British democracy. It is also curious to note, after a century of Progress, that the self-avowed disciples of Karl Marx in Eastern Europe have succeeded in building a society which is no less divided against itself than that of Disraeli's Victorian England. Of course, one might argue that Leninism is not compatible with Marxism, or that Marxist-Leninists are not proper Marxists; and one can debate whether or not the exact relationship of the communist élite to the means of production permits them to be labelled a true 'ruling class' in the Marxian sense. That is for Marxists to decide. But it is undeniable that what Milovan Djilas named the 'New Class', and what others have called 'The Bureaucratic Leviathan', constitutes the most characteristic feature of the supposedly classless societies of Eastern Europe.[5] In Djilas's own country, Yugoslavia, or in the USSR, where communist regimes *do* enjoy a measure of popular support, the existence of these two nations, the bureaucrats and the subjects of the bureaucrats, provides food for thought. In Poland, where the regime has virtually no legitimacy, it is the source of common oppression.

For the first thing which Poles have had to realize in recent years is that the agents of their oppression today are not weird-looking foreigners wearing a *pickelhelm* or a Tartar cap. The oppressors are Poles like themselves, instantly recognizable by their dress, their manner, and their jargon, but men and women in the main part from their own towns and villages, from their own families. The line which divides the oppressor from the oppressed runs through the blood and bone of Polish society, and often enough, in the event of divided loyalties, through the heart and soul of an individual person. One of the principal products of a generation of Communism is this division between the 'power' (*wladza*) and 'society' (*spoleczeństwo*), between the bosses and the people, between 'them' and 'us'.

In the early days after the war, the new Establishment was cobbled together from the most variegated elements. There were a few hundred survivors of the pre-war Polish Communist Party, among them Gomułka, who had the good fortunate to be in a Polish prison during Stalin's purge of the KPP. More numerous were Soviet citizens of Polish origin, former employees of various Soviet agencies. Among these were Bolesław Bierut—not his original name—who had headed the Polish section of the OGPU and had worked for Comintern; Jakub Berman; Stanisław Radkiewicz, Beria's deputy in Poland; Aleksander Zawadzki, Bierut's successor as Polish President, who, as an 'unfrocked' Colonel of the NKVD, had once served sentence in the Oneglag prison camp in northern Russia; Karol Świerczewski (pseudonym 'Walter'), a Red Army General of Polish origin who had fought in the Spanish Civil War; and Wanda Wasilewska, daughter of a prominent pre-war Polish politician and by 1944 wife of a sometime Commissar for Foreign Affairs of the Ukrainian

SSR. There were also Polish communists brought in from the West, intellectuals like Oscar Lange from America, or Polish workers active in the European Resistance, like Edward Gierek. Most numerous of all, however, were the 'acting Poles', the so-called *POPy* (Persons fulfilling the duties of Poles), mainly Russians or Ukrainians, who were dressed in Polish uniforms and drafted into Poland in their thousands. It was a source of ribald humour when an officer or a manager, officially presented as an active 'Polish patriot', proved incapable of speaking grammatical Polish. Then there were the Poles recruited and trained from the vast pool of wartime refugees and deportees in the USSR. Some, like Wojciech Jaruzelski, joined the military: others undertook civilian careers. Here, the largest single group was made up of Polish Jews, who were judged unlikely to sympathize with the Polish population at large, and who were drafted in force into the security organs. They were the principal cause of later anti-Semitic tendencies within the Party. Last of all, there was the large number of representative figure-heads, chosen for their names or for their prestigious connections, real or invented, with pre-war bodies. Edward Osóbka-Morawski had left the Polish Socialist Party during the war, to form a breakaway pro-communist faction, the RPPS. Michał Rola-Żymierski, a pre-war legionnaire and General who had studied at the École de Guerre in Paris, had been cashiered on charges of graft. General Zygmunt Berling, a lieutenant-colonel of the Polish Army before the war, was the only senior serving Polish officer to accept wartime service under Soviet command. Andrzej Witos, the half-brother of the leader of the pre-war Peasant Movement, had left that movement in 1928. Bolesław Piasecki had been head of the pre-war Fascist 'Falanga'. Dr Emil Sommerstein had been a Zionist deputy to the Sejm. These men, hardly any of whom had a respectable political pedigree in Poland, formed the vanguard of the new élite. It was not an auspicious beginning.

Naturally, in the course of four decades, the original vanguard was expanded out of all proportion by local recruitment. Party membership reached one million in 1948, the year of the PZPR's formation, and almost three million in 1980, or about 12 per cent of the adult population. The recruits came overwhelmingly from the ambitious sons and daughters of an indigent peasantry, from families with no previous political orientation. For them, the Party provided the chance of education and of rapid social advancement—the chance, in fact, to cease being peasants. Recruitment from the industrial working class was also high during the 1950s, but has been gradually falling ever since. Recruitment from the intelligentsia, as distinct from internal recruitment from within the families of educated Party members, has always been marginal. In recent years, the tendency of the Party to supply its own recruits has markedly increased, deepening the gulf between the élite and society as a whole, and moving towards the creation of a self-perpetuating ruling caste. It is true that the sons and daughters of high officials, sickened by their elders' corruption and cynicism, have also supplied a steady flow of principled dissidents; but it is none the less true, by virtue of their parents' status, that they have had access to the best education, the most comfortable material conditions, and the most attractive and promising careers.

Not surprisingly, the nature of the communist system feeds the mechanisms of negative selection. Firstly, since the basic requirement of all recruits is unquestioning subservience to Party discipline, it follows that enterprising, imaginative, or eccentric personalities are disadvantaged from the start. Even if they join the Party, they are unlikely to make much headway. Secondly, since the dogmas of official ideology cannot be challenged by junior comrades, there is little place for the open, intellectual, or enquiring mind. Excessive cleverness is liable to be rewarded by expulsion. Thirdly, since the Party's system of promotion is based on the patronage of the higher organs over the lower, advancement depends not on one's devotion to the Party's finer principles but more on ingratiating oneself with the immediate whims of a superior boss. Scruples tend to keep one chained to the lower rungs of the ladder. Yet that is not the whole story. It would be absurd to suggest that a body of some three million educated men and women could be entirely devoid of intelligence. Intelligent comrades *do* occur, and they *do* gain promotion; but they can only advance by concealing their personal views, their criticisms of the system, and their contempt for less gifted colleagues. In other words, the aspiring comrade may be intelligent or honest, but not both. Add to that the specific conditions in Poland, where membership of the communist party carries the mark of social stigma, and yet another barrier emerges—the barrier of social sensitivity. There is no point in joining the Party if one is going to pay too much heed to the feelings of one's relatives and friends. All in all, the resulting picture is extremely bleak. The workings of negative selection over a whole generation have resulted in a nation governed by its most unworthy elements. It is probably a simplification to say that the political Establishment in Poland consists of a leadership drawn from dishonest opportunists and impervious scoundrels, and a membership marked by lack of imagination, stupidity, and toadyism; or that the rest of Polish society is unfailingly creative, brilliant, scrupulous, honest, and socially alert. That is surely an exaggeration. Another characteristic of the communist machine is its inefficiency, and one cannot guarantee that it will produce the type of leaders which it clearly deserves. But this much is incontravertible. The average level of culture, intelligence, and probity in the Polish communist Establishment lies far below standards prevailing elsewhere amongst educated Poles in general—in the Church, in the arts and sciences, or in the professions. It is no mean reproach even to democratic countries that the best talents do not always seem to be reproduced in a nation's leaders. But for a nation to be ruled by men of inferior calibre in perpetuity, and without hope of redress, is a living insult.

The small band of intellectuals who joined the communist movement did not flourish for long before falling foul of their political masters. In the early years after the War, a number of Marxist-Leninist enthusiasts took their chance, and set about their self-appointed task of revolutionizing Polish cultural and economic life. Oskar Lange and his disciples in Economics; Adam Schaff and the brilliant young Leszek Kołakowski in Philosophy; Stanisław Arnold and Celina Bobińska in History; Stefan Żółkiewski, Pawel Hoffman, Jan Kott, Mieczysław Jastrun, Kazimierz Brandys, and Adam Ważyk in Literary Studies; Roman Werfel and Jerzy Borejsza in the realm of cultural bureaucracy, went about the business of applying the

new ideology to Polish conditions. They realized that they
represented a tiny minority in educated circles as a whole; but
they felt that they represented the future. They included
people who were capable of attending cultural committee
meetings with an ode to Stalin in one hand and a symbolic
revolver in the other. They probably faced the greatest
challenge in the literary field, since Polish Literature was the
most developed branch of the national culture; and Żółkiewski's journal, *Kuźnica* (The Smithy), dating from 1945,
was the flagship of the new trend. The journal's name, which
was taken from that of Hugo Kołłątaj's circle during the
Polish Enlightenment, revealed that its contributors saw
themselves as a select, rationalist élite fighting against the
remnants of reactionary idealism and clerical fantacism. They
were the apostles of a new brand of communist Positivism (see
p. 357–8), fervently opposed to Romantic patriotism, and
convinced that social and political progress depended on
rebuilding Polish culture from its foundations. Jan Kott's
tract *Mitologia a realizm* (Mythology and Realism, 1946) laid
down the guide-lines for making the Marxist 'Laws of History'
the basis for all literary and cultural values. Żółkiewski,
promoted to head the Party's Department of Culture, founded
the influential Institute of Literary Research (IBL) in 1948,
and in 1957 served as the first editor of *Polityka*. Ignoring the
thinly disguised hostility of the traditional Polish intelligentsia, they none the less persisted with their *rewolucja łagodna*,
their 'Gentle Revolution', which was supposed to transform
Polish attitudes by force of persuasion and example. In effect,
by proclaiming the first priority of 'maintaining a correct
political stance towards present reality', they quickly lost
public interest, and turned themselves into mere sounding-
boards for Party policy. They also found that the Party
leadership was suspicious of their experiments and bright
ideas. Those of them who tried to uphold an independent line
found themselves denounced and expelled as 'revisionist'
renegades. The Party did not practise gratitude. One by one,
they fell from favour, left the country, or joined the growing
ranks of the dissidents. In the span of twenty years, the
communist movement in Poland alienated almost all the
prominent intellectuals who had originally tried to serve it.

Despite the Party's open adherence to the theory of the 'Dictatorship of the Proletariat', the central institution of that dictatorship, the *nomenklatura,* remains strictly secret.[6] In fact, in terms of the Polish Constitution, which guarantees the equality of citizens, it is strictly illegal. As reorganized in 1972, the Polish *nomenklatura* is operated by the cadres department of the central Party Secretariat, and consists of two separate lists—one, a list of reserved posts in the state and party bureaucracies, the other, a list of people exclusively entitled to fill those posts. The former is known, and has been published outside Poland; the latter has never been revealed, but it is thought to contain between two and three hundred thousand names from every conceivable walk of life. These are the dictators, the self-appointed bureaucrats who collectively control the means of production, the agencies of coercion, and the media of information, of the entire country. In practice, since they appoint the key secretaries of the Party's regional, city, and rural committees, they also control the corresponding *nomenklatura* lists of the lower levels. Although one rightly tends to think of the *nomenklatura* as a magic circle of top bosses, there is not a cleaning superviser or a park keeper in the land whose job, directly or indirectly, does not fall within its purview. Membership of the magic circle carries important privileges—higher salaries, preferential pensions, special identity cards, access to education, private Party health clinics, holiday homes, car pools, luxurious family housing, foreign travel, and foreign currency, and most lucratively, the ability to exact favours with impunity. According to rules published in the *Dziennik Ustaw* (Law Calendar) of 1972, many of these privileges were invested not just in the incumbents themselves but in their spouses and relatives.

Any description of the communist Establishment, however, must not be confined to the Party members *per se*; and it must also take account of numerous factions. In the notorious 'non-party' sector, it must be deemed to include the Party's immediate allies in the Front of National Unity (FJN), the leaders of the SD and the ZSL; the leaders of the Party-sponsored, non-Party social organizations such as the *Liga Kobiet* (Women's League), the ex-combatants' League of Fighters for Freedom and Democracy (ZBOWID), or the

PAX Organization of progressive Catholics; a wide range of non-party professors, specialists, and cultural figures, who owe their positions to the Party in return for services rendered; and, if President Bierut can be emulated, a number of well-camouflaged Soviet officials, who can stay hidden as non-party 'sleepers' until their country needs them. Within the political arena, the patronage groups probably carry more weight than the more obvious institutional interests or the shifting membership of ideological centres. Such is the system, that men who owe their careers to the patronage of a particular leader—Gomułka, Gierek, and now Jaruzelski, or perhaps to a particular regional boss or Politburo member, have the most reason to stick together. Until the emergence of the military dictatorship in 1981, ambitious members of the Armed Services or the Security organs were as likely to be competing for favours as to be acting in concert. With the imposition of Party discipline in the wake of each major crisis, the ideological centre associated with each of the losing factions would tend to be pruned. Yet, despite the periodic prunings certain tendencies have succeeded in preserving separate identities. The Polish Stalinists, once associated with the Natolin faction of 1956 and more recently with the Katowice Forum or the journal *Rzeczywistość*(Reality), have always commanded a following. Their fellow radicals, the communist Nationalists, who originated with the wartime Partisan Faction of General Moczar, made their abortive bid for power in 1968. They have been responsible for repeated anti-Semitic campaigns within the Party—even when no significant number of Jews remained; and have now surfaced once again in the Patriotic Association *Grunwald*. Whilst sharing the Stalinists' dogmatic version of Marxism-Leninism, they tend to be covertly anti-Soviet, pressing above all for a Polish Party for Polish communists. Their support lies among the faceless lower ranks, whose virulent resentments they foster. In contrast, the milder, reforming, intellectual factions, (who are often erroneously dubbed 'liberals' in the West) can conveniently be divided into reformers of phoney or of genuine stamp. The former, who are careful not to overstep the bounds of Party discipline, first emerged in the shade of Gomułka's 'October', and are led by arch-trimmers best represented at present by Mieczysław Rakowski, Vice-Premier and for twenty-five years editor of *Polityka*. The latter, the guardians of the comrades' guilty conscience, charge the Party with abandoning its principles. In the 1960s they included rebels such as Kuroń and Modzelewski. Władysław Bieńkowski, sometime Minister of Education, Stefan Bratkowski, Chairman of the Union of Journalists until recently, and the Experience and the Future Group (DiP) have assumed similar positions over recent years. They usually pay for their temerity with expulsion.

The common attitudes of this large and diverse Establishment, therefore, centre less on politics in the narrow sense than on social issues. Firstly, they all insist on their absolute right to govern. They behave as if the state, and all its inhabitants, were their private property. When in 1981 the public debate on the nature of the 'leading role' of the Party called the *nomenklatura* into question, an official spokesman characteristically declared that 'there is no room for discussion on this point'. Secondly, they instinctively close ranks in face of any outside threat. Although they can fight vituperously among themselves, and conduct purges, and turn on comrades who fail to conform, they absolutely refuse to allow any independent inquiry into their affairs. Explanations of past mistakes are always attributed to the shortcomings of individuals, never to the rottenness of the system as a whole. Going on past form, the various inquiries and tribunals concerning the admitted crimes and corruption of the Gierek leadership may result in some specific prosecutions but not in any general conclusions. Thirdly, they treat the individual citizen with unconscious, unstinting contempt. The idea that the Party's deliberations should be governed by the wishes and aspirations of ordinary people strikes them as bizarre. For, as Rakowski revealed in one of his *port-mortem* interviews after the December coup, SOLIDARITY's fundamental mistake was to imagine that it could unseat the Party. To the likes of Rakowski, Polish society is a horse, an animal to be mounted and ridden; and the Party is the rider. (It was Stalin's own metaphor.) Fourthly, they have adopted a life-style which apes the habits of the old ruling class, and sets them apart from the people in general. They wear slightly old-fashioned

executive suits reminiscent of ageing Western businessmen;
they speak to each other as *Wy* (You), and to the public in
jargon-ridden clichés; they are driven around by chauffeurs in
private limousines with tinted glass and lace curtains; and
their favourite pastime is hunting—hunting in private Party-
owned forests and reserves. Fifthly, they are ashamed of
themselves. They conduct their business behind closed doors;
they transmit their orders by telephone, leaving no trace in the
files; they keep the files hidden behind the stifling walls of the
Censorship; and they have never had the nerve to make their
privileges legal. As Bieńkowski has been forced to admit, they
are agents working 'in a foreign environment'; and in their
heart of hearts, they know it. It must put a monumental strain
on their nerves.

Now, since December 1981, the traditional communist
Establishment has been pushed aside by a small military
residue in their midst who had not lost the will to act. They
must be angered at the reminder of their own failure, yet
relieved to be saved from the people's revenge. They are
unlikely to reassert themselves in the near future against their
new masters, and would be well advised to ponder the entry in
the *Great Polish Encylopaedia* under the entry *nomenklator;*

A slave in ancient Rome . . . who had the duty to remind his master
of the names of persons with whom to exchange greetings. It was
particularly important in office-hunting in the Republican period. . . .

More to the point, perhaps, they should ponder the origin of
the word *nomenklatura* in Polish usage. It is a Latin term,
referring to the lists of named properties of the great feudal
magnates, and by extension to the tenants who possessed those
properties.[7] Here one can see the true cultural ancestry of
modern communist society. Anything further removed from
socialism, as the rest of the world imagines it, would be hard to
conceive. The Party bosses treat the state as their private
property, in the manner of medieval barons; and they treat
the common citizens as the chattels of their fief. The gulf
between the ruling élite and the masses is wide, and getting
wider. The existence of the 'two nations' is already a reality.

*   *   *   *   *

The emotional consequences of this social schism are far-reaching indeed. One sociologist has likened Polish society to a married couple which is condemned to go on living in the same house even after being divorced. Some sort of practical arrangement, or at least a truce, is essential if they are to avoid the round of endless rows and daily hell. The picture is convincing, until one wonders by what logic they must inevitably go on living together. If their own interests are to be considered, one might reasonably consider a separation. After all, their forced marriage was never a union of true love in the first place. To insist on indefinite cohabitation, irrespective of human feelings, is to invite an eventual tragedy.

Yet, saddled with its ruling Establishment, Polish society has reacted with extraordinary restraint. Although violence may yet be the response of a desperate people to the violence of the authorities, so far the thirty-three million have not turned in anger on the three million bureaucrats in their midst. Despite recurrent clashes—in 1956, 1968, 1970, 1976, and 1980-1—the toll of victims has probably not exceeded five or six hundred in thirty-six years:which is deplorable, but by standards elsewhere in the world, not excessive. On this front, if anyone wants to repeat the hoary slander of Poles being a nation of trouble-makers bent on political suicide, let them examine the record. Naturally, there have been good reasons for the post-war generation's restraint. The Church's influence on the masses is strong; and the Church has consistently preached the path of spiritual suffering in preference to that of revenge. Among the educated classes, which have grown far more numerous, there is the traditional solace of the national literature, with its ready-made dream world for willing escapees; and there is the vibrant world of the Polish arts—from an avantgarde theatre to a musical scene of great competence and variety. More particularly, the post-war years have been crammed with upheavals of every sort. Even if Poland had led a quiet existence, it would have taken decades to recover from the agonies and blood-letting of the Second World War (see Chapter II); but the survivors were granted no respite to settle down quickly. The resettlement schemes of 1945-7 threw millions into cities and provinces in which they were total strangers. The massive industrialization projects of the Six-Year Plan of 1950–5 and subsequent Five-Year Plans brought still more millions of men and women flooding into the new towns and factories from the countryside. In the quarter century from 1945, an overwhelmingly rural, agrarian society was transformed into a predominantly urban one—52 per cent by 1971; and that, at a time when the unprecedented post-war birth-rate, reaching 30.7 per thousand in 1950, filled Polish homes with babies. In other words, the typical Polish family of the 1950s and 1960s consisted of two young parents, both of them working long hours for a pittance, struggling without support of grandparents to rear two or three young children in the cramped and primitive accommodation of a half-finished housing estate, in a new town or suburb to which they were only party acclimatized. This was not the setting for complaints and rebellion, but for a heroic battle to survive. Only in the 1970s, when the Recovered Territories had been repopulated, when the birth-rate and the march to the towns had decelerated, and when rising wages brought an interval of relative prosperity, could the post-war generation begin to reflect on its predicament. Only at the very end of the period, when the economic crisis set in with a vengeance, could it realize how many of its sacrifices had been in vain.

One must also recognize the overpowering sense of helpless dependence which ordinary men and women feel towards the communist state and its Party bosses. In all the main sectors of employment, the communist state is a monopoly employer. It owns all production enterprises, all services, all transport, all the administrative offices. What is worse, the same Party bosses who run the places of employment also control the provision of housing and education: the pension and insurance schemes and other social services; the police, who supervise obligatory registration; and the courts, where in theory any doubtful cases may be tried. Against this massive concentration of social power, the individual worker has little chance of self-defence. In the bad old days before the War, when evil squires and black-hearted mill owners exercised similar monopolies within their particular localities, the disheartened worker could at least move on, and seek employment elsewhere. Nowadays, he does not even possess that option. For in the next town, in the next province, he would find the same Party organization, the same Party-run unions, the same Militia keeping the same sort of records of domicile, employment, and offences. In short, he must bend his neck to the Party authorities at every turn, or risk being deprived, not just of his livelihood, but of all other social benefits. For crossing his foreman, or displeasing his director, he and his family can be turned into virtual outlaws overnight. Once he is 'handed his cards', or as the Polish expression has it, given his *wilczy bilet,* his 'wolf's ticket'; he is free to roam the woods like a hunted animal. He is a pariah. The number of occupations open to self-employment in Poland is extremely limited. There are a few specialized craftsmen—such as watchmakers or car mechanics; there are a few retail outlets, such as small private restaurants and souvenir stalls; there are private artists—writers, painters, sculptors, musicians; and there are the famous *badylarze* or 'market gardeners', who have become ostentatiously prosperous in recent years. Apart from that, if one seeks independence, one has little choice but to enter holy orders or to start farming. Yet even on his own farm, the peasant lives at the mercy of the state land registrar, the state price commission, the state taxman, the manager of the state-run machinery depot, and the state-run village store. Perhaps the best-placed class are the so-called *chlopo-robotnicy,* the 'peasant-workers' who contrive to keep the family plot whilst holding down a job in a factory. Many such families living on the fringe of the great industrial regions, have the best of both worlds—a high cash income all the year round, a cheap supply of home-grown food, and an independent base. They are prosperous and relatively secure.

In the last resort, however, no one in communist society escapes the tyranny of the inconvertible currency. Those same Party planners who fix both incomes and prices, and hence the standard of living, have also decreed that no Polish money shall circulate outside the country or be freely exchanged. The State authorities buy the workers' labour for soft currency, for zlotys; but are free to sell the fruits of that labour on the world market for hard currency—for dollars, DM, sterling, or yen. In this way they determine not just the official rate of exchange, which can be endlessly manipulated, but also the real costs of labour. The Silesian miner whose coal is exported to West Germany for Deutsche Marks is not paid in money which can be freely converted into that currency. Even if he toils for fifty years, he will never have the means to order a Volkswagen from Germany in return for digging the Germans' coal. Polish workers are paid in a state currency which can only be spent on goods that are produced, priced, and distributed by the State. In short, they are the victims of a massive deception, where workers are paid not in real money, but in tokens on the company store. According to the textbooks, the 'truck system' was one of the most vicious abuses of primitive Capitalism. In England, it was denounced as an unprincipled form of exploitation, and was abolished in Parliament by the Truck Act of 1831. It is now a mainstay of the wage policies of the communist states. When Silesian miners under SOLIDAR-ITY dared to demand that their wages be paid in dollars, not złotys, they were making a very practical suggestion. But they were also challenging the foundations of a system which exploits its dependent workers in almost every detail.

Even so, SOLIDARITY did not choose to gain its ends by sudden or drastic means. It saw itself as a 'self-limiting revolution' from the start, fully responsive to the constraints of Poland's special political situation. It steered clear of Soviet interests, ensuring, for instance, that the Soviet Union's lines of communication to East Germany were never once inter-rupted. It accepted the Party's 'leading role' within the framework of the initial Agreement. After the collapse of the old Central Council of Trade Unions (CRZZ) in December 1980, it made no effort to create a similar monopoly position for itself, allowing other Party-dominated Industrial Unions (BZZ) and Autonomous Unions (ZZA) to set themselves up in competition with it. Similarly, in the student world, the new pro-SOLIDARITY Independent Student Association (NZS) operated alongside the official and formerly monopolistic SZSP. Rural SOLIDARITY operated alongside smaller, rival organizations in the countryside. At first SOLIDARITY showed no interest in the crucial self-management issue, which did not feature in the twenty-one points agreed at Gdańsk. Indeed it was a plan for economic reform from the government which in January 1981 produced the earliest self-management proposals. Predictably, these called for workers' 'participation' rather than for workers' control. At this juncture, SOLIDARITY did not care to respond. But, in March, the spontaneous formation of *rady pracownicze* (employees' councils) in major factories and of a separate *Sieć* or Network of SOLIDARITY's local factory organizations pushed the matter forward; and in May, SOLIDARITY's national executive adopted the concept of Workers' Self-Management in principle. As local sparring continued, and in the absence of any overall compromise, the Party's retreat accelerated, and SOLIDARITY found itself drawn in spite of itself on to the sacred territory of the *nomenklatura*. In the Spring, free elections in the Universities returned a crop of non-Party rectors and deans. In Bielsko-Biała, a corrupt *Wojewoda* (Provincial Governor) was driven out by a concerted unofficial strike. In July, the whole staff of Polish Airlines (LOT), including the Party organization within it, went on strike in protest against their Ministry's imposition of an Air Force officer over their constitutionally elected president. In August, a referendum at the giant Katowice Steelworks voted to oust a high-handed director who had closed down the works newspaper. In October, the Ponar Factory at Żywiec set an ominous precedent by voting to remove the entire Party organization from the factory premises. Yet there was still no lead from the Government. The diehards in the Party were insisting on everything or nothing, and were able to block any concessions or any clear statement of an official policy. The rising chaos suited their purposes very well. It gave cover to the Coup, whose preparations advanced with every day. And SOLIDARITY, driven to desperation, never once resorted to violence.

The Church, too, eagerly sought compromise. Cardinal Wyszyński welcomed the birth of SOLIDARITY and gave it his blessing; but he also helped the Party in its hour of distress. In the tense days of August 1980, after Party Secretary Gierek's appeals had fallen on deaf ears, it was the measured tones of the Primate which calmed the people. After this crucial broadcast, the Church was granted its long-standing request to hold a weekly televised Mass—a request consistently blocked by the Party since the inception of the television service in 1956. (SOLIDARITY's similar request for its own weekly television programme was never conceded.) The Church's connections with SOLIDARITY were very close. Wałęsa himself is demonstratively Catholic in all his actions. He signed the Gdańsk Agreement with a huge pen topped with the picture of Pope John Paul. His immediate advisers included many prominent Catholics like Tadeusz Mazowiecki, sometime editor of the Catholic journal, *Więź* (The Link) who edited the Union's own weekly, *Tygodnik Solidarność*. He paid extravagant homage to the Pope, during a much publicized visit to Rome in January 1981. At the same time, the Church took care to keep its lines open with the Party. It is highly significant that the Pope adopted the catchword of 'Odnowa' (Renewal) which at that juncture was the Party's main slogan. Cardinal Wyszyński's successor, Józef Glemp, has pursued the same aims, though not always with the same sureness of touch. Glemp's initial response to the December Coup, which some people thought to sound like a plea for peace at any price, has been rephrased in subsequent declarations. In this, the Primate's personal consultations with the Pope, and with the Pope's successor at Cracow, Cardinal Franciszek Macharski, have no doubt served to redress the balance. The Church longs for social harmony and reconciliation. It is opposed to any idea of overthrowing the state by force. But as the guardian of the nation's conscience it could not give its seal of approval to a regime which exploited the people so cynically before 1980, and attacked them so brutally in December.

In the course of 1980–1, a yawning gulf was revealed between the communist Establishment and society at large on every major issue that was aired. The Party's half-hearted atheism jarred against the people's Catholic piety; its Leninist autocracy against the spontaneously chaotic democracy of SOLIDARITY's meetings. Its view of education, as a training ground for obedient robots, was challenged by demands for unshackled knowledge and the development of the whole person. Its view of Polish History as the heroic march of the working class towards the inevitable creation of the People's Republic contrasted with the public's awareness of successive disasters and oppressions. The Party media were still turning out old war films and hackneyed books on the people's struggle against Fascism; the people were listening in their tens of thousands to SOLIDARITY-sponsored lectures on all the things they had a right to hear—the Miracle of the Vistula, Józef Piłsudski, the Katyn Massacre, the Warsaw Rising. Its view of the Arts as a vehicle for official culture; its view of sport, as a means for proving the superiority of 'Socialism'; its view of tourism and foreign travel as group activities for officially approved purposes—all these bore no resemblance to society's ideas of free expression. On almost every score, the Party's claims were shown to be *pozorny* (superficial): what the people wanted was something *autentyczny* (genuine). The Party claimed to be 'democratic', 'socialist', and 'patriotic'; and to be made up from the 'best representatives of the working class'. What the people were demanding was genuine democracy, genuine socialism, genuine patriotism, and some genuine representation.

In these conflicts, the moral dimensions of Poland's tragedy were made fully evident. It is not the case that Poles are inherently more sensitive to moral issues than other nations: still less that their conduct is somehow morally superior. Far from it. If anything, the stresses and strains of life in Poland produce a greater incidence of moral failings, petty crime, and social evils than in more fortunate lands. But that is simply to state the problem. The citizens of a country, in which the difference between the moral values held by society and those propagated by a monopoly state is so extreme, are bound to suffer from extreme moral pressures. In a communist state, it takes a very strong character to stay loyal to one's friends and upbringing at the expense of one's career, to refrain from the pilfering of state property (in which Party officials set such a fine example), or to resist the accepted norms of communal drinking and alcoholism. At every turn, the temptation is there is to gain advancement by informing on one's colleagues, to overcome the housing shortage by bribing the foreman of the state building-yard, or to surrender to despair with a bottle of *wódka*. Even Poland's admirers must admit that all minor forms of treachery, corruption, and social irresponsibility are rife. In such a debilitating atmosphere, it is not easy for an honest person to know where his loyalties should lie. If a husband wishes to provide better conditions for his family, he knows that he can do so by joining the Party and forgetting everything that his pious mother told him about his soul and his conscience. If a wife wants to help her husband, she knows where to ingratiate herself. If teachers want to keep their jobs, they often have to impart information which they know to be untrue, or to suppress what they know. If students wish to pass their exams, they must limit their remarks to what the examiners are empowered to accept. If a worker feels inclined to produce anything more than the minimum required, he has to accept that the benefit will accrue not to himself but to the foreman or the factory manager. If the Party functionary has genuinely joined the movement in order to serve his fellow men and the ideals of socialism, he must undertake to abandon all expression of those ideals in the interests of Party discipline. What a cruel world! And whom is one to believe? Under some dictatorships, where all sources of information are successfully controlled or where a social consensus has been established, people do not suffer so much from the agony of conflicting authorities. But in Poland, where the Church says one thing and the State the other; where one's grandmother inevitably contradicts one's teacher; and where parents conceal their employer's views from their children—every man and woman is reminded of right and wrong much more frequently and much more forcefully. Because of their country's tragic history, Poles face more moral choices more acutely not only in comparison to citizens of democratic countries—who are generally left to their own damnation— but also to their counterparts in other communist countries. Poland's moral agony derives less from the communist dictatorship in itself, than from the fact that the Soviet brand of Communism is designed to tear Poland away from all its most cherished values and traditions. That, no doubt, is why Poland has produced a rich crop of grafters and scoundrels together with some of the finest men and women one might ever hope to meet.

The gamut of emotions invoked by Poland's tragedy runs from anger and frustration to cynicism and despair. Poles are obliged to watch their country torn apart for no good reason, to see their hopes repeatedly dashed. They find themselves governed by disreputable leaders. They live in growing poverty in spite of their rich human and material resources. They stand in line for hours for their daily bread. After four decades of back-breaking reconstruction, they see their country bankrupt. Once again, they have to suffer the jibes about the *polnische Wirtschaft,* the chaotic Polish economy, and wonder if they really are so congenitally incompetent as their super-efficient German neighbours would like to maintain. They suffer the indignity of receiving foreign charity, like the poorest countries of Asia and Africa, and worst of all, they are blamed for it all themselves. To the underlying question of why Poland must bear such indignities, the only possible answer is that the interest of the Soviet Union requires her to do so. The essence of Poland's modern experience is humiliation.

CHAPTER II

THE LEGACY OF DEFEAT

Poland's Wartime Experience, 1939–1947

2,078 Days and More

In those vast chains of events which took the Second World
War into every continent of the globe except Antarctica, it
was easy to lose sight of the War's Polish overture. British
soldiers fighting in the North African desert and the jungles of
Burma, American marines on the heights of Iwo Jima, or
Russians in the rubble of Stalingrad, can hardly have
imagined that they were fighting, among other things, over
the fate of Poland. But Poland was the first link in the first
chain; and the issue of Polish independence was never
dropped from Allied war aims. Of course, after the brief Polish
Campaign of September 1939, the ambitions of the Axis
Powers spread ever wider into the new war zones of Western
Europe, the Mediterranean, and South-East Asia. After the
formation in 1941 of the Grand Coalition of Britain, the USA,
and the USSR, attention centred on the titanic contests in
Russia and in the western Pacific. For the Allied Powers as a
whole, the main issue of the War by now was to force the
unconditional surrender of Nazi Germany and of Imperial
Japan. For the Poles, however, the main issue remained that
of their own country's future. For nearly six years, Poles
fought and died and waited in the hope that, from the welter
of competing claims and interests, they would regain that
same independent Republic so brutally destroyed at the
outbreak of War in 1939.

Wartime in Poland lasted longer than for any other country in Europe (except Germany). Between the commencement of the Nazi attack at dawn on 1 September 1939 and the final capitulation of the Nazi Reich on VE Day, 9 May 1945, there stretched over two thousand days of violence and suffering. In proportion to its size, Poland incurred far more damage and casualties than any country on earth.

The loss of over six million Polish citizens from a total population in 1939 of thirty-five millions represented a casualty rate of 18 per cent, compared with 0.2 per cent in the USA, 0.9 per cent in Great Britain, 2.5 per cent in Japan, 7.4 per cent in Germany, 11.1 per cent in Yugoslavia, and 11.2 per cent in the USSR. Poland became the killing-ground of Europe, the new Golgotha. Yet even in 1945 peace was not fully restored. Fighting in the backwoods continued for a further two years. The final shot of the aftermath of war was not fired in Poland until the summer of 1947.

During all this long agony, Poland's predicament was principally determined by the state of relations between her two mighty neighbours. When Germany held the upper hand over Russia, Poland fell under Nazi sway. When Russia held the upper hand over Germany, Poland fell under Soviet sway. When Germany and Russia agreed to collaborate, as happened during the first two years of the war, Poland fell under a double tyranny.

1 The Era of the Nazi–Soviet Pact, 1939–41

The outbreak of war was made possible by a secret protocol of the Pact of Non-Agression between the Nazi Reich and the Soviet Union, signed in Moscow by Ribbentrop and Molotov on 23 August 1939. By this protocol, the two contracting parties envisaged a joint attack on Poland and the Baltic States, and the division of their territory between them.[1] Without the assurance of Soviet collusion, the *Wehrmacht* could not have risked a unilateral attack on Poland. Whatever his motives at the time, Stalin was no less responsible for the outbreak of war than Hitler.

The September Campaign in Poland was fierce, but brief. Isolated from the direct assistance of their French and British

allies; surrounded on three sides, by German forces in East
Prussia and Slovakia as well as on the western frontier; and
vastly outmatched in manpower and equipment, the Polish
Army had little hope of victory. Also threatened, as it proved,
by the Soviet Red Army in the East, it had little chance even
of protracted resistance. Even so, the Polish forces performed
well. They exceeded their original objective, which was to
hold the *Wehrmacht* in check for fourteen days until France
could mobilize her divisions on the Maginot Line and launch
an invasion of the Rhineland. In many instances, as in the fort
of Westerplatte near Danzig, in the nineteen-day siege of
Warsaw, or in the rearguard battle of Kutno, they fought with
skill and heroism. Colourful stories about sabre-swinging
cavalrymen charging the steel hulls of Panzer tanks hardly do
justice to the record. The Poles inflicted over 50,000 casualties
on the *Wehrmacht*, and were still fighting hard when the entry
of the Russians on 17 September sealed their fate. Their
performance was certainly more creditable than that of the
British and French forces when they in their turn faced the
German *Blitzkrieg* eight months later. Meanwhile, in September, the Western Allies had not fired a shot in Poland's
defence. The last Polish unit in the field capitulated at Kock
on 6 October.

As a result of the September Campaign, the whole of
Poland passed under the occupation of Nazi and of Soviet
forces. The Polish Government and High Command took
refuge in Romania, and on 30 September, a new Government was constituted abroad under General Sikorski, first in
France, and later in England. On the western side of the
Nazi–Soviet demarcation line along the Bug and the San, the
Germans established a 'General Government' with its headquarters in Cracow. Many districts of pre-war Poland,
including Suwałki, West Prussia, Wielkopolska, and Upper
Silesia were directly incorporated into the Reich. On the
eastern side of the demarcation line, in 'western Byelorussia'
and 'western Ukraine', the Soviet authorities staged bogus
plebiscites to demonstrate the people's wish for annexation
into the USSR. The district of Wilno (Vilnius) was gener-
ously handed to Lithuania in anticipation of the Soviet
Army's attack on that country eight months later. Poland

was neatly partitioned. In the opinion of its conquerors, so ably expressed by the Soviet Foreign Commissar, Molotov, 'it had ceased to exist'. The arrangements were crowned by the German–Soviet Treaty of Friendship of 28 September 1939, which also provided for the joint action against the expected Polish Resistance.[2]

In this era of close Nazi–Soviet collaboration, both partners pursued similar policies towards their Polish charges. Both sides were guilty of atrocities. The Germans shot 20,000 civilian hostages in Bydgoszcz alone, and burned synagogues; the Russians massacred prisoners in the gaol of Vinnitsa. Both sides subjected the population to police screening and registration, segregating it into descending categories of undesirability. The Gestapo followed racial guide-lines, consigning some two million Polish Jews to closed *reservaten* or ghettoes, and dividing the Aryan population into *Reichsdeutsch* (German citizens born in the Reich), *Volksdeutsch* (German nationals), and *nichtdeutsch* (everyone else). In the Extraordinary Pacification Campaign *(A Baktion)* of 1940 some 15,000 Polish priests, teachers, and political leaders were transported to Dachau, or shot in the Palmiry Forest. The first experiments were made in euthanasia, in the selection of children for racial breeding, in slave-labour schemes, and in gas chambers. The NKVD followed guide-lines based on their own idea of class analysis, assigning some two million people associated with the professions or with pre-war state employment to forcible deportation. Both sides arrested many thousands of political prisoners, and when convenient exchanged them. The Gestapo received German 'criminals' and Jewish agitators in return for communists and Ukrainians. Both sides engaged in trade—Russian oil flowing into Germany through Poland in support of the invasion of France and the Battle of Britain. Both sides were as happy to make frontier adjustments, such as the Soviet purchase of Suwałki, as they were reluctant to interfere in each other's military adventures. Hitler did not intervene in Stalin's attacks on Finland, the Baltic States, and Romania. Stalin did not intervene in Hitler's conquest of Denmark, Norway, Holland, Belgium, Luxemburg, and France. Each side, in massive propaganda campaigns, praised the achievements of the other. Each side was working with equal vigour for the reduction of the Poles to the condition of a leaderless, friendless nation.

Indeed, in the light of the subsequent reversal of policy, it could be argued that at this stage the Soviet terror in many ways exceeded that of the Nazis. The Stalinist regime had a head start on the Nazis in the techniques and logistics of terror, having built up the necessary machinery during the recent purges in its own country. At a time when the Germans were still refining their preparations for Auschwitz or Treblinka, the Soviets could accommodate a few million Polish and West Ukrainian additions to the population of their 'Gulag archipelago' with relative ease. Although they preferred to condemn their victims to a long slow death from cold and starvation, in contrast to the Nazi methods of summary murder—and who is to say which was the more humane? —the effect was much of the same. Of the estimated two million Polish civilians deported to Arctic Russia, Siberia, and Kazakhstan in the terrible railway convoys of 1939–40, at least one half were dead within a year of their arrest.[3]

The Soviet crimes of this vintage are symbolized by the fearful name of Katyn—a name which clearly arouses as much guilt in the Soviet Union, as revulsion in the outside world. Katyn Forest near Smolensk in Byelorussia marks the site of a mass grave where the corpses of some four-and-a-half thousand Polish officers were unearthed by German investigators in April 1943. They formed just one part of a much larger group of over 15,000 Polish officer-prisoners, professionals and reservists, who had disappeared from Soviet captivity in the Spring of 1940, and whose fate was otherwise unknown. They were almost all educated professional men—doctors, civil servants, teachers—and each one had his hands tied behind his back, and a German bullet in the base of his skull. The Soviets announced that the crime had been committed by the Nazis. But to any impartial observer, who is prepared to

consider circumstantial evidence in addition to the known
facts, there can be no reasonable doubt about Soviet
responsibility. It may well be that the crime was somehow
organized by the NKVD and the SS in concert—which might
explain the Soviet Union's reticence to mention Katyn in
conjunction with Stalin's many other admitted 'errors'.* It
may even be true that it resulted from some terrible
bureaucratic mistake—as Stalin himself once hinted. But
Soviet reactions after the War do not inspire confidence. The
removal of Katyn from the investigation of Nazi war crimes at
the Nuremberg Trials, and the extraordinary selection of the
nearby village of 'Khatyn' *(sic)* for the site of the national war
memorial of Byelorussia, both point to an elaborate cover-up
operation. So long as the crime of Katyn remains unconfessed,
unexplained, and unexpiated, Poles will remember it as the
symbol of Soviet oppression, past and present.[4]

2 The Nazi Supremacy, 1941–3

Operation BARBAROSSA, Hitler's attack on the Soviet
Union, which was launched from the *Wehrmacht*'s positions in
Poland on 22 June 1941, ended the Nazi–Soviet Pact in one
mighty and treacherous blow. It drove the Soviets from
eastern Poland within two weeks, and extended the Nazi
realm into the depths of Russia. For the next two years, the
Nazi grip on Eastern Europe was complete, and even then was
slow to crumble. The Germans' New Order in Poland could
be constructed without serious disturbance. The General
Government, now enlarged to include the District of Galicia
with the city of Lemberg (Lwów), was to serve as the principal
laboratory for the Nazis' ambitious social experiments.

According to the outlines of the *Generalplan-Ost*, the Nazis
aimed to redistribute the entire population between the Oder
and the Dnieper. German settlers were to be introduced by the
million. The Poles were destined either for Germanization
where suitable, or for expulsion beyond the Urals. The
residual Slavs were to be turned into a pool of half-educated

---

*According to the German–Soviet Friendship Treaty, agents of the Nazi Reich
were authorized to operate on Soviet territory. (See note 2.)

Map 3.   The German Occupation (1939–45)

slave labourers. Inferior or useless human beings—Jews, gypsies, recalcitrant prisoners of war, imbeciles, and invalids —were to be eliminated.

One encouraging change, from the Polish point of view, took place in Soviet policy. Having worked with Hitler in the joint suppression of all things Polish, Stalin now turned to the Poles for a common front against Germany, and proposed an alliance with Sikorski. Diplomatic relations were established on 30 July 1941 and a military convention signed on 12 August. The USSR stated its readiness to form a Polish Army in Russia, to grant an Amnesty to all Polish internees (for crimes never committed), and to annul the provisions of the Nazi–Soviet Pact regarding Poland. *Pravda* even announced that the western frontier of the USSR, as fixed in 1939 in conjunction with Hitler, was not necessarily final. Constant difficulties arose on every simple issue of Polish–Soviet relations, especially over arrangements for the Poles in Russia; and no satisfactory explanation was forthcoming to queries about the 15,000 missing officers. But, at the height of German arrogance in Poland, it was far preferable for the Poles to be pitted now against just one enemy instead of two.

German resettlement schemes were already under way in West Prussia, where 750,000 Polish peasants had been expelled to make way for Germans transferred from the Baltic States. Now the same methods began to be applied in central Poland, notably in the region of Zamość. In 1942–3, over 300 villages were cleared in this region alone. There remained 400 villages intact simply because the SS could not spare the manpower to clear them. The evictions were attended by unspeakable burnings, beatings, and butchery. The well-known fate of the one Bohemian village of Lidice, where 143 men were murdered by a Nazi reprisal order, was visited on Poland not once, but hundreds of times over.

The network of Nazi concentration camps proliferated throughout the General Government where the SS and the Gestapo could operate with total impunity, beyond the law of the Reich and free from the influence of the *Wehrmacht* in the front-line military zones. Apart from numerous prisoner-of-war camps, where mortality was also high, there were penal-investigation camps, labour camps of various kinds, and from

1941 onwards the death camps. In this last category, one
must include Maidaneck, Sobibor, Treblinka, Dora, Plas-
chau, and above all Birkenau, the extension of nearby
Auschwitz. Each of these enormous installations was designed for the sole purpose of killing human beings *en masse*
in the most efficient manner possible, and was supported by
hundreds of collecting centres all over Poland. They made
the early concentration camps within the Reich itself, at
Dachau or Buchenwald, pale into insignificance. They provided the last resting-place for nine or perhaps ten million
people, over half of them Jewish, transported to their deaths
from all ends of occupied Europe. Inside the camps, every
brand of unspeakable bestiality flourished. Outside, in Polish
town and villages, the Nazi terror turned street executions,
hangings, collective reprisals, and murder for pleasure, into a
commonplace.[5]

Fortunately, the Final Solution of the so-called Jewish
problem is the one aspect of the overall complex of crimes
against humanity in wartime Poland which has been properly
recorded and documented.[6] If all the other crimes and acts of
genocide were as well known and published, the world would
be better informed. Oddly enough, though, the actual
decision to launch the Final Solution sometime towards the
end of 1941 has never been precisely documented. But its
results were all too plain to see. The Jewish community, which
had been isolated in the ghettos for a couple of years, was
already wasting away from disease, malnutrition, and starvation. Now it was to be crowded into cattle-wagons, street by
street, town by town, and sent to the gas-chambers. It took
only twenty minutes between the arrival of a train load to be
undressed and 'disinfected' and the arrival of the special
detachments to strip the corpses of hair, gold fillings, and
personal jewellery at the entrance to the crematorium. Hair
mattresses, bone fertilizer, and soap from human fat were
delivered to German industry with Prussian precision. Gold
was delivered to the Reichsbank by the ton. The last of the
ghettos to be broken up, at Litmannstadt (Lódź), was empty
by August 1944. By then, Poland's Jewry had been virtually
wiped out. Although several hundred thousand Polish Jews
had escaped to the Soviet Union, the only Jewish survivors in

Poland itself were hiding in barns and attics or living in fear of betrayal under false identities.

At the height of the mass murders, the Rising in the ruins of the Warsaw Ghetto in April 1943 proved that Poland's Jews would not go to deaths unsung and unavenged. Like the last stand of their forebears against the Romans at Masada, the heroism of the Jewish Battle Organization set an example that all could honour and respect. A handful of youths and girls, armed with hand-guns, grenades, and home-made bomb launchers held a brigade of SS infantrymen at bay for three weeks. Seven thousand fighters were killed; a similar number were incinerated in their hide-outs; the remaining fifty-six thousand were transported to Treblinka. This was the largest single act of Resistance until the outbreak of the main Warsaw Rising fifteen months later.[7]

It is often asked why so little help was extended to Polish Jewry in the hour of its distress. The question can only be put by people with no conception of the circumstances in occupied Poland, which bore little relation to the relatively genteel condition of occupied Denmark, France, or Holland. The antagonisms between Christians and Jews, which undoubtedly existed in Poland, were largely irrelevant. The Jews had been segregated since the winter of 1939–40, since when all normal intercommunal contact had been lost. The Polish population at large lived under the formal threat of instant execution for the entire family of anyone found sheltering, feeding, or helping Jews. In this light, it is as pointless to ask why the Poles did little to help the Jews as to enquire why the Jews did nothing to assist the Poles.[8]

In any case, the Polish Resistance was inevitably slow in forming. Although the foundations for an organized underground Resistance were laid before the end of the September Campaign in 1939, the military and civilian branches of the movement did not begin to function on a widespread scale until the end of 1942. On the military side, the Home Army (AK) with its main allies, the Peasant Battalions (BCh) and the nationalist National Military Organizations (NOW), grew into a force of some 400,000 trained and armed soldiers, far outnumbering their diminutive communist rival, the People's Guard (GL). The growing incidence of ambushes, train derailments, and sabotage led in due course to open confrontations with the German military in a countryside where huge tracts of hill and forest were ruled by partisan leaders. On the civilian side, a plenopotentiary Delegate of the Polish Government co-ordinated the work of political representatives and directed the efforts of welfare, educational, propaganda, and intelligence agencies. Poland organized a remarkable underground state, operating under the noses of the occupying power. The illegal press blossomed. Needy citizens were given aid, in kind, or with duplicate ration cards. The Council of Assistance for Jews (RPZ) was created in September 1942. Polish lessons, banned in school above the elementary grade were provided by a Secret Teaching Organization (TON). University tutorials were held in 'flying' classes. Degrees were awarded. Underground courts passed sentence on collaborators and speculators; and sentences were executed by a conspirational gendarmerie. National art treasures were spirited to safety. Polish slogans and posters were painted on walls. Military intelligence was passed to London. Industrial production was constantly interrupted. Underground agents even penetrated the camps, spreading information and planning incidents.[9] Despite its isolation from Allied supply lines, the Polish Resistance could fairly claim to be the largest and most elaborate movement of its kind in Europe.

3 *The Soviet Advance, 1943–5*

News of the Soviet victory at Stalingrad, and the turning of the tide on the Eastern Front, sounded the knell of the Nazi empire. Eastern Europe, yearning for the day of deliverance, was filled with an air of rising expectancy. But in Poland the prospect of liberation by the Soviet Army aroused mixed feelings. For one thing, the Russians were old enemies, and knowledge of their methods and mentality was bound to raise suspicions. Memories of the Polish–Soviet War of 1919–20 were still fresh. (See pp. 116–8.) For another, Stalin took the first opportunity presented by his new-found strength and confidence to sever his links with the Polish Government. On 5 April 1943, as soon as news of the Katyn massacre had broken, he denounced the agreements made with Sikorski two years earlier. In Poland itself, it emerged that he was breathing new life into Polish communist movement which refused to harmonize its activities with the main Resistance organizations. Stalin's plans were far from clear; but it was evident from this point onwards that the Soviet Advance would bring serious complications. No Pole could view the collapse of the Nazis with anything but joy. Very few awaited the Soviet Liberation without deep anxiety.

To make matters worse, at the very time when the political situation was entering the critical phase, Poland was deprived of its most able and respected leader. On 4 July 1943, General Sikorski was flying back to England from a visit to Polish troops in North Africa. His Liberator aircraft, piloted by a Czech, Lt. Prchal, touched down for a scheduled stop at Gibraltar. At about 11.03 p.m. it took off again, but never gained height, plunging into the bay beneath the Rock. Sikorski, his daughter, and most of the passengers were either killed on impact, or drowned when the Liberator sank. The cause of the crash, confirmed by the pilot, who survived, lay in the malfunction of the elevator controls.[10]

The rift between Poland and the USSR threatened to split the Grand Coalition. Some scholars see it as the origin of the later Cold War.[11] Britain and America continued to regard the Polish Government in London as their first and staunchest ally; whilst the Russians, having severed diplomatic relations, began to smear the Polish leaders publicly as 'reactionaries' and 'Fascist collaborators'. (This last epithet was produced when the Polish Government asked the International Red Cross to investigate the Nazis' disclosures about Katyn.) Behind the scenes, Stalin was keeping his options open, searching, as he told President Beneš, for 'a Pole one can talk to'. He did not commit himself irrevocably to the Polish communists until June 1944, on the eve of the Warsaw Rising.[12] But the fact is that there were no Poles in the Government camp whom Stalin could have 'talked to' in the way he wanted. The rift could not be repaired. Reluctantly, and with fulsome protestations about their equal esteem for both of their Slavonic allies, the Anglo-Americans were driven by force of circumstance to lean towards the Russian side in the Polish–Soviet dispute. At a time when the second front in

Western Europe had not yet been opened, and when the Soviet Army was carrying the main burden of the fighting against Germany, Churchill and Roosevelt were in no position to risk a breach with Stalin over the Polish issue. Although they reserved as many points as possible for future settlement, they had no means of insisting that the Grand Alliance adopt the Polish version of Poland's future. In the first of the meetings of 'The Big Three', held at Tehran at the end of November 1943, it was agreed that post-war Europe would be divided into 'zones of influence'—Western and Southern Europe for the Anglo-Americans, and Eastern Europe for the Russians. This implied that Poland would fall under Soviet occupation and control. It was also agreed that the post-war Polish–Soviet frontier should follow the line once put forward in 1920 in a long-forgotten proposal by the former British Foreign Secretary, Lord Curzon. Few cared to notice that the Curzon Line was essentially the same as the Nazi–Soviet Demarcation Line of 1939 and as the old boundary between the Tsarist Empire and the Congress Kingdom. In this way, in the absence of any Polish representative, Stalin persuaded the Allied Powers to adopt the Russian imperial view of Poland's national territory. At this stage, the Polish Government was not even informed of these crucial decisions, which had been made over its head. They were to be told of the *fait accompli* at a moment more convenient for the Allies. A lamentable precedent was set for future Allied decisions on the Polish Question at Yalta and Potsdam.

The crucial issue of the definition of Polish territory affected every subsequent event, including the Liberation itself. In the Polish view, the Liberation of Poland began on 4 January 1944 when the Soviet Army drove the Germans across the pre-war frontier in Volhynia. In the Soviet view, already confirmed by the Big Three at Tehran, Poland's former eastern provinces were now officially part of the Soviet Union. This meant that the local Polish Resistance movement, which came out of the woods to help the Soviet Army's offensive, could be declared an 'illegal' movement and be safely arrested by the NKVD for opposing Allied policy. In Volhynia, and later in Wilno, Lwów, and Białystok, Home Army units who

had first suffered terrible casualties fighting alongside the
Russians to drive the Nazis from their native land were
rewarded by a free passage to Soviet prison camps. In the
Soviet view, the Liberation of Poland could not begin until
the Soviet Army entered what the Soviet Government said
was Polish territory—namely when it crossed the River Bug
on 19 July 1944.

From the start, therefore, the Liberation of Poland took
place on Soviet terms. The Soviet Army brought a ready-
made pro-communist administration in its baggage, in the
form of the Polish Committee of National Liberation
(PKWN), and on 22 July proceeded to instal it, unelected,
and unconnected with the legal Polish Government, in the
city of Lublin. (See p. 92–100.)* The Lublin Committee had
no right to assume the functions of a provisional government,
and had no known measure of popular support. But since
anyone who openly opposed it was promptly removed by the
NKVD, it was able to operate quite freely. In the ensuing
months, as the Eastern Front lurched inexorably westwards on
the last onslaught against Germany, the Soviet Special Forces
were able to purge the Polish population of all the most active
political elements. As the front line advanced, the Resistance
groups were arrested or disarmed, one by one. In every town
and village, mayors and elders and factory managers were
replaced or confirmed according to their performance under
Soviet interrogation. Workers and peasants were invited to
hold spontaneous demonstrations in favour of 'People's
Power', on pain of their jobs or their land. Landowners and
entrepreneurs were told that their property or their businesses
had been confiscated or requisitioned. Recalcitrant individuals of all classes were simply removed. Meanwhile, in the hunt
for suspected collaborators, for German males of military age,
for former members of the *Volksturm* and the *Hitlerjugend,* and
for ex-officials of all Nazi organizations—all of whom could be
assaulted or killed without special licence—the Soviet soldiery
in the rear areas were free to decide for themselves who was, or
was not, the enemy. The Russian liberators were both

*Hence the adoption of 22 July as the so-called 'National Day' of the People's
Republic, and the suppression by the communist regime of Poland's traditional
National Day of 3 May.

welcomed and feared. Hence, in the space of a few months, Poland was rendered incapable of contesting the Soviet take-over in any concerted manner.

Warsaw, the capital city, provided the one place where an independent Polish administration might have been established. For in Warsaw the Home Army Command possessed a concentrated underground force of some 150,000 armed men, hidden by a fiercely patriotic population, and straining at the leash for the order to fight. In July 1944, in the flood of that same offensive which brought the PKWN to Lublin and the leading units of the Soviet Army to the banks of the Vistula, General Bór-Komorowski, the AK Commander, was weighing the pros and cons of the most tragic Polish decision of the War. He knew that everyone amongst his advisers wanted the capital city to be liberated by Polish military action, and that everyone wanted to see the liberated city in the hands of an administration loyal to the Polish Government. He also knew, in the atmosphere of suppressed excitement, that the citizens might rise against the hated Germans of their own accord. So it all turned on the timing. If he gave the order too soon, the Germans would still have the strength to crush the Rising regardless. If he gave the order too late, the Soviets would enter Warsaw unopposed, and would install the PKWN on the coat-tails of their victory parade. The only moment for a successful Rising would lie in a short interval of two or three days, after a new Soviet advance had committed the German garrison to withdraw but before the advancing Soviet troops had actually arrived in strength. On 20 July, news of the attempt to assassinate Hitler in his headquarters at Rasten-berg in nearby East Prussia, suggested that the *Wehrmacht* was cracking; and the evacuation of German civilian offices in Warsaw seemed to signal the start of their retreat. On the 19th, Moscow Radio broadcast an appeal urging the Varso-vians to rise. A Soviet armoured division crossed the Vistula and set up a bridgegead at Magnuszew forty miles to the south. On the 31st, when a patrol of T34 tanks was sighted from Praga, in the eastern suburbs of the capital, it seemed inconceivable that the decisive moment had not arrived. At 5.30 p.m. Bór-Komorowski gave the order: 'Tomorrow at 17.00 hours you will start Operation Tempest in Warsaw.'

The consequences were unmitigated tragedy. Even as the AK
were taking their guns from their hiding-places, and gathering
in cellars and Warehouses, the German Ninth Army was
moving across the Vistula bridges to launch a counter-attack
against the Soviets. The German garrison in Warsaw was
strengthened by the dispatch of the SS *Viking* Panzer Division,
the SS *Herman Goering* regiment, by units of military police,
and by the infamous Dirlanger and RONA Brigades. This
force, commanded by General von dem Bach-Zalewski and
containing a strong admixture of penal battalions, convicts,
and desperate ex-Soviet Volunteers, was given the chance of
smashing the Rising in isolation. Stalin denounced the leaders
of the Home Army as 'a handful of power-seeking criminals',
and withheld Soviet assistance. For sixty-three days, the
fighting raged with unprecedented savagery whilst the Soviet
Army, one mile away across the river, looked on in virtual
passivity. A quarter of a million civilians died, from shelling,
from dive-bombing, or from wholesale massacres, Sporadic
supply drops by British and American planes sent from Italy
brought little relief. An unsupported attempt to cross the river
by a Polish unit under Soviet Command was doomed to
failure in advance.[13] Block by block, street by street, sewer by
sewer, the AK was being squeezed with appalling losses into a
tiny enclave in the city centre. Bór-Komorowski capitulated
on 2 October. The surviving inhabitants were evacuated.
Hitler ordered that Warsaw be 'razed without trace'. It was
the end of the old order in Poland. After that, the Home Army
was broken, and no one was left to challenge the communists
effectively. The Nazis had done the Soviets' work for them.[14]

During the final stage of the Liberation, which started with
the great Soviet winter offensive of January 1945, the German
retreat turned rapidly into a rout. The hard-pressed *Wehrmacht*
occupied a series of defensive positions—on the Pomeranian
Wall in February, and in selected 'fortresses' like Breslau or
Glogau, which were ordered to fight to the last man. But the
Soviet tide, assisted now by two full Polish armies, washed
over and around these obstacles with impunity. Berlin was in
their sights. All organized administration collapsed. The
transport system was overloaded to breaking-point. The roads
were crammed with refugees. Rumours of massacres in East

Prussia precipitated a general exodus. Thousands perished in the woods and on the Baltic beaches, and on the frozen wastes of the Frisches Haff. In the bay of Danzig, the sinking of an evacuation ship, the *Wilhelm Gustloff* by a Soviet submarine, the greatest maritime disaster in world history, was hardly noticed. Further west, in Pomerania and Silesia, the Soviet authorities formally encouraged plundering. Although these provinces were already earmarked for Polish ownership, the Soviets subjected them to a devastation unparalleled elsewhere in Europe. Soviet reparation squads dismantled entire factories, entire railways, and carried them off to Russia as booty. Entire cities, like Danzig or Neisse (Nysa), were emptied of their movables, and burned to the ground. The German civilians who had stayed behind, especially the women, were shown no mercy. Group rapes were the order of the day. No one who has read the depositions of the survivors of this terrible visitation can fail to be impressed by their pointless sufferings, and by the general coincidence of their individual stories.[15] Here was Russia's revenge for the Nazis' devastation of Russia.

In the midst of the chaos, the Allied leaders assembled to finalize their arrangements for post-war Europe. On the Polish issue they had little chance of deflecting the Soviets from Stalin's chosen solution. With the A-Bomb still untested, and with the prospect of colossal American casualties in the expected assault on the main Japanese islands, the US Administration had to humour Stalin in order to secure Soviet participation in the final stage of the War in the East. At Yalta between 4 and 11 February 1945, they confirmed the Curzon Line frontier agreed at Tehran, and approved in principle that Poland's loss of territory in the East should be compensated by the award of former German territory in the West. They insisted that representatives of the parties supporting the Polish Government in London should join members of the Soviet-sponsored administration in Warsaw (the RTRP) to form a united Provisional Government of National Unity (the TJRN). (See p. 5.) As a result of this decision, the London Government was condemned to lose its accreditation, and its right to appoint a Polish representative to the founding conference of the United Nations.[16] At Potsdam, between 17 July and 2 August, the Allied leaders heard evidence from a Polish communist delegation supplied by the Soviets, but not from any more representative body. They then fixed Poland's western frontier on the Oder and western Neisse: approved the plan for the expulsion of all Germans: and made their famous declaration about 'free and unfettered' elections. (See p. 5.) With that, they left Poland to the mercy of the Soviets.

4 *The Postscript of War, 1945–7*

Although the Second World War formally ended for Poland, as for the rest of Europe, with the capitulation of Germany in May 1945, the internal struggle continued for many long months. The civil war continued where the international war left off. Armed opposition to the new order centred on three separate underground organizations—the right-wing National Armed Forces (NSZ);[17] the Freedom and Independence Movement (WiN),[18] which was partly raised from the ranks of the disbanded Home Army: and the Ukrainian Insurrectionary Army (UPA). The NSZ, active in the Holy Cross Mountains, ceased to resist by the end of 1945, when its last brigade forced their way through Czechoslovakia to meet up with US forces. The WiN which was strongest in the vicinities of Bialystok and Lublin, and which had links with the former National Democratic orientation, held out to February 1947, when 40,000 men laid down their arms in a formal amnesty. The UPA, cornered in the Bieszczady Mountains of the South-East, survived until July 1947. Trapped in a three-cornered offensive by Soviet, Polish, and Czechoslovak forces, most of these Ukrainians paid with their lives for their belief in 'neither Hitler nor Stalin'. The overgrown cemeteries and dilapidating Uniate churches of their razed villages bear witness to their fate to this day. In addition to such incidence of organized resistance, many remote rural districts in Poland steadfastly refused to recognize the new authorities. In the Podhale region round Zakopane, for instance, the gravestones of assassinated officers of the Citizens' Militia attest to the ferocious resentments of the local highlanders led by 'Captain Fire' (Józef Kuraś) throughout 1946 and 1947. In a very real sense, therefore, the Second World War in Poland was not concluded by the political conferences at Yalta and Potsdam. It was concluded on the ground, in the woods and the hills where it had raged with sporadic violence ever since 1939. The last shot of the War was not fired until nearly three years after the ruins of Warsaw had been reoccupied, and a prostrate country had commenced the arduous task of reconstruction.

Poland's economic recovery was severely hampered by political considerations. Although huge deliveries of relief from America were made by the UNRRA agency in 1945–6, the Soviet Union prevented its clients in Eastern Europe from receiving Marshall Aid. The direct looting and dismantling of property which characterized the Soviet Liberation was replaced by more systematic exploitation. According to the notorious Soviet–Polish Frontier and Reparations Agreement of 16 August 1945, for example, Poland was obliged to deliver thirteen million tons of coal per year in the period 1946–50 at a price, 1.3 US dollars per ton, which was only one sixth of the world price. This tribute was imposed on a country that had lost 60 per cent of its industrial capacity.

The Poland which emerged at the end of this terrible ordeal differed from its pre-war predecessor in several fundamental respects. It possessed a different territory, having been bodily moved from 150 miles to the West—as Churchill had once showed Stalin using three matches on the table, 'like a company of soldiers taking *two steps to the left, close ranks*'.' It possessed quite different economic resources, having exchanged the primitive rural districts of the East for the rich industrial and seaboard districts of the former German lands. It possessed a different society, with entirely different ethnic composition, religious affiliations, and class structures. The Jewish, German, and Ukrainian communities, forming over a quarter of the pre-war population, had been murdered or banished; the intelligentsia had been decimated, the propertied classes dispossessed—all as a result of war itself, not of some post-war social revolution. Above all, Poland possessed a different standing in the world. In place of its full pre-war independence, in whose defence the War was supposed to have been fought, it was granted no more than the outward trappings of sovereignty. It was restored to its separate

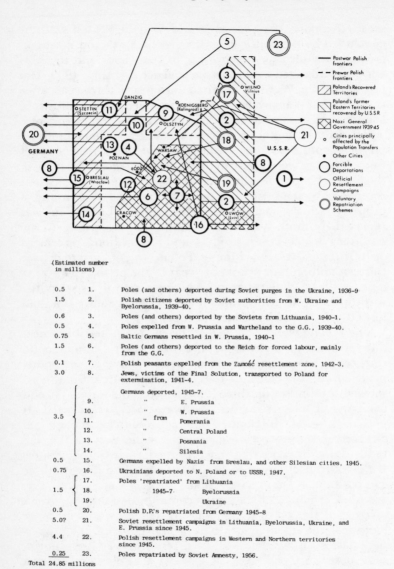

(Estimated number in millions)

0.5	1.	Poles (and others) deported during Soviet purges in the Ukraine, 1936-9
1.5	2.	Polish citizens deported by Soviet authorities from W. Ukraine and Byelorussia, 1939-40.
0.6	3.	Poles (and others) deported by the Soviets from Lithuania, 1940-1.
0.5	4.	Poles expelled from W. Prussia and Wartheland to the G.G., 1939-40.
0.75	5.	Baltic Germans resettled in W. Prussia, 1940-1
1.5	6.	Poles (and others) deported to the Reich for forced labour, mainly from the G.G.
0.1	7.	Polish peasants expelled from the Zamość resettlement zone, 1942-3.
3.0	8.	Jews, victims of the Final Solution, transported to Poland for extermination, 1941-4.
		Germans deported, 1945-7.
	9.	" E. Prussia
	10.	" W. Prussia
3.5	11.	" from Pomerania
	12.	" Central Poland
	13.	" Posnania
	14.	" Silesia
0.5	15.	Germans expelled by Nazis from Breslau, and other Silesian cities, 1945.
0.75	16.	Ukrainians deported to N. Poland or to USSR, 1947.
	17.	Poles 'repatriated' from Lithuania
1.5	18.	1945-7 Byelorussia
	19.	Ukraine
0.5	20.	Polish D.P.'s repatriated from Germany 1945-8
5.0?	21.	Soviet resettlement campaigns in Lithuania, Byelorussia, Ukraine, and E. Prussia since 1945.
4.4	22.	Polish resettlement campaigns in Western and Northern territories since 1945.
0.25	23.	Poles repatriated by Soviet Amnesty, 1956.

Total 24.85 millions

Diagram A. Population Transfers (1936–56)

existence as a state, whilst being politically shackled to the Soviet Union. (See page 29–43.) This dependent status, this stunted and unwanted first fruit of the war for Polish independence, is something which apologists for the People's Republic are pleased to call 'victory'.

Cuckoo in the Nest

According to the authorized version propagated in the present-day Poland, Polish politics during the Second World War was characterized by 'a dialectical process of revolutionary polarization'. The two opposing polar extremes of political life—the 'reactionary' camp of the 'Government-in-Exile',* and the 'progressive' camp led by the communists—entered a phase of intensifying antagonism, where the fortunes of the dominant 'reactionaries' gradually waned whilst those of the subordinate 'progressives' gradually waxed. At the start of the War, up to 1941, the progressives hold an admittedly inferior position; in the central phase, in the era of the Polish–Soviet alliance, 1941–3, they achieve a state of equilibrium; in the final phase, after 1943, they assume the inevitable ascendancy. In the course of the process, the dominant and the subordinate elements have neatly exchanged roles; the 'reactionaries' become subordinate, and the 'progressives' dominant. The natural conclusion of the process, governed by the scientific laws of history, demands that the 'reactionary' element be eliminated, and that the progressive element take command of the new 'socialist stage' launched by the 'Revolution'.

Viewed in the abstract, this alleged dialectical process undoubtedly possesses a certain mathematical elegance. Examined at close quarters, however, it can be seen to have been constructed from a number of false premises. If one tests the various labels against reality, one finds them signally inappropriate. One has to conclude for example, that the Polish 'Government in London', being mainly supported by parties in opposition to the pre-war regime, was not particularly reactionary; that the genuinely progressive forces of

*Although the legal Polish Government was necessarily stationed abroad, it did not become a true 'Government-in-Exile' until it lost accreditation in 1945.

Polish politics—the radicals, socialists, and peasants—were largely to be found in the Government camp; and that the communists, far from being the accepted leaders of the progressive groups, were their sworn enemies. The co-ordinating centre of the communist movement was also abroad, in 'exile', just like the Government. One of the greatest flaws is to be found in the fact that at the start of the alleged process, in 1939, the Polish communist movement could hardly be judged to have played even a subordinate role in political life, because at that particular juncture it did not actually exist. Not only were the non-Government progressive forces not there to be led; the communists were not there to lead them. In this light, the idea of the political contest between the foreign forces of reaction led by Sikorski and the native forces of progress (led by someone who can never quite be named) is revealed as the figment of someone's ideological imagination. Obviously, some other convincing analysis needs to be considered. There was no 'Polish Revolution'.

The wartime Polish Government came into being on 30 September 1939 in France, was legally constituted on the initiative of the President of the Republic, Władysław Raczkiewicz. Its head, General Władysław Sikorski, held ideal qualifications for both his military and his political duties. He had a distinguished career behind him as a front-line general in the Soviet War of 1919–20, and he had served as Minister of Military Affairs and as Prime Minister in the coalition governments of 1922–3 and 1923–4. More importantly, although an associate of Józef Piłsudski in his early years, he had broken with Piłsudski's group during the Great War, he had stood aloof from Piłsudski's dictatorship in the years after the May Coup of 1926, and he had played a part, together with Wincenty Witos and Ignacy Paderewski, in the oppositional Morges Front of the late 1930s. (See p. 127.) He was a proven parliamentarian, a liberal by inclination, a distinguished author, and a figure of international reputation. Like Churchill, who assumed office in Great Britain at almost exactly the same time, he could fairly be described as the 'man of destiny'. He believed passionately in Poland's independence, but had no time for narrow party politics or for rigid ideological dogma. He longed for a better Poland after the

War, a Poland of greater security, greater prosperity, and greater social justice, and he was prepared to make compromises, even with Stalin if necessary, to achieve it. His detractors have described him as vain, overtolerant, and indecisive at critical moments; but to label such a man 'reactionary', or even a conservative, is a travesty.

The political complexion of the wartime Polish Government was limited only by its commitments to the principle of Independence, to the war against Poland's invaders, to the Constitution, and to the territorial integrity of the Republic. Anyone who accepted these principles—and they included the overwhelming majority of Poles at home and abroad—was free to participate in its numerous organs and agencies. For obvious reasons, the political emphasis moved away from links with the pre-war regime which had been discredited both by its internal policies in the last years of peace (see p. 127–9) and by the uninspiring conduct of its leadership during the September Campaign. Almost all the leading personalities and parties connected with the wartime Polish Government, like General Sikorski himself, had either fallen foul of the Sanacja regime or had actively opposed it. Both August Zaleski, the Foreign Minister 1939–41, and General Kazimierz Sosnkowski had once been close associates of Piłsudski the former as Piłsudski's emissary in London during the First World War, and as Foreign Minister in Warsaw from 1926–32, the latter as Piłsudski's chief associate in the Legions and in the Soviet War of 1919–20. But both had parted company with their former chief, Zaleski, over issues of international policy, Sosnkowski over the May Coup of 1926, when he had actually attempted suicide. The two successive presidents of the National Council (RN), Ignacy Paderewski, the musician, and Professor Stanisław Grabski, an economist, were both independent figures of irreproachable reputation. The four main political parties reflected the radical priorities of the day. The National Movement (SN), headed by Dmowski's political heir, Tadeusz Bielecki, represented the 'right-radical', nationalist trend. The Labour Movement (SP), led by people such as Cyryl Ratajski and Stanisław Jankowski, was composed of a relatively recent amalgam of Catholics and non-socialist syndicalists, and was dominated by the proletarian wing of the old Christian Democrats. The Peasant Movement (SL), led by Stanisław Mikolajczyk, and the historian Professor Stanislaw Kot, represented the centrist sector of peasant politics at the head of the largest single class of Polish society. The Polish Socialist Party (PPS), headed by Tomasz Arciszewski and Adam Ciołkosz, both ex-defendants in the notorious Brest Trial of 1931–2 (see p. 125), and by the Freedom, Equality, and Independence Group (WRN) of K. Zaremba and Kazimierz Pużak, followed the mainstream of non-Marxist Polish Socialism. These dominant trends filled the entire spectrum of native Polish politics in the 1940s, excluding only the insignificant extra-parliamentary fringe groups of the far Left such as the communists or the Polish Workers Socialist Party (RPPS), and the equivalent fanatical fringe of the far Right, such as the minute Fascist 'Falanga'. Poland's ethnic minorities—Jews, Germans, and Ukrainians—did not form a separate Minority Bloc as in pre-war politics, but were adequately represented by individual politicians. The Government itself was led by General Sikorski, with only one serious challenge to his Premiership before his tragic death in July 1943: thereafter by Mikolajczyk to November 1944, and then by Arciszewski.

The Polish Government's military forces were scattered the length and breadth of Eurasia; and it took an immense feat of organization to co-ordinate their activities and replenish the depleted cadres.[19] In the initial period following the September débâcle, the main concentration of some 85,000 men arrived in France from units gradually released from internment in Romania and Hungary. Sikorski's 'Polish Army in France' included two infantry divisions, the Podhale Rifle Brigade of General Bohusz-Szyszko, the Armoured Brigade of General Stanisław Maczek, and an Air Force Division of fighter squadrons. It served under French command at Narvik and in the French Campaign of May–June 1940. Another concentration, the 'Polish Army of the Levant' consisting principally of General Kopański's Autonomous Carpathian Brigade, had assembled in French Syria. The remnants of the Polish Navy—three destroyers, and two submarines, which had escaped from the Baltic with incredible ingenuity—together with the Merchant Marine, were already in British ports. The fall of France caused near-catastrophe. Despite his intimate connections with the French command, Sikorski declined Weygand's order to capitulate. Most of the Polish units in France were taken into German captivity; but some crossed into neutral Switzerland or Spain, and approximately one-third succeeded in extricating themselves by a hair-raising evacuation to Great Britain. The Polish Air Force Division escaped via North Africa. Kopański's Brigade defied its French superiors, and marched from Syria into British Palestine.

All of the survivors of the Polish Armed Forces were now under British command—Churchill, Sikorski, and de Gaulle sharing the distinction of being the only Allied leaders who 'fought on'. Yet they all needed a long period of recuperation, which the soldiers were granted but the airmen and sailors were not. In the Battle of Britain in the autumn of 1940, Polish fighter pilots eventually made up 20 per cent of the RAF's strength. Two exclusively Polish Squadrons—302 (Poznań) and 303 (Kościuszko)—alone accounted for 109 Luftwaffe 'kills' (12 per cent of the total); and their 'loss–kill ratio' of 1 : 9 was unsurpassed. The Polish Navy was sent off immediately on Atlantic patrol. The Army was rebuilt more slowly.

In 1941, the Polish–Soviet military convention permitted the formation of the 'Polish Army in Russia' under General Władysław Anders. This decision launched one of the epic odysseys of modern warfare, worthy of Xenophon's 'Ten Thousand'. Polish refugees and deportees who had withstood the rigours of Stalin's Arctic camps or of Siberian exile drifted into the collecting centres at Buzuluk on the Volga and at Yangi-Yul in Uzbekistan, and in March 1942, after endless obstructions by the Soviet authorities, crossed in British-controlled Persia. From there, the civilians were transferred to safety in India or Africa; the young men and women of military age were sent to Palestine for training. Many Polish Jews (Corporal Begin among them) opted to stay in Palestine, eventually to fight their British protectors and to launch the state of Israel.[20] But the merger of the main body of Anders's Army with Kopański's Brigade produced the 'Second Corps' which moved on to Cairo and joined the British Army in North Africa. In the next three years, fighting in the ranks of

Montgomery's Eighth Army, the Second Corps covered itself
with glory— at Tobruk (1943), at Monte Cassino (1944), and
at Bologna (1945).

Meanwhile, the Polish 'First Corps' of General Marian
Kukiel was stationed in Scotland. At first, an excess of officers
and too few men caused difficulties; and the island of Bute
(known to the Poles as 'the island of snakes') was incongruously designated as a Polish political detention district. Later,
through re-equipment and recruitment, five full divisions
emerged. The Polish Parachute Brigade, under Brigadier-
General Sosabowski, took part in the ill-fated landings at
Arnhem. The First Polish Armoured Division of General
Maczek played a crucial role at the Falaise Gap in the break-
out from the Normandy beaches, and ended the War
accepting the surrender of Wilhelmshaven.

No one can question the fact that the Polish Armed Forces,
in total some 228,000 men under arms by 1945, set an
outstanding example of duty and sacrifice in the Allied defeat
of Nazi Germany. No Pole who loves his country can fail to
honour their memory.[21]

The Polish Government's links with Poland were close and,
until the entry of the Soviet Army in 1944, growing closer.
The Government Delegates in Poland—successively Ratajski,
J. Piekalkiewicz, and Jankowski—established an underground Council of Ministers together with an embryo
underground parliament. The Home Army and its associates
possessed an efficient radio network and a clandestine courier
service which usually enabled them to clear their plans and
orders with Polish HQ in England. The extraordinary feat of
intercepting, dismantling, and delivering the entire working
parts of a German V2 rocket shows just how sophisticated the
link between England and Poland had become.[22] The link
only began to falter after the failure of the Warsaw Rising.
Yet, if doubts remain about the cause of this faltering link, one
should ask what prevented the Polish Government from
maintaining contact with Poland throughout the Nazi Occupation, but not during the Soviet Liberation. The Polish
Government paid a high price for its inability to work with the
Soviets, not least during the Warsaw Rising; and some of its
members were happy enough to acquiesce in the deadlock.

But co-operation requires both sides to co-operate, and not the best will in the world could have swayed Stalin's total determination to deny the Polish Government all recognition and, by ruthlessly eliminating its representatives in Poland, to sever its lines of communication to the Polish people. The Polish Government lost out in Poland less through its own failings, than through the violence and chicanery of the Soviets.

The international dealings of the Polish Government were based on the British alliance of 1939, and on the democratic principles of the Atlantic Charter of 1941; yet they foundered on exactly the same Russian rocks. Sikorski's initial relations with Churchill were so close that the only attempt by his colleagues to unseat him was launched (in July 1940) on suspicions of a Churchillian plot. His relations with the Americans were very cordial, especially after his meetings with Roosevelt in 1941 and 1942. His relations with Beneš, the leader of the Czechoslovak Government-in-Exile, promised to heal the ancient rift between the two neighbours, and produced plans for a post-war Polish–Czechoslovak Federation.[23] In each of these cases, however, the success of Polish policy in the first phase of the war was dashed by the rise of the Soviet factor in the second phase. None of the Allied leaders could continue to support the policies of the Polish Government if such support risked a breach with the Soviet Union. Churchill and Roosevelt had to rely on Stalin for completing the strategic plans of the Grand Alliance. Beneš relied on Stalin for his hopes of returning to Prague.[24] Ineluctably, therefore, through the logic of Stalin's exclusive grip on the future of Eastern Europe, all of Poland's main allies were constrained to suppress their sympathies for the Polish cause and to bow before the Soviet juggernaut. Apart from the very smallest fry among the Allied Powers, such as the leaders of the Baltic States, Norway, and Holland, General de Gaulle was probably the only figure in Allied London who held true to his Polish friends. The Free French had much in common with the Polish Government and had the same good reasons to despise the machinations of the Big Three.[25] Though they, too, were excluded from decisive deliberations affecting their future, they at least gained the satisfaction of returning home in triumph at the end of the War. For France, unlike Poland, was liberated by Montgomery and Patton, and not by Zhukof and Rokossowski.

Opposition to the Polish Government came more from disaffected circles among the *émigrés* than from opinion at home. Of course, there was no means of canvassing Polish opinion during the Occupation, but there is no evidence to suggest that any significant group contested either the legality of the Government or its policies. The most furious attacks on Sikorski came from Bielecki and Sejda, the nationalists, who felt that he was too liberal in his social stance and too eager to do business with Stalin. Opposition in Poland itself did not really exist until the prospect of a Soviet victory of Eastern Europe had to be taken into account and the Polish communist movement had been re-activated.

At the outbreak of war in 1939, the Polish communists were in the middle of the most agonizing episode of their pathetic history. They laboured under every conceivable disadvantage. They were predominantly, though not overwhelmingly, Jewish in origin, and were popularly perceived accordingly as a minority interest. As atheists, they earned the anathema of the Jewish no less than of the Catholic leaders; and, having supported Soviet Russia at the time of the Soviet invasion of Poland in 1920, they were widely regarded as traitors. They had two deputies in the *Sejm* of 1922, but thereafter none. Having decided to support the May Coup in 1926, and being dispersed by Piłsudski's gendarmes for daring to do so, they became the laughing-stock of political circles. Their relations with the Soviet comrades were even worse. Having strong leftist and international traditions, they held more to the memory of Róża Luksemburg than to that of her erstwhile partner and co-founder of the movement, Feliks Dzierżyński. In the internecine struggles of the CPSU, they had sympathized with Trotsky rather than with Stalin, and their links in Moscow were mainly with the Comintern organization. Most ominously, they were suspected by Stalin to be infiltrated by the Polish counter-intelligence service and a danger to Soviet security. When the Stalinist purges reached their height, they were obvious candidates for proscription. The Communist Party of Poland (KPP) disappeared from the list of Comin-

tern's affiliated parties. The Party's leaders—Adolf Warski
Józef Unszlicht, Maria Kostrzewa, Maksymilian Horwitz,
Juliusz Leński, Stanisław Bobiński— were all liquidated. The
membership, whose last recorded total in 1937 stood at 3,927,
was virtually wiped out.[26] At a stroke, forty years of
communist idealism, which had begun in 1897 with the
founding of the parent party, the Social Democracy of the
Kingdom of Poland and Lithuania (SDKPiL), was cynically
crushed. In this one action, the Soviets killed far more Polish
communists than the Nazis could ever have laid their hands
on. The survivors, who included a few individuals escaping
the Purge by accident and others 'preserved on ice' by the
Soviet security organs, could barely have reached four figures.
The remaining activists could have been assembled in one
small room. They had no party, no significant support among
the Polish population, and no expectation of anything but a
swift death if they were caught either in the Nazi or in the
Soviet zones of occupation. Even their bitterest enemies must
pity their condition, and admire their devotion. But the idea
that this tiny band of unfortunates had any serious role to
play in Polish politics at this stage is absurd.

The reactivation of the Polish communist movement was a
direct result of the German invasion of Russia and of Stalin's
consequent change of heart. Up to that point, having
physically annihilated both the cream of the Polish 'bourgeoisie' and the 'avante-garde' of the working class, Stalin cannot
possibly have harboured any plans for restoring Poland. Now
he needed all possible help from the Poles. His recognition of
the Polish Government (in London) was matched by his
revival of interest in the Polish communists. Stalin had clearly
been reconverted to the concept of a separate Polish state,
though he would never concede the principle of genuine
independence. This is the point at which the seeds of post-war
communist Poland were sown. At the end of 1941, Comintern
reopened its Polish section and the air waves were graced by a
new station called 'Radio Kościuszko'. Political planning
followed two parallel tracks—one in Poland itself under the
noses of the German Occupation, the other in Moscow.

In Warsaw, on 5 January 1942, a clandestine meeting was
held between a handful of survivors of the old KPP and a

small 'inititiative group' · smuggled in from Russia. They constituted the core of a new communist Party which they called the Polish Workers Party (PPR). After the deaths in mysterious circumstances of its first two leaders, Marceli Nowotko and Paweł Finder. Władysław Gomułka emerged as its guiding spirit from 1943 to 1948. (See p. 4–6.) The Party's first Manifesto in November 1943, entitled *O co walczymy?* (What are we fighting for?), stressed the twin goals of national independence and social revolution, thereby breaking with the internationalist ideology of the KPP and initiating the characteristic blend of Nationalism and Leninist Socialism.

At this same time, in Moscow, the Polish Bureau of the CPSU set up a body called the Union of Polish Patriots (ZPP) under the chairmanship of Wanda Wasilewska (see p. 74). Their aim was to create a vehicle for Soviet control over all the new Polish organizations, both military and civilian, which were then in the making. The Union's choice of name—which caused great offence amongst Polish circles at home*—none the less revealed its essential function. The ZPP was designed not so much to strengthen the Polish communists as to attract all Poles irrespective of their political connections who could be induced to serve under Soviet orders. In this scheme, the PPR was intended to play only a subordinate role. Stalin had given ample proof of this contempt for foreign communists, whom he thought unreliable. The first priority of the Soviet authorities was to build up a select group of Poles whose prime loyalty lay with the USSR rather than with Poland. In this selection, they were bound to prefer weak-minded turncoats or opportunists, who could be blackmailed with their past, to the iron-hard devotees of international communism. It was for this reason that all the committees and governments which made their appearance under Soviet auspices from 1944 to 1948, from the PKWN to the TRJN, were dominated by non-party figures. Ever since, the name of 'patriot' has been debased in the Polish language to mean little more than

---

*The 'Patriotic' label was 'borrowed' without attribution from the *Rada patriotyczna* (Patriotic Council) set up in 1940 by former members of the Morges Front, and closely associated with the Polish Government in London. In the First World War, there had been a pro-Piłsudski organization called the 'Union of Patriots'.

'Russian stooge', just as the label of 'demokrata' is nowadays applied to someone who pushes to the front of a food queue. A permanent wall of suspicion was set up in the Polish communist movement between the few original idealists and the many servants of Moscow.

The communists' allies in the shadowy world of wartime Poland were few and far between. None of the major parties would have anything to do with them. Of course, in building their claim to be the 'avant-garde of all progressive forces', they put equally inflated labels on the individuals and factions who joined them. Osóbka-Morawski, who was packaged as 'a leading pre-war Socialist', was in fact a minor clerk in a Warsaw Co-operative Housing Organization. His 'party', the RPPS, was not a continuation of the mainstream PPS, but a tiny splinter group. He was not, as claimed, a former executive member of the PPS. Andrzej Witos and Jan Czechowski were packaged as 'leading members' of the Peasant Movement. They were nothing of the sort. Their 'opposition wing' of the SL was a movement of their own creation. A self-styled group of 'non-party Democrats' appeared, headed by Wincenty Rzymowski, as did groups of 'progressive' writers, trades unionists, co-operativists, fighting youth, Jews, partisans, women. None had any independent standing. Many of the new activists, from Bierut and Żymierski (Łyżwiński) to Jerzy Borejsza (Goldman) or Stanisław Kotek (Agroszewski), could not be freely identified by the public because of their use of pseudonyms. In 1944, a rash of newspapers emanating from liberated Lublin and using titles such as *Rzeczpospolita* (The Republic), *Robotnik* (The Worker), *Zielony Sztandar* (The Green Flag), violently attacked the Polish Government whilst blatantly plagiarizing the names of the Government Parties' official organs. Overall, the operation to construct a broad 'progressive coalition' was a brilliant success on paper; but it had very little genuine substance.

For much of the war, the links between the communists in Poland and their patrons in the USSR were extremely tenuous. Despite the relative proximity of Soviet territory, there were few safe refuges in the Polish countryside, and very little Soviet air support. The Polish communists could

communicate with Moscow less easily than the Home Army
with London. Indeed there is good reason to believe that
Gomułka's comrades had no desire to consult with Moscow
too often. At critical moments they announced that their
radio transmitter had broken down, or that the codes were
lost, and did as they pleased. During one such interval, during
the New Year of 1944, they set up their own 'National
Homeland Council' (KRN), which was the first formal
attempt in Pland to bypass the administrative organs of the
Polish Government. The members of the two main centres of
the Polish communist movement, in Warsaw and in Moscow,
were not properly integrated until the arrival of the Soviet
Army brought them together in the PKWN in July 1944.

The communists' links with the Home Army and other
underground formations were limited to local, tactical co-
operation. They joined forces during the Warsaw Rising,
where they fought bravely alongside the AK; but elsewhere
they were involved in bloody clashes with the NSZ and the
NOW. On no account were they prepared to commit
themselves to any action implying recognition of the Polish
Government.

Their links with the outside world were non-existent. Prior
to June 1945, none of their self-proclaimed institutions was
recognized by any foreign power other than the USSR.

The military forces of the communist movement grew from
modest beginnings in 1943 to impressive proportions by 1945.
The PPR's own 'People's Guard' (GL) started life in obscurity
as the Party's private militia. But following its transformation
in January 1944 into the 'People's Army' (AL), it quickly
assumed wider ambitions and began to form partisan brigades
in all the main regions of Poland west of the Bug. Politically
subordinated to the KRN, and commanded by Franciszek
Jóźwiak (Colonel 'Witold'), it gave an apprenticeship to
several prominent post-war figures including Mieczysław
Moczar ('Mietek'), commander of the Łódź region, and
Marian Spychalski, later Marshal of Poland and President. At
the height of the struggle against the Nazi Occupation, there
were more people attached to the communists' partisans than
to the Party itself. Simultaneously in the Soviet Union, a new
regular Polish army was being formed under Soviet auspices.

Although the Soviet authorities had kept this option open ever since 1940, when the NKVD won over a small group of Polish Officer-prisoners headed by Colonel Zygmunt Berling, their first attempt foundered. Having failed to bring Anders's Army under Soviet control, they had been happy enough to see it depart. Their second attempt was obliged to wait until the diplomatic break with the Polish Government in April 1943. The 'Polish Armed Forces in the USSR' commanded by General Berling made their appearance three days later, when the formation of the First Kościuszko Division was gazetted by Tass. In the course of next summer, the Polish base on the River Oka south of Moscow saw three infantry divisions and one armoured brigade in formation and training. The Kościuszko Division met its baptism of fire at the Battle of Lenino in October 1943 in the body of Zhukov's sector of the Eastern Front. The composition of this Polish force was peculiar in several respects. Firstly, owing to their subordination to the Union of Polish Patriots, the political departments were one step removed from the immediate control of the NKVD, and provided a happy hunting-ground for a coterie of radical Polish communists with distinctly revolutionary ideas. These 'men from the Oka', including figures like Roman Zambrowski, Hilary Minc, and Edward Ochab, were destined to add a special flavour to the Polish Party in the 1950s. Secondly, owing to the inexplicable shortage of trained Polish officers, the greatest part of the officer corps had to be seconded from the Soviet Army. Although several of the leading names such as Karol Świerczewski, Aleksander Zawadzki, or Antoni Siwicki were Polish by origin, very few had ever seen Polish service and many of them were unable to speak anything but Russian. The bulk of the soldiers were Polish, however, being drawn from the still considerable pool of Polish refugees and deportees in Russia. Their numbers were expanded rapidly, from some 78,000 in 1944 to over 400,000 in 1945, as soon as conscription could be introduced in the liberated areas. The final stage of organizational evolution occurred on the crossing of the Bug in July 1944 when 'Berling's Army' of the ZPP was merged with the 'People's Army' of the PPR. The resulting 'Polish Army' (WP) remained under the operational control of the Soviet High

Command, but its political organizations were subordinated to the PKWN. It stayed in the front line throughout the last year of the War, one element ending up in Bohemia, the other in Berlin where it eventually raised the Polish flag on the Brandenburg Gate. This is the progenitor of the post-war armed services of the People's Republic.[27]

By the final phase of the fighting, therefore, the pro-Soviet Camp in Poland was made up of several distinct components. Yet at each stage of the amalgamation the chains of command followed an invariable pattern. Each military formation was supervised from within by political departments which took their orders from a superior civilian organization. Each civilian organization, whether the PPR, the ZPP, the KRN, or the PKWN, was in its turn a creature of the Soviet authorities. The pattern of civilian mergers is also interesting. Every time that the Polish communist element attempted to establish a measure of autonomy, it was overtaken shortly afterwards by the imposition of a watch-dog group sent from Moscow. In 1942–3, Gomułka's group in Warsaw had to admit Bierut and his associates, specially flown in to help them. Gomułka and Bierut's KRN, which operated fairly independently in Poland in the first half of 1944, was obliged in July 1944 to join forces with the PKWN, and later the TRJN, both dominated by Osóbka, Rola, and the Soviets' closest agents. No sooner had the PPR reasserted its position after the war, and taken the leading position as the nucleus of the PZPR, and of the new one-party state, when it was knocked down once again by the arrival of Marshal Rokossowski, yet another of those Poles in Soviet service, who were the ultimate masters of the process all along. One may despise the Soviets' manipulative techniques; but one is forced to admire their ingenuity. Layer after layer after layer of interlocking political control mechanisms enables Moscow to hold its dependants in check at every turn. And if one check snaps, there are plenty of others in reserve. Moscow's allies are not merely held by a collar round the neck; they are held by a leash on the collar, a chain on the leash, a handler on the chain, a collar and lead on the handler, a handler's handler, and, for safety's sake, a muzzle on the mouth, blinkers on the eyes, and a set of trip-wires fastened to the paws and tail. In the parlance of Soviet dog-handling, they call it 'fraternal assistance'. Only capitalist dogs can run.

The final denouement between the pro-Soviet camp and the followers of the Polish Government was staged in the hour of Europe's victory over Nazism. The men and women of the Polish Resistance, who had fought against Nazi tyranny for longer than anyone else, were crushed whilst the rest of the Allied Powers were celebrating the victory. And they were crushed by one of the Allied Powers. With the Home Army broken by the Warsaw Rising; the *émigrés* in London hopelessly split by Mikołajczyk's decision to join the communists in Warsaw; the hopes of the Government camp brutally dashed by the Yalta agreement; and the whole of Poland prostrate beneath the Soviet Army, there was no objective need for the Soviets to be vindictive. Poland had been handed to them on a platter. Yet the well-tried canons of Soviet political culture demanded that the fallen opponents be ritually degraded and scourged. In June 1945, admidst the founding festivities of the United Nations and on the eve of the last meeting of the Big Three at Potsdam, the leaders of Poland's wartime Resistance were put on trial in Moscow as war criminals. Men who had fought the Nazis for longer than any of the Allies, and in conditions of the utmost hardship, were publicly branded as diversionists and subversionists and charged with collaborating with the Nazis and with opposing the Allied struggle against Germany. In the Moscow Trial, sixteen leaders of the Polish Government camp, including the last GOC of the Home Army, General Okulicki, the last Delegate, J.S. Jankowski, and prominent figures from the Socialist, Peasant, Labour, and Nationalist Parties, were given punitive sentences of imprisonment and penal servitude. Several of them were destined to die in Soviet detention. Of all the moral surrenders demanded by the Grand Alliance of the Western democracies with the Soviet Union, none was more obscene than this. The euphoria of Victory could be forgiven; the immense admiration of the British and American public for the heroism and sacrifices of the Soviet armies was entirely proper; but the act which publicly disgraced and humiliated some of the founding members of the anti-Nazi alliance in the interests of political revenge, places a blot on the conscience on everyone who watched in silence. For if other moral outrages of that era (such as the forcible repatriation of Russian Cossacks and Soviet prisoners) were conducted in secret, the Soviets' suppression of the Polish Resistance movement was widely publicized in a blaze of propaganda. The proceedings of the Moscow Trial were openly published in English in London for all the world to read.[28]

The fate of the Polish Government and its loyal adherents was painful in the extreme. The Home Army was formally disbanded in February 1945. Those of its members who decided to fight on in the ranks of the NIE and WiN organizations (see p. 80) did so without guidance from above. Tens of thousands of them were arrested by the Soviet security organs, and forced to sign pledges of loyalty. Many were deported to camps in the USSR, where some still remain to this day. The more prominent among them, having lingered in gaol in the company of Nazi war criminals and other 'enemies of the people', were tried and condemned in secret in trials continuing into the 1950s.[29] A few of them accepted service in the People's Republic, *either* for an easy life *or* sometimes in a conscious attempt to influence the new institutions from within. The Polish Government itself remained in London, but lost all major diplomatic accreditation as soon as Great Britain and the United States recognized the Soviet-backed TRJN in Warsaw in June 1945. At that point, but not before, it became the *Rząd Emigracyjny*, the '*émigré* Government', severed from its homeland and condemned to the endless vigil of permanent exile. Its presidents have duly succeeded each other—W. Raczkiewicz (1939–47), August Zaleski (1947–72), S. Ostrowski (1972–9) and from 1979, Edward Raczyński—and in strictly legal terms it can still claim to be the rightful government of Poland. Its seat still functions at the *Zamek* at 43 Eaton Place; a Council of Ministers still meets; and the *Dziennik Ustaw* (Calendar of Statutes) is still published. Until a serious dispute in 1954 with General Anders and the Polish Military mandarins, it remained the focus of the Polish life abroad. The Polish Armed Services were held for a while on the British military establishment—the First Corps in Germany, the Second Corps in Italy. When demobilization was finally ordered in

1946, all Poles who were serving under British Command were given the choice between a free passage to Poland and resettlement in the United Kingdom or the British Commonwealth. About 105,000 (42 per cent) opted to return. The other 144,000 (58 per cent) chose to stay. (Many whose home towns had now been incorporated into the USSR could not have returned in any case.) Joined by their children and womenfolk, shipped to Britain from Africa and India, and swelled by a large influx of Polish 'displaced persons' from Germany, they constituted the core of the new Polish exile community in the West. Aided in their problems of assimilation, education, employment, and welfare by the British-sponsored Polish Resettlement Corps (1946–50), by social and cultural bodies created by the Polish Catholic Mission and the ex-Combatants Association, and by a large measure of sturdy self-help, they settled down to life in their adopted country. After one whole generation has passed, few of them can doubt their acceptance by British society. The ageing veterans of the wartime exodus are still demonstratively Polish, as anyone can see by a visit to the *Ognisko Polskie* (Polish Hearth Club) in Kensington or to the nearby Polish Institute and Sikorski Museum. The young people, British-born from Polish parents, are reaching out to bridge the gap between two cultures. Life in British exile has its compensations. But no one can pretend that this is the fate for which these dutiful Poles left their country in 1939 or for which the War was fought.[30]

Meanwhile, in the new Poland, the adherents of the Moscow camp had taken the reins of government. In the eyes of the overwhelming majority of the nation, they were usurpers, the agents of a foreign power which had helped them steal the birthright of their real leaders. At all events, their success was not the product of a natural political process. It was not determined by the internal interplay of the aspirations, interests, and organized groups within Polish society. Rather it was determined by the interplay of external forces—by the division of Europe between the victorious Allied Powers, by the stranglehold of the Soviet Army on Eastern Europe, and by the Soviet Union's masterly exploitation of Poland's wartime distress. For the Moscow Camp in

Poland, though stamped with the name of 'People's Power,* and the 'union of all progressive and anti-fascist forces', was nothing of the sort. It was a cuckoo's egg, placed by stealth in the Polish nest, and left to hatch. In the fullness of time, like all voracious cuckoos, it forced its fellow fledglings to starve, cast them out, and took the nest for itself.

Bitter Harvest

Modern warfare, which often afflicts civilians more grievously than soldiers, is a terrible experience; and it has become a commonplace to assert that War has no victors, only losers. Certainly in terms of human suffering there is nothing to choose between the maimed, the war widows, the orphans, and the homeless of one side or the other. In material terms, also, it is hard to distinguish between the gains of the victors and the penalties of the vanquished. Forty years after the Second World War, West Germany and Japan possess the two of the most stable and dynamic economies of the world; whilst the economies of the USA, Britain, and France seem to lurch from crisis to crisis. In the communist world, the productivity, technological advancement, and agricultural output of East Germany or Hungary have far outstripped the USSR, which enjoys the lowest living standards of the entire Soviet Bloc. Many people in the capitals of the wartime Allies must conclude that to have 'won the war' may well have proved a major handicap. But wars are not fought just for motives of material gain. They have much more to do with power, with the right to control one's destiny, and with the great motors of the psychopathology of nations—insecurity, ambition, aggression, and prestige. It is on these moral and political issues above all that the main balance sheet of wars must be judged. For Poland, on the balance sheet of the Second World War, the losses far exceed the gains.

Poland's greatest loss, final and irrecoverable, was the loss of its six million dead—almost one in five of the pre-war population. This gaping wound in the living flesh and blood

*The label of *Polska Ludowa* (People's Poland) was 'borrowed' by the communists without attribution from the propaganda of the non-communist peasant movement within the wartime Resistance.

of the nation, which eliminated the entire natural increase of the inter-war period, took three decades to heal, and has left permanent scars and disfigurations. For the hand of death did not fall evenly on all sections of the population. It fell most heavily on those elements most difficult to replace. It fell most frequently on the youth—on the young men and women who fought and resisted; on the trained and educated classes, who were selected for elimination by the genocidal planners of the occupying powers; and on the brave and the active, who did not care to serve the tyrants in silence. In the nature of things, these victims were the future leaders of the nation, whose energies, brains, and character should have been used to build a better Poland. Without them, if for no other reason, post-war Poland was condemned to be run by people of lesser calibre. In the fumes of the Nazis' Final Solution, the wartime holocaust also consumed the greater part of Polish Jewry—almost one half of the total victims. No one can contemplate this particular crime with anything but horror. Some people, perhaps, in Israel as well as in Poland, whilst abhorring the Nazis' practices, would argue that the resultant separation of two embattled and antagonistic communities has been mutually beneficial. The outbreak in 1946 of a stage-managed pogrom in Kielce would appear to support this view. Others might contend that Poland's divorce from its former Jewish citizens has deprived it of cultural variety and human talents which it could ill afford to lose.

By one means or another, Poland was further deprived of several million other subjects, who, if not actually killed by the War, were separated from their homeland for ever. The political exiles of the Government camp—the soldiers, civil servants, politicians, and writers, and all their depen-dants—numbered many hundreds of thousands. They had formed the core of the ruling élite—the nation's reserve of political experience. Similarly, the deportees and the slave labourers who survived the ordeal of transportation to Germany or Russia, were often obliged to make a new life abroad. The Poles who stayed in Western Europe or in Siberia for reasons of health, marriage, bureaucratic obstruction, or sheer despondency, were even more numerous than the voluntary exiles. Poland's German and Ukrainian minorities—the one expelled in accordance with the Potsdam Treaty, the other decimated by virtue of a private agreement between the Soviet authorities and the PKWN—left huge areas of the country to be repopulated and redeveloped by imported strangers. No country could experience such acts of demographic surgery without developing symptoms of profound shock.

In all these cases, the psychological context of Poland's human losses was particularly severe. Other countries who lost millions during the Second World War were helped to bear the agony by an awareness of clear moral explanations. The Russians mourned their war-dead in the sure knowledge that their sacrifices had turned the Soviet Union into one of the world's superpowers. The British and Americans, whose democracies survived the War intact, could believe that the men and women who died in defence of freedom had not died in vain. The Germans and the Japanese could at least explain their agony by blaming the wartime leaders whose folly had led them to disaster. But the Poles, whose death-toll was the greatest of all, had to mourn without comfort or consolation. Unlike the Russians, they could take no pride in the power and glory of a military triumph, or in the stamina of the socialist order. Unlike the Anglo-Americans, they could not look to the survival of pre-war freedom and democracy. Unlike the Germans or Japanese, they could not even blame their leaders, since the Polish Government had not started the War and had not abandoned the struggle. Poland's dead had perished honourably, but to no obviously worthwhile effect.

Equally, Poland's territorial loss could not be measured in miles or acres. Nor could territorial compensation in the West make up, in anything but material terms, for the 'unrecovered' provinces in the East. Clearly, the industrial value of Danzig, Stettin, and Breslau was greater than that of Wilno, Brześć, or Lwów. The agricultural resources of Pomerania or Lower Silesia far exceeded those of Lithuania or the Pripet Marshes. But a people's attachment to its native soil is not determined by any fondness for statistics. The loss of territory is not just a geographical phenomenon, a change on the map. It is an assault on a nation's body, on its established lifelines and traditions. When accompanied, as in Poland's case, by wholesale transfers of population, it involves the painful separation from all that one holds most dear. Poles who moved in 1945 or 1946 from Lwów to Breslau (renamed Wrocław), or from a hamlet on the Niemen to a farm by the Oder, may or may not have been improving their chances of a prosperous life; but they were *not* 'returning home'. They were embarking on an involuntary journey into the unknown, full of anxiety and apprehension. The move may have been necessary, and in some cases was even welcome. But it was not easy. The process of tearing up a family's roots and of putting them down elsewhere is a searing experience at the best of times. Multiplied by millions, it administered a jolt to Polish society which sent it reeling for decades.

Of course, it would be idle to pretend that Poland could have been reconstructed in 1945 without some adjustments to its pre-war territory. Intercommunal violence of the most frightening kind to which the Polish minority had been subjected in Volhynia and Byelorussia during the War, had convinced many Poles that their possession of the eastern provinces presented something of a doubtful blessing; whilst the hope of acquiring the districts of predominantly Polish settlement in Germany—especially in Opole Silesia, in Poznania, and in West Prussia—was shared by almost all Poles without exception. After much bitter experience, many thinking people were prepared to concede that the rule of a Polish minority over Lithuanians, Byelorussians, or Ukrainians in the East was no more defensible than the rule of the German minority of over Poles in the West. The principle of balanced frontier changes, accompanied by territorial compensation, was not itself in dispute. Even the Polish Government in London, which felt duty bound for the fate of all parts of the pre-war Republic, was not entirely opposed to negotiations on this sensitive subject. Although individual politicians may have stridently denounced all thoughts of conceding even an inch of former Polish territory, and although the official line of the Polish Government was to postpone the discussion of territorial changes until the intended post-war Peace Conference, the fact is that both Sikorski and Mikołajczyk conducted lengthy negotiations about Poland's future frontiers. The source of the trouble lay less in the idea of change than in the methods of procedure, and above all, in the absence of trust between the various parties concerned. For if the Polish Government was reluctant, hesitant, and suspicious, the Soviet Government showed itself to be brutally inflexible. Once Stalin was assured by 1943 that the Soviet Army would overrun the whole of Eastern Europe, he repeatedly refused to countenance any solution of the Polish frontiers other than that which he dictated. The Kremlin was adamant that the Allied Powers should restore the western frontier of imperial Russia, as agreed with the Nazis in 1939 and now conveniently called the Curzon Line. Soviet diplomats in London and Washington so harassed their British and American colleagues on this point that a breach in the Grand Alliance was threatened. Churchill and Roosevelt felt constrained to impose the Russian solution on their Polish allies for the sake of winning the war. The total intransigence of the party with the strongest cards inevitably led to a settlement by *diktat*. What was worse, in those few areas where the 'Curzon Line' was open to interpretation, the Soviet side declined to make any gesture of magnanimity towards the feelings of its Polish opponents. The fate of the city of Lwów was one main case in point. Unlike Wilno (Vilna, Vilnius) in Lithuania, Lwów (Lvov, Lviv, Lemberg) had never been part of Russia or the Soviet Union, and, although it formed a Polish island in a sea of Ukrainian settlement, there was no doubt that its population was predominantly Polish. It lay less than fifty miles East of the main area of ethnic Poland beyond the River San, (see Map 2), and there was a serious question mark over the alleged desire of the Ukrainian peasants in the intervening districts to be incorporated into the collectivized farms of the Soviet Ukraine. Even the Polish communists from Gomulka to Oskar Lange, who talked to Stalin about it in May 1944, were largely agreed on a Polish Lwów.[31] As the records of the Tehran Conference now show, the British Foreign Secretary, Anthony Eden, was prepared to support the Polish claim. But his Soviet counterpart, Molotov, attacked the proposal with fury. Significantly, and perhaps symbolically for the fate of Eastern Europe, throughout the heated exchange between Eden and Molotov, President Roosevelt slept in his chair.[32] As a result, the Poles were denied the one token concession which could have restored equanimity in Allied counsels and which could have sweetened the tenor of Polish–Soviet relations after the war. In the end, Poland was awarded far more German territory in the West than she could possibly have wanted, whilst receiving nothing, not an acre, of her historic lands in the East. Whatever might have happened, the territorial settlement was bound to have been painful. Yet Soviet insensitivity made it far more painful than was strictly necessary. In Poland, the pain and the resentment have continued to fester to the present day.

The ferocity of Soviet attitudes on the territorial issue was symptomatic of their approach to most of the other associated problems. The Soviet Occupation of Poland, and the reign of terror of the Soviet security organs, meant that the Soviet view of each and every detail could be enforced throughout public life. Yet Western observers, such as they were, do not seem to have noticed what was happening. Indeed, the mentality of Soviet officialdom and of its Polish Stalinist imitators was so alien to Western modes of thinking, it was not to be expected that Western diplomats and reporters should rapidly comprehend the full extent of Poland's torment. In the experience of the British or the Americans, politics is customarily treated as a sport akin to tennis or cricket, where one's 'Right Honourable' opponent is never quite one's enemy: where the accepted rules of the game enable one to distinguish cheating and fouling from 'fair play' (if not always to prevent them); and where, in any case, the main tournament is always replayed every four or five years. To such people it was virtually impossible to conceive of the Soviet attitude to a fallen foe. For, by the Stalinist code of conduct, one's opponent had to be forced to confess the heinous crime of his opposition; the accepted rules authorized one of the players to cheat and to foul without redress; the game was never replayed; and to ensure that the victory was permanent, the victor was allowed to deprive the vanquished of the means of remembering their conflict. Not surprisingly, therefore, it was two or three years before the first informed Anglo-American protests about Poland were made, and even then, amidst the prevailing disinclination to cast aspersions on the honour of

our wartime Allies, they were thought to be rather exaggerated.[33] In the process, the Soviet Union was free to punish
Poland at will, and to blacken the name of her wartime Polish
ally with impunity. The remnants of the Home Army were
not simply suppressed; they were put on trial as 'bandits',
'smugglers', or 'Fascist collaborators'. Returning Polish soldiers and airmen, who had fought for the Allied cause at Monte
Cassino or in the Battle of Britain, were arrested as
'imperialist agents'. The Polish Government in London was
not merely ignored; it was officially declared to have been
'illegally' convened by the 'Fascist' constitution of 1935. Ex-
premier Mikołajczyk, who had dared to participate in
Warsaw politics, was not merely obstructed; he was denounced in Parliament as a spy. The Poles who chose to stay
in the West were treated as outcasts and pariahs. Contact and
correspondence with the Polish *émigré* community became a
treasonable offence. Poles who had fought for the Allied cause
in the ranks of the Soviet front, were welcomed home as
heroes. Those who had died in the West, as comrades of the
British or Americans, could not be honoured even in their
death. Gravestones, obituaries, and memorial notices making
any reference to the Polish Government, the Home Army, or
to foreign service were simply removed bv agents of the state
police. Children in school were told how the War had been
won by the Soviet Union alone, whils: the Western Powers
stood by in calculating idleness. Teachers were forbidden to
mention the names of Sikorski or Anders, whilst careless talk
of the 17th of September or of Katyn could lead to instant
arrest. Parents who knew a fuller version of the War from their
personal experience, were fearful of telling their families.
Foreign visitors to Poland were taken to the Warsaw Ghetto,
to the Pawiak Prison, or to Auschwitz with alacrity; but there
were no conducted tours round relics of the Warsaw Rising or
round the Bieszczady Mountains. Historical Museums made
exclusive reference to the achievements of the communist
underground and the People's Army. Historical monuments
were raised exclusively to the 'victims of Nazi aggression'.
Every Polish town had its War Memorial to the heroes of the
Soviet Army of 1944–5: none to its own sons who died in the
service of their country in 1939. In all journals, books, films,

plays, and programmes, the Censorship enforced the same invidious standards. For the dozen years from 1944 to 1956, when Poland was governed by resident Soviet satraps, the memory of Poland's role in all those aspects of the Allied Victory not directly connected with the Soviet camp was systematically erased from the record. Even now, after nearly forty years, no full and balanced account of the Second World War has ever been published in Poland.

The effect of this massive deprivation on Polish consciousness was one of prolonged trauma. Not only were Poles condemned to bear the deaths of their 'lost generation' in silence, and to overcome their separation from the 'lost provinces'; they were even expected to sever their ties with their friends and relations abroad: to renounce their friendship with wartime Allies in the West; to suppress their admiration for the wartime Resistance movement; to pay extravagant tribute, in words and in kind, to the Soviet liberators; to blame their misfortunes on themselves; and, in the cruellest cut of all, to pretend that their tragedy could somehow be counted a victory. This, for the Polish nation, was equivalent to the destitution of a tortured prisoner who is forced to watch as his tormentors destroy his children, his property, his companions, and eventually his own memory and his self-respect.

With the benefit of hindsight, it is not difficult to see how far the post-war settlement of the Polish question deviated from the ideals, for which the Western Allies had professed to be fighting. For Poland, the Atlantic Charter remained a dead letter. The principle of a war without territorial expansion was ignored. The Soviet Union succeeded in persuading the British and the Americans to acquiesce in the essence of the Nazi–Soviet Friendship Treaty of September 1939, together with the demarcation line to the west of Lwów and the suppression of the Polish independence movement. It succeeded in extending Poland's acquisition of former German territories beyond the limits which anyone else thought reasonable or necessary. And it succeeded in disregarding the democratic safeguards which the Western Allies had introduced into the Yalta and Potsdam agreements. Once the official documents of the crucial wartime episodes were published in the 1950s and 1960s, the earlier protests made by opponents of the Polish settlement were largely vindicated. But by that time, when the outbreak of the Cold War had killed the original intention of reviewing post-war dispositions in a comprehensive Peace Conference, Poland's destiny had passed beyond recall.[34] It is often said that 'possession is nine tenths of the Law'; and so it proved in Poland. The Soviet Union was in possession of Poland from the moment that the Soviet Army moved into Eastern Europe in 1944–45; and no formal opportunity has ever been given for the finer points of the issue to be disputed.

Fortunately, however, all was not lost. The Polish peasantry survived the War largely intact, and, in the unprecedented birth-rates of the post-war years provided the biological reserves from which Poland's depleted substance could be replenished. The Polish Emigration abroad preserved a fuller record of the Second World War than officially exists in Poland. Its memoirs, recollections, and publications infiltrate across the Censor's screen and are serving even now to enrich the consciousness of a younger generation eager for knowledge. The Polish Church survived, tempered by a martyrdom shared with the people, and strengthened as the torch bearer of the national identity. The name of Maksymilian Kolbe, the martyred priest of Auschwitz who willingly stepped forward to offer his life to save another's, became the symbol of the sacred union of Church and Nation. In all the important branches of cultural life—in literature, science, the arts, music, drama, scholarship, enough knowledgeable people survived to guard the treasures of an ancient culture and to convey its traditions to posterity. In face of these survivals, the military and political triumph of the Soviet camp may yet prove to have been a superficial and temporary episode in Poland's thousand-year history. The wounds were deep, but total destruction was defied. A long period of convalescence was essential. The seeds of certain regeneration were saved from the bitter harvest of defeat.

CHAPTER III

THE LEGACY OF DISENCHANTMENT

Poland's Experiment in Independence, 1914–1939

One Generation

In August 1914, when Europe entered the ordeal of the Great War, Poland did not exist in any practical sense. 'Poland' could not be found on the map of Europe: between twenty and thirty million people who might have called themselves Poles lived as subjects of the Russian Tsar, the German Kaiser, or the Emperor-King of Austria; and there was no one alive who could remember the time when Poland had been an independent state. Warsaw and Wilno (Vilna) were provincial cities of Russia; Danzig (Gdańsk) and Posen (Poznań) were flourishing cities of Prussia; Kraków and Lwów (Lemberg) were part of the Austrian Empire. The 'Polish Question', one of the recurrent bones of nineteenth-century contention, had all but disappeared from the diplomatic agenda. Yet the Great War was destined to transform the map of Europe, and to rescue the Polish Question from oblivion. The transformation of Eastern Europe was as rapid as it was unexpected. By pitting the three great Empires against each other, the War assured their mutual destruction. Within five years, an independent Poland was reborn; and within seven years, it had fought off a series of attacks from its mistrusting neighbours and established its frontiers. Yet in twenty-five years it was dead. The whole experiment in modern independence, from start to finish, lasted just one generation.

1 Poland's Rebirth during the Great War, 1914–18

The revival of the Polish Question arose quite logically from
the need of the combatant powers to win and maintain Polish
support for their war effort. The bulk of the fighting on the
Eastern Front was bound to take place on territory largely
inhabited by Poles, and mass conscription had brought
millions of Polish soldiers into each of the armies. As long as
the empires of Eastern Europe had been at peace, they had a
common interest in suppressing the Polish issue; as soon as
they were at war, they were compelled to compete with each
other for Polish sympathies. Hence, it was only a matter of
months before the first ambiguous proposals about Polish
autonomy had been raised into a public discussion about
Polish independence. The process resembled nothing so much
as a political auction, where, owing to the system of alliances,
the Western Powers, too, were obliged to join the bidding. The
opening bid was made already in August 1914 by the
Russians, whose commander on the Eastern Front, the Grand
Duke Nicholas, promised the abolition of existing frontiers
and the creation of a 'reborn Poland', 'free in her own faith,
language, and self-rule' under the sceptre of the Tsar. Owing
to the Russians' retreat, this manifesto remained a dead letter.
But the precedent was there. When the German and Austrian
armies overran the whole of Russian Poland in the course of
their great summer offensive in 1915, the Central Powers
could not settle for less than the Russians. After much
deliberation, the German and Austrian Emperors declared on
5 November 1916 that a Polish Kingdom was to be restored
within the conquered territories. Pending the settlement of the
legal and territorial framework and the nomination of a King,
the infant kingdom was to be administered by a collective
Regency Council subject to the military occupation authorities. Obviously, the next move had to come from the West. In
January 1917, President Wilson of the USA raised the stakes
by talking in his State of the Union Speech about 'a united
Poland'. Two months later, the new Provisional Government
in Russia issued a Proclamation on Polish Independence, and
appointed a Liquidation Commission to prepare the transfer
of Tsarist assets in Poland to Polish ownership. Until this

point, Britain and France had kept quiet about Poland out of respect for their Russian ally. But once the Provisional Government in Petrograd had conceded the point, there was no cause for further hesitation. 'Poland' was recognized as one of the Allied powers, and Polish independence was adopted as one of the Allies' war aims. Although some confusion prevailed, the thirteenth of President Wilson's Fourteen Points of 8 January 1918 which demanded 'a united, independent, and autonomous Poland, with free, unrestricted access to the sea' was widely taken as a clear statement of Allied intent. Poland was still under German control; but it was taken for granted that an Allied Victory over Germany would result in the immediate replacement of the puppet Polish Kingdom by an independent Polish State.

Thanks to years of ferment before the War, Polish political organizations, and Polish military formations, sprang up on all sides. On the political front, the growing prospects first for autonomy and then for independence inspired a froth of activity. In Cracow, from 1914 to 1917, there was a Supreme National Committee (NKN) dedicated to forming a united Poland under Austrian auspices, and the Polish National Organization (PON) of Józef Piłsudski, dedicated to fighting for Polish independence by more direct means. In Warsaw in 1914, then in 1915 in Petrograd, in 1916 in Lausanne, and from 1917 in Paris, there was the Polish National Committee (KNP) of Roman Dmowski, which progressed from its original demands for Polish autonomy under Russia to its later claims to be the sole repreentative of the future Polish Government. In London, during 1915–17, there was a Polish Information Committee (PKI), opposed to Dmowski's line; and in Vevey in Switzerland, there was Paderewski's Polish Relief Committee (CAP) which had strong links both with the KNP and with Polish-American organizations in the USA. Each of these bodies acted independently, and each cherished its own vision of how the new Poland was actually going to be delivered. On the military front, the changing fortunes of the War encouraged the formation of a wide variety of Polish units. First and foremost there were Piłsudski's Legions, the military wing of the PON in Austria, and the associated but necessarily clandestine Polish Military Organization (POW) in Russia. The former, consisting of three brigades, fought with distinction in the ranks of the Austrian Army until disbanded somewhat abruptly in 1917. The latter, which ran Piłsudski's intelligence and special operations network behind the Russian lines, continued to function in secret throughout the War. In the Tsarist Army, there was a small volunteer 'Puławy Legion' recruited by the KNP. In France, there was the Polish Army of General Haller, which was formed in 1917 from Austrian and German ex-prisoners-of-war, and which saw action on the Western Front. In Warsaw, in the new Polish Kingdom, there was a small local force incongruously named the *Polnische Wehrmacht.* Both the American and the Canadian armies encouraged volunteer recruitment amongst Polish emigrants in North America.

Generally speaking, Polish political groupings during the War were divided between those of the 'activists' led by Piłsudski, who had hoped to win Polish Independence by making his Legions indispensable to the Central Powers, and those of the 'passivists' led by Dmowski, who sought to gain their ends by diplomatic means and by association with the Allied Powers.

In Poland itself, the backdrop to these developments was one of death and unparalleled destruction. It is often forgotten that the damage to life and property on the Eastern Front was almost as great in 1914–18 as in 1939–45. Yet, with some two million Polish conscripts serving in the armies of Russia, Germany, and Austria at any one time, and with the greatest battles raging in the heart of the Polish provinces—at Tannenberg, Łódź, Gorlice, Przemyśl, and in Brusilov's offensive towards the Carpathians—it was inevitable that Polish casualties were high. Polish military casualties topped the million mark, including 450,000 dead. Civilian casualties were much higher. Galicia was declared a disaster area in the first months of the fighting. When the Russian Army withdrew in 1915 behind its screen of 'scorched earth', it drove almost one million people from their homes. The horrors of the refugee problem were compounded by a typhoid epidemic, and in 1918 by the arrival of the world pandemic of influenza. All in all, calculations based on the territory of the inter-war Republic reveal that a population of 30.9 million in

1914 had fallen by 4.6 million by 1919,—a decrease of 14.9 per cent.* Add to that, the requisitioning by vast armies in the field; the destruction of roads, railways, and bridges; the elimination of entire towns and villages by modern artillery; the displacement of industrial machinery and the deliberate firing of the oilfields—the cost in lives and livelihoods was incalculable.

The German contribution to Polish Independence is also frequently underrated. Of course, the German military authorities, who ruled in Warsaw from August 1915 to November 1918, had no special love for Polish national politics; and their plans for Poland's future were severely limited. There was never any willingness to unite the conquered Polish provinces of Russia with the Polish provinces of Germany or Austria; and the restoration of the puppet Kingdom of Poland was never intended as a stepping-stone to Independence. Yet the General-Gouvernement of those years cannot be compared in anything but name to its Nazi successor of 1939–45. General von Beseler was no Hans Frank. Whatever their ultimate intentions may have been, the Germans laid the foundations on which Polish independence was later built. It was a German decision to permit the public celebration of the Polish National Day on 3 May 1916 for the first time since 1862, and hence to foster the growth of national feeling. It was German policy which proposed to introduce a Polish administration into the Kingdom, and restored the Polish language in official usage. A Council of State with a premier and twelve ministries began the task of creating Polish educational, financial, military, and social institutions. In March 1918, the Germans were bitterly condemned by the Poles for signing the Treaty of Brest-Litovsk with Soviet Russia—a treaty which would have left the Polish Kingdom stranded indefinitely in its hapless condition of a truncated German puppet state; but the fact remains that, without the steps taken by the Germans in Poland during the War, the task of creating an independent Polish state at the end of 1918 would have been much more

*This figure compares with *c.*18 per cent for 1939–45 losses (see p. 100), which includes over three million Polish Jews killed by the Nazis' 'Final Solution'.

daunting. When the German Army chose to withdraw from
Warsaw on Armistice Day, 11 November 1918, for reasons of
largely German concern, it was the German-appointed
Regency Council which was left in control; and it was to Józef
Piłsudski, purposefully released from a German gaol one week
previously, that the Regency Council decided to entrust its
powers.

It is fair to say that the particular way in which Poland was
reborn in November 1918 was accurately foreseen by no one.
The Allied Powers had been expecting that they would
organize the new Republic under Western patronage, and
were outraged that the Germans should have produced
Piłsudski out of the hat at the last minute. The Polish
National Committee in Paris was mortified that its man,
Dmowski, was pipped at the post. The Russians, whether
'Whites' or 'Reds', were fully engrossed in their Civil War, and
had little influence on developments in Poland one way or the
other. Even Piłsudski himself, who had correctly prophesied
that Germany would defeat Russia only to be defeated in turn
by the Western Powers, was in no position to control events.
Having failed to use the Legions as a political instrument
against the Germans, and having refused in July 1917 to swear
an oath of allegiance to the Kaiser, he had remained ever since
in Magdeburg Castle as a German prisoner. When he was
released from Magdeburg and put on a train for Warsaw on
10 November 1918, he must have realized that his hour had
come; but he must also have known that he was only free to
take his chance by favour of the German Intelligence Service.
At that time it so happened that the interests of Józef
Piłsudski, the prophet of Polish Independence, coincided with
the interests of imperial Germany, which wanted to forestall
an Allied take-over in Poland. Like Lenin, whom the Germans
had sent home in a sealed train eighteen months earlier in
similar fashion, Piłsudski was sent to Warsaw for a purpose.
Like Lenin, he 'found power lying in the street', and simply
picked it up.

Poles may be forgiven for believing that in 1918 they had
'fought their way to independence'. But that was not the case.
They certainly did a lot of fighting during the Great War, and
they did gain their independence. But the two were not

causally connected. The vast majority of Polish soldiers had fought in each of the opposing armies of the Eastern Front, and their military efforts only served Polish interests in the sense that they added to the mutual exhaustion of the partitioning powers. The only Polish formations to have separate national political aims, Piłsudski's Legions, were broken up before their goal was achieved. Polish Independence came about through a combination of circumstances largely beyond direct Polish control. To many, it looked like a miracle, even a fluke. The Poles were not given the opportunity to fight for it directly on any large scale. But once they had it, they fought for it and defended it with immense courage and determination.

2 Birth Pangs of the 'Second Republic', 1918–21

The Republic of which Piłsudski took control on 11 November 1918, and was declared the Chief of State of on the 14th had no frontiers, no established territory, no government, no constitution, and no international recognition. It existed, but no one could clearly define its nature or extent. Most Poles agreed, however, that it was the reincarnation of the old Republic which had been destroyed at the end of the eighteenth century. For this reason it is known in Polish History as 'the Second Republic'. The task of establishing its territory and institutions lasted nearly three years; and the birth pangs were attended by many lusty screams.

The establishment of Poland's frontiers in the period of 1918–21 is one of the most complicated episodes of modern European History, and misunderstandings abound. Despite the claims of many textbooks, the Peace Conference in Paris played only a secondary role. Most of Poland's territory was won by force of arms in a series of local wars conducted in defiance of the Peace Conference. The heartland of the new Republic—the German and Austrian zones of occupation (Warsaw and Lublin), Western Galicia (Kraków), and, following the Posnanian Rising of December 1918, Wielkopolska—was secured before the peacemakers even assembled. Several peripheral areas in the East and South—the Lithuanian frontier, the eastern borderlands beyond the Bug, Eastern

Galicia (Lwów), and Cieszyn Silesia—were being disputed whilst the Conference was still deliberating. In effect, the only part of Poland's territorial problems whose settlement can be attributed to the Peace Conference was the new western frontier with Germany. The Allied Powers played the decisive role in the Treaty of Versailles (June 1919) in awarding West Prussia (the so-called 'Corridor') to Poland and in withholding Danzig; in organizing plebiscites in East Prussia (July 1920) and Upper Silesia (May 1921); and in dividing the Duchy of Cieszyn (July 1920). The rest of the Poles were left to fend for themselves. (See Map 4.)

Of the six border wars of these three years,—against Germany (in Posnania and Silesia), Czechoslovakia, Lithuania, the western Ukraine, and Soviet Russia—the Polish–Soviet War of 1919–20 alone held implications of more than local importance.[1] Although the war began almost by default, as the Polish and Soviet armies moved into vast areas recently evacuated by the Germans, it was clear that the future of the eastern borderlands was not simply a matter of territorial possession. For the Bolsheviks, in the full flush of their revolutionary enthusiasm, the advance to the West was an ideological necessity to ensure the survival of their Revolution in Russia. For them, Poland was 'the Red Bridge' which had to be crossed in order to link Russia with Germany and the advanced industrial countries of Europe, where the revolution ought by rights to have been launched in the first place. For the Poles, and for Piłsudski in particular, the conflict with Soviet Russia provided the test of whether the Tsarist Empire could be rebuilt by the Bolsheviks and whether the nations of the borderlands could resist Russian imperialism in its new, 'socialist' guise. Piłsudski's dream was to create a federation of independent national states from Finland to Georgia whose common fear of Russia would inspire them to help each other. In the event, neither Lenin's nor Piłsudski's dreams were realized. The Red Army did not succeed in its drive to cross Poland and link up with the West; and the Federation of the Borders also remained a dead letter.

The fighting lasted for nearly two years. In 1919, when the Red Army was still preoccupied with the Civil War, the Polish Army pushed eastwards, taking most of Lithuania and

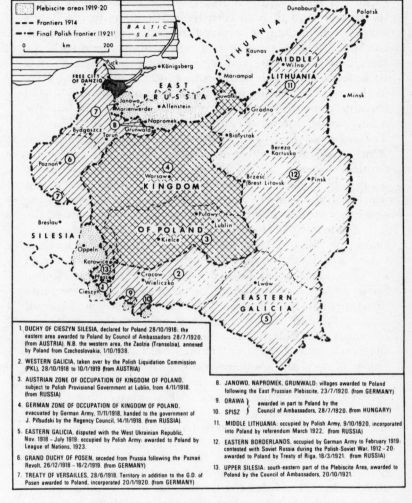

Map 4.   The formation of the Second Republic (1918–21)

Byelorussia. Piłsudski's refusal to assist Denikin in November 1919, when the Russian 'Whites' stood within an ace of capturing Moscow, undoubtedly helped the Bolshevik 'Reds' to triumph and then to turn their attentions to the Polish front. In 1920, the war involved colossal forces on both sides. In April, with a view to cementing his alliance with the Ukrainian Directorate and to outflanking the massive Soviet strike force forming in Byelorussia, Piłsudski marched on Kiev in the south. Then, in June, the arrival of Budyonny's 'Red Cavalry'·army drove the Poles out of Ukraine; and in July, the main Soviet offensive was unleashed in the North by Tukhachevsky from the Berezina. Within six weeks, the Red Army stood at the gates of Warsaw. Lenin was calling for ruthless victory, and a Polish Revolutionary Committee headed by Feliks Dzierżyński, the chief of the *Cheka*, was waiting in the wings to assume power. The Communist press, and other optimists in Germany, had already announced the fall of Warsaw. At which point, the Polish Army delivered a shattering blow which no one had expected to succeed. Piłsudski's flank attack from the south split the Soviet advance, and severed Tukachevsky's communications. Three Soviet armies disintegrated. One large group was driven into internment in East Prussia. The rest fled. Budyonny was all but annihilated in the 'Zamość Ring'. Trotsky, the Soviet Commissar for War, blamed the lack of co-ordination between the northern and southern commands. Tukhachevsky in the North blamed the southern command. Stalin, in the south, blamed Tukhachevsky. The fact is, the Red Army had suffered the only unredeemed defeat in its distinguished history. Lenin, admitting his error in having wrongly expected the Red Army to be welcomed in Poland, sued for peace. Negotiations were pursued at Riga, in neutral Latvia. Just before the fighting ceased on 18 Octover, Piłsudski seized his beloved Wilno from the Lithuanians. The Treaty of Riga of 18 March 1921 divided the Borders between Poland and the Soviet republics, established diplomatic relations, and completed Poland's territorial struggle on a note of satisfaction.

The population of the Second Republic was rich in variety but poor in economic resources. Approximately two-thirds were Polish by language, the other third consisting mainly of

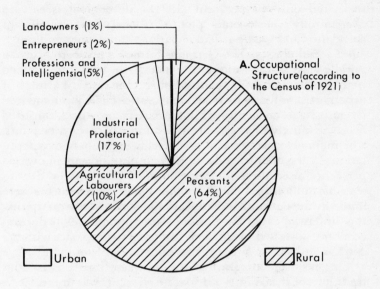

Diagram B.   Polish Social Groups (1921–31)

Ukrainians (15 per cent), Jews (9 per cent), Byelorussians (5 per cent), and Germans (2 per cent). Almost three-quarters lived in the countryside as peasants or agricultural labourers, only one-quarter in the cities. The industrial proletariat registered only 17 per cent (1921). Although it is easy to oversimplify the overall picture, there was a significant correlation between particular national minorities and particular social classes. The Germans formed a prosperous urban middle class in the western provinces. The Jews were typified both by a small and wealthy bourgeoisie and by a mass of urban artisans living by trades and crafts. The Ukrainians and Byelorussians, concentrated in the eastern provinces, consisted overwhelmingly of the poorest and most backward peasants. The main obstacle to social progress lay in rampant overpopulation. In less than two decades, a natural increase of over 33 per cent raised the population from 26.3 million in 1921 to over 35 million in 1939. Although great improvements were made in the cultural and educational spheres—by quartering the illiteracy rate, for example—an underdeveloped rural economy possessed insufficient resources to keep pace with the extra mouths or to support modern standards of living.

The task of integrating the peoples, institutions, and traditions of the country's disparate elements was immense. In 1919–20, there were six different currencies in circulation; five regions maintained separate administrations; there were four languages of command in the Army; three legal codes; and two incompatible railway gauges. Poles who had lived all their lives in Russia, Prussia, or Austria had developed quite distinct habits, and could not adapt to each other overnight. The apocryphal story of the ex-Austrian officer who had to consult his French Army manual before telling his ex-Russian infantrymen how to load their ex-English ammunition into their ex-German rifles had more than a grain of reality.

Political life reflected the fragmentations of Polish society. (See pp. 129–32 below.) In January 1919, the rift between Piłsudski's government in Warsaw and Dmowski's Polish National Committee was temporarily healed by a series of compromises. Dmowski was installed as the Chief Polish Delegate to the Peace Conference; Ignacy Paderewski, the concert pianist, was imported to Warsaw to serve as the first

parliamentary Prime Minister; parliamentary elections produced a working legislature; and the Polish Republic was
formally recognized by the Allied Powers. At the height of the
Soviet War in 1920, the government passed for a time under
the control of a supreme Council of State Defence (ROP); but
by March 1921, in the same week as the signing of the Treaty
of Riga, a new Constitution was inaugurated. The constitutional commission relied heavily on the model of France's
Third Republic; but the reduction of the powers of the
President, engineered by Nationalists fearful of Piłsudski's
election, and the absence of a strong civil service, combined to
deprive Poland of the French system's redeeming virtues. A
plethora of political parties was condemned to compete
without any hope of producing a clear majority. The
sovereign Sejm found difficulty both in expressing its will and
in enforcing its statutes. The omens were not favourable.

In foreign policy, the new Poland stood haughtily aloof and
isolated. There was no hope of close ties with her two great
neighbours, since both Weimar Germany and Soviet Russia
fiercely resented Poland's resurgence; and there was little
chance of uniting with the lesser states of Eastern Europe.
Poland's continuing dispute with Lithuania over Wilno
obstructed any common front with the Baltic States. The
Bolshevik conquest of independent Ukraine and Georgia put
paid to the idea of a federation of border nations; whilst
Poland's traditional sympathy for Hungary inhibited both the
development of links with Romania and Polish adherence to
France's 'Little Entente'. The failure of the Western Powers to
support Poland effectively during the Soviet War had cooled
relations with London and Paris; whilst the USA, whose credit
was high as a result of the work of the post-war American Relief
Mission, had retreated from an active policy in Europe. The
military conventions signed with France and Romania were
strictly limited in scope. Less by design than by force of
circumstance, Poland was obliged to shift largely for itself.

3 *The Constitutional Period, 1921–6*

The widespread failure of parliamentary systems in Eastern
Europe after the First World War, like their failure in Africa

after the Second, seems to indicate some general truth. Western democracy, which grew slowly in Britain or America in a context of security and prosperity, cannot be easily transplanted into the turbulent affairs of new states. In the years after 1918, country after country in Europe fell prey to dictatorships of various sorts. Starting with Mussolini's 'March on Rome' in 1922 and culminating in Franco's invasion of republican Spain in 1936, the European democracies fell like skittles before the onslaught of the dictators. In Central and Eastern Europe, the parliamentary regime lasted longest in Czechoslovakia, for twenty years to March 1939. In Austria it lasted nineteen years; in Germany, sixteen years; in Yugoslavia, nine years; in Poland, just seven.*

The Polish coalition governments of 1921 to 1926 operated in an atmosphere of frustration and violence. They resulted from the inability of any one party to overcome the spoiling activities of its opponents, and in turn gave rise to a number of deplorable deformations. Neither the socialists on the Left nor the radical nationalists on the Right could gain the upper hand, and power fell to the political middlemen of the Centre. Corruption of both the political and the material kinds came to the fore. Figures such as Wincenty Witos, the leader of the moderate wing of the Peasant Movement, who headed three separate governments in those years, could only solve the deadlock in parliament by ignoring or betraying their own electoral platforms. Ministers who held office for only a few months at a time could not pursue any consistent policy; whilst discontented underlings sought to cut corners by bribery and embezzlement. The underlying frictions were revealed during the tragic presidential election of 1922. Piłsudski, the prime contender, was offended by the constitutional limitations placed on the office, and had refused to stand. The minority electors lined up against the Nationalist candidate. The successful contestant, Gabriel Narutowicz, a distinguished scientist, was denounced by the Nationalists for being elected by 'non-Polish votes' and was assassinated at a

*The Sejm operated in 1919–21 on an *ad hoc*, pre-constitutional basis, and from 1926 to 1939 under the unconstitutional limitations placed on it by the Sanacja regime.

show. If such dissensions could occur at the top, it was not hard to imagine what passions were raging below.

A series of feeble governments was faced by a long list of intractable problems. Agrarian reform did not produce the desired effects. In 1919, the Sejm decided to break up all large estates of more than 400 hectares. In July 1920, with the Red Army advancing on Warsaw, it determined to buy surplus land for redistribution at half its market value. In 1925, it finally set an annual target of 200,000 hectares to be purchased by the state and parcelled out among the poorest peasants. State finance was in chaos. Poland, like Germany and Hungary, experienced several years of catastrophic 'hyperflation', in which the rate of the Polish mark against the US dollar rocketed from 1:9 in 1918 to 1:15 million in January 1923. Minimal stability was only achieved in 1924 by the reforms of Władysław Grabski, and the establishment of the new złoty currency managed by a new Bank Polski. The budget could not be balanced until 1926. Up to that point, there could be no prospect of large-scale foreign investment, industrial recovery, or expansion of the primitive economic infrastructure. Most ominously, the Army was reluctant to submit its affairs to civilian control. With Piłsudski sulking in retirement, and the officer corps openly contemptuous of the politicians' ineffectual wrangles, the stage was well set for a mutiny.

Even so, the achievements of those early years are easily forgotten. Starting with the core of institutions left by the Germans' Polish Kingdom, a modern state had to be built in haste in the most adverse conditions of war and economic disruption. The creation of an army, a legal system, an educational system, a civil service, a parliament and country-wide political parties, a financial system, state industrial and commercial sectors, a united transport and communications network, together with the training of the personnel to run them, must be regarded as a major success in each instance. The survival of these institutions attests to the fact that the period of parliamentary rule was not entirely fruitless.

4 *The Sanacja Regime, 1926–35*

Piłsudski's motives in overthrowing the legal government of the Republic, over whose rebirth he had so recently presided, have been much debated. It seems that he had no burning desire to regain the reins of power, and no clear plans of how to do so. He resisted all pleas to allow himself to be reinstated as the formal Head of State. On the other hand, he was concerned by the Locarno Treaty of 1925 which had pointedly omitted any guarantee of Poland's frontiers, and he was seriously worried by the corruption and (in his view) the incompetence of the parliamentary leaders. He deeply resented civilian interference in 'his' Army, and in particular was determined to stop Witos from forming yet another Centre–Right coalition. So, on the morning of 12 May 1926, when a couple of mutinous legionary regiments appeared before his home at Sulejówek, he went along with them; and later, when challenged by the President of the Republic, Stanisław Wojciechowski, in a dramatic personal meeting in the middle of the Poniatowski Bridge over the Vistula, he refused to withdraw. Fighting with troops loyal to the President broke out that same afternoon. Piłsudski was constrained to settle the issue by force of arms.

The May Coup of 1926 shocked Poland to the core. Only eight years after gaining their independence from the foreign oppressor, Poles had taken up arms against each other. The Polish Army, the pride of the nation, was split down the middle. Piłsudski was opposed by many of his former associates, like General Sikorski or President Wojciechowski himself. He was supported by the Left, including the communists, who feared a similar take-over by the Nationalists. The overall balance of forces had not been in Piłsudski's favour, since the President and the Government retained the loyalty of the bulk of the Army and of most citizens. But the issue was determined by a critical strike by the socialist Union of Railwaymen. Having lost a number of strongpoints in central Warsaw, including the airport and railway station, the Government was unable to bring in reinforcements by train, and within three days Piłsudski's men had captured all the key buildings and officials. On 14 May, both the President and the Premier were forced to capitulate, and to resign from office. For the remaining nine years of his life, Józef Piłsudski was to be the unchallenged ruler of Poland.

The regime installed by the May Coup defies easy classification. It took its name from the slogan of *Sanacja*, meaning a return to (political) 'health', and was guided by a vague, if forceful, ideology, akin to Moral Rearmament, which imagined that the evil in men's souls could be scrubbed clean by military spit and polish. (According to its many critics, it blended the philosophies of Nietzsche and Kant— *nicze* in Varsovian slang meaning 'rubbish', and *kant* meaning a 'swindle'.) It was not at all Fascist in its leanings, since the only Fascist sympathizers in Poland were to be found among Piłsudski's opponents; and it was not a formal dictatorship. The parliament, the political parties, and the opposition all continued to function. Piłsudski was content to direct affairs from behind the scenes: to mask his personal rule with a parliamentary façade: and to cow the opposition by strong-arm police methods and harassment. His main instrument at the outset was the so-called Non-Party Bloc for Co-operation with the Government (BBWR), which was designed to win popular support by manipulating the electoral system. When this failed, the opposition was attacked more directly. To his lasting credit, Ignacy Daszyński, the socialist Marshal of the Sejm, refused in September 1930 to open the House in the presence of armed officers, when, following a Convention of People's Rights called to Cracow to mobilize protest, the leaders of the Centre-Left opposition were arrested. Their detention in the fortress of Brest was followed by a lengthy trial, by harsh sentences of imprisonment, and in March 1933 by the suspension of the nationalist opposition's Camp of Great Poland (OWP). By that time, the Sanacja regime was embattled on numerous fronts. Rebellious peasants in the countryside were brutally pacified. Separatist Ukrainians were harried without mercy. Polish society, like the European scene in general, was starting to polarize. If the parliamentary regime had been somewhat chaotic, the Sanacja was downright clumsy. One blithe spirit described the May Coup as 'an attack by bandits on a lunatic asylum'.

The Army inevitably advanced in social and political stature. Its role in education, and in moulding the outlook of hundreds of thousands of young conscripts, exerted a great force for cultural assimilation. The officer corps offered a career open to merit, and for that reason thought of itself as a force for democracy. At the same time, political loyalty to Piłsudski represented the touchstone of success. Military men, and legionary officers in particular, moved into the civil service and into government circles in large numbers. Army colonels appeared in all high places—Colonel Józef Beck as Foreign Minister from 1932, Colonel Walery Sławek, as Prime Minister on several occasions and as manager of the BBWR, Colonel Adam Koc as Leader of the BBWR's successor, the Camp of National Unification (OZON). Piłsudski himself retained the two key posts—Inspector-General of the Armed Forces and Minister of War.

Apart from the Army, Piłsudski was only really enthusiastic about Foreign affairs. He looked on the world through sceptical eyes, and taught that Poland must count on her own strength. Faced with the rise of Stalinist Russia on one border, and with Nazi Germany on the other, he formulated 'the Doctrine of Two Enemies'. Poland was to uphold proper relations with both neighbours, but to ally with neither. To this end, he signed two ten-year pacts of non-aggression—one with the USSR on 25 January 1932, and its sequel with Nazi Germany on 26 January 1934. Recognizing the menace of Hitler's dynamic expansion, he tried to sound out the Western Powers on the subject of a joint preventative war, but was rebuffed in horrified silence.

Piłsudski's Poland had several redeeming features. On the surface at least, it exuded a spirit of debonair confidence. Polish cultural life saw an explosion of literary and artistic talent. Economic life, if not prosperous, was at least stable. The złoty stayed on the gold standard. Political repression did not affect the mass of the population. There was no enforced ideology. The great Marshal was the object of much adulation and much genuine affection.

Yet the system, like the Marshal himself, was seriously ill. Social distress in the countryside was acute. Unemployment in Polish industry during the Depression reached 40 per cent. Intercommunal antagonisms, and rising anti-Semitism, caused great anxiety. A new constitution, unveiled in April 1935, moved in the direction of intensified authoritarianism. The ills of society were being suppressed, not treated. One month later, when the Marshal died of cancer, the nation's grief was mingled unmistakably with foreboding.

5 The Road to Disaster, 1935–9

Poland's predicament in the late 1930s was far from enviable. A seat between Hiter and Stalin provided the least comfortable location on the globe. To combine with one or the other was equally distasteful, and equally dangerous. To do nothing was to tempt fate. To rely on the Western Powers or on the 'Collective Security' system of the League of Nations was less than reassuring. As Piłsudski had warned, and as the Munich Agreement over neighbouring Czechoslovakia amply demonstrated, the British and the French seemed content to appease the aggressors at other people's expense. Furthermore, the effects of the European crisis were compounded by the longering effects of the World Depression. The Polish economy was incapable of generating the resources which might have permitted military modernization and rearmament on a scale commensurate to the¹ Army's needs. In such a pass, it is doubtful whether the Poles were fully masters of their fate or really responsible for their downfall.

On the internal front, the Sanacja regime witnessed a distinct closing of the ranks. The 'Government of the Colonels', dominated by General Sławoj-Składkowski as premier and Marshal Edward Śmigły-Rydz as Commander in Chief, strengthened military control. The Piłsudski-ites without Piłsudski were not averse to reconciling the differences with their Nationalist rivals, and encouraging the OZON's increasingly chauvinist excesses. With the example of Czechoslovakia before them, they were obsessed with the idea of national unity. The German minority in Poland was rapidly turning to Nazism. The Jews were fearful of persecution and harassment. The Ukrainians were seething with discontent. Many Poles were defensive and assertive. Several nationalist splinter groups and Fascist gangs made their appearance. The Church was being dragged into politics. Too many Catholic priests were being carried away by the nationalist tide. The Army was reformed within the bounds of its resources. Poland's first economic plan, which established the Central

Industrial Region (COP) together with a state-controlled armaments industry, took a belated step towards greater self-sufficiency.

The real source of anxiety, however, lay abroad. After the Rhineland in 1936, Austria in '37, and Czechoslovakia in '38, it was fairly predictable that Hitler's venom in 1939 would next be turned on Poland—as indeed it was. Throughout those years, Colonel Beck continued Piłsudski's policy of even-handedness, whilst' trying to offset the growing danger of encirclement by Germany. His ultimatum to Lithuania in March 1938, and his inglorious invasion of the Zaolzie district of Czechoslovakia during the Munich Crisis in October of the same year, are often described as the actions of a petty-minded opportunist, meanly settling old scores against his neighbours in distress. They could also be seen as attempts to forestall German penetration into areas vital to Poland's defence. Beck was no less steadfast in resisting Nazi overtures for a common attack against the Soviet Union, as in resisting Western demands to admit Soviet troops into Poland for the containment of Germany. The Western appeasers were still thinking that Europe's tranquillity should be bought by someone else's sacrifice. In March 1939, the game entered its terminal phase. Hitler's cynical invasion of Czechoslovakia removed the ambiguities of his previous assertions, and Great Britain was moved to offer its famous Guarantee of Poland. Both Hitler and Stalin recognized the Guarantee as a piece of empty bluff, knowing full well that the British possessed neither the planes, the ships, nor the soldiers which could possibly protect Poland from attack. Hitler proceeded immediately to denounce the Polish–German Pact of Non-Aggression, and to prepare for war. Stalin sensed that his safest course of action lay in an accommodation with the Nazis. When Molotov replaced Litvinov in May, all the pre-conditions of a Nazi–Soviet Pact had been brought into place. Although the Western Powers continued the motions of Collective Security, the game was already up. With a Franco–British military mission still nominally negotiating in Moscow, the Soviets were already negotiating with Berlin. In July, Ribbentrop let it be known in the Kremlin that there was 'no problem' that could not be amicably resolved. The Nazi–Soviet 'trade talks' rapidly changed gear. The essence of the deal was that each side could pursue its aggressive designs without the interference of the other, on condition that their respective spheres of expansion were kept apart. The Germans had designs on Western Poland, and in due course on Western Europe and Scandinavia. The Soviets had designs on Eastern Poland, the Baltic States, and Bessarabia. A public pact of Non-Aggression bvetween Nazi Germany and the Soviet Union was signed in Moscow by Ribbentrop and Molotov on 23 August 1939. A secret protocol defined the territorial arrangements including the prospective partition of Poland along the rivers Narew, Vistula, and San. It was Poland's death warrant. Notwithstanding the renewal of the British Guarantee, Hitler was free to lanch the attack on Poland with impunity. He ordered the *Wehrmacht* to march within the week. It marched on 1 September.

For the sake of precision, it is important to state the true nature of Poland's demise in 1939. The Second Republic was frail; but it did not die of natural causes. Poland was foully murdered by two assailants acting in collusion. The spirit and vigour with which she defended herself during that vicious assault suggests that recovery from her infirmities was perfectly possible. She was not given the chance to recover.

But the result was incontrovertible. The Second Republic was dead. Within one quarter of a century after 1914, Polish independence had been conceived, born, raised, nurtured, killed, and buried.

The Duel: Dmowski versus Piłsudski

Any full description of the political spectrum in pre-war Poland would require a small encyclopaedia. The proliferation of interests, movements, parties, factions, coalitions, parliamentary circles, youth sections, military wings, community groups, regional associations, trade unions and co-operative societies, fringe lobbies, and debating clubs (most of which seemed to change their names at regular intervals), was enough to confuse the most persistent enquirer. Yet the confusion is somewhat reduced if one pays attention to three distinct types of political groupings.

Firstly, there were the three great institutions of Polish society—Church, Army, and Intelligentsia, which played a vital, if informal role, in political affairs. They were far from uniform in outlook. The Church was characterized both by an arch-conservative hierarchy and by the lesser clergy, who were often very radical. The Army contained a mixture of the traditional officer class (largely from the Austrian or Tsarist Service) and of young ambitious social climbers with strong democratic tendencies. The Intelligentsia displayed a wide variety of attitudes, from religious pietism to social anarchism. (See Chapter IV, pp. 262–67.)

Secondly, there were the four main political movements—Socialists, Nationalists, Peasants, and Christian Democrats—each of which was strongly represented in Parliament, and each of which spawned a string of central or regional parties and factions. All four of them had emerged in their modern form at the turn of the century, but had not been able to organize fully-fledged, nation-wide parties until Independence was gained in 1918.

In order of seniority, the socialist movement, whose principal organization, the Polish Socialist Party (PPS) was founded in Paris in 1892, combined strong interests in non-Marxist socialism and in national independence. It had split in 1906 between the mainline PPS-*Rewolucja* (Revolution), which held that no social progress could occur without national independence, and the PPS-*Lewica* (Left) which considered national politics to be secondary to social change. The former, largely based in Russian Poland, had been matched by lesser counterparts in Prussia and in Galicia. The latter had moved increasingly towards internationalist, Marxist socialism, and in 1918 had joined with the tiny Social Democratic Party of the Kingdom of Poland and of Lithuania (SDKPiL) to launch the Polish communist movement (KPRP and from 1926 the KPP).

The Nationalist Movement, in contrast, was violently opposed to socialism of all hues, and treated class conflict as something to be superceded, not fanned. Its main areas of interest lay in ethnic issues, economic development, and international affairs. It had begun life in 1893 with Dmowski's National League, which in turn gave rise to the National

Democratic Movement (SN-D) in 1897, to the People's National Union (ZL-N) in 1919, to the National Movement (SN) in 1928, and to the Camp of Great Poland (OWP) in 1926–33. It was generally known as the *Endecja* or 'National Democracy', and its right-radical ideology exerted an influence far beyond the bevy of parties it directly inspired.

The Peasant Movement (PSL), founded at Rzeszów in Galicia in 1895, represented the most numerous class of Polish society; but its influence was greatly weakened by a tendency towards constant fragmentation. The main PSL-*Piast* party from Galicia was widely suspected of being controlled by the clergy and by the wealthier farmers, and had parted company from the more radical PSL-*Lewica* (Left) in 1914. A separate PSL-*Wyzwolenie* (Liberation), also very radical, had operated in Russian Poland. The attempt to keep these various elements in line in the 1920s was thwarted by the secession of an offshoot Peasant Movement *(Stronnictwo Chłopskie)* between 1926 and 1931; but was repeated again in the 1930s.

The Christian Democratic Movement or *'Chadecja'* had originally come into being in 1902 in Prussian Poland, where the proletarian character of Polish society, especially in Silesia, had promoted its characteristic blend of Catholic philosophy and social action. Its associated parties included the Polish Movement for Christian Democracy (PSChD), and from 1937 the Labour Movement (SP).

Each of these main movements possessed particular regional 'fortresses'—the socialists in Lódź and Warsaw, the Nationalists in Poznań and Lwów, the peasants in Kraków and the South, the Christian Democrats in Upper Silesia— but all operated on a country-wide basis after 1918.

Thirdly, there was a whole kaleidoscope of the organizations serving each of the national minorities. Some of these, such as the *Rat der Deutschen in Polen* or the local Jewish *kahal* (communes), which were supported by the Government, exercised essentially social, cultural, or religious functions. But others were more explicitly political. A 'Bloc of Minorities' operated in the Polish Parliament. The Germans in the western provinces ran their own socialist party, the DSAP, and their own nationalist party, the *Jungdeutsche Partei*. Polish Jewry could boast almost as many parties as voters, and it is

interesting to note how, *mutatis mutandis,* the four main
tendencies mirrored the experience of their Polish counterparts. The *Paole Zion* (Workers of Zion) was stretched, like the
PPS, to reconcile its nationalist and its socialist interests. The
Bund (Jewish Workers League), like the Polish communist
movement, was internationalist and Marxist in flavour, but
split between its pro-Soviet and non-Soviet wings. The Zionist
movement, whose very first conference in 1884 had convened
at Katowice, suffered, like the Polish National Democrats,
from an ambivalent relationship with its religious authorities.
The *Agudat Israel* (Union of Israel), the conservative Judaic
party, combined, like the Christian Democrats, strong religious affiliations with social action among the masses. The
Byelorussians, in contrast, were represented exclusively by a
peasant-based organization, the *Hramada* (Commune) which
was broken up by the police in 1928 and driven underground.
The Ukrainians in Poland inherited a wide range of political
parties from their Galician days—the Ukrainian Social
Democratic Party (USDP), the Ukrainian Peasant Socialist
Federation *(Sel Rob)*, the Ukrainian Socialist Radical Party
(USRP), and the Ukrainian National-Democratic Union
(UNDO). Increasingly, however, intercommunal tensions
gave prominence to the illegal Organizations of Ukrainian
Nationalists (OUN) which as from 1931 indulged in a
widespread campaign of terrorism and sabotage.

Lastly, there were a number of vociferous groups on the
political fringe. On the Right, there was the Fascist *Falanga*
(Phalanx), an offshoot of the Nationalist OWP. On the Left,
the communist KPP, (see p. 130), was an offshoot of the
socialists.

Not surprisingly, given the immense complexity of antagonisms and affiliations, the Polish political arena gave great
scope to enterprising individuals. Especially in the 1920s, the
Sejm was full of colourful personalities—Ignacy Daszyński
(1866–1936), the silver-maned socialist veteran, who closely
resembled his namesake, the first Premier, Ignacy Paderewski;
Wincenty Witos (1874–1945), the Peasant leader in smock
and breeches; Father Eugeniusz Okoń (1882–1939), a fiery
priest devoted to Land Reform; Wojciech Korfanty
(1873–1939), the ex-Prussian deputy and Christian Democrat,

who led the three Silesian Risings of 1919, 1920, and 1921; Róża Pomerantz Meltzer, Poland's first woman deputy in 1919; and Yitzhak Gruenbaum (1879–1960), the Zionist leader. In the 1930s, the men who made their mark were more memorable for their military medals than for their sophisticated philosophies. Yet the Senate was adorned with figures of genuine distinction, from Michał Bobrzyński (1849–1935), the historian to Wojciech Korfanty (1873–1939), the Silesian leader; and the political press from the dailies such as the *Kurjer Warszawski* or the *Ilustrowany Kuryer Codzienny* in Kraków to the quality monthlies such as the *Przegląd Współczesny* (Contemporary Review), was full of life and humour. No one can claim that pre-war Polish politics was as dull or as bereft of individual talent as the post-war period. Equally, no one could claim that any of the lesser personalities could be compared in stature to the two men whose personalities and ideologies dominated the scene from beginning to end. These two were Roman Dmowski and Józef Piłsudski.

Dmowski and Piłsudski had several things in common. In an age of nationalism, and in the era of national independence, they both gave pride of place in their thinking to the concept of the nation. They both transcended party politics, both commanding wide followings far beyond the parties from which their early careers developed. They were both self-declared democrats who had little patience with democracy in practice. Each regarded the other as the devil incarnate. Apart from that they were as different as chalk and cheese.

Roman Dmowski (1864–1939), quite simply, was the father of modern Polish Nationalism.[2] Born into a struggling suburban family in Praga, he graduated from a Russian *gimnazjum* in Warsaw, and completed his studies in the natural sciences at the (Russian) University of Warsaw. His social origins were those of the new assertive Polish bourgeoisie of the late nineteenth century, whose ambitions were frustrated by the closed nature of the imperial regimes of the partitioning powers and by competition with the numerous non-Polish elements of urban society. His lifelong commitment to Polish politics was ignited in 1892, when he was imprisoned in the

Warsaw Citadel and sentenced to banishment for his part in
organizing a patriotic student demonstration in honour of the
Third of May. After a brief association with 'Zet', the youth
section of the Polish League, and a formative visit to Western
Europe, he returned to Poland in April 1893 as one of the
founding members of the National League, quickly establishing himself as its chief publicist and ideologist, and editor of
the *Przegląd Wszechpolski* (The All-Polish Review). As an
author, he gained widespread recognition with his *Młodzież
polska* (Polish Youth, 1895) with his *Myśli nowoczesnego Polaka*
(Thoughts of an up-to-date Pole, 1903), which examined the
changing interests and attitudes of contemporary society, and
above all with *La Question Polonaise* (1906), which helped to
revive interest in the Polish factor in international affairs both
at home and abroad. During the 'revolution' of 1905-6, his
National Democratic Party gained prominence as a alternative to socialism. He even visited Japan in order to scotch the
scheme for raising a Polish Legion from Russian prisoners of
war in Manchuria, only to run into Piłsudski on the street in
Tokyo. In the following years, as a deputy to the Russian
Duma in St. Petersburg and chairman of the Polish Circle, he
advocated a gradualist approach to national politics, aiming
to win concessions by close collaboration with the Tsarist
authorities. In 1911, he earned considerable notoriety by
organizing the boycott of Jewish enterprises in Warsaw, as a
result of which, at the next election, he lost his deputy's seat.
During the Great War, as chairman of the Polish National
Committee, he chose to work for the Polish cause in
conjunction with the Allied Powers, calculating that his
contribution to an Allied victory over Germany would be
rewarded by the creation of a Polish state under Allied
auspices. That was not to be. His initial reliance on Russian
patronage was nullified by the Germans' rapid successes on
the Eastern Front; and in 1916 he switched his attentions to
the new diplomatic opportunities in London and Paris. Yet
the Allied Government grew sceptical of his promises, and in
the last weeks of the War he was still in the West, in
Washington, still uncertain whether the Allied Powers would
install his Committee as masters of the new Poland. Following
Piłsudski's unexpected triumph, he undertook the task of

being Chief Polish Delegate to the Peace Conference, remaining at hs post for the next two years. He served briefly as a member of the ROP in the summer of 1920 during the Soviet War, but any prospect of his gaining power through Piłsudski's mistakes was ended by the Battle of Warsaw. He was greatly distressed by the parliamentary disputes, preferring to write in seclusion than to wrangle in public. His works from those years included *Polityka polska a odbudowanie państwa* (Polish politics and the reconstruction of the state, 1925), an apologia for his work during the War, and a prophetic little article called *'Piasek w maszynie'* (Sand in the engine, 1925) which correctly predicted the May Coup. He emerged in the autumn of 1923, to head the Ministry of Foreign Affairs in Witos's second coalition cabinet. Although he retained a powerful influence over the nationalist movement, his only descent into party politics was to form the Camp of Great Poland in 1928. Although he was the person to whom the Right constantly appealed for protection from Piłsudski, he never again attained high office. He preferred to operate behind the scenes; but no one doubted that he was one of the pillars of opposition to the Sanacja regime. He was frequently absent abroad, notably in North Africa, vainly seeking a cure for worsening arteriosclerosis. He died in January 1939 in retirement, and was buried before a great crowd of admirers in the cemetery of Bródno in Praga, next to his mother. The Government was not represented at the funeral.

Józef Piłsudski (1867–1935), quite simply, was the champion of modern Polish independence.[3] Born into an impoverished noble family in Lithuania, he graduated from the Russian *gimnazjum* in Vilna, and began his studies in medicine at the University of Kharkov. His social origins were those of the broken remnants of the old Polish nobility and intelligentsia, whose dreams were shattered by the repressions of the imperial regimes. His lifelong commitment to Polish politics was ignited in 1887 when he was sentenced to five years' penal servitude in Eastern Siberia for his brother's part in organizing an attempt to assassinate the Tsar. After a brief flirtation with theoretical socialism, and the first of several visits to Western Europe, he returned to Poland in 1893 as one of the founding members of the PPS, quickly establishing himself as

editor of *Robotnik* (The Worker) and as a tireless militant of the
revolutionary underground. As an activist, he seems to have
had a particular interest in historical issues, and concentrated
all his efforts on the practical problems of national liberation.
He began his literary career with a little history of the
notorious 'Tenth Pavilion' of the Warsaw Citadel, where he
himself was imprisoned in the winter of 1901, having been
arrested in Łódź in possession of an illegal printing press and
a false passport. During the 'revolution' of 1905–6, his PPS
battle-squads took the lead in the wave of strikes and terrorist
incidents. He even visited Japan, to press his scheme for
raising a Polish Legion, only to run into Dmowski on the street
in Tokyo. In the following years, as an outlawed terrorist and
then as a political refugee in Galicia, he opted for the military
solution to Poland's problems, aiming to organize an armed
force which could be used at an appropriate moment to wring
concessions from the Tsarist authorities. In 1913 he earned
considerable prestige by putting his 'riflemen's association' on
manœuvres, and by lecturing abroad. During the Great War,
as *Komendant* of the Legions, he chose to fight for the Polish
cause in conjunction with the Central Powers, calculating that
his participation in a German victory over Russia would give
him the means for creating a Polish state on his own terms.
That was not to be. His initial usefulness to his German
patrons was nullified by their excessively rapid advances on
the Eastern Front, and in 1916–17 he switched his attentions
to the political opportunities in the new Kingdom of Poland,
where he briefly served as Minister for Defence. Yet the
German Government grew sceptical of his motives, and in the
last weeks of the War he was still imprisoned in Magdeburg
Castle, still fearful that the Allied Powers would install
Dmowski's National Committee as masters of the new Poland.
Following his unexpected triumph, however, he threw himself
into the task of defending the Republic (and his own position)
from all comers. He served as Chief of State and Commander
in Chief through the first four years of independence; and any
prospect of his nationalist rivals gaining power from his
mistakes during the Soviet War was ended by the Battle of
Warsaw. He withdrew in 1923, greatly distressed by the
parliamentary disputes, preferring to write in seclusion than

to run for the presidency. His works from those years include *O wartości żołnierza Legjonów* (On the value of the legionary soldier, 1923); *Rok 1920* (The Year 1920, (1924)); *Moje pierwsze boje* (Memoirs of a revolutionary, 1925); and *U źródeł niemocy Rzpltej* (On the sources of the Republic's impotence, 1924), which throws light on his state of mind prior to the May Coup. When he re-emerged in 1926, it was to stop Witos's attempt to form yet another coalition cabinet with the nationalists. Although he retained strong sympathies for the socialist movement, he never rejoined the PPS. Although he was repeatedly pressed to 'accept the crown', his only descent into formal office was to hold the Premiership temporarily for a short period in 1926–8 and again in 1930. He preferred to operate behind the scenes, but no one doubted that he was the boss of the Sanacja Regime. He was frequently absent abroad, notably on Madeira, vainly seeking relief from worsening stomach cancer. He died in May 1935 in harness, and was buried with all the pomp of state in the crypt of Wawel Cathedral in Cracow, next to the kings of Poland. Dmowski was not invited to the funeral.

Of the two men, Dmowski had the stronger claim to a coherent ideology and to a consistent entourage. His associates—Zygmunt Balicki and Jan Popławski in the early years; Zygmunt Wasilewski (1865–1948), and Zygmunt and Marian Seyda later on—shared the same basic ideas, and applied them both in their private speeches and writings and in the strong nationalist press. Piłsudski, in contrast, showed greater reluctance to formulate theoretical propositions, and, by shifting his ground on several occasions, tended to alienate many of his associates. The close colleagues of his socialist period such as Leon Wasilewski (1870–1936) or Stanisław Wojciechowski (1869–1953) had largely parted company with him by the time of the May Coup, if not before. His closest associates in the Sanacja regime—such as Walery Sławek, Adam Koc, or Józef Beck—were all military men with strong legionary connections. Even so, the clash of principle between the two camps was deep and genuine and was not merely the product of personal animosities. The issues which they contested so fiercely over forty years covered the whole gamut of domestic and international affairs, and explain why the debate between their respective admirers and detractors has continued to the present day.

The concept of the nation*—that is, the nature of the national community—was the central issue for people actually engaged in forging one. In Piłsudski's view, the nation was a product of history, a community sharing the same values and loyalties, though not necessarily the same ethnicity or origins. Within such a nation, there was room for many nationalities so long as each of the constituent parts stayed loyal to the whole. His model for a 'multinational nation' was undoubtedly drawn from the old Republic of Poland–Lithuania (see p. 316), although it had much in common with the British and American ideas on the subject. In Piłsudski's eyes, ethnic and cultural variety within the nation should be a source of strength and vitality. In Dmowski's view, however, the nation was a natural phenomenon, the result of the God-given division of mankind into distinct entities each possessing its own exclusive language, territory, and history. With his training in biology, and his tendency towards social Darwinism, he came extremely close to thinking of the nation as a race, a biological kinship group possessing its own 'blood' and its own genetic 'stock', and having a corporate existence and identity far superior to those of its individual members. By this reckoning, most of the evils of modern Europe could be blamed on the indiscriminate mixing of the peoples in the dynastic empires. The primary task of contemporary statesmen lay in unscrambling the mixture into its constituent parts, and separating them out on their individual territorial reservations. There was a strong belief in the 'once and forever' nation, which had always existed irrespective of political circumstances, and which possessed an inherent corporate 'right' to control its own land, people, and destiny. Individual rights should be subordinated to the collective. Ethnic or cultural variety within any given community could only be a source of friction and injustice. (There could not, by definition, be ethnic variety in one *nation.*) Although Dmowski would have been the last to admit it, his model for this ideal

---

*nation in the European, not in the American sense. See *God's Playground*, Vol. II, pp. 9–11.

derived from the earlier German nationalists of the *Blut und Boden* school, the original purveyors of the myth of the mystical link between 'the blood and the soil'. By the same token, one might fairly suspect Dmowski of subconsciously wishing Poland to resemble that powerful, prosperous, ethnically cohesive, and reunited imperial Germany which, consciously, he so much feared and hated. These sentiments, of course, form the common coin of most modern nationalisms whether in imperial Germany, Fascist Italy, or Begin's Israel—and by European standards of the early twentiety century Dmowski's opinions were hardly original. What he did was to apply the general nationalist theories of his day to particular Polish conditions. It was highly significant that Piłsudski could boast of not being a member of the Polish nation—which he once derided as 'a nation of morons'—but a Lithuanian of Polish culture; whilst Dmowski spent most of his career calling on his compatriots to combat the 'alien elements' within their midst.

National Independence also provided a bone for constant contention. For Piłsudski, Independence became the first and essential pre-condition for all purposeful political activity; and for this reason, between 1908 and 1918, he devoted himself to that one sole aim. If a nation were not free and independent, its energies would be used not for its own benefit but for the benefit of its masters. Social, cultural, and economic activities could only bear fruit after independence, not before. For Dmowski, independence was more of an ultimate goal than an immediate necessity. Although he had Darwinian visions of a vicious international jungle, where nations have to fight or perish, he strongly believed that a nation was not worthy of independence until its material resources and spiritual consciousness had been raised to a viable level. For this reason, prior to 1917, he had been content to settle for Polish autonomy as a first step on the road. He also believed that mere independence in itself was no guarantee of a nation's success. If independence were to arrive before the nation had solved its internal problems and provided itself with a sound economic base, a solid cultural system, and above all, a homogeneous society, it could not expect anything but trouble. Hence his reservations about the

Second Republic. Dmowski's criticisms of the Sanacja regime were undoubtedly fired to some extent by personal pique; but they were informed by a conviction that no one in the Piłsudski camp could comprehend the extent of radical reform essential for the nation's survival. For Piłsudski, independence was a jewel of infinite worth; for Dmowski, it was an item of doubtful value, unless it was supported by other more solid social and economic foundations.

Opinions about political methods were bound to differ. Piłsudski believed that the world was ruled by brute force and that fundamental changes could only be obtained, or essential interests defended, by the willingness to use violence, terror, and military power. In his revolutionary days, he had been no stranger to the bomb plot or the mail-train robbery. As a politician, no less than as a military strategist, he was a master of the *fait accompli*. He looked on international as on internal politics as a trial of strength, in which one's adversary would only listen to sense when compelled to do so. Dmowski was appalled by such suggestions. He always considered that the terrorism and revolutionary talk of his socialist opponents had increased the repressions which they sought to overthrow. Risings and plots were worse than a waste of time; they diverted people's energies from the really effective, if less sensational, methods of national regeneration. He saw politics as a battle of interests, a game of skill, which one could only enter if one possessed the necessary equipment. Politics, for both men, was a game for a select, dedicated élite, but it made no sense for Piłsudski if one sat down at the table without a gun in one's pocket. For Dmowski, it made no sense if the players simply intended to shoot down their opponents, or worse still, if one was inadequately supplied with skill and ammunition.

There was a striking contrast too, in emotional modes of political action. Piłsudski was a warrior, who appealed to the chivalry of combat, who dared to challenge the oppressor to a fight to the death. He had a strong attachment to honour, and, if military weakness obliged him in his early days to indulge in the conspiratorial methods of the underground, he felt no sympathy for moral compromise or political subterfuge. When in 1917 the German Governor of Warsaw offered him the tempting prospect of ruling Poland under German auspices, his reply was absolutely uncompromising: 'Germany would gain one man', he said, 'but I would lose a nation.' Dmowski's approach was more flexible, more malleable. Although he appealed to honest virtues like hard work and religious piety (which he rated much more highly than warfare), he also played on people's weaknesses, on their fears, insecurities, and prejudices. He was a dealer in myths and fantasies, in stories of Jewish plots, of nests of freemasons, or of the marvels of the German intelligence system. Piłsudski cast caution aside and set the example of relying on emotional security gained from a clear moral commitment—come hell or high water. Dmowski taught Poles the advantages of prudence and restraint, whilst urging them to be on their guard against the dark unseen forces of the invisible enemy. From the emotional point of view, Piłsudski's stance was strong and simple, appealing to the moral sense of the individual. Dmowski's stance was more complicated, giving emphasis to the corporate rights and interests of society as a whole.

Polish democracy, after a century or more in abeyance, was bound to be something of a doubtful quantity. In the early twentiety century no Poles had any practical knowledge of democracy beyond the very limited experience provided by the provincial Diet in Galicia, the imperial Reichstag in Berlin and Vienna, or the Tsarist Duma in St. Petersburg; whereas every Pole had learned the ingrained habits of opposition. Even in the best of circumstances, the transition from imperial rule to constitutional democracy was bound to be fraught with danger. As it was, both Dmowski and Piłsudski lost patience with the system at an early juncture; but they did so for different reasons. Dmowski felt aggrieved that the wishes of 'the Polish majority' could be frustrated by the votes of the non-Polish Bloc of Minorities. For, if the nationalists and their allies on the Right commanded 'a majority of the majority' within the Polish-speaking, Catholic population, they could not match the combined strength of the Left and the national minorities. Whatever pretensions he may have professed about constitutional liberalism, Dmowski's feeling that one-third of Polish citizens were somehow disqualified from full civil rights because of their ethnic origins, was extremely illiberal. In the mid-1920s, he openly praised Italian Fascism. Although he was a nominal member of the Sejm, he never participated in its proceedings. Piłsudski's objections were more pragmatic. The Polish parliament was a talking shop which could produce neither continuous policies nor responsible leaders. Polish democrats were corrupt and disorderly, and in need of discipline. Piłsudski solved the problem by bringing in the Army. For Dmowski, although he undoubtedly felt the same call for some form of supra-parliamentary paternalism, the military solution was a betrayal of the nation, a resort to 'Prussianism'. Yet his inability to organize any coherent alternative either to the parliamentary regime of the 1920s or to Piłsudski's semi-dictatorial regime after 1926, effectively excluded him from government. On this score, his supporters felt that he showed far too little ambition.

Social, economic, cultural, and diplomatic affairs, therefore, all had their part to play in Dmowski's broad schemes. Without proper attention paid to all the facets of national reconstruction, national politics would inevitably be reduced to a senseless series of tricks and brawls. Piłsudski, however, characteristically absorbed himself increasingly in military affairs—in questions of external security, internal stability, and in army training, in wars and the prospect of wars. For this reason, if for no other, he was condemned to lose the confidence of his original socialist comrades as of his permanent nationalist opponents. In the 1930s, some of the lesser figures of the Sanacja camp, like the Jędrzejewicz brothers, Janusz and Wacław, or Kwiatkowski, the economist, endeavoured to make amends for the narrow interests of the regime as a whole.

History and historical symbols exerted a powerful spell over the architects of modern nationhood. Dmowski looked back with nostalgia to the idyll of primitive Piast Poland of the early medieval period when the ancient Polish tribes, uncorrupted by alien influences, were supposed to have spent all their time fighting the German foe. His friend, Popławski, is credited with the authorship of the so-called 'Piast Concept'. (See Chapter V, below.) Dmowski's brightest heroes were the Polish warriors who had broken the Teutonic Knights at

Grunwald in 1410. He strongly favoured the recovery of the Polish provinces of Prussia, the cradle of the Polish state, and their reunion with the Polish provinces of Russia and Austria. Yet he was no advocate of an ethnic Poland in its narrowest limits. His idea of a 'Greater Poland' laid claim to the eastern as well as the western borderlands—and conflicted with similar schemes harboured by Poland's neighbours for a 'Greater Germany' or a 'Greater Ukraine'. Piłsudski, in contrast, looked back to the Republic of Poland-Lithuania, and the 'Jagiellonian Concept'. (See Chapter V, below.)

Religion played a prominent part in Polish life, and spilled over into politics. Dmowski regarded Roman Catholicism as the national religion, an essential attribute of Polish identity, as of the 'Latin races' which he so much admired. For him, a 'non-Catholic Pole' was virtually a contradiction in terms. His deep devotion to Catholicism earned him, on the one hand, the vociferous support of the militant clergy and, on the other, the undying distrust of the non-Catholic minorities. It also protected him and his followers from bending more openly to the seductions of Fascism (of the Italian not the German brand) with which they might otherwise have toyed rather more seriously.[4] Piłsudski had no strong feelings about religion. Although born a Catholic, he had registered as a nominal Protestant, and had married in a Protestant chapel, simply to reduce the attentions of the Tsarist police. For him, Polish identity had little to do with religious affiliations, and was open to Christians and Jews, Catholics and Protestants, believers and non-believers alike. His tolerance in religious matters, and his alienation from the Church, earned him on the one hand the support of the national minorities, and, on the other, the lasting suspicion of the militant Catholic clergy. It also gave him and his followers a high standing on the Left of Polish politics, since the Left invariably saw the Church as one of the chief bastions of the Right and of conservatism in general. Dmowski classed Piłsudski among the traitors to Polish culture, a rootless and unprincipled opportunist, 'a great sinner'. Piłsudski thought of Dmowski as a fountain not of Christian charity but of hate, and a sower of discord.

The Jewish Question aroused great passions in Poland, though surprisingly little violence. Dmowski clearly believed in the myth of the great Jewish conspiracy, and urged his compatriots to defend themselves against it. He was the author of several anti-Jewish boycotts, and a strident advocate in the 1930s of the *numerus clausus* in Polish education. He even saw the Jewish lobby at work behind Poland's difficulties in foreign affairs, blaming Lloyd George's decisions at the Paris Peace Conference, for example, on the unseen hand of World Zionism (in that particular case on the influence of Lewis Namier). Piłsudski was not impressed by such fantasies, and constantly urged reconciliation between Poles and Jews. All the organizations associated with him—the PPS, the Legions, and the early Sanacja regime—welcomed Jewish members. Dmowski was a professional anti-Semite; Piłsudski, if pressed on the point, would not have objected to the label of 'philo-Semite'.

All debates about Poland's international relations were dominated by her unenviable location between Germany and Russia. Poland's strategic predicament was essentially the same in 1900, on the borders of imperial Germany and Tsarist Russia, as in 1921 in the space between the Weimar Republic and Soviet Russia, or in 1934–9 between Hitler's Third Reich and Stalin's USSR. In each of the crises of these years, the Poles had three basic choices: either to side with Russia against Germany; to side with Germany against Russia; or to stay neutral, and risk the retribution of Russia and Germany together. Dmowski consistently held that the main threat came from Germany. Infinitely impressed by Germany's economic power and cultural supremacy in central Europe, as well as by the Prussian military tradition, he felt that backward Russia was no match, and that the Slavonic nations would have to form a common, anti-Teutonic front for their mutual protection. He felt a natural affinity for the Latin nations, especially Italy, and he was no great admirer of the Russians. In his student days he had fought an energetic campaign against the Russification of the Vistula provinces. He simply felt that in face of Germany Russia presented the lesser of two evils. His strategy was greatly embarrassed first by the collapse of his Tsarist patrons in 1915–17, and then by the rise of godless Bolshevism with which Catholic Poland could not easily co-operate. But he never wavered in his belief in the primacy of the German menace—a belief which received added impetus after 1933 from the rise of Nazi Germany. In these convictions, it was entirely logical that he should have drawn his strongest support from those western provinces of Poland, especially Posnania, which were most exposed to German revanchism and most conscious of German influences. Piłsudski, in contrast, the Lithuanian, consistently held that the main threat came from Russia. Infinitely impressed by the scale of Russia's manpower and natural resources, and by the uncompromising nature of her political ambitions, he felt that Germany's technological and industrial advantage would not last for ever and that time was limited for the peoples of Eastern Europe to form a common anti-Russian front for their mutual protection. He was no great admirer of the Germans, whose arrogance he resented, though his long exile in Galicia had given him some sympathy for the Austrians. He shared the Austrians' fear of Russia, and their distaste for the humiliating necessity to rely on German strength. In turning towards the Germans, therefore, he simply felt that Germany presented the lesser of the two evils. His strategy was somewhat upset first by the Germans' excessive success in 1915–18 and then by the rise of Nazism, with which his leftish Sanacja regime could not easily co-operate. Yet he never wavered in his belief in the primacy of the Russian menace—a belief which received added impetus after 1929 from the rise of Stalinism. In those convictions, it was entirely logical that he should have drawn his strongest support from those eastern provinces of Poland, especially in Lithuania and Byelorussia, which were most exposed to Soviet revanchism and most conscious of Russian influences. Dmowski was an unashamed 'westerner'; Piłsudski the archetypal *kresowiec*, the 'easterner'.

Attitudes to Germany and Russia largely determined attitudes to Poland's smaller neighbours and to the Allied Powers of the West. Dmowski, the Germanophobe and Latinophile, felt sympathy for Czechoslovakia and for Czech links with Russia, and also for Italy. He had much in common with Beneš, whose career as an Allied client installed in Prague had been the one intended for himself in Warsaw. He had very close ties with the Quay d' Orsay, and every intention of making Poland the eastern bastion of the French plan to encircle Germany. He was a natural proponent of the 'Little Entente'. Piłsudski, the Russophobe, felt no sympathy for Czechoslovakia, or for Czech links with Russia, nor indeed for Beneš, whom he heartiy despised for being a malleable puppet of Allied and Russian interests. In the eyes of London and Paris, Piłsudski could never fully redeem himself for having fought during the Great War on the side of the Central Powers; and he returned Allied suspicions in full measure. He constantly suspected the French of expecting Poland to fight for France without committing themselves to fight for Poland, and wanted nothing to do with the 'Little Entente'. He felt at home in Bucharest, and Budapest, as he did with the Finns, Estonians, Latvians, Ukrainians, Cossacks, and Georgians; but his unrequited quarrel with the Lithuanian nationalists, who had committed the unforgivable sin of seeking Russian aid in attempts to recover Vilnius (Wilno), prevented him from ever realizing the border federation of his dreams.

The extraordinary symmetry in the antagonisms of Dmowski and Piłsudski suggests that their careers and opinions were the product of forces much deeper than the antipathies of two prickly personalities. Indeed, the fact that a nation of over thirty million people could have been so preoccupied by them, to the neglect of so many other important men and issues, supports the proposition that their rivalry reflected similar deep divisions within Polish society itself. The extent, and the perfect balance in the list of their differences and connections, is truly remarkable. The usual labels of 'Nationalist Camp' and 'Independence Camp' are inadequate abbreviations for the complex mix of principles on both sides. One suspects that the two men incarnated most of the contradictory elements of Polish life inherited from the long period of the Partitions (see Chapter IV below), in which they both grew up and which they both served, in their different ways, to overcome.

The Republic which developed amidst the cross purposes of the two contenders conformed to the plans of neither the one nor the other. Inter-war Poland was not the mononational, ethnic Poland of which Dmowski dreamed, nor was it part of the federation of free peoples for which Piłsudski had hoped. Indeed, each man helped to frustrate his own particular solution. It was Dmowski who laid claim at the Peace Conference to the Polish frontiers of 1772, thereby presuming the inclusion of millions of non-Poles in the eastern provinces; and it was Piłsudski, who, for all his misgiving, finally accepted the Treaty of Riga, which partitioned Lithuania, Byelorussia, and Ukraine and turned the population of the borders into subject peoples.

Of course, in terms of political power and short-term success, Piłsudski won the duel with Dmowski hands down. At each of the critical moments in their long careers, Piłsudski came out on top. During the 'revolution' of 1905–6, he gained the reputation of a fearless patriot, whilst Dmowski was made to look a spoiler and a compromiser. In the Great War, his campaign for Independence did in fact precede Independence—although it did not cause it singlehandedly—and Dmowski's initial plans for autonomy under Russia were made to look faint-hearted. In 1916–17, he operated in Warsaw whilst Dmowski was still abroad, and in 1918 took over the reins of government conclusively during the Republic's formative years. In 1919–20, in the Soviet War, he was hailed as the saviour of Poland, the champion of the country's deliverance, whilst Dmowski took a back seat in obscurity. In 1926, he reassumed power in an imperious manner which thrust Dmowski into the role of one of the many rival opponents scrabbling helplessly in the political undergrowth. Whether by preference or design, Dmowski never exercised executive power for any length of time; Piłsudski, once in full control, never relinquished it.

In the long term, however, and particularly in the realm of political ideas, Dmowski's success was far greater than his rivals would care to admit. As soon as the Marshal was dead, the Sanacja regime began to mend its fences with the nationalists, and many of the new accents, heard in 1935–9, can be traced to Dmowski's influence. The heightened Nationalism, the harassment of the minorities, the anti-Semitism, the concern for economic planning, the recognition of the German menace, and the *rapprochement* with the Western Powers were partly just signs of the times; but they all involved conscious changes of policy and of emphasis which Dmowski, in his retirement, must have greeted with warm approval. Even within their author's lifetime, Dmowski's nationalist ideas had begun to overtake government thinking. Little could he have dreamt that at the end of the Second World War, which he did not live to see, an important selection of his ideas would be adopted by a communist Party installed in Warsaw by the Soviet Union.

The duel of Dmowski and Piłsudski did not die with them, therefore. Quite apart from the *émigrés* of pre-war vintage who continue the battle in the pages of *Myśl Polska* (Polish Thought) and of *Niepodległość* (Independence), as if the 'Endecja' and the 'Sanacja' were still engaged in current politics, the figures of Dmowski and Piłsudski still tower above all other contributors to modern Polish attitudes. Almost fifty years after their world was destroyed, they still arouse admiration and controversy. They have strongly influenced attitudes both in the communist élite and in Polish society at large. In the era of SOLIDARITY, the 'post-Endeks' and the 'neo-Piłsudski-ites' could be encountered in almost every political discussion; and in the KPN and KOR, they provided the two main strands of open opposition. (See p. 17.) The sound of Dmowski's nationalist slogans is still mingled with the rumble of the Marshal's guns and with the insistence on the moral imperative.

*   *   *   *   *

Memories of Independence

The continuing fascination of the Second Republic for Poles in the post-war period lies in the fact that the generation of 1914–39 had the unique distinction of realizing, however briefly, the dream of more than two centuries. Born in the darkest days of foreign domination, when hopes for the survival of Poland's separate identity were fading, the leaders of inter-war Poland none the less achieved the apparently impossible. For this reason, if for no other, their deeds and their ideas have been studied and pondered both by Poland's new communist rulers, who desperately needed to win a measure of popular support and legitimacy, and by the great mass of the communists' opponents who still harbour hopes of breaking the nation's chains once more.

The marriage of pre-war Nationalism with post-war Marxism-Leninism within the ideology of the PZPR may seem to be a subject worthy of sarcasm; but it does possess a compelling logic when examined in detail. It would be hard to deny that the sudden conversion of the Polish communist movement to Nationalism, after four decades of condemning Nationalism as the most loathsome of all evils, smacks slightly of insincerity. It was no less remarkable than the transformation of the Jewish Saul into the Christian Paul. At the same time, one must admit that it happened in conjunction with the reappearance in Polish political life of several objective factors which had helped to shape Dmowski's philosophy in the first place. In the 1940s, as in the 1890s, many people in Poland—and not just the communists—were forcibly impressed by the primacy of the German menace; by the need to collaborate with Russia or perish; by the 'alien' forces threatening to engulf Polish culture; by the perception of a hostile Jewish element (in this case within the Soviet-backed security organs); by the necessity to give priority to economic reconstruction; by the rise of a new bourgeoisie; and by the pointlessness of armed resistance. What is more, the prevailing atmosphere within the Soviet Bloc as a whole was quite receptive to the nationalist mood. Gone were the days of the old Bolsheviks when the Soviet Union had been the leader of leftist internationalist Marxism. Just as Stalin had promoted a right–radical reaction within his own Soviet establishment during the 1930s, and had openly appealed to Great Russian chauvinism during the War, so Stalin's protégés in each of the countries occupied by the Soviet Union were encouraged to utilize the latent forces of local nationalism in a bid to strengthen their hold over the populace. In Poland, where the old KPP had never commanded any strong support, the communists had only two native traditions to choose from—the Russophobe, multinational, insurrectionary, Piłsudski-ite tradition of Independence, or the Russophile, anti-Semitic, conciliatory, Dmowski-ite tradition of Nationalism. For them, with Stalin leaning over their shoulder, the nationalist option was absolutely obvious.

Most importantly, perhaps, the Polish communists needed Nationalism for their own private, recondite purposes within the Party itself. Quite apart from the wish to strengthen their own Polish identity against that of their Russian masters, they needed a nationalist 'base' on which to build the dialectical materialist interpretation of Polish History. For, if the changing economic relations of the historical base are to determine the development of social forces and the character of the political and cultural 'superstructure', by means of the ceaseless dialectical process, it follows that the base *must* have continuity; it *must* have an unbroken existence if the theory is to be credible. Unfortunately, in the absence of a continuous state history—which modern Poland, unlike modern Russia, did not possess—the only conceivable historical base for Polish Marxism–Leninism had to be provided by the 'once and forever nation' lifted in its entirety from the Nationalists' writings. It is some sort of a compliment to the perspicacity of Dmowski's thought that many of his ideas had to be appropriated by the ideological engineers of a Party ostensibly hostile to his memory, and that these ideas constituted the only element in the communists' platform acceptable to the Polish masses. For the historian of ideas, it is a delicious paradox that the Polish nationalist tradition proved attractive first to Piłsudski's heirs in the late Sanacja regime and then to the Polish Stalinists of the post-war era. Dmowski, the political leader who failed to form his own government, became a pillar of government philosophies. Piłsudski, the specialist in seizing power, became an outcast, and in the eyes of the communist propagandists, a pariah.

Strangely enough, the adoption of nationalist ideas by the communists coincided with the removal of the ethnic minorities, and the transformation of Polish society. Stalin's radical influence on the Polish communist party was matched by his fabrication of a mononational Poland. The unexpected revival of Dmowski's ideas in post-war ideology was attended by the attainment, in an equally unforeseen manner, of his fondest ethnic dreams—of a Poland inhabited exclusively by Poles. At first sight, the success may appear total; but on reflection it is less so. For one thing, the communists rejected as much of Dmowski's overall philosophy as they stole; and if

they shared such things as his ethnic vision or his insistence on
collaboration with Russia, they certainly did not share his
views on the eastern borderlands or on Poland's Catholic
heritage. The graft was less than complete. Dmowski may
have heirs in the PZPR; but he also has admirers among some
of the PZPR's most fervent (Catholic) opponents. Apart from
that, it is doubtful whether the emergence of an ethnic Poland
has actually furthered the cause of Nationalism. On the
contrary, the realization of the nationalists' principal plans
has robbed them of their cause. Nationalism has lost its point.
So long as Poland was 'full' of Germans, Jews, or Ukrainians,
it made some sense to defend one's precious heritage against
them. But now that the minorities have gone, the old slogans
no longer have a purpose. There is no real internal enemy
against whom to direct one's venom. The anti-Semitism of the
PZPR could only be directed against the handful of Jews in its
own ranks, and even that grew stale after repeated purges.
Nationalist slogans, as propagated by the Party, may have
helped to calm the desperate insecurities of an uprooted Polish
population and to assure them that at last they had a land of
their own to enjoy. But as the post-war generation took root,
these assurances have grown increasingly unnecessary. If
Polish society today believes in the presence of 'the enemy
within', it identifies that internal menace above all with the
communists, not with mythical 'Zionists' and infiltrators; and,
since it certainly believes in the 'enemy without', it has
undoubtedly come to identify the external menace more with
Russia than with a divided Germany. And that, already, is
Piłsudski's domain.

For all its obvious faults, the Second Republic is greatly
admired in contemporary Poland. For anyone under the age
of fifty, it is an item of ancient history; but it is well within the
memory of the older generation, and the basic facts cannot be
concealed even by the most assiduous propagandists of the
communist regime. Comparisons with present-day circumstances are not unfavourable. The faults do not seem so
glaring to contemporary eyes. Piłsudski's military dictatorship
looks mild and ramshackle in comparison to the elaborate
dictatorial machine set up by the communists. The measures
taken against the opposition in the 1930s bear no resemblance

to the brutal repression of the wartime Resistance in the 1940s. The notorious Brest Trial of 1931–3, held in open court and fully reported in the press, was a model of public justice compared to the secret political trials of the Stalinist era. The one notorious internment camp at Bereza Kartuska was a minor aberration against human rights compared to scores of similar camps opened by General Jaruzelski in 1981. In relation to later disasters, the virtues of pre-war Poland look particularly beguiling. In the 1950s, no efforts were spared by Party propagandists to blackwash the 'Fascists and bourgeois criminals' whose narrow class-based policies were supposed to have wreaked such havoc on the Polish people. But nowadays, even the communists realize that they have much in common with their predecessors in the Sanacja. They share similarly intractable social and economic problems—backward agriculture, a lame industrial sector, and an over-mighty bureaucracy; and their standing in public esteem is lower even than that of the 'Government of Colonels'. After forty years of communist rule, most ordinary Poles have reached the point where anything condemned by Party propaganda must surely have merit for them. They admire the brilliant scientific and artistic life of the pre-war era, when a thousand talents could flourish freely. They admire the rich variety of social life, which has since sunk for ever beneath the Party's insistence on drab conformity and 'socialist norms'. They admire the feeling for quality and style in the artefacts and manners of the 1920s and 1930s. They even admire the political scene, where the socialists were true socialists, the military were proper soldiers, the communists were genuine Marxists, and the Zionists were real Jews. They admire the Second Republic's obstinate defence of its freedom, and its honourable defeat. Above all, they adore Piłsudski—not for his socialism, about which they know little, not for his dictatorship, which does not affect them, not for his revolutionary career—but for one thing only: that he was the last of Poland's leaders to defeat the Russians in battle.[5] All of this they value, with its warts and wrinkles, because it was theirs. They love it with a fierce pride, like defensive parents who still love the memory of a prodigal son.

The cultural life of inter-war Poland is especially admired. The two decades of the Second Republic saw a veritable explosion of creativity. In the pure sciences, the Warsaw School of Analytical Philosophy under Jan Łukasiewicz (1878–1956), the inventor of 'Polish Notation', and the Lwów School of Mathematics, headed by Stefan Banach (1892–1945), a pioneer of Functional Analysis, could fairly claim to be in the forefront of world learning. In the social sciences, figures such as Edward Loth (1884–1944) in anthropology, Michał Kalecki (1899–1970) in economics, or the magnificent Jan Baudouin de Courtenay (1845–1929) in linguistics, were counted among the founding fathers of their disciplines. In the arts, everything from the Contemporary Music Society of Karol Szymanowski (1882–1937) to the Warsaw PEN Club founded by Stefan Żeromski and the leading theates under directors such as Leon Schiller (1887–1954) or Stefan Jaracz (1883–1945) played a part in European, and not merely in national activities. Warsaw's brilliant intellectual circles were enlivened by an artistic avant-garde of great sophistication, such as the poets of the Skamander Group, and by a number of outstanding and outrageous, multi-talented bohemians. Leon Chwistek (1884–1944) made his name successively as a painter, a mathematical logician, and then as a philosopher of aesthetics. Stanisław Ignacy Witkiewicz (1885–1939), generally known as 'Witkacy', first made his living as a fashionable portrait painter; but then moved into futuristic novels, into philosophy, and into the 'theatre of the absurd'. His suicide on 17 *(sic)* September 1939 is still regarded in intellectual circles as a symbol of the tragic fate of Polish culture in general. Yet the real achievement of the interlude of academic and intellectual independence was to train a generation which could still learn from contact with the surviving masters of the nineteenth century, but which would live to transmit the traditional values of Polish culture to the new society of the post-war world. They were the vital bridge between the old and the new. In the 1920s and 1930s, writers and poets, who had spent their formative years in the eras of Positivism or Modernism, mingled with apprentices of the trade who would later have to cope both with the horrors of the War and Occupation and with the onslaught of official communist 'Socialist Realism'. Among the established writers, Włady-

sław Reymont (1868–1925), a Nobel Prize-winner, Stefan
Żeromski (1864–1925), and Juliusz Kaden-Bandrowski
(1885–1944) were still at work and in circulation; among the
poets, Kazimierz Tetmajer (1865–1940), Jan Kasprowicz
(1860–1926), Karol Hubert Rostworowski (1877–1938);
among the critics, Stanisław Przybyszewski (1868–1927), and
Zenon Przesmycki (1861–1944). At the same time, many of
the younger adepts were learning their trade in this most
stimulating of environments. Despite the fearful decimation of
the Polish intelligentsia during the War, many would survive
to become household names in contemporary Poland. Some of
them, such as Kazimierz Wierzyński (1894–1969), Jan Lechoń
(1899–1956), Witold Gombrowicz (1904–69), or Czesław
Miłosz (born 1911) chose to live and write in emigration.
Others, like Leopold Staff (1878–1957), Julian Tuwim
(1894–1953), Antoni Słonimski (1895–1976), Jarosław
Iwaszkiewicz (1894–1980), Maria Dąbrowska (1889–1965),
Konstanty Gałczyński (1905–53), or the pre-war communist
Władysław Broniewski (1897–1962) survived in Poland or
returned home to provide the living link with former days.
They were the guardians of the nation's storehouse of
independent ideas and cultural excellence. These were the
people who surmounted the traumas of the War and its
aftermath, and who convinced the new Poland, hungry for
reassurance and for a sense of continuity, that all had not been
lost.

Mingled with the admiration for pre-war Poland run
feelings of infinite loneliness. The inter-war years saw Poland
take its place as part of the Western world, only to be brutally
separated from its Western friends by force. The twenty years
of independence raised hopes that Poland's fundamental
cultural ties with the West, which were still unshaken, would
be matched by practical links of mutual aid and free
intercourse. After more than a century, when the Poles had
been obliged to live in the alien environment of the East
European empires, it seemed that their love affair with the
West might at last be consummated by marriage, and that
Poland would be welcomed into the family of Western
nations. Instead, those brief hopes were crushed, and Poland
was driven back into the uncongenial, Eastern world of the

Soviet Bloc. From the standpoint of unimpeded contacts with Rome, Paris, London, Munich, or Washington, Poland's position in the late twentieth century is no better than it was a hundred years ago. It is as if the Polish slave girl, dreaming of her handsome liberator, had actually made her escape from the harem, only to find that the man of her dreams was unable either to help her or to prevent her recapture by the agents of her cruel máster. The bitterness of slavery is all the more painful, if accompanied by the crushing or false hopes and the broken promises of false friends. The drama reached its climax in the first week of September 1939. Exuberant crowds surrounded the British and French embassies in Warsaw, warmly singing 'God Save the King' and roaring the 'Marseillaise'. The Western Powers had declared war on Nazi Germany. Poland had powerful friends who were springing to her defence, and honouring their obligations. Just for those few days, perhaps for two weeks in the span of two centuries, the Poles felt that they were not alone. But that is as far as the consolation went. The Western allies did not declare war on the Soviet Union when the Red Army invaded Poland on 17 September; and they did nothing to prevent the partition of the country by the Nazis and Soviets just as they did nothing to oppose the Soviet take-over in 1944–5. It seems after all that the Poles really are alone in the world. Their enemies are strong, and near at hand; their friends are indecisive, and far away. Of course, many Poles blame themselves. In bouts of self-criticism, they argue that the Second Republic, with its interminable quarrels with its neighbours and its abandon-ment of constitutional government, was not worthy of Western support. Communist apologists argue that Colonel Beck's rejection of Soviet assistance, in favour of Western promises, received its rich deserts. Explanations vary; but the fact remains that the Second Republic was abandoned to its fate. The West could not be counted on. The pain of rejection and of separation is still very real.

Anger and resentment with respect to Poland's neighbours are felt even more keenly. Whatever Poles may feel about the shortcomings of their pre-war and wartime relationships with Britain, France, America, or the Vatican, no one pretends that these failures in any way compare with the tragedy of Poland's treatment at the hands of Hitler and Stalin. There can be no comparison between the regrets over faint-hearted friends and the traumatic revulsion directed against Poland's executioners. It may seem unreal that in the middle of the twentieth century, in the centre of the world's most developed continent, two of history's most vicious regimes could calmly destroy an established European state with impunity, or, at the end of the War to preserve Freedom, that due restitution against both assailants could not be made. But that is the reality which every Pole has to face. What is worse, like the victim of rape who is charged with contributory negligence by talking beforehand to the rapist, Poles have to listen to learned historians explaining how the leaders of pre-war Poland contributed to their own disaster—as if Beck's contacts with the Reich in 1937–8 constituted a culpable 'dalliance' similar to the Nazi–Soviet Pact, or the rejection of the offer to station Soviet troops in Poland somehow justified the subsequent Soviet attack. Anger aroused by memories of the crime is compounded by resentment caused by specious explanations. Whom is to be protected, they ask, if the motives of a crime cannot be sought in the pathology of the criminals involved?

In the last resort, no amount of analysis can completely overcome the legacy of disillusionment. Fatalism and self-doubt are the inevitable companions of personal tragedy. Frequently in Poland one hears that 'independence will always escape us', or 'Poles are incapable of keeping their own house in order', or 'we will always be rebels and never our own masters'. It can all be illustrated from fact. At the outset of the inter-war period, there were many plausible critics who loudly proclaimed that an independent Poland would not be a viable proposition; and they were not confined to Germany or Russia. J.M. Keynes was one of many such prophets of doom,[6] and David Lloyd George was another. They argued at length that Poland had ineffectual economic resources, or inadequate military strength, or insufficient political experience to withstand the resurgence of her two great neighbours. When their prophecies were fulfilled, they were quick to rub salt in the wound, and to explain how Poland had deserved her fate.[7] Needless to say, *ex post facto* developments do not necessarily prove the original arguments to have been correct.

No one in 1918–19 could have predicted the rise of Hitler or Stalin, let alone of both; and a sanguine assessment of independent Poland's economic, military, and political difficulties did not warrant the conclusion about inevitable collapse. Still less can one accept the view that the destruction of independent Poland in 1939 somehow justified Poland's dependent status after 1945. If that were the case, one would have to question the post-war independence of all other European countries, from Austria and Czechoslovakia, to Norway, Denmark, Belgium, Holland, France, and Greece which had collapsed, like Poland, under the pressure of wartime aggression. Poland's post-war status was not fixed by the rights and wrongs of the Second Republic but by the constellation of international forces in 1944–5, and by the rise of the Soviet Union as the imperial power in Eastern Europe. Even so, the tragedy of the Second Republic cannot be avoided. It is a brute fact of history that independent Poland was poor, weak, divided, and friendless, and that in the maelstrom of the European crisis, it did not survive. Poles cannot brush these stark realities aside, and have been told for decades that the whole inter-war experiment was a terrible mistake. Only the strongest minds and the bravest hearts can resist the overpowering emotion of disenchantment.

CHAPTER IV

THE LEGACY OF SPIRITUAL MASTERY

Poland during the Partitions, 1795–1918

123 Years

After the destruction of the old Polish Republic in 1795, the Republic's former citizens found themselves in an alien world. Their involuntary subjection to the Partitioning Powers was bitterly resented, especially in the ruling nobility; but it was a fact that none of them could change. By an additional Treaty of 1797, the Powers had even agreed to abolish the very name of 'Poland'. Although several attempts were made in succeeding years to restore Polish statehood, none of the ephemeral creations of Napoleonic and post-Napoleonic diplomacy was endowed with true sovereignty or succeeded in reuniting all the Polish people under one rule. Neither the Duchy of Warsaw (1807–15), nor the Congress Kingdom (1815–64), nor the Grand Duchy of Posen (1815–48) could be rated higher than autonomous dependencies of foreign governments. The tiny Republic of Cracow (1815–46) was hardly more than a curiosity, a temporary aberration of the feuding diplomats, a toy, whose nominal independence was cynically ignored. The famous kingdom of Galicia, whose autonomy under Austrian rule in the second half of the nineteenth century played such a vital role in Polish life, covered only a small part of the Polish lands. Many of the former Polish provinces never gained control of their own affairs, even for a few short decades. The overwhelming experience for all Poles during five long generations was one of foreign rule, and political oppression.

In one of the religious metaphors much loved by the
Romantic poets, Poland had been crucified, and its body had
descended into the Tomb, awaiting the Resurrection.
Whereas most European countries basked in the Age of
Improvement, of Expansion, and of Empire, the nineteenth
century for Poland was the era of effacement—'the Babylonian Captivity', 'the Sojourn in the Wilderness', 'the Journey
through Hell', 'the Time on the Cross'.[1]
   Poland's political demise has serious consequences for the
historian. In the absence of a Polish state, there could be no
question of a separate Polish economy,[2] or of separate Polish
social structures. The socio-economic development of former
Polish society became an integral part of the economics and
sociology of Russia, Prussia, or Austria. The concept of an
organic Polish historical process based on Poland's separate
socio-economic progress is a figment of the modern imagination.
The realm of Politics, too, was greatly diminished. Except in
those limited periods when the leaders of the Duchy of Warsaw
or of the Congress Kingdom were able in a limited way to pursue
their own policies, or when there was a limited revival of Polish
institutions in Galicia, the history of Polish diplomacy, of Polish
government, of the Polish Army, of Polish law and constitutional relations, even the Polish Question itself, which provided
a major topic for discussion in the period up to 1864, faded
thereafter from view. Polish History in the nineteenth century
cannot be approached with the same enquiries that one applies
to the state histories of Britain, France, or Russia, or to the
histories of those more fortunate countries like Germany and
Italy, which actually won their statehood. For most of the peiod,
'Poland' was just an idea—a memory from the past, or a hope for
the future. Hence, the essential sources of its history have to be
sought less in social, political, and economic affairs than in the
realm of culture, literature, and religion—in short, in the world
of the Polish spirit, which enabled men and women to live their
lives in their own way in spite of the established order, and often
in defiance of the law.

1 *Under the Shadow of France*

In the Revolutionary Era, the conservative monarchies which
had recently partitioned Poland were consistently opposed to

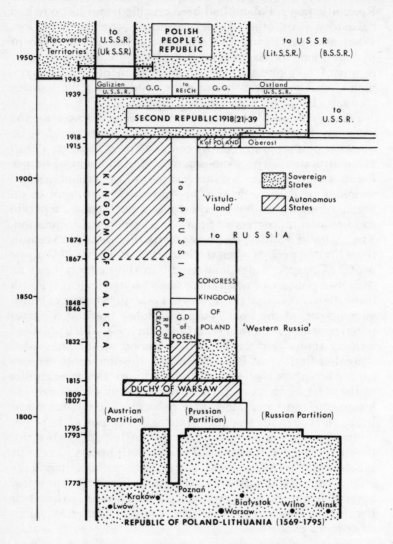

Diagram C.   The Successor States of Poland–Lithuania

the new ideas emanating from France. So the Poles and the French were natural partners. However, by the time that the French armies actually entered central Europe in 1805–6, the Polish Republic had already been destroyed, and the Franco-Polish alliance could never be established on a formal, interstate basis. The Third Partition of 1795 preceded Napoleon's victory at Austerlitz by just ten years, and in the intervening decade Poles could only serve the French cause as *émigrés* and as individual volunteers. Even so, they rallied to the French colours in their thousands. Their inimitable code of honour and sacrifice was taken up by the Polish Legions of the Army of Italy, by the Polish lancers of the Imperial Guard, and above all by the noble figure of Marshal Poniatowski.

The Polish Legions were first created in 1797 in Italy from Polish prisoners and deserters of the Austrian Army, and were commanded by General Henryk Dąbrowski. In all, three Legions were raised. They marched under the French tricolour, but wore distinctive Polish uniforms with the slogan, *Gli uomini liberi sono fratelli* (Free men are brothers) on their shoulder flashes. They fought in the battles of Trebbia (1799), Marengo (1800), and at Hohenlinden (1801). Their belief, that by serving Napoleon they were somehow fighting for the re-creation of Poland's independence, is clearly expressed in their melancholy song, *Jeszcze Polska nie zginęła*:

> Poland has not perished yet
> So long as we still live.
> That which foreign force has seized
> We at swordpoint shall retrieve.
> March, march, Dąbrowski!
> From Italy to our Polish land.
> Let us now unite the nation
> Under Thy command.*

In reality, their hopes were misplaced. The Legions never reached Poland. Instead, they were left on garrison duty in conquered Italy, before being sent to their deaths in Napoleon's German wars and in the chaos of the Haitian expedition. Kościuszko was proved correct. As an exile in Paris, the last

---

*Dąbrowski's 'Mazurek' has been the Polish national anthem since 1926.

military leader of the old Republic could have led the
Legions, but he had refused. In a prophetic pamphlet entitled
Can the Poles win back their Independence? (1797), he argued that
the Poles could count only their own strength and resources.
Bonaparte, he claimed, was 'a tyrant' whose only aim was to
satisfy his own ambitions.

When Napoleon created the Duchy of Warsaw in 1807,
however, hopes rose once more. The Duchy was confined to
the lands of the former Prussian partition, although in 1809 it
absorbed Cracow and Lublin. It had its own Polish administration, its own parliamentary Constitution, its own Army
under Poniatowski, and it received the Napoleonic Code; but
it was also subjected to an absentee Duke (the King of
Saxony), who was entirely answerable to French orders, and to
the twin burdens of crushing war taxes and of a colossal
French garrison. Although important reforms were introduced—in the decree on personal liberty which abolished feudal
servitude, and in the fields of culture and education—the
weight of Napoleon's military schemes hung round the
Duchy's neck like a millstone.

The future of the Duchy depended largely on the outcome
of Napoleon's relations with Russia. Tsar Alexander's Polish
minister and confidant, Prince Adam Czartoryski, had long
been pressing his master for an accommodation; but events
moved inexorably towards a decisive conflict. Napoleon called
the war of 1812 his 'Polish War', and in crossing the frontier of
the Russian Empire the *Grande Armée* was in fact restoring the
historic border of Poland and Lithuania, annulled in 1795.
Inexorably, the Russian victory spelt disaster no less for the
Polish cause than for that of Napoleon. Poniatowski's heroic
conduct of the rearguard on the retreat from Moscow was but
the prelude to the destruction of himself and his men at the
Battle of the Nations before Leipzig. When the defeated
Napoleon drove through Warsaw without paying so much as
a farewell call on his Polish mistress, Maria Walewska, it was a
sign that he had no more time for Poland either. The Russian
Army was not far behind. Nearly twenty years of Poland's
affair with France ended in bitter disaster. The Partitions
were to be reinstated—in a slightly different form, but with a
heightened sense of finality.

2 *The Vienna Settlement, 1815–30*

At the Congress of Vienna in 1814–15, as at Yalta and
Potsdam in 1945, the Russians' physical occupation of the
Polish lands proved the decisive factor in negotiations on the
Polish question. Although both Castlereagh and Talleyrand
submitted memoranda in favour of an independent Poland, it
was clear that the Western powers could not push the matter
to the point of war; and Napoleon's escape from the isle of
Elba forced them into compromise. The Tsar was to extend
his dominions into central Poland, including Warsaw; but in
his new territories he was to rule over a separate Polish
kingdom endowed with a modern, liberal constitution. The
Prussians were to keep the western areas of their former Polish
acquisitions, now organized as the Grand Duchy of Posen
(Poznań). The Austrians were to keep the bulk of Galicia with
its capital of Lwów (Lemberg). Since no agreement could be
reached on the assignation of Cracow, the city was set up as a
sovereign Republic. In all areas, the principle of local Polish
autonomy was solemnly confirmed, and the settlement was
declared permanent and immutable. In fact, within a very few
years, the Polish clauses of the Treaty of Vienna were
overturned with impunity. The constitution of the Congress
Kingdom was suspended in 1832; the Republic of Cracow was
absorbed into Galicia after 1846; and the autonomy of the
Grand Duchy of Posen was finally abolished in 1848. The
Partitioning Powers began to undermine the inconvenient,
constitutional safeguards of the settlement almost as soon as
they had been erected. In the age of Metternich, constitutions
and civil liberties in eastern Europe were regarded as a
dangerous disease, and the Poles were suspected of being the
main carriers of contagion.

The Congress Kingdom of Poland served as the focus for
Polish national aspirations for barely fifteen years. It had
inherited many of the institutions of the Duchy of Warsaw,
including an elected Diet, a separate Army, the Napoleonic
Code, and its own Polish administration. At first, with the
adjoining Polish provinces of the Russian Empire still basking
under the benevolent influence of Prince Czartoryski in
Wilno, there were hopes that the historic union of Poland and

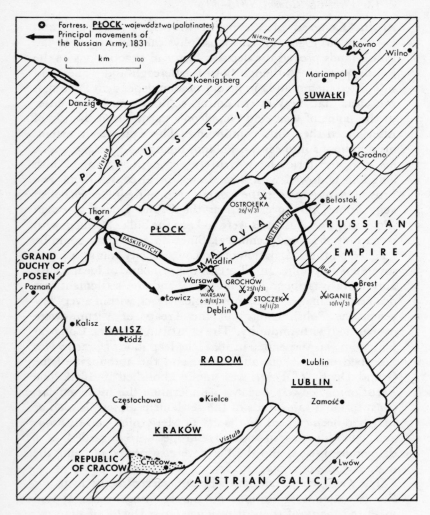

Map 5.   The Congress Kingdom, and the November Rising

Lithuania might eventually be restored. The Government in Warsaw consolidated the educational system, and endeavoured to imitate Prussian methods of state initiative in economic affairs. The establishment of Warsaw University (1816), of the metropolitan Archbishopric of Warsaw (1818), and of the Polish Bank (1828) aimed to consolidate the foundations of a modern, national state. Yet the supreme authorities in St. Petersburg had other ideas. Under Alexander I, the vicious campaign of police repression which harried the Polish elements in Lithuania in the early 1820s did not reach the Kingdom; but the supposedly 'liberal' Tsar did not hesitate to withhold publication of the budget, to annul the election of troublesome deputies, or to suspend the Diet by decree. Under Nicholas I, who succeeded in 1825, the mask was cast aside. Nicholas I, an arch-autocrat by temper and intent, had no stomach for his role as constitutional king of Poland; and the Polish connections of the Decembrist Revolt in Russia made him ultra-suspicious of his Polish subjects. His arbitrary interventions in the running of the Kingdom's police, army, and courts indicated the new priorities, whilst the wholesale arrests and vindictive prosecutions undertaken by his 'Third Section' mocked the Kingdom's constitution. For two or three years prior to the ill-fated attempt to assassinate the Tsar's brother and Viceroy, the Grand Duke Constantine, in November 1830, many Poles feared for the future. The outbreak of the November Rising gave Nicholas the opportunity he needed; and his fellow monarchs in Prussia and Austria were tempted to follow suit. The Russian Army's invasion of the Kingdom in February 1831 spelled the end of the brief constitutional era throughout the Polish lands.

In the world of the arts and sciences, the first three decades of the nineteenth century saw the culmination of the Polish Enlightenment. Most of the leading figures in Warsaw during the Napoleonic period and in the early years of Congress Kingdom could remember the ideals of the last king of Poland, and had lived through the disasters of Kościuszko's Rising and the final Partitions. (See pp. 306–10.) Many of them were deeply impressed by the social, legal, and educational reforms of the revolutionary movement, though appalled by its fanaticism and its violence. Stanisław Staszic

(1755–1826), the president of the influential Society of the
Friends of Science (1808); Stanisław Kostka Potocki
(1755–1821), active under the Duchy and the Kingdom;
Prince Ksawery Drucki-Lubecki, a dominant minister in the
1820s, and Prince Czartoryski himself, were all sons of the Age
of Reason. Some of their younger colleagues were repentant
Jacobins. In politics, they were moderates, compromisers; in
religious matters, sceptics; in artistic taste, classicists. Their
main concerns, like those of the *philosophes,* were with scientific
knowledge, secular education, and social and economic
improvement. The Congress Kingdom, which itself incarnated
a rational compromise between the clerical and military arch-
conservatives of the pro-Tsarist camp and the ex-progressives
of the pro-French orientation, was to be the arena where
Reason and Enlightenment could prevail. It did not last long.

3 *The Romantic Age of Insurrections, 1830–64*

In 1830, a general revulsion against the stifling constrictions of
the European order was signalled by the July Revolution in
Paris and by the secession of Belgium from the United
Netherlands. England was in the throes of Catholic Emancipation and the Reform Bill. In Poland, the November Rising
heralded a whole chain of insurrections and conspiracies
which was to persist for over thirty years. Plot followed plot, as
each abortive adventure was followed by harsher and harsher
repressions. The Russo-Polish War of 1831 encouraged the
monarchs of eastern Europe to adopt common precautions
against Polish subversion; whilst the *émigré* plotters aimed at a
general rising to be launched simultaneously in each of the
three Partitions. But no effective co-ordination was ever
achieved. Poland's participation in the 'Springtime of Nations' in 1848 was greatly reduced by the premature outbreak
of a Rising two years earlier, which had provoked the frightful
Galician Jacquerie of 1846 and the Berlin Trial of 1847. In
1863–4, the second great January Rising in Russian Poland
was due to be crushed in isolation. In this generation, there
were Poles on every barricade in Europe, from Munich to
Transylvania, from the Roman Republic to the Paris Commune. But the tangible benefits for Poland were meagre.

In this entire series of events, the original November Rising of 1830–1 was perhaps the most tragic.[3] On this occasion, the original explosion could have been most easily controlled, whilst the objective chances of reconciliation were at their greatest. Of course, the attempted assassination of the Tsar's brother was a serious matter; but the subsequent dethronement of the Tsar by an infuriated Diet might well have been avoided if Nicholas had taken the advice of his loyal Polish ministers. As it was, the 'Nebuchadnezzar of the North' was bent on retribution. The Tsar would not hear of concessions, and appealed instead to force. (See p. 192.) Even so, the Army of the Congress Kingdom was well armed and well trained; and in the early battles of the Russo-Polish war the invading Russians suffered severe set-backs. Later, Polish resistance was undermined by indecisive generals, by political divisions between the 'Whites' and the 'Reds', and by the lack of foreign support. After the Battle of Ostrołęka in May, the Russian invasion force gathered strength. Warsaw was captured by storm in September; the Constitution was suspended. All officers who had served the National Government were automatically cashiered and deprived of their property. All remaining Polish soldiers were drafted into the Russian Army for service in the Caucasus. Field tribunals condemned all rebels and their families to penal servitude in Russia, and some 80,000 Poles walked in irons to Siberia. Thousands more fled into exile. The inevitable cycle of repression and resistance had begun with a vengeance. The Tsar's victorious general, Ivan Paskievitch, stayed on for twenty years as military Governor and 'Prince of Warsaw'.

The January Rising of 1863–4 had far less chance of success. Preceded by several years of patriotic demonstrations, and by reform petitions presented to the new 'Tsar-Liberator', Alexander II, it was generated by the continuing refusal of the Tsarist establishment to make anything but superficial concessions. It was sparked off by the Tsar's Polish minister, the Marquis Wielopolski, who tried to silence his opponents by subjecting them to forcible conscription. By this time, the Congress Kingdom no longer possessed any representative institutions, and had no army. So the conflict could only take the form of a guerrilla war, fought in the countryside between

Europe's largest professional force and the amateur volunteers of an unseen, underground National Government.[4] Amazingly, the insurrection persisted in the hills and forests for sixteen months, before the last 'Dictator' of the Rising, Romuald Traugutt, was unmasked and hanged. Once again Poland felt the merciless bludgeon of Russian revenge. The Congress Kingdom was dissolved, and merged with the Empire as 'the Vistulaland'.* Siberia welcomed its next massive influx of Polish deportees. The tribunals and the official hangman preyed once more on a prostrate population.

Both in 1831 and in 1863, parts of Lithuania rose in solidarity with Poland. Wilno stood by Warsaw. The idea of the historic union was still alive. Volunteers from Posnania and Galicia crossed the frontier to join the insurrectionaries. The bonds of the common culture and loyalty had not yet been broken. But the logistics of joint action were all but insuperable.

In both the great Risings against Russia, the politics of national liberation were compounded by the struggle for social reform. Serfdom was still intact in most parts of the Polish lands, and radical politicians had long argued that the independence of the nation as a whole could only be won in conjunction with the emancipation of the peasantry. In 1830–1, the Rising is generally judged to have lost much of its potential support by the reluctance of its propertied leaders to appeal to the peasants. By 1863, when the Tsar had already conceded his commitment to Peasant Emancipation, the insurrectionaries had learned the lesson also. In the end, to drive a wedge between the Polish peasant and the incorrigible Polish nobility, the Tsar was obliged in the decree of April 1864 to grant Emancipation on more favourable terms than in any other part of the Empire.

---

*A certain ambiguity surrounds the abolition of the Congress Kingdom after 1864. The Tsars did not resign their title as 'Kings of Poland', although there were no more coronations. Despite the Russification of most of institutions, certain peculiarities, such as the civil code inherited from the Duchy of Warsaw, did remain. Technically, the date of abolition could be taken as 1874 when the office of Viceroy was replaced by that of Governor-General. The name of the kingdom of Poland was revived on the same territory by the German authorities in 1916–18.

In the cultural field, the era of the Polish Risings coincided almost exactly with the heyday of Polish Romanticism. Unable to conceive their world on the rational and harmonious lines of the Enlightenment, Polish writers and artists turned instead to the exploration of the Spirit, to the evocation of the inner nature of things. Not surprisingly, the first steps of the Polish Romantics were taken in Lithuania, in the 1820s, where the collapse of the old order was felt most sharply and most precociously. It was no accident that the towering triumvirate of Polish Romantics—Adam Mickiewicz (1798–1855), Juliusz Słowacki (1809–49), and Zygmunt Krasiński (1812–59)—all came from Lithuania. Their ideas were nurtured by familiarity with Western precursors, notably Lord Byron, but were reinforced by fundamental native contributions to philosophy, historiography and literary theory. These men and their literary confrères drew on a remarkable store of erudition and theoretical preparation. Like their contemporaries in western Europe, they were fascinated by folklore, by historical traditions, by medieval legends, by the supernatural, by the emotional extremes of ecstasy and agony, by human Love and Death, by heroes and heroines larger than life, by the cult of Freedom; and they added a specifically Polish note of Catholic piety. All the main countries of Europe passed through the Romantic experience; but in Poland it was particularly intense. Arguably, it has provided the largest single ingredient of modern Polish culture. Indeed, since the oppressive hothouse conditions which fostered Polish Romanticism in the first place have continued in many respects to the present day, the Romantic tradition still reigns supreme in the Polish mind.[5]

4 *The Age of Organic Work, 1864–1905*

The failure of the January Rising, and the terrible ordeal inflicted on its participants, led to a reappraisal of political attitudes. Although the aims and ideals of the insurrectionaries were still widely admired, it was generally realized that appeal to force was impractical in prevailing circumstances.

Their critics included the conservative 'Stańczyk Group' in Cracow, and the so-called 'Warsaw Positivists', who argued that the cultural and economic resources of the Polish nation were as yet too underdeveloped to sustain an independent state. In order to take their place among the modern nations of Europe, the Poles must first improve the trade and industry of the Polish provinces, build towns and railways, and raise the literacy and national consciousness of the population. The leaders and writers who emerged after 1864 were well aware of the rapid progress being made at that time in western Europe, and especially in Germany, and taught their compatriots to compete, if they were to stand any chance of ultimate survival. After the Romantic interlude of conspiracy and resistance, they revived the attitudes prevalent in Poland during the Enlightenment and the early years of the Congress Kingdom, and they popularized the slogan of 'Organic Work'. (See pp. 189 below.)

In this same period, attitudes in Russian and Prussian government circles took a distinct turn in the direction of official nationalist doctrines. The Russian Empire was strongly influenced by Pan-Slavism, and began to believe more seriously in its alleged mission as the natural leader, liberator, and protector of all Slav peoples. The Kingdom of Prussia played the leading role in the formation in 1871 of a united German Empire, and was justly proud of the pre-eminence in Europe of German industry, German universities, and the German Army. In both countries, officialdom abandoned the old idea that loyalty to the monarch was a sufficient test of civic respectability. They now demanded that all their subjects be transformed into 'true Russians' or 'good Germans'. Russification and Germanization, backed by the full coercion of the State, threatened to deprive the Poles of their very identity. Hence the intensifying struggles over control of education, the use of language, and the position of the Polish Catholic Church.

In the Russian Empire, the political defeat of the Polish element contrasted sharply with its social and economic advancement. Once the old tariff barriers were removed, the products of Polish industry could penetrate the vast Russian market at will. As a result, the stresses and benefits of the industrial revolution and the railway age reached the Polish cities of the Empire well in advance of their arrival in central Russia or Ukraine. A new assertive Polish bourgeoisie appeared, contemptuous of the old rebellious nobility and conscious of the profits of the Russian connection, but equally impatient of the crudities and brutality of Russian rule. Compared to the decades before 1864, the Poles under Russian rule were relatively cowed and quiet, and undoubtedly more affluent; but the modest rise of prosperity could not indefinitely compensate for resentments caused by the presence of a colossal garrison, the despotism of petty officials, and the irrational hostility to all things Polish. A considerable number of Poles, especially in the professional and technical classes, played a prominent role in the Empire; the masses remained sullen or apathetic to the supposed advantages of the Tsar's beneficence.

In Prussia, where the progress of urbanization and industrialization had promised to Germanize the Polish population in a natural and painless manner, the blockheaded policies of an insensitive Government provoked a bitter conflict. Bismarck's *Kulturkampf* of 1872 may have been principally directed against the German Catholics of the Rhineland and Bavaria; but it turned every Polish Catholic of Posnania and Silesia into a potential rebel overnight. Similarly, the ill-conceived Prussian Colonization Commission (1886–1913), which aimed to strengthen the German element in the East, actually had the opposite effect. By the end of the century, the sturdy Polish peasantry of Prussia, mobilized by a militant Catholic clergy, was thoroughly disaffected, and, as the school strikes of 1901–7 indicate, was determined to defend its Polishness with a will. The Germans of the *Deutscher Ostmarkverein* were determined to thwart Polish aims. Polish–German attitudes, once quite sympathetic, were now antagonistic.

In Galicia, however, the Austrian authorities showed no desire to imitate their Russian and Prussian counterparts. Forced by the Austro-Hungarian *Ausgleich* of 1867 to abandon the idea of a unitary Empire, the Habsburgs were content to win the loyalty of their Polish subjects by granting them regional autonomy. Galicia was far and away the poorest of the three partitions, with little industry and acute over-

population in the countryside. It was controlled for the
most part by conservative Polish landowners whose manipu-
lations of the provincial Diet were a standing joke. But a
relaxed and nonchalant atmosphere gave scope for cultural
enterprise. In the re-Polonized universities of Cracow and
Lwów, in the Polish Academy of Learning (1872), in the
mildly censored theatres and publishing houses, in the Polish
School Board, the 'organic work' of the Poles in Galicia
redeemed the constrictions on Polish culture in Prussia and
Russia. For this reason, Galicia has been labelled Poland's
'Piedmont'.

In all three partitions, the conflict of the Polish national
movement with the ruling powers was complicated by the
emergence of other rival movements, which were no less
hostile to the Poles than they were to the imperial authorities.
Every ethnic group in eastern Europe, it seemed, was
demanding its civil rights, its own educational system, its own
religious freedom, and in most cases, its own fantastic version
of an exclusive national homeland. In Russia, especially in
Wilno, the Poles ran up against the Lithuanians; in Austria,
against the Ukrainians of eastern Galicia, and the Czechs. In
most of the cities, they began to encounter militant Zionism.
No common front could be established. The mutual antagonisms of the various nationalities enabled the empires to
divide and rule without serious challenge.

In the era of Positivism, Polish literature continued to
flourish. The social novel, notably in the works of Bolesław
Prus (1847-1912), took precedence over the poetry and drama
of the Romantics. Prus had no time for the Risings, or for the
political heroes. Positivist historians, too, like Korzon and
Smoleński, abandoned the study of narrow political history,
with its obsessive interest in the Partitions, and turned instead
to social and economic themes, and to the analysis of 'the
nation'. Yet the theoretical distinction between Positivism
and Romanticism was not always easy to sustain. Many of the
'organic works', undertaken to educate and inform the new
generation, like the historical paintings of Jan Matejko
(1838-93), or the historical novels of J. I. Kraszewski
(1812-87) and Henryk Sienkiewicz (1846-1916), contained
more than a touch of Romanticism.

5 *The Growth of a New Society, c. 1890–1918*

The long European peace, which followed the Franco-Prussian War of 1870–1 and the Congress of Berlin in 1878, saw few international upheavals; but fundamental social changes gradually made themselves felt, in Poland as elsewhere. The emancipation of the serfs, which had been completed in 1864, released a growing stream of rural migrants into the towns and factories to join the nascent working class, although the great mass of the indigent peasantry still survived in the villages through the traditional methods of subsistence farming. The new bourgeoisie pushed its way forward to the distaste of the old nobility and the ex-noble intelligentsia, whilst an over-mighty bureaucracy of petty officials, many of them of foreign origin, moved into the Polish cities on government service. The artisanate, strongly Jewish in composition, was squeezed towards pauperization by the competition of new techniques and larger enterprises. Everywhere, a rocketing birth rate led to severe demographic pressures. The trickle of economic migration, first of seasonal workers travelling to Germany and later of permanent emigrants leaving for western Europe and America, grew in due course into a veritable flood. (See pp. 254–61 below.)

In the last decade of the nineteenth century, most of the new social forces found expression in new, spontaneous political movements. The Polish Socialist Party (PPS), founded abroad in 1892, operated mainly in the cities of Russian Poland—in Warsaw, Łódź, Białystok. The Nationalist Movement, launched one year later in 1893, drew its strongest support from the peripheral provinces—in Poznań, Wilno, and Lwów. The Peasant movement was based from 1895 in Galicia, whilst the Christian Democratic movement, from 1902, drew its principal support from the Catholic proletariat of Silesia. To begin with there was no established forum where all these parties could compete; but their very existence heralded the reassertion of Polish political life which even then was gaining momentum. (See pp. 129–35.)

Meanwhile, responding to the demands for extending popular suffrage, the imperial governments made cautious provision for representative assemblies. Elected Polish deputies made their appearance in the German *Reichstag* in Berlin, from 1871,* in the Austrian *Reichsrat* in Vienna from 1867, and in the Russian *Duma* from 1906. Their activities exerted distinctly centrifugal pressures on the overall Polish scene; but from the Polish point of view it was important that Polish issues, ignored for decades, could at least be publicly aired. Violent tensions lay only half concealed and a series of violent episodes—the school strikes in Posnania, the 'Revolution' of 1905–6 in Russian Poland, and the assassination of the Governor of Galicia in 1908—created an atmosphere of apprehension where the ruling establishments felt inclined to retract previous concessions in order to avoid further troubles.

This changing world of the *fin de siècle,* where the changes seemed agonizingly slow compared to the rock-like inertia of established politics, artistic taste, and social attitudes, provided the soil of frustration from which there sprang the defiant outgrowth of Modernism. The movement was born of the feeling, since progress was an illusion and reform a charade, that the creative artist could still justify his existence by the boldness of his symbols and the bravura of his style. In this respect, Polish Modernism echoed the Art Nouveau, 'Art for Art's sake', and Secessionist movement at points further west. Its outstanding personality was Stanisław Przybyszewski (1868–1927), critic and publicist, ideologue of 'Young Poland', and its greatest talent, the Cracovian, Stanisław Wyspiański (1869–1907), painter, illustrator, poet, and dramatist. (See pp. 231–33 below.) The high point of the Academy of Fine Arts in Cracow (ASP) dates from this time.

In 1914, on the eve of the Great War, the Polish nation had passed the danger of extinction, though there was no clear way forward on the political front. Thirty years before, Polish sympathizers had feared that the Polish nation would succumb to the onslaught of Russification and Germanization. In 1897, the French dramatist Alfred Jarry, looking for an absurd scenario in a country that didn't exist, had written his notorious stage direction 'En Pologne, c'est-à-dire nulle part'. Now, for all its shortcomings, the Polish national

---

*Polish deputies had taken part in the *Landtag* (Diet) of the Kingdom of Prussia since 1848.

movement was showing signs of real achievement. The newly educated masses were conscious of their Polish identity; Polish political life was adopting contemporary concerns; and Polish cultural life was as vibrant as ever. When in 1914–18 the world of the Empires fell apart with frightening rapidity, the Polish nation proved sufficiently mature to seize its destiny.

By Word and by Deed: The Polish Cause

Polish History in the nineteenth century is particularly complicated because most of its constituent subjects have to be reconstructed from separate and contrasting experiences under each of the three partitioning powers. Even within the orbit of Russian, Prussia, Austria, or briefly of France, the Polish experience varied widely from region to region, and from period to period. Developments in Warsaw, in the Congress Kindom, have constantly to be contrasted with those in Wilno or Kiev, just as life in Prussia followed a different path in the Grand Duchy of Poznań from that in Breslau or Danzig. In all three partitions, the political and cultural environment of the 1880s or 1890s differed sharply from that of the 1850s or the 1820s. Generalizations are difficult to make, and it is very easy for the historian to sink into the minutiae of local or provincial life. In the absence of a sovereign Polish state, and with the constant fragmentations of such state structures that did exist, social and economic themes can rarely be satisfactorily pursued in any specifically Polish context; whilst for most of the time Polish politics is narrowed either to the level of the parish pump or else to the two great themes of the age—the preservation of national identity, and the restoration of national independence. Throughout these five generations, Polish History loses much of its material substance, and retreats into the realm of ideas, plans, dreams, and prospects. Right from the start, the subject seems tailored for the Romantics, with their contempt for material things and their preoccupation with the world of the spirit. Polish Literature is a surer guide to the essential features of the age than is Sociology or Economics.

Owing to the specific circumstances of the Partitions, the link between Politics and Literature in Poland was exception-

Map 6.   Eastern Europe *c.* 1880

ally intimate. Of course, in any country, political life is always influenced to some extent by the books which people read; and it would be strange if Literature did not contain a political element of some sort or other. In nineteenth-century England, from Wordsworth's *Prelude* with its echoes of the French Revolution to Kipling's *Recessional* with its sublimation of the British Empire, the connections of politics and literature can be observed at every step. The same is true in France, Germany, or Italy, from Chateaubriand to Zola, from Heine to Nietzsche, from Alfieri to Croce. Even in Russia, where the nineteenth century saw the flowering of one of the world's great literary traditions, literature had a strong, if concealed political flavour, from the early Pushkin to Maxim Gorky. Pushkin wrote several fiercely political poems, some of them, like *To the Slanderers of Russia*, on themes closely connected with Poland. Tolstoy's *War and Peace* contains a vast panorama of Russian History, and of social reactions to political events. Dostoevsky made little attempt to hide his fervently conservative views, and all his novels can be read as a commentary on his fears of social disorder, anarchy, and nihilism.

In Poland, however, national Politics and national Literature were smelted in the same fierce fire, and were fused into an amalgam of such unusual intensity that often the one could no longer be recognized from the other. In a land where all forms of open political activity of a national character were gradually suppressed, poetry and fiction were mobilized as the most convenient vehicle of political expression. Polish politics, driven from the public arena by an army of police and censors, took refuge in the metaphors of the poets and the allegories of the novelists. It developed its own vivid literary code, a corpus of symbols and conventions which assumed a life of their own. For this reason, nineteenth-century Polish Literature, which in quantity, variety, and artistic accomplishment, was comparable to all the great literatures of Europe, has proved markedly unsuitable for export, and largely untranslatable. But in Poland, its role was paramount. It quickly became a great fortress, a cultural Fort Knox, impregnable because its invisible walls could not be breached by guns and search warrants. Indeed, in a society where political activism was

usually judged an indictable crime, it began to assume the role
of a political surrogate, a substitute for 'normal' political
discussions and activities. In Poland, Literature did not
merely *reflect* Politics as it did elsewhere; it threatened to
replace it. For long stretches of Poland's 'Babylonian Captivity', in the lonely watches of Poland's political night, the
'Word' was at least the equal of the 'Deed'.

Although it is an over-simplification to maintain that the
Partitions deprived all Poles of all their political rights and
freedoms, it is none the less true that for most Poles, in most
regions of the Polish lands, and in most periods of the
nineteenth century, political deprivation was an established
fact. In other words, there were very few people in Poland, in
very few places and in very few instances, who could aspire to
cultivate their native political traditions without serious fears
of harassment and violence. Absolute Governments could
never be absolutely successful in putting their absolutist ideals
into effect; just as Autocrats could never rule entirely by
themselves; and the authority of authoritarian states could
never pass entirely unchallenged. In the contemporary era, the
so-called totalitarian regimes, whether Fascist or Communist,
can never exercise total control over their subjects in the
intended manner. But by and large the proscriptive powers of
the ruling Empires of Eastern Europe, with their vast armies
of policemen, informers, bureaucrats, frontier guards, censors,
dependent legislators, and subservient judges, was, and still is,
immense.

The scope for minority politics was minimal. No independent or unapproved political activity designed to strengthen
the national, Polish interest, as distinct from the power of the
State, could flourish for long. As the old institutions were
suppressed one by one, no new national institutions could take
their place. The old traditions could not be applied to and
tested against new circumstances. The Poles had to live off
their memories, and their day-dreams. Political deprivation—with all the social, economic, legal, and cultural
consequences which flowed from it—was a major fact of life.

Throughout the world, faced by a system with pretensions
to absolute power, the individual citizen possesses very limited
political choices. Logically speaking, since pluralist tendencies

are actively suppressed, the existence of absolute authority leaves only four possible courses of action open. The ruling regime can be loyally accepted; it can be resisted by illegal means (but not legally 'opposed'); it can be drawn into some form of a bargain or compromise with its subjects; or it can be evaded. From the viewpoint of the individual Pole, as a subject of the Tsar, the Kaiser, or the Emperor-King, loyal acceptance of the claims of the Government generally required a straight rejection of national politics. Illegal resistance ran the risk of summary punishment; the art of compromise and of political bargaining ran the risk of denunciation by Government and people alike; and the art of evasion involved anything from the pretence that the Government did not really exist, to leaving the country for good. Since the absolute claims of the partitioning powers dominated all aspects of political life, so political attitudes were dominated not so much by social philosophies or by sectional interests (though they were not unimportant), but rather by people's varying reactions to oppression. As a result, Polish politics, from the mid-eighteenth century to the present day, have been dominated by four distinct traditions—the traditions of *Loyalism, Resistance, Conciliation,* and *Emigration.* The terminology has varied; but the basic concepts have not changed. In relation to the first three, home-based, traditions, many Poles would recognize the labels of Collaboration, Idealism, and Realism, or sometimes Loyalism, Romanticism, and Positivism; whilst others according to their particular convictions might prefer the equivalents of Treason-Independence-Collaboration or Surrender-Fanaticism-Sobriety. In the eyes of the ruling Empires, the three main traditions represented the paths of Duty, Rebellion, and Moderation. For outsiders, the trouble is that no Pole will ever admit to following any other tradition than 'Patriotism'.

Loyalism*—in the sense of loyalty to the ruling Power—has acquired such a negative connotation in Poland that many Polish analysts forget even to discuss it. Loyalism lies beyond the pale of patriotic respectability, and any Pole who

---

*In Polish, *Lojalizm*; 'in partitioned Poland, faithful subjection to the partitioning powers, *wiernopoddaństwo*', *Słownik Języka Polskiego* (1963); similar to American and Irish republican, but not to British usage.

expressed unreserved support for the powers that be could expect to be ostracized by his compatriots. Yet it is undeniable that the existence of Polish Loyalists can be observed at almost any time in the last 200 years. Understandably enough, the degree of loyalty covered a wide spectrum. At one extreme, there were Poles who became such enthusiastic neophyte converts to the cause of their political masters that they renounced their Polish origins altogether. Such was Stanisław-Szczęsny Potocki (1751–1805), one of the Confederates of Targowica who, in the aftermath of the Third Partition, declared: 'Poles should abandon all memory of their fatherland; I am a Russian forever.' Another was Tadeusz Bulgarin (1789–1859), editor of *The Northern Bee,* who became one of the most vociferous advocates of official *Russian* nationalism under Nicholas I. Feliks Dzierżyński (1877–1926), founder of the Soviet *Cheka,* and Konstanty Rokossowski (1896–1968), Marshal of the USSR, followed similar paths in the Soviet, as opposed to the Tsarist, services. At the other extreme, there were Poles whose Loyalism was limited by all sorts of personal restrictions and prevarications. They included a numerous body of 'crypto-patriots', men and women who had been obliged to serve by force of circumstance but who were biding their time for the moment when they could show their true colours and openly rebel. These, in deference to Mickiewcz's hero, Konrad Wallenrod (see p. 216), were the 'Wallenrodists'. In the eyes of the Establishment, they were a Polish fifth column of secret enemies operating in its midst. Most typical, perhaps, was the Loyalist who, whilst exercising unwavering support for the political programme of the Establishment, retained a sentimental attachment to Polish traditions and Polish culture. In this, the broadest category, one must include both General Krasiński and Henryk Rzewuski.

Wincenty Krasiński (1782–1858), a professional soldier and an aristocrat of the old school, was born a subject of the last King of Poland, and served each of the succeeding regimes with unstinting devotion. As one of his biographers remarked, his career under Napoleon during the Duchy of Warsaw, under Alexander I during the Congress Kingdom, and under Nicholas I in the Russian Empire was marked by *ta sama, afiszowa gotowość do służby* (an unchanging and ostentatious willingness to serve). At each stage, he collected a profusion of titles and honours, being an imperial count first of France and then of Russia. At each stage, he ensured that his possession of the family estates at Opinogóra in Volhynia, where he built a vast neo-gothic palace, were confirmed in entail. As a soldier, he progressed from being a gentleman-comrade of the national cavalry in 1791, to the rank of colonel in the French service in 1806: to Général de Brigade and Commander of the famed *Chevaux légers* of the Imperial Guard: and eventually to Cavalry-General of the Russian Army. As a trusted politician, he rose from Marshal of the Polish Diet in 1818 to be Senator of the Kingdom, Senator of the Empire and member of the imperial Council of State, and eventually in 1855–6 to be acting Viceroy in Warsaw. At each stage, he provoked accusations of needless servility. On these grounds he was slighted by Marshal Poniatowski. He was execrated by Polish opinion for his dissenting vote against leniency in the Treason Trial of 1828, and for his desertion of the November Rising. Krasiński displayed the usual virtue and vices of his class. He fought with valour, especially at Eylau and Wagram, and in the Peninsular War; he was a highly cultivated man, the leader of a distinguished literary salon in the 1820s, and a minor author, who wrote, among other things, a work on Provençal literature; yet he had no patience with radical politics or social reform. In the campaign of 1812, his lancers were used to pacify Ruthenian serfs who had rebelled against their lords. Most interestingly, as father of the poet, Zygmunt Krasiński, he went to great lengths to prevent his only son from falling into the evil ways of Polish patriotism. Zygmunt was banished from Poland to keep him out of the November Rising, and was subsequently supported abroad in the nomadic, bohemian life of an archetypal Romantic exile. Father and son, the pillar of Tsarism and the rebel artist, met each year in Karlsbad, Lugano, or Nice, where the aristocrats of Europe took the waters. There can be little doubt that the excessive conformism of the parent explains the exaggerated unconventionality of the child.[6]

Henryk Rzewuski (1791–1866), a man of the same social origins and of the same generation as General Krasiński, shared many of his opinions. He was an unremitting advocate of Russian political supremacy, and, rarity of rarities, a Polish Pan-Slavist, who eternally regretted the date of his birth on 3 May 1791. Yet Rzewuski was also an active proponent of Polish culture. A disciple of de Maitre, he propagated the most ultramontane brand of Catholicism, and as author of the popular *Pamiątki Soplicy* (Memoirs of Soplica, 1839), he was widely admired for these nostalgic evocations of old Polish life. This combination of political Loyalism with sentimental patriotism caused few problems in Rzewuski's day, when the ruling powers did not demand cultural and ideological conformity from their loyal subjects. At the end of the century, in the then prevailing climate of Russification and Germanization, it had become quite impossible.

In contrast to Loyalism, the tradition of *Resistance*** has been so closely associated with Polish attitudes that many commentators see it as the only tradition worthy of mention. It was the political companion of Polish Romanticism. The impression is sometimes given that twenty million Poles spent the entire nineteenth century sitting behind assorted barricades at home and abroad. Needless to say, this view involves a slight overstatement. What is more, Resistance was conceived in a variety of forms. At one end of the scale, the iron-hard devotees of Insurrection were prepared to use all possible means, including violence and military force, to further the national cause. In the nature of things, they were few in number, but great in resolve and prestige. Their associates, the political dissidents who backed them with everything except guns and bombs, possessed fewer opportunities or perhaps a milder temper. These were the underground publicists, the uncensored poets, the secret educators. At the other end of the scale, the cautious advocates of passive resistance limited their activities to acts of insubordination, or just to a congenital disinclination to co-operate with the authorities. In time, as the national struggles of eastern Europe intensified, they probably encompassed the majority of the Polish population.

---

*In Polish, *opór*. This term has only come into general usage in the mid-twentieth century, especially during the Second World War. In communist terminology, it refers exclusively to resistance against the Nazis. In the early nineteenth century, *Patriotyzm* (Patriotism), and later *Niepodleg łość* (Independence) or *Aktywizm* (Activism) had similar connotations, and were the usual expressions in everyday use.

They were admirers of the insurgents and readers of dissident literature. It stands to reason that a majority of Poles, with families to support and parish priests to heed, could not be permanently engaged in conspiracy, insurrection, or illegal publishing; but that stubborn, unspoken will to resist, the refusal to 'bend the neck', passed deeply into the Polish psyche. As successive governments have discovered to their cost, one can take a Pole to the water but one cannot make him drink. Stubbornness was bred by the political environment.

Also, since most modern movements of national liberation have their 'military' and 'political' wings, together with the passive support of their national population, one might be led to conceive of the Polish tradition of Resistance as something very similar to that of the modern IRA or the PLO. If so, one misreads the authoritarian social context of nineteenth-century eastern Europe in which the Polish tradition was forged. In Tsarist Russia, or in the Austria of Metternich, and to a lesser extent in Bismarck's Prussia, the authorities made no distinction between different degrees of resistance, nor between the different methods employed. There was no appreciation of a 'legal opposition', let alone of 'non-violent' resistance. There was no chance of working openly within the law by some glib, public rejection of one's private sympathies for terrorist colleagues; there was no opportunity for stating one's case in public. Except in Prussia, where the *Rechtstaat* survived, there was no point in appealing to the Law. There was no tolerance shown to prisoners of conscience, no hope of intervention from Amnesty International. The Absolutist empires demanded absolute obedience, and any form of resistance met with the same implacable reaction. If the Poles could not all be professional insurrectionaries, therefore, they were nearly all suspected of latent treason. Under such pressures, and hardened by the horrors of twentieth-century occupations, they developed a sense of social solidarity which the comfortable inhabitants of modern democracies (including the comfortable and disaffected) find hard to comprehend.

The devotees of *Insurrection*,* the most consequential branch

*In Polish, *Powstanie* (Rising) or less frequently *Insurekcja*; 'taking up arms in the name of Freedom'. *Słownik Języka Polskiego* (1902).

branch of Resistance, whose tradition stretched in unbroken
line from Kościuszko to Piłsudski, dedicated their lives to fight
for the Polish cause at all costs. Over the generations, they
produced a crowded gallery of adventurers, folk heroes, and
martyrs. They were men and women, careless of their own
safety, who fought against tyranny wherever it was found,
under their banner 'FOR YOUR FREEDOM AND OURS', the
original prototypes of the international revolutionaries and
anarchists of a later age. In the eyes of some of their more
sober-minded compatriots, they were dangerous, suicidal
fanatics, and to the authorities, simple terrorists. Yet not even
their enemies could deny that they were often people of
principle, moved by deep moral convictions. In the long
intervals between their open insurrections, they formed a
network of secret brotherhoods, which were sustained by a
band of daring and devoted women, who acted as their
messengers, gun-runners, and teachers, and by sympathizers
and fellow conspirators among the *émigrés*. The more famous
of their organizations included the republican *Deputacja* in
Paris, which mounted Denisko's expedition to Poland in 1797;
the Polish Legions of the Napoleonic period; the Belvedere
Group, which unleashed the November Rising of 1830; the
National Patriotic Society of the 1820s; the Polish Democratic
Society (TDP) of 1832–46; the 'Reds' of Warsaw's City
Committee who launched the January Rising of 1863; the
'revolutionary wing' of the PPS, whose 'battle squads' led the
struggle in 1905–7; Piłsudski's Legions of the First World
War; and the Home Army of the Second. Among the best-
remembered names are those of Józef Bem (1794–1850),
artillery officer in the Russo-Polish War of 1831 and
commander of the Hungarian Insurrectionary Army in
Transylvania in 1848–9; Henryk Kamieński (1813–66), the
theoretician of 'the People's War'; Ludwik Mierosławski
(1814–78), who graduated from the Carbonari and the TDP
to the Berlin Trial of 1847, to the risings of Poznania,
Palermo, and Baden-Baden in 1848, and eventually to a brief
moment of glory as 'Dictator' of the January Rising in 1863;
Edward Dembowski (1822–46), a social revolutionary who
identified the nation with the whole of the population, and
who was killed in 1846 by the first Austrian volley in Cracow;

Ludwik Żychliński (1837–91) another prominent insurgent of 1863 who also fought with Garibaldi and the American Union Army and who survived a stretch of penal servitude in Siberia to return home and write his memoirs; Jarosław Dąbrowski (1836–71), who ended his days as commander of the forces of the Paris Commune: Romuald Traugutt (1825–64), the last Dictator of the January Rising; and Ignacy Hryniewiecki (1855–81), known as 'Ivanovitch', a Polish member of the Russian 'People's Will', who hurled the bomb that killed both Alexander II and himself in St. Petersburg on 13 March 1881.*

Prince Józef Poniatowski (1763–1813), although not an insurrectionary himself, nephew of the last King of Poland and Marshal of France, embodied most of the ideals which inspired the later insurrectionaries. As a professional soldier in an age of political turmoil, Poniatowski repeatedly faced the soldier's fundamental moral dilemma: to serve or not to serve. In the end, he consciously chose a hero's death rather than be subjected once again to the same agonizing decision. Together with Kościuszko, he had a commendable record in the Russo-Polish War of 1791–2, and in the National Rising of 1794; and his was an obvious and popular appointment to be commander of the Army of the Duchy of Warsaw. In the intervening years, he tarried long before throwing in his lot with Napoleon. In the campaign of 1809 against Austria, Poniatowski showed his mettle as a subtle and flexible strategist, repeatedly outwitting a more powerful enemy. In the campaign of 1812 against Russia, at the head of the Fifth (Polish) Corps of the *Grande Armée,* he accepted the two most arduous commands—that of the avant-garde on the advance to Moscow and of the rearguard on the retreat. His unit, though depleted, was one of the few to reach Warsaw intact. He gathered his reserves together, and withdrew into Germany. Here, for the fifth or sixth time in his career, he spurned Russian offers of clemency. Unlike many of his fellow Polish generals in Napoleon's service—Krasiński, Zajączek, Dąbrowski, Kniaziewicz, Chłopicki—Poniatowski had no desire to

---

*In the interests of equity, one should also mention that it was also a Pole, Leon Czolgosz, who assassinated President Mckinley of the USA on 6 September 1901, although not apparently for political reasons.

live to serve the Tsar. At the Battle of the Nations near Leipzig
on 19 October 1813, he was caught in the thick of the French
defeat. Trapped in a bend of the River Elster by Prussian and
Russian forces, the hopeless position of his Polish lancers on
that day was symbolic of Poland's historic fate. There was no
question of surrender or retirement. Mortally wounded by
three bullets, Poniatowski summoned up his final strength,
spurred his horse into the river in a flurry of sniper fire, and
sank beneath the stream. His death is often quoted as yet
another example of suicidal, and pointless, Polish courage. Yet
it was a step entirely consistent with his intolerable predicament; and it was not taken in vain. Napoleonic service had
demanded years of devotion and blood-letting, and a painful
change of loyalties—a change which his old comrade in arms,
Kościuszko, had consistently declined. To have changed his
loyalties once again was all too worrying for an infinitely
weary and honest man. Like much of his generation, he had
hoped; he fought; he served; and he only found rest in
honourable defeat. His motto—*Bóg-Honor-Ojczyzna* (God-
Honour-Fatherland)—has inspired all those of his compatriots who were determined to resist to the end, and for whom
death and defeat were not marks of failure.

Emilia Plater (1806–31) could not have been more different
from Marshal Poniatowski in outward characteristics; yet she
too was a person whose example fortified the insurrectionary
tradition. A woman of the most determined Polish breed, she
fought as a man in the ranks of the November Rising, and
gave her life for the cause. She was born in Lithuania into the
aristocratic clan of Plater de Broel, a distinguished family of
Westphalian origin which had settled in Livonia, and which
had been thoroughly Polonized across the centuries. In the
early nineteenth century, there were Platers in all corners of
Poland, and in every branch of government and the arts.
Ludwik Plater (1774–1846), a pioneer of forestry science, was
Director of the Crown Estates of the Congress Kingdom, and
a Senator. His brother, Stanisław Plater (1784–1851) had
settled in Posnania, and was a geographer and military
historian. Adam Plater (1770–1862) was a naturalist of
distinction, whilst Władysław Plater (1806–89), sometime
Polish soldier, is remembered as founder of the Polish

Museum at Rappersville in Switzerland. In such company, the young Emilia could hardly be other than an aesthete and a patriot. Her cultural energies centred on the study of Ruthenian folklore in her native Lithuania. Her patriotism was aroused by an incident in 1823, when her cousin, Michał Plater, was drafted into the Russian Army for daring to celebrate the Third of May in public. When the November Rising broke out in 1830, she raised a partisan band from the local peasants and joined her uncle, Cezar Plater (1810–69)— later the President of Polish Literary Society in Paris—in the Lithuanian campaign of General Chłapowski. She served at first as a 'gentleman' volunteer, and later as a captain in the Twenty-fifth Regiment of Infantry. She fought in three pitched battles against the Russian Army, before retiring across the Prussian frontier in an attempt to break through to Warsaw. She expired in December 1831 at the age of twenty-five in a peasant's cottage, apparently from sheer exhaustion. Herself a devotee of the new Romantic trend, she was immortalized by Mickiewicz in *Śmierć pułkownika* (The Death of the Colonel). The poem describes the deathbed scene, and the wonderment of the local peasants when they are permitted to view the body:

> But look! This soldier, though dressed in soldier's clothes,
> Has the fairest face of a maiden, and a woman's
> Gentle breast. These mortal remains
> Are those of the rebel leader, the virgin-martyr,
> The girl from Lithuania—Emilia Plater!

Gustaw Ehrenberg (1818–95) was less of an active insurrectionary—since he was too young to participate in 1830–1 and was still under arrest in 1863–4—and more of a political dissident, although he was an associate and sympathizer of the insurrectionaries. As a poet, whose fervent Polish patriotism was combined with uncompromising social radicalism, he composed popular verse denouncing Tsarism and Serfdom with equal ferocity, and was treated by the authorities as an incorrigible subversive. His savage parodies of the landowning classes made him very popular in later times, and one of his poetic tirades about the November Rising, *Szlachta w roku 1831*

(The Nobility in 1831), was set to music, and became one of
the favourite anthems of the Polish communist movement:

When the people went forth with the sword to the fray,
The gentry were chatting in parliament.
When the people declared 'We shall conquer or die',
The nobles were counting their rent.
The cannon at Stoczek were captured by youths
Whose arms had been tanned at the plough,
Whilst the gentry in town were smoking cheroots
As they talked and debated, and furrowed their brow,
On the problems of weighing the means and the ends,
And their hopes of appeasing their Muscovite friends. . . .

(Not every line of the anthem finds its way into present-day
Party songbooks.) It was grossly unfair to suggest that the
Polish gentry declined as a class to fight against Tsarism. It
was the most active element. And it is a pity that few of the
people who sing Ehrenberg's words today are told that their
author, who spent over half his life in exile in Siberia for his
pains, was the natural son of a Russian Tsar.

The tradition of *Conciliation** arose from the constant need
to forge a working compromise between the opposing camps
of Loyalism and Resistance, between the immovable object of
absolute Government and the unstoppable force of popular
demands. In Polish society, the role of political conciliator and
arbitrator has often fallen to the Roman Catholic Church,
although in the nineteenth century the Church hierarchy,
whose appointments were controlled by the state, enjoyed less
public confidence than it does today. The conciliators had to
demonstrate sufficient loyalty to the regime to avoid suspicions of wishing to overthrow the established order, and at the
same time sufficient concern for national traditions to make
them credible representatives of the people. They constantly
ran the risk of denunciation by one side or the other, either for
excessive impertinence or else for excessive subservience. They
steered a dangerous course between the Scylla of official

---

*In Polish, *Ugoda.* The Polish term has a more active sense than a mere
'compromise'. The verb *ugodzić się* means 'to strike a bargain', and *ugoda* has the
connotation of a painful, provisional arrangement between two irreconcilable
extremes.

displeasure and the Charybdis of popular rejection. They differed from the Loyalists in their insistence that national traditions must find some sort of expression in political organizations and in legally sanctioned institutions; and they differed from the Resisters, in accepting the established regime as a permanent and unchallengeable reality. For this reason, they have always called themselves 'realists', although their emphasis on social and cultural work and on economic progress, especially after 1864, gave them the labels of 'positivists' and advocates of 'organic work'.* Their venom was largely reserved for the insurrectionaries, whose conspiratorial activities on behalf of national independence they regarded as negative, suicidal, and hopelessly 'idealistic'. In the purely political sphere, they were minimalists by necessity, with no greater aim in immediate view than the gradual recovery or expansion of limited autonomy. In non-political spheres, however, they could be highly ambitious, believing that Poles could only begin to think of independence when their cultural and economic prowess was equal to that of their neighbours. If politics is indeed 'the art of the possible', then the conciliators were indeed the only true politicians on the Polish scene. The strategy of Conciliation was first pursued by the last King of Poland, Stanisław-August, in the first twenty-five years of his reign. It was revived by the men who sought to give effect to the Vienna Settlement, and in particular by the leaders of the Congress Kingdom in the period 1815–30; it came back into fashion after the collapse of the January Rising in 1864, when it provided the dominant mode of Polish politics for the rest of the century. In this last period, it reaped few benefits in Russia, where the resurgence of reactionary Tsarism left little room for manœuvre, and scored only marginal gains in imperial Germany; but in Austria, it achieved a working alliance between the Habsburg Monarchy and the Galician Poles which lasted right until the end of the Austrian Empire itself in 1918. Apart from Stanisław-August,

*The modern Polish term *organicznikowstwo* (the Organic Approach) is sometimes used to denote the common denominator, akin to conciliation, possessed by the anti-insurrectionary trend in Polish politics throughout the period from the late Enlightenment to the late nineteenth century. *Pozytywizm* (Positivism), in its broadest, non-specific sense, is also popularly used for the same purpose. (See pp. 200–2 below.)

its leading practitioners included Prince Drucki-Lubecki, the Marquis Wielopolski in the years 1861–3, and, at the turn of the century, Roman Dmoswki.

Franciszek-Ksawery Drucki-Lubecki (1778–1846), the younger son of an ancient Polish family from Byelorussia, must be regarded as the conciliator *par excellence*. He never wavered in his loyalty to the Romanovs, whom he served as soldier, diplomat, and administrator; but equally, he never wavered in his belief that his Polish compatriots could not be ruled by coercion alone and that they must be granted a wide measure of autonomy. In this respect, his abortive scheme to revive the separate constitutional status of the Grand Duchy of Lithuania—which was overtaken by the war of 1812—is less known than his career as the Minister of Finance of the Congress Kingdom from 1821 to 1830. Lubecki was trained in the imperial cadet corps in St. Petersburg, and fought under Suvorov throughout the Swiss and Italian campaigns of 1798–1800. On leaving the Russian Army, he soon emerged as the provincial Marshal of the Nobility of the Grodno *gubernia*—a post which brought him to the attention of the imperial Court and which on several future occasions made him a natural choice for the Governorship of various western provinces. During Napoleon's invasion of Russia, he stayed loyally at the side of Alexander I, and showed no interest in Napoleon's claims to be the liberator of Poland. For six years after the Napoleonic war, he built up his reputation as a financial wizard, working as a diplomat and negotiator in the liquidation of post-war international debts. Up to this point his experience of Polish affairs was limited to the few months in 1813–14 when he had acted on the Tsar's Provisional council for the Duchy of Warsaw, and when he had been coldly received by the Varsovians for his alleged servility to Russian interests. Lubecki's mettle as a man who could stand up to bullying Tsarist bureaucrats was only revealed when he arrived in Warsaw for the second time in 1821, to put some order into the Kingdom's chaotic economy. 'Poland', he declared, 'will not perish because of its finances'. He quickly realized, however, that the financial chaos formed part and parcel of a wider, political, problem where the calculated hostility of senior Russian officials was undermining all efforts to put the affairs of the Kingdom on to a viable footing. He also decided that the Tsarist bureaucrats could only be beaten by people prepared to use the same arbitrary methods. As a rationalist, and an admirer of Joseph II, he had no sympathy for the independent aspirations of the Catholic Church in Poland; and he was no great respecter of constitutional niceties. Despite his constant battle with Novosiltsov, the Tsar's personal representative in Poland, Lubecki did not hesitate to approve the latter's repressive police decrees, or to present his budget, illegally, without reference to the Diet. Yet as the only man in Warsaw who could argue with the Grand Duke Constantine on equal terms, and as one of the very few Poles with direct access to the Tsar in St. Petersburg, he could fight his corner with spirit; and he gradually cleared away the obstacles to orderly administration and economic progress. He failed in his impudent attempt to extract reparation payments for Poland against the costs of the Russian Occupation of 1813–15, but his campaign to limit Russian Protectionism in trade matters paid dividends. He balanced the budget, ended the tariff war with Prussia, opened the tariff frontier with Russia, laid the foundations of agricultural recovery, and of state-supported industrialization. Corazzi's grand design for the new Bank of Poland, erected in 1828 alongside his own Ministry of Finance, is a lasting monument to his achievement.

Lubecki's role in the crisis of 1830 merits close examination, since it exactly illustrates the eternal dilemma of all would-be conciliators in the moments when major political decisions were made. When the conciliator's balancing act was brought to an end by the outbreak of the November Rising, he was forced like everyone else in Poland to make his choice between the merciless demands of the Autocrat and the hopeless demands of the people. In effect, after one last courageous bid to conciliate, he returned to the path of unconditional Loyalism, and his influence in Poland was lost forever. In the fateful night of 29–30 November 1830, Lubecki was called away from his vigil at the bedside of a dead son; but none the less he took energetic steps to contain events. He urged the Grand Duke Constantine to crush the outbreak whilst it could still be presented as a minor mutiny, and whilst General

Krasiński still held the forces to act. He was instrumental, together with Czartoryski, in forming the Provisional Government, made up of loyal conservatives and a token sprinkling of radicals; and later in installing the 'Dictatorship' of General Chłopicki. In the pre-telegraph age, it was inevitable that these moves be made without the formal consent of the Tsar, and it was a mark of the greatest magnanimity on the part of the Polish leaders that the Grand Duke was allowed to withdraw the Russian garrison from Warsaw with its colours and its prisoners intact. At this stage, Lubecki seems to have felt that it was better to negotiate with the Tsar from a position of strength and with a show of goodwill; and he left for St. Petersburg on 12 December in optimistic mood. His interview with the Tsar cured him of all such illusions. Nicholas made it clear that he could only receive Lubecki as a loyal minister, not as a spokesman for the Polish 'mutineers', and that the unconditional submission of the Polish Government and Army was the sole matter for discussion. To his credit, Lubecki had the temerity to tell the Tsar to his face that such an unyielding demand would be 'unacceptable' to the Poles; but those words were his last contribution to the conversation. The Tsar was set on revenge. Russian Autocracy was determined to bring Polish constitutionalism to heel. The role of Conciliation was at an end. Lubecki wrote to Chłopicki, urging him after all to try to suppress the Rising with Polish troops, since that was the only way to avoid Russian intervention; but he can have had little faith in this advice. In due course, he submitted to the Tsar, and was appointed to the imperial Council of State. The Loyalist who had dared to work for Conciliation was forced to revert to Loyalism. Conciliation, it seems, faced with Autocracy, could be no more of a permanent solution than Insurrection.

If Lubecki approached Conciliation from the starting-point of the public servant, his colleague and close acquaintance, Stanisław Staszic (1755–1826), moved towards similar conclusions essentially from the position of a distinguished private citizen. Staszic, a product of the Enlightenment and a disciple of the physiocrats, from whom the later positivists drew much of their inspiration, had made his name as philosopher, translator, publicist, and scientist in the last decades of the old

Republic. (See pp. 306–10.) As a member of the burgher estate, excluded from the Diet for most of his early career, he probably felt the political oppression which followed the Partitions less keenly than many of his noble contemporaries. In his *Przestrogi dla Polski* (Warnings for Poland, 1790) and other political writings, he certainly made no secret of the failings of Polish society. 'There is no such example', he wrote, 'of a people counting nearly twenty million and settled on the most fruitful land, and endowed by Nature with all resources, who await slavery with such complacency'. From his Polish translation of Homer's *Iliad* to his pioneering survey of Polish geology, he displayed that ceaseless intellectual energy, practical approach, and capacity for selfless labour which the positivists came to see as the supreme national virtues. When the noble monopoly of landowning was abolished, and he was free to buy an estate near Hrubieszów, his first act was to free the serfs and to grant them the land in communal tenure. As President of the Society of the Friends of Science, founded in Prussian Warsaw in 1800, he was the acknowledged Father of modern Polish learning, fittingly giving his name to the palace which has been adopted as the seat of the Polish Academy of Sciences. Although in later life, in the Duchy of Warsaw and in the Congress Kingdom, he accepted minor public office, he confined his involvement to the educational and economic spheres, maintaining a sceptical stance towards the blessings of politics. On the central issue of the relationship between the individual and the state authorities, and in particular between the Poles and their Russian masters, he is often given the credit for the phrase which became the watchword of the realists: 'We are ready to be your brothers, but not your slaves'. Unfortunately, as Polish conciliators have repeatedly found to their cost, it takes two partners to keep that sort of a bargain.

The tradition of political *Emigration**—as distinct from the separate phenomenon of economic migration (see pp. 254–61)—is the logical product of the limitations of all other alternatives. When the possibilities of Loyalism, Resistance, and Conciliation have been exhausted, the politically active

---

*In Polish, *wychodźstwo* or, more usually nowadays, *emigracja*.

Pole had nothing left but to emigrate. Political Emigration did not imply attachment to any particular philosophy or tradition, but only to the conviction that effective political action at home was impossible. Indeed, in conditions prevailing for much of the nineteenth century, political activism was often rewarded by imprisonment in distant parts of the ruling Empires or by forcible deportation. In 1848, for example, hundreds of Poles implicated in the 'Revolution' in Cracow were forcibly expelled by the Austrian authorities to the USA, just as tens of thousands of Poles were forcibly deported to Siberia after each of the Risings against Russia. The usual choice, therefore, lay between being driven to leave the homeland under one's own steam, or waiting to be transported under guard. From the mid-eighteenth century onwards, wave after wave of political *émigrés* has flowed out of Poland to east and west, draining the country of its most active talents and swelling the *émigré* communities abroad. Strong Polish contingents were established at an early date at points as far apart as Irkutsk and Constantinople, as well as in Switzerland, Britain, or America, or most importantly in Paris and Rome. Even larger numbers made the involuntary journey across the frontiers from one sector of partitioned Poland to another, most typically to seek refuge from Tsardom in Prussia or Galicia. The earliest of the great Polish *émigrés* was the former king, Stanisław-Leszczyński, in his Duchy of Lorraine (see p. 306); but his successors were legion. The ex-confederates of Bar, the tide of *émigrés* in the Napoleonic Era who fled the collapse of the Old Polish Republic; the 'Great Emigration' to France in the aftermath of the November Rising; the victims of 1848, 1863, and 1905; and in our own century the tidal waves of the two World Wars, have restocked the Polish settlements abroad in ever-increasing numbers. Political Emigration has become a permanent part of the Polish condition.

Of all the Polish *émigrés*, no one better illustrates the finest qualities of the political exiles than Julian Ursyn Niemcewicz (1757–1841). As a writer with an astonishing literary range, and an active statesman both before and after the Partitions, he cultivated that quintessentially Polish combination of Literature and Politics; as an involuntary exile during two long and quite separate periods of his life, he demonstrated the cyclical nature of the *émigré* tradition. As an anglophile and a fervent admirer of the United States, who spent several years both in England and in America, he deserves to be better known to the Anglo-American public. In the first half of his long life, Niemcewicz experienced the whole sad story of the Polish Enlightenment and Reform movement from beginning to end. He could remember the disgrace of the First Partition of 1773; and in the terminal crisis of the old Republic twenty years later, he was pushed inexorably from the stance of a liberal publicist to that of constitutional reformer, and eventually to that of soldier-insurrectionary. In the space of five frenzied years, he wrote two of the most influential works of the age—the drama *Powrót posła* (The Return of the Envoy, 1790) and the satirical *Biblia targowicka* (The Targowica Bible, 1791)—he worked in the Great Sejm as deputy for Livonia, as a leading protagonist of the Constitution of 3 May; and he served in the Army as Kościuszko's adjutant. He was wounded and captured with Kościuszko at the battle of Maciejowice on 10 October 1794, and imprisoned with him in the Petro-pavlovsk Fortress in Petersburg. This first period of exile was dominated by seven years spent in America where he became a lifelong friend and correspondent of Thomas Jefferson. In the second half of his career, Niemcewicz experienced the same sad cycle of events. He returned to Poland in 1807, and was appointed secretary to the Senate of the Duchy of Warsaw. His phenomenal literary output, which included a string of comedies, an operatic libretto about 'Queen Jadwiga', a 'History of Sigismund III' in three volumes, the ever popular *Śpiewy historyczne* (Historical Ballads, 1816), and a series of precocious novels in the style of Walter Scott, made him a national celebrity. He was the obvious choice to succeed Staszic in the presidency of the Society of the Friends of Science. In 1831, he was sent to London as an ambassador-emissary of the National Government, after which, being sentenced *in absentia* by a Russian court, he had no hope of return. He travelled widely in England and Ireland as well as on the continent, but settled among the Great Emigration in Paris. His copious memoirs, patiently compiled during his old age, read like an encyclopaedia of the times. His last verse, composed only ten days before his death, can be read as a comment on all his peers:

O Exiles! whose earthy wanderings are ne'er complete
When may you rest your sore and weary feet?
The worm has his clod of earth. The wild dove has its nest.
Everyone has a home: but the grave, for a Pole, is the only
place of rest.

Curiously enough, in the best Polish tradition, political emigration did not necessarily require foreign residence or travel abroad. Since the Polish nation passed the best part of three centuries in the trip of regimes which have not permitted freedom of movement, and which have actively obstructed foreign travel by only issuing passports to approved persons, it has often proved impossible for would-be *émigrés* to leave the country. In any case, the general consensus of opinion has always discouraged the departure of anyone who was not actually compelled to leave. Families were reluctant to see their friends and loved ones depart for good, whilst political leaders frequently deplored the drain of the nation's life-blood. Voluntarily emigration was easily equated with desertion. For many Poles, therefore, political emigration had to be practised at home, in a conscious act of denial of the political realities of the day. People could live in Russia or Prussia or Austria, and could be coerced into that minimal degree of political conformity which would keep them in employment and out of prison. But they ostentatiously refused all forms of public service, and all but the most token forms of co-operation with officialdom. In their private lives, in the intimacy of their friends and relations, in the company of trusted companions, they led a double existence of fervent patriotism and secret Polishness. To their way of thinking, which was the practical application of the purest Romanticism, their bodies were captive, but their spirits were free. Poland was a prisoner, but its soul was unbound. This *emigracja wewnętrzna* (spiritual or literally 'internal' emigration) was a widespread phenomenon, internal in both the geographical and the psychological sense. It is impossible to quantify, since it was in essence a covert and highly personal operation. But there can be little doubt that it was far more common than political emigration in its overt form. For all the tens of thousands of Poles who were forced by political circumstances to leave their country and live abroad, there have been millions who stayed at home but emigrated in their hearts. Mickiewicz provided the guidebook to this spiritual journey in his *Books of the Polish Nation and Pilgrimage* (1832). 'He who would follow Freedom', he wrote, echoing Christ's commands to his disciples, 'let him leave his homeland, and risk his life. For he who lives in the Fatherland, and accepts Slavery, shall lose both his life and the Fatherland.' Surely, Mickiewicz was hardly calling for mass emigration overseas and the depopulation of Poland, but rather for people to free themselves from the spiritual slavery of the existing social and political order.[7]

Clearly, any description of political attitudes which confines itself to theoretical categories must be subject to serious objections. Polish political life was far more fluid and sophisticated than any brief summary of the basic vocabulary might suggest. No individual could ever conform exactly to the specifications of a pure type. Most politicians frequently changed their positions and hedged their bets, whilst others, whether through ignorance or cunning, proved capable of expressing mutually contradictory opinions at one and the same time. One has only to examine the careers of the most prominent Polish figures of the nineteenth century to see that the opinions of youth rarely coincided with the convictions of old age. The world in which they operated as mature statesmen was no longer the world which they had known as students or aspiring débutants. Men such as Czartoryski or Wielopolski who were active in politics for half a century or more would have been less than human, not to say totally insensitive, if their views had not evolved with the times.

Adam Jerzy Czartoryski (1770–1861), for example, a man with an extraordinary breadth of experience, moved progressively through each of the main positions of the Polish political scale. Sent to St. Petersburg during the events of 1795 as a hostage at the Russian Court, he became a personal confidant of the young Alexander I, and in the first decade of Alexander's reign served as one of the Tsar's leading ministers and chief adviser on foreign affairs. Despite his constant concern for the Polish Question, and his attempts to persuade the Tsar to take some bold initiative in favour of the Poles, Czartoryski must be viewed in this period as essentially a political loyalist. In the following decades, however, freed from the constraints of the highest office, he rapidly emerged as a bold practitioner of Conciliation, and an inspiration for the work of the later positivists. As author of the liberal constitution of the Congress Kingdom, he could fairly claim to have struck the most favourable bargain which any Polish conciliator ever induced a Russian Tsar to sign. From 1803 to 1822, as Curator of the Wilno School District—a vast area covering most of the ex-Polish provinces in Lithuania, Byelorussia, and Ukraine—he guided the most important cultural and educational project of the day. In that brief interval, which spanned the turmoil of Napoleon's collapse and the post-Napoleonic settlement, Wilno carried the torch of Polish culture, salvaging many of the ideals of the old Education Commission and sowing the seed for the most brilliant intellectual harvest of the century. Yet in 1830–1, Czartoryski found himself cast in the role of insurrectionary, indeed of President of the rebel National Government in Warsaw. For all his aristocratic connections and conservative temper, he could not bring himself to condone the Tsar's primitive vendetta, and saw active resistance as the only way to bring his former Russian colleagues to their senses. Thus, when the November Rising was crushed, he was left with no alternative but to flee the country, and to become a political *émigré*. For thirty years, Czartoryski's residence in the Hotel Lambert in Paris formed the hub of the Great Emigration—at once the focus of intense diplomatic activity and the symbol of Polish aspirations.[8] Like any politician and statesman, Czartoryski was subjected to many jibes and criticisms, especially from compatriots with a more radical social outlook; but his record of accomplishment was second to none. Loyalist, Conciliator, Insurrectionary, and *Émigré*, Czartoryski proved himself a great patriot, a distinguished servant of the Polish cause.

Aleksander Wielopolski (1803–77), the Marquis Gonzaga-Myszkowski, experienced similar swings of fortune and conviction. A far more choleric person than Czartoryski, he was given to more trenchant opinions and more extreme reactions; and he has aroused much greater controversy amongst historians. Wielopolski's political career began during the November Rising, when, as a young man of twenty-seven, he was sent to London in the steps of Niemcewicz as an emissary-ambassador of the National Government. The disillusionments of that mission, in which he saw the hypocrisy of the Western powers at first hand, led to the bitter realization of Poland's isolation and to a complete reversal of his attitude towards the partitioning powers. In 1846, appalled by the conduct of the Austrian authorities during the Galician Jacquerie, he turned to Russia as the only worthy master of the Polish nation. In his anonymous *Letter of a Polish nobleman to Prince Metternich'*, he made a public appeal to the Tsar to accept the willing and unconditional submission of his compatriots. 'Once we were yours by right of conquest and from fear, like slaves ... But today, ... we submit to you as a free people, voluntarily and by God's favour, and we accept His sentence. We reject ... everything which is pompously called "the right of nations." ... We make no conditions.' Nicholas I did not even read this appeal; but later, Alexander II took note of Wielopolski and picked him in 1861 as the chief agent of his reform programme in Poland. For three of the most turbulent years of the century, buffeted on the one hand by the rising demands of patriotic opinion and on the other by the disapproving looks of his Russian colleagues, Wielopolski strove to introduce the reforms whilst upholding law and order and keeping the Autocracy intact. After the interminable ice age of Nicholas's reign, the milder climate of Alexander's rule was certainly welcome. Wielopolski's reforms—the reinstatement of Polish education, and the first decree of emancipation, among others—were widely acclaimed in Poland; and his personal courage, which he proved on one occasion by interposing himself between a line of sabre-waving Cossacks and the taunting ranks of a patriotic demonstration, was beyond question. But the 'thaw', which he sought to control, turned into a flood which swept him away. Polish opinion about him is as divided in the history books as it was in clubs and circles of 1863. Wielopolski is still judged harshly by those who see him as a loyalist tool of Russian oppression, masquerading as a patriot and reformer in order to strengthen the foundations of Tsarism; and he is admired by others as a courageous conciliator, a determined realist, who failed through no fault of his own. At all events, the youthful insurrectionary of 1830 had certainly been transformed by 1863 into an unequivocal opponent of all resistance. His fate, which condemned him to the obloquies of both Poles and Russians, perfectly illustrates the impossible (yet necessary) task of reconciling Polish and Russian interests. When Wielopolski joined the Polish Resistance, he suffered humiliating defeat; when he offered his services to Tsardom, he was snubbed and then manipulated; when he tried to build a bridge between the two sides, he was destroyed. This frequent reversal of individual roles, and the seemingly inevitable collapse of whatever stand was taken, is the surest evidence of the surging pressures at work in the Polish political maelstrom.

Not surprisingly, the main political debate in Poland has concentrated ever since the Partitions on the question of combating foreign oppression. It rests on the assumption that Poland's internal affairs are dominated by external pressures, and that Poland's loss of independence—unlike other states in decline such as Spain or Sweden, which escaped much more lightly—can only be explained by her geopolitical position and by the nature of her neighbours. This so-called *prymat polityki zewnętrznej* (primacy of external relations) does not merely refer to the need for foreign diplomatic support, but rather to the recognition that nothing fundamental can change in Poland without fundamental transformations on the international scene. In the initial phase, in the century beginning with the First Partition in 1773, Poland's external predicament was fixed by the network of alliances and rivalries between Russia, Prussia, and Austria. From 1871, with the rise of the German Reich and the eclipse of Austria, it was dominated by the duel between Russia and Germany; and from 1945, with the final defeat of Germany, it has been determined by the policies of the Soviet Union.

The great divide in the Polish political debate has always lain between the Romantic-Insurrectionary-Idealist Camp on one side, and the Positivist-Conciliatory-Realist Camp on the other. It cut right through the middle of all the other social and political groupings in Poland, splitting the social classes, such as the nobility or the peasants, into insurrectionary and anti-insurrectionary elements; splitting the political parties such as the PPS or the PSL into 'national revolutionary' or 'non-national revolutionary' factions (see pp. 130–31); and splitting the three main 'orientations'—the Russophobe, Prussophobe, and Austrophile—into 'active' and 'passive' wings. It virtually ignored any phenomena, such as Loyalism or Emigration, which could not be used as grist for the patriotic mills of the two contestants, and it developed a bewildering profusion of relative labels and epithets which can only be understood in relation to the viewpoint of their users. The typical Polish Romantics, for example, always claimed that they were just as 'realistic' as their positivist opponents, only that they had a different conception of reality. The typical Positivist would always claim that he was no less in favour of Polish Independence than the Romantic, only that he differed on the ways and means of achieving it. In Polish usage, the common labels of 'Romantic' and 'Positivist' came to possess rather wider meanings than the literary and philosophical terms from which they derived; whilst the opposing concepts of 'Idealist' and 'Realist', widely employed in European political philosophy as descriptive instruments, came to acquire subjective colourings in Poland equivalent to 'utopian' or 'capitulationist'. Two things, however, are certain. Firstly, arbitrary attempts by modern ideologists to apply their own jargon of 'Left' and 'Right', or 'progressive' and 'reactionary', have only added to the confusion. Secondly, notwithstanding the war of epithets, it is important to see that this traditional Polish debate is not particularly unique. It is nothing more than a local variant of the age-old dispute between the Platonists and the Aristotelians. As Albert Sorel once put it, politicians must be divided between those 'who seek to change the world to suit their ideas' and those 'who seek to modify their actions to suit the world'. Sorel was not thinking of Poland—he was writing about Montesquieu at the time—but his insight into one of the universal dichotomies of political life can be used to explain the contrast between the

Polish political Romantics and the Polish political Positivists as well as any other.[9]

Polish Romantic ideology was first expounded in allegorical language by the great poets of the early nineteenth century. The seminal text is to be found in Mickiewicz's *Księgi narodu i pielgrzymstwa polskiego* (Books of the Polish Nation and Pilgrimage, 1832):

In the beginning, there was belief in one God, and there was Freedom in the world. . . . But later the people turned aside from the Lord their God, and made themselves graven images, and bowed down. . . . Thus God sent upon them the greatest punishment, which is Slavery.

And the Kings, renouncing Christ, made new idols which they set up in the sight of the people, and made them bow down. . . . And the nations forgot that they had sprung from one Father. Finally in idolatrous Europe, there arose three rulers, a satanic Trinity—Frederick whose name signifieth 'Friend of Peace', and Catherine, which in Greek signifieth 'Woman of Purity', and Maria Theresa, who bore the name of the immaculate Mother of our Saviour. Their names were thus three blasphemies, their lives three crimes, their memories three curses. And this Trinity fashioned a new idol, unknown to the ancients, and they called it POLITICAL INTEREST. . . .

But the Polish nation alone did not bow down . . . And Poland said, 'Whosoever will come to me shall be free and equal for I am FREEDOM.' But the Kings, when they heard it, were frightened in their hearts, and they crucified the Polish nation, and laid it in its grave, crying out 'We have slain and buried Freedom.' But they cried out foolishly. . . .

For the Polish Nation did not die. Its Body lieth in the grave; but its spirit has descended into the abyss, that is into the private lives of people who suffer slavery in their own country. . . . For on the Third Day, the Soul shall return again to the Body; and the Nation shall arise, and free all the peoples of Europe from slavery.

Here, in all the majesty of its biblical cadences, was that strongest of all Romantic metaphors, of 'Poland, the Christ of Nations'. Kazimierz Brodziński (1791–1835) expressed the same thought in simpler words:

> Hail, O Christ, Thou Lord of Men!
> Poland in Thy footsteps treading
> Like Thee suffers, at Thy bidding;
> Like Thee, too, shall rise again.

In the hands of the poets, the concept of the nation was not merely idealized; it was sublimated, projected into the realms of religious mysticism. Indeed, the religious overtones of Romantic politics grew so intense that they threatened to supersede the teachings of Roman Catholicism. (See p. 263.) The practices of Andrzej Towiański (1799–1878), for example, who founded a mystic, adventist sect among the Polish *émigrés* in Paris in the 1840s, lay far beyond the pale of the Church; still they matched the temper of the time and attracted the support of both Mickiewicz and Słowacki.

Yet the principles of Polish Romanticism were constructed on much firmer foundations than the poetic licence and mystical fervour of some of its enthusiasts might suggest. An explicit link between Romantic Literature and insurrectionary politics was expounded at an early date in the reflections of Maurycy Mochnacki (1804–34). Mochnacki's key work, *O literaturze polskiej* (On Polish Literature, 1831) was completed at the height of the November Rising, and clearly stated that the moral force of a nation as expressed in its arts and culture was the nation's surest weapon in the struggle for survival. Poetry and Resistance were partners in the common cause. 'It is time to stop writing about art. . . .' he said, '. . . our life is already poetry. From now on, our metre will be the clash of swords, our rhyme the roar of guns.' At the same time, Polish Romantic philosophers and historians were playing a prominent role in the general European predilection for messianic theories, all of which were adapted in their different ways to explain how the agonies of the present could be resolved into the perfections of the future.[10] In 1822, Józef Gołuchowski, (1797–1858) a Professor at Wilno, published a volume of metaphysics entitled *Die Philosophie in ihrem Verhaltnis zum Leben* whose German title betrayed its derivations but whose exploration of intuition and of the indestructibility of the soul were well matched to Polish concerns. In 1831, J. M. Hoehne-Wroński (1778–1853), a veteran *émigré* of Dąbrowski's legions, published his *Prodrome du Messianisme,* where he predicted the advent of an 'Intellectual Age' of mankind's perfection and fulfilment. Wroński's emphasis on rationality and intelligence, combined with his arguments about a systematic 'law of creation' and about human immortality, spanned the gap between Kant and Hegel, linking the Enlightenment of his youth with the Romanticism of his maturity. In 1838, August Cieszkowski (1814–94) published his *Prologomena zur Historisophie,* the first of several works devoted to a much more consciously religious brand of messianic philosophy. Cieszkowski's 'Era of the Holy Spirit' could be seen in some ways as a Catholic version of Wroński's intellectual utopia, and as such was more attuned to Polish thought. His chief work, *Ojcze Nasz* (Our Father), published posthumously in 1900, showed the stamina of Romantic productivity and, whilst helping to reconcile radical national politics with Catholic belief, did much to combat the Romantics' earlier reputation for violence. Unlike Mickiewicz, Cieszkowski did not pray for a 'universal war of liberation'. In fact, Cieszkowski mapped out some of the common ground between the Romantics and their Positivist rivals, and served as a healing influence. Cieszkowski, one of Marx's fellow students at Berlin, had started off as a left-Hegelian philosopher who, by turning metaphysics to the service of social action, must be regarded as one of the precursors of early Marxism. Yet his deep convictions about the divine mission of the Catholic Church and the primacy of human will soon led him into different paths; and it is most appropriate that this most original of Polish Romantic philosophers, like Polish Romanticism itself, should have been thoroughly imbued with Christian values. In contrast, the historian Joachim Lelewel (1786–1861), a man of no less influence in his day, stayed much more closely within the secular sphere. A professional colleague of Gołuchowski's at Wilno; a ministerial colleague of Lubecki and of Czartoryski in the National Government of 1830–1; and a sometime associate of Marx in their obscure *émigré* International Democratic Society, Lelewel was a militant republican and an agnostic. Yet his *Dzieje Polski potocznym sposobem opowiedziane* (Poland's Past Recounted in a Familiar Way, 1829) became a political bible for the thousands of Polish insurrectionaries and *émigrés* of his generation. Lelewel invented a theory about primitive Slavic self-government, whereby the Poles were seen to possess a natural predilection for Democracy, and where the whole of their history could be interpreted as an unrelenting struggle for Freedom. He divided Polish History into alternating periods of Liberty and Servitude, the last of which, the servitude of the Partitions, was due to prepare the way for the era of universal liberty. In this process, the role of the Polish Nation was that of a chosen 'ambassador to humanity' whose sufferings were meant to inspire a world seduced by the lure of power and success. In short, quite unconsciously and independently, Lelewel had invented a close historio-philosophical parallel to Mickiewicz's allegory of Poland as the 'Christ of Nations'.[11]

Polish Positivist ideology was expounded at a slightly later date, but with no less thoroughness. Like Romanticism, it could trace its origins to the pre-Partition era and it owed a particular debt to the Enlightenment. Yet it took its main inspiration from mid-century disillusionment with insurrectionary politics and with the apparent failure of the Romantics' prophecies. Its leading proponents were repelled by the endless catastrophies, violence, and fantasies of the Romantics, and called instead for a more cautious, constructive, and pragmatic approach to the nation's ills. Hence the emphasis on Education, on Self-Improvement, on Science, on Economics, on Social Reform, and above all, on Work. They drew their conclusions from the practical policies of Conciliation as practised by Stanisław-August, Lubecki, or Wielopolski, and turned them into a coherent system of values and ideas. Although they affected to despise the role of poetry for its associations with Romanticism, their clearest manifesto was penned in verse by Karol Świdziński (1841–77), a repentant survivor of both the January Rising and the Paris Commune:

Forward Through Work

. . .
The strains of the harp are not for you,
No cavalry charge, no flash of lightning,
No eagles soaring on the wing,
Neither sabre, nor spear, nor arrow.
What you need is unremitting toil,
The food of the mind, the bread of the soul. . . .
What have you ever gained by your whirling swords?
Just a couple of notches in the mildew of History.

What benefit came from your lutes and your poetry?
The world will doze through a million chords.
Young comrade, one fights
Not by the sword, but by other lights,
Head down, poring o'er the page
Of wisdom. There your heart can gauge
The true current of affairs;
And from the harvest of our forebears
Can learn to understand and love
Everything which makes it good to live.

Świdziński's sentiments were as far removed from the Romantics, as was the quality of his verse. But his priorities were
perfectly clear: Work before Battle, Science before Art, careful
Study before rash Action; and they matched the mood of his
contemporaries. They were echoed in the opinions of far more
distinguished literary figures, among them other repentant
insurrectionaries such as J. I. Kraszewski or Adam Asnyk, but
most notably the influential journalist Aleksander Świętochowski (1849–1938) and the novelist, Bolesław Prus
(1847–1912). Świętochowski, who rose to prominence after the
January Rising and who used the pen-name of 'the Ambassador of Truth' after his journal *Prawda* (Truth), was regarded as
the prophet of Positivism for over half a century, and lived to
see both its rise and its fall. A graduate of Wielopolski's Main
School in Warsaw, with a doctorate in moral philosophy from
Leipzig, he can only be compared to Staszic or Niemcewicz for
the sheer quantity and variety of his writings. Journalist,
social reformer, dramatist, poet, novelist, historian, he
touched on every conceivable topic from the emancipation of
women to the history of the peasantry, from Jewish culture to
mass education. Yet his views were remarkably consistent. In
an article of 1871 entitled 'My i Wy' (You and Us), he stated
his belief that the break with Poland's Romantic past was
irreparable. 'Between our two camps', he wrote, 'all the
bridges have been burned, all the dykes are breached.' In
another article of 1872 entitled 'Abstenteizm', he launched the
slogan of 'Organic Work', borrowed from Herbert Spencer. In
his *Wskazania polityczne* (Political Indications, 1882), he summarized the programme of social and economic action which

he felt an era of stability and prosperity would facilitate, and which he briefly tried to put into practical effect as president of the Society of Polish Culture (TKP) in the last years before the World War. It was a minimalist programme, which paid little attention to political methods and had no timetable. Like all his colleagues in the positivist camp, Świętochowski was convinced that the supremacy of the partitioning powers could not be challenged. The Polish cause could only be pursued from within the reigning system. All patriotic enterprises must be compatible with the law and institutions of the ruling empires. Any attempt to resist the authorities, or to change the system, would be counter-productive. 'Historical necessity', wrote Antoni Wrotnowski (1823–1900), a prominent financier who dabbled in politics, 'does not permit the Poles to seek independent statehood, since independence is an unattainable goal, which could not be realised even by the greatest sacrifices of a united society or by their most energetic efforts.' In this case, Polish political aspirations had to be cut to size. Grandiose schemes, plans for risings and revolutions, and demands for conditions similar to those prevailing in western Europe, were out of the question. 'We do not believe in revolutions', Kraszewski wrote, 'nor in those radical utopias which are supposed to transform society overnight and to cure all social ills by some unspecified panacea . . . What we believe in is that slow, gradual progress which by raising the morale of individuals, and the standards of education, by urging people towards work, and restraint, will enable us to effect the most surprising transformations of the social order by evolutionary means.'

The shift in political attitudes was mirrored by a parallel shift in literature, philosophy, and the arts. The great novelists who dominated the positivist era—Kraszewski, Prus, Eliza Orzeszkowa (1842–1910), Sienkiewicz (1846–1916), Zygmunt Miłkowski (1824–1915), Władysław Reymont (1868–1925), Stefan Żeromski (1864–1925)—turned their talents in the main to social and psychological themes, and to literary realism. In general, they avoided overtly political subjects, although it would be a gross overstatement to imply that political content was lacking. Prus, for example, grew increasingly political in his later years. His novel *Faraon*

(Pharaoh, 1897), a masterly analysis of power politics in
Ancient Egypt, is filled with echoes of Tsarist Russia. His story
Dzieci (Children, 1908) is an undisguised attack on the
revolutionaries of 1905. The colossal output of historical
novels launched by Kraszewski and Miłkowski and crowned
by Sienkiewicz in *Ogniem i Mieczem* (By Fire and Sword, 1884),
Quo Vadis? (1896), and *Krzyżacy* (The Teutonic Knights, 1900)
was based on the use of the techniques of literary realism for
increasingly non-positivist purposes. Sienkiewicz's declared
intention of *krzepienie serca*, of 'raising people's spirits' by
stirring tales of the Swedish Wars, the early Christians, or the
struggle against the Teutonic Knights, could not fail to revive
his readers' resentments against current political oppressions.
Among the philosophers, the Positivists could claim fewer
original talents than their messianist predecessors; though
Comte had his followers in Poland in men such as Józef
Supiński (1804–81) and Julian Ochorowicz (1850–1917),
whilst the works of the English ₁empiricists and evolutionists
were made available by early translations of Mill, Spence, and
Buckle. 'A Positivist', wrote Ochorowicz, 'is a name we give
anyone whose statements are supported by evidence which
can be checked, a person who does not discuss doubtful
matters without qualifications and who never talks of things
which are inaccessible.' This type of approach was tailor-made
for leading a change of direction in historiography. Among
the historians, the polemics of the Stańczyk Group of Cracow
led by Józef Szujski (1835–83) and later by Michał Bobrzyński
(1849–1935) challenged the reputation of Lelewel, and opened
the way for the Warsaw School led by Tadeusz Korzon
(1839–1918) and Władysław Smoleński (1851–1926). These
Varsovians, who gladly accepted the 'positivist' label, were far
less pessimistic about Poland's past than the Cracovians,
though they shared the contempt for the 'idealized' history of
the Romantics. In particular, they denounced the Romantics'
obsession with political events as the sole theme of historical
research, and they rejected the notion that history books
should be written for moral or didactic purposes. 'The
question is determined by one's overall concept of Science',
'Smoleński argued, 'and Science has no other task than the
verification and explanation of phenomena. For the botanist,

it is quite irrelevant whether the characteristics of a particular plant may be applied in medicine or in gastronomy. Similarly, for the historian, there is no obligation to draw (political) lessons from the past.' Having said that, Smoleński passed to his famous denunciation of political history, which in Poland was still preoccupied with the causes and effects of the Partitions:

> To take the fall of Poland as the foundation of one's view of the past is a complete and utter error. . . . There is no scientific reason why the disappearance of the state should be seen as the cardinal event of our entire history . . . It would be understandable for the theme of decline and fall to dominate the history of the state, but not the history of the nation which is the primary subject of historical research and which did not cease to exist because of the loss of political independence. . . . The organism we call the state is not the centre of all aspects of life, and its history is not the quintessence of the past. In addition to creating its own state, the Polish nation left a legacy to civilisation which survived the Fall; and this is the main theme of [our] History.

Like other writers and thinkers of the Positivist camp, historians like Smoleński would have strenuously denied that they were influenced in any way by political considerations. Yet the political context of their work is undeniable. By defusing the supercharged themes of Independence and Statehood, they inevitably undercut the ground of their Romantic, insurrectionary opponents, whilst hoping to create that calm and restrained intellectual and social atmosphere in which Positivist politicians were trying to operate.

The Positivists' quarrels with the Romantics, therefore, ranged over every branch of intellectual life. Quite apart from the obvious differences in political aims, methods, and priorities, they differed fundamentally in matters of historical analysis, artistic taste, and psychological temperament. Where the Positivists looked with detachment, though not indifference, on Polish History, the Romantics saw the injustices of the past as the guiding light of the present and the inspiration of the future. Where the Positivists busied themselves to improve the details of their daily existence, the Romantics felt that a stateless nation had nothing concrete worth improving. As the slogan of the Hotel Lambert declared, *"istnieć a dopiero potem jak istnieć"* (First we must exist, before deciding how to exist). Where the Positivists followed the dictates of science and of realism in the arts, the Romantics cultivated the workings of the imagination. Whilst the Positivists took 'Reality' to apply to the material, observable world—including the everyday world of life under the Partitioning Powers—the Romantics took Reality to include the world of the spirit—the world of fancy, of the Poland 'which had not perished'. What the Positivists called Realism, the Romantics called 'defeatism' and 'appeasement'. What the Positivists said was the maximum, the Romantics judged less than the minimum. What the Positivists held to be moral courage, the Romantics held to faint-heartedness. What the Romantics thought to be courage, the Positivists thought was suicide.

Yet this dialectical war of contrary values had its advantages. Despite the quarrels, the interminable dialogue between the Positivists and the Romantics kept both traditions alive, and enabled them to complement each other. Neither side was free to establish a monopoly, and each was kept within the bounds of credibility. Polish Romanticism, if it kept the idea of the Nation alive in the darkest days of oppression, was not allowed to lose itself entirely in utopian dreams. Polish Positivism, if it built up the nation's economic resources and cultural organizations, was not allowed to decline into sterile materialism. At each stage of the struggle, a new synthesis could be reached, a fresh balance between the two extremes could be struck. By the end of the century, when both Positivism and Romanticism were permanently established as the twin beacons of the national consciousness, extreme positions were much harder to maintain. Stanisław Wyspiański, the brightest star in the firmament of Polish Modernism, combined his bent for neo-Romantic poetry with a Galician disdain for Romantic politics. (See p. 232.) Roman Dmowski, the scourge of insurrectionary activists, found himself in 1917 at the head of a Polish Army in France. Józef Piłsudski, the revolutionary conspirator, found himself as the Head of a Polish state. The Positivists could fairly claim to be the guardians of Poland's Body, the Romantics to be the guardians of her Soul. And at the end of their separation, on the Third Day of 11 November 1918, Body and Soul were reunited.

The dynamics of the debate between the Romantic and Positivist camps is sometimes seen as the cause of the characteristic cyclical rhythm of Polish politics, where one of the two camps would gain the upper hand for a season, only to decline in due course and give way to the other. Certainly, a generational cycle was observable in Polish political life long before modern theorists thought of giving such phenomena their scientific blessing. There is no doubt that the wheel of political fortune in nineteenth-century Poland revolved with a regularity beyond the bounds of mere coincidence; and strong credence must be given to the idea that the regular alternation of the two dominant ideologies was closely associated with the rise and fall of successive generations. In the context of the Absolutist empires, all independent political ventures were doomed to failure, and neither of the two main variants of Polish politics could produce sufficient results to convert a majority of young people to the convictions of their elders. As a result, neither Romantics nor Positivists could ever enjoy a run of more than three or four decades before disillusionment and failure destroyed their supremacy, and gave an opening for the revival of their opponents. The main Romantic generation, fired with contempt for the failed compromises of the preceding, conciliatory era, held sway in Poland from the November Rising of 1830 until 1864—a period of thirty-four years. The main Positivist generation, fired by embarrassment at the collapse of the January Rising, held the field at least until the 1890s, and arguably until the outbreak of the Revolution of 1905—a period of forty-one years. In its turn, 1905 marked the emergence of a new Romantic generation, whose growing devotion to the cause of national Independence bore fruit in 1918, and whose supremacy lasted until the final defeat of Independence in 1944. Taken as a whole from 1795 to 1918, the period of Partition saw four complete revolutions of the generational cycle—each of which averaged roughly thirty years. Historians, of course, are congenitally suspicious of theories. Many will challenge the details of any overall scheme; and all of them will reject the notion that the generational cycle could work with the mathematical accuracy of a Swiss watch. Some would debate whether the first thirty-five years of Partition, from 1795 to 1830, should be regarded as a single, essentially conciliatory era with insurrectionary interludes, or whether they formed two distinct, but shorter cycles divided at 1812 or 1815. Some would question whether the Revolution of 1905 could farly be classed as a turning-point of the same significance as the Risings of 1794, 1830, or 1863. Such bone-picking is unavoidable. What is important is not the identification of exact turning-points—although that is sometimes possible—but the identification of the alternating trends for which contemporary Polish commentators had much sharper antennae than their plodding historical successors. It is of little moment whether the close of the great Positivist era should be precisely dated to the revival of the patriotic demonstrations of 3 May 1891, to the formation of the PPS in 1892 or of the National Democrats in 1897, or the the first outbreak of revolutionary violence on the Grzybowski Square in Warsaw on 13 November 1904. It is of great moment to know, in the estimation of all sides of opinion, including Dmowski as well as Piłsudski, that the political situation in 1905 was fundamentally different from that of the positivist supremacy ten or twenty years before. After all, the members of any new generation do not all come to maturity at exactly the same time, and any generational cycle must necessarily be driven by the combined effects both of the sudden and arbitrary impact of political events and of the more gradual, continual replacement of the ageing by the young. A decisive moment of change in public opinion can only occur when an absolute majority of adults is too young to remember the formative experiences of the preceding period.

What is more, there is no logical reason to confine the workings of the generational cycle to the Period of Partition. If, in the case of Poland, the characteristic political cycle was put into motion not merely by the loss of statehood but rather by the earlier intervention of foreign powers, then it must be seen to begin at the start of the eighteenth, not the nineteenth century, and must be expected to continue as long as foreign oppression persists. In this light, the Romantic and Positivist generations of the mid-nineteenth century must be seen not merely as the successors to the generations of Stanisław Leszczyński and Stanisław-August, but also as the precursors of the generations of Władysław Gomułka and Lech Wałęsa. The modern political cycle in Poland may well have been turning not just for four or five generations, but for eight or nine. By this beguiling reckoning, with nine generations at thirty years per generation stretching from the Battle of Poltava to the birth of SOLIDARITY,* the modern political tradition in Poland is considerably senior to the Constitution of the United States, and is only marginally junior to the parliamentary democracy of the United Kingdom.

The imprecision, not to say the *imponderabilia,* of Polish politics was increased by the habit, indeed the necessity, of conducting the debate in indirect terms, and most typically by literary methods. Polish literature was not concerned exclusively with politics by any means; its scope stretched far beyond the political sphere into everything from lyricism to social farce; but the fact remains that literature served as the most common surrogate for political debate. Western analysts, who are accustomed in their own countries to examining electoral returns, opinion polls, reliable statistics, checkable government statements, and a press constrained by nothing more than the laws on libel, obscenity, and official secrets, find great difficulty in comprehending the closed world of Eastern Europe, where, except for a fitful interval between the two World Wars, such things have rarely existed. They have to learn to decipher a new mode of veiled expression where hints, oblique references, allegories, and omissions speak louder than superficial content, and where the standard techniques of scientific research no longer apply. In Poland, nineteenth-century conditions brought the art to a high pitch of tuning, and taught people to read political meaning into the most innocent material. By the same token, Polish writers had to be aware that their literary products would not be read literally, and developed a sixth sense for satisfying both the censors and their readers. As honest political comment became increas-

*Calculating 270 years from 1980 puts the starting-point at 1710, the year in which, thanks to the Russian victory at Poltava, Stanisław Leszczyński was dethroned in Poland and August II restored. The formal establishment of the Russian protectorate over Poland can be dated to the Silent Sejm of January 1717 (see p. 303).

ingly inhibited, as the masterpieces of national literature had to published increasingly abroad, and as the Polish language itself came under official attack, so political comment assumed ever more devious forms. Books published abroad carried greater credibility than home productions; and fiction outpaced fact. Fictional characters aroused the same controversies as historical figures.

Some of the fictional characters, of course, were idealized versions of real people. Jan Kozietulski—the hero of Somosierra, General Sowiński, the hero of the *Reduta Ordona* of 1831, 'Brother Mark', and even 'Konrad Wallenrod', all fit into that category. Others were inventions of the literary imagination. Yet in the minds of educated Poles, they belonged to the Polish political gallery as surely as Poniatowski, Lubecki, or Czartoryski; and no survey of the political scene would be complete without them.

Jan Kozietulski, the champion of Napoleon's 'Chevaux Légers', must surely be one of the historical figures most often subjected to the flights of artistic fancy. Dubbed by his French companions in arms as 'the bravest of the brave', his feats were seized on by Polish painters, sculptors, poets, and novelists as the symbol of national courage and determination. Every schoolchild in Poland has heard Maria Konopnicka's verse, read aloud in reverential tones:

A wtem Napoleon	Then Napoleon turned to his lancers.
Na Polaków skinął:	And begged his Poles to save the day.
Skoczył Kozietulski,	So up jumped Kozietulski,
W czwórki jazdę zwinął.	To draw them up in fourfold array.
Na wiarusów czele	At the head of his old companions
Jak piorun sie rzucil,	Like a thunderbolt he struck,
Wziął pierwszą baterię,	And stormed the first emplacement,
Ale już nie wrócił.	Nor thought of turning back. . . .[12]

Inevitably, perhaps, Kozietulski also became the target for droves of sceptics and debunkers. His feat of taking the Spanish guns by storm at Somosierra, in an uphill attack under close fire from batteries entrenched in a narrow defile, has been downgraded to an act of pointless folly; and his achievement of opening the road to Madrid for an entire army, at the cost of fifty-seven casualties, has been compared to the Charge of the British Light Brigade at Balaclava half a century later. His personal failings have been unearthed in persistent attempts to destroy the legend. Of course, the real Kozietulski (1781–1821), who resigned his colonel's commission in the Army of the Congress Kingdom amidst investigations into regimental embezzlement, was not the unblemished superman of the fictional hero. Yet the motives of his detractors are as suspect as those of his beatifiers. Kozietulski was a symbol of the activist and insurrectionary wing of Polish politics, and by discrediting the symbol the detractors no doubt sought to undermine the Romantic tradition as a whole. Tennyson could write an epic poem how 'the Five Hundred rode on' without rocking the foundations of Victorian England; but Polish comments on Somosierra are contributions to the central arguments of the national political debate. In their modern emanations, they have much more to do with judgements on Józef Piłsudski, Monte Cassino, or the Warsaw Rising than on the Peninsular War. Tennyson's lines—'Their's not to reason why, their's, but to do and die'—referred to the fate of just one unit. Equivalent Polish lines are taken to refer to the fate of the entire nation. Kozietulski's charge at Somosierra was not only magnificent; it also made good military sense. But the question of individual sacrifice and courage subsequently became submerged in the broader issues of national honour and national survival.

Zbyszko the Knight, the hero of Sienkiewicz's novel *Krzyżacy* (The Teutonic Knights, 1900), had no basis in fact, but was the result of a foray into medieval romance for the purpose of combating the pretensions of Wilhelmian Germany. In the nineteenth century, the wars and legends of the Teutonic Knights were as popular among Polish writers as they were in Germany, although each side used them for opposite purposes. Sienkiewicz's tale, like those of Gustaw Freytag, mirrors the antics of the imperial court at Marienburg (now Malbork), where the Kaiser used to appear in the full regalia of the Grand Master, surrounded by medieval ladies and by courtiers replete with spears and basinets. Sienkiewicz, whilst reversing the roles of heroes and villains, borrowed some of the Wagnerian melodrama. The Knights, wearing black armour and the sinister sign of the black cross, are simply the champions of Evil. Zbyszko, their Polish rival, is fighting for the Good. As one critic has remarked, the cast resembles 'incarnate absolutes', not real characters. To the outsider, they look for all the world like the 'goodies' and 'baddies' of an east European 'B Western'. To the Polish reader, however, they were the symbols of a national ordeal which at the time was in progress in deadly earnest and which in the Second World War was to gain added poignancy. Himmler, dressed up as 'Henry the Fouler'* in the dark rites of his black-suited SS Guard at Quellenburg, in conscious imitation of the Kaiser at Marienburg, showed that the game was still for real. Many Poles certainly thought so, and read their antidote with relish. Zbyszko stands for Virtue and true chivalry. His two wives—Danusia, who is killed by the Knights, and the beautiful, athletic, resourceful Jagienka—stand for Poland. The tale is one of courage but, above all, of survival. After 600 pages of derring-do, Zbyszko is building his castle of stone. Jagienka has borne him twins. The clan of the Hail-stones, with their emblem of the Blunt Horseshoe, is going to survive. The age-old German foe is thwarted.[13]

Konrad Wallenrod, the main subject of a much earlier verse-novel published by Mickiewicz in 1828, moves in that same world of pseudo-Teutonic romance, but with rather more conviction. The work was conceived as an essay in the Byronic style, full of weird happenings and violent emotions. It was not rated highly by its author, who subsequently disowned it as 'no more than a political pamphlet'. The political element was one reason for its lasting success, however, for it skilfully set the mode for contemporary comment to be camouflaged in the exotic settings of distant places and ancient times. (The camouflage was good enough to mislead some of the initial critics, like Mochnacki, who judged it to be nothing more than a rather unconvincing example of the Gothic Revival.) Wallenrod, a taciturn, angst-ridden knight, whose deeds of selfless valour are rewarded with the chief command of the Teutonic Order, is based on the life of a real historical personage from medieval Prussia; but the historicity is slight

---

*More usually, Henry the Fowler (*Heinrich der Vogelfänger*), Emperor of Germany, 876–936 AD.

and incidental. From the promptings of a venerable Lithuanian bard called Halbran, the Grand Master learns the secrets of his orphan's past. Wallenrod, too, it appears, is a Lithuanian, carried off as a child by the Knights in one of their brutal raids, and brought up from infancy as a Prussian. His own name, it seems, was 'Alpha', and his mission, henceforth, hidden in the deepest recesses of his heart, is to avenge the wrongs of his people. Unbeknown to his fellow knights, the Grand Master is working and waiting for the Order's defeat. In the final battle, the ranks of the Knights are decimated, and Wallenrod, at their head, is destroyed. The psychological study of a man driven to self-destruction by the progressive revelation of his inner nature rises far above the conventional demands of romantic heroics. The moral study, of a man driven into dishonourable means for the sake of an honourable goal, and systematically planning to sacrifice himself in atonement for his past misconduct, explores a theme of universal appeal. The political study of a man torn between the longing for open rebellion and the advantages of opposition from within, presents the fundamental dilemma of all political rebels. Halbran, the bard, whose songs recall the forgotten deeds of a conquered nation, personifies Literature and History as guardians of the national conscience

Oh, Song of the People, You, ark of the flood,
Which joins the distant shores of former and modern times.

Wallenrod, the Grand Master and chief dissident locked in one person, embodies the fate of a captive nation which is forced to choose between its conflicting loyalties. Wallenrod is trapped through no fault of his own, but gradually realizes that it is impossible to remain both a loyal servant of the Order and a true son of his people. Having fixed his goal, he then determines the means, committing himself to lesser evils in order to attain the greater Good. The traitor-hero can only resolve his agonies in an act of noble self-sacrifice. His fate is symptomatic of a society ruled in a state of undeclared war by a regime leaving no common ground between absolute obedience and absolute enmity. For this reason, the term *wallenrodyzm* (Wallenrodism) has passed into the Polish language. In general usage, it has a similar meaning to

'Machiavellianism', where 'the end justifies the means'. In its precise connotation, however, it denotes a particular brand of calculated 'political action: 'a two-faced attitude, characterised by apparent servility towards an enemy whom one intends to betray and destroy.' It is a concept which makes every Polish Loyalist suspect in the eyes of his political masters. The reading of *Konrad Wallenrod* was widely credited with inspiring the November Rising. The conspirators of the Belvedere Group, among whom were a number of literati, certainly accepted the attribution. One of them, Ludwik Nabielak (1804–83),* is often credited with the saying, famous in its day, that 'The Word became Flesh, and Wallenrod became Belvedere.' Literature directly contributed to political action.[14]

Gustaw-Konrad, the central figure in Mickiewicz's most ambitious work, the poetic drama *Dziady* (Forefathers Eve, 1832) shares Wallenrod-Alpha's double nature; but it would take exegetic skills far beyond those of a visiting British historian to unravel even the basic outlines of this immensely sophisticated literary creation. Suffice to say that, in one of his emanations, 'Konrad' appears as a recognizable human being, a political dissident and insurrectionary, rotting in his chains in a Russian cell and reflecting on the injustices of his country. His patriotic soliloquies from prison are delivered as the Tsarist governors of Wilno dance with their Polish lickspittles to the music of a grandly satirical Ball. In one of his other emanations 'Gustaw' appears in a more ambiguous form, part Man and part Phantom, a Hamlet and a Shakespearian ghost compounded into one. Here his soliloquies and his conversations with a priest range over all the great mysteries of human existence—Love, Death, Creation, and the individual Soul. It is these scenes which give the drama its name, for they are set in the old priest's cabin in Lithuania on Halloween, when preparations for the Christian feast of All Saints' Day become confused with the pagan rites of Lithuanian ancestor worship. The priest, a Uniate widower, is sitting down at the table with his two sons amidst the flickering candles of the winter

---

*The apotheosis of Nabielak's Romantic career was reached some dozen years later, when, as an *émigré*, he was appointed Director of the Municipal Gasworks in Barcelona, Spain.

evening, when the shadowy 'Gustaw' emerges from the gloom, dressed in sackcloth and ashes, bleeding from a self-inflicted wound to the heart, and (in an echo of Palm Sunday) carrying a bough of spruce. In the ensuing dialogues, the priest acts as the rational foil to Gustaw's apparently irrational questionings, drawing out a narration of the emotional and political tragedies which have brought the young visitor to the act of suicide. One partner of the dialogue, the priest, who constantly tries to bring it down to 'reality', to everyday problems, is seen by Polish audiences as the spokesman of 'Positivism'; the other, 'Gustaw-Konrad', who talks on a higher plane of the 'invisible bonds that bind' is seen as the arch-advocate of Romanticism, of spiritual values. Amateur programme notes do no justice to a towering masterpiece which owes much to its author's deep knowledge of European literature as well as to his reactions to Russian oppression in Poland. The Tsarist censorship ensured that *Dziady* could not be performed in the nineteenth century at home; but its text, smuggled into Poland from abroad, was well known at an early date. If Konrad Wallenrod played his part in launching the November Rising, Gustaw-Konrad made a lasting contribution to the intellectual fare of all subsequent generations of Polish Romantics.

Gustaw's allegorical metamorphosis into Konrad foreshadowed other, still more remarkable, supernatural feats performed by the mystical heroes of Juliusz Słowacki—or, to be precise, the heroes of Słowacki's final mystical period.[15] More than any of his contemporaries, Słowacki pursued the exploration of the spiritual world with the most relentless consequentiality; and since the 'life of the spirit' is generally taken to be the hallmark of Romanticism, he must be judged the most Romantic of the Romantics. Like Mickiewicz, he abandoned the conventional Catholicism of the Church and was influenced by the mystical sect of Andrzej Towiański; but his thought is saturated by ideas and allusions deriving from the Christian distinction between 'The Body' and 'The Soul'. The watershed of his short career was reached during the composition of a philosophical treatise entitled *Genezis z ducha* (Creation through the Spirit, 1844) where he developed a system of 'spiritual evolutionism' reminiscent possibly of

Dante's *Divine Comedy* and anticipating the later writings of
Teilhard de Chardin. The universe was created by God at the
request of the spirits who urged him to give them material
form. Matter was thus created, but in such primitive,
imperfect form that the spirits within were required to
transform and improve themselves by incessant struggle and
thereby to undertake the long process of self-perfection and
the return towards God. At each stage of the struggle, the
spirits grow weary as their material form decays, only to be
revitalized by some God-sent cataclysm, which gives them the
renewed impetus to assume a new form and gain new energy.
The decay of the old form was a necessary condition for the
birth of a new and higher one; the process of perfecting the
spirit could only be achieved by the cycle of death and
regeneration of the material body. According to Słowacki, this
process of the destruction and reincarnation of forms is subject
to a general Law of Transformation which applies no less to
natural science and to political history than to human beings.
'There is a spiritual commonwealth in material form', he
wrote, 'of which you're not aware. There is also a spiritual
hierarchy struggling against a material hierarchy on the earth
and it is their conflict which gives rise to all wars, riots, and
revolutions... These wars will not cease until all material
forms have been constructed in accordance with the spiritual
hierarchy... It is for the same reason that old and decayed
nations have to be cured by revolutions...'. Needless to say,
Słowacki's system ran parallel to much of Hegelian thought,
not to mention the Marxists' Spiral of Progress'; although he
admitted no intellectual debt except to the French transfor-
mists, and he attributed spiritual progress not to logic but to
moral sacrifice. In practical terms, it meant that wars and
insurrections were necessary trials for the advancement of a
nation's spirit, just as pain, suffering, and death are necessary
trials for the salvation of an individual's soul. Taken literally,
this Romantic philosophy could be used to justify Polish
insurrections as worthy and necessary events, irrespective of
their outcome. Romantic Poles, like pious Muslims or
Japanese kamikaze, could cheerfully believe that their death
in the Holy War could lead to a better life for themselves and
their people. They might even be convinced that Russian or

Prussian bullets did not kill; and it seems that on one occasion Słowacki actually tried to persuade his compatriots to put the idea to the test. In April 1848, in the year before his own early death, he travelled with some companions from Paris to the Rising in Poznania, where he addressed a band of insurgents hesitating before the walls of a huge Prussian fortification. 'Sir', he is supposed to have told one ditherer, 'we shall capture the *Kernwerk* with our knives. All that is needed is a little faith.' Or again, 'What's the matter with you? Do you imagine that you still need guns, regiments, or officers? I'm telling you that you don't, that the day has come for holy anarchy.' In the mean time, having thought better of leading the attack on the fortress in person, he concentrated his own efforts on poetry designed to reveal the hidden spiritual side of reality which lay beyond outward appearances. 'The world is like a carpet seen from the reverse side', he once wrote to his mother, 'and all we see are threads which appear and disappear without rhyme or reason. On the other side, however, there are beautiful flowers and coherent patterns.' The task which he set for himself was 'to look on the world from the side that God sees it'. To this end, he created a marvellous collection of forceful, poetical figures among whom 'Brother Mark' and the 'King-Spirit' are outstanding.

Brother Marek, the Preacher of Bar, was one of those real historical figures, like Kozietulski, sung and idealized in countless literary evocations. The Confederation of Bar of 1768–72 (see p. 310), one of the earliest Polish risings against Russian oppression, is often regarded as the first manifestation of modern Polish nationalism, and was treasured by the Romantics of a later age for its combination of religious fervour and patriotic sacrifice. The Revd Marek Jandołowicz (1713–99), the Superior of the Carmelite Friary at Bar, an associate of Pułaski and chaplain to the confederates, was known in his own day as a charismatic preacher and faith healer. During the storming of Bar in 1768 he roared defiance at the Cossacks, cross in hand on the battlements. He survived years in solitary confinement under . Russian arrest, and eventually returned to his monastery. Until the middle of the following century, his undecayed body became an object of popular pilgrimage. In Słowacki's portrait, Brother Marek is

credited with visionary powers, foretelling the future death of
Poland and her resurrection 'like a phoenix from the ashes'.
This particular story was hardly original, since it had been
circulating in an apocryphal work long before Słowacki
borrowed it and incorporated it into his drama in 1843; but
Słowacki gave it that poetic power which ensured its
immortality. Set against the company of the confederates
themselves, whom Słowacki paints in tones of stark simplicity,
the words of the visionary prophet ring out with immense
power and majesty. The preacher's audience possess the
unquestioning piety to believe against all reason in the
triumph of their cause:

> Without cannon, without swords, but through Faith alone
> The Lord God shall conquer on our behalf.

The preacher, welcoming the inevitability of death, turns the
ramparts of Bar into a Polish Calvary:

> May God allow that sometime it be told
> How on this spot, where we were killed,
> The Patron of the Nations was also put to death,
> How here, where the saviour of Poland
> Knelt for the first time before misery
> For the sake of the world's peoples, stands a new Calvary.
> Gentle Sirs! Here is a site of fame.
> This is the place, and Bar is its name.

There was no attempt to sophisticate the Confederates, who,
in actual fact, were a curious mixture of patriots and
scoundrels. There was no attempt to enter the complexities of
their politics, which were mixed up not just with the Polish
revolt against Russia, but also with the revolt of the Ukrainian
Peasants against their Polish masters. Brother Marek spoke
with the voice of prophecy, and Bar was the home of
martyrdom.*

Król-Duch (King-Spirit), Słowacki's most ambitious figure,
forms the centre-piece of an epic in the same genre as Hugo's

---

*'BAR—a town and centre of the Bar district of the Vinnitsa oblast of the
Ukrainian SSR, situated on the River Rov, 6 km from the railway junction of Bar,
14,000 inhabitants (1968). Machine construction, sugar refinery, distillery, garment,
furniture and jam factories. Bar received its present name in the sixteenth century.'
Bol'shaya Sovietskaya Entsyklopediya, 1970, vol. 2.

Légende des Siècles. It is a poetical essay on Polish History, viewed, as Słowacki would have put it, 'from God's side of the carpet'. From this, it emerges that Poland's 'royal spirit', always expressed in the First Person of the poet himself, is the guide of all Christian nations on their road to Perfection, to Jerusalem the Beautiful. The Spirit is presented in a succession of different metamorphoses, each of which is based on the great warriors of Poland's past—Popiel, Mieczysław, Bolesław Smiały—whose ordeals are the price of progress and perfection. In other words, Poland's suffering makes sense. It has a purpose. If elsewhere Słowacki and Mickiewicz elaborated the image of Poland, 'the Christ of Nations', and Lelewel wrote of Poland, the 'Ambassador to Humanity', the King-Spirit can perhaps be likened to Dante's 'Virgil', the poet-guide of Christian pilgrims on their journey through Hell and Purgatory in the hope of Heaven.

The prophet *Wernyhora* must be seen in many ways as a partner for Brother Mark. He, too, was supposedly a real personage, who appeared on the historical stage during the same period of the Confederation of Bar, and whose prophecies were embellished by a long line of poets, novelists, and painters. But Wernyhora was a Ukrainian Cossack, not a Pole, an Orthodox, not a Catholic; and his call was made for the harmony of peoples, not for the rights of one nation. At the height of the troubles in the Ukraine in 1768-9, where he opposed the Cossack insurgents, and when Poles, Ukrainians, and Jews were the common victims of communal massacres, Wernyhora appealed to them all from his island refuge in the middle of the Dnieper. 'Let us love one another', he was reported to say, 'for we are all children of the same Mother.' This proclamation of Poland as the Mother of many nationalities became a rallying cry not only for the early Polish Romantics, but equally for the later federationists; and it provided a starting-point of claims for the restoration of Poland within the frontiers of 1772. The earliest documentary formulation of Wernyhora's prophecies, in a manuscript now in the Jagiellonian Library, has been dated to 1809, many years after the prophet's death; and its wide circulation during the 1830s can be traced to the deliberate propaganda of the National Government of 1831 and of the subsequent TDP.

But the call for 'the ancient frontiers' obviously reflected deeply-held feelings, and explains the persistence of Wernyhora's appeal throughout his lengthy literary and artistic career. Wernyhora was the main subject of a popular historical novel published in Paris in 1838 by Michał Czajkowski (1804–86), who later, as Sadik Pasha, led the Ottoman Cossacks in Turkey. After that, he appeared in Siemieński's work *Trzy Wieszczby* (Three prophecies, 1838) in the company of Brother Marek and the sixteenth-century Abbot of Jędrzejów; in Mickiewicz's lectures at the Collège de France; in three works by Słowacki; in Matejko's famous portrait of 1883; and eventually in Wyspiański's *Wesele*. In Ukrainian folklore, where ultra-nationalist intrusions erased all former thoughts of Poland as the 'one Mother' of many children, the Cossack prophet could only be remembered as a minor figure of the wars against 'the Polish lords'; but for the Poles he became a symbol of the rebirth of the old Republic, a beacon of hope for a

> Poland, free within her furthest extremities,
> Joining once more the shores of the two seas.[16]

The heroes of Mickiewicz, Słowacki, and other Romantic writers made their entrée mainly in the 1830s and 1840s, and made their greatest impact on the generation in the January Rising. In due course, in the aftermath of the Rising's suppression, a new breed of heroes and heroines made their appearance.

Ślimak, the peasant, the anti-hero of Prus's novel *Placówka* (A place to Work, 1885) possesses none of the qualities of his Romantic predecessors. The name itself, which means 'Snail', makes light-hearted fun of his obstinate character in true Dickensian style, with its overtones not only of a creature withdrawn into its protective shell but also of the fable of 'the tortoise and the hare'. The Poles who run fastest in the national cause will not necessarily be the ones to win the race. Ślimak, a lonely widower, lives on his own outside the village, on the top of a draughty hill which is almost impossible to cultivate, but which is ideally suited to the windmill planned by his German neighbours. He watches the squire sell the manor to the Germans in a moment of generosity during the county ball; but he himself grimly scorns all offers to sell his own little plot. He survives the death of his wife, and the burning of his farm; but nothing can persuade him to cede his land. His only supporter is the village priest, who suffers great remorse for dallying with the ladies of the manor and for neglecting the peasants. The story has a happy end with Ślimak still in possession of his farm, remarried and expecting an heir, and triumphant over the departure of his German neighbours. Ślimak's village is clearly a microcosm of rural Poland, and his victory is one of native grit over oppression and adversity. (It is the proletarian counterpart to Zbyszko's aristocratic castle.) Despite the colouration given to it in Prussia, and in People's Poland, the novel was not primarily intended as an anti-German polemic. The action takes place in the Congress Kingdom, where Ślimak's neighbours had to be described as Germans in order to placate the Tsarist censor. In any case, the Germans' virtues of hard work, austerity, sound management, and social solidarity are given their full credit. In his private correspondence, Prus explained that old Poland had benefited from German colonization for centuries, and that the answer to the new 'German Problem' did not lie in mindless hatred of everything Germanic, but rather in learning from the Germans' own success. Prus wrote openly and with appreciation what the later Nationalists merely feared in secret. Ślimak is an arch-product of Positivism, but not of Nationalism in the narrow sense.

Wokulski, the central figure of Prus's best-known novel, *Lalka* (The Doll, 1890), is inseparable from the rich social panorama in which his career is presented. In contrast to Ślimak, Wokulski inhabits the new urban world of late nineteenth-century Poland where the simple Positivist slogans of the previous decades are beginning to lose their appeal. Polish society, like the broken doll, is in a state of decay. The old values have gone, and simple solutions no longer work. My aim, Prus wrote, was 'to present our Polish idealist on the background of social disintegration', in a century 'which began with chivalry and dedication, and has ended with capitalism, corruption, and the pursuit of lucre'. Wokulski begins adult life as an oppressed shop assistant, is drawn into political conspiracy, and then, after a sobering interlude as a convict in Russia, becomes a respectable bourgeois citizen—a scholar, merchant, and financier. His friends and acquaintances cover the whole spectrum of standard Polish attitudes, from the anachronistic Romantic, Rzecki, still living out the Napoleonic epic, through Dr Szumann, the assimilationist Jewish doctor, to Ochocki, the Positivist, an enthusiast for science and education. Each if them finds his efforts frustrated; and none can achieve a sense of satisfaction and fulfilment, least of all Wokulski, whose hopeless love for an aristocratic woman can never lead to reciprocation and marriage. This psychological cul-de-sac, vividly expressed in Wokulski's over powering feelings of life's senselessness, was to be resolved by the shift in attitudes already under way in the political radicalism and artistic rebellion of the turn of the century. In the narrow, literary context, *Lalka* marked the transition from Positivism to Modernism. In the broader historical context, it anticipated the revival of Polish political life, the formation of modern parties, and the onset of the turmoil and tension in Eastern Europe which led to the Great War.

Benedykt Korczyński, the head of the family featured in Orzeszkowa's novel *Nad Niemnem* (On the banks of the Niemen, 1887), has something in common with both Ślimak and with Wokulski. Like Ślimak, he leads a desperate struggle on the verge of bankruptcy to preserve his family's estate from foreign creditors; and like Wokulski, he grows disillusioned and embittered. His private life in marriage with a hysterical, uncooperative wife is as painful as his public life as an ex-insurrectionary from the January Rising. His inner struggles have given him an impediment of speech; and any attempt to talk about the Rising evokes a meaningless stutter. Korczyński, however, is a member neither of the peasantry nor of the bourgeoisie, but of the famous petty *szlachta,* the ex-nobility so proud, so poor, and so prolific, which thronged the confines of Poland and Lithuania. (The social setting, in fact, on the banks of Mickiewicz's home river, full of the 'health, happiness, and hope of my childhood', is identical with that which Mickiewicz had immortalized fifty years before in *Pan Tadeusz,* in his idyll of old Polish life at the manor of Dobrzyń.) The unhappy Korczyński is sinking in a sea of troubles—in arguments with his children, who reproach him for his antiquated social aloofness and political apathy, and in disputes with his neighbours, a family of even poorer and pettier nobles, whom he is determined to sue in the courts. His son, Witold, is a radical, a socialist; his neighbour, Anzelm Bohatyrowicz, was a friend of his dead brother; and to cap it all his ward, Justyna, makes friends with Bohatyrowicz's son, Janek. Gradually, the friendship of the young people of both houses, crowned by the marriage of Justyna and Janek, breaks the obstinate enmity of their elders, and reveals the calamities which had so embittered them. In a final scene of reconciliation in the depths of the Lithuanian forest, the youngsters discover the graves both of their relations killed in the Rising and of the pioneer-ancestors who first settled the neighbourhood many centuries before. From the viewpoint of the Tsarist censorship, Orzeszkowa sailed dangerously close to the wind, and many of her political and historical statements had to be made by allusion. But from the viewpoint of her Polish readers, the combination of nostalgia for the past and faith in the generation of the future has ensured the novel's unflagging popularity until the present day. Indeed, Orzeszkowa continues to have her imitators, and the inhabitants of Korczyn their modern descendants. In the 1960s, a Polish radio serial called 'In Jeziorany'—in the genre of the BBC's record-breaking programme, 'The Archers' of Ambridge—described the life of a village whose chief inhabitants bore a striking resemblance to the inhabitants of Korczyn. In the 1970s, a best-selling novel by Edward Redliński called *Konopielka* describes the social salvation of a contemporary Korczyński—suitably transmogrified into 'Kaziuk', a peasant living on the Polish side of the Lithuanian border—who is rescued from his antisocial ways by contact with bright-eyed, forward-looking youngsters. In the 1880s, Orzeszkowa's Positivism was an innovation, a revelation. In the 1960s and 1970s, its bowdlerized offspring provided a convenient element for the artistic fare of latter-day communist propaganda.

Stanisław Połaniecki has been one of the most controversial figures in Polish Literature ever since his appearance in 1895 in Sienkiewicz's Novel, *Rodzina Połanieckich* (The Połaniecki Family). Yet, to anyone unfamiliar with Polish conditions, he might seem a particularly harmless, not to say colourless individual. He is certainly the antithesis of the dashing, romantic heroes—like Zbyszko, or Wołodyjowski with whom Sienkiewicz's name is usually associated. Połaniecki is simply a Polish bourgeois of the late nineteenth century, a practising Catholic, a social conformist, a man absorbed in his business affairs and in the comfortable routine of domestic life. His one great aim is to buy back the estate of his wife's parents, which has been lost through the neglect of her disorderly and unreliable relations. He is a kind father to his children, an artistic philistine, and an unfaithful husband on occasion; but, overall, he has no strong virtues and no strong vices. His motto is 'Let philosophical systems go their way, but the Mass must always be celebrated.' If ever there was a Polish non-hero, here it is. Of course, that was the point of the novel. Sienkiewicz played to his audience with masterly precision, endowing Połaniecki with all the negative qualities, or rather with a lack of all the favourable qualities, which Polish patriots held most dear. He was supposedly an example of Positivism, but an example of which dedicated Positivists could hardly be proud. He was a Pole and a Catholic, but one whose smug brand of patriotism and religion drove Romantics and left-wing radicals into paroxysms of fury. Połaniecki was prosperous, but his prosperity was intended exclusively for his private benefit; he possessed the means, but not the intelligence or the temperament, to interest himself in cultural affairs; above all, he was religious, a loyal son of the Polish Church; yet he viewed his Catholicism as nothing more than the ritual confirmation of his own, material success. He was immediately the focus of furious debates between the Polish conservatives and the radicals, the yardstick for social and political attitudes of the day. When in 1908 Father Gnatowski (1855–1925), a conservative, clerical literary critic from Lwów, ventured to express the view that Połaniecki was a worthy man whose idea of civic virtue was based on honest gain and landed property, Wacław Nałkowski (1851–1911) took violent exception:

You make out that land-grabbing is a civic virtue. Is the land going to save you? The foundations of national life are not built on land, but on great hearts and great minds, of the sort which you yourselves do not possess . . . It is built on minds that are not restricted to the bounds of the parish, and are not hemmed in behind the Chinese wall of 'our father's faith,' but on minds that are open to the whole world and to the future, on minds that are capable of receiving new faith in humanity. . . . The human beings of tomorrow will turn in disgust from animals and shit-shovellers of Połaniecki's type. There'll be no place for such crude atavists. Not even the land will save them . . .[17]

Nałkowski's emphasis on the 'national mind' lay very much in the Romantic line of thought, and his assault on Połaniecki's mean materialism exactly expresses the Romantics' low view of the Positivists' priorities. More specifically, by choosing to vent his wrath on conservative Catholicism and on the obsession with Land and Property, he was fixing his sights on the new bourgeois Nationalism to which the old Positivism was yielding at that very time. It is no accident that Dmowski's National Democratic movement, with its strident appeals to defend the 'national Church' and the 'national Territory,' was rising to prominence at the time of Nałkowski's tirade, and that Nałkowski himself should have been associated with the opposing, socialist circles. In this context, the figure of Stanisław Połaniecki was not quite so innocent as first appeared. It challenged the readers to align themselves on one side or the other of the main dividing line of Polish patriotic opinion, and has continued to act as a touchstone of that division ever since. Typically enough, at the height of the Gierek regime in the 1970s, the Party ideologues, who control the media, selected the 'Połaniecki Family' as the subject of their most extragavant television serial. Nothing illustrates the bank-ruptcy of Polish Communism more exactly than their choice, without the slightest hint of satire, of a comfortable, conform-ing Catholic clan of the archetypal Polish bourgeoisie to be held up for emulation by the citizens of the People's Republic.

Old *Skawiński* is the subject of Sienkiewicz's short story *Latarnik* (The Lighthousekeeper, 1882), one of those unforget-table gems, which still brings tears to the eyes of its readers. Skawiński is an ageing exile in America, a veteran of the November Rising, of the Carlist Wars in Spain, of the Springtime of Nations in 1848, and of the American Civil

War, who has found employment for his final years as the
keeper of a lighthouse on the stormy coast of Panama. He lives
the life of a hermit, completely cut off from all human
company, except for the creoles of a nearby fishing village.
His memories of Poland are all but fading away, until one
afternoon, as a complete surprise, he receives a parcel of
books; and among the books is *Pan Tadeusz*. Alone in his tower
beside the ocean, with a hurricane brewing outside and the
lamp sputtering from the gusts, he sits down in the evening to
read. From the very first line, he is gripped with tears and
excitement. 'Oh Lithuania, my homeland', he begins, 'you are
like health. Only he who has lost you can truly know your
worth. . . .' After that, he cannot put the book down,
entranced by the poetry and overcome by nostalgia. He reads,
and reads, and reads until he falls into a deep sleep of
exhaustion; and for the first time ever he forgets to tend the
Light. Then to his horror, when he wakes, he learns that a ship
has been driven onto the rocks below. Struck with remorse, he
braves the fury of the storm and brings the stranded crew
safely to shore. But he has committed the cardinal crime of all
lighthousekeepers. He forgot the Light. He is held responsible
for the shipwreck, and is summarily dismissed. Homeless and
friendless, hanging his head in shame, but clutching the
beloved book to his breast, Old Skawiński walks out into the
wind and the rain to end his days as the eternal wanderer. End
of story. At one level, 'The Lighthousekeeper' can be read as a
straightforward tale of great power and pathos. It has all the
ingredients of a Romantic masterpiece—honour and shame,
heroism and agony, hurricanes, oceans, and man's destruction
by the forces of Nature. At the same time, and especially in the
eyes of the Polish reader, it can be read as an allegory, whose
moral seems to be far removed from the ideals of the Polish
Romantics. Skawiński's career is a parable about Polish
History in the course of the nineteenth century. After a
lifetime of sacrifice, fighting in interminable wars of liberation
at home and abroad, the old man is destitute. He finally
settles down to secure and useful work in his old age, only to
lose his head and his livelihood through reading Romantic
literature. The result of his folly is a catastrophe which
endangers the life of others as well as his own. Explained in

PLATE 1. PEOPLE'S POLAND (Andrzej Krauze)

PLATE 2
THE AUTHORITIES

(a) Political–Military: General
Wojciech Jaruzelski

(b) Spiritual and Popular: Pope John
Paul II and Lech Wałęsa

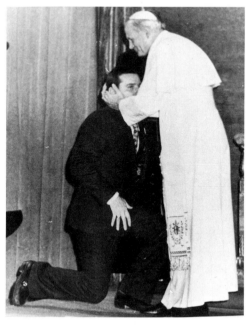

PLATE 3
WARTIME LEADERS

(a) General Władysław Sikorski:
Prime Minister and Commander-in-
Chief

(b) Wanda Wasilewska and General
Berling: Moscow's 'Patriots'

PLATE 4
RIVAL TRADITIONS

(a) Roman Dmowski (1864–1939): the
Nationalist

(b) Józef Piłsudski (1897–1935),
Champion of Independence: Marshal
Piłsudski on 'Kasztanka' (Wojciech
Kossak)

PLATE 5
SYMBOLS FROM THE
PAST

(a) The prophet Wernyhora
(J. Matejko): symbol of
resurrection

(b) The jester Stańczyk
(J. Matejko): symbol of cynicism

PLATE 6. HISTORICAL INSPIRATION

The Battle of Somosierra, 9 November 1808 (January Suchodolski): Kozietulski's lancers inspired by a vision of Father Marek on the battlements of Bar

PLATE 7. OPPRESSION AND RESISTANCE

(a) Cossak Patrol, 1880 (J. Chełmoński)

(b) Monte Cassino, 1944 (E. Mesjasz)

PLATE 8. CONSTITUTIONAL PRINCIPLES (Andrzej Krauze)

(a) The Leading Role of the Party (1981)

(b) The Soviet Alliance

this way, 'The Lighthousekeeper' has been seen as one of the cleverest manifestos of Polish Positivism, which uses Romantic techniques in order to discredit Romanticism. But the conclusion is not so sure. Is Skawiński to be blamed for reading his copy of *Pan Tadeusz*? Is Mickiewicz to be blamed for having written it? Notwithstanding the shipwreck, does Skawiński regret having opened his parcel of books? Hardly so. Skawiński's portrait is deftly sketched with the greatest tenderness and sympathy. He is a humble as well as a noble man, who is willing to work as well as to fight, and his mistake could easily have been made by any sensitive person of feeling. He is a human being, with a heart as well as a mind and a sense of duty, and for that he is not censured. Poland, one might conclude, was not to blame for its past, nor for its humanity. Poland, without its culture and traditions, would have no hope, nothing to keep it alive. Yet Poland's traditions were dangerous. They were heady medicine that could easily lead to disaster. In short, one would not wish Poland to change; but one must realize that it constantly pays a high price for its weaknesses, and its ultimate destiny is uncertain.

At this point, it is possible to understand why Henryk Sienkiewicz has remained the most popular author in the vast Polish repertoire. Sienkiewicz only really broke on to the international scene with *Quo Vadis*? (1896), a novel about the early Christians in Rome which could appeal to the whole of Christendom and not just to his Polish audience. But his feeling for the Polish pulse was unmatched. He could write 'for the heart', like the Romantic masters, or 'for sober thought', like a Positivist. He could conjure up personalities, from Zbyszko the Knight to Połaniecki, the bourgeois: from Wołodyjowski to Skawiński, which between them explored all shades of Polish opinion. He united both main strands of literary taste, in forceful prose, and in dazzling images. He described the Polish condition as no one before or since; and, above all, he did not condemn it.

By the turn of the century, the established equilibrium had begun to distintegrate as much in literary and artistic taste as in diplomatic, political, and social affairs. The arrival of Modernism, at the end of a whole generation dominated by Positivism, formed a fitting counterpart to the Franco-

Russian Alliance, the upsurge of political parties, and the growth of new social classes. Amidst the changes, it was a time for taking stock, for looking back over the previous century as well as for striking new poses; and in this stock-taking Stanisław Wyspiański (1869–1907) acted as the chief artistic accountant. Wyspiański possessed a keen sense of History, and in Cracow, in Galicia, the freedom to operate without serious restrictions. He was a man of many talents—playwright, poet, theatre director, painter—and, in his determination to be original—a Romantic trait in itself—he frequently defied all classification. Yet his principal concern was to revive, rework, and reinterpret the Romantic repertoire. As theatre director, he staged a series of memorable productions including, in 1901, the première of *Dziady*. As a playwright, he took a number of standard Romantic themes, notably medieval chivalry and modern insurrections; but treated them in ways which would have surprised, if not actually offended the Romantics. *Warszawianka* (La Varsovienne, 1898) and *Noc Listopadowa* (November Night, 1904) were both fantasies spun round the November Rising of 1830. *Legion* (The Legion, 1900) fantasized on the military activities of Mickiewicz in Italy in 1848–9. *Wyzwolenie* (Liberation, 1903), which centred on the opening of Cracow's municipal theatre, propagated the Romantic theme of poetry as the guardian of the Nation's future, whilst vehemently combating the Romantic idea of national salvation through suffering. Yet Wyspiański's masterpiece was undoubtedly *Wesele* (The Wedding Feast, 1901), which was based on a real event in his life, (and which Andrzej Wajda was later to make into a prize-winning film.) When one of his fellow Cracovian poets married a local peasant girl, Wyspiański attended the week-long festivities at the bride's home at Bronowice, near Cracow; and the occasion provided the setting for the dramatic action. The play contrives to combine and contrast an elaborate historical pageant of the Polish wars of independence with serious reflections on the divisions of contemporary society. As the music of the wedding dances grows wilder, the guests more and more inebriated, and the distinction between fact and fiction more blurred, a succession of visitors from the great events of Polish History make their appearance: first Stańczyk, the royal jester; than a Knight and Hetman of the

Noble Republic, and finally Jakub Szela, the perpetrator of the massacres of 1846, and Wernyhora. They symbolize Poland's greatness and decline. At the same time, the Cracovian intellectuals constantly try to strike up a conversation with their peasant hosts, only to discover how little they have in common. The political message was depressingly clear. Poles may have shared a splendid past; but they did not possess either the means or the incentive for fresh patriotic ventures. Much of the dramatic material in *Wesele* is arch-Romantic; yet the conclusions were decidedly un-Romantic. Life was no longer simple. The politics of Polish Literature, with its weary-wise air of *fin de siècle* decadence, had ripened, like the old century, into full maturity.[18]

The constant interaction between the 'Word' and the 'Deed', between Romantic thought and political action, between History and Literature, permeated nineteenth-century Poland at every level. The Word inspired the Deed; the Deed inspired a new Word; and the new Word inspired a further Deed; further deeds inspired further words . . . and so, *ad Libertatem*. Polish writers of the Romantic tendency have always maintained not only that great Literature made a contribution to the Risings, but that it actually precipitated them. They see Literature not just as a necessary precondition, but as the prime mover. They talk of the 'pre-eminence of poetry in Polish political culture' and explain how it provided 'a practical programme' for young people's political calculations. Romantic poetry, write Janion and Żmigrodzka in their discussion of the period between November and January, 'supplied young people with models of personal behavior, with a repertoire of gestures, with a vocabulary for verbalising their mental experiences and organisational activities, with stereotypes both of their own and the enemy's camp, and with a vision of the coming struggle and the coming victory. Formulated originally as the dreams and longing of their creators, and since then systematically banalised by over a century of usage, the poets' words concerning "the government of souls" and the "fatal power of poetry" served a very real function in their own day in the life of the avant-garde of their generation.' 'Poetry created a world of spiritual freedom for them, together with a purpose, and a method of bearing the burden of a terrible reality.'[19] The Romantic story-line returns time and again to illustrate this mechanism, usually in guise of a bard or prophet whose Delphic ramblings galvanize the hero into action. Halban in *Wallenrod* is an obvious example. Contemporary memoirs support the contention. In 1830–1, insurgents relate how they were won over to the cause by reading Mickiewicz: 'We cast aside the sword of the Archangel', they wrote in a reference to one of the scenes of *Wallenrod,* 'and took up our own.' Soldier-poets were as common in the Polish Army as military policemen in the opposing Russian ranks—Wincenty Pol (1830–70), Józef Bohdan Zaleski (1802–86), Seweryn Goszczyński (1801–76), Siemieński, Magnuszewski, the brothers Borkowski, Gaszyński, Gosławski, Garczyński . . . Ludwik Nabielak, the Belvedere conspirator, relates how he came up to Warsaw from Galicia expecting to devote himself 'to the trade of Apollo' only to find himself within a day or two in a soldier's uniform. They saw themselves as the knights of today, setting off to kill the Dragon or Bear and to rescue the national Maiden. In 1863–4, the insurgents paid homage to Słowacki. 'In the climate of opinion preceding the January Rising', Janion and Żmigrodzka write, 'Romanticism of the mystical vintage achieved its widest social response and played a specially important role. . . . [Słowacki's] mystical works formed the setting for the conduct of the new generation in the course of its historical testing-time; his personality moulded it; and his statements during the Springtime of Nations in 1848 were well known to all his admirers.'[20] To sober historians of the present day, such claims by literary colleagues no doubt smack of poetic licence. For analysts who seek only political and socio-economic causes, the outbreak of the January Rising can be explained in full without regard to marginal literary factors. The striking thing is that the sober, scientific, positivist analysts of the 1860s, who actually witnessed the January Rising, did not attempt to minimize the role of literature. They did not take the side of Professor Kieniewicz. On the contrary, they singled Literature out for special emphasis. By attacking the Romantic poets with such vehemence, they paid them the inestimable complement of recognizing their great impact. The Positivists did not deny the crucial role of the Romantics and their Literature. What they did was argue that the Romantic role had been harmful and destructive, and that it should be avoided in the future. In other words, both main camps in mid-nineteenth-century Poland could agree on the vital link between the Word and the Deed. If this were not so, they would hardly have spent so much of their time compiling, reading, and debating the largest literary corpus in eastern Europe.

Nothing confirms the link more clearly than the biography of Polish Literature's most prominent personality—Adam Mickiewicz. Mickiewicz was a born poet, who wrote compulsively, who composed the supreme masterpiece of Polish poetry—Konrad's 'Great Improvisation' from *Dziady III*—in a single night, and whose forty-five years were all too short for the talent within him. Yet he was unceasingly torn between his duty as a poet to write and his duty as a patriot to involve himself in practical action. His idyllic early life as a boy in the Lithuanian countryside, and then as a student and teacher, was rudely interrupted by his arrest in 1823 for membership of a secret society, and by five years' exile in central Russia. But when he sailed from eastern Europe for good in 1829, never having set foot either in Warsaw or Cracow, his relief at leaving Russia was less in his mind than his horror at living the life of a helpless exile. Mickiewicz's translation of 'Childe Harolde's Farewell' was inspired not by his expulsion from Poland, but by his departure from St. Petersburg. 'To lose my way among foreigners', he wrote for Konrad, 'in a crowd of non-acquaintances! And I poet, of whose song no-one understands anything.' At the time of the November Rising, Mickiewicz was staying in Italy and stung by Gosławski's poem addressed 'To A.M., amusing himself in Rome during a national war'. After that, he was intent on redeeming the fault, and threw himself into political as well as literary activities. In 1844, his lectures at the Collège de France were suspended for political reasons, and in 1848 he left for Rome to organize a Legion to fight against Austria. For nearly two years, his five hundred volunteers fought in successive Italian revolutions, in Milan, Leghorn, Genoa, and Rome, only to be disarmed by the French, when they suppressed the Roman Republic, and expelled to Greece. In 1853, after the outbreak of the Crimean War, he set off once more, this time to Constantinople as a military agent of the Hotel Lambert. He organized a regiment of Ottoman Jews to fight against Russia, and was struggling with plans to raise yet another Polish Legion, when he died of cholera in a dingy tenement on the shores of the Bosphorus. (Meanwhile, his younger brother, Aleksander Mickiewicz (1801–71), continued to work as Professor of Roman Law at Kharkov in the Ukraine.) The poet's remains were brought back to Paris, and eventually transferred to Wawel Castle in 1890. His complete works were published in Magdeburg in 1855, but not in Poland until after Independence. The first statue to his memory was erected in Poznań in Prussia in 1857, but not in Warsaw or Cracow until the centenary of his birth in 1898, and not in Wilno until 1922. Mickiewicz, in the words of his biographer, was 'the bard of the Polish Nation, and a pilgrim for the freedom of Peoples'.

The Polish record, both in Word and in Deed, was impressive, therefore Polish authors overstate their case when they claim that Romanticism in Poland was unique in its inspiration of armed revolution.[21] There have been plenty of other Romantics—from France, Germany, Italy, Hungary, Ireland, and even England, who were prepared to die for their cause. Lord Byron, dead at Missolonghi in the War of Greek Independence, is hardly to be forgotten. The wars of the Risorgimento in Italy were saturated with Romanticism; and, though blessed with the priceless advantage of foreign assistance, they involved even larger operations than the Risings in Poland. Even so, as the Romantics would have been the first to insist, success was not to be measured by the number of soldiers in the field or by the fickle fortune of battle. Success was to be measured by the exercise of will and by the survival of the nation's spirit.

1 *The Impotence of Diplomacy*

The 'Polish Question', like its partner 'The Eastern Question', occupies a prominent place in almost every standard textbook on European Diplomatic History; and nothing better illustrates the self-centred approach of most Western historians than their emphasis on this one aspect of Polish affairs which

did least to alter Polish conditions. Throughout the nineteenth century and beyond, the statesmen of the Western
powers harboured the illusion that diplomatic action might
induce the empires of Eastern Europe to modify their policies.
The flood of memoranda, projects, and diplomatic notes on
Poland, which began during the Napoleonic War, did not
slacken until the 1860s, and started to race again during each
European crisis of the twentieth century. Many Poles shared
the same illusion. It was a firm belief of the Romantic period
that insurrectionary movements in Eastern Europe should be
supported by complementary diplomatic initiatives on the
international front from the West. Czartoryski's Hotel Lambert, which functioned from 1831 to 1870, embodied this
belief. According to the oldest joke in the ambassadorial
repertoire, an essay competition on the subject of 'Elephants'
produces a poem from the French candidate on 'Les Amours
de l'éléphant'; a treatise from the German candidate on 'Der
Elephant und die Philosophie'; an essay from the English
candidate on 'Elephants and Cricket'; and a tirade from the
Polish candidate entitled 'Elephants' miconceptions concerning the Polish Question'.

Yet the fact remains that very few, if any, of the diplomatic
memoranda concerning Poland's future ever exerted a decisive influence on the course of events. During each of the great
continental wars, the territory of partitioned Poland formed
an area of actual or potential instability; and at each of the
great peace conferences, at Vienna in 1814–15, and at Paris in
1919–20, as at the allied consultations at Yalta and Potsdam
in 1945, Poland's future was the object of intense negotiations.
In between the wars and conferences, from Prince Czartoryski's Memorial of 1803 to the project for Polish–Czechoslovak Federation in 1943, formula after ill-fated formula was
invented in attempts to control the instability and to reconcile
the demands of the Polish people with the interests of the
ruling powers. For 150 years after the Partitions, the Polish
Question was a conundrum that could never be solved to the
satisfaction of the main parties. Over the years it has
generated mountains of archival material and oceans of
secondary literature. But almost all the diplomatic initiatives
remained sterile. At Vienna, for example, there was no way

that Castlereagh and Talleyrand could have persuaded Alexander I to relinquish his grip on a country long since occupied by the victorious Tsarist Army. When the diplomats finally arranged for the Tsar to rule in Warsaw as the constitutional King of Poland, their modest success was hailed as a major triumph. When the constitution was unilaterally suspended by the Russians only seventeen years later, they protested in vain. At Paris in 1919, there was no way that the Allied statesmen could have persuaded Józef Piłsudski to relinquish power in Poland, although they strongly suspected Piłsudski of being a pro-German interloper. They had no means to enforce their numerous declarations on any Polish issue except the western frontiers, and that through their hold on Germany and Czechoslovakia, not on Poland. The history of the Allied plebiscites in Poland was little more than a fiasco. The critical disputes with Lithuania, Soviet Russia, and the Ukraine were settled by force of arms, without allied mediation. At Yalta and Potsdam, there was no way that Churchill and Roosevelt, by diplomatic means, could have persuaded Stalin to relinquish his grip on a country long since occupied by the victorious Soviet Army. When they finally arranged for the Soviet-backed regime to submit itself to popular elections, their marginal success was hailed in the West as a major triumph. When the elections were shamelessly rigged less than two years later, they protested in vain. At each of these decisive moments, matters were not decided at the conference table, but by the local situation on the ground and by the men who held the reins of practical power. At moments of lesser importance, diplomatic action counted for even less. Throughout the modern period, in fact, notes, protests, and rejoinders about Poland fell thick as autumn leaves. But Eastern Europe lay beyond the reach of Western influence, and Poland's political and military masters could ignore Western rhetoric with impunity.

The nineteenth century is often seen as the high point of European Diplomacy, the heyday of the 'Concert of Europe'. The fact is, Poland was largely excluded from that Concert. At some diplomatic festivals, like the Congress of Vienna, Polish interests were raised, only to meet with rebuff. On most occasions, however, as at the Congress of Paris in 1856 or the

Congress of Berlin in 1878, they were not even mentioned. A firm precedent was set whereby Western Diplomacy might talk about Poland or might keep silent, but could not be expected to inspire practical action.[22]

2 *The Military Tradition*

Few nations in the last three hundred years have seen more military action than the Poles. In the eighteenth, as in the twentieth century, the Polish lands regularly provided the arena for Europe's wars on 'the Eastern Front'. In the nineteenth century, they supplied the armies of three martial empires with countless officers, volunteers, and conscripts. Yet no nation has reaped fewer rewards for the sweat and blood expended. As often as not, the Polish soldier has followed foreign colours. When marching under the Polish flag, he has met, almost invariably, with defeat. It is a sad fact, but Poland was obliged by circumstances to act as one of Europe's principal nurseries of cannon-fodder.

The Polish military establishment, hamstrung as from 1717 by externally imposed restrictions, led a fitful existence until the fourth decade of the nineteenth century. The armies of the old Republic, reformed in 1788, never achieved their goal of a standing force of 100,000 men, since the Russians and the Prussians were not in the habit of encouraging competition; but after their disbandment they supplied the pool of professional soldiers which subsequently made up the backbone of the Polish Legions (1797–1802), the Army of the Duchy of Warsaw (1807–13), and the Polish Army of the Congress Kingdom (1815–31). In this period, Napoleonic influence was at its height. The introduction of six-year conscription in 1807, affecting every man in the Duchy of Warsaw between the ages of twenty-one and twenty-eight, brought military training and experience for the first time to the broad mass of the population, and played its part in launching the cult of Napoleon in Poland. The French also brought the idea of the 'nation in arms', discrediting the traditional view of the army as mob of brutalized serfs in uniform, marching under compulsion to the orders of gentlemen-officers in powdered wigs. The clash of values between the ex-Napoleonic officer corps of the Congress Kingdom and their more conservative Russian commanders goes far towards explainin the military unrest in Poland which preceded the November Rising, and which contributed to the Tsar's decision to disband his Polish Army for good.

After that, in the eighty-six years from 1832 to 1918, no formal Polish army of any great consequence existed. The various military enterprises which were undertaken, whether in the risings of 1846, 1848, or 1863, lacked any potential for concerted and consolidated action. They belonged to that romantic world of amateur, partisan warfare where it is more important to play the game, and to stay in the field, than to think of winning. The various Polish units which came into being—from Mickiewicz's Legion in Italy and Bem's Army of Transylvania, to Czajkowski's Polish Cavalry Division with the Turks in the Crimea, the guerrilla bands of the January Rising, and eventually Piłsudski's Polish Legions (1914–17), the *Polnische Wehrmacht*, and Haller's Polish Army in France (1917–19) in the First World War—were ephemeral affairs, which never managed to survive for more than three or four years. One should not belittle their achievement. It was a marvel of determination and dedication that they existed at all. But they cannot be compared in scale, or in social impact, to the Polish contingents throughout the nineteenth century in the armies of Russia, Prussia, and Austria.

In the circumstances, no permanent military institutions, no Polish professional tradition, was able to develop. Repeated defeats repeatedly slighted the competence of each generation in the eyes of the next. Momentary hopes were usually followed by bitter disillusionment. The officer corps, the regimental units, the military colleges of the early nineteenth century, like those of the Second Republic, were dispersed before they could bequeath their traditions to their successors. What did develop, however, was a strong belief in the private virtues of the individual Polish soldier. Stamina and fortitude in adversity, the ability to improvise, devotion to one's comrades, and carelessness for one's own safety, were traits which won the admiration of all the armies where Poles have served. These qualities are celebrated in the vast repertoire of Polish military folklore. They are to be found in the lively mazurkas of the Lancers, in the innumerable versions of the 'Uhlan's Farewell', and above all, in the haunting words of the March of Piłsudski's Legions—*My, Pierwsza Brygada* (We of the First Brigade):

Legiony to—żołnierska buta;	The Legions stand for a soldier's pride.
Legiony to—ofiarny stos;	The Legions stand for a martyr's fate.
Legiony to—żebracka nuta;	The Legions stand for a beggar's song.
Legiony to—straceńców los,	The Legions stand for a desperado's death.
My, Pierwsza Brygada,	We are the First Brigade.
Strzelecka Gromada,	A regiment of rapid fire.
Na Stos, rzuciliśmy,	We've put our lives at stake.
Swój życia los,	We've willed our fate.
Na stos, na stos.	We've cast ourselves on the pyre.

As Piłsudski himself freely admitted, when he founded the Legions, there were only two things in prospect: 'either death or great glory.' He fully expected the former.

Piłsudski's attempt to put an independent Polish military force back on to the international scene looked ridiculous to many of his contemporaries, and the experiment did not quite work out as he might have expected. The original Union of Active Struggle (ZWC) of 1908, financed by a mail-train robbery in Lithuania, led first to the 'Riflemen's Associations' formed in Galicia in 1910–13, and then, at the outbreak of War, to the open formation of the Legions under Austrian auspices. The pathetic picture of their *Komendant* (recorded by Piłsudski's friend, the writer Żeromski) 'living in a hut in Zakopane in his underwear' in 1909, and the equally pathetic advance of the first cadre company across the Russian frontier near Kielce on 6 August 1914, carrying saddles on their shoulders in the hope of finding horses, did not inspire much confidence. The Polish population of Kielce did not welcome Piłsudski's riflemen, fearing the intervention of 'our boys' (meaning the Tsarist Army); and the subsequent battles of the Legions in the ranks of the Austrian Army were soon lost amidst the colossal movements of the main combatant forces on the Eastern Front. The Legions were forcibly disbanded in July 1917 without having achieved their goal. Yet to judge the brief career of the Legions in purely factual terms is to miss the main point. Their sacrifices, indeed their sheer impudence, rekindled the feeling that the benefits of independent Polish action were not entirely illusory, and that the Polish Republic may yet be reborn. Their military achievement was marginal; their psychological impact was crucial.

The same can be said of the Polish Army in France. Formed in 1917 from a mixture of Polish prisoners of war captured on the Western Front and of Polish American volunteers, it was commanded by an ex-legionary officer, General Józef Haller (1873–1960) who had fled internment by the Austrians and reached France via Murmansk. Its baptism of fire took place in Lorraine in the autumn of 1918, but it could not contribute to the Polish cause in any direct way until its transfer to Poland after independence was already achieved. Yet the mere knowledge of its existence gave a great surge to Polish morale. Its arrival from the West in May 1919, in elegant blue French uniforms and armed with the most modern weapons—an experience which was denied to its counterparts of the Second World War—was an occasion for great pride and rejoicing.

Piłsudski's reflections on military affairs during the terminal phase of the Partitions throws interesting light on the Polish predicament. He naturally took a close interest in international developments, making detailed studies of the Japanese victory over Russia in 1904–5 and of the Balkan Wars of 1912–13. (He actually visited Tokyo in 1906, with a view to forming a 'Legion' under Japanese command from the thousands of Polish conscript-prisoners.) In February 1914, at the Geographical Society in Paris, he presented a lecture which correctly predicted the imminence and general outlines of a World War, in which Germany and Austria were to defeat Russia only to be defeated in turn by the Western Powers; but he did not foresee exactly how the War would be exploited to Poland's advantage. His main preoccupations, however, were with military History—and with two aspects of military history in particular—Napoleon, and guerrilla warfare. Napoleon's career attracted his attention principally on account of the stress which Bonaparte laid on the moral factor in battles; guerrilla warfare because it offered him the only realistic means for confronting the professional armies of Eastern Europe in the foreseeable future. In this connection, Piłsudski's high estimation of the Boers' resistance to the British Army in South Africa took second place only to his unlimited admiration for the Polish insurrectionaries of 1863–4. His works on the January Rising still form one of the standard academic introductions to the subject. Unlike many of his contemporaries of the Positivist generation, Piłsudski firmly believed that the moral credit generated by military action could influence the course of events in the desired direction, irrespective of the immediate outcome of battle; and, in this belief, he was a pure Romantic. 'Defeat', he once said, 'is to rest on one's laurels. Victory is not to submit even when conquered.' At his wish, the grave in the Rossa Cemetery in Wilno which received the remains of his mother together with those of his own heart, was inscribed with lines by Słowacki:

KTO MOGĄC WYBRAĆ, WYBRAŁ ZAMIAST DOMU
GNIAZDO NA SKAŁACH ORŁA. NIECHAJ UMIE
SPAĆ GDY ŹRENICE CZERWONE OD GROMU
I SŁYCHAĆ JĘK SZATANÓW W SOSEN SZUMIE.
TAK ŻYŁEM.

(Whoever had the choice, would choose an eagle's nest on the cliffs in place of a home. May he know how to sleep, though his eyes be red from the thunder, and listen to the cries of the wild spirits in the murmur of the pines. That is how I lived.)[23]

3 *The Alienation from Authority*

Political authority was perceived as an alien imposition in partitioned Poland on several counts. Foreign rule was hardly objectionable in itself; since in the past the citizens of Poland–Lithuania had freely elected foreign rulers more frequently than native ones. Europe at the turn of the eighteenth and nineteenth centuries was full of foreign monarchs; and the Poles would have been extraordinary in that age to have rejected their rulers simply on the grounds that they were not Polish. But they had their reasons. Firstly, the monarchs of Russia, Prussia, and Austria were representatives of dynasties which had harassed the old Republic throughout the previous century, and were already regarded as hereditary enemies prior to the Partitions. The German Kings of Prussia, the German Habsburgs of Austria, and the German Empress of Russia had assumed power in Poland at the end of a long series of assaults and humiliations. Their rule was associated from the outset with force and fraud, and their pious claims to divine legitimacy only served to add insult to injury. Secondly, the establishment of foreign rule was accompanied by the influx of large numbers of foreign troops and foreign officials, who treated their new Polish subjects with fear and contempt. With the sole exception of the Congress Kingdom between the coronations of 1818 and 1829, there was no serious attempt to endow the Polish provinces with even the trappings of a sovereign court and government. Instead they were ruled from afar, from St. Petersburg, Vienna, or Berlin, like colonial dependencies, with the same lack of sensitivity to local feeling that the Spaniards showed in America or the French in Africa. Thirdly, despite the relatively advanced state of Polish culture and literacy, the partitioning powers increasingly insisted on cultural conformity in addition to political obedience, gradually introducing German or Russian as the sole language of government. Practices which were received in other parts of the world, and in other parts of the East European empires as a sign of progress and modernization, were received in Poland as signs of regression. Lastly, and most importantly, the political culture of the three Empires—autocratic in Russia, authoritarian in Prussia, and absolutist in Austria to 1848—bore no relation to the ancient democratic, individualist traditions of Poland–Lithuania. There was no common ground where the new regimes might easily take root. The Poles had been conditioned for centuries to treat the pretensions of central authority with healthy scepticism, and latterly with derision. (See Chapter V.) As a result, they were predisposed to reject outright the infinitely greater pretensions of foreign Tsars, Emperors, and Kings. From the viewpoint of the partitioners, Poland was probably the least propititious country in Europe on which experiments in enlightened despotism might have been practised. From the viewpoint of the Poles, the Partitioning Powers were seen as illegitimate from the start, and with the sole exception of Austrian Galicia after 1867, never gained any viable measure of legitimacy in twelve decades. The great majority of Poles remained in a state of perpetual alienation from their governments throughout the nineteenth century.

One process which well illustrates this alienation was the compulsory registration inflicted on the former inhabitants of Poland–Lithuania in the years immediately following the Third Partition of 1795. The nobles were told to register their certificates of nobility, which few possessed; and most of them were promptly deprived of their noble status on the spot. The burghers were asked to submit their city charters for confirmation, which may or may not have been forthcoming. The clergy were obliged to register as state employees, and the peasants as state taxpayers. The Jews, who had enjoyed communal autonomy under the old Republic, were required to register for the first time as citizens of the state. Since Polish Jewry had not previously been accustomed to the use of surnames, they found that registration could only be effected by accepting a surname issued at the whim of some petty official. In Warsaw, which from 1795 to 1807 was the chief town of 'South Prussia', the Prussian Registry was run by E. T. A. Hoffmann, better known for his 'Tales':

> Mr. Hoffmann does not receive clients every day, since he is usually occupied with his writing; and when he does condescend to see them, he is in such a hurry that one is not allowed to ask him about anything. Before dinner, on an empty stomach, he issues serious or melancholy surnames, after dinner more amusing ones.
>
> In the office, Hoffmann sits with his back to the window looking fiendish. He has a long, stringy neck wrapped in a Turkish scarf, and a large head of tangled hair. He glares at the client in deathly silence, and then shouts out the first word which comes to mind. This word, which the clerk enters into the Register, becomes the client's official surname. At the end, Hoffmann says when the certificate is to be collected, and calls for the next customer. . . .
>
> Today being Friday, we learned that Mrs. Hoffmann, who is a Polish Catholic, had served him pike in parsley sauce for dinner; so he has been handing out nothing but the names of fishes. . . . Last Sunday, he was given a bouquet of roses after conducting the local choir; so all day Monday he handed out the names of roses. Everyone was reasonably satisfied, except for the merchant who is now called Mr. ROZENMADCHEN. On another occasion having visited the district of Warsaw where cage-birds are sold, he came back to the office and created a mass of VOGELS. Once, when Hoffmann had

been playing the organ in church, he issued a string of surnames with a religious flavour, such as HELFGOT, HIMMELBLAU, KADZID LO (Incense), PANIEBOŻEDOPOMÓŻ (Help-Us-Good-Lord), BOŻAKRÓWKA (Ladybird, or literally 'God's Cow'), and so on.

Or again, one night Mr.Hoffmann went drinking with a Prussian Colonel. In the morning he ordered cold water to be poured over his head, arrived in the office in a fine humour, and started issuing military surnames such as FESTUNG, FOJER, PISTOLET, SZYSPULVER, TROMMEL, TROMPETER, HARMATA. That's as far as he got, because the rest of his clients fled.

Antics of this sort were hardly designed to inculcate confidence and respect.[24]

The disrepute of political authority was reinforced by the fact that other forms of existing authority, in the social and religious spheres, remained essentially intact. The pattern of land ownership, for example, was altered, but not overturned. Although foreign officials were often rewarded by land grants in the Polish provinces, and state-sponsored colonists encouraged, especially in Prussia, the state-owned sector did not assume massive proportions, and the overall pool of Polish-owned land was not seriously diminished. The greater part of Polish nobles who lost their noble status had been landless in the first place, and the harshest campaigns of sequestration for political purposes affected Polish landowners in outlying districts of Lithuania and Ukraine, rather than in Prussia, Galicia, or the Congress Kingdom. As a result, by and large, the Polish landowning class was able to hang on to most of its estates, and together with them the right to jurisdiction over most of the serfs. In the era after Emancipation, the Polish squire may have forfeited many of his former legal powers; but he still retained much of his traditional social authority within the village. The traditional influence of the Roman Catholic clergy in spiritual matters was also upheld. The clergy were subject to closer administrative control, and forfeited much of their landed property; but their hold over the masses had never been primarily due to economic factors, and tended to increase when ever they shared the people's distress. As respect for the state fell, respect for the Church rose. Where state officialdom fought a losing battle to bolster its prestige, the ancient authority of squire and priest actually bloomed once more. The aura of political oppression swelled the sense of social solidarity, irrespective of class; and social solidarity in turn improved the climate for political opposition. The ruling class (associated with service of the state) looked increasingly like a thin layer of parasites living off the body of Polish society.

Of course, the existence of an 'alien' ruling class, identified by service of the alien state, did not mean that Poland was ruled exclusively, or even largely, by foreigners. On the contrary, the number of Poles who served the Partitioning Powers, in every branch of their armies and bureaucracies, steadily increased as time went by. The first Poles had entered the service of the Partitioners in the 1770s, after Byelorussia, Royal (West) Prussia, and Galicia were taken from the Republic; and by the time of the Third Partition they were already quite numerous. There were Poles (like Lubecki) in the Byelorussian regiments of Kutuzov's armies; there were Poles in large numbers with the Austrians in Italy. Poles in the uhlan regiments, and amongst the famous Pomeranian grenadiers, of the Prussian Army. There were Poles in each of the Russian armies, which occupied the Duchy of Warsaw in 1813, which suppressed the November Rising in 1831, which garrisoned the Congress Kingdom thereafter. Alexander II commended his Polish soldiers for their steadfast service in the Crimea; Bismarck made special mention of *his* Polish soldiers for their devotion to duty in Schleswig-Holstein, at Sadova, and at Sedan. Poles fought against Poles at Borodino; at Waterloo (when Blücher's cavalry met Napoleon's Imperial Guard); at Sadova; and in almost every trench of the Eastern Front of the First World War (just as Poles holding Tobruk for the British Eighth Army in 1943 found that there were Poles in Rommel's Afrika Korps). The opportunities for advancement were relatively good in Russia, where the Tsarist establishment's dislike for Catholics was offset by its shortage of educated recruits. Poles, like Finns and Baltic Germans, served in every corner of the Russian Empire from Archangel to Alaska. Polish political convicts dragged in chains to Siberia could find that the governor of the province, or the commander of their camp, was a Polish compatriot; Polish *émigrés,* who had to visit Russian embassies and consulates all over the world, found that they were received by Polish functionaries of the Tsarist diplomatic service. Polish conspirators plotting and demonstrating in the streets of Warsaw or Wilno found that the policeman who arrested them or hit them over the head with his truncheon was just as likely to be a Pole as a Russian or a Cossack. A recent study of the personnel of the hated Tsarist Gendarmerie introduced into Warsaw in 1832 shows that the majority of both officers and men were Polish by nationality.[25] (The ZOMO has its ancestry.)

Here was a phenomenon with far-reaching social and moral implications of the most divisive nature. Although the regimes of the Partitioning Powers in some ways showed the features of an imperialist colonial-style 'occupation', they did *not* resemble, for example, the Nazi army of occupation of 1939–45, where the overwhelming majority of soldiers, policemen, and officials in Poland were Germans from Germany, and foreigners in every sense. In the nineteenth century, the ruling powers were alien in nature, and alienated psychologically from the Polish population; but they were staffed and supported to a degree rarely admitted in modern history books, by the sons, friends, and relatives of the oppressed people. Polish society, like many Polish families, was split down the middle, not so much by a conflict of nationality as by a conflict of loyalties. A large part of the occupying parasites were locals. Pole was turned against Pole, friend against friend, children against parents. As a result, in their endless search for conformity and obedience, the political authorities had endless scope for using coercive methods in conjunction with moral intimidation. Careerists, informers, and the black sheep of every family could thrive in ways inapplicable to a united society confronted by a foreign enemy. Blackmail, threats, bribery, inducements, dark hints about the safety of loved ones, were the order of the day. Political authority in partitioned Poland stank with an odour of moral putrefaction undetectable by the receptors of political science, and unimaginable either in democratic countries or in states with a native authoritarian tradition.

It is here that the outsider can begin to understand

the intensity of the moral conflict within Polish society, and the reasons why many thinking Poles felt that their moral and spiritual heritage, rather than their material resources, were the nation's last line of defence. It is this aspect of Polish life which explains the corresponding intensity of the Romantic tradition, whose emphasis on fortifying the 'spirit' of the nation, even at the cost of military and political disasters, begins to look more realistic. Cyprian Norwid, writing in 1852, expressed the problem succinctly:

> Ogromne wojska, bitne generały,
> Policje—tajne, widne, i dwupłciowe,
> Przeciwko komuż tak się pojednały?
> Przeciwko kilku myślom . . . co nie nowe.

(Enormous armies, brave generals, police forces—secret, or open, and of both sorts, against whom are they ranged? Against a few ideas, which are not new.)

These lines, directed at the regime of Prince Paskievitch in 1831–55, would make fair comment on all of Paskievitch's successors—on General Hurko in the 1890s, on Marshal Rokossowski in the 1950s, on General Jaruzelski in the 1980s. As one observer has rightly remarked, it makes the most fitting epitaph imaginable for SOLIDARITY.[26]

Clearly, though, the political alienation of the Poles from their rulers had its negative consequences for the population as well as for the government. Although in the circumstances it must be seen as a necessary mechanism for self-preservation, it can hardly be judged a healthy state of affairs. It was a form of civic malady, of social deformation, appropriate no doubt to the twisted world of Russian Tsarism, but quite inappropriate to a nation supposedly preparing itself for independence. It fostered all the spoiling habits of opposition and resistance whilst hampering the constructive skills of political negotiation and responsible administration. It boded ill for the day when Polish Independence actually arrived, and an alienated nation would be required to govern itself. It certainly formed the background to the factiousness and lack of co-operation between the parties which blighted the experiment in parliamentary democracy in the early 1920s. Józef Piłsudski knew from his own career how pressing the problem was. In April 1921, when he was awarded the honorary degree of Doctor of Laws by the Jagiellonian University in Cracow, Piłsudski thanked his hosts for the award, then proceeded to tell them how misguided their good intentions were. He hailed from a country, he said (meaning Russia), where 'lawlessness was the law', where the authorities used the law for their own convenience, and where he had been obliged to become 'a professional criminal'. He had never pursued his original intention of studying law, but had turned instead to a soldier's life of licence and brute force. 'Imagine my horror', he later confided, when as Chief of State he asked for the services of a legal attorney, and 'they gave me a man whose name was *Car*'.*[27]

4 *The Spread of National Consciousness*

Nationalism—the most powerful of modern political beliefs —is generally reckoned to have its roots in the French Revolution. The slogans of *Liberté, Égalité,* and *Fraternité,* which destroyed the social and political barriers of the *ancien régime,* left Europeans free to seek new identities derived from membership of their 'nation' or 'nationality' or 'national group'. The new 'national consciousness' based on ethnic, linguistic, or historical criteria gradually replaced older patterns of group identity based mainly on religion, dynastic loyalties, or social estates. Amidst the changing landscape of the nineteenth century, Britain and America stood on the conservative side of the argument, which, led by the dynastic monarchies, continued to hold that it was natural for 'the state to forge the nation', and not vice versa. The USA favoured national self-determination for the tribes of Europe, whilst vehemently denying any such right for the ethnic groups or secessionist regions of North America. Great Britain, slowly, came to accept national self-determination for the peoples of the continent, but not for the nations of the British Isles or the British Empire. The French, who led the fashion for 'the nation to forge the state', exported their ideas first to the Italian Risorgimento and eventually to Germany; but

*Stanisław Car (1882–1932). *Car* is the Polish spelling for 'Tsar'.

they declined to apply them to Brittany or to the subjects of the French Republic overseas. Only in the twentieth century was Nationalism allowed to reach Asia and Africa, where it has since become entangled in the same inconsequentialities and hypocrisies that marked its progress through Europe.

In the Polish case, Nationalism certainly received a boost from Poland's close contacts with France during the revolutionary era. Yet it had its origins still earlier. Poland's long subjection to Russian tutelage throughout the eighteenth century (see pp. 305–6 below) aroused precocious feelings of national resentment at a time when France itself was still in the grip of the *ancien régime*. Polish Nationalism, which made its first unmistakable appearance during the Confederation of Bar, received its principal stimulus from the Partitions themselves. The conscious drive towards a national state, and towards the creation of a nationally conscious population, had begun even before the First Partition of 1773, while the old Republic was still alive, and it proceeded unabated for almost two hundred years. The most significant steps along the way occurred in the nineteenth century.

From its origins in the ideology of the Polish *Szlachta*, the concept of the Polish nation spread wider and wider until it encompassed all classes of society. In the mid-eighteenth century, it had only referred to the 'nation of nobles' who ruled the old Republic and who were the only people to think of themselves as Poles. (See pp. 331–35.) In 1791, it was expanded to include the burghers, enfranchised by the constitution of 3 May, and in 1794, with Kościuszko's Manifesto of Połaniec, it made its first step towards the inclusion of the largest social class, the peasants. From then on, it took seventy years until the last serfs were freed of their feudal dues in Poland, and probably another couple of generations before the last Polish-speaking peasants realized that they, too, were Poles. The progressive awakening of national consciousness among the masses occurred at a different tempo in each of the three Partitions, and in different districts within each Partition; but how it looked to one person who experienced it is well described in the memoirs of Jan Słomka (1842–1929), a peasant from the district of Tarnogrod on the Galician bank of the Vistula. Słomka, who was born a serf, passed, as he relates, 'From Serfdom to Self-Government' in one lifetime. As an illiterate young man, he had no idea that he was a Pole. The peasants on that part of the Vistula called themselves *Mazury* or 'Mazovians',* he said, and only the gentlemen were regarded as Poles. On learning to read, however, and by participating in the work of the Peasant Movement in Galicia, Słomka because enthusiastically aware of his own Polish identity. He became a pioneer of rural education, and ended life as the respected mayor of his village, decorated by the Sanacja Regime for distinguished services. When he was born, only a small minority of the population of the Polish lands would have consciously belonged to the Polish nation; when he died, the great majority would have done so.[28]

If the social base of Polish nationality was vastly expanded, therefore, one must not forget that at the same time the ethnic base was considerably narrowed. The old Republic had been a multi-religious, multilingual state (see pp. 316–22); but after the Partitions much of the old sense of common belonging was lost. Each of the various religious and linguistic groups tended to drift apart. With time, nationalist ideas caught hold on the German, Ruthenian (Byelorussian and Ukrainian), Lithuanian, and Jewish communities, as well as on the Poles. Each community began to think of itself as a separate nation, distinct from the Poles, and to gravitate towards its kinsmen in other parts of Eastern Europe. In 1650 or 1750, a Protestant or Orthodox nobleman could have considered himself as good a Pole as the next one, even if his mother tongue were German or Ukrainian; yet in 1850, his descendants would have been considered very quaint and old-fashioned to persist with such an idea. In 1798, the German-speaking burghers of Danzig, who had remained loyal to the King of Poland for almost 350 years, rebelled against their incorporation into Prussia. By 1898, their descendants were among the most fervent advocates of German nationalism, and of adherence to the German

*On this point, Słomka was mistaken. *Mazury* referred to the inhabitants of Mazuria, not of Mazovia. Its use three hundred miles to the south probably derived from a Mazurian colony, established conceivably at the Reformation. Mazuria lay within the Duchy of (East) Prussia, and most Mazurians became Polish-speaking Protestants. Mazovia, in contrast, was joined to the Kingdom of Poland in 1527; and the Mazovians were noted for their fanatical Catholicism.

Empire. In the 1930s, they were converted wholesale to Nazism. In short, national identities changed with the changing times. The Polish nation was increasingly confined to the Polish-speaking, Catholic core. What is more, many families of Polish origin, especially those in Prussia who moved to the German-speaking towns, lost all memory of their former Polish connections, just as many families of German or Ukrainian origin were being Polonized. Whilst the Polish nation received many new recruits, it also lost a large part of its former membership; and the ruling powers were only too eager to encourage the losses.

The overall picture, in fact, was exceedingly complicated. In quantitative terms, Polish national consciousness did not diminish. There were far more people who regarded themselves as Poles in 1900 than in 1800. But the understanding of their Polishness was so varied, so fragmented by competing loyalties and by conflicting social, economic, and political interests, that it provided no certain basis for concerted action. Polish nationalism was smouldering steadily, burning itself out in some areas whilst spreading into others. But it could not hope to burst into open flame so long as the stifling restrictions of the three empires remained intact. Germanization and Russification were also proceeding apace. The issue hung in the balance. A body of die-hard Polish patriots continued to believe that victory would somehow be theirs; but many sanguine observers, including some who were deeply sympathetic to the Polish cause, felt it unlikely that Polish identity could survive indefinitely. In 1886, the literary critic Georg Brandes, who visited Warsaw, sensed an impending crisis. 'For a hundred years', he wrote, 'Poland has served as the anvil of three great powers, and has borne the blows of the enormous hammers without being crushed. Before very long, either the hammers will be stopped, or this culture will be annihilated.' The hammers were stopped in 1918, just in time.

The fact is: the modern Polish nation is the end-product of modern Polish Nationalism. Its growth proceeded erratically over two centuries, and its ultimate success was far from certain for most of its recent History. The exact date at which it assumed a preponderant role in the affairs of the Polish lands is a matter for dispute. Some historians see the decisive moment in 1864, when an important measure of social emancipation coincided with the national demonstration of the January Rising. Others would delay it to the rebirth of the Polish state in 1918. Yet the most rigorous analyst would insist that the national process could not be regarded as complete until a homogeneous Polish population, uniformly conscious of its national identity, took undivided control of its own national territory. That point was not reached until 1945.

Ironically, if the Second Republic possessed political sovereignty but not a nationally uniform population, the People's Republic possesses a truly national society, but lacks full sovereignty. In this sense, the campaign for national self-determination in Poland is still incomplete.

One must also note the tone and style of Polish national consciousness. Although in some instances it could take pride in the common European heritage shared with other neighbour nations, it was often marked by a narrow egocentricity. Inflamed by foreign oppression, it was easily seduced into a way of thinking which held everything foreign to be hostile and inferior and everything Polish to be above criticism. Oppression bred truculence; and the truculence of the fanatical element among Polish nationalists did much to bring Poland into disrepute.

5 *The Émigré Tradition*

Emigration from the Polish lands, which reached its peak at the end of the period of Partition, must be attributed to a wide variety of interrelated causes. The standard division between political emigration on the one hand and economic emigration on the other is a useful starting-point for enquiry; but it does not provide any complete or clear-cut explanation of the subject. All political exiles are affected by the material circumstances of their departure, just as every economic migrant adds to the political and cultural consequences of mass movements of people. The *émigrés* who stayed abroad because their lands and property had been sequestrated, or because they lost their source of livelihood in a home district annexed by a foreign power, were reacting as much to economic as to political factors. The starving migrant who blames his poverty on the neglect or mismanagement of the ruling Government is making a political comment no less than an economic decision. Furthermore, once abroad, political exiles, economic migrants, and refugees of all sorts tend to coalesce into a distinct community, whose common bonds are as important as their varied motivations, and whose very existence, irrespective of their origins, exerts a powerful influence on the parent nation back home.

The history of economic migration from Poland, though not so ancient as that of political emigration (see pp. 193–97), is every bit as complicated. It started as a seasonal movement between one neighbouring locality and another, most typically of peasants from Galicia or Congress Poland seeking work on the vast estates of Prussia or eastern Germany; and it grew in the course of the nineteenth century into a transcontinental, and intercontinental flood. Its main roots lay in the grinding poverty of the Polish countryside, whose rural society possessed few sources of employment other than subsistence farming, and whose over-population reached terrifying proportions; but many of its irregular rhythms and 'fevers' owe more to psychological fantasies and to collective hysteria than to the strictly economic conditions prevailing on the day of departure. Paradoxically, it was the relatively fertile farming districts, such as lower Silesia or western Galicia, which were in the greatest danger of over-population, and which therefore provided a disproportionate number of migrants in periods of dearth and famine. Similarly, it was the most developed regions of western and southern Poland, in Prussia and Austria, which were first affected by peasant emancipation, and which were free to release their surplus peasants at the earliest date. The poorest and most backward Polish provinces, in central Poland and in the Russian Empire, provided a relatively modest supply of migrants. The march of the Polish peasants from the countryside to the new industrial towns began, in Silesia and Posnania, at the end of the eighteenth century. The flow of Polish workers to industrial regions further afield, first to the Ruhr and later to Belgium and France, began in the first half of the nineteenth century. Overseas emigration, largely to North and South America, was essentially a feature of the fifty years preceding the First

World War. According to one reliable estimate, some 3.6 million people left Poland in the period between 1870 and 1914—31 per cent from Galicia, 33 per cent from Prussian Poland, and only 36 per cent from the largest of the Partitions in Russia. The conditions which provoked this exodus were often harsh indeed. The 'Galician Misery', well documented and publicized in Szczepanowski's study of 1887, became proverbial. According to another statistic, over 400,000 peasant holdings in Galicia in 1902 were so small that they could only supply food for the average family for three months of the year. Approximately one-quarter of the population of Galicia is thought to have emigrated in the three years, 1911–14, overwhelmingly to the booming cities of the American mid-West. Equally interesting, however, are the social and psychological factors which have to be considered to explain the characteristic cycles, waves, and rushes of economic migration. The classic study of *The Polish Peasant in Europe and America* by Thomas and Znaniecki, which is based on an analysis of the correspondence between Polish migrants in the USA and their relatives back home, shows that there was a constant flow of information and opinions between the two terminals of migratory movement. Travel tickets, job contracts, or just letters of encouragement sent from the USA to Poland, set up the frequent occurrence of 'chain migration', whereby successive members of a Polish family or village would pull their friends and relatives after them. Remittances of money, regularly dispatched by the Polish worker abroad to his dependants at home, formed an important element of the family budget, and kept the two ends of the arrangement in touch. Exaggerated publicity about the opportunities for employment and prosperity abroad, the activities of unscrupulous agents, or intergovernmental labour contracts could spark off a sudden exodus, inexplicable in purely local or economic terms. At the peak of the 'Brazilian Fever' of the 1890s, one agency contracted with the government of Brazil to supply 50,000 colonists from Germany and Russia, and within weeks had registered over 100,000 volunteers from the Polish provinces alone. Four border counties of the Congress Kingdom were threatened with total depopulation at a stroke. It would appear that the motions of economic migration were as complex, as repetitive, and as tidal in character as those of its political counterpart.[29]

The nationality factor in Polish Emigration possessed an immense range of nuances, which are often misrepresented in modern studies. At the point of departure, in any town or district in the Polish lands in the nineteenth century, an emigration agency, whether official or clandestine, would be approached by applicants of several different nationalities. In Prussian Poland, it would be approached by Poles and Germans in roughly equal numbers; in Galicia, by Poles, Ukrainians, and Jews; in Russia, by Poles, Jews, Lithuanians, and Byelorussians. As often as not, these nationalities travelled abroad together in one body—not as a national group, but just as one of the mixed consignments of migrants of every conceivable nationality which trekked out of Eastern Europe in all the third-class compartments and steerage holds of westbound transport. Although the fact is not now widely advertised, the first Polish settlers in Texas, for example, the founders in 1854 of Panna Maria in Karnes Country, travelled to New Orleans from Silesia in the company of Silesian Germans bound for a nearby destination. Only at the point of arrival did they go their separate ways. Most typically, on arriving in the unfamiliar environment, each immigrant would be taken in hand by his own relatives or by compatriots who spoke the same language. The Jews would be met by their *landsmen*, and taken off to the nearest Jewish reception centre. The Germans would be met by Lutheran pastors. The Poles would be welcomed by Catholic priests and directed to the nearest Polish parish. The Ukrainians would head for an Orthodox or Uniate community. In this way, people who in Poland might have been neighbours and acquaintances were separated on the spot, literally on the dockside, and were quickly turned into strangers. Official immigration records usually show their citizenship—Russian, German, or Austrian —but not their nationality; yet within hours of their arrival they were attached to a distinct national group, with its own cultural life and its own organizational structures, to which they would belong, in many cases, to the end of their lives. In the industrial suburbs of Europe, and even more in the ethnic jungles of America, national identities were inflated, and intercommunal antagonisms sharpened. Memories of common origins were blurred. In the Polish communities abroad, the identity of Pole and Catholic was even more exclusive than at home; and Polish Nationalism of the narrow, intolerant, ethnic variety was even more widespread than in Poland.

The Polish Emigration in France was undoubtedly the senior *émigré* community in the nineteenth century. Until the installation of Polish miners in the Pas de Calais in 1919–20, it was largely political in character. The Hotel Lambert, the Bibliothèque Polonaise, the Société Littéraire were institutions of major importance. With Adam Mickiewicz at the Collège de France, and with Słowacki, Niemcewicz, and Czartoryski strolling down the boulevards, for thirty or forty years after the November Rising Paris was a more significant centre of Polish culture than Warsaw or Cracow.

The American *Polonia** developed rather later, and its numerical preponderance was not established until the beginning of the twentieth century. Until the Second World War, it contained relatively few political *émigrés*; yet it contained a disproportionate number of 'the wretched refuse' —to quote the Statue of Liberty—of Europe's most 'teeming shore'. Whole suburbs of Pittsburgh, Detroit, Cleveland, or Buffalo were solidly Polish in character. Chicago boasted more Polish citizens than any city in the world except Warsaw. The influence of the Polish clergy was paramount; although a conflict with the anglophone Irish establishment of the Catholic Church in America led to the formation in 1875 of a breakaway, schismatic Polish National Church. Polish Americans were among the most disadvantaged of American immigrants—the 'white niggers' of the northern states; and they were not quick to overcome their disadvantages.[30]

The Polish exiles of Siberia and central Asia deserve a chapter to themselves. In origin, they were convicts and deportees rather than *émigrés* or migrants; but in the long run their fate was not dissimilar to either. As often as not, after serving their sentence of penal servitude, they were forbidden to return to Poland, and they remained in their thousands in

---

*Polonia, the Latin name for 'Poland' used by the Catholic Church for all Polish communities abroad, is usually associated nowadays with non-political migrant groups rather than with political *émigrés*.

the farthest wildernesses of the Russian Empire. Their earliest predecessors were Polish prisoners of war dispatched to the East in the early seventeenth century; and every generation of Polish prisoners and deportees since then has reported its contacts with the remnants of previous deportations. Until the building of the railways in Russia in the mid-nineteenth century, they were forced to travel in the terrible convict wagons or even to walk all the way from the Vistula to the Yenisei or the Lena in chains.* Many of them died on the journey. It is impossible to estimate their total numbers, although they probably formed the largest category of political exiles in Tsarist Russia. (Of Siberian exiles under the Tsarist regime, 90 per cent were relcalcitrant peasants and common criminals, deported by administrative decree.) It is curious to note that a Tsarist encyclopaedia admits that, in 1880, 75 per cent of the population of Irkutsk was Catholic. It is also significant that educated Polish exiles provided a major contingent of the intelligentsia of Siberia, such as it was. Scientists such as Bronisław Piłsudski (1866–1918), brother of the Marshal, who wrote the first ethnographic survey of Sakhalin and Kamchatka; and a long line of Polish explorers starting with the famous Maurycy Beniowski (1746–86), served to open Siberia to modern knowledge. These days, their contribution is rarely remembered.[31]

Owing to the great variety of their circumstances—and the great variety of social class, educational level, and political affiliations—every Polish community abroad was rent by a series of repeated schisms and factions. The educated 'politicos' felt little in common with the peasant immigrants, especially if they had to soil their hands in the same dirty workshop. The leaders of each generation of 'politicos' were divided between the aristocratic conservatives and democratic radicals, and yet were united by their resentment against new arrivals with new ideas and new connections. In the Great Emigration, Prince Czartoryski's position at the Hotel Lambert was challenged by republican 'reds', like Lelewel or Stanisław Worcell (1799–1857); yet both their positions were

*Prince Roman Sanguszko (1800–81), an ex-officer in a Tsarist Guards Regiment, was specially sentenced to walk in irons to his Siberian exile. He returned to Poland after fourteen years, and lived to be eighty-one.

overwhelmed by the next influx of *émigrés* from the January Rising who had an entirely fresh complexion and different interests. It would be tempting to suggest that the political *émigrés* adhered predominantly to the Romantic outlook, having failed to reach a personal *modus vivendi* with the ruling Powers in Poland; and that the economic migrants, in their urge to work hard and better themselves, belonged predominantly to the opposite, Positivist, and later Nationalist, camp. If so, there were many exceptions. Perhaps the most prominent of Polish *émigrés* in mid-century America, Adam Gurowski (1805–66), a veteran of the November Rising and of the TDP, turned out in later life to be a great admirer of Russia and Tsarism. His prophetic work, *American and Europe* (1857), predicted that the USA and Russia were destined to surpass the degenerate powers of Europe and to divide the world between them. One should also remember that thousands of Polish Americans, whose families had emigrated in large part for economic reasons, were prepared none the less to make the supremely Romantic step—of volunteering to fight for Poland in Haller's Army in France.* Just as the theoretical distinction between political and economic emigration was easily blurred in practice, so the equally seductive distinction between Romantic and Positivist frequently breaks down when applied to particular instances.

From the viewpoint of Poland, however, the mere existence of a numerous Polish Emigration outweighed all the short-comings, or achievements, of its individual members. Like the Roman Catholic Church, the Emigration had its faults; but with a solid base abroad, immune from the pressures of the political authorities in Poland, it could play a role in Polish life of incalculable importance. In the political sphere, it provided the only forum for free debate and critical analysis of all Poland's problems. With the perpetuation in Poland of alien, imperial regimes with little provision for democracy, it fulfilled the function of the principal, if absent, opposition. In the economic sphere, it provided a much needed source of foreign income, and, eventually, of trade and enterprise. In

---

*They also were influenced no doubt by the none too Romantic prospect of being drafted into the US Army.

the cultural sphere, it ensured that free expression could be given to the full variety of ideas, arts, and genres on which a living culture depends. In the period of Partitions, a large part of the classics of Polish Literature could only be published in emigration. Lastly, in the moral sphere, the Emigration bestowed a measure of prestige and respectability on Polish nationality which was officially forbidden in Poland. Nineteenth-century Poland produced a great number of talented artists, musicians, and scientists, who, if they had only performed at home, would only have been known to the world as talented figures in the life of Russia, Germany, or Austria. As it was, because they made their reputations abroad and could freely advertise their Polish connections, they were widely known as 'Poles'. The roll of honour was spread far and wide: Paweł Strzelecki (1796–1873), Australian explorer; Ignacy Domeyko (1802–89), pioneer of Chile; Frederyk Chopin (1810–49), composer; Sir Casimir Gzowski (1813–91), Canadian architect; Ernest Malinowski (1818–99), railway pioneer in Peru; Helena Modjeska (1840–1909), actress; Karol Rołów-Miałowski (1842–1907), Cuban revolutionary; Jan de Reszke (1850–1925), operatic tenor; Joseph Conrad (Korzeniowski, 1857–1924), English novelist; Ignacy Paderewski (1860–1941), pianist; Marie Curie-Skłodowska (1867–1934), physicist; Guillaumo Apollinaire (Kostrowicki, 1880–1918), French poet; Sir Lewis Namier (1880–1960), British historian; Bronisław Malinowski (1884–1942), social anthropoloogist. A nation which continued to produce people of this calibre could hardly be said to have disappeared.

Poles abroad no doubt made a worthy contribution to the life of their host countries. Yet their contribution to the survival of their own nation sometimes consciously, sometimes unconsciously, was even greater. However strong, or tenuous the link, they continued to be part of Poland. As Pope John Paul was to tell their heirs and successors in London at the end of the twentieth century:

What I say flows from a keen sense of History. You who have created the... *Polonia* of today are not in my eyes first and foremost emigrants. First and foremost, you are a living part of Poland, which, though torn from its native soil, does not cease to be itself.[32]

A year earlier, when the Pope visited France, he was received by the Cardinal Archbishop of Paris, Jean-Marie Lustiger. What could be more symbolic of their common predicament when it is realized that both Pontiff and Archbishop were Polish *émigrés*!

6 *The Cultural Imperative*

Once it became clear that Poland's political demise could not be quickly reversed, and that the Poles had to prepare for a siege lasting into the indefinite future, cultural affairs assumed prime importance. Opinions regarding the efficacy of diplomatic action, political strategy, or social and economic policy were often divided; and serious differences arose regarding the content of education; but few people doubted that Polish culture constituted the nation's chief treasure and its last line of defence, to be preserved at all costs. Throughout the nineteenth century, attention centred on two issues: national education and the role of the intelligentsia.

Education came to the forefront of Polish concerns at the time of the First Partition, and remained there for the duration. (The creation of the National Education Commission in 1773 was the price which the Sejm of the old Republic exacted for consent to the treaties of Partition.) As in the military sphere, the problem was how to create permanent institutions and to train a pool of professional people who could ensure the transmission of Polish culture from one generation to the next. The task was daunting; and the struggle in each of the Partitions became very fragmented. But in the end, where the generals and military planners failed, the educators triumphed. Polish culture, Polish educational enterprise, and the Polish intelligentsia survived, bruised but intact, from the Partitions to the 'explosion' of Independence in 1918.

The way in which this was achieved can best be likened to a relay of Olympic runners, where each man carries the torch of learning for a stage before passing it on, exhausted, to the next runner. The institutions of the National Education Commission, and the two reformed Universities at Cracow and Wilno, barely survived the Third Partition. The Commission was summarily disbanded, its staff and schools dispersed by the new authorities. But an important part of its resources was salvaged by the Wilno School-Board, which flourished in a vast area covering all the western *gubiernas* of Russia during the first two decades of the nineteenth century. The University of Wilno, where Mickiewicz studied and Lelewel taught, and the distinguished gimnazjum at Krzemieniec in Podolia, where Słowacki was educated, took up the running at a time when the Jagiellonian University had been Germanized by the Austrians, and Warsaw was in the hands of Prussia.[33] The educational system of the Duchy of Warsaw, launched in 1807, was further expanded under the Congress Kingdom, together with the new University of Warsaw (1818), only to meet its end in 1832 after the November Rising. By that time, however, the Jagiellonian University had been re-Polonized in the Republic of Cracow; and the Polish schools of the Duchy of Posen were enjoying a brief lease of life. From 1854 to 1861, Polish education was at its lowest ebb. There was no institution of higher learning and no state-approved schooling in Polish. But church schools and private schools were not yet persecuted, and the Polish educational system in Galicia emerged just in time to beat the *Kulturkampf* in Germany and the drive for total Russification in Russia. In the eight years of its existence from 1861 to 1869, the *Szkola Główna* (Main School or *École Normale*) in Warsaw, whose distinguished pupils included Prus, Sienkiewicz, Świętochowski, Ochorowicz, Baudouin de Courtenay, Piotr Chmielowski (1848–1904), Bronisław Chlebowski (1846–1918), Adolf Dygasiński (1839–1902) and Wiktor Gomulicki (1848–1919) succeeded in carrying the torch until the Jagiellonian University was re-Polonized for the second time in 1870, and in handing over the relay to the Galicians for the next forty years. Galicia's economic poverty was a scandal, and its political system a joke; but in educational matters it was rich. Until the reopening of Polish Education under German auspices in Warsaw in 1916, Galicia's Polish educators enjoyed a virtual monopoly, and they ran the long, final leg with courage and distinction.

The supreme achievement of Polish education, despite the need to flit from perch to perch, was to preserve a unified cultural community bestriding the frontiers of the three empires. There was no continuity in Polish politics in the nineteenth century: no national economic system, no social structures that were exclusively Polish—but there was always at least one academic and educational centre which could propagate Polish culture for the citizens of all three Partitions. When Wilno was the main centre in the teens and the twenties, young men from Prussia or Austria went to Lithuania for an education; whenever Warsaw could function, Polish families from Russia, Prussia, or Galicia sent their sons (and a few of their daughters) to the Congress Kingdom; when Cracow and Lwów were left as the two twin bastions of Polish learning, they sent them there. One should not underestimate the great influence on nineteenth-century Polish culture of the great German and Russian universities. In terms of numbers, there were probably more Poles educated 'abroad'—at Berlin, Breslau, Jena, Göttingen, or Heidelberg, at St. Petersburg, Dorpat, and Kiev, at Vienna and Salzburg or at technical institutes such as the popular Mining College at Graz, or indeed at the Russian University of Warsaw, 1869–1915—than at all the Polish universities put together. At the same time, the persistence of the national sector enabled Polish culture to keep pace with the times, to absorb new knowledge, especially in philosophy and the natural sciences, and to preserve the national identity. No one can have failed to be moved by the scenes at the Jagiellonian University at the end of the summer term in July 1914, when many of the students, who were reserve officers in the Russian, German, or Austrian Army, took their leave of each other under the shadow of impending war.[34] They knew that within a matter of weeks, if not days, they would be exchanging machine-gun fire instead of student greetings, intellectual arguments and girl-friends. Edward Słoński (1872–1926), who served in the Legions, composed perhaps the best-known verses of the final years of Partition on this very theme:

> Now I see the vision clearly,
> Caring not that we both will be dead;
> For *that which has not perished*
> Shall rise from the blood that we shed.

Słoński, even then, may have entertained hopes of Independence. But 'that which had not perished' referred more certainly to the Polish national community, united by its common culture, than to any particular political programme.

Although modern Polish scholarship tends to emphasize the intensifying educational struggle between the state authorities and the advocates of national culture, the parallel conflict between secular and religious education was equally important, at least until the last quarter of the century. The National Education Commission had been given its chance in 1773 by the Vatican's abolition of the Jesuit Order; and the Church never relinquished its efforts to recover the lost ground. In the Duchy of Warsaw and the Congress Kingdom the war between the secular educators and the clericals reached a peak when Stanisław Potocki (1775–1821), the author of *Podróż do Ciemnogrodu* (A Journey to Ignoranceville, 1819), was dismissed from his ministerial post. In that era, the Church still maintained an arch-conservative stance in social affairs, and generally sided more with the ministers of the Tsar than with Polish liberal educators.[35] It was only at a much later date, when the Church's own schools were attacked by the state, that the clericals found common cause with the national educators. In the era of the *Kulturkampf* and the school strikes in Prussia, when Catholic primary schools and even school prayers came under fire, and when General Hurko was closing down private convent schools in Russian Poland, the Church was obliged to reverse its previous stance and to join forces with its former opponents.[36]

The educational environment in Russian and Prussian Poland at the end of the century had to be seen to be believed. The Ministries in Berlin and St. Petersburg were intent on eradicating Polish culture in the shortest time possible. The Polish language was not to be spoken on pain of expulsion. Polish books were banned. Polish teachers had to speak to Polish children in Russian or German, on pain of dismissal. In Warsaw in the 1880s the absurd decision was taken—as a special concession—to permit the study of selective works of Polish Literature, but only on condition that it was undertaken as part of the Foreign Language curriculum, with all textbooks, commentaries, and discussion in Russian. The young Maria Skłodowska remembered the tension in her Warsaw school room in 1878:

On the threshold, laced into his yellow pantaloons and blue tunic appeared M. Hornberg, inspector of private boarding-schools. Hornberg advanced towards the teacher:

—You were reading aloud, mademoiselle. What was the book?

—Krylov's *Fairy Tales.* [A Russian classic] We began them today Hornberg opened the lid of the nearest desk, as casually as he could. Nothing. Not a paper, not a book. . . .

—Your prayer, he snapped.

Maria recited 'Our Father' in an expressionless voice. One of the subtlest humiliations was to make Polish children say their Catholic prayers in Russian. . . .

—What is the title of the Tsar in the scale of dignities?

—*Vyelichestvo* [Majesty]

—And what is *My* title?

—*Vysokorodye* [High born]. . . .

—And who rules over us? . . . Who rules over us?

—His Majesty, Alexander II, Tsar of All the Russias. . . .

Not surprisingly, Polish educators, teachers, and children sought every possible means, legal and illegal, to circumvent the official stranglehold. This was the era of the craze for Self-Education, of popular library associations disguised as welfare societies, and of the famous underground 'Flying University'. Polish experience in clandestine education was to stand the nation in good stead in later times when it was confronted not with the likes of Hornberg, but with his Nazi and communist successors.

The Polish intelligentsia* was the social class, or rather the functional group, on which the educational and cultural activities of the nation came to depend. In eastern Europe, the intelligentsia was assumed to be politically disaffected, and it was very often excluded from any form of public service, employment, or expression. For that reason it possessed very different traditions and habits from 'the educated class' of Western societies and from trendy 'intellectuals' in democratic countries who could parade their grievances without fear of arrest or harassment. In origin, it owed a great deal to the *déclassé* nobility, the largest educated element in old Poland

*Intelligentsia: Despite its obvious Latin derivation, the word was not first used by the Poles, but was borrowed by them from the Russian. In the *Słownik Języka Polskiego* of 1898, it is spelled in the Russian way as 'inteligiencja'; *klasa ludzi światłych* (the class of enlightened persons).

(see pp. 331–5); but it soon lost any particular social or economic characteristics. Unlike other social classes in nine-teenth-century Poland, the intelligentsia has to be defined by the function which its members perceived for them-selves—to guard, treasure, and expand Polish culture. Owing to the striking contrast between the cultural climate in Galicia and in the other partitions, there was a striking difference between the affable, academic, and articulate *inteligent* of Cracow or Lwów at the turn of the century, and the radical *révoltés* of Warsaw and Wilno, or the educated Catholic circles of Silesia or Poznań. The archetypal Cracovian 'Professor of Romanticism' would have quickly found his way to the police station in Russia or Prussia, where the inimitable humour of a Boy-Żeleński was equally out of place:

> For many long years by Heaven aided,
> Our nation preserved its mighty sway
> At whatever point, they were not needed,
> The Polish hussars charged into the fray. . . .
> At last, even Heaven's forbearance was rattled.
> Our conduct had Providence thoroughly riled.
> The Almighty declared, 'I'll slaughter such cattle;
> The merest sight of them drives me wild. . . .'

The high services of Tadeusz Boy-Żeleński (1874–1941) to Polish culture are beyond dispute. Among other things, he translated virtually the whole of the French classics into Polish, single-handed, in over one hundred volumes; his doggerel verse on the stage of the 'Green Balloon' Cabaret was composed no doubt as light relief from his daily toil as a physician; and he was destined to be killed by the Nazis. But his style and temperament were inseparable from Galicia.

In Russia, the Polish intelligentsia had to resist pressure of a far more painful kind. If terrorism and political activism were for the few, cultural activism was for the many. Thousands of young people, who recoiled from violence, none the less found a mission in life by fighting for Polish culture. They instinctively sensed a new ethos in which the traditional language and values of Polish society would be swamped by the brainwashed products of state-controlled, mass education. They included the pioneers of Women's Emancipation, who were to supply them with their largest legion of recruits, and the pioneers of rural education among the peasants. In Russia, if the typical Polish 'patriot' at any time up to 1864 had been a young man with a sabre or revolver in his hand, the typical patriot at the turn of the century was a young lady of good family with a textbook under her shawl. This generation of the *niepokorni*, 'the unsubdued', went forth as missionaries into their own land. They were as determined to manufacture 'true Poles' as the state authorities were intent on training 'real Germans' or 'good Russians'; and they had an utter idealist contempt for the *ludzie-byki* (Ox-people) who were incapable of patriotic sentiment and the *ludzie-świnie* (The Swine-people) who, though intelligent, had betrayed the national culture. They had to contend on the same ground and with the same human material, not only against authorities, but often enough against the Church, against public indifference and reticence, and against the rival national missionaries of the local German, Jewish, or Ukrainian movements. Many worked in anonymity and obscurity; but others, like Jadwiga Szczawińska (1863–1910), the founder of the Flying University, and her philosopher husband, Jan Władysław David (1859–1914), are well remembered. In the end, their cause prevailed.[37]

Overall, therefore, the nineteenth century saw the triumph of Polish culture over great adversity. In Prussia, where illiteracy was virtually eliminated, universal state education may have taught Polish children to read German, but it did not stop them from transferring their skills to Polish matters. In Russia, a high rate of illiteracy among the peasants protected the masses from Russification. In Galicia, the Austrian authorities gave up their earlier opposition to Polish culture altogether, and let it roll. By 1918, the task of the Polish educators was far from complete; but enough had been done to give the new Polish Republic a solid cultural base.

7 *The Religion of Patriotism*

'Patriotism', said Dr Johnson, 'is the last refuge of scoundrels'; and his much quoted remark well illustrates the confusion with which the subject is usually surrounded. For patriotism, or 'love of one's country', is universally thought to be a virtue, even among people who oppose their country's social or political system. It turns out that Dr Johnson was venting his wrath not on patriots in general, but on a small cabal of the King of England's ministers who happened to call themselves 'the Patriots'. The good Doctor was fully in favour of patriotism (except perhaps when practised by the Scots), and he loved his country, England, dearly.

In Johnson's day, in the mid-eighteenth century, the Poles already had a reputation for exaggerated pride in their country; and it is true that a large part of the Polish nobility were wedded to so-called 'Sarmatism'—the belief that traditional Polish ways were superior to those of all other nations. 'If you should ask a Polander what he is', wrote Daniel Defoe, 'he would tell you he is a *gentleman of Poland*; and so much so do they value themselves upon the name that they think themselves... above the rules of honour.' Of course, Defoe's complaint was directed as much at the Polish nobility's arrogant belief in its 'blue blood' as at its national chauvinism. Patriotism, in its modern ethnic sense, had not yet been invented.

As in so many areas, the real change in Polish patriotic attitudes was provoked by the Partitions. As all the modern nations of Europe were inventing their flags, their emblems, and their national anthems, the Poles were being told that all the symbols of their own nationality were illegal and subversive. The royal throne of Poland and the royal insignia were carried off to Russia in 1831, never to return. The Polish flag and coat of arms, with its crowned white eagle, was gradually modified, and eventually banished. With the singing of patriotic songs a treasonable offence, the intoning at the end of the Mass of Feliński's hymn 'Boże coś Polskę' in Russia, and of Ujejski's 'Z dymem pożarów' in Galicia, was all that could be permitted; and, even there, the words had to be judiciously censored. Even worse, all subjects of the Tsar, Emperor, or Emperor-King were required to salute the standard of Russia, to praise the black eagle of Prussia, or to begin each school-day with a rendering of 'God save the Emperor' to Haydn's tune, 'Österreich'.* No doubt to outsiders

---

*—better known as 'Deutschland, Deutschland über alles'.

all these details look rather petty. To most Britishers or Americans, who are free to stand up to 'God Save the Queen' or 'The Star-Spangled Banner' or to remain seated, who can salute the Union Jack or Old Glory with pride (or burn it in protest), it is hard to imagine one's feelings if coerced to pay respect not merely to one's own country's symbols but to someone else's. All modern countries have developed their patriotic mystique, with their own rites and rituals. But in Poland, all 'normal' manifestations of patriotism were officially repressed, and driven underground. As a result, Polish patriotism became the object of an intense, secret, and highly developed mysticism. It possessed its Scriptures, in the writings of the Romantics; its 'Fathers of the Church', in the great poets; its Martyrs, in the victims of the Risings; its theologians, in the messianic philosophers and literary critics; its priesthood, in the intelligentsia; and a large number of Faithful. Not surprisingly it also had its apostates and agnostics, and, in the Positivists, its schismatics, its 'protestants'. To call it a Religion may seem like a metaphor worthy of the Polish Romantics themselves; but the term is hardly misplaced. It was based on a system of irrational beliefs whose acceptance demanded an act of Faith; and its beliefs were intended as a guide to everyday living in a hostile, and equally irrational world.

Poland's Romantic Religion was developed, not unnaturally, from the country's traditional Catholic, Christian Faith, which it reflected in several important respects. Its theology of the 'national spirit' ran parallel to that of the Christian 'soul'; its dogma of future 'Independence', of which there were few concrete signs on earth, resembled the doctrines of 'eternal life' and of the 'resurrection of the body'; its interpretation of the Partitions was inspired by the Crucifixion. It also drew heavily on secular mythology, on medieval tales, and supernatural folklore; but its main inspiration remained Christian. Indeed, in the period of its greatest intensity between the two great Risings, it began to assume the proportions of a coherent sect. The image of 'Poland—the Christ of Nations' had distinct overtones of blasphemy, if taken literally; and several leading apostles, including Mickiewicz and Słowacki, abandoned the Catholic Church altogether. In the circumstances, it was bound to arouse the suspicions of the Hierarchy, and to cause a major *crise de conscience* throughout the Catholic ranks. (See below.)

In the nature of things, Polish Patriotism could adopt few formal rites or public ceremonies. Its mysteries were private and intimate. An active insurrectionary described how she was initiated at the tender age of seven:

My grandmother was a woman of great intelligence and strength of character ... Patriotism was the main motor of her life ... and in the conspiratorial work of the January Rising she had played a prominent part ... The Rising's failure caused the greatest trauma of her life. Henceforward, she always wore the same black dress, and on her finger a ring decorated with a white cross in pearls on black enamel.
—It's a ring of mourning for those who died, she said.
But when I asked to put it on my finger, she shook her head.
—You can only wear it when you're a real patriot ...
—And what does that mean, Grandma, 'being a patriot'?
—A patriot is someone who loves Poland above everything else in the world, and will abandon everything, even life itself, for her Freedom ...
—I want to fight for Poland, Grandma, I said, only half comprehending.
After a while, my grandmother's eyes flashed.
—Yes ... Do you promise to fight for Poland, my child?
—I promise, Grandma. I repeated, enthralled by the ominous feeling.
Then she caressed me, and placing the ring on my finger, held it there tightly.
—Now there, run along ... But don't forget, and don't tell a soul.

Thus, in 1889, did the young Ola Szczerbińska (1882–1963), begin a revolutionary career which was to involve her in the same gun-running escapades as her grandmother. Her husband, Józef Piłsuduski, recalled similar childhood experiences. Polish Patriotism, it seems, made the same rigorous demands as those of Christianity—'Leave all, and follow me.'[38]

The central article of belief lay in the power of the spirit. All the great Romantics celebrated the supremacy of the invisible spiritual world over the visible, material world. For them the spirit of things was real; the body, the outward clothing, was a sham. In *Dziady III,* in the moment of the metamorphosis of Gustaw into Konrad, the Ghost intones:

Oh Man, if only you knew what power is yours!
When the invisible thought flashes in your mind
Like a spark in the mist, it can scatter the clouds;
It can make the rain, the thunder, the whirlwind. . . .
Oh People! Each one of you, imprisoned and alone,
By faith and thought could raise, or dash, a throne.[39]

Later, in his 'Great Improvisation', Konrad marvels at his creative, poetic powers, God-given but equally divine; and he calls for the *Rząd dusz,* the mastery of the Spirit:

Grant me Mastery of the Spirit!—How I despise
That dead construction which by vulgar men is called the world,
And which they praise from habit. Although I have not tried,
It could be overturned at a stroke by my very word.
Thus in myself, if there should only be the Will,
I feel the power that could a hundred stars instil
With fire, another hundred quench by bended concentration.
For I am immortal! And within the wheel of creation,
Others, too, are immortal. . . .[40]

Mickiewicz, in the heat of poet inspiration, expressed what all Romantics believed. The apparently impossible was possible.

The ultimate goal was Freedom—but freedom of the spiritual, not the worldly kind. The Romantics were not concerned with the form and constitution of the future Poland, which remained a very vague concept until Dmowski and Piłsudski unwrapped their rival visions at the turn of the century. In so far as they thought of such concrete details at all, they looked back to the old Republic of Poland–Lithuania, and to the constitution of 3 May which still lay within living memory until the 1840s. Political theory and constitutional law were simply not their *métier.* What they had in mind was much closer to a secular version of the 'City of God', or to Blake's 'New Jerusalem', than to anything historical. The paradise of perfect Freedom was to be enjoyed by nations and by individuals alike, and Poland was simply the first of many, the leader of a numerous pilgrim band. Nations which failed to follow Poland, even though like England and France they were 'children of Freedom', would be cast into the outer Darkness, and paradise would be built 'from the stone of

Muscovites and Asiatics'. People who sought their rewards on Earth would lose their hope of Freedom forever:

And JESUS said, 'He who would follow me, let him leave his father and mother' and risk his soul. And the pilgrim of Poland says 'He who would follow Freedom, let him leave his homeland and risk his life.' For he who lives in the Fatherland, and accepts Slavery, simply to save his own life, shall lose both his life and his Fatherland. But he who leaves the Fatherland, and risks his life in order to defend Freedom, shall gain both the Fatherland and eternal life.[41]

There is no reason to suppose that 'leaving one's Fatherland' meant travelling abroad. The journey to Freedom was a spiritual journey: and the 'Fatherland regained' was a paradise of the spirit.

The sceptics—and they were many—usually employed the well-worn arguments which all rationalists direct against systems of belief. The Positivists shared the common mid-century preference for Science over Religion, thinking the two to be incompatible. They saw, and feared, the emotional force of Romantic Patriotism, which threatened to upset their longing for orderly progress and calculated policy. They despised its enthusiasms, its lack of caution, its ability to mislead simple people, its disregard of consequences. They attacked the Romantics for being 'impractical', 'unreasonable', and 'unrealistic'. They thought of themselves as frightfully modern, and of the Romantics as old-fashioned fanatics, devoid of 'understanding'—rather as the aces of the Enlightenment thought of the mystics and marvels of the Age of Faith. In short, they held a narrow view of Reality, bounded by what was visible and immediately verifiable, and incapable of appreciating a Reality which included spiritual, emotional, imaginative, and creative elements as well as the mundane and the materialistic. The Positivists' successors, the Nationalists, inherited the materialism, the pragmatism, and the caution; but they added a whole new mythology of their own about Blood, Land, and History. (See pp. 133 ff.) In this last regard, they must be seen as a sect within the Sect, accepting the Romantics' fundamental belief in the nation, but endowing it with special dogmas of their particular invention. At the same time, they veered back in the direction of traditional Catholic observances, thereby helping to bridge the gulf between Romantic Patriotism and traditional Catholicism.

In the last resort, and much to the Positivists' surprise, the ultimate test for Romantic Patriotism was the same as that for all religions, the test of practicality. Its critics had to ask whether or not it met the everyday needs of ordinary people. And in this regard, it passed the test with flying colours. Romanticism had its drawbacks, and its tragedies; but time and time again, it has proved that Poles, like all human beings, have spiritual as well as material needs; that a full sense of fulfilment and satisfaction does not come merely from order and prosperity: that, in spite of everything, Polish Man does not live from Bread alone.

8 *The Divided Conscience*

As the modern Polish Nation coalesced in the course of the nineteenth century, the average man and woman found themselves torn by three conflicting loyalties. Since most of them were baptized and practising Catholics, they felt a sense of duty to the Church; since an increasing number had become conscious of their Polish nationality, they felt a sense of duty to the Nation; and since all of them were subjects of Russia, Prussia, or Austria, they were constantly told that they must feel a sense of duty to the State. Each of these three duties made separate calls on their consciences, and pulled them in different directions. Inevitably, since all three sources of authority made claims of an absolute, dogmatic nature, where compromise over matters of principle was judged impossible, the task of reconciling them in any lasting form was logically impossible. This conflict has always lain at the root of the intense moral environment of Polish life, and has posed a problem which every individual conscience must resolve as best it can. When historians write that Poland has been a 'symbol of moral purpose in European life', they are not making a judgement on the private morality of Polish people, but rather on the heightened moral pressures under which Poles have been obliged to live for the last three centuries.

The nature of state authority in eastern Europe was such as to grant the minimal degree of latitude to the individual citizen, and to arouse the maximum degree of alienation amongst its Polish subjects. (See above, p. 243.) If Tsarist Russia had ever succeeded in implementing its intended constitutional reforms; if Prussia and Prussian Germany had practised something more than 'façade democracy' or had possessed the tolerance and confidence of more firmly established states; and if the united Austrian Empire had collapsed somewhat earlier—then life in the Polish lands might have been easier. But these things did not happen. In its formative years, the modern Polish nation was forged under the triple hammers of the Tsarism of Nicholas I, the Absolutism of Metternich, and the ambitions of Bismarck. The heat of the process was necessarily intense; but the resultant alloy was hard. With hindsight, it is tempting to imagine that alienated authority commanded little respect, and was incapable, therefore, of inflicting much emotional distress. Poles felt free, one might suppose, to resist or to cheat the state without any pangs of conscience. But there was more to it than that. For one thing, state officialdom could bring immense pressures to bear on any individual, by threatening his livelihood and by harassing his friends and family. Everyone who has lived in a police state knows what 'the friendly word in one's ear' from the local official can mean. For another, the State could pressurize the Church to take a loyalist stand in political affairs, and could thereby use the Church's moral credit for its own nefarious purposes. In the nineteenth century, the Roman Catholic Church was less able to withstand these pressures than it has since become (see Chapter V, pp. 412–15); and the power of the State to hurt Polish consciences by indirect means via the Church should not be underestimated. The disgust and mental confusion aroused, when patriotic Poles had to listen to their Bishop's pastoral letter urging them to love and honour the Tsar, still more when they heard their friends and heroes excommunicated from the pulpit, is not hard to imagine.

The nature of the Church's authority also caused severe problems. Although the Roman Catholic Church had long since lost its powers of civil coercion, its dogmas of absolute obedience and, after 1870, of papal infallibility, were no less unbending than those of Tsarism. Catholics who resented the workings of the Tsarist censorship could hardly oppose it in principle, since the Church operated a censorship of its own. Whilst the state censors banned the works of Mickiewicz or Słowacki, the Church Index still upheld its ban on the works of Copernicus. Some works, like those of the pan-Slav historian Wacław Maciejowski (1793–1883), found themselves on the Index for being too favourable to Russian, or Orthodox views; others, such as Mickiewicz's treatise 'On Messianism' (1848), were banned by the censorship and the Index alike. If the Roman Catholic Church in Poland had retained more of its traditions from the age of Catholic Humanism and Protestantism in the fifteenth and sixteenth centuries, and if the clergy had felt less threatened by the decline in the Church's power and by local competition from Orthodoxy, Lutheranism, and Judaism, then life for the Poles might have been easier. But those things did not happen. In its formative years, the Polish nation had to live not only with the secular despots, but also with a brand of clerical despotism that has passed into History very slowly. Słowacki's notorious description of a Polish patriot's reception in the Vatican was written with a view to satire, if not parody; but it contained more than a grain of truth:

SWISS GUARDSMAN: Count Kordian, a Pole!

POPE: Welcome, kinsman of Sobieski. . . . Daily, I thank God that the Russian Emperor . . . is ever most favourably disposed to the Catholic religion.

PARROT: (raucously) *Miserere*

KORDIAN: Holy Father, I bring you a sacred relic, a handful of earth from a place when then thousand men, women, and children were murdered. . . . without the blessing of the sacraments. Treasure it with the presents of the Tsars, and give me in return just one tear. . . .

PARROT: *Lacrymae Christi.*

POPE: Down Luther, down! What, my son? Have you not seen . . . the Circus and the Pantheon? . . . Let the Poles pray to God, reverence the Tsar, and hold fast to their religion.

KORDIAN: But what of this handful of bloody earth? . . . What shall I tell my friends?

PARROT: *De profundis clamavi*

POPE: Down Satan, down! My Son, may God guide thy steps, and grant that thy people cast the seeds of Jacobinism from their

>bosom, and devote themselves to the worship of God and the
>cultivation of the soil....
>
>KORDIAN: (throwing the earth into the air.) I scatter the ashes of
>the martyrs to the four winds. I return to my native land with a
>sorrowful heart.

The Church in Poland was not devoid of Christian charity, as
some of its atheist enemies have declared; but it had to carry a
terrible cross of institutional inertia, clerical prejudice, and
doctrinal rigidity.

The nature of Polish Patriotism compounded the problems
still further. (See above, pp 268–74.) Polish Patriotism was not
merely a reaction to secular oppression; it was a reflection in
many ways of religious attitudes. It professed a belief in the
absolute Good of the freedom of the Nation, and in that belief
its priorities were at variance both with the State and the
Church. The absolute State could not envisage the idea of
political opposition, let alone ideas of absolute political
freedom; and the absolute Church could not accept that the
Good lay anywhere but in the salvation of souls. For
individual Poles, who were involuntary subjects of the State
yet who wanted to be active servants of the Nation as well as
faithful children of the Church, the resultant agonies of
conscience were obvious. Once the difficult decision was taken
to reject the authority of the State and to run the risks of
political activism, there still remained the yet more painful
choice between Patriotism and Catholicism. Karol Baykowski
(1823–1904) for example, a conspirator and terrorist, explained his conscious choice in favour of patriotism. 'I am a
Christian', he wrote, 'therefore, I ought to have observed the
law of Christ to the last iota; but I am a Pole, so I ought to use
all means for freeing my country from the foreign yoke. . . . For
the liberation of the fatherland, or rather for avenging its
oppressors, one had to be ready to sacrifice not just one's life,
one's family, one's property, and one's personal career, not
only one's honour and reputation in the eyes of the world, but
even one's conscience and the salvation of one's soul. Having
taken the patriotic ideal to heart, however, I then proceeded to
feed it with everything to hand, including the Holy Scriptures.'[42] Baykowski was an honest man in that he made his
choice with open eyes, and did not hide the adverse

consequences. Later on, in the disillusionment of exile, he rejected both his patriotic past and his Catholic faith, and became a leading exponent of Tovianism. The moral price of a clear decision was always high.

For the Polish dilemma could never be satisfactorily resolved one way or the other. Poles who opted for political Loyalism (see pp. 179–82), or for uncritical Catholicism were made to feel guilty by their betrayal, or their neglect, of the Nation. Those who opted for Patriotism felt guilty either from remorse at the cost of their sacrifice or from their defiance of the Church. Those who avoided all decision, and did nothing, felt guilty from a feeling of cowardice. Whichever decision was taken, it could not hold for long. Individual Poles were pushed back and forward from one untenable position to another. The guilty Loyalist turned on his hated masters from prolonged humiliation; the disillusioned patriot turned conciliator or loyalist. The well-intentioned Catholic rushed back and forth between the State authorities and the suffering Nation, and was able to satisfy neither. The person of passive disposition, who carefully avoided involvement in one of the Risings in order to save his skin, felt obliged to take part in the next. So long as the State was illegitimate in the eyes of the people; so long as the Poles were both Catholic and patriotic; there was no hope of relief, no chance of a simple solution.

What the Romantic Patriot and the Catholic devotee shared, of course, was a belief in the primacy of spirituality. The patriot could engage in violent and disastrous ventures because he believed that the Nation's Spirit was indomitable, that sacrifice and suffering produced a moral victory. The Catholic would shrink from violence and politics because he feared for the safety of the patriots' souls. But both of them would agree that life promised rewards much dearer than mere political order or material success. Those Poles, who were more patriotic and less Catholic, would press for action; their brothers and sisters, who perhaps were more Catholic and less patriotic, would urge restraint. Yet everyone in the argument could accept without question that the clue to Poland's future, as to the purpose of their own lives, lay in the exercise of spiritual mastery.

CHAPTER V

THE LEGACY OF AN ANCIENT CULTURE

Poland before 1795

A Historic Nation

During the nineteenth century, the concept of 'the historic nation' was one of the basic tools of the historian's trade. Developed by Hegel, and refined by Marx, it referred to that select company of nations which were qualified, through their achievements in a broad range of political, military, economic, social, and cultural spheres, both for the sovereign control of their own state and for an independent role in world affairs. It implied the existence of a second category of 'unhistoric nations', whose deficiencies in one or other of the necessary accomplishments condemned them to a subservient position and eventually to assimilation and extinction. Under the influence of the popular theory of Evolution, the fate of nations on the international scene was likened to that of biological species in the natural world, where only the fittest can survive and where the unadapted must expect to perish. Historians and statesmen could never fully agree as to which nations were best qualified for which category. (There is a natural tendency for people to assume, since one's own nation possesses 'a manifest destiny', that one's neighbours can be safely consigned to oblivion.) Yet it was generally accepted that the historical process in modern Europe had produced a number of anomalies which needed to be corrected. Whilst few questioned the historic role of Britain or France or Russia, it was widely admitted that the emergence of the German Empire or of a united Italy was fully consistent with the natural order. The rights and claims of the Greeks, the Czechs, or the Irish were more open to debate.

In this continuing debate, Poland's position has been particularly controversial. On the one hand Poland's detractors could point to a long list of 'historic' deficiencies—to the alleged oppressions of the Polish nobility, to the economic regression of the seventeenth and eighteenth centuries, and above all to the 'Anarchy' of the old Polish political order. Led by the court historians of St. Petersburg and Berlin, from Karamzin to Treitschke, they made sure that everyone in Europe had heard of the tyrannical *szlachta*, their ridiculous *liberum veto*, and their appalling *Polnische Wirtschaft*. On the other hand, Poland's proponents, including Michelet, Macaulay, and Marx, were less impressed by Poland's shortcomings than by the blatantly false testimony of her enemies. To their way of thinking, it was as absurd to assign the Poles to the same category as the Basques, the Bretons, or the Bulgars, who had no modern experience of a separate political existence, as it was to regard their demise at the hands of the three most reactionary empires of Europe as an example of the onward march of civilization. As Marx was the most eager to assert, the Poles were the victims of a historic 'crime' and the restoration of Poland was a pre-condition for Europe's peaceful development. After all, in Marx's day, Russia was by far the most backward country in Europe, just as old Prussia had been the most retarded province of Germany; and the rise of these two powers to supremacy had to be attributed much more to brute force than to high culture. To Marx and his liberal contemporaries, the continuing alliance of the conservative monarchies of eastern Europe, whose fortunes had been assured by the Partitions of Poland, represented the main obstacle to European progress. For them, in their broad vision of the past and the future, the claim of the Poles to be one of Europe's historic, but temporarily deprived nations, was as clear as that of the Germans or the Italians. The arguments, for and against, have been reproduced and redebated in all the international crises of the last hundred years in which the fate of Poland has been at stake.[1]

Whatever one's opinion, certain facts are beyond discussion. Poland's tenacious traditions were not just the product of modern politics or of recent misfortunes. They are not the inventions of nationalist fantasies. They are grounded in an age-old association with Western Christendom, in familiarity with all the great experiences of European history—Renaissance, Reformation, Baroque, Enlightenment; in close contact with all the great powers of the continent—with the Holy Roman Empire, France, Hungary, Sweden, and the Ottomans; and above all, in centuries of independence and of the uninterrupted promotion of the native Law, Language, and Literature. In short, they are the fruit of more than a thousand years.

1 *Prehistory*

The great Polish plain, which merges to the East of the Oder and the Vistula into the limitless steppes of Eurasia, was one of the main routes of entry for Europe's primitive migrants. From the Old Stone Age in the 180th millennium BC to the dawn of recorded history in the tenth century AD, it provided the staging post for wave after wave of nomads, raiders, and settlers. For longer or for shorter periods of time, it provided a home for the most assorted mixture of peoples—from the nameless tribes of the pre-Christian era, known only from their archaeological remains, to the shadowy pagans of the Dark Ages. Among its inhabitants, who followed a more sedentary way of life, were various brands of Balts, Celts, Germans, and Slavs; amongst the nomads were the Scythians, the Sarmatians, the Huns, and the Mongols. It stands to reason that the human stock of the region must have been highly diverse. What is more, once the invasions from the steppes began to slacken towards the end of the first millennium—the Magyars in the ninth century were the last to settle—the main tide of movement in central Europe began to flow for several centuries in the opposite direction. As the French pressed for the Rhine, so the Germans recrossed the Elbe and entered the Baltic; the Poles pushed eastwards into Lithuania and Ruthenia; and the Russians breached the Urals and headed for the Pacific. It is not good form in modern Poland to recall that the Slavs took part in this great *Drang nach Osten* (The Drive to the East) no less than the Germans; but it is undeniable that the eastbound migrations of the early Middle Ages, which brought Dutchmen, Germans, Czechs, and Jews into Poland's western provinces, took Polish colonists into more easterly provinces, to mingle there with Letts, Litts, Ruthenes,* Romanians, and Tartars. The net result for historic times was a magnificent patchwork of peoples speaking a babble of languages and professing a profusion of faiths. Ethnic variety must be seen as one of the hallmarks of Poland's population until very recent times.

In this light, it may seem strange that serious scholars should disregard the obvious richness and complexity of primitive settlement in favour of simplistic theories supporting the exclusive claims of immemorial possession by just one ethnic group. Yet central European prehistory is plagued by ethnocentric theories. In this, the findings of the contemporary Polish 'Autochtonous School', which sees the territory of the present People's Republic between the Oder and the Bug as the fixed and exclusive homeland of the *Praslowianie* (the 'early Slavs'), are highly reminiscent of the work of its predecessors in the old Prussian School, who designated the selfsame area as the ancestral homeland of the *Früostgermanen* (the 'early east Germans'). The habit of referring to its one chosen group as 'autochtones', or 'the indigenous people', or 'the native population', and to all the others as 'aliens', 'foreigners', 'transients', or 'invaders' is as misleading for the general reader and it is unconvincing for the specialist. One can only conclude that the study of Prehistory is still strongly influenced by the national prejudices of researchers, and, worse still, by the demands of official censors. It is an unusual situation to say the least. There can be a long prehistory of England before the English, of France before the Franks, of Bohemia before the Czechs, even of Russia before the Russians, but not, it seems, of Poland before the Poles.

---

*The forebears of the modern Byelorussians and Ukrainians—not to be confused with the Great Russians (Muscovites). Russian scholars have traditionally claimed that the Ruthenes were no more than a minor branch of the Russian nation: and to confuse the issue, in Tsarist times Ukrainians were officially referred to as 'Little Russians'.

In actual fact, the long process, whereby the Slavonic, Polish-speaking element rose to a dominant position within the population at large, is clouded with obscurity. There is no general agreement as to the location of the Slavs prior to their irruption into the Balkans in the sixth and seventh centuries; and there is no sure record of their presence to the East of the Elbe and the Oder before the eighth century. According to non-Polish authorities, there is little reason to put a Slavonic tag on the 'Lusatian Culture' of the Vistula Basin in the Iron Age, and still less to identify the ancient Vandals as Slavonic 'Wends'. As far as the post-Roman era is concerned, it is clear that the forebears of the Poles must have been living somewhere on the Eurasian continent; but it is not proven at what point or in what circumstances they diverged from the parent Slavonic community, to which they were undoubtedly related. Equally, it is not entirely improbable that the 'proto-Poles' had already begun to settle somewhere in the lands between the Baltic shore and the ridge of the Carpathians. But their arrival would in no sense discount the presence of the Goths on the lower Vistula, of Balts to the East of the Vistula delta, or of the Celts in Silesia and in the environs of modern Cracow. There is no cause to suppose that one particular ethnic group could ever have enforced exclusive possession of so large an area; and in primitive conditions, cultural and linguistic assimilation must have proceeded with minimal speed. The name of *Polska* (Poland) does not emerge until the very threshold of historic times in the tenth century, and then only as the domain of just one small Slavonic tribe, the *Polanie* ('the people of the open fields'), settled on the banks of the Warta in the vicinity of modern Poznań. The exact relationship of those *Polanie* to other Slavonic tribes, and perhaps to their non-Slavonic neighbours as well, is the subject of no certain knowledge.

For modern governments, which appeal to prehistorians for evidence to justify modern territorial settlements, and for modern citizens who gain a sense of reassurance by learning about their ancestors, the tentative conclusions of responsible scholarship in this field may be less than satisfactory. Yet for all but the most interested parties, the common practice of supplementing inconclusive fact with attractive fiction, or the habit of researching the prehistory of one group to the exclusion of all the others, belongs more to the imaginary arts than to science.[2]

2 Piast Poland

The legend of Piast—the peasant boy, whose future election as ruling prince was prophesied by two tall strangers—is one of those curious items of Slavonic folklore with great political potential. It is on a par with the story of Lech, Czech, and Rus—the three Slav brothers who set out through the primeval forests as progenitors of the Polish, Czech, and Ruthenian nations; of Princess Wanda, who drowned herself in the Vistula rather than marry a German knight; or of King Krak, who ingeniously slew the dragon of Wawel Hill by putting fire in its belly and forcing it to drink the river water till it burst. All these legends, and more besides, were written down by the early Polish chroniclers in the twelfth and thirteenth centuries; but they clearly date from a much more remote era, long before the adoption of Christianity. Piast, if such a man really existed, most probably lived in the middle of the ninth century and ruled as the tribal chief of the Polanians. He would have been a contemporary of Charlemagne's sons; of Alfred of Wessex; of the Macedonian Emperors of Byzantium; and possibly of Rurik the Viking, another semi-legendary figure who is credited with the founding of Kievan Rus. At all events, whatever his origins, Piast was to launch a dynasty that ruled for five hundred years, and eventually united the scattered Slavonic tribes of the area into one Polish Kingdom.

The House of Piast emerged from the mists of prehistory in AD 965, when Prince Mieszko I (died 992) accepted Catholic baptism, married a Czech princess from Prague, and introduced literate, clerical scribes into his court. His son, Bolesław Chrobry (Boleslaus the Brave, 992–1025), a warrior in the grand style, whose armies reached both Prague and Kiev, had the distinction of being the first of several crowned Polish kings. The regal crown, sent by the Pope from the Vatican, was the symbol of Poland's formal recognition as a member of

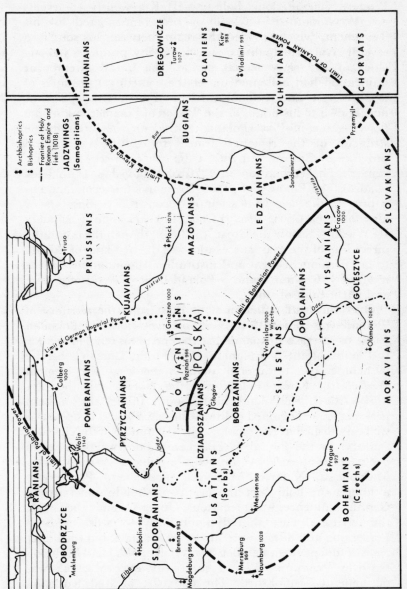

Map 7.   The Realm of the Early Piasts (10th to 11th Centuries)

Western Christendom. Bolesław III Krzywousty (Boleslaus the Wry-mouthed, 1102-38) is best remembered for his Testament, which divided the realm between his sons into several rival principalities. As with many primitive monarchies of the early feudal period, the initial attempt at unification had collapsed under the centrifugal pressures of local interests and regional war-lords. For the next 182 years, now known to historians as the 'Period of Fragmentation', the power game in Piast Poland centred on the interminable struggles of the regional princes to capture the capital province of Cracow and with it the title of *princeps* or 'senior prince'. The coronation in 1320 of Władysław I Łokietek (Ladislas the Elbow-high, 1306-33) marks the second, and as it proved, the successful attempt to construct a consolidated kingdom, the *Corona regni Poloniae*. Łokietek's son, Kazimierz III Wielki (Casimir the Great, 1333-70), though the last in the direct line of the Piast succession, was the first king of Poland to lay permanent legal and institutional foundations for the monarchy. Casimir found a Poland built of wood, it is said, and left it built of stone.

Over this half millennium of Piast rule, the territory of 'Poland' was subject to considerable evolution. The Polanian *Polska* of Mieszko I expanded at the end of his reign to include the lands of the Vistulanian tribe round Cracow, thereby launching the traditional division between the original *Wielkopolska* (Great Poland) in the North, and the new *Małopolska* (Little Poland) in the South. In fact, the southern province quickly gained political supremacy, and Cracow was well established as the royal seat by the middle of the eleventh century. In the Period of Fragmentation, the Polish realm consisted in theory of six main provinces—Wielkopolska, Małopolska, Kujawy, Mazovia, Silesia, and Pomerania; although the hold over the last two, already under strong German influence, was precarious. Under Casimir the Great, the territorial base shifted significantly towards the East. Pomerania and Silesia were finally abandoned; but the buffer zone of independent fiefs between Wielkopolska and Małopolska was incorporated, and suzerainty over Mazovia was permanently established. The conquest of Red Ruthenia (1349), and of distant Podolia on the Dniester (1366), took the

Poles over the continental watershed on the route to the Black Sea coast.

Of course, in the depths of Europe's medieval backwoods, nominal control over territory mattered much less than real control over people. In feudal practice, the 'Polish obedience' carried much more meaning than the Polish frontiers. Thus, as the ruling princes took measures to strengthen and increase the population, Polish society, too, was subject to change. In the early centuries, social structures reflected the military priorities of a warlike society, with the social élite centred on the *drużyna* or 'bodyguard' of the princely courts: a broad warrior class holding land in return for service; and, at the bottom of the scale, the mass of dependent slaves and peasants. By the thirteenth century, however, the modest advance of agricultural techniques had made systematic rural colonization a worthwhile venture, whilst the decline of former insecurities encouraged the growth of trade. As a result, a free peasantry was already coming into existence. Rulers encouraged the foundation of new settlements, releasing land in the countryside to villages enjoying the favourable terms of 'German Law', and granting charters to new cities incorporated under the Law of Magdeburg. The municipal corporations of Wrocław (1242), Poznań (1253), and Cracow (1257) all date from this time. Although much of the colonization involved Slav colonists, Poland also saw a massive influx of migrants from over-populated districts of northern Germany and the Netherlands. Most Polish towns came to be dominated by German-speaking burghers, whilst whole areas of Pomerania, the Neumark, and Lower Silesia were settled by German peasants. Jewish liberties, first confirmed by a charter of 1265, and later much expanded by Casimir the Great during the time of the Black Death, witnessed the growth of Europe's most important Jewish refuge.

Poland was taking its place in the community of Catholic nations. Initially, much friction had been caused by the Piasts' ambiguous relations with the German Emperors, some of whom, like Otto III (died 1003), were friends and allies, whilst others, like Frederick Barbarossa (died 1190), endeavoured to enforce their intermittent claims to suzerainty. But close ties with Bohemia, which in 1293–1306 led to a brief union of the Czech and Polish thrones, served to keep the Empire in check. Generally speaking, medieval Poland's relations with Germany were far more peaceful and beneficial than modern propagandists would like to believe. More serious was the creation of the State of the Teutonic Knights in Prussia. Invited to Poland in 1226 by Conrad of Mazovia, who sought their help in his quarrel with the pagan Prussian tribes, this Order of unemployed crusaders soon turned its nominal mission for converting the heathen into a major campaign of subjugation and conquest. Within a hundred years, the Knights controlled most of the Baltic coastland, linked Prussia with Livonia, and in 1308 captured the port of Gdańsk (henceforth 'Danzig'), the key to the Vistula. Yet their depredations were mainly directed towards the East, and cannot be compared to the two great Mongol invasions of 1241 and 1259 which cut a swathe of destruction right through the heart of Poland and into Silesia. It was these same Mongol invasions which finally destroyed the unity of Kievan Rus, and created the opening for Poland's main eastward expansion. The Piasts had always enjoyed close family ties with the ruling houses of the Ruthenian principalities; and there were many instances of intermarriage. But these ties also furnished the pretext for meddling, and in 1340 for Casimir the Great's expedition against Red Ruthenia. For under Casimir, Poland was at last becoming a power to be reckoned with. The 'Congress of Cracow' of 1364, which treated five crowned kings and five ruling dukes to an extravagant programme of feasting and jousting, marked Poland's modest entry into the world of international diplomacy.

Casimir's long reign was most distinguished for his activities on the domestic front. The codification of Polish law undertaken as from 1347, in the style of a Hammurabi or a Justinian, summarized all the legal customs and practices of the past and provided the foundation for all future legislation. The construction of more than fifty stone castles provided the basis for a permanent system of fixed defence. The introduction of a new silver currency, based on the *grzywna* (mark), greatly facilitated the growth of trade. The formation of a new corps of royal officials, including a central secretariat and the regional *starostas,* served to counterbalance the older system of less controllable castellans and palatines. The founding of the Cracovian Academy in 1364 (later renamed the Jagiellonian University) created a safe and independent environment where higher learning could flourish. What is more, Casimir expressed his confidence for the future in the most solid material form. Cracow gleamed with the fresh white stone, bright red bricks, and the Gothic architecture of a score of magnificent projects. St. Mary's Church, the Cloth Hall, the *Ratusz* (City Hall), a new Royal Castle on Wawel, the third Cathedral, the model suburb of Kazimierz—all bear witness to the Great King's energy and vision.

In this gradual rise of Piast Poland, from prehistoric obscurity to medieval splendour, the role of the Roman Church must be regarded as decisive. Although the Slavonic tribes north of the Carpathians had been in contact with Orthodox missions from Byzantium at an earlier date, the official adoption of Roman Catholic Christianity represents the most momentous event of Polish history. Mieszko's baptism in AD 965 was the first step in the formation of the single most important element in modern Polish culture. The ecclesiastical province of Poland, the See of Gniezno, which was founded in AD 1000 during the Emperor Otto's visit, provided a permanent link with Rome and with the wider world of Catholic Christendom. Having survived destruction by the great pagan rebellion of 1037, it provided a stronger bond of continuity in the life of the nation than the fluctuating rule of the Piast princes, or the fragmented history of the Piast state. The clergy gained full jurisdiction over its vast landed property at an early date, and emerged as the first independent social estate. The cathedral chapters freed themselves from princely control. The story of St. Stanisław of Cracow, 'the Polish Becket', who was murdered in 1079 on the orders of an arrogant king, suggests that the authority of the bishops was equal, if not superior, to that of the secular ruler. Bishop Stanisław's oppressor was driven into exile; and in popular belief, the dismembered limbs of the martyr's body were miraculously rejoined, as a symbol of the future harmony and reunification of the Polish kingdom. Sceptical commentators are quick to denounce a clever piece of clerical propagan-

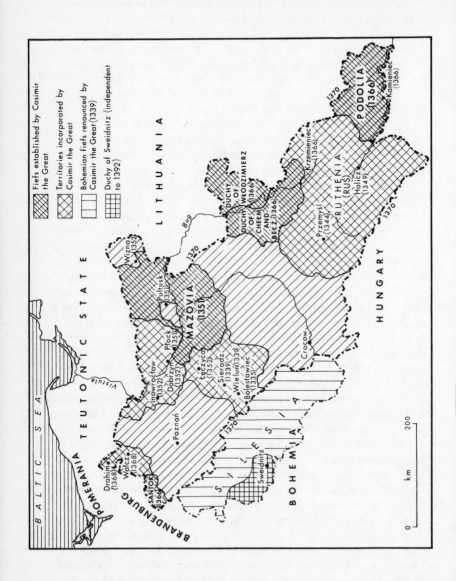

Fiefs established by Casimir the Great

Territories incorporated by Casimir the Great

Bohemian fiefs renounced by Casimir the Great (1339)

Duchy of Sweidnitz (independent to 1392)

BALTIC SEA

Vistula

POMERANIA

TEUTONIC STATE

LITHUANIA

Bug

1320

BRANDENBURG

Drahim (1368)
Wałcz (1368)
SANTOK (1365)

Inowrocław (1352)
Dobrzyń (1352)

Płock (1351)
Pułtusk (1351)

Wizna (1352)

MAZOVIA (1351)

DUCHY OF WŁODZIMIERZ (1366)

DUCHY OF CHEŁM AND BEŁZ (1366)

Krzemieniec (1366)

Poznań

Łęczyca (1352)
Sieradz (1339)
Wieluń (1339)
Bolesławiec (1335)

Cracow

Przemyśl (1344)

RUTHENIA (RUS)

Halicz (1349)

PODOLIA (1366)

Kamieniec (1366)

1370

1370

1370

SILESIA

Sweidnitz

1370

BOHEMIA

HUNGARY

0   km   200

da—which it was—but they omit to explain why the legend met such a receptive audience. For the Church stood at the centre, not just of politics, but of medieval consciousness. It provided the ideology which explained the links not only of the King to his Crown, but also of every man and woman to their ruler and to the universe. It was the fount of all knowledge. It provided the literate clerks who ran the chancelleries, and the Latin language with which all educated men worked. It enjoyed a monopoly in formal education. Its monasteries were the research laboratories of the day. Its prelates combined the powers of barons, ministers, and diplomats. Its friars and nuns were the teachers and social workers. Its faithful, who accepted the Faith with a finality inconceivable in the present age, comprised the overwhelming mass of Poland's population. It is usually said that Piast Poland adopted Christianity. It may be more accurate to say that the Catholic Church adopted Poland.

3 *The Jagiellons, 1385–1572*

Following the death of Casimir the Great, the royal succession passed first to Casimir's nephew, Louis of Hungary, and then to Louis's daughter, Jadwiga of Anjou, who was crowned king *(sic)* in Cracow in 1384. After Jadwiga's marriage to Jagiełło, Grand Duke of Lithuania, and her premature, childless death fourteen years later, it passed to the issue of Jagiełło's later marriages in direct descent. In this way, Poland was ruled in personal union with Lithuania for 187 years. One single political marriage, subject to all the accidents of human frailty, had none the less decided the fate of two nations for centuries to come. Poland's earlier dynastic unions with Bohemia (1293–1306) and with Hungary (1370–85) had been but fleeting episodes. The link with Lithuania was to prove one of the formative experiences of Polish History.

Medieval Lithuania was the last pagan country in Europe, and at the time of the Polish union, one of the most expansive and dynamic. Throughout the fourteenth century, Lithuanian expeditions had been fighting their way south from their ethnic heartland on the River Niemen, overturning the Ruthenian princes, and seizing everything that the Mongols disrupted or broke. Where Casimir the Great had merely nibbled, the sons of Gedymin gorged. Lithuania stretched out from the Baltic to the confines of the Crimea, from the Bug to the Don. It encompassed the entire basin of the Dnieper, including Minsk, Smolensk, Kiev, and Ochakov (Odessa). Its ruling caste consisted of warrior *boyars*, abjectly obedient to the absolute will of their Grand Duke. Its population consisted largely of Ruthenian Slavs, Orthodox Christians. Its economy depended heavily on slave labour, and on seasonal looting. Its official language was *ruski* (a form now known as Old Byelorussian), and its patron was Pierkun, God of the Thunderbolt. By joining with Poland, the Lithuanians opened the door to many changes. Their pagan religion was abolished, the sacred oak groves ritually felled, and the people baptized in legions. Their closed world was thrown open to Western influences, and their *boyars* began to demand the same rights and privileges as the Polish nobility. In due course, all but the lowest levels of society were thoroughly Polonized—both in language and in outlook. The 'Polish connection' in Lithuania came to have the same connotation as the 'British' connection in Scotland. The 'Lithuanian connection' in Poland brought still further enrichment of its rich multinational heritage.

Yet the horizons of the Jagiellonian dynasty were not confined to Poland and Lithuania. Within Jagiełło's own lifetime, the pride of the Teutonic State, whose ambitions prompted the Union in the first place, was severely trimmed. At the Battle of Grunwald in 1410, the victory of the Polish–Lithuanian host marked the beginning of the Teutonic Order's long decline. After that, the Jagiellons took to the European stage with a will. They were twice pressed by the Hussites of Bohemia to accept the crown of St. Wencelas; and two of their number became kings of Hungary. Jagiełło's second son, Kazimierz Jagiellończyk (Casimir IV, 1447–92), was known as the 'Father of Europe'. His children included one saint, one cardinal, four kings, and the matriarchs of three ruling Houses. His grandchildren included the last Grand Master of the Teutonic Order and progenitor of another famous dynasty, Albrecht von Hohenzollern. Sigismund I (1506–48) was married to a Sforza, and saw the Renaissance

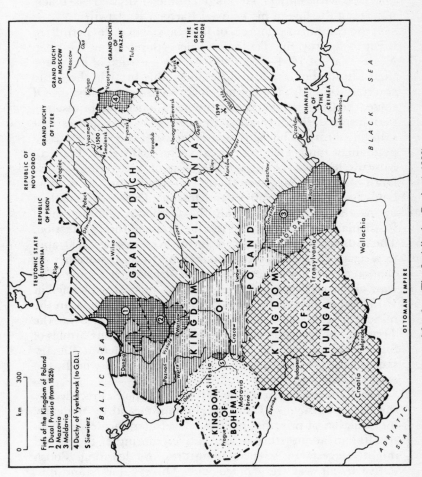

Map 9. The Jagiellonian Realm (c.1500)

bloom. Sigismund-August (1548–72), the last of the male line, was persuaded to marry two Habsburgs in a row, but could not live with either. He died childless, dressed in black, mourning the loss of his beloved Barbara Radziwiłł.

If the combined resources of Jagiełło's twin states permitted them to destroy the Teutonic Order—the decisive 'Thirteen Years' War' of 1454–66 ended with the partition of Prussia—their Lithuanian responsibilities inevitably brought them into confrontation with the Grand Duchy's eastern neighbours. Of these, the Crimean Tartars represented a perennial nuisance, and inspired the formation in the 1490s of Poland's first standing army. The Muscovites, in contrast, represented a permanent and growing threat. The self-styled Tsars of Moscow had set themselves the tasks of 'recovering' all the lands of ancient Rus, even though no significant part of those lands had ever been subject to Moscow. They set themselves up as the 'protectors' of all the Orthodox population of Ruthenia, even when the Orthodox declined such protection. The Muscovite army marched for the West in May 1500, and, in a sense, has never stopped marching since. It sustained its campaigns with savage tenacity for decades at a time. The wars of Ivan III were mainly aimed at Smolensk, which fell in 1513. Those of Ivan IV were directed against Livonia. In the middle of the sixteenth century, the spectacle of Ivan the Terrible, the quintessence of barbarity, battling the armies of Sigismund-August, the ideal of a mild and tolerant Renaissance prince, was truly the scene from a war of worlds, the clash of East and West.

The Renaissance struck deep roots in Poland. Preceded by the strong ferment of Catholic Humanism and by the early introduction of printing, its ideas penetrated far deeper than the Italian architecture or derivative painting of the period might suggest. In science, literature, and learning, Polish native talent was truly precocious. Three names stand out. Nicolas Copernicus (1473–1543), who discovered the earth's motion round the sun, caused the most fundamental revolution possible in prevailing concepts of the human predicament. Jan Kochanowski (1530–84), an exquisite poet in the mould of Petrarch or du Bellay, was the leader if not the founder of the vernacular tradition in Poland, and hence of the senior branch of Slavonic literature. Kochanowski's Psalter did for Polish what Luther's Bible did for German. Jan Zamoyski (1542–1605), chancellor and Hetman, was a student of Roman history and the chief architect of Poland's 'noble democracy' (see p. 333 ff.). All three men were graduates of Cracow and Padua; all three were accomplished classicists and translators; all three were devoted public servants; all three took a serious interest in a wide range of arts and sciences, and in education. All, it is not too much to say, were prime examples of Renaissance Man—*l'uomo universale*. They were the pinnacle of the best educated, and probably the most inspiring generation of Polish History.

The Reformation, too, reached Poland with no mean impact. Lutheran doctrines immediately won over the German burgher element, especially in the cities of Royal Prussia—Danzig, Thorn, Elbing. They also delivered the *coup de grâce* of the Teutonic Order. In 1525, when his knights converted to Lutheranism *en masse,* Grand Master Albrecht von Hohenzollern was obliged to convert the Order's remaining territory of (East) Prussia into a secular fief of the Polish Kingdom. Calvinism, in contrast, which arrived in the 1550s, attracted large numbers of the Polish nobility, including many of the most powerful Lithuanian magnates. By 1572, the Protestants commanded an absolute majority among the lay members of the Senate. A few years earlier, a schism in the Polish Calvinist movement gave rise to the 'Polish Brethren' —otherwise known as Arians, Anti-trinitarians, Racovians, and Socinians—who were destined to exercise a profound influence on radical theology throughout Europe in the following century. If the Calvinists' 'Brest Bible' of 1563 marked a milestone in popular vernacular publications, the Racovian Catechism of 1601 was perhaps the most progressive theological tract of the age. In addition, Poland offered a haven for numerous refugee sects—including the Hussite 'Czech Brethren' from Bohemia, Anabaptists and Menonites from the Netherlands, German Schwenkfeldians from Silesia. A country which had long since grown accustomed to the peaceful coexistence of Catholicism, Orthodoxy, Armenians, Judaism, and Muhammadanism, was unique in Europe. Poland alone, in a continent torn by Wars of Religion, could

have produced the epoch-making Statute of General Toleration promulgated by the Confederation of Warsaw in 1573.
Isolated acts of fantaticism could still occur; but no general
campaign of persecution was possible. Poland truly deserved
its name as 'a land without stakes'. Protestant writers such as
Mikołaj Rej (1505–69), Cyprian Bazylik (1535–92), Stanisław Sarnicki (1532–97), or Andrzej Wolan (1530–1610)
polemicized with the main Catholic stream. The Reformation
complemented the Renaissance to form Poland's *Złoty Wiek*
(The Golden Age).

4 The Noble Republic, 1569–1795

Like the Piasts before them, the Jagiellons were cut down in
their prime for want of an heir. Foreseeing the predicament,
Sigismund-August spent his declining powers in transforming
the fragile personal union of Poland and Lithuania into a
permanent constitutional union. At the Treaty of Lublin
(1569), the assembled Polish nobles and Lithuanian princes
called into being a united, but dual state, in which the *Korona*
(Kingdom) and the Grand Duchy were to keep their separate
laws and administrations, but were to be jointly governed by
an elected King and a common *Sejm* (Diet). They called the
new creation their *Respublica* or *Rzeczpospolita,* the united
Republic of Poland–Lithuania. At the request of the nobility
of the Ukraine, fearful that the Lithuanian princes might
reject the Union, the southern provinces of the Grand Duchy,
including Volhynia, Kiev, and the Cossach *Sicz*, were incorporated into the Kingdom. At the insistence of Zamoyski, who
steered the detailed negotiations which followed the death of
Sigismund-August in 1572, the kings were henceforth to be
elected *viritim,* that is, directly, by the mounted assembly of
the entire nobility. What is more, they were not to be crowned
until they had sworn to uphold a lengthy covenant, whose
articles guaranteed the principle of toleration, the practice of
free royal elections, the regular convocation of the Sejm, the
surveillance of royal policy by sixteen resident senators, the
nobility's personal privileges, the nobility's right to approve
taxes, declarations of war, and foreign treaties, and finally, the
nobility's Right of Resistance. For its day, on the eve of the

Age of Absolutism elsewhere in Europe, this was an extreme form of democracy. The noble citizens of the Republic were to be its masters; the king was to be their servant. The King of Poland, in fact, was less of a limited monarch, like the kings of England or Sweden, and more of a manager under contract.

The supremacy of the *Szlachta* (the Nobility), which had been maturing throughout the Jagiellonian period, was evident no less in the social than in the political sphere. It could be traced back to the Statute of Košice of 1374; to the famous statute of *Neminem captivabimus* of 1434 (the Polish equivalent of Habeas corpus); and to the decisive parliamentary statute of *Nihil novi* of 1505. In their slogan of *Nic o nas bez nas* (Nothing concerning us can be settled without us), the Polish nobles of the sixteenth century had anticipated the ideals of the Glorious Revolution of 1688 in England, and of the American Revolution of 1776; and in their saying that '*Polska nierządem stoi*' (Poland stands by the lack of government) they gave a foretaste of Henri Thoreau, Proudhon, and Bellegarrigue. They were extreme devotees of individual freedom and civil liberty—for themselves. Like the slave-owning Fathers of the American Constitution, or the original inventors of democracy in ancient Athens, they saw no contradiction between a political system based on the liberties of the ruling estate and a social system based on the complete subjugation of the lower orders.

The rise of the nobles' legal privileges in Poland coincided almost exactly with the rise of serfdom. The *Szlachta* always insisted on the legal equality of everyone in their own order, irrespective of wealth or power. They made no distinction between the great magnates, the middle stratum of landed nobility, or the growing mass of the landless and impoverished 'noble rabble'. At the same time, they insisted on the exclusive nature of their privileges, holding the absolute right of life and death over the serfs tied to their land. The clergy, the city burghers, and the Jews, whose separate legal positions were protected by royal charters, formed separate social estates enjoying a wide measure of autonomy, and largely exempt from direct noble control; but these formed only a small part of the population as a whole; and, with the exception of the noble Bishops in the Senate, played little part in the

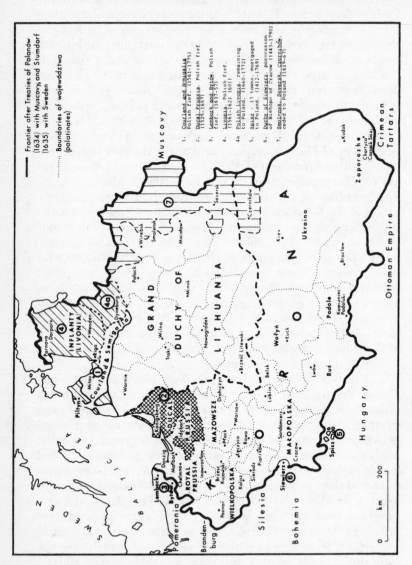

Map 10.   Poland–Lithuania at its Greatest Extent (1634–5)

institutions of the Republic's central government. By comparison with other European states, where the nobility formed only 1 or 2 per cent of society, the Polish *szlachta,* at 8–12 per cent, was extremely numerous, and formed by far the largest franchised class in Europe. Yet the contradiction between its libertarian politics and its conservative social traditions was due to cause serious tensions, especially with the passage of time.

Over the 223 years from its inauguration to its destruction, the Republic was ruled by eleven elected kings, each reigning for an average of some twenty years. Of the eleven, no less than seven were foreigners—Henry Valois (1574); Stefan Batory (1576–86); Zygmunt III Vasa (1587–1632); and his two sons Władysław IV (1632–48); and John Casimir (1648–68); August II (1697–1706, 1710–33); and August III (1733–63). These included one Frenchman, one Hungarian from Transylvania, three from the Swedish House of Vasa, and two from the Saxon House of Wettin. Only four of the eleven—in Michał Wiśniowiecki (1668–72), John Sobieski (1674–96), Stanisław Leszczyński (1704–10, 1733), and Stanisław-August Poniatowski (1764–95)—were native Poles. Taken as a whole, they present a random selection of talent, mediocrity, and nonentity. In the nature of things, as elected individuals, they could never inherit much of a corporate tradition, and they stood or fell according to the exigencies of their day and their personal qualities. They included one homosexual, one religious enthusiast, one glutton, one father of over 300 children, and one confirmed bachelor (also a father); two of them were distinguished soldiers, two of them fled the country (one did so twice), and two of them were forced to abdicate; none was assassinated. By general assent, the foreigners could claim both the most successful among them—Stephen Bathory; and the most ineffective—August III; the natives includes both the most famous—Sobieski; and the most maligned—Stanisław-August. As was the case with the Kings and Queens cf England over the same period, they did not invite any general conclusions.

In many spheres, however, it is not difficult to conclude that Polish life witnessed severe and prolonged deterioration. After two centuries of tribulations, the general condition of Poland's economic, social, religious, literary, constitutional, military, and foreign affairs was weaker towards the end of the eighteenth century than it had been during the Republic's early years at the end of the sixteenth.

The Polish economy, whose prosperity had been built on the Baltic Grain Trade and on the growth of towns and internal commerce, began to show signs of regression as early as the 1620s, and was shattered by the two decades of war in the 1650s and 1660s. Thereafter, the Baltic Trade dwindled; the cities withered; and the impositions of the manorial system were relentlessly increased in a vain attempt to offset the vicious spiral of decline. Judged by the usual indices of productivity, trade turnover, diet, clothing, or housing, the standard of living of the average inhabitant of the Republic was much lower in 1750 than in 1550.

Polish society saw the gradual ossification of the rigid system of estates. Social mobility between the peasantry, the burghers, and the nobles virtually ceased. If the earlier period was marked by the rise of the *Szlachta* within a society as a whole, the later period was marked by the rise within the ruling *Szlachta* of an all-powerful oligarchy of magnates. By the mid-eighteenth century, a handful of magnatial families —the Radziwiłł, Potocki, Branicki, Czartoryski, Zamoyski, Lubomirski, and Sapieha broods among them—had cornered most of the hereditary offices of state and had accumulated landed fortunes larger than that of the Crown itself. They ran the provincial noble dietines as English aristocrats ran their rotten boroughs. They treated the lesser nobles as clients, and by patronizing the Jews as agents and allies, they undermined the rights of the cities. Their private 'states-within-the-state', populated in some cases by hundreds of thousands of serfs, exceeded the dimensions of many a German principality or of an English county, sustaining self-sufficient economies and private armies. They pursued a life-style of luxury amidst the prevailing penury, and their suspect loyalty to the Republic was an obvious target of foreign intrigue.

Religious conflict was not avoided, despite the continuing validity of the Statute of Toleration. The Counter-Reformation, launched in Poland in 1565 with the introduction of the Jesuits, succeeded in reconverting large numbers of Protestants, especially among the Calvinist nobility. Its leading figures, like Piotr Skarga (1536–1612), Zygmunt III's confessor, openly preached against the sin of tolerance. The creation of the Uniate Church,* at the Union of Brest in 1596, created a lasting schism in the Orthodox community and the disaffection of many powerful groups such as the Dnieper Cossacks. The restoration of the Orthodox hierarchy in 1632 did little to heal the rift, and the disaffected Orthodox fell increasingly under the spell of the Moscow Patriarch. Step by step the Catholic supremacy in Poland was being reconstructed. The Polish Brethren and the Czech Brethren were banished in 1658 on the grounds of alleged treason; and the last Calvinist delegate was expelled from the Diet in 1718, The Lutherans of the North held firm, but the notorious 'Bloodbath of Thorn' of 1724 showed that deep animosities still swirled beneath the surface. A concerted effort by the Prussians and Russians to inflame the issue of the religious 'dissidents' in Poland only served to entrench the Catholics' demands for conformity. Polish Catholicism assumed an air of intense fervour, and the Marian Cult flourished. The Jews of the Republic continued to multiply, but two exceptional massacres at the hands of Cossack rebels—one in 1648, and the other in 1769, did little to increase their hopes of security. The appearance in the eighteenth century of Jewish sectarianism, notably of the Frankists and the Chassidim, increased antagonisms still further. The religious communities of Poland–Lithuania were not embattled against each other to the extent that prevailed, say, in Ireland, or in France prior to 1685; but they did not find much common cause.

Polish literature in the aftermath of the Golden Age passed through two distinct phases—the earlier phase given the misleading title of Baroque (since it had only limited connections with the Baroque style of western Europe), and the later one called 'Sarmatism'. The Polish Baroque, which encompassed the seventeenth century, had lost the spontaneous gaiety and lyricism of the Renaissance. In part it abandoned the vernacular, and it took to devotional writing, to epic history, to social criticism, and to satire. Skarga's

---

*The Greek Catholic Confession of Slavonic Rite in union with Rome.

Żywoty Świętych (Lives of the Saints) was the best seller of the century. Piotr Kochanowski (1566–1620), son of Jan, and translator of Tasso, maintained his father's Italian interests, whilst the Latin verse of Szymon Starowolski (Starovolscius, 1588–1656), and particularly of Maciej Sarbiewski (Sarbievius, 1595–1640), was read far beyond Poland. Samuel Twardowski (1600–60) or Wespazjan Kochowski (1633–1700) both versifiers and chroniclers, could only have local appeal. The Arian, Wacław Potocki (1621–96), author of the celebrated *Wojna chocimska* (The War of Chocim) shared a bitter sense of irony with the two Opaliński brothers, Krzysztof (1610–56) and Łukasz (1612–84). Baroque architecture, the outward sign of the triumph of the Counter-Reformation, made a lasting mark.

Polish Sarmatism, the characteristic style of the Saxon era, wallowed sentimentally in the Republic's alleged glories and achievements, and is generally thought to have little literary or artistic merit. Allied to the fashion for oriental dress and decoration, it reinforced the conservative tendencies of the *Szlachta* and the belief in the superiority of their 'Golden Freedom' and their noble culture.

Polish constitutional theory made little progress after 1573, and the stresses of putting the theory into practice resulted first in repeated chaos, and eventually in total paralysis. The Right of Resistance and the Principle of Unanimity were both explicit in the Law and customary procedures of the *Szlachta;* but both led in time to deformations and excesses. The Zebrzydowski Rebellion of 1606–9, the first general confederation of the nobility against the king, did not lead to any resolution of the deep issues involved. No one could question the *Szlachta*'s right to oppose a tyrannical king. At the same time, no one knew how to stop the right being invoked for trivial purposes. Further chaos returned during Lubomirski's Rebellion of 1664–7, and by the end of the century political factions were turning to armed confederation as a matter of first resort. The principle of unanimity suffered a similar fate. Originally conceived as a means of assisting debate and of assuring general consent, it was perverted in due course by individuals seeking private advantage. In 1652, the first appeal to the *liberum veto*—the right of any one man to reject the legislation of the Diet—was the work of a client of Prince Radziwiłł, and caused amazement when ruled legal; but it soon led to the realization that anyone could terminate the sessions of the Diet at will. In the reign of August III, only one session of the Diet succeeded in passing any legislation at all, in a span of thirty years.

Constitutional paralysis paved the way for financial ruin, for military impotence, and for foreign invasion. If taxes could not be raised, the Republic's armies could not be maintained, and the Republic's enemies could do as they pleased.

None the less, Polish military prowess held its own for most of the seventeenth century. Reformed by Bathory and reconstructed by Władysław IV, the Republic's armies were the equal of their contemporaries at least until the Great Northern War. Bathory's victorious campaign in Russia (1579–82); Żółkiewski's advance to Moscow (1610–12); Koniecpolski's spirited defence of Prussia against Gustavus Adolphus (1626–9); Czarnecki's remarkable recovery against Charles X (1656–60); Sobieski's defeat of the Turks at Chocim (1673); and above all, the stupendous charge of Sobieski's winged Hussars at the Siege of Vienna (1683); all attest to the valour and technical competence of Polish arms. Thereafter, the military establishment collapsed. In the Great Northern War (1700–21) a divided Republic was no match for Charles XII or Peter the Great. The Russian-sponsored Silent Sejm of 1717, which limited the Republic's forces to a meagre 24,000, left it virtually defenceless. Polish armies played no significant part in the War of the Polish Succession (1733–5), the War of the Austrian Succession (1740–8), or the Seven Years' War (1756–63), most of whose eastern operations were disputed on Polish territory.

Poland's foreign relations followed surely in the path of her military decline. The struggle to check the Hohenzollerns' relentless drive for independence in Brandenburg–Prussia was abandoned in 1657 at the Treaty of Wehlau. The interminable duel with Sweden, which began with the Livonian Wars and was compounded by the Polish Vasas' dynastic claim, came to an end in 1660 in stalemate, at the Treaty of Oliwa. The still longer feud with Muscovy reached a similar state of apparent deadlock and mutual exhaustion at the Truce of

Andrusovo in 1667. At this very point, when the Republic seemed to have reached a *modus vivendi* with each of her traditional opponents of the previous century, she was attacked for the first time in nearly fifty years by the Turks. And the Turkish challenge was to have momentous consequences. For Sobieski's strategic decision to concentrate all his resources on the Turkish threat, at the cost of all of the Republic's other foreign concerns, was a certain invitation for later disasters. Sobieski may have scattered the Turks, and recovered the province of Podolia, which was returned to Poland by the Treaty of Karlowitz (1699); but in so doing, he saved Vienna, and exhausted his troops in the Austrians' recovery of Hungary. He surrendered his original intention of bringing the Prussians to heel; and he was forced to leave the Muscovites in their possession of Ukraine (1686). The costs far outweighed the gains. The Habsburg realm, in control of Hungary, was revived as a great power. The Prussians proceeded to gain international recognition for their independent kingdom (1701); and the Muscovites, in possession of Ukraine, were set to build the Russian Empire. These three powers, Austria, Prussia, and Russia, were destined to dominate eastern Europe in the following century, and, irony of ironies, to partition the Republic between them. Sobieski, in fact, was the last of Poland's sovereign statesmen. Sobieski's successor, August of Saxony, was a mere suppliant of Peter the Great, to whom he owed his throne on more than one occasion. The Russian Protectorate in Poland, installed after the Battle of Poltava, was never relaxed thereafter, and independent Polish diplomacy virtually ceased.

In this long and pathetic saga of failure and decline, many historians have seen the unhappy reign of John Casimir Vasa (1648–68) as the critical point of no return. Certainly, the concentration of so many catastrophies in those two turbulent decades weakened the Republic immensely. The Cossack Rebellion (1648–57) of Bohdan Chmielnicki was the first step in Poland's loss of the Ukraine. The depredations of six invading hordes—Cossacks, Swedes, Muscovites, Transylvanians, Tartars, and Brandenburgers—caused destruction of life and property comparable to that of the Thirty Years' War in Germany. One-quarter of the population was lost; the economy broken almost beyond recovery. The confusion and civil strife of Lubomirski's Rebellion merely completed the mood of apathy and despair. The year 1667—in which Lubomirski defeated the royal army, when the king decided to abdicate, and the Truce of Andrusovo left the Ukraine in Muscovite hands—is often seen as the moment when the scales of power in eastern Europe tipped irrevocably away from Poland's favour. Yet categorical judgements of this sort are easy to make with hindsight. If Poland's decline was set in motion in the mid-seventeenth century, one must not conclude that eventual destruction was inevitable. All was not yet lost. Poland's powers of regeneration had been shown to be remarkable. Her potential resources, once mobilized, were still considerable. Even in the Saxon Era, when the cultural and economic decadence of the country was at its lowest ebb, and when the magnates held the central government in virtual abeyance, there were clear signs that the Polish reformers posessed the means and the will for their country's reinvigoration. The chances of survival had obviously been reduced by the accummulation of past misfortunes; but the Republic's fate was not yet decided.

The central issue of Polish History in the eighteenth century, therefore, is less concerned with the incontestable facts of the Republic's decline than with the reasons for its failure to recover. In recent years, historians have tended once again to emphasize the internal factors, and point to the economic débâcle, to the oppressions of the magnatial oligarchy, and to the incompetence of the monarchs. Certainly, Sobieski bears a heavy responsibility for the neglect of urgent problems. During his reign, the *liberum veto* began to be used at regular intervals, unpaid soldiery mutinied with impunity, and the magnates of Lithuania, embroiled in a private civil war, virtually seceded from the life of the Republic. Sobieski scourged the Turks; but he could not control his own subjects. August II, too, was hamstrung by the turbulence of the Great Northern War, and by his dependence on Russian patronage. Under the Wettins, the politics of Warsaw took second place to Dresden; just as Dresden's policies were decided by those of St. Petersburg. In this context, Poland's internal stagnation can hardly be divorced

from the Republic's subordination to foreign interests. Poland–Lithuania did not recover, because it was not the
concern of her political masters to allow her to do so. The
troubles of the Great Northern War marked the true
beginning of Poland's modern history, when the country's
sovereignty was irretrievably lost. The Silent Sejm of 1717
marks the point when Peter the Great guaranteed the existing
constitution, and imposed a protectorate over Polish life
which could effectively obstruct all movement towards
Reform and independence. Henceforth, at critical moments,
the Russians strengthened their grip. In 1733, they drove out
the legally elected King, Stanisław Leszczyński, for the second
time, and restored the rule of their passive, docile Saxon
clients in the person of August III. Under the Russian
protectorate the need for radical Reform became ever more
pressing; but the chances of achieving it became ever more
remote.

5 The Partitions of Poland—the Reign of Stanisław-August, 1764–95

Textbooks of European History generally present the last part
of the eighteenth century as 'the Age of Enlightened
Despotism'. The absolute monarchs of the leading East
European states—particularly Catherine, Empress of Russia,
Frederick, King of Prussia, and Joseph II, Emperor of
Austria—cultivated a special relationship of mutual admiria-
tion with Voltaire and other leading *philosophes* of the French
Enlightenment. Yet sceptical spirits may find some difficulty
in understanding how any statesman or philosopher could
contrive to be both 'enlightened' and 'despotic' at one and the
same time. (One might venture the opinion that 'Enlightened
Despotism' is an involuntary oxymoron.) Certainly one's
doubts must be increased by an examination of Polish History
during this period, for in Poland, the interests of Reform and
of the Enlightenment were diametrically opposed to those of
the despots of St. Petersburg, Berlin, and Vienna.

The Polish Enlightenment had a direct link with France in
the person of Stanisław Leszczyński (1677–1766), sometime

king of Poland, father-in-law of Louis XV, and for the last thirty years of his life, Duke of Lorraine. From his brilliant court at Lunéville, he promoted the cause of Reform in Poland in the pit of Saxon decadence, and in 1749 published *Głos wolny wolność ubezpieczający* (A Free Voice insuring Freedom), the most influential tract of the age. In succeeding years, Leszczyński inspired numerous disciples and admirers, among them Stanisław Konarski (1700–73) the educationist, and the last Polish king, Stanisław-August, who carefully nurtured the ideals of science, constitutional government, secular education, and economic improvement. Stanisław-August's swift election in 1764 was supposed to serve the interests of the Russian Empress, his former lover. Instead, to the Empress's growing alarm, it served the cause of Reform. The king gave practical encouragement to radical thinkers, many of whom attended his 'enlightened' Thursday luncheons. Franciszek Bohomolec (1720–84), an ex-Jesuit, was editor of *Monitor,* a weekly journal crammed with the new French ideas. Bishop Ignacy Krasicki (1735–1801), the King's chaplain and a satirical poet, was also an associate of Frederick the Great. Bishop Adam Naruszewicz (1733–96), the king's historian, devoted himself to preparing the first national history. Hugo Kołłątaj (1750–1812), Rector of the Jagiellonian University, was a prime mover in the campaign for constitutional change. Stanisław Staszic (1755–1826) another lapsed priest, scientist, and philosopher, carried their ideals beyond the Partitions. (See p. 192.) Julian Ursyn Niemcewicz (1757–1841), dramatist and novelist, survived them all and lived to participate in the Romantic Age. In outline, the task before them was stark but simple: to catch up on a century of stagnation and lay the foundations of a modern state. Yet the obstacles were enormous. Arrayed against them were all the forces of inertia—the fanatical conservatism of an ignorant *szlachta;* the factional concerns of the magnates; the conservative hierarchy of the Church; the military commanders of the Republic; and behind them, the armies and diplomacy of the Republic's despotic neighbours. If Stanisław-August, despite his links with the Empress Catherine, was the leader of Reform in Poland: the Empress, despite her links with the

Enlightenment, was the paymistress of Poland's conservative establishment.

Catherine's hope was clearly to keep the Republic in its place of the last fifty years—as an impoverished and enfeebled client on Russia's western border, a convenient and inexpensive buffer against the European powers. To this end, the court of St. Petersburg took the precaution of buying the obedience of the Republic's highest officers. The Hetmans,* the Primate, the Marshal of the Diet, were all Russian pensioners. It also took care to trumpet its support for the privileges of the *szlachta* and the principles of the noble democracy including the *liberum Veto*. This support rang hollow in the mouth of Europe's most extreme Autocracy; but it suited its purpose of keeping Poland weak and divided. The Russians possessed both the political means to minimize the chances of Reform in Poland, and the military means, if the frustrated reformers turned to resistance, to defeat them by force. At first sight, therefore, it looked as if they could preserve their Polish protectorate in perpetuity. The trouble was that, by obstructing even moderate reform, they repeatedly drove the reformers into rebellion; whilst, by sending their armies into Poland to crush the rebellions, they threatened to upset the whole balance of power in eastern Europe. Hence, to have a free hand in Poland, they were obliged to calm the fears of the Prussians and Austrians by agreeing to territorial compensations. Essentially, the three Partitions of Poland in 1773, 1793, and 1795 were not planned in advance. They were made necessary by the Russians' compulsive desire to crush Reform at all costs, and they were sops to obtain the acquiescence of Berlin and Vienna. In the end, of course, the Empress Catherine found that she had no protectorate to protect. Her policy was not so successful after all.

In the first round, in 1764–73, the pattern began with the King's attempt to implement a programme of reform at the first Diet of the reign. The abolition of the *Liberum Veto* was thwarted by the threat of its use. The attempt to install an

---

*Military Commanders—one for the Army of the Kingdom, the other for the Grand Duchy, each with his own deputy or *hetman polny*.

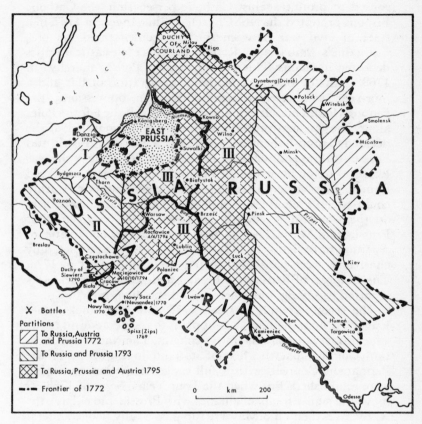

Map 11.　The Partitions of Poland (1773–95)

excise system, as the basis of state finance, was thwarted by the
Prussians' retaliatory bombardment of the new Polish custom
posts on the Vistula. When the religious dissidents were
roused to protest against Catholic persecution, the Catholic
Bishops protested that the Church was in danger. In 1767, in a
state of civil war between the two confederated factions,
Catherine's Ambassador Repnin had his ecclesiastical critics
deported in chains. This was the nadir of Polish 'anarchy'. In
1768, with the outbreak of the Confederation of Bar and a
four-year war directed against Russian oppressions, the
Empress found herself in a pretty dilemma. If she left the Poles
alone, the Russian protectorate would be dismantled; if she
decided to punish them, she would risk a war with Austria and
Prussia. In the end, in order to crush the Reformers, she was
forced to resign herself to the Prussian plan of Partition. Freed
from its involvement on the Turkish front, Catherine's army
could sweep Poland clean, and annex a few Polish provinces
on the way. But Frederick the Great must be given West
Prussia, and Maria Theresa must have Galicia. The treaties of
partition were signed in 1772. The Polish King and Diet, duly
chastened, were persuaded to put them into effect in 1773.
The Empress of Russia had breakfasted, Edmund Burke was
reported as saying, but where would she dine?

The second round, between 1773 and 1793, took rather
longer. At first, the King was at pains to restrict reforms to the
educational and administrative spheres. The National Education Commission, the first of its kind in Europe, and the
Permanent Council, with a full range of civilian ministries,
were established. But when the Four Years' Sejm of 1788–92
moved to sign a treaty of alliance with Prussia and enlarge the
Army, and then on 3 May 1791 to pass a fully fledged liberal
Constitution, the limit of Russian patience was passed. The
Empress told her Polish Hetmans to form the Confederation
of Targowica and with Russian help to overthrow the
Constitution. She bought off the Prussians with the promise of
Danzig, and took Byelorussia and Volhynia for herself. On
this occasion the hesitant Austrians received nothing. Suvo-
rov's Russian Army, despite a threefold superiority over the
Republic half-trained recruits, took over a year to suppress a
spirited defence organized by Kościuszko and Poniatowski.

Finally, a desperate king changed sides and called for surrender. In 1793 at Grodno, in the last session of its history, and abjectly cowed by Russian guns, the Sejm was called on to annul the Constitution, and to acclaim the Second Partition.

The third and final round was short and intense. Despairing of peaceful Reform, Tadeusz Kościuszko launched the National Rising of 1794 to right Poland's ills. General Suvorov arrived shortly afterwards to put the Rising down. Kościuszko read the 'Act of Insurrection' in Cracow's city square. Warsaw hanged its spies and collaborators. In one glorious battle, at Racławice, the national forces, aided by peasant scythe-men, were triumphant. But the issue was not long delayed. Suvorov stormed Praga, the eastern suburbs of Warsaw, and put its inhabitants to the sword. The capital surrendered. The King was deported, and told to abdicate. The rump of the Republic was divided into three. Warsaw fell to the Prussians; Cracow and Lublin to the Austrians; and Wilno to the Russians. The Partitions were complete. The Republic of Poland-Lithuania had ceased to exist. Poland of the Enlightenment had been killed by Despotism.

Writing some thirty years after the destruction of the old Republic, Adam Mickiewicz evoked the primeval forests of his native Lithuania and 'the giant oaks of centuries' which weaken and split and eventually crash to the ground that fed them. Old Poland was such an ancient oak—weakened and split. But it did not topple of its own accord. It was felled by the axe.

The Life and Death of Old Poland

History, which is the study of mankind in Time, is often said to teach us nothing. It is certainly a poor guide for snap predictions. Pundits and journalists who wish to know what will happen in the next six months need not bother. Yet time brings change, and change brings the prospect of growth or decay. Everything in the human condition, as in the physical world, is in motion and flux, nothing stands still for long; at any given moment, any given human being or institution is either on the path to its prime or on the road to ruin. For the one thing that History does teach is that all power is transient, all success emphemeral. All states and kingdoms, like all men and women, are mortal. Though some may hope for an exception to the rule, all will pass away. The captains and commissars, who imagine themselves and their systems to be eternal, will sooner or later depart. Their pomp will surely be one with the dust of Nineveh and Tyre. If the final Apocalypse of world civilization has not by then occurred, in the form of Nuclear War, today's proud empires will be replaced in the fullness of time by the next generation of polities and philosophies.

This spectacle of the life and death of empires is the central theme of all political history, and has attracted the attention of the greatest historians. Edward Gibbon, composing his final paragraphs amidst the ruins of the Coliseum, after a lifetime spent in the writing of the *Decline and Fall*, presents a scene almost as moving as the last years of the Roman Empire itself. As Ferdinand Lot wrote in the same connection, 'the tragedy of a world which did not wish to die presents a spectacle as entrancing as anything which the historian or sociologist is ever likely to see'. In this context, the death of old Poland in 1795, after eight hundred years of life, is one of the most poignant moments of Europe's past. Like the death of an aged person, ripe in years and achievement, it is as inspiring in its memories, as it is pathetic in its reality. It prompts the same sort of reflections as those other great moments of irrecoverable change—the fall of Constantinople in 1453; the death of the last Inca in 1531; the collapse of the *Ancien Régime* in France in 1789; the arrival of Commodore Perry's 'black ships' in Japan in 1853; the removal of the Romanovs in the February Revolution of 1917; the departure of the last British Viceroy from Delhi in 1947. . . .

From Vico to Arnold Toynbee, historical theorists have grappled with these cycles of events; and it is not the case that today the theme is entirely ignored. Karl Marx, the single most influential historian of modern times, based his philosophy of historical materialism on the concept of a spiral of change, and Marxists are eager to point out the fascinating parallels between the constant motion of physical matter, in dead atoms and living cells alike, and the constant motion of human affairs. Yet for reasons both of convenience and of theory, many contemporary commentators seem to have lost the balance and the wisdom of the earlier masters. Some of them, like the political scientists with their static models and 'systems analysis', seem to have lost the sense of Time altogether; whilst others, transfixed by the political priorities of the day, are servile worshippers at the shrine of endless advancement and success. No doubt the Marxists, with their cult of technological progress and their belief in economic motivation and quantitative improvement, have made an important contribution to the present state of affairs; but the real culprits are the political propagandists, the penmen of every regime of every hue and bias, who are paid to suggest that their masters' regimes are immortal. Just as the history textbooks of our grandfathers' era were filled with chapters on 'The *Rise* of Prussia' or 'the *Growth* of the British Empire', so today the school-books of our own generation are filled with the 'Making of America' or, in the Soviet Bloc, with 'the Building of Communism'. No publisher in Berlin or London in 1883 would have offered a large advance for a popular book on 'The decline of Germany' or the decay of Great Britain (Oswald Spengler had to wait until 1920); just as no enterprising historian is going to get a commission from Washington on 'the Unmaking of America' or from the Ministry of Education in Moscow on 'The Dismantlement of the USSR'. Success, and the history of success, is good political business; failure, and the history of failures, is not. Individual authors in the West may be free to risk their hand at pessimistic ventures if they so wish; but they are unlikely to receive official encouragement, and in the Soviet Union they are forcibly repressed. André Amalrik, a qualified historian, who dared to write an essay entitled *Will the USSR survive till 1984?* was rewarded with six years in a labour camp. Indeed, there is every likelihood that the present troubles of the Soviet Union will push the Censors into reducing the coverage of the Russian Revolution, lest young people get ideas—just as in Poland in the era of SOLIDARITY the official censors discouraged popular histories of the Polish communist move-ment with its record of plotting, agitation, and strikes. Every regime in the world wants to foster a mood of progress and

optimism—hence in large measure the attraction of Marxism.
But surely, for a rounded view of Man's predicament, one
needs to match the success with the failures, the triumphs with
the disasters, the rises with the falls. In modern European
History, the Decline of Spain and Austria merits the same
space as the unification of Germany and Italy; and the
Partitions of Poland require the same emphasis as the
'Expansion of Russia'.

In Poland itself—a country where power and prosperity
have long since disappeared—no such admonitions are
necessary. Polish historians have been consumed by the story
of the Partitions. The collapse of old Poland, with its causes
and conclusions, has been the reigning obsession of Polish
historiography right to the present day. The Romantic
School, headed by Lelewel in the 1830s, argued that the old
Republic had been destroyed by external agents and believed
that its inner, spiritual resources would enable it to revive.
The Cracow School in Galicia—led by the Stańczyk Group in
the 1860s—argued that it had been destroyed largely by its
own failings, and implied that it could never resurrect. The
Warsaw School of Positivists, led by Korzon and Smoleński
after 1864, turned to the analysis of social and economic
questions, in the belief that the clues to the problems of the
past, like those of the present, could best be found in the
material sphere. The Diplomatic School, led by Askenazy and
Handelsman, revived the question of external relations,
hinting, by their concentration on the consequences of the
Partitions during the Napoleonic Period, that the crucial
element in Polish affairs lay in her choice of allies. All these
classical schools of Polish historiography were strongly
grounded in an awareness of the links of the Past with the
Present, and all have had their devoted continuators. Over the
years, the 'Pessimists' (in the Cracovian sense) and the
'Optimists' (in the Varsovian tradition) have fought the issue
to a close draw. The prophets of Doom, and the merchants of
Hope, are nicely matched.

In recent years, the official Communist School of Polish
historiography has met with great obstacles in its efforts to
reach a new and final synthesis. As Marxist-Leninists, they
adopted an interpretation based on socio-economic analysis

—and as such developed the work of the traditional Positivists. As neo-Nationalists (see p. 326) they also needed to stress the grievances and oppressions of the Polish people, and as such took a leaf from the traditional Romantics. Indeed, their mix of Varsovian positivism with a streak of Romantic messianism must be regarded as something of a theoretical *tour de force*, since it met their own recipe for obligatory Optimism whilst blending important elements of the national tradition. Unfortunately, in practice, and on the one key issue of Polish History, it has proved itself less than adequate. No amount of socio-economic analysis can explain why the old Republic could not have been reformed and modernized, instead of being devoured by its neighbours. Nor can it explain, after the separate socio-economic base had been destroyed by the Partitions, why Poland continued to exist as a spiritual and cultural community. Present-day Polish historians are no nearer a final consensus than their predecessors. They still have the corpse of old Poland in their theoretical mortuary; but no amount of internal dissection has convincingly determined the cause of death.[3]

The fate of Poland, in fact, prompts reflections on the deepest aspects of history and human mortality. In weighing the arguments over the internal and the external causes of the Partitions, over the relative impact of political, material, and cultural factors, the historian is drawn ever deeper into enquiries about the essential attributes of human society, indeed of human nature. If Poland were indeed destroyed, how then could it later be revived? If Poland did resurrect, then surely something must have survived its physical destruction. In short, when the Body Politick dies, what is it exactly, if anything, that remains? To these questions, as old as Plato, the Marxists have no clear answer. The Catholics will argue by analogy from the fate of an individual sinner, and will talk of the nation's 'soul'. The Romantics talk of Poland's 'Spirit'. All serious men must wonder. At all events, the puzzle is more convincing than the official legend of the Long March of the Polish nation on the road to the People's Republic. When active, in the lengthy span of its lifetime, old Poland played a prominent part in the pageant of Europe's historic nations. When destroyed, as the Dead Man of Europe, it still had a part to play. Evidently, there is life after Partition.

Lasting Traditions

Most of the institutions of the old Republic died with it. The Polish Monarchy, the Royal Court, royal elections, the Crown estates and monopolies; the *Korona* and the Grand Duchy, and their frontiers; the Diet, Senate, and Chamber of Envoys, and the provincial dietines; the Constitution, *Pacta Conventa*, the Law, tribunals, and law courts; the Polish administration, offices of state, and regional officials; the armies of the Republic and the Hetmans; the Polish diplomatic service, such as it was; the National Education Commission; the old Polish currency; the separate status of the Nobility and the Jews; the Republic's coat of arms, with the crowned white eagle of Poland and the horseman of Lithuania—all these, and more besides, were banished once and for all. A few institutions—the Primacy of the Polish Church and the united Polish See; the city charters; the Polish schools and universities, if not the educational system; the system of weights and measures—were left alone in 1795, only to be remodelled or abolished at a later date. Everything, in the palaces of the magnates as in the cottages of the serfs, was subjected to profound change. Yet the inhabitants of the former Republic survived its fall, and with them many of the more intangible elements of old Polish life—their culture, languages, religions, social and political attitudes. These survivals formed the living bridge between Poland's ancient Past and her uncertain Future.

1 The Multicultural Heritage

To the objective observer, the most outstanding feature of pre-Partition society in Poland-Lithuania was its multicultural character. Within the confines of the old Republic, there flourished a profusion of peoples, a riot of religions, a luxuriance of languages. Polish noblemen and Slavonic peasants mingled with German burghers and with Jewish or Armenian merchants. People prided themselves in their descent, real or imagined, from Sarmatians or Chazars, or from Dutch, Swedish, Italian, or Scots immigrants. The Roman Catholic majority was surrounded by a colourful array of sects and faiths—by Calvinists, Lutherans, Arians, Unitarians; Orthodox, Uniates, and Old Believers; by orthodox Jews, Karaim, Chassidim, and Frankists; by Armenian monophysites and by Tartar Muslims. The official languages of Polish and Latin in the kingdom were matched by *ruski* and Polish in the Grand Duchy. Vernacular speech was conducted in anything from the four main regional dialects of Polish, plus Kashub and *góralski,* (the highland brogue) to Ruthenian in its northern (Byelorussian) or southern (Ukranian) forms; Lithuanian, Latvian, and (to 1600) Prussian; *platdeutsch* in the northern cities, Yiddish, Tartar, or Armenian. The royal court was Italianate under Bona Sforza and Sigismund-August; Francophone under Henry Valois, Latinophone under Bathóry, and Germanophone under the Vasas and the Wettins. The liturgical languages in use included Church Latin, Old Church Slavonic, High (Lutheran) German, Hebrew, and Arabic. Documents were written in a variety of alphabets including the Roman, Cyrillic, Hebrew, and Arabic. Even the calendar showed marked variations. In a city like Wilno, for example, when the Poles celebrated the Constitution of 3 May AD 1791, the Orthodox were still on 22 April, the Jews were in the month of Iyyar after Passover in the year 5552 AM, and the Tartars were in the eighth month of the year of Hegira 1205.

The cultural variety of old Polish society encouraged a number of specific attitudes. It prepared the ground, if not for universal tolerance, then at least for practical toleration. It promoted an environment of cultural 'cross-fertilization', where open-minded people could learn from their neighbours; and it encouraged a strong tradition of education, where each of the communities had to emulate the others in the excellence of their schools and academies. In the period after the Partitions, when each of the peoples developed their own exclusive national movements, it fostered a deplorable degree of animosity; but it also convinced the opponents of Nationalism that the cultures of eastern Europe must either learn to co-operate or perish.

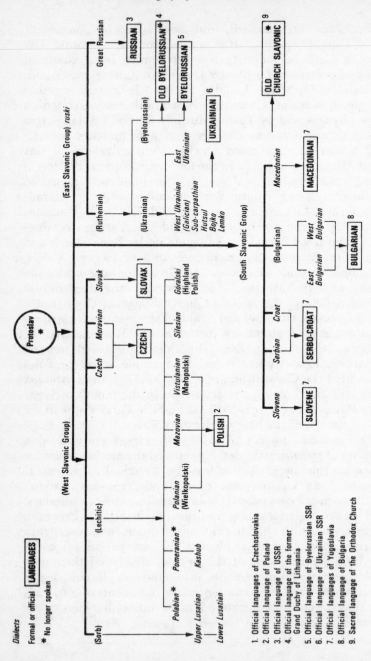

Diagram D.   The Slavonic Languages

Dialects

Formal or official   LANGUAGES

* No longer spoken

1. Official languages of Czechoslovakia
2. Official language of Poland
3. Official language of USSR
4. Official language of the former
   Grand Duchy of Lithuania
5. Official language of Byelorussian SSR
6. Official language of Ukrainian SSR
7. Official languages of Yugoslavia
8. Official language of Bulgaria
9. Sacred language of the Orthodox Church

Protoslav *

(West Slavonic Group)

(Lechitic)

Polabian *
Pomeranian *
Kashub
Polanian (Wielkopolski)
Mazovian
Vistulanian (Małopolski)
Silesian
Góralski (Highland Polish)

POLISH 2

Czech
Moravian
Slovak

CZECH 1

SLOVAK 1

(Sorb)

Upper Lusatian
Lower Lusatian

(East Slavonic Group) *ruski*

Great Russian

RUSSIAN 3

(Byelorussian)

OLD BYELORUSSIAN * 4

BYELORUSSIAN 5

(Ruthenian)

(Ukrainian)

East Ukrainian
West Ukrainian (Galician)
Sub-carpathian
Hutsul
Bojko
Lemko

UKRAINIAN 6

(South Slavonic Group)

(Bulgarian)

Macedonian

MACEDONIAN 7

West Bulgarian
East Bulgarian

BULGARIAN 8

Croat
Serbian

SERBO-CROAT 7

Slovene

SLOVENE 7

Macedonian

OLD CHURCH SLAVONIC * 9

The educational tradition in Poland had a long and sturdy history of social service and independent scholarship. The Jagiellonian University, founded in 1364, was the second most ancient seat of higher learning in central Europe after Prague. In the fifteenth century, one of its early Rectors, Pawel Wlodkowic (Paulus Vladimiri, 1370–1435), was sufficiently sure of his theology and canon law to challenge the prevailing opinions of the papal and imperial experts at the Council of Constance; whilst Wlodkowic's successors, including a long line of rectorial prelates from Cardinal Oleśnicki (1389–1455) to Archbishop Jan Laski (1456–1531) and Bishop Tomicki (1464–1535) nurtured the growth of Catholic Humanism and patronized the fine arts. Archbishop Grzegorz of Sanok (died 1477) at Lwów and Bishop Lubrański at Poznań founded secular academies of lasting influence. In the sixteenth century, however, the Catholic monopoly was broken. The Protestant schools established such high standards that their clientele crossed all denominational barriers. The University of Königsberg (1545), the great German gimnazjum at Danzig, the Calvinist Academy at Pinczów, known as the 'Sarmatian Athens', even the sectarian colleges of the Hussites at Leszno or the Arians at Raków, attracted pupils not only from the Catholic nobility but also from abroad. In the Jewish community, the Talmudic Schools of Cracow, Lublin and Wilno were renowned across Europe and produced a wealth of publications. Chancellor Zamoyski's private academy at Zamość (1583) was a model experiment in Renaissance learning. Its professorial staff numbered Jews, Armenians, and Turks among the scholars, as proof of the breadth of its founder's vision. Quite clearly, the Catholic Church was obliged to respond in kind. As from 1565 at Braunsberg (Braniewo), more than fifty Jesuit colleges were established in the Polish See— from Breslau in the West and Perejeslaw in the East, to Dorpat in the North and Kamieniec in the South—and their success goes far to explain the general advance of the Counter-Reformation. Renowned no less for their academic excellence than for their religious piety, they served as the parent foundations of later universities—at Wilno, Lwów, and Dorpat. They also provoked a parallel revival of learning among the Orthodox. The Academy of

Peter Mohyla at Kiev (1632), the first seat of higher learning in the East Slav world, was destined to play a seminal role in the modernization of Russian Orthodoxy, and had modelled its programme on the local Jesuit college when Kiev was still a city of the Polish kingdom. In later years, the relative importance of Jesuit education declined, especially with the introduction of the Piarists and of the Bernadine friars (Observantists). When the Jesuit Order was disbanded in 1773—in Poland though not in Russia—many of its former pedagogues joined the teaching staff and the textbook committees of the National Education Commission. Similarly, when the National Education Commission was abolished by the Partitioning Powers, the majority of its schools were quickly revived in the educational systems of the Duchy of Warsaw, of the Congress Kingdom, or of Prince Czartoryski's Wilno School Board in the western gubernias of the Russian Empire. Ancient foundations such as the gimnazjum at Chelmno in Prussia, or its modern counterpart at Krzemieniec in Volhynia, managed to preserve their traditional Polish identity well into the nineteenth century. The Jewish schools, too, persisted in their endeavours despite the political changes. The *yeshivot* (religious schools) of the Jewish Pale, which was carved from the former Polish provinces of Russia, were renowned throughout world Jewry. The scriptural emphasis of the Chassidim, and the new secular schools of the *Haskalah* (Jewish Enlightenment), at opposite ends of the Jewish spectrum, both served to maintain a high level of Jewish literacy. Throughout the Polish lands, in fact, respect for education was part of the way of life. It is not surprising, therefore, that when Russifiers and Germanizers set to work, as they thought, to 'civilize' their new subjects, they came face to face with unexpected problems. In terms of culture, the Prussian schoolteacher or Russian inspector, sent out like naïve missionaries from Berlin or St. Petersburg, often found that they had much to learn from the natives. Eventually, from the great educational battleground of nineteenth-century eastern Europe, the champions of native culture emerged bruised but unbowed.

Cultural cross-fertilization took many forms. It could be observed, in scholarship, where reflections on the religious or social ideas of one community could inspire the writings of another. (To cite just one famous example, Izaak of Troki's *Fortress of Faith* (1585), which Voltaire later discovered and claimed to be the intellectual fount of the Enlightenment, was the result of a Jewish scholar's fascination with the work of an Arian professor, expelled by the Jagiellonian University, who settled among the Karaim of Lithuania.) Not unnaturally, in a society of such variety, there was a long tradition of bilingual or multilingual writers expressing themselves in two or more languages. Latin literature survived alongside the various vernaculars almost until the Partitions; whilst in the later period Polish was often preferred for the début of writers who graduated with time to some other idiom. The Lithuanian literary revival was first patronized by the Polish bishops of Wilno and Samogitia, just as the Yiddish literary revival was launched by men who began their careers writing in Polish. The beginnings of Modern Ukrainian Literature, in the figure of Taras Shevchenko (1814–61) and his contemporaries, owed a great debt to Polish Romanticism. For centuries, and right up to the Second World War, Poland was a country where different cultures could compete and coexist. Just as the Renaissance printers of Cracow produced not only a wealth of precious *incunabula* in Polish and Latin, but also the first book printed in Cyrillic, the first book in Hungarian, and early books in Romanian, so in the era of the Partitions, Poland gave rise to important works by German and Russian, as well as Polish writers. Few students of modern European literature realize that the *Tales* of Hoffmann were composed in Warsaw, or that Warsaw was the birthplace both of Alexander Blok and Isaac Bashevis Singer. Just as Polish noblemen flocked in their thousands to the universities of Padua, Paris, and Bologna in the sixteenth century, returning home filled with the ideals of the Renaissance, so in the nineteenth and early twentiety centuries, young Poles were sent in their tens of thousands to the schools and universities of Germany and Russia—to Berlin, Heidelberg, Göttingen, and Jena, to Petersburg, Dorpat, Kiev, and Kharkov—returning home with a firsthand knowledge of German philosophy, Russian literature, or modern technology. The Poles lived at the crossroads of Europe. Even in the lowest points of its political misfortunes, Poland could hardly decline into a total cultural backwater.

It would be idle to suppose that Poland's multinational heritage has produced anything approaching unruffled fraternal harmony. The internecine quarrels, and mutual intolerance of the various national movements of the former Polish lands, from the mid-nineteenth to the mid-twentiety century has been one of the scandals of the continent. The self-righteous pettiness, narrow-minded arrogance, and ill-tempered dogmatism of Polish, Ukrainian, Jewish, German, and Russian Nationalists—all convinced of the superiority of their own 'threatened' culture—do not strike the outsider as particularly cultured in tone. Yet it must be realized in the midst of all the disputes that many people did strive to preserve the ideals of intercommunal harmony and of a multicultural society. There were men and women who looked forward to a time when the positive virtues of the old Republic's cultural variety could be restored. Not surprisingly, in searching their history for a suitable model, they hit on the Poland of the Jagiellons, when their multinational ideals were first supposed to have taken root.

The 'Jagiellonian Concept' was the brain-child of the politicians of the early Romantic Era, and found its most popular expression in the prophecies of Wernyhora. (See p. 223.) It was adopted, above all, by the Piłsudski camp. It had its roots in the attempts to reunite Poland and Lithuania and Ukraine, during the November and January Risings, and gave rise in its turn to Piłsudski's abortive schemes in 1918–21 for a Federation of the Border Nations. It foundered on the reefs of the artificial segregation of the peoples of the area after the Second World War. But it may yet stage a come-back. The nations of eastern Europe no longer suffer from the frictions of competing for survival on the same patch, and with the decline of communist-sponsored Nationalism, they may revive the memory of a common heritage as a spur to their common liberation. Many of the key documents of the Jagiellonian era, from the magnificent preamble to the Act of Horodło in 1413 to the moving testament of Sigismund-August in 1572, talk of the 'love, harmony, and unity' of the different communities of the realm. These words were not mere slogans, and in a

Christian environment can provide lasting inspiration. Now that the old divisive generation of pre-war Nationalists is dying out in all the countries of the Soviet Bloc, a new generation devoted to mutual understanding could conceivably emerge. The first steps of Polish–Lithuanian reconciliation have been made on the basis of their common Catholicism; whilst moves have been made in the Emigration to foster Polish and Ukrainian *rapprochement*. The multicultural harmonizers of today have many precedents on which to draw from the Past.

2 The Ethnic Core

Owing to the disservices of Nazism and Fascism, racial history enjoys little respectability among contemporary scholars; and it is a matter of speculation whether the present advances in human genetics may ever influence historiography. But it is undeniable that biological concepts have played a major role in past debates on historical development, not least under the influence of Darwinism in the late nineteenth century. One has only to look into the first volume of the *Transactions of the Royal Historical Society* (1883) in London, which contains a lurid examination of the superior contribution to British civilization of the Anglo-Saxon over the Celtic strain, to realize that racial analysis was not the exclusive preserve of continentals or individuals like Gobineau or H.S. Chamberlain. What is more, it is undeniable that the traditional idea of national communities being based on kinship has more than a grain of truth to support it. Whatever reservations one likes to make—that the genetic stock of any nation is constantly subject to change and addition; that new nations (like America or Australia) can be forged from people sharing widely differing racial origins; or that language and culture can be transferred from one nation to another without regard to their racial affinity; it still remains true that the sense of modern nationhood has been greatly strengthened by the awareness of ancient hereditary bonds based on the 'the mother tongue', on generations of interbreeding, and hence on common biological descent. Most important perhaps is the fact that ordinary people gain a sense of pride and security by hearing of the deeds of their 'forebears' and 'ancestors', irrespective of the scientific validity of the alleged ancestral link. The greater their sense of insecurity in the modern world, the greater is their need to belong to some real or imagined 'national family' with common 'roots' and common 'blood'. Certainly, with respect to European History, the exclusive racial basis of modern nations has been thoroughly discredited. But the more fashionable concept of 'Ethnicity', which combines linguistic, cultural, and environmental as well as hereditary factors, has many proponents. The new 'ethnic core' sounds less offensive than the old talk of 'racial genealogy', 'tribal roots', or 'our ancient kith and kin'.

In Poland, as in most central and east European countries, the growth and evolution of the ethnic core has always attracted much scholarly attention. In the days of the noble democracy, great efforts were made to prove that the 'Polish nation' of noblemen possessed different racial origins from the mass of the population. Popular mythology held that they were the descendants of the noble Japheth, as distinct from the ignoble 'sons of Ham'. (*Cham* (Ham) has become a synonym in the Polish language for ignobility of both the moral and social varieties.) Sixteenth-century authorities like Marcin Bielski (1495–1575) maintained that they were descended from the warrior Sarmatians, whose prehistoric conquest of the docile Slavonic tribes justified the subsequent supremacy of the *Szlachta*. In the nineteenth century, scholars paid much more attention to the Slavonic connection. Once the pioneer philologists, such as Vostokov and Miklosič, had established the common origins of the Slavonic languages (see Diagram D), scholarship was only one step away from the conclusion that all the Slavonic-speaking peoples possessed common racial origins. The conclusion had obvious political potential, and both Poles and Russians disputed their 'natural right' to the leadership of the Slavonic peoples. In Russia, Pan-Slav theories became an integral element of Russian Nationalism. For the Poles, in contrast, Pan-Slavism came to be seen as a mortal danger, since it implied that their association with the Russians and their submergence in some vast Slavonic family dominated by the Russians could be part of a natural historical process. Not even cultural Slavophilism could win many Polish adherents. As a result, Polish delegates to the various Slav Congresses of the nineteenth century—Prague (1848), Moscow (1867), Prague (1908), Petersburg (1909), Sofia (1910)—regularly took a dissenting opinion from that of the Russian, Ukrainian, Czech, or South Slav delegates, and earned Poland the label of 'the Judas of the Slavs'. Polish scholars, whilst not rejecting the Slavonic connection outright, have tended to minimize the importance of the alleged common racial factor and to maximize cultural, religious, and environmental differences. The work of Franciszek Duchiński (1817–93), author of *Peuples aryans et tourans* (1864), influenced Ukrainian as well as Polish views on these matters. It assaulted the very foundations of Pan-Slavism by arguing that the Great Russians were not true members of the Slavonic race, since they were the descendants of the Slavicized Finnic and Hunnic peoples just as the Bulgars were a Slavicized Turkic tribe. By this reckoning, it was the Poles, not the Russians, who should be seen as the natural leaders of the Slavonic world.[4]

In more recent times, several Polish political movements have seen fit to adopt variations on the ethnic theme as part of their official ideology. The first of these were the Peasant Movement and the National Democratic Movement; surprisingly enough, they were joined later on by the post-war Polish Communist movement.

At the end of the nineteenth century, when Polish politicians were dreaming of restoring national statehood, there were many different opinions as to the model on which the future Polish state should be based. If the Piłsudski Camp backed the Jagiellonian Concept, the peasant leaders headed by Bolesław Wysłouch and the nationalists of Dmowski's persuasion had other ideas. For reasons of its supposed ethnic purity, they latched on to the primitive state of the early Piasts as the sort of Poland which they wanted to create in a modern version—the Poland of Mieszko I and Bolesław Chrobry; the Poland of the early Polish tribes as yet undiluted by German colonists, Jewish refugees, or Ruthenian conquests; the Poland of their ancestors, whom, it was claimed, held absolute right of possession to their Polish land. This Piast Concept, first propagated by Wysłouch, and popularized in the 1890s by

Jan Popławski (see p. 137), became a standard goal of the Nationalists' ideology.[5] It was reinforced by their strong admiration for the undivided Catholicity of Piast Poland, and for the Piasts' resistance to German imperial claims. It stood far apart from Pan-Slavism, since its stress on the unique nature of Polish ethnicity hindered any thoughts of assimilation or even 'Slavonic convergence'; but it certainly favoured the notion that the Poles should take their place as equal partners in the age-old struggle of the Slavs against the Teutons. For these same reasons it possessed powerful attractions for the Polish communists in the post-war period.

The communists' adoption of the Piast Concept was dictated no less by their own inclinations than by the logic of the international situation. They desperately needed to justify the annexation from Germany of the Western and Northern Territories (see p. 103), and in so doing to appear as the champions of Polish national interests. The Piast connections of medieval Silesia and Pomerania suited their purposes exactly. At the same time, they needed to assert their own identity, to dispel their reputation as Russian puppets dressed in Polish uniforms, and to present themselves as the avant-garde of the ancient Polish nation with its distinct ethnic composition and its own national territory. Notwithstanding the recent struggle with the Nazis, racism lurked close to the surface of Stalinist communism, whose mass deportations of the late 1940s were designed (like the similar programmes of the Nazis) to segregate the various peoples of the Soviet empire into their designated reservations. Yet this segregation served the Polish communists very well. It provided a necessary base for the new Marxist–Leninist interpretation of Polish History (see p. 314); it strengthened their control over a disoriented and uprooted population; and it distanced them in some degree from their Soviet masters. Thanks to their conversion to the idea of the ethnic core, communist propagandists could claim that the People's Republic was the natural culmination of a thousand years of Polish History. Their adoption of the crownless Piast eagle was no accident.

Less open to doubt is the plain fact that the position of the Polish-speaking element in the Polish lands has risen over the centuries from one of uneasy partnership with various other peoples, to one of absolute supremacy. In Mieszko's time, the 'Poles' were just one tribe among scores of others; in the old Republic before the Partitions, two-thirds. In the People's Republic, they are 99 per cent. Spontaneous developments have been aided by artificial 'social engineering'. The end result is that the 'ethnic core' has grown into a monopoly community. A wholly Polish Poland has lost the need to worry about its ethnic roots.

3 The Polish Language

In a sense, the Polish language has followed a longer career than any other element of Polish history. It is older than the Polish Church, older than the. Piast state, older than the very idea of 'Poland'. It is the only certain and continuous link between the Poles of today and the 'proto-Poles' of Slavonic prehistory.

Within the span of recorded history, however, the Polish language for long took a secondary place. All the official documents of medieval Poland were written in Latin, and there is no documentary trace of written Polish before a handful of isolated phrases appeared in the text of the 'Bull of Gniezno' of 1136. The earliest literary fragment composed entirely in Polish is the hymn *Chrystus z martwych wstał* (Christ rose from the Dead), dating from 1365. Polish letters were largely the devotional preserve of women (who were not taught Latin); and by the fifteenth century, devotional material in the vernacular was fairly common. The hymn of the *Bogurodzica*, sometimes described as the most ancient Polish poem, was not written down until two or three centuries after its original composition. It was sung by the Polish knights on the eve of the Battle of Grunwald:

Bogurodzica dziewica,	Virgin, Mother of God
Bogiem sławiena Maryja,	Maria honoured by God,
U twego syna Gospodzina,	Your Son's patroness,
Matko zwolena, Maryja,	Maria, chosen Mother,
Zyszczy nam, spuści nam.	Assist us!
Kyrieleison.	Kyrie Eleison.

Prior to this time, the entire development of the language—including its divergence from common Slavonic, its strong debt to medieval Czech, and the growth of its regional dialects—can only be reconstructed by deduction and guesswork.

Following the Renaissance, however, Polish came into its own. Mikołaj Rej reminded his countrymen that 'they were not geese, but had a tongue of their own', and the advice was heeded. Although the Latinists fought a long and doughty rearguard action, especially in the crucial field of Church-sponsored education, Polish gradually adapted itself to use in all branches of government, commerce, science, and culture. By the time of the Enlightenment, its eventual triumph was guaranteed. The schools of the National Education Commission, which stepped into the gap left by the disbanded Jesuits, were entirely based on secular and vernacular studies. The Four Year Sejm saw a massive output of legal bills and political tracts all written for the first time entirely in Polish. Oddly enough, the refinement of the Polish language progressed further in Lithuania, than in Poland itself. In the Kingdom, where many of the peasantry were frequently Polish-speaking themselves, the educated gentleman could best emphasize his quality by cultivating his Latin. But in the Grand Duchy, where the masses spoke Latvian, Lithuanian, or Ruthenian, a proper command of the Polish language became the mark of gentility and of social accomplishment. It was no accident that in the Romantic period Lithuania and Ukraine produced rather more great Polish writers than Poland itself. At a time when the Russian government was often using French; when Russian literature was in its very earliest stages; and when the Lithuanian or Ukrainian languages were hardly used for literary purposes at all, Polish was the main vehicle of high culture and educated social intercourse from the Warta to the Dnieper. In that vast region, Polish performed the same function which German was assuming in the similarly vast dominions of the Austrian Empire in the Danube Basin and the Balkans.

This long formative period, in which the Polish language grew slowly to maturity in a multicultural environment, endowed it with certain specific characteristics. For one thing, the syntax was standardized at an early date in the hands of classical grammarians, thereby widening its scope as an educational instrument and as agent of intercommunity relations. Standard Polish crystallized during the Renaissance, so that every generation of educated people has had easy access to its literature ever since. For another, Polish vocabulary was continually enriched by a vast range of calques and loan-words, particularly from classical and Church Latin, but also from German, French, and Italian. Polish never knew the cramping native purism which stunted the growth of many other languages of the region. Polish exuded Westernisms, and served as the natural vehicle in the East for Western cultural taste and values. If the Baroque period brought an excess of *makaronizm*—the garbled admixture of Polish and Latin—the native idiom was strong enough to reassert its integrity during the Enlightenment. When Samuel Bogumil Linde (1771–1847), the Polish 'Johnson', published his great Dictionary in 1807–14, he recorded a language which was already an all-purpose cultural instrument—well ahead of Russian, and arguably on a par with German. The capacity of such a language to resist the onslaught of the official Russifiers and Germanizers was clearly much greater than that of the typical plebeian vernaculars of other East European nations.

Not surprisingly, therefore, a native knowledge of the Polish language was destined to become the touchstone of Polish national identity. Under the old Republic, the loyal German burghers of Danzig or the Ruthenian noblemen of Ukraine might well take pride in their Polishness in spite of an inadequate grasp of the Polish language; whilst millions of Polish-speaking peasants felt no sense of solidarity with the 'noble' Polish nation. By the end of the nineteenth century, all this was changed. In modern times, it is as hard to conceive of native Polish-speakers who do not consider themselves to be Poles, as it is to think of a Pole who cannot speak Polish.* On

---

*One can find exceptions in Polish Jews, whose mother tongue is Polish but who regard themselves as Jewish, not Polish nationals. There is also the curious case of the descendants of Poles deported to Siberia, whose families have adopted the Russian language, but who still claim to be Soviet citizens of Polish rather than Russian nationality.

this score, the Polish experience contrasts very sharply with that of the English-speaking world, where Irishmen, Scots, Australians, or Americans may all be native speakers of English, but would violently object to being described as Englishmen. In Poland, language, even more than birth or religion, is the essential ingredient of Polish nationality. In Julian Tuwim's memorable phrase, 'the language is the homeland'—the *ojczyzna-polszczyzna*.

4 Polish Literature

Owing to the early maturation of the language, the corpus of Polish literature assumed impressive proportions long before the demise of the old Republic. Prose, poetry, and drama all had an extensive repertoire covering at least three centuries of development. What is not always realized is that the range of literary genres stretched far beyond the creative and imaginative arts. *Belles-lettres,* in the broadest sense, had a long pedigree. Quite apart from the primitive chroniclers, Polish historiography had an unbroken line of achievement from the great Jan Długosz (1415–80), father of the art, through his continuators Marcin Bielski (1495–1575) and Marcin Kromer (1512–89), and the epicists of the Baroque, right up to Bishop Naruszewicz. Polish memoirs, whose earliest known practitioner was Janko of Czarnków (d. 1387), the Vice-Chancellor of Casimir the Great, flowed in a continuous stream from the Renaissance to the Enlightenment. Memoirists of note included the inimitable Jan Chryzostom Pasek (1636–1701), Marcin Matuszewicz (d. 1784) and Jędrzej Kitowicz (1728–1804). The body of Polish devotionalia and hymn-writing, launched with the numerous thirteenth-century hagiographies and confirmed in the *Kazania Świętokrzyskie* (Holy Cross Sermons) of the fourteenth century, was continually expanded. Kochanowski, Skarga, Kochowski—all contributed. The magnificent hymns and carols of Franciszek Karpiński (1741–1825), which most Poles learn by heart with their catechism, were the culmination of an immemorial tradition. All these works of the pre-Partition era were the solid blocks of Poland's literary foundations, which were as broad as they were deep.

Polish history itself, already recorded and analysed by its early devotees, provided an inexhaustible mine of raw material for the talents of later generations. That vast, glorious and pathetic pageant of princes, saints, warriors, martyrs, heroines, traitors, and humble serfs and historians— so inadequately sketched in the preceding pages—has provided much of the inspiration of modern artists. The Romantic poets and dramatists, the historical novelists, the historical painters, balladeers, and librettists, the historical symbolists and expressionists, even the proponents of historical materialism —all would have been impotent without the rich fund of Poland's recorded past on which they drew.[6]

5 The Noble Ethos

Of all the products of Polish life before the Partitions, the Polish nobility—the *Szlachta* and all their works—might seem to have been the most discredited. The *Szlachta*'s knightly code had not helped them to fight and repel the Republic's enemies. Their peacock pride in a supposedly exclusive ancestry was grotesquely unsuited to their miserable decline. Their social ideals of brotherly love and equality ill fitted their continuing support for serfdom. The political philosophy of their 'Golden Freedom' resulted in common anarchy. Their richest brethren, the noble magnates, were usually foreign pensioners, and not infrequently traitors. Their poorest brethren, the noble rabble, were poorer than many a Jew or a peasant. The *szlachta* were the laughing-stock of Europe, the butt which every radical wit from Defoe to Cobden could mock. If, in Carlyle's cruel words, their noble Republic was 'a beautifully phosphorescent rot-heap', then they were the parasites who swarmed upon it. One might have supposed that the ideals of the *szlachta* were supremely redundant, and would have been quietly forgotten at the first opportunity. In fact, though the legal status of *szlachta* was annulled in 1795 by the partitioning powers, its ideals lived on. The *kultura szlachecka* (the noble ethos) has become one of the central features of the modern Polish outlook.

As it happened, the annulment of *szlachta*'s legal status rendered a signal service to their reputation. Although a fair number of the wealthier Polish noblemen were able to register as members of the Russian, Prussian, or Austrian nobility, the great majority were excluded. Henceforward, it could be said that the oppressions of the landowning class were not due to the native nobility but to the injustices of foreign rule. The mass of the *déclassé* nobility shared the misfortunes of the common people, and, as the main educated element, could act as their tribunes. What is more, in mourning the fate of their own defunct estate, they could interpret the attacks on their own battered ideals as an assault on the beliefs of the entire population. In this way, the ex-*szlachta* became the pioneers of the new intelligentsia; the former 'noble nation' was transformed and expanded to include all social classes of the new, universal Polish nation; and the *kultura szlachecka*—with its ideas of exclusivity, equality, unanimity, resistance, and individualism—continued to provide the guide-lines for Polish social and political thought. In the old days, only the *Szlachta* could address each other as *pan* (Lord) or *pani* (Lady). Nowadays, it is the normal form of address for everyone.* Two hundred years after the former abolition of the *Szlachta* most people in Poland are content to think of themselves as honorary nobles.

The *Szlachta* undoubtedly thought they were a race apart from mankind. Nowhere in Europe was the mystique of 'blue blood' more cherished than in Poland, and later commentators have talked of 'Noble Racism'. This 'Vanity of Birth', wrote Daniel Defoe 'is carried [in Poland] to a monstrous extravagance.' Great efforts were made both to protect the noble estate from the ignoble impurities of mesalliance and to weed out bourgeois or Jewish impostors. Of course, once the noble estate was dissolved, there was nothing left to protect. But the habit of regarding one's ancestry not merely as a source of personal pride but also as proof of collective superiority, may well have been transmitted from the 'noble nation' to at least one branch of modern Polish opinion. The 'vanity of birth' was certainly an important plank in the platform of the Nationalists, and may conceivably be the

---

*The only exception is that of the Polish communist party, whose members address each other in the Russian fashion either as *Wy* (you) or *Towarzysz* (comrade).

source of the superiority complex which some Poles display with respect to their more·proletarian neighbours.

More attractively perhaps, the *Szlachta* were devoted to the principle of treating each other as equals. All noblemen called each other 'Brother'. Except for the princes of Lithuania, whose titles had to be confirmed to gain their acceptance to the Union of Lublin, all titulation in the old Republic was legally banned. All noble citizens, irrespective of wealth or office, enjoyed the same civil liberties, and full equality before the Law. Phrases implying that some nobles were more equal than others—such as 'magnate' or 'lesser nobility'—were struck from the record of the Diet. No one could seriously contend that all members of the *Szlachta* were equal in all respects, since the gamut of wealth and power was enormous. But the legal fiction of equality was an important social lubricant, which added greatly to the sense of solidarity within the broad mass of the nobility as a whole. After the partitions, the ex-nobles shared the 'democracy' of the oppressed and the deprived—where the old ideal could be preserved in new forms. Certainly the popular democracy of contemporary Poland has more to do with the belief in the equal worth of every individual than with any practical experience with constitutional theory and procedures.

The *Szlachta* also recognized the equality of the sexes, at least in the vital sphere of property law. Unlike many European countries, where women were virtually the chattels of their husbands or families, Polish noblewomen could hold property in their own right. For this reason, if for no other, the strong-minded female, secure in her own inheritance, is a well-established personality of Polish history and literature. In the era of the Partitions, when the menfolk were obliged to seek employment in 'foreign service' or to join the 'foreign' army, it was the strong-minded Polish women, the mothers and grandmothers who brought up the children at home, who proved to be the guardians of the nation's most precious property—its culture.

In all their counsels, the *Szlachta* laid great store by the principle of unanimity. Neither the central Diet nor the regional dietines could pass a resolution unless it gained the consent of all persons present. The resolutions of the Sejm did

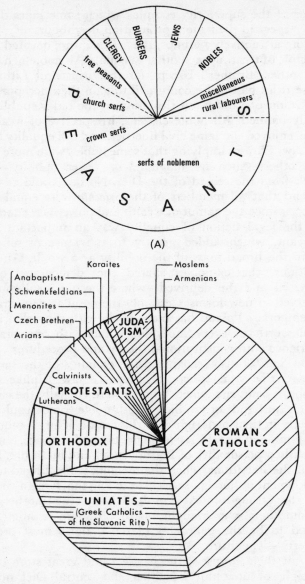

(A)

Karaites
Moslems
Armenians
Anabaptists
Schwenkfeldians
Menonites
Czech Brethren
Arians
JUDA-ISM
Calvinists
PROTESTANTS
Lutherans
ROMAN CATHOLICS
ORTHODOX
UNIATES
(Greek Catholics
of the Slavonic Rite)

Diagram E.   (a) The Social Estates of Poland–Lithuania (16th Century)
                (b) The Religious Communities of Poland–Lithuania (1660)

not gain the force of law until confirmed by the vote of the individual dietines. Behind the principle, and its logical product, the *Liberum Veto*, lay the conviction that any good law must have the consent of all those whose duty is to enforce it. Predictably enough, the application of the principle led to interminable debates, and to frequent delay or deadlock. But it also had a positive side. It gave a strong sense of commitment to any consensus that was actually reached. It encouraged the nobleman to stand by his word, once given, and to defend his commitments as a matter of honour. This 'honourable' tradition of unanimity was a natural ally of the West European concept of liberal government by consent. It goes a long way to explaining why Poles in the nineteenth century instinctively rejected beneficial reforms when imposed 'from on high', and why, having identified an injustice, they would fight against it to a man. Their critics call it a fanatical penchant for trouble-making; their admirers call it a fine sense of responsibility.

The *Szlachta*'s Right of Resistance was enshrined in the fundamental constitutional covenants of every royal coronation. The loyal citizen possessed not merely the right, but the duty to overthrow an unjust ruler. The practice of Confederation—the formation of an armed league to correct a breach of the constitution—was an established part of political life. Without doubt, it was used to excess by unscrupulous politicians and by foreign intriguers. (It was even used by the Four Years' Sejm as a device to ensure that the calling of confederations could be legally abolished!) But it was supported by deep convictions and ingrained attitudes, and needless to say, it provided a perfect training ground for resistance to the imposed rule of foreign regimes. The Confederations of the seventeenth and eighteenth centuries were the natural antecedents to the Risings of the nineteenth and twentiety centuries. The new insurrectionary was the old confederate writ large.[7]

The common denominator to all these ideals of the *Szlachta* lay in their unwavering belief in the value of the individual person. Materialists may wish to attribute this belief to the inbred confidence of a class who were absolute masters over their estates and the affairs of their localities. The nobleman

was *Pan sobie*, a 'lord unto himself', an individual of infinite
worth who naturally saw the same merit in all his (noble)
equals. Others may wish to give more weight to the influence
of Christian theology, and the doctrine of the individual soul.
It would be certainly worth while to ask whether the *Szlachta*'s
massive conversion to the Reformation in the middle of the
sixteenth century did not have some connection with the
Calvinists' teaching on the predestination of a chosen élite and
their emphasis on the individual's direct access to God. One
might even enquire with some profit how far these Protestant
inclinations survived in the prejudices of the *Szlachta* after
their wholesale reconversion to the Catholic Church. At all
events, Individualism lay at the heart of the noble ethos. Once
the legal and social barriers had been dismantled in the
nineteenth century—and particularly after the Emancipation
of the Serfs, it could spread into the wider strata of Polish
society as a whole. To a nation oppressed by the limitless
power of foreign States, the preservation of the individual's
dignity gained paramount importance. It was all that could
be hoped for. In the centuries of the Noble Democracy,
individualism had been the preserve of a jealous élite,
incomprehensible, even offensive, to the population at large.
In the era of Partition, it became the watchword of an
embattled population, irrespective of social origin, but equally
oppressed by the alien tyrannies of the three great Empires.
Russia, Prussia, and, to some extent, Austria before 1848 were
living embodiments of the all-powerful State. Poland became
the symbol of the oppressed individual.

6 Church and People

Almost at the end of the old Republic, the Polish Church
suffered a series of tragic shocks. The last Primate of
Poland–Lithuania, Archbishop Michał Jerzy Poniatowski
(1736–94), the King's brother died apparently by suicide.
There were doubts whether the Head of the Polish See could
be buried in consecrated ground. During Kościuszko's Rising,
several Polish bishops were hanged by the mob for treason.
One of Poniatowski's predecessors, Archbishop Gabriel Podoski (1719–77)—one of the Empress Catherine's most dis-

reputable appointees and the chief advocate of preserving the *Liberum Veto* in the Sejm of 1767—had died in exile in France; but his bones were disinterred by a revolutionary mob in Marseilles and cast into the sea. It seems that the affairs of the Church were as rotten as those of the State.

In the eighteenth century, the Roman Catholic Church in Poland had not enjoyed the same degree of security as other established churches in Europe. The challenge of the Reformation had been successfully countered; and the Roman doctrines regained their former supremacy. All the elected kings were loyal sons of Rome, and one or two, like Zygmunt III, had been convinced clericalists. The Bishops sat in the Senate; the Primate ruled as *Interrex* (Acting King) during every interregnum; and the clergy had been strengthened by the continual arrival of new religious orders. The Bonifraters arrived from Spain in 1608, the Lazarists of St. Vincent de Paul from France shortly afterwards: the Reformists in 1622, the Piarists in 1642, the ascetic Cameduli in 1612. Two exclusively Polish Orders, the Marian Fathers (1673) and the Sacramentalist Sisters (1683), reinforced the growing Marian Cult. In 1717, the year of the Silent Sejm, the ceremonial coronation of the Black Madonna of Częstochowa as 'Queen of Poland' indicated the clergy's determination to keep its hold over the faithful despite the country's political decline. Yet many limitations remained. Ever since 1565, when the diocesan courts were forbidden to prosecute noblemen in matters of morals or religion, the Church had been incapable of enforcing canon law against all but the most obscure offenders. The landed wealth of the Church had regressed, whilst all the leading benefices had fallen into the disposal of the great magnatial families. At the royal elections, the Bishops' regular support for their favourite Habsburg candidates was regularly thwarted. The rift with the Orthodox was growing deeper in face of Russian provocations; and the burden of defending the threatened Uniate Confession was growing heavier. The Lutherans were abetted by the king of Prussia. The Jews were increasing fast, and the sensational conversion of the Frankists in the 1760s caused as much embarrassment as rejoicing. The loss of the Jesuits in 1773 was a serious blow to religious education. Poland's detractors in

Protestant Europe thought of it as a fanatical papist stronghold. But from the viewpoint of the Church's Hierararchy, heresy, dissidence, and apathy were rife. There was nothing approaching a Catholic monopoly. The Polish Bishops must have looked with envy at their counterparts in Spain or Italy, or even in the Catholic principalities of neighbouring Germany.

In many respects, however, the strength of the Catholic faith was sounder than the fabric of the Church. The invasions of Poland by Protestant Swedes and Orthodox Cossacks and Russians in the wars of the seventeenth century, and again during the campaigns of the Great Northern War, greatly stimulated the country's Catholicity. Later on, the depredations of the Prussians and Russians, and their support of the dissidents, served the same purpose. By the time of the Confederation of Bar, when many of the confederates took the field in defence of the Catholic religion, the notion that Polish patriotism was necessarily associated with Catholic loyalty was well on the way to general acceptance. Under the blows of political disaster, where the Church faltered, the Faith took heart. One might almost believe that Polish Catholicism was preparing itself for the ordeal of the Partitions. Hard times and persecution rallied the Faith, even when the Hierarchy reeled.

The prowess of Catholic learning is generally ignored by modern scholars. Yet the picture where Polish clerics confined themselves to their port wine and their prayers and left the discussion of social, political, or artistic matters to secular writers is quite misleading. The scope of Catholic intellectual interests was enormous. A clear majority of the Republic's writers and thinkers were men in holy orders, and quite a number of them were high-ranking prelates. The pioneer Bishops of Catholic Humanism had many successors. The brightest star in this firmament was undoubtedly Stanisław, Cardinal Hozjusz (Hosius, 1504–79), Bishop of Warmia and sometime president of the Council of Trent, whose *Confessio fidei catholicae christiana* (The Christian Confession of the Catholic Faith, 1553) ran into a score of editions published at all ends of Europe. It was one of the seminal texts of the Counter-Reformation. His predecessor as Bishop of Warmia,

Jan Dantyszek (Dantiscus, 1485–1548), Latinist and diplomat, was crowned poet laureate of the Empire. Once the theological battles with the Protestants relaxed, Catholic authors paid great attention to social and educational issues. Mikołaj Łęczyca (Lancicius, 1574–1653), Provincial of the Jesuits in Lithuania and a convert from Calvinism, was a bold advocate of interdenominational tolerance—the so-called *Concors discordia* (The Agreement to disagree). Stanisław Papczyński (1631–1701), founder of the Marian Order, wrote a whole library of books on ethics, rhetoric, philosophy, history, literature, and mysticism. Provocative in its own day, his *Prodromus Reginae Artium sive Informatio Tyronum Eloquentiae* (A Preface to Eloquence, 1663) dared to criticize many of the main institutions of contemporary society—from the *liberum veto* and serfdom to the cult of property and noble birth. Quoting Cicero, in imitation of the Protestant Rey, he told his noble readers that nobility derives from virtue, not blood. In his political works, he outlined the perversions of the worthy principles of individual freedom and unanimity which even at that stage augured disaster. Among the reformers of the Enlightenment, Stanisław Konarski (1700–73) was General of the Piarist Order and founder in 1740 of the Collegium Nobilium, Warsaw's most modern school. His tract *O skutecznym rad sposobie* (Concerning an Effective Method of Government, 1763), exerted a marked influence on the projects of Stanisław-August's reign. Finally, there was that remarkable bench of enlightened bishops—Stanisław Załuski (1695–1758) Bishop of Cracow, a Polish physiocrat; his brother, Józef Załuski (1702–74) Bishop of Kiev, founder in Warsaw of the first public library in Europe;* Władysław Lubieński, Archbishop of Lwów, geographer; Adam Naruszewicz (1733–96), Bishop of Smoleńsk, historian; and Ignacy Krasicki (1735–1801), Bishop of Warmia, satirist and social critic. When one realizes that most of the other leading names of the Enlightenment—Kołłątaj, Staszic, Bohomolec, Świtkowski, Albertrandy, the Skrzetuski brothers, Jezierski, Ostrowski, Bogusławski, Dmochowski—belonged to priests

---

*The Załuski Library, looted by the Russians in 1795, formed the core of the imperial collection in St Petersburg, now the Saltykov-Shchedrin Library.

(or ex-priests), one begins to see the true proportions of the Catholic contribution to Polish intellectual progress. The headlines may have been won by a handful of disreputable prelates like Podoski, or the Kossakowski brothers, who were hanged during Kościuszko's Rising as Russian collaborators; but the solid achievements of the Church's writers and thinkers assured lasting reputations.

During the era of Partitions, the rift between the conduct of the Church as an institution and the attitudes of the faithful was further underlined. In Orthodox Russia, in Protestant Prussia, and even in Catholic Austria, where the Jozefine spirit lingered long in ecclesiastical affairs, the Polish Church was beset by suspicion and hostility. The Primatial See of all-Poland was discontinued; vacancies were often left unfilled for want of politically suitable candidates; and in Russia, all the Church's affairs were subject to state administrators and to police supervision. Courageous priests who protested against injustice risked their careers and their liberty. Several thousand Polish priests were deported to Siberia over the decades, among them in 1863 Bishop Krasiński of Wilno and Archbishop Feliński of Warsaw. In 1831, the Austrians expelled the Bishop Skorkowski of Cracow, and kept his see vacant for forty-eight years. In 1873, the Prussians imprisoned, and later exiled Archbishop Ledóchowski of Gniezno. What was worse, the Vatican showed little interest in defending its Polish subjects. In its horror of radical social ideas, the Vatican consistently supported the conservative monarchies of Eastern Europe. Successive Popes were so eager to reach agreement with the Tsars, and to enshrine their agreements in the Concordats with Russia, that each of the Polish Risings was formally condemned by Rome. In 1832, Pope Gregory XVI excommunicated the insurgents of the November Rising, just as his predecessor had condemned Kościuszko. The bitter scene from Słowacki's drama *Kordian,* where an inane Pope with a parrot on his shoulder ignores the pleas of his Polish petitioner, reflected many people's feelings. It seemed to many that the Church was more concerned to preserve itself than to defend the faithful. (See p. 412 below.)

The *rapprochement* of the Church with the people, which began in the late nineteenth century and has steadily progressed ever since, can be attributed to many factors. Firstly, due credit must be given to the devotion of the lowly parish clergy, who did not follow in the hesitant steps of the Hierarchy. Radical priests, like Piotr Ściegienny (1801–90) of Lublin, exiled to Siberia for social agitation, redeemed the Church's faltering reputation as the 'Good Shepherd', the fold of charity and compassion. Secondly, in conjunction with the wider revival of Polish life in Galicia, the reinstated Archbishopric of Cracow formed a focus round which ecclesiastical reform could coalesce. Three powerful, impressive, and long-lived Cracovian prelates—Cardinal Albin Dunajewski (1817–94), Cardinal Jan Puzyna (1842–1911), and, above all, Cardinal-Prince Adam Stefan Sapieha (1867–1951)—gave a sense of direction and continuity that had been lacking since the loss of the old Primacy. Thirdly, the Roman Church developed its own brand of 'Modernism'—a movement which was concerned, above all, with applying Catholic doctrine to the social ills of the day. At the turn of the century, the forward-looking element in the clergy promoted the rise of Catholic education associations, Catholic welfare societies, Catholic trade unionism, Catholic publishing and an independent Catholic press, a Catholic co-operative movement, Catholic intellectual clubs, and Catholic political parties. The Christian–Peasant Party (SCh-L) in Galicia, the Christian Democratic movement in Prussia, and the Association of Christian Workers in Russian Poland were all important signs of the times. Lastly, and perhaps most importantly, during the high water of Imperialism and Nationalism, the Polish clergy and the Polish people were thrown together in the common struggle to resist the attacks both of hostile bureaucracies and of hostile national minorities. Common distress created the sense of a common purpose.

In the twentieth century, the Roman Catholic Church in Poland found its footing once more after a further cycle of confusion and political disorientation. National independence endowed the Church with many basic institutions. The Primacy of the reunited Polish See, restored in 1919, was held in turn by Cardinal Edmund Dalbor to 1926, and by Cardinal Augustyn Hlond OJB to 1948. The Catholic University of Lublin (KUL), founded in 1918, provided a necessary haven of higher learning for the network of seminaries and schools. The Concordat of 1925 restored Poland to the community of fully autonomous Catholic nations. Confiscated Church property was restituted. Compulsory religious education was introduced in state schools. Yet many frictions persisted. The March Constitution had failed to make Roman Catholicism the established official religion of the Second Republic. The Church received no more than 'the leading place among religious denominations enjoying equal rights'. The Sanacja regime, and Piłsudski's leftist entourage in particular, was anticlerical by temperament, whilst the nationalist opposition, arrogating to itself the voice of all true Catholic Poles, inevitably dragged the Church into the political arena. The adherence of a significant section of the Catholic clergy to the more strident voices of Nationalism embroiled the Church in exchanges of uncharitable recriminations with equally militant Ukrainian Uniates and Jewish Zionists. The Promised Land of independence was not free from the quarrels and bickerings of Freedom. Only with the horrors of the Second World War, when clergy and people were put to a test surpassing all previous ordeals, was the undivided Catholicity of the Polish nation finally secured.

It is an unlikely story. Poland's oldest institution took almost a thousand years to reach its absolute supremacy. On the eve of the Second Partition in 1793, the Roman Church could speak for perhaps 54 per cent of the population of the old Republic. In 1931, in the Second Republic, it spoke for 65 per cent. Since the War, in the People's Republic, it speaks for 96 per cent. Poland's historic claim to be 'Semper Fidelis', to be the undivided champion of the Catholic Faith, has had its moments of exaggeration; but its present claim to be the most Catholic country in Europe is hard to refute.[8]

7 *The Bond with the West*

Whatever one's definition of Europe—whether it is the old idea of Christendom, or the modern concept of a geographical continent stretching from Gibraltar to the Caucasus; and whatever one's definition in Poland—whether it was the ancient realm of the Piasts of the Jagiellons, or the united

Republic of Poland–Lithuania, there can be no dispute that historic Poland always lay on Europe's eastern confines. On one or two occasions, Polish scholars have made out a case for placing Poland not in 'Eastern Europe' but in the centre. In this case, most of their compatriots felt as uneasy belonging to a *Mitteleuropa* dominated by Germans and Austrians as to the Eastern Europe of Mongols, Muscovites, and Muslims. Yet by no stretch of the imagination could the Poles claim that their country lay in the western half of Europe. At the time of Mieszko's baptism, Piast Poland formed the eastern extremity of Christendom on the edge of the pagan world. Under the Jagiellons, the frontier beyond the Dnieper bordered the steppes of the Golden Horde and the nomad peoples of Asia. In Sobieski's day, Poland shared a long frontier with the Ottoman Turks. Geographically, Poland belongs and always has belonged to the East. In every other sense, its strongest links have been with the West.

Poland's Western connection was forged in large measure by its loyalty to the Roman Church. The watershed of Christendom between Western Catholicism and Eastern Orthodoxy ran along the borders of the Piast kingdom, and right through the middle of Poland–Lithuania. Poland's adjacence to the Muslim world led her, like Hungary, to claim the title of *Antemurale Christianitatis,* the 'Bulwark of Christendom'. Poland's Catholicism determined that all her elected rulers came from the West; that all her cultural ties lay with the Latin world; that her closest political connection would be with the Empire, her immediate neighbour; and, in the age of faith, that most of her sympathies lay with the Catholic peoples of the West rather than with the pagans, schismatics, or infidels of the East.

The Western connection was strengthened by trade and politics. Although Poland's overland trade on the Black Sea route, and the fur trade with Muscovy should not be ignored, the main axis of Polish commerce lay westwards on the roads to Germany or on the Baltic sea lanes to Holland, France, and Spain. What is more, the consuming Franco–German struggle in central Europe, which ran for centuries, repeatedly drove the Kings of France to seek an eastern Polish ally to complete the encirclement of Germany. France's first venture in this direction with Henry Valois in the sixteenth century was repeated intermittently with the Vasas and with Sobieski in the seventeenth century, and with Stanisław-Leszczyński and the Confederates of Bar in the eighteenth. France's special relationship with Poland already had a pedigree of 250 years before it was cemented in perpetuity by the Napoleonic Legend. Napoleon's high reputation in Poland, which was richly undeserved (see p. 162), derived from the one fact that he stood to save the Poles from Russian captivity. All subsequent Polish dalliances with the Western powers—with France, Britain, and eventually the USA—have been inspired by the same motive—in 1831–2, in 1863–4, in 1914–18, and in 1939–45. But the Western powers are far away, and have never been able to give Poland any substantial practical help.

The contrast between Poland's fierce attachment to the West and the West's feeble response to Poland prompts one or two serious reflections. At one level, it suggests that the hard-pressed Poles have been rather more true to their principles than the decadent Western democracies have ever been. At another level, it suggests that in the long run spiritual ties based on a common culture and a common religion are more decisive than the immediate concerns of commercial profit or political advantage. Poland's physical separation from the West has done nothing to dampen the Polish admiration for all things Western. Separation, it seems, makes the Polish heart grow fonder. Unfamiliarity precludes contempt. The repeated failures of the West to come to Poland's aid have undoubtedly caused pain; but they have not diverted the Poles' instinctive Westward gaze.

In comparison, Poland's much closer physical contact with the East has done little but to sharpen existing antagonisms. Ancestral memories of the Huns and the Mongols have been invoked on every occasion that the Russian armies have marched on Poland from the East; whilst the traditional horror of the medieval Schism has been perpetuated by modern revulsions against the state-backed Orthodoxy of Tsarism and the obligatory atheism and Marxism–Leninism of the Soviet Bloc. Recurrent violence only drives the resentments deeper. Yet the depth of Poland's rejection of her Russian neighbour can only be gauged in full by the absence of any redeeming features, by the almost total lack of any mitigating emotions. Poland's extended confrontation with the Tartars, whose incessant raiding across the centuries took tens of thousands of Poles into slavery and ruin, did not prevent the Polish nobility from dressing in Tartar style or cultivating Tartar horsemanship. Poland's long wars with the Turks did not discourage a strong taste for Persian rugs and oriental fashions. A weakened Turkey eventually became a weakened Poland's ally. But Poland's age-old contact with the Russians has brought nothing but bitterness and mutual mistrust. For the Pole, few things from Russia have any value—neither its shoddy manufactures, nor its ideology, nor even its superb dance, art or sport. For the average Russian nothing ever came out of Poland except trouble. The antipathies are reflexive. The Poles expect the Russians to bully them; and the Russians expect the Poles to resist. Russia is East, and Poland is West; and never, it seems, the twain shall meet.

Poland's Westernism, therefore, is fundamental and compulsive. It differs both in kind and degree from the Westernizing trends which most other East European countries have experienced. Russia's own Westernizers, for example, from Peter the Great to the advocates of *Détente*, have always been an intellectual minority, obliged to assure their compatriots that the imports and ideas of the West will not harm the country's native products and traditions. In Russia, the dominant Easternizers, the Slavophiles, the majority which prides itself in their barbarian 'Scythian past', have always held their own. In Poland, in contrast, the dominant Westernizers have hardly any native opponents with whom to contend. True Polish Russophiles—as distinct from politicians who reluctantly argue for a *modus vivendi*—do exist; but they are as rare as Polish teetotallers. For the Poles, the West is a dream, a land beyond the rainbow, the lost paradise. The Poles are more Western in their outlook than the inhabitants of most Western countries.

8 Diversions from the East

For the first 500 years of the current millennium, Poland lay on the very edge of the civilized world. Beyond the eastern

borders lay the *Dzikie pola*, the 'wild plains', the open steppes
of Eurasia. The affairs of the kingdom were no more affected
by events beyond the settled frontier among the Tartars,
Muscovites, and Ruthenians, than the progress of the
American colonies was affected by the wars of the Sioux and
the Apache. Not until Muscovy was established as a powerful
and expanding state in the fifteenth century, did 'the Eastern
factor' begin to impinge in any systematic way. Yet earlier, in
1251, an event occurred which set a long-standing precedent.
In that year, when much of eastern Europe was being ravaged
by the Mongol Horde, Genghis Khan died of a fever in distant
Mongolia. The horsemen of the Horde departed as swiftly as
they had arrived, recalled to the homeland to ensure their
share of the great Khan's inheritance. Poland was saved at a
stroke. A chance event on the confines of China diverted
developments on the confines of Europe.

In more modern times, the Ottoman Turks provided the
most frequent source of oriental diversion.[9] Whenever Poland
was hard pressed by the Habsburgs, or by the Muscovite
Russians, the Poles would fervently pray for a Turkish
campaign in the Balkans or on the Black Sea coast. From the
Battle of Mohačs in 1526 to the Treaty of Adrianople in 1829,
the Ottomans provided the only regular counterbalance to
Poland's more immediate eastern neighbours, and increasingly the only hope of relief. By the eighteenth century, during
the Russian Protectorate in Poland, the Turkish mechanism
had assumed a fixed pattern. So long as the Russian armies
were engaged on the Turkish Front, they could not descend in
force on Poland. Russo–Turkish Wars provided the only
intervals when the Polish reformers could act. War clouds over
Constantinople spelt fair weather for Reform in Warsaw. The
Confederates of Bar took the field under cover of the
Russo–Turkish War of 1768–74; the Four Year Sejm was
made possible by the Russo–Turkish War of 1787–91, the
Duchy of Warsaw aided by the Russo–Turkish War of
1806–12. The anger of Nicholas I was delayed by the
campaign of 1827–9. By the same token, whenever the
Russians and the Turks made peace, the Poles had reason to
tremble. Peace on the Bosphorus spelt war on the Vistula. The
Treaty of Kuçuk Kainardzi in 1774 was the necessary adjunct

to the First Partition: the Treaty of Jassy, in 1792, was the signal for the Second. The Treaty of Adrianople, in 1829, marked the end of Turkish resistance and the start of an era when the Russians could occupy Poland without looking over their shoulders. (Mickiewicz's attempt to form a Polish Legion in Turkey during the Crimean War in 1854–5, and to restart the old mechanism, did not succeed.) Touchingly enough, the Ottomans did not forget their link with Poland. The 'Sick Man of Europe' remembered the Dead. Throughout the nineteenth century at the gatherings of the Diplomatic Corps of the Sublime Porte, the Ottoman *chef de protocol* would call on His Excellency, the Ambassador of Lechistan, to step forward, and an aide would announce his regrets for the ambassador's temporary indisposition.

As Asia has developed, Poland has looked for relief from Russia's more distant Asian neighbours. Russia's war with Japan provided the backdrop for the 'Revolution' of 1905, and the occasion for both Dmowski and Piłsudski to visit Tokyo. In the late 1930s, the Soviet war with Japan in Mongolia restrained Stalin's hand, until the truce of 13 September 1939 opened the way for the implementation of the secret protocol of the Nazi–Soviet Pact and the subsequent destruction of Poland. In 1956, Chairman Mao is said to have cooled Krushchev's anger in the quarrel with Gomulka—though he did not save Hungary—whilst the running Sino-Soviet dispute of the 60s and 70s may have helped to keep Soviet intervention in eastern Europe to a minimum. It takes no great strategic subtlety to see why President Carter's Polish-born adviser Zbigniew Brzeziński knew how to play the 'China Card' in 1978, or why Lech Wałęsa's only trip outside Europe in 1981 was to Japan. As the storm clouds gather in Warsaw over the relics of SOLIDARITY, the Poles once more wish all success to the Afghan fighters and long for a Soviet embroilment with China or Iran. It may seem a far cry; but it is not entirely fanciful to suggest that the stay of execution of the Polish People's Republic may hang on Soviet negotiations with Peking, or on events by the banks of the Ussuri and on the heights of the Hindu Kush.

9 Political Corruption

Careerism, like acne and halitosis, is one of these perennial
plagues of the human condition which are almost too banal to
bear mention. There is not a country in the world which does
not have its 'careerists', 'sycophants', and 'opportunists', not a
language which lacks its own special idiom for 'the gravy
train', 'jobs for the boys', *protezione, protekcja.* Polish vocabulary
is rich in this field. Yet surely it would be adding insult to
injury to suggest that poor suffering Poland has been more
susceptible to this plague than other more fortunate lands. At
least one can confirm that Poland has no monopoly.

Certainly, particular disorders of the body politick are
aggravated by the particular conditions of an unhygienic
political habitat. Careerism is encouraged by economic
regression, where the ruling élite controls the distribution of
shrinking rewards ever more effectively; by despotic regimes
which thrive on flattery and a monopoly patronage, and by
rigid social systems which inhibit the mobility of talent.
Russia's protectorate in eighteenth-century Poland exactly
fitted the prescription on all these points. Several specific
features, however, deserve special emphasis. For one thing, the
old Republic possessed very few of the standard structures of a
modern state. There was no professional army worth the
name, no professional local government, and until 1775 no
permanent ministries. Apart from the Church and to a limited
extent the royal court, the usual channels for advancement in
the public service for ambitious young men simply did not
exist. Almost all the paths of promotion lay in the private
control of an ultra-conservative magnatial oligarchy. Careers
could be made, but only by people prepared blindly to uphold
the existing system. For another thing, the magnatial oligarchy itself set an example of blatant careerism by seeking and
receiving the favours of foreign powers, principally of Russia.
The Ambassador of the Empress Catherine had only to suborn
the loyalty of a handful of magnatial office-holders—the
Primate, the Hetmans, the Treasurer, the Marshal of the
Sejm—and the whole Republic lay at her mercy. In view of
the Russian stranglehold, the careerist was obliged either to
collaborate with the conservative pro-Russian party or to

forgo his career. In short, careerism in Poland was not merely an instrument of political sclerosis, it was tinged with tension. Reformers and patriots in Poland did not have prospects.

The careerist collaborators of the old Republic make a sorry list—Primate Podoski, the Bishops Massalski and Kossowski, the three rebel Hetmans—Feliks Potocki (1751–1805), F.K. Branicki (1730–1819), and Seweryn Rzewuski (1743–1811), who headed the Confederation of Targowica, have been already mentioned. But none was more disgraceful than 'Prince' Adam Poniński (1732–98). Poniński first found his niche as Master of the Royal Kitchens under August III, but on the accession of Stanisław-August passed from the Saxon to the Russian service. By agreeing to serve as Marshal of The Diet of 1773 which approved the First Partition, he secured himself a fortune. The Empress Catherine rewarded him with the title of Prince, with a chivalrous award in the Order of the knights of St. John, with ample grants of land, and with the lucrative office of Treasurer. From St. Petersburg's perspective, Poniński's career was a small price for the dismemberment of his country. Not surprisingly, the brief reign of the reformers during the Four Years' Sejm declared him confiscate. But the Confederates of Targowica moved swiftly to his reinstatement. A regime that was based on careerism and collaboration instinctively looked to its own.

In the years that followed, the scandal could only be compounded. The destruction of the Polish Republic meant that no career could be made except in the pay of foreign and reactionary monarchies. All forms of public service—in the Russian Bureaucracy, in the Prussian Army, or at the Austrian court—were felt, to a greater or lesser degree, to be acts of betrayal, even when conducted in the most decent and modest fashion. And few Poles could escape the pressures. Most people had to make a livelihood in systems where the all-powerful state offered the best prospects of employment. Most young men were conscripted to the Army, where they had to swear the oath of loyalty to the Tsar or Kaiser. Everyone had to pay their taxes. Everyday living during the Partitions became tainted by the moral doubts previously reserved for the worst brands of careerism. Unprincipled opportunists gained the benefits not merely of material prosperity but also the respect and prestige due to pillars of law and order. Men and women who stood too hard on their principles were cast into the wilderness of penury, unemployment, and even prison. Such, in Mickiewicz's words, was 'the fate of people who suffer slavery in their own country'. Corruption in all its forms—the corruption of political principles and loyalties; financial corruption; and, worst of all, the corruption of a nation's moral integrity—became a public issue of lasting import. It has surfaced at every point where the nation's ills could be freely debated—not just in 1791, but equally in 1830, in 1863, in 1926, and above all in 1980. The Confederates of Targowica have had their latter-day successors in the PKWN of 1944, and in the PKWN's communist heirs. Adam Poniński has its contemporary counterparts in Osóbka-Morawski, Piotr Jaroszewicz, and Maciej Szczepański, Esq.

The two main psychological consequences of this specifically Polish brand of careerism are curiously contradictory. The Polish careerist, who can win everything except social esteem, carries a heavy burden of guilt. On this point, he is to be pitied much more than his counterparts in authoritarian countries like Russia or Japan, where the representatives of state power are traditionally respected, or those in open, capitalist societies such as the USA, where the self-seeking careerism of private entrepreneurs is generally thought to work for the common Good (in the material, if not necessarily in the moral sense). In Poland, the rift between the careerist establishment and the public is a running sore, a national scandal which constantly decries the inability of 'Poles to talk with Poles'. As a result, the guilt-laden Polish careerists are constantly urged to temper the severity of their regime, to fudge, and delay and deliberately forget, to interpret their orders in the mildest form possible. In a word, they are born procrastinators, often of a very sophisticated sort. What is more, they can rationalize their procrastination with the excellent argument that they are protecting their compatriots from people much worse than themselves. If it were not for them, Poland would be left at the mercy of those frightful Russian barbarians (or German ruffians) who, as everyone knows, would use the knout, the firing-squad, the psychiatric ward, or the mass deportation order with no compunction at all. In fact, if only the blockheaded public would realize it, they, the much maligned Polish servants of St. Petersburg or Moscow (or Berlin), are Poland's real patriots, the true realists, the only 'responsible' people in the land. How many times across the last two centuries have these pleas been heard? How many crocodile tears have been shed by Polish collaborators wounded to the quick by the ingratitude of an uncomprehending nation? The more intelligent among them are alive to their servile condition, and feel the pain more keenly. They are the pliable Greeks in a world ruled by cruel Roman savages, whom they serve with infinite regret and infinite agility. Their crumpled faces tell the story, from Poniński to Rakowski. What can be said in their favour is that Warsaw under Drucki-Lubecki or Wielopolski was a more comfortable place than Warsaw under Paskievitch or General Hurko. Polish Stalinism avoided the mass purges of Soviet Stalinism. Better the ZOMO than the Cossacks, the Gestapo, or the KGB. It is a shocking thought for visitors from democratic societies, but political corruption Polish-style can take pride in the occasional saving grace. In the long dark vigils of Poland's servitude, it has offered a flickering glimmer of humanity.

On the other hand, in moments of crisis, the corruption of Polish politics has introduced an element of great instability. Under pressure from popular resentment, the brittle careerist Establishment can crack. Servile regimes, carefully constructed with impressive façades of monolithic power, prove on the inside to be rotten to the core. Time and again, the Russians have toiled to build their protectorates in Poland on solid, native foundations, only to find that their house of cards has crumbled and collapsed. They lost faith in the decadent Saxons; they were deeply offended by Stanisław–August, a product of the court of Petersburg, who turned out to be a reformer, and by Prince Czartoryski, a minister of the Tsar, who turned up as president of an insurrectionary National Government and leader of the anti-Tsarist Polish Emigration. They were outraged by the conduct of the Congress Kingdom which repaid their liberality with repeated Risings; they were appalled by Joseph Piłudski, a product of the Russian revolutionary underground, who took up arms against the land of Lenin; they were let down by Gomułka, who had to be removed at one point for 'national deviationism'; and there can be little doubt that they are thoroughly disgusted with the Polish United Workers' Party of Gierek, which collapsed in 1980–1 under the weight of its own inefficiency and unpopularity. In the Russians' view, the Poles are, and always have been, eternally *nieblagonadzczhni*—incurably 'unreliable'. And they don't seem to understand why. Yet one need not look very far. Those same guilt-laden careerists on whom the Russians have largely relied are not monsters, idealists, or calculating traitors. They are ordinary men and women led imperceptibly into corruption by the prevailing circumstances of the established order. So long as the political warfare is confined to insults, black looks, and minor skirmishes, they stick at their desks and their commands; but as soon as it turns into open violence, they are likely to desert. After all, as they have had to tell themselves throughout their careers, they did not join the public service in order to fight with their friends and relations. In the moment of truth, they usually turn out to be Poles like everyone else. The pent-up fury of frustrated patriots and reformers is joined by the pent-up guilt of their erstwhile, half-hearted tormentors; and the Polish insurrection is born. The ranks of successive Risings have been swelled by Poles who for years had borne their humiliation under a mask of servility or indifference. The lifelong collaborator is suddenly converted into a burning revolutionary.

Yet, conversely, the opposite is also true. The overwhelming force of Poland's oppressors has always led to the crushing of each successive attempt to break free from their control. The sons and daughters of collaborating parents rush to the banner of Polish freedom, only to suffer defeat, amidst death and destruction. The youthful insurrectionary matures into the convinced careerist. The disillusioned revolutionary becomes a pillar of law and order. Józef Zajączek (1752–1826), Kościuszko's Jacobin adjutant, ends up as the Tsar's Viceroy; Aleksander Wielopolski, an agent of the November Rising, volunteers for service as the leading agent of Tsarism (see p. 198); Bolesław Piasecki of PAX turns full circle from pre-war Fascist to post-war Soviet supporter. Sudden conversions are a symptom of Poland's unenviable moral pressures, and there are few Polish families who escape from the indignity completely. Careerists, collaborators, and converts, no less than the paragons of pure patriotism, are victims of that same corrupting oppression under which most Poles have lived for the best part of three centuries. Lord Acton rightly confirmed that 'Absolute Power corrupts absolutely.' It corrupts both rulers and ruled. Polish traditions have not escaped the Corruption; even if the Absolutism is not their own.

*   *   *   *   *

When the Third Partition was complete in 1795, and the name of Poland was removed, the Partitioning Powers undoubtedly felt that time was on their side. In time the Poles would accept their lot, and eventually merge into the population at large. Each of the East European monarchies were dynastic states that had grown over the recent centuries by annexing a broad selection of conquered peoples and provinces. Both Russia and Austria were zoological gardens of nationalities, and Prussia had a long tradition of absorbing and welcoming colonists and immigrants. There seemed no obvious reason at the time why the Poles should prove more hard to absorb than the others. But they did. Jean-Jacques Rousseau had wisely counselled the Poles on this point. 'If you cannot prevent your enemies from swallowing you', he wrote, 'at least you can prevent them from digesting you.' It was a prophetic statement. The Poles have proved more resistant to digestion than anyone else. The reason lay in the thousand years' history of their ancient culture.

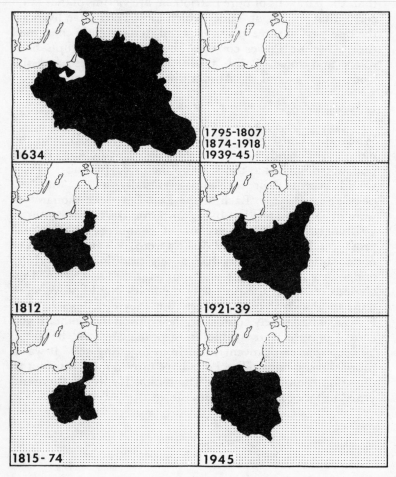

Map 12.   Poland's Changing Territory

CHAPTER VI

ECHOES

The Past in Poland's Present

The Polish troubles have lasted so long—the duel with Russia
is now in its ninth or tenth generation—that the existence of
many recurrent factors is often taken for granted. Poland's
traditional culture is so deeply ingrained that the role of the
Catholic Church or the pro-Western sympathies of the Polish
population hardly need to be discussed. Indeed, these things
are so obvious, that many leading experts, when discussing the
present situation, forget even to mention them. No one expects
the Catholic, pro-Western, individualist Poles to turn atheist,
Slavophile, or submissive any more than Russia can be
expected to be anything but autocratic. Other factors do vary,
however. The ruling political regime, the rise and fall of
institutions, the economic environment, the international
situation, and the leading personalities of the day, are always
changing. Any realistic analysis of current affairs involves an
exploration of the ever-shifting blend of the old and the new.
The Present is never an exact reproduction of the Past; but
echoes of the Past always reverberate through the developments of the Present.

*   *   *   *   *

1 The Impasse of Polish Communism

Critics of the Polish Communist movement often dismiss it
out of hand. According to them, it is a foreign growth,
transplanted into Poland by Soviet political gardeners, and
unrelated in any way to the traditional, native products of the
Polish habitat. This view, common enough in the early post-
war years, has been strengthened by recent events, where the
corruption and feebleness of Polish Communism has been
revealed for all to see. Yet the argument is overstated. The end
result is hardly in doubt; but there was a season when it
looked for a while that Polish Communism might have been
taking root, and when Polish Communists seemed to be
adapting themselves to national political traditions. Whatever
one may think about the involuntary imposition of Communism on to Poland in 1944–5—and that, too, is hardly open to
discussion—none the less, it is inaccurate to regard all Polish
communists exclusively as Soviet creatures from start to finish.
There was a tiny, but genuine Polish Communist Party before
the War (see p. 132); and there were significant numbers of
bright-eyed enthusiasts in the post-war era who were eager to
give the new 'socialist' ideology its chance. Their views, and
their disillusionments, deserve consideration.

In the circumstances prevailing at the end of the War, with
Poland under continuing Soviet occupation, it was inevitable
that the Comrades be widely regarded as mere Soviet puppets.
Gomułka loudly complained to his Politburo in April 1945
that the population at large thought of the PPR as nothing
more than 'an agency of the NKVD'. It is also true that many
of the more dogmatic Comrades believed that Soviet-style
Communism represented a radical new departure in world
civilization, and as such should not be expected to possess any
of the characteristics of the Poland's discredited and reactionary past. The brave new world of the People's Democracy had
no need to learn from any such meaningless abstractions of the
bourgeois order as the 'national tradition' or the 'national
culture'. As soon as the new socio-economic foundations were
constructed, Polish society would automatically develop a
new, socialist culture where any reference to preceding
religious or spiritual values would be superfluous. To put it

crudely, to extend Stalin's own metaphor, the Polish cow could be redesigned as a horse, and made to carry the saddle. It was ten years at least before the experience of Stalinism cured most of the ruling élite of such naïveties.[1]

At the same time, one has to recognize the existence of a strong pragmatic trend within the ranks of the post-war Comrades. Right from the start, one wing of communist opinion accepted the proposition that the building of socialism in Poland would have to take account of local conditions, and that 'the Polish Road' would not necessarily follow the Soviet route in every detail. With Gomułka at their head, they stood up for their convictions to the point of being purged and imprisoned; and in 1956, they gained supremacy in the Party for the next twenty-five years. Concurrently with developments in the political leadership, the new caste of communist intellectuals made its appearance, intent on applying the formulae of Marxism–Leninism to Polish conditions and on forging a specifically Polish brand of 'scientific' socialism.

For a dozen years or so, from the early fifties to the mid-sixties, their battles with the Party dogmatists and Soviet clones brought real vigour to the communist camp. Whether consciously or unconsciously, they had latched on to one of the central issues of traditional Polish politics, and had launched themselves into a communist brand of Organic Work, adapting and applying new social and cultural ideas to protect Poland from losing its separate identity. Whether they liked the label or not, they were Positivists in the traditional Polish sense—positivists of a totally new variety, but positivists all the same. They saw themselves as opponents not only of the Romanticism of the previous generation, which had ended so tragically amidst the ruins of the Warsaw Rising, but also of the servile Loyalists in the Party who danced at every step to the Soviet tune. They provided the only spark of life that the post-war Polish Communist movement has ever shown.

Oddly enough, therefore, the supremacy of the Soviet Union inspired within the ranks of the Polish Comrades representatives of each of the traditional positions of Polish politics developed during the Partitions. (See pp. 179–97.) Communist Loyalism was ably represented by Bierut, Minc,

Zambrowski, Rokossowski; Communist Positivism was represented by Gomułka, Gierek, and the generation of 1956. But
where, one might ask, were the communist Romantics, and
the communist *émigrés?* The communist Romantics, in the
best Romantic, revolutionary tradition, were dead. The
idealists of the KPP, who had dreamed not of a national but
of an international social revolution, had been cut down in
1938–9 in a massacre of sufficient proportions to discourage all
imitators. They had been crushed by the sheer impracticality
of their position, which vastly overrated both the receptive-
ness of Polish society and the benevolence of their foreign
patrons. As for the communist *émigrés*, one did not have to
wait too long before they, too, made their appearance. Each of
the crises of People's Poland has debouched its wave of ex-
communist expellees and refugees. The great, non-communist
Emigration of 1939–45 has been topped up in 1948, 1956,
1968, 1970, 1976, and 1980–1 by the arrival of the Party's
latest cast-offs. In some cases, as with the arrival of Leszek
Kołakowski or Włodzimierz Brus, the economist, the Emigration has been enriched and enlivened. Oxford's gain has been
Warsaw's loss. In other cases, best left in decent silence, former
Party devotees and executioners, who themselves fell victim to
the dictatorial machine of their own making, have arrived in
the democratic West complaining of everything from unfair
dismissal to racial discrimination. Robespierre, as someone
has said, at least had the decency not to blame the guillotine.

Naturally, it would be wrong to suppose that the communist positivists were the only, or even the most numerous
positivists of the post-war generation. As always, the viability
of the positivist strategy depended on the ability of representatives of the official camp to strike their bargain with
conciliators who came forward in the name of Polish society.
In 1956, as in the nineteenth century, the bargain was struck
under the aegis and arbitration of the Roman Catholic
Church; and the national communist regime launched by
Gomułka depended on the tacit alliance between a wide
variety of Party, pro-Party, non-Party, and even anti-Party
elements. So long as this alliance held, and the Party elements
held the upper hand, the regime could survive. Unfortunately,
as tends to be the case with dictatorships, the regime began to

destroy the very people on whom it most relied. It turned out that the Polish communist movement, in the best tradition of Autocracy, could only tolerate toadies, not free-minded allies. The first shift occurred in the mid-1960s when Gomułka purged the so-called 'revisionists', including Kołakowski, thereby depriving the Party of the only major group of communist intellectuals respected by society at large. This process came to a head in 1968. The second shift occurred in the mid-70s, when Gierek gradually lost the confidence of the remaining non-Party allies. This process began in 1975–6, with the proposals to amend the Constitution, and culminated in 1980 with the birth of SOLIDARITY. In 1965, the communist regime in Poland had still possessed a *modus vivendi* with its reluctant subjects. By 1976 it had lost it; and had no other aim but to keep itself in power. By 1981, it had lost the means to survive by anything but military coercion. The experiment in communist positivism was breaking down. Polish Society, in the generation of SOLIDARITY, saw the first stirrings of the revival of Romanticism. To the historian, or to anyone else with a sense of Poland's past, it has all the aura of a latent tragedy, *déjà vu*. In the space of thirty-five years, the political scene had turned full circle. The native resources of Polish Communism were almost exhausted.

In this context, it must be admitted that the December Coup was intended to preserve the positivist position which had dominated the ruling Establishment ever since 1956. The authors of the Coup must have been alarmed no less by the prospect of a revival of idealism in the Party—which in communist terms would have meant a return to dogmatic Stalinism—than they were by the Romantic tendencies developing within SOLIDARITY. They were faced by the polarization of attitudes on both sides, and acted to preserve their hold on the middle ground. If they were to fail, they knew that the only option remaining would be a move towards the servile Loyalism inherent in direct Soviet intervention in Polish affairs. Even during the State of War of 1982, the official media continued to call for a 'return to positivism' and to advocate the virtues of 'quiet, modest, devoted, work'. The trouble was, these same slogans had been broadcast throughout the 1960s and 1970s by communist leaders, who were now thoroughly discredited, and it was doubtful if many ordinary Poles would be willing to give the communist version of positivism a further chance. What is more, from the viewpoint of Marxism–Leninism, communist Positivism was an absurdity, disliked by the hard-line Comrades in the Party at home, and incomprehensible to the Comrades in Moscow. Faced with the talk of 'positivism' in the Party press, the Warsaw correspondent of the Soviet *Literaturnaya Gazeta* completely misunderstood the specific Polish usage of the term, and bitterly complained to his readers about the Polish Comrades' adoption of the philosophy of Auguste Comte! The impasse was complete.

One last figure deserves a footnote. The position of General Jaruzelski was shot through with contradictions and ambiguities, and his personality remained an enigma. In the eyes of the population at large, he was a prime example of pro-Soviet Loyalism, the man who had crushed SOLIDARITY and who had ended hopes for reconciliation between the ruling Establishment and Polish society. At the same time, in the eyes of the Polish communists, he was the agent of moderation and positivism, who had saved them both from SOLIDAR-ITY and from Soviet retribution. In the eyes of the outside world, he appeared to be a man with no clear political profile. The figure behind the smoked spectacles seemed to be deliberately hiding behind his mask, uttering little more than clichés about his desire 'to serve the nation in its hour of need'. This was not Socialism with a Human Face, nor even Socialism with an *inhuman* face; it was Socialism with no face at all. Humourless, expressionless, listless, the General behaved in public, and spoke on television, with all the lack-lustre of an automaton. Everyone who had known him at various stages of his career made the same report: that his true feelings and convictions had always been concealed, that he was a man 'enclosed in himself'. It was a great puzzle, and there was a great debate as to whether or not, under the cloak of his Soviet-style uniform, he really possessed the heart of a Polish patriot. It emerged that he had been carried off to the Soviet Union as a boy during the deportations of 1939–40, and that he had been reared and trained under Soviet supervision since adolescence. It seemed hard to believe that a person with such a history might not harbour some secret resentments and that he could be whole-heartedly devoted to the Soviet cause. He had the curriculum vitae of a janissary; but none of the fire of a fanatical Turk. He had the air of a Soviet agent, and the reputation at home of a Polish conciliator. There he was, the Grand Master of the Polish Order' of Black Knights, the chief of the ZOMO—and a potential Wallenrod. (See p. 216.)

Little is known about the biography of the real Konrad Wallenrod. It is known that he served as Grand Master of the Teutonic Order for three years, from 1391 to 1394, and that at the end of his rule he led the Order to defeat. But what his motives were, or how the defeat was accomplished, History does not exactly tell.

2 The Military Establishment

The Polish Military Tradition, though different from that of nations with a continuous state history, is very long (see pp. 239–42); and, when the Army assumed power in December 1981, some observers expressed the opinion that the Poles' traditional respect for their soldiers had asserted itself over their habitual contempt for civilian politicians. The Army's publicity machine made a strong bid to reinforce such sentiments. Television newscasters appeared in smart military uniforms, as did old Party journalists, re-dressed and redescribed as 'reserve officers' of the Army's information service. Most Western commentators, too, were eager to emphasize the distinction between the 'respectability' of the Armed Services and the disrepute of the hated and corrupt Party. Some even went so far as to compare General Jaruzelski's regime in Poland with that of General Pinochet in Chile or of the military Junta in Argentina.

Comparisons with the perennial military revolutions of Latin America may not be entirely wide of the mark, in the sense that the Polish Army felt compelled to fill a political vacuum. Yet Jaruzelski, a lifetime communist, did not act to overthrow the communist Establishment but to preserve it, and to give it the chance of regeneration. He acted within the broad framework of the Soviet system, not against it. Even so, the projection of the Military to the forefront of the political stage was an event of momentous significance for the whole Soviet Bloc. According to the Leninist rules, it should not have been necessary or possible. Yet it happened. It can only be appreciated by a close examination of the whole, elaborate, politico-military complex.[2]

In theory, the Armed Forces of the Polish People's Republic conform in all important respects to the Soviet model, and have nothing in common with their predecessors in pre-war and wartime Poland. In the official view, they are an integral part of the new socialist order, which has made a radical break with the past, and which has no connection with Piłsudski's pre-war Polish Army or with the Home Army of 1939–45. They grew from the Polish forces organized by the USSR, starting in 1943 (see p. 94), and from the armed guard of the wartime communist movement. Although a certain number of pre-war officers and men volunteered or were impressed into service at the end of the War, most of these were dismissed during the 1950s; and by 1973 only 2 per cent of the officer corps had pre-war military experience of any kind. From 1949 to 1956, during the formative period of military expansion, the Polish Armed Forces were directly subordinated to the command of Marshal Rokossowski and his Soviet advisers. Since 1956, the prime condition of their relative autonomy from Soviet tutelage has been absolute conformity to the Soviet alliance, based on shared military doctrine, integrated commands, joint exercises, standardized training and equipment, economic co-operation, and rigorous political controls.

Polish military doctrine, as developed in the late 1950s in conjunction with the Soviets, centred on the concept of 'coalition warfare'. This postulated a threat of invasion by NATO and assumed that any independent role for Polish forces against such a threat would be pointless. It aimed to ensure that any warfare between NATO and the Warsaw Pact would take place on 'an external front' beyond Polish territory—presumably in Germany. From this, it follows that Warsaw Pact operations would be offensive, rather than defensive in nature. The Polish forces, therefore, were designed to make a major contribution to the projected campaign to encircle and overwhelm NATO defences between the Elbe and the Rhine. All fifteen of Poland's front line divisions, including the airborne and seaborne assault divisions, were permanently designated to the strategic reserve for this 'external front'; and constituted almost one-third (fifteen out of fifty-one divisions, or 29.4 per cent) of the Warsaw Pact's attack force. The HQ of the Warsaw Pact's Northern Group of Forces is located in Poland, at Legnica in Silesia. The Polish Navy, which possesses no capital ships, was limited to the support role for projected landings on the Baltic coast of North Germany and Denmark; whilst the formidable Polish Air Force, which was equipped with swing-wing SU-20 fighter-bombers as well as with squadrons of MIG 21s and 17s, was devoted to the interceptor role against prospective NATO counter-attacks. As from 1962, the Polish Air Defence Forces were organized as an integral element of the unified Warsaw Pact air defence system. However, some greater sensitivity to Polish national sentiment was evident in the Warsaw Pact's apparent acceptance of the additional concept of a 'Polish Front' whereby ten of Poland's fifteen divisions would fight together under Polish command on a separate, central sector of the Pact's advance into Germany. This concept conflicted with the more usual practice of designating non-Soviet forces to integrated 'multinational Fronts' under Soviet command; and it is doubtful whether the Soviet military fully shared Polish views on this subject.

In conjunction with Poland's massive contribution to the Warsaw Pact's 'external front', Polish strategists in the 1960s developed the complementary concept of 'the Defence of National Territory (OTK)', on 'the internal front'. This postulated a threat from NATO air strikes and missile attacks behind the main battle front, and laid strong emphasis on anti-nuclear Civil Defence. It also justified itself on the grounds that OTK forces could facilitate the transit of Soviet units from the USSR to Germany, and could quell any local threat to Soviet lines of communication. Inevitably, since the main component of Poland's armed forces would be serving abroad in wartime, it assumed that the entire civilian population would have to be trained for mobilization on the home front. In 1967, a new law on national defence embodied the main provisions. The OTK forces, made up of the WOW, the WOP, and the LOK, were separated from the main operational forces of the strategic reserve, and two separate Chief Inspectorates came into being—the *Chief Inspectorate of Training of the General Staff* responsible for the operational forces and the wartime 'external front', and the *Chief Inspectorate for the Defence of National Territory* responsible for the OTK and for the peacetime 'internal front'. A new network of regional military commands was created at the provincial *(voivodship)* level, and renewed emphasis placed on civil defence, territorial units, and the paramilitary volunteer reserve. Although civilian unrest was not a problem at this juncture, the insulation of the internal security forces, and the distancing of the main part of the Armed Services from involvement in internal political affairs, was to have important implications in the future. (As a matter of curiosity, the forces of the pre-war Polish Army were also divided into two separate establishments and designated to two parallel functions—the *tor wojenny* (the wartime track) and the *tor pokojowy* (the peacetime track). Without inside information, it is impossible to say whether the Polish planners of the 1960s were aware of the precedent or not.)

Owing to Poland's membership of the Warsaw Pact, the supreme command of the Armed Forces enjoys only limited scope for independent initiative. The permanent allocation of the main body of Poland's front line troops to the 'external front' means that their orders ultimately derive not from the Polish General Staff but from the Commander-in-Chief of the Warsaw Pact Joint Armed Forces—since 1977, Soviet Marshal V. G. Kulikov. The head of the Chief Inspectorate of Training (General Staff), the most influential of the deputy defence ministers, also serves as a joint deputy commander of the WPJAF and hence is directly dependent on the Soviet Commander-in-Chief. The Polish Chief of Staff, together with other deputy defence ministers, is subject to the Military Council of the Warsaw Pact; just as the Polish Minister of National Defence answers to the Pact's Committee of Defence Ministers, and the Polish Party Secretary to the Pact's Political Consultative Committee.

In this set-up, the Polish General Staff might appear to be almost superfluous; but it retains important functions. The

General Staff acts as a co-ordinating body between the 'external front' sector and the internal OTK sector; and brings together the individual service chiefs, who exercise control over the utilization of their particular services. No one has forgotten that in 1956, despite Marshal Rokossowski's presence as Polish Defence Minister and Commander-in-Chief, General Komar was able to order the KBW to resist the threatened Soviet attack on Warsaw; whilst General Frey-Bielecki and Admiral Jan Wiśniewski put the Air Force and the Navy on a war footing. Warsaw Pact control is far-reaching, but it is not total.

Joint manœuvres of the Warsaw Pact provide a well-tried instrument for strengthening the concept of coalition warfare and for testing the responsiveness of the USSR's allies. They were formally instituted in 1961 and have continued at regular intervals ever since. They took place on Czechoslovak territory in July 1968, immediately prior to the invasion of that country, and were held on Polish territory in 1980, 1981, and 1982. As from 1970, the forces of the Polish OTK Command have also conducted their own, separate exercises—which is one reason why their deployment for the December coup in 1981 did not arouse undue suspicions.

Standardized training, and standardized equipment and supplies, characterize all the armed forces of the Warsaw Pact—and the standards are set by the Permanent Secretariat of the Pact in Moscow. Although each member country is expected to contribute certain specialized items—Poland supplies armoured vehicles, small arms, naval vessels, ammunition, communications equipment, chemical products, and so on—the overwhelming mass of military equipment and of military fuel comes from the Soviet Union. The USSR's allies are given to complaining that Soviet clients in Vietnam, the Middle East, or southern Africa enjoy preferential treatment in the supply of the most modern Soviet weaponry; but their deepest resentment centres on the fact that by withholding spare parts, key supplies, or vital devices, the Soviet Union can render much of their existing equipment inoperative. Poland's tank regiments, for example, are almost completely dependent on the Soviet oil pipeline; whilst it is believed that Polish missile units do not possess their own warheads and that the

Polish parachute division does not possess adequate transport aircraft. Officer training follows a similar pattern. Although the days of Russians dressed in Polish uniforms are past (see p. 34), no senior Polish officer progresses beyond the rank of colonel without an extended course of further training in a Soviet military academy.

As in all countries of the Soviet Bloc, the Polish military establishment possesses its own 'private' economic sector, which is integrated with the vast and privileged military-industrial complex of the Warsaw Pact as a whole. Details of these relationships are the subject of high secrecy; but it is generally believed in the West that the economic affairs of the Warsaw Pact are organized along the same lines, and in conjunction with, the 'specialized allocation system' adopted by Comecon. Indeed, it is reasonable to suppose, since the secret military economy enjoys precedence over the public economy within each member state of the Soviet Bloc, that the economic planning of the Warsaw Pact enjoys precedence over the civilian planning of Comecon. Co-ordination is reportedly achieved through Comecon's confidential Military–Industrial Committee. Thanks to the mechanisms of a command economy, which can impose priorities from on high, no serious complications were encountered, so long as the economy of Poland, and of the Pact as a whole, continued to show a health growth rate.

Ideological conformity is an essential attribute of the Soviet-style military system. The Armed Services are conceived as an active element in 'the building of Communism'. In Poland, however, the obligatory baggage of Marxism–Leninism has always been yoked to a strong load of Nationalism, especially after 1956—thus reflecting trends in the Party as a whole (see p. 326). At least in its public manifestations, the Military's Nationalism has always followed the communist 'Patriotic' formula rather than 'patriotism' as understood by the population at large. The organs of military propaganda, such as the army newspaper *Żołnierz Wolności* (Soldier of Freedom), eternally insist that Polish independence and Polish patriotism are synonymous with the Polish–Soviet alliance. They are very keen to demonstrate their pride in Polish military history; and the publishing house of the

Ministry of Defence (MON) has sponsored much interesting work in this field. Yet a customary glance at a list of published titles shows how biased and selective the military propagandists are. Inordinate prominence is given to the victorious phase of the War against Germany in 1943–5; work on medieval knights, on wars against Swedes and Turks, on Hussars, Napoleonic Legions, insurrectionary guerrillas, the Paris Commune, or the Spanish Civil War, is clearly encouraged; but important topics such as the German defeat of Russia on the Polish front in 1914–17, the Polish victory over Soviet Russia in 1919–20, or the initial period of the Second World War from 1939 to 1941, are conspicuously neglected. The ordinary Polish soldier, browsing in his billet or studying for his political exams, is led to believe that Germany alone is Poland's eternal enemy; that NATO is on the brink of attacking the Warsaw Pact; and that Poland's only safety lies in her unshakable alliance with the benevolent and invincible Soviet Union. Polish conscripts were required to swear an oath of loyalty not merely to Poland and the Commander-in-Chief but to socialism and the People's Republic.

Political control over the Armed Services was designed to operate both vertically, through three or four separate chains of authority, and horizontally through political organizations implanted at every level from the General Staff to the battalion and the company. Prior to 1981, the Chief Political Administration (GZP) of the General Staff functioned simultaneously as a Department of the Party's Secretariat and as a division of the Ministry of National Defence. In this way, it ensured the subordination of the General Staff to the highest Party and State authorities. It ran the Military Political Academy—the Alma Mater of all officers, and the pinnacle of all military education; it stood at the head of the political departments whose officers doubled up with all field commanders and supervised the work of all military personnel; it organized the Party cells, which functioned in all military branches and units; and it headed the Military Youth Organization (ZMW) which had the task of indoctrinating the rank-and-file conscripts. Its work was overseen by its senior partner in the Party's Secretariat, the innocuously named Administrative Department, which managed the *nomenklatura* of the General Staff on behalf of the Political Bureau, co-ordinated military affairs with those of the police and intelligence services, and ran the Military Security Service (WSW). This last body—the Party's armed service within the Armed Services—should not be confused with the WOW. It served as a form of military police for political matters, and existed for the purpose of eliminating dissent from within the Military. Hence, from top to bottom, and from side to side, the military machine was designed to be the Party's humble and obedient servant.

Some Western authorities have suggested that the Soviet military was not content to exercise indirect restraint over its Polish allies through this elaborate chain of commands and controls. After the withdrawal of Rokossowski, key appointments in the Polish military machine were said to be still reserved for Soviet officers; whilst particular specialist security services, such as the Military Counter-Intelligence Service, remained in the hands of the Soviet KGB. A high-ranking Soviet political officer was permanently attached to the Polish Ministry of Defence. In this way, the Soviets would have possessed an effective reinsurance policy. Deficiencies or irregularities in the Polish Military could be spotted in good time, and nipped in the bud.

None of these dispositions, of course, had much to do with Poland's own native military tradition. Soviet military planners could take pride in creating a Polish Army of a new type. In theory, at least, they could be satisfied with their handiwork. Over the years, however, a number of discrepancies have crept into the system—almost all them attributable to the nature of Polish society within which the Soviet-style Polish Army is expected to operate.

The Polish Military has been repeatedly disrupted by political factionalism in the ruling Party and by shifts in organizational policy. Following the expulsion of Rokossowski's Soviet advisers, the Polish Armed Services were racked throughout the 1960s by the campaign of General Moczar's 'Partisans', whose avowed aim of cleansing public life of 'alien' elements and 'Zionist agents' attracted many sympathizers. The campaign, which had covertly anti-Soviet as well as overtly anti-Semitic overtones, culminated in 1967–8 in the purge of fourteen generals and 200 colonels. But it did not result in Moczar's victory. The ousted officers were replaced by reliably pro-Soviet, but factionally neutral professionals of whom General Jaruzelski, appointed Defence Minister in April 1968, was archetypal. Further upheavals were caused by attempts to restructure officer training. Technological advances in modern warfare made it imperative that military training should include a much larger technological component. Between 1958 and 1974, the number of officers with higher degrees of the physical sciences or engineering rose from 17 to 40 per cent. To keep pace with technical modernization, the curriculum of the trainees of the political departments was also altered, to give them the ability to talk with their military commanders on equal terms. Inevitably, the purely political component of training was greatly reduced in all branches of the Services. The habitual mistrust between the old-style 'commissars' and their professional military colleagues was significantly blunted; whilst the antagonism between the modernized Military and the unreformed Party apparatus was significantly sharpened. Thus in the 1970s a running battle began between civilian comrades in the Party Secretariat who wanted to maintain direct Party control over the Chief Political Administration, and military comrades in the General Staff who wanted to protect themselves from the influence of an indecisive and increasingly corrupt Party leadership. Following the catastrophe of 1970, when regular army units were ordered by the Party to fire on Baltic rioters, the higher ranks of the Armed Services felt increasingly disinclined to rescue the Party leadership from the results of its crass follies. In 1976, General Jaruzelski, rightly or wrongly, was credited with the dictum that 'Polish soldiers do not shoot Polish workers'; and the Army's stand on this occasion provides the best explanation of Gierek's sudden reversal of his offending price policy. After that, as the civilian apparatus of the Party steadily fell victim to creeping paralysis, the standing of the Military steadily increased. With the Party Secretariat issuing few firm directives to its representatives in the Armed Services, the officer corps was gradually left in charge of its own affairs. It is reasonable to suppose that the General Staff won the battle for control of the Political Departments. For the first time in the long history of a Communist Army, the Polish officer corps was master in its own house. By 1980, when the Party apparatus was approaching the point of collapse, the Polish Military was already in a position to arbitrate with the Kremlin over Poland's fate. These developments were the necessary pre-condition for Jaruzelski's 'Coup' in December 1981.

In the late 1970s, therefore, when lowly researchers in the West had dared to enquire whether the Polish Military was not gaining the upper hand within the communist regime, they were solemnly told by their senior professors that such things under Leninism were impossible. Yet they were proved right. In normal times, the military element is the junior servant of the senior, civilian, element of the communist system. But in abnormal times, when the civilian apparatus ceases to function as intended, the Military is duty-bound to assume the leading role. In Poland, the Party Dictatorship was obliged to hand over to a Military Dictatorship; and the civilian politicos gave way to their military colleagues. Henceforward, it was the army officers who gained the final word in relations between the Armed Services and the Party. General Jaruzelski successfully demonstrated the first law of Leninism—that a ruling communist clique, whether in mufti or in uniform, never voluntarily surrenders power to its popular opponents, even if the Party itself is crippled in the process.

Yet it is important to recognize that the Polish military establishment is not a simple monolith. It is a complicated amalgam of numerous specialized services, each with their own interests, their own *esprit de corps,* and their own idiosyncratic attitudes to the country's problems. One may safely assume that the professional security forces, the WOW and the WSW, like their counterparts in the civil Militia, the ZOMO, were effectively immunized against the SOLIDAR-ITY virus, and had been conditioned by intensive political and psychological training to accept action against political 'hooligans' as part of their routine. It is interesting to recall that in 1956 the KBW was no less responsive to the order to crush the Poznań rioters in June, than to confront the Soviet invaders in October. In 1970, the mistake of using the regular conscript troops of the local Gdańsk Military Region, instead of an élite security brigade from Warsaw, was never properly explained; but it had very serious consequences. It caused immense resentment in the officer corps, and was followed by a spectacular drop in officer recruitment; and it raised the spectre of mutiny. The lesson was certainly well heeded in December 1981, when the frontal assaults on strikers and demonstrators were left to the ZOMO, with Army details held in reserve for patrol and cordon duties. For there can be no question that regular army units reject the callous indifference to popular feeling so ostentatiously cultivated by the security forces. No less than 73 per cent of total military manpower consists of raw young conscripts, who come into the service at the age of eighteen, thoroughly inoculated by their mothers, their friends, and their parish priests against everything which their political officers are going to tell them. Lech Wałęsa was a conscript corporal in the Polish Army, and was described by his former commander as a good soldier; yet one can see what the Army's political training did for *him*. As from 1982, and for four or five years ahead at least, every conscript intake will consist overwhelmingly of former members or sympathizers of SOLIDARITY. The Army Command will have a difficult choice: either to curtail conscription (as it did in 1981) and renege on its obligations to the Warsaw Pact; or to continue conscription at its normal level and dilute the Army's reliability with every new intake.

At the other end of the scale, the officer corps is characterized by particularist attitudes and inter-service rivalries. It is common knowledge that élite formations such as the Parachute Division feel undisguised contempt for the political, security, and police services. This was publicly demonstrated in the disturbances of March 1968 when young 'red berets' of the garrison in Cracow took sides against the Militiamen besieging a recalcitrant student hostel. Feelings of this sort must abound in all the most self-respecting units. The more educated the officer, the greater is his pride in his technical or professional proficiency, and the deeper his distaste for the sordid political purposes which the Armed Services have been required to serve.

In which regard, special note might be taken of the Polish Air Force, whose aloofness from recent political events was very striking. One can reasonably expect the Air Force to steer clear of civil unrest. No one in his wildest fantasies was likely to suggest that SOLIDARITY strikers should have been bombed and strafed from the air. But one cannot conclude that the Air Force is immune from the emotions of society as a whole. Polish airmen may be the most professional among professionals, but even they must have their sensitivities and their memories. They can hardly forget that the finest hour in the history of their service was in the Battle of Britain in 1940, or that those same Polish heroes returning home from the RAF were treacherously shot or imprisoned on fictional charges of treason and espionage. Just as the aloofness of the Armed Services as a whole gave them a position of supremacy over a divided Party apparatus in the late 1970s, so the aloofness of the Air Force could give it a position of supremacy within an officer corps torn by the strains of Martial Law and the war against SOLIDARITY. After all, everyone in Poland has been preoccupied with the possibility of a Warsaw Pact invasion, and the Air Force is the only arm of the Polish services to possess a significant deterrent. The Kremlin could hardly want to launch its campaign to liberate Poland from counter-revolution by bombing the bases of Poland's interceptor squadrons.

On the economic front, the anxieties of the Polish Military were rising throughout the 1970s. According to Western experts, the proportion of Poland's GNP devoted to military expenditure peaked in 1970, and has been falling ever since.[3] Gierek's economic strategy, to meet consumer demands and to modernize industry through foreign loans and imports, was clearly undertaken to the disadvantage of the military interest. An increase in civilian expenditure automatically involved slower growth for the military budget; whilst the Armed Services could not benefit in any direct way from Western loans or from Western (strictly non-military) technology. Although military expenditure seems to have moved modestly ahead in simple accounting terms, in relative terms it suffered a drastic set-back. As a result, Polish military programmes fell seriously behind schedule: Polish deliveries of military supplies to Warsaw Pact partners began to dwindle; and the first strains between General Staff and Party leadership made themselves apparent. After 1975, when

Gierek's strategy began to head for disaster, the distress of the military economy was doubly compounded. As the Polish Government edged towards bankruptcy *vis-à-vis* its Western creditors, so the Polish Military edged towards the point of incapacity in its obligations in the Warsaw Pact. There could be no hope of salvation unless the Party leadership were removed, and the country's entire economic priorities remodelled. That calculation alone must have tempted the Polish generals (and behind them the Soviet Marshals) to consider the overthrow of the PZPR. But worse was to come. In 1980–1, support for SOLIDARITY spread quickly among the workers of the military–industrial sector. The armaments factories at Stalowa Wola and at Radom—which had been picked on for special punishment in 1976 because of their military connections—were militant centres of SOLIDARITY activism. When all the other institutes of higher learning in Poland were conceded the right of free elections, the Government denied this concession to the Radom Politechnic, and doggedly upheld the continued appointment of its rector, Colonel Michał Hebda, against all protests. Unknown to the public at large and certainly to the Western press, the Radom Politechnic was the principal scientific and technical training ground for employees of the military-economic sector, and Rector Hebda was a military, not an academic, appointee. On this issue, which brought the general academic strike to a head in November 1981, SOLIDARITY thought it was fighting for academic freedom. The military was fighting for the survival of its economic autonomy. This incident, more than any other, alerted the authorities both in Warsaw and in Moscow, to the fact that SOLIDARITY had begun to sap the hidden foundations of communist power. If by that stage the Kremlin had still needed to be convinced of the coming military take-over, the news from Radom must have swept all remaining doubts aside.

The net result of the Military's experiences, therefore, was to turn the generals into advocates both of reform and of caution. On the one hand, they realized better than anyone else that the established system of corrupt Party rule was on the road to ruin, and that it had to be revived by new political and economic measures. On the other hand, they knew from their own soldiers that any attempt to impose reforms of an extreme ideological nature would provoke a violent popular reaction, and that the distasteful and uncertain task of suppressing any major disturbance would fall on them. In this way, General Jaruzelski emerged as the natural ally of the moderate trimmers and centrists of the Party, like Rakowski and Barcikowski. He was the natural ringleader, to hold the balance between the radical neo-Stalinist reformers and the ultra-conservative bureaucrats. As the Party machine gradually ground to a halt, the General Staff had little option but to substitute itself for the Political Bureau, and to suppress SOLIDARITY. At the same time, it was careful to use a minimum of force, and to keep the door ajar for future reform. To this extent, from the communist viewpoint, the Military Take-over must be rated a brilliant move. It saved the regime from total collapse; it obviated the necessity for fraternal assistance from the USSR; it restored confidence that Poland would fulfil its role in the Warsaw Pact; and it rescued a demoralized Party from fratricidal strife. As a stopgap measure, it worked wonders.

None the less, as the creators of the first military regime in the communist world, the Polish generals must soon have become desperately conscious of their delicate predicament. Having committed the cardinal sin of 'Bonapartism', they would be pressed to step down at the first opportunity. Indeed, there is little reason to doubt that most of them would have loved to return to soldiering forthwith and to hand back politics to the politicians. Yet they were hooked on the tangled horns of several interlocking dilemmas. They were faced with disasters at every turn. If they proceeded to a prompt dialogue with the Church, and with the representatives of the post-SOLIDARITY opposition, they laid themselves open to charges from Moscow of betraying the socialist camp. If they followed the advice of the Party hard-liners to enter on a programme of doctrinaire reform, they risked an outburst of popular violence. If they relinquished power to a Party apparatus devoid of authority, they invited a return to the chaos of 1980–1. If they were to hang on to power indefinitely, they would arouse the suspicions both of their own Party comrades and of the fraternal parties of the Bloc. If they did nothing—which must have been very tempting—they would have let the country sink even deeper into political paralysis and economic penury. The negative proscriptive powers of the Military Regime had already been demonstrated; and its capacity for positive constructive action was known to be minimal. Yet its ability simply to depart from the scene, and to wash its hands of politics for good, must also have been in doubt. The Polish Bonapartists had none of Bonaparte's military talents and few of his political ambitions; but they were stuck with their responsibilities. How they must have longed for an Isle of Elba, or for a lifetime's retreat on St. Helena!

Step by step over the last decade, every member of the Polish Military has been made aware of the dubious rationale on which his very existence has been based. In 1970, the Treaty with West Germany, which ended Polish fears for the security of the Oder–Neisse Line, removed Poland's need for an indefinite military alliance with the USSR. In the mid-70s, the fiasco over the Civil Defence programme showed that no one in Poland, not even the Party leadership, seriously believed in the danger of an imminent NATO attack. The recurrent political crises—in 1970, 1976, 1980, 1981—in which the Army was repeatedly asked to bail out the Party, taught them how heartily the communist system was loathed by the nation at large. Most ominously, since 1981, when tens of thousands of soldiers were brought out from the seclusion of their barracks, and placed on patrol in the streets or on guard duty in the mines and factories, almost every serviceman in Poland was personally subjected to the silent, contemptuous glances of his compatriots. From the dimmest recruit, to the most die-hard general, the awful realization must slowly have dawned. If Poland was not threatened by West Germany—which seemed to be sending rather a lot of free food parcels—and if it was not going to be attacked by NATO; and if the Soviet-backed communist system was not the protector of the Polish people, but its oppressor, then for what purpose did the Armed Services of the People's Republic exist? Such thoughts, in official jargon, smacked of 'anti-socialist' and 'anti-Soviet' delusions; and Anti-Sovietism was a still more heinous crime than Bonapartism.

For obvious reasons, the process of ferment in the Armed Forces was bound to proceed more slowly than that in the civil population at large. For most of their careers, professional officers were shielded from the stresses and strains of public discontent. They enjoyed reserved housing, reserved stores, and reserved recreation centres. Their families did not have to stand in bread queues, and did not feel immediate resentment against the regime from which their special privileges derived. In any case, for many years after the War, the German menace was genuinely feared in Poland, and there were genuine hopes in a radicalized society that Communism might bring some real benefits. Only the direct involvement of the Armed Services in political affairs could trigger the disillusionment which other sections of society had begun to feel at a much earlier stage. In this process, the December Coup of 1981 must have provided the key experience. Until 1981, the military chiefs could have felt fairly confident that the security forces could cope with a limited operation of repression. After 1981, they could be fairly certain that the Armed Services as a whole could not be ordered to crush any major popular outburst in the future. Poland's 'Army card' had been played; it could not be played again. In any future confrontation between the communist Establishment and the people, the Polish communists would have no recourse but to call for rescue from the Soviet Army. At which point, and not before, the world would learn the truth about who in the Polish Military was a covert Soviet surrogate and who was a genuine Polish patriot.

Even so, there have been so many veiled hints about a possible Soviet invasion, that anyone with the slightest sense of History must have been constantly reminded of all those occasions in the past when the Russians marched into Poland for real—in 1944–5, in 1939, in 1919–20, in 1863, in 1831, in 1813, in 1794, in 1791–2, in 1768–72, in 1710, in 1706, in 1655, in 1632. . . . . Although the most recent of those invasions do not figure prominently in the textbooks of the Military Political Academy, all the earlier ones do. Traugutt, Bem, Sowiński, Kościuszko, Poniatowski, are all heroes of the official military pantheon; and they all made their names by fighting against the Russians. Nor can one seriously doubt that every Polish soldier, irrespective of his political views, has a sneaking admiration for Piłsudski and heartfelt pangs of conscience for the victims of Katyn. As from December 1981, the false historical propaganda of the last thirty years lost its relevance. In the hearts and minds of all those Polish servicemen who could be faced at any time with the agonizing choice between assisting a Soviet invasion of their country or of resisting it, Poland's genuine military tradition has suddenly acquired very special significance.

In the meantime, outside observers must content themselves with the intriguing puzzle of the mechanisms through which the leaders of the Military Regime have undertaken to govern the country. General Jaruzelski, as chairman of the WRON, Commander-in-Chief of the Armed Forces, First Secretary of Party, Prime Minister of the State Government, and Minister of National Defence, certainly amassed more benefices than the average Renaissance Cardinal; but it was never publicly advertised how the various institutions under his control related to each other. The Political Bureau of the Party, formerly the supreme decision-making body, was not abolished, though its membership was changed. The Central Committee continued to hold occasional meetings. The Party Secretariat presumably continued to function; but it was hard to believe that it could still give orders to the Army. The Council of Ministers continued to minister, although several ministries were axed; and the Sejm, unchanged in composition since 1979, actually accelerated the passing of new laws. The President of the Republic, and his Council of State, who had approved the emergency decree of 13 December, were left in place. The WRON was put in charge of the State of War, and all the duties deriving therefrom; but there was no evidence that it had formally usurped the powers of the Political Bureau or of the Council of Ministers. So where, other than in General Jaruzelski's person, was the centre of power located? A personal dictatorship would have been as unsuited to the General himself, who did not have the manner of a Tito or a Ceaucescu, as it was to the communist system as a whole. One can only surmise; but the kernel of Jaruzelski's Military-Party cabal seems to have resided in a shadowy body, sometimes referred to as the Committee for the

Country's Defence (KOK). Just as in an orthodox communist system, the official State Government does not care to advertise its subservience to the Party's Political Bureau, so in this new variant of Leninism 'the Crow' took pains to conceal its subordination to 'the Cock'. The existence of this confidential but crucial policy-making Committee was divined by specialists who comb the communist press for signs of such developments; and it was thought to consist of equal numbers of generals from the WRON and of civilian members of the Political Bureau. Its meetings were supposedly held under General Jaruzelski's chairmanship. In this case, Jaruzelski's sixth and unacknowledged appointment would have been his most important. Like Poland's more famous military dictator, he preferred to exercise his dictatorship from behind the scenes, and to maintain the façade of existing institutions. Apart from these coincidences, however, and the fact that both men happened to seize power at exactly the same point in their careers, at the age of 58, the parallel between Wojciech Jaruzelski and Józef Piłsudski stops there.

3 Workers' Control

The sudden suppression of SOLIDARITY in December 1981 took almost everyone by surprise (see p. 16); and it is a bold soul who would now claim with hindsight that he had foreseen it all. The very existence of SOLIDARITY engendered a spirit of hope amongst everyone except the communist Establishment; and that hope was successfully exported to Western observers. In 1980 and 1981, nobody wanted to listen to those few eccentric prognosticators who dared to warn of coming disaster. Yet in retrospect, if one examines the record of workers' movements under Soviet Communism over a longer period, the fate of SOLIDARITY does not appear to be in any way unusual or extraordinary.

The advocates of Soviet Communism, of course claim not only that their philosophy is socialist in nature, but also that it is the only true form of 'socialism'. The CPSU rules in the name of 'the workers and peasants'; and in the Soviet Union, the first 'Workers' State', the cult of the heroic worker, the avant-garde of the proletariat, is to be seen at every corner. The entire symbolism of Soviet ideology—the 'hammer and sickle'; the Stakhanovites; the cultural 'shock brigades'; the whole repertoire of 'Socialist Realism' is built round the motif of 'the Worker'. Indeed, one of the three founding decrees of 1917—for Bread, Peace, and Work—was launched under Lenin's slogan: 'All power to the Workers.' For the millions of people, inside the Soviet Union and out, who take these symbols and slogans at face value, it is hard to understand why the Soviet leaders, or the leaders of a Soviet ally, should have to contemplate the suppression of a genuine workers' movement.

Yet the historical record, both in the communist movement of the USSR and in that of the USSR's Polish neighbour, is crystal clear. Leaving aside the suppression of the Social Revolutionary Party in Russia, which the Bolsheviks claimed was neither social nor revolutionary (because it was not controlled by the Bolsheviks), the very first movement within the Bolshevik camp to be forcibly suppressed was that of Tomsky's so-called 'Workers' Opposition'. Tomsky had argued in favour of workers' control to be exercised through autonomous trade unions; but at the first opportunity after the Civil War, at the Tenth Congress of 1921, Tomsky found himself vilified by Lenin and block-voted out of any position of influence. There was no ambiguity about Lenin's view of 'workers' control': the Party must control the workers. Since then, every attempt by Soviet workers to run their own affairs has been ruthlessly stamped out. Workers, in their capacity as workers, play no part in the Soviet system. In Poland, the picture has hardly been much happier. Leaving aside the suppression of the KPP, which Stalin held to have deviated from genuine communism (because it did not respond swiftly enough to Stalin's demands), there is no instance where the ruling Polish communist movement has tolerated for long, let alone initiated, an organization based on the principle of workers' control. The scheme for workers' self-management launched in 1957 in the afterglow of Gomułka's October was never allowed to achieve its original aims. The independent role of the Workers' Councils created on that occasion was swiftly muffled by their absorption into Party-controlled

Committees of Workers' Self-Management (KSR). 'Self-management' in the language of the Party turned out to mean 'management by the Party'. Thereafter, prompted no doubt from Moscow, the PZPR learned its lesson. No more experiments were permitted. In 1970–1, following the Baltic riots, Gierek's promises to give the workers a greater say in the decisions which most closely affected them, were quietly ignored. Similar demands in 1976 went unheeded. The Independent Trade Union Movement from which SOLIDARITY eventually sprang, and which had existed in embryo since 1976, was forced to operate in the underground in complete obscurity, and on an illegal basis. When the representatives of the PZPR signed the Gdańsk Agreements in August 1980, and when the Warsaw District Court formally registered 'SOLIDARITY' as a legal organization on 10 November 1980, they were breaking the established norm of all official conduct in the Soviet Bloc. In that context, it should not have been so surprising that SOLIDARITY was due to be suppressed. On the contrary, it was surprising that SOLIDARITY contrived to last so long.

In September 1982, nine months after the December Coup, the Military Regime introduced a statute formally terminating all existing trade unions, and introducing a project for new, factory-based unions. An official propaganda campaign urged the workers to join; but hardly anyone bothered to do so. The prevailing view, solicited from the shipyard workers of Gdańsk by Western reporters, was 'either SOLIDARITY or nothing'. If the Polish workers were not to be allowed to control their own unions, they were not disposed to fall once more for the communists' blandishments. One of their lasting achievements in 1980–1 was to show the whole world that in communist parlance 'Workers' Control' means 'Control of the Workers by the communists'.

4 Poetry in the Shipyards

Despite widespread reporting, much of the cultural content of the SOLIDARITY era was lost on the outside world. Western reporters, whose knowledge of trade union disputes centred on the social and economic issues most familiar in their own countries, did not always reach out beyond and beneath the material aspects. When they did, they tended to notice the all-pervasive religious element, which could hardly be avoided; and, quite rightly, to stress the role of the Roman Catholic Church. But often, whether through the language barrier or from their own predisposition, they failed to catch the subtler literary and historical allusions which in their way were equally significant. 'Poetry-reading in Poland' did not make such good headlines in the foreign press as a riot or a demonstration; and the text of a Polish poem, hastily typed and cyclostyled on the backs of office paper, was much harder to decipher than the mass of more readily intelligible political slogans, cartoons, or appeals.

Yet for the people involved, for the millions who supported SOLIDARITY, it is arguable that the cultural element in all its aspects, including the religious services, lectures, film shows, concerts, and cabarets, as well as the purely literary events, was cherished no less fervently than the demands for union rights, increased wages, or improved factory conditions. Workers in the West, who live in democratic societies where most of their freedoms are respected for most of the time, feel little need to press their unions for cultural fare, since every family is free to cultivate, or to ignore, the cultural activities of its own choice. In the communist world, however, where all Culture is supposed to be a branch of official propaganda, workers' needs are rather different. Workers show genuine excitement and enthusiasm at the prospect of a dramatic performance or an informal poetry reading, with its promise of the forbidden fruit of double meanings and ambiguous images. (It is no accident that the largest popular audience in the world for poetry is to be found in the Soviet Union.) In Poland, where the independence of the Church has tradition-ally provided an umbrella for a measure of cultural freedom, the social demands for free expression might have been judged less urgent. None the less, they were made all the same with great force, and no picture of the era is complete without them.

Most remarkably, the main initiative in the cultural sphere seems to have come less from the professionals than from the common people themselves. There was a spontaneous outburst, a vast manifestation of the thirst of the masses for genuine and unfettered culture. Of course, professionals like Andrzej Wajda, the film-maker, who were quick off the mark, made a valuable contribution. The public screening of Wajda's *Man of Iron* as from July 1981, often in conjunction with its predecessor *Man of Marble,* left an indelible impression on its millions of viewers. After that, popular awareness of the manipulation of ordinary working people by the Party, and the resultant demoralization and brutalization of society, knew no bounds. Lecturers, actors, musicians, artists often contributed their services free, in support of SOLIDARITY-sponsored events. Yet the real marvel of the day was set by the spontaneous participation of countless young men and women, often lacking in formal education, whose sensitivity to cultural values might not previously have been noticed. It was not altogether unexpected in Catholic Poland that strikers should pray, among other things, for the Party and Government, or that youngsters with guitars should gather to sing their versions of Western protest songs of the 1960s. 'LET US PRAY FOR THOSE IN AUTHORITY, AND FORGIVE OUR ENEMIES' and 'WE SHALL OVERCOME' were standard parts of the repertoire. Students of the Politechnic might post a poem in the street to touch passers-by for donations to their strike fund. But when dockers and miners showed that they knew their Mickiewicz and Słowacki, and sought to circulate the classics of Polish literature at their meetings and demonstrations, it must have surprised and delighted even the most sceptical professors. For a while, poetry came into the open in Poland's steelworks, mines, and shipyards.

The first sign of the phenomenon appeared before the gates of the Lenin Shipyard during the original strike of August 1980. A scrap of paper, attached to the makeshift wooden cross commemorating the victims of ten years before, bore an eccentric but recognizable quote from Byron's poem *The Giaour:*

> For Freedom's Battle once begun,
> Bequeath'd by bleeding sire to son,
> Though baffled oft is ever won . . . .

Significantly enough, as a sign of non-violence, the word for 'bleeding' was omitted; the word 'oft' was translated as 'one hundred times', and there were various other inconsistencies. The poem was wrongly attributed to Krasiński, although the original Polish translation had been undertaken by Mickiewicz. But no matter, some unknown striker, or possibly a huddle of eager strikers behind the gates, had racked their brains to recover those most appropriate lines of Romantic poetry that had first reached Poland more than 150 years before. Their mistakes are proof of their spontaneity.[4]

Elsewhere, on the walls of the besieged shipyard, the strikers hung posters and slogans addressed to the crowds of wives and sweethearts standing in support outside. The most frequent posters carried the words of an anonymous verse, *Farewell, my lass, our country calls me away!*, popularized during the November Rising. Again, the textual accuracy left something to be desired; but the meaning was absolutely exact:

> PAMIĘTAJ ŻEŚ POLKA
> O POLSKĄ SPRAWĘ WALKA.
> OBOWIĄZEK JĄ BRONIĆ
> TO TWOJA RYWALKA.

> Oh why beats your heart, why tears in your eye?
> I owe you my Love, owe my country, my Life.
> Think who you are, and think of our Duty.
> Your rival, my girl, is Poland's Liberty.[5]

During the long summer days of the strike, actors from the local *Wybrzeże* (Coastland) company, were called to the shipyard to entertain the workers with readings of Mickiewicz, Słowacki, Norwid. Their Director was overwhelmed by the reception:

We were rather fearful about employing our usual, professional routine, but it turned out that the texts were marvellously received. Mickiewicz's *Books of the Polish Pilgrimage* made an impact on the listeners as if it had just come hot from the author's pen. In the auditorium where we had to perform, there was a constant clatter of typewriters, and telex machines. But during 'Father Peter's Vision' everything fell silent. People openly wept . . . We were begged for encores. . . . I talked to the workers myself, and it appeared that they really need great literature and great poetry.[6]

In December 1980, when the permanent monument to the workers was unveiled, poetry entered the scene once more.

The unveiling ceremony, attended by Church and State dignitaries and a guard of honour of uniformed commandos, began with the singing of *Rota* (The Oath), the defiant anthem of the Poles in Prussia composed by Maria Konopnicka. Despite the flurries of winter snow, it was sung with all the fervour that it had evoked seventy years before when it was first heard in public at the unveiling of the Grunwald Monument in Cracow by Ignacy Paderewski:

> We shall not yield our forebears' land
> Nor watch our language muted.
> Our Nation is Polish, and Polish our folk,
> By Piasts constituted.
> By cruel oppression we'll not be swayed.
> May God so lend us aid.[7]

The melody possesses all the *hwll* of a Welsh hymn. (*Rota* for the Poles is what *Cwm Rhondda* is for the Welsh.) Then the sash was pulled, and the monument's plaque revealed. Under the towering crosses, and the anchor of the Home Army, words from a poem by Czesław Miłosz were carved in bronze:

> You, who wronged a simple man,
> Bursting into laughter at the crime,
> And kept a crowd of fools around you,
> Mixing good with evil to blur the line,
> Though everyone bowed down before you
> Saying Virtue and Wisdom lit your way,
> Striking gold medals in your honour
> And glad to have survived another day,—
> Do not feel safe. The poet remembers.
> You can slay him, but another is always born.
> The words are written down, the deed, the date.
> You could have done better with a winter's dawn,
> And a rope, and a branch bent down beneath your weight.[8]

In such a context, there could be no doubt to whom the poem referred.

Czesław Miłosz (born 1911), together with John Paul II and Lech Wałęsa, was one of the faces which most strongly makred the Polish renaissance of 1980–1. Having lived in exile for nearly thirty years, Miłosz was Poland's greatest living poet; but until he was awarded the Nobel Prize for Literature in 1980 his works had remained on the Party's Index. Suddenly the ban was broken, and the demand for his poems outran all possibility of supply. A Pole from Lithuania, a man stamped with the excellence of pre-war education and refinement, and a non-communist Marxist, Miłosz defied all the narrow dogmas of official ideology. His triumphant return to his homeland in 1981 came second only to that of John Paul II two years earlier. His meeting with Wałęsa, at the Catholic University of Lublin, was a delightfully enthusiastic romp, a living demonstration of the alliance between the intelligentsia and the proletariat. Later, he returned once more to exile in California.

By general consent, however, the most popular poetry of the entire SOLIDARITY era belonged to Juliusz Słowacki. For reasons which literary historians will no doubt dissect at their leisure, the hard-headed, hard-hatted workers of the Polish labour force felt the greatest affinity with the works of the most Romantic of the Polish Romantics. At all the mass rallies and ceremonies, not merely in Gdańsk, but equally on 3 May throughout the country, at Wałęsa's recital of Kościuszko's oath on the city square in Kraków, the most widely circulated handbills carried Słowacki's renderings of the songs of the Confederates of Bar from *Ksiądz Marek* (see p. 221):

> We'll never submit to be allies of kings,
> We'll ne'er bend our necks to power and might.
> For only from Christ do we take our commands,
> We are Servants of the Virgin![9]

In one form or another, these lines have been sung in Poland for over two hundred years. They are part of the national heritage. They cannot be erased by truncheons and water-cannon.

SOLIDARITY even inspired its own breed of poets. Time is too short for the literary world to have sifted the products of genuine talent from the mass of amateur ephemera; but the intensity of feeling, and the awareness of the national tradition, were to be met with at every hand. The habit of expressing political attitudes in Romantic verse, and the wish to sample the outpourings of the versifiers on walls, lamp-posts, and broadsheets, were everywhere in evidence. Typically, perhaps, when the students of the Warsaw Academy of Fine Arts joined the national educational strike in November 1981, only days before the declaration of the State of War, their appeal for donations to the strike fund was accompanied by a long poem pasted to a billboard outside the academy's locked gates:

Polonia Resurrecta

My country, of joyful promise and sorrowful Springs,
My country of greying birch trees,
My country of the Vistula, flowing slowly,
My country of church bells, singing in tears,
My country bearing shame in patience . . .
This is not the Poland desired by our forebears.
This is not the land of which they dreamed.
For Poland, You are a City of the Dead;
Poland, You are a tomb for the living.
Your nation, oh Poland, is a half-cremated corpse,
And your body an unfulfilled vision.
Yet the day at last will dawn
When that dream will become reality, . . .
When the Word will be reborn,
When superfluous words will be banished,
When everyone will say what they feel,
What they love, and what they need.   (Mirosław Biskupski)

Above all, the mood of the moment was caught in popular songs—in new defiant words set incongruously to old melodies, in fierce parodies of official anthems, and in angry doggerel and sentimental lament. Sometimes, the wrath of the people found voice in bitter refrains—'Let the red rabble tremble', 'Only one verdict fits', 'Thirty-six wasted years'. But most frequently, it broke surface in a great chorus of assertion of the nation's history and of their ancient sense of longing:

When the Tsar was cast down from the schoolroom wall,
And Father Ściegienny was saying his prayers,
And Old Drzymała and his cart stood their ground,
And Norwid was writing his verses with pride,
Every man who could carry a sabre on high
Would form a legion, or an Army, and cry:
   'So that Poland may be Poland, So that Poland may
   be Poland',
   Żeby Polska była Polską, żeby Polska była Polską.

5 Underground Resistance

Poland has been occupied so often in the last two hundred years that passive resistance and clandestine activities come to the population as second nature. The State of War declared in 1981 revived all the habits learned under Stalinism and the German Occupation. Young people ask their parents how the wartime Resistance tried to outwit the Nazis, and fathers tell sons what grandfather had recalled of the Tsarist *Okhrana*. The battle of wits between the forces of order and an alienated population is older than anyone can remember, and it is fought instinctively—not with bullets, but with signs and symbols. What was more natural, when the ZOMO appeared on the streets of Warsaw, then the crowd of onlookers should have chanted 'GE-STA-PO, GE-STA-PO'.*

Once SOLIDARITY was forced into illegality, the organization's leaders were obliged to rethink their strategy and tactics for the duration of the State of War; and on 30 March 1981, *Tygodnik Mazowsze* (Mazowsze Weekly), one of the many uncensored journals still circulating in the underground, published three connected articles all devoted to this theme.[10]

The first of the articles, written by Jacek Kuroń and smuggled out of his cell in Białołęka Prison, advocated the creation of an underground state, 'a well-organized resistance movement'. Entitled 'A way out of the impasse', it argued that a concerted effort to drive the authorities into a new agreement was the best way to stem the drift towards violence. It appeared to envisage a mounting campaign of local diversions, centrally directed, which in the course of 'a dozen weeks' or so would lead to a decisive showdown with the Military Regime. It also recommended a public declaration to the effect that the strategic and military interests of the USSR would be safeguarded.

The second article, entitled 'Walka pozycyjna' (Trench Warfare), was written by Zbigniew Bujak, the head of the Warsaw branch of SOLIDARITY still at liberty. Bujak criticized Kuroń's analysis on the grounds that it greatly

---

*The analogy was somewhat exaggerated. No one in wartime Warsaw publicly taunted the Gestapo for long, and lived to tell the tale.

underestimated the power of the military-police state and that it would only lead to vicious retaliation from the authorities. Instead, he proposed a strong, decentralized movement using a variety of techniques, and committed to 'the principle of avoiding head-on conflicts with the Government'. He called on his supporters to set up all manner of independent social, cultural, and economic activities without reference to official bodies. These self-help committees, informal trade union groups, underground publishing houses, independent literary and artistic circles, and clandestine educational associations, would form the basis of 'an underground society'. Bujak did not promise rapid success and he did not rule out the possibility of an eventual Rising; but he supposed that a period of 'long, hard, and demanding work' would best prepare the nation for whatever lay ahead.

The third article, entitled 'A Third Alternative', was signed by Wiktor Kulerski, one of Bujak's colleagues in the Warsaw underground. Kulerski was equally critical of Kuroń's thesis, but based his conclusions on an assumption regarding 'the gradual decomposition of the system'. Since direct opposition strengthens the government apparatus, the best way forward would simply be to ignore it. He advocated 'evolution, not revolution'. Sharing Bujak's view of an informal, decentralized 'pluralist movement', he envisaged a situation where the communist regime would eventually rot away—'where the government will control the empty shops, but not the market: places of employment, but not people's livelihood: the state media, but not information: printing houses, but not important publications: post office and telephone services, but not communication: the schools, but not education.' Kulerski realized that the success of his programme, which would eventually leave the communist Government in charge of a hollow shell of inoperative institutions, might well oblige the Soviet Union to intervene. In that case, he argued, the Polish people would have been much better trained in the arts of survival than if they spent their time in futile resistance.

All three articles mirror arguments which took place in the wartime Underground in Poland at the beginning of the Nazi Occupation in 1939–40. The advocates of early confrontation, of gradual mobilization, and of social survival all had their counterparts in the counsels of the Home Army. General Jaruzelski's 'State of War' was received as just another round in the endless struggle against alien opposition; and majority opinion as always was looking to a campaign not of weeks or months, but of years.

The true impact of underground Resistance can best be viewed from the other side of the fence—through the eyes of the Military Commissars who had to deal with it. As luck would have it, an extensive speech on the subject, delivered in April 1982 by Colonel Wiślicki, a commissar assigned to oversee the personnel of Polish Radio and Television, was secretly recorded and published. It admirably reveals the nature of the problem:

Some Comrades say that this *Solidarność* was a kind of paper tiger that was destroyed overnight on December 13th, and that it is no longer dangerous. . . . Such certainty has led some of us to declare that in principle we have won and that it is time to celebrate our victory—time to curtail or abolish the State of War, that everything is back to normal. This is the attitude of those Comrades who have installed themselves in their official armchairs under large potted palms . . . and under the protection of the Military. Such a view of the situation is quite wrong . . . and very harmful.

Should any one of you ask how long the State of War will last, I think the question is quite simple, but the solution is quite difficult. The State of War in Poland will last until the Party is reborn. And I'm not thinking about the Party's bureaucracy . . . but about the rank-and-file members in the large enterprises. . . . Political pluralism is out of the question. Any sort of opposition, more or less organised, is out of the question. . . . I'm not talking about acceptance—we can't expect that from society. We are far from being accepted. So when answering the frequently asked question—'how long will the State of War last?'—we can answer: it will last a long time, and for that at least the Army is ready.

In this context, there are other problems linked with our ideological influence on society. Lately, we have noticed a great upsurge in the activities of the anti-socialist element within the country. After the initial shock caused by the introduction of the State of War—I have to admit, incidentally, that its introduction was much easier than we expected, and . . . many fewer victims than we expected—the enemy is beginning to pull itself together . . . The question of SOLIDARITY is linked with the question of the trade union movement, and for the time being no one has any idea what to do with the trade union movement. . . . The Prime Minister said in the Sejm that trade unions will be what the working-class wants them to be. Personally . . . I have serious doubts if . . . the working-class's wishes would be compatible with the proper functioning of the state.

But what are we seeing now? We see that SOLIDARITY . . . is getting better and better organised. . . . All sorts of bulletins that appear as periodicals, issue after issue, point to a well functioning organisation. . . . The articles in these illegal publications . . . forbid terrorist-type activities. In his interview for American TV, Bujak said that SOLIDARITY members should organise passive, not active resistance . . . First of all, work should be slowed down because if people do this in the right way, they avoid repression. . . . Another guideline is that in extreme circumstances strikes should be organised—but in a sporadic fashion . . . Let's say for example that some enterprise starts a strike, then the riot police arrive to break it up . . . Then, after the riot police leave, the strike can start again. Some calls are for visible actions that will prove SOLIDARITY is still around: turn off your lights at a given hour, light candles. . . . Another directive is against any kind of co-operation. They call for the collection of evidence against 'collaborators'. . . . They say, for example, if a military commissar gives an order, demand a detailed explanation and pretend you don't understand. If you think the order makes no sense whatsoever—obey at once. And so on. The situation is very complex. We're far from celebrating our victory. . . .

Someone asks, *Why haven't they caught Bujak yet? What the hell is the Ministry of Internal Affairs doing?* We have no information from comrades who are dealing with this. . . . If Bujak and the others are in a monastery, which is quite likely, or in a convent, it would be necessary to organise a company or a battalion to break up the whole place. I don't know if the internal and international repercussions would justify the effort . . . Anyway, if we don't know what trade unions will be in the future . . . how can we know if this son of a bitch Bujak won't come in handy one day . . . I'm not so sure at all. Personally, I don't know what sort of game the security apparatus is playing.

Comrade, why aren't the police arresting all those people who switch off their lights and light candles? It is not as easy as all that. First, this is a common occurrence, and secondly Jaruzelski stated that the State of War is in force in Poland, but that no rights have been suspended. So what right have you to enter homes and ask people why they switch off their lights. They switch them off because they feel like it . . . Well, Comrades, they do have the right. . . . Take Świdnik, for example. People go for a walk during the television news. They walk round peacefully, and what can you do about it? Send for the riot police? You can't do that—that would be an escalation of terror.

You talk about verifying people. We are verifying people whenever we can, and so what? We check a SOLIDARITY member, saying that he doesn't work well. . . . And when he comes to us and declares he's giving up his membership, you'll tell him . . . 'you're fired.' The same applies to the academic community. . . . One has to think of the consequences. The verifications cause a great stir in those circles, and I don't know whether an academic wouldn't be more dangerous if chucked out of the university so that he might organise without our control. . . . Well, I don't have an answer to that.

Another topic . . . is the issue of the Church. So I think the Church is a time-bomb. To me it is clear that the Church's activity all in all is decidedly anti-State at this time. It is decidedly aimed against the current system in our country. But in the Church's hierarchy there are differences of opinion. The most—shall we say docile,—is Glemp, who supports some dialogue with the Government. . . . Macharski represents a more radical attitude though not an extremist one. As far as, er, what's his name, Gulbinowicz is concerned, he represents the very extreme in the Church. . . . It wasn't by chance that it was these three who went to see the Pope. . . . As for the rank-and-file clergy, their activities more often than not are decidedly anti-State. . . . The pastoral letter dated January 19th, which was to be read in all churches . . . was an exceptionally perfidious letter, calling . . . for armed resistance. Well, perhaps not directly, but there were statements which could be interpreted in such a way. . . . All the cribs in the churches now have a uniquely political character. Religious symbols of the Home Army, emblems of Fighting Poland, banners spattered with blood and so forth. Just as it was during Hitler's Occupation. I repeat: I don't know if this time-bomb will explode, but we must be vigilant, because they are very cunning.[11]

Here was the authentic voice of the Military Regime in 1982. Here was no expectation that Party rule could soon be restored, no pretence of popular support, no idea how resistance could be overcome. Although Colonel Wiślicki was sceptical of the Prime Minister's wish to accede to the wishes of the working class, he was clearly reluctant to resort to the harshest means of repression. On the practical questions of arresting dissidents, or exacting *weryfikacje* (Loyalty Oaths), he showed himself to be a classic Polish fudger (see p. 350). His harshest words were for the Church; but he had no suggestions of how best to deal with it. He repeatedly made reference to the ironic historic parallel with the Nazi Occupation. In every phrase, he exuded that characteristic outlook of Jaruzelski's Military Regime which mixed tough talk with a large measure of practical restraint; and he was settling into an unlimited tour of duty.

After only six months of Martial Law, the underground struggle between the regime and the resistance was already reaching stalemate. Of the three variant programmes floated by SOLIDARITY leaders in March, Kuroń's was soon proved mistaken. Bujak and Kulerski, in their strategies for passive resistance, were nearer the mark. As the summer and autumn wore on, as demonstrators were dispersed without excessive violence and leading underground activists (notably Frasyniuk in Wrocław on 5 October) were picked up by the police, Kulerski's provisions for unlimited survival seemed the most realistic of all. General Jaruzelski may have expressed his condolences in person to the family of the youngster killed by a plain-clothes policeman in Nowa Huta in November; it was evidence of his attention to public relations, but not of a change of heart. Like the military commissars, whom they defy, the leaders of the underground resistance were settling down to a long assignment. Their fathers had survived a far harsher state of war between 1939 and 1945, and their fathers' forebears had survived a siege lasting throughout the nineteenth century. The feeling was there, that one way or another, they, too, would survive.

All along, the main danger had been that the suppression first of peaceful opposition and then of passive resistance would inaugurate an era of Terrorism. Having resorted to violence themselves, the communist authorities exposed Poland to the possibility of retaliation in kind. It was the logical consequence. God knows, there were enough terrorists in the world's news to fill the heads of Poland's frustrated young men with ideas; and there were enough terrorists in Polish history, subsequently enshrined as national heroes, whose example could make terrorism patriotically respectable. The distinction between terrorists and freedom fighters has nothing to do with the nature of their activities, and everything to do with the viewpoint of their enemies or admirers; and Polish society, driven to desperation by an unyielding regime, would be only human if its long-standing hostility to terrorism were to change into admiration for freedom fighters. If it were an act of great patriotism for Lieutenant Piotr Wysocki to plot the assassination of the Grand Duke Constantine in 1830, it would be hard to condemn a similar attempt against the Soviet Ambassador in 1984 or 1985. If the underground 'gendarmes' of the January Rising in 1863–4 were justified in knifing and hanging agents of the Tsarist police, it would be hard to tell the determined young men of the 1980s that it would be wrong to cut the throats of SB or ZOMO agents; and if it was in order for Ignacy Hryniewiecki to hurl the grenade which killed Tsar Alexander II (and himself), it would be equally in order for some contemporary Polish youth to try to plant a car bomb in Mr Andropov's limousine. These are the very 'heroes' whom communist textbooks have eulogized, and it would be a sad irony if some Polish student were actually to take them seriously. But terrorism has to be preceded by 'expropriation', since every terrorist cell has first to lay its hands on funds for financing its activities. On this score, Poland has plenty of folk heroes, from Janosik, the 'Robin Hood' of the Tatra Mountains, who tormented the Austrians in the eighteenth century, to men of our own time. Of the two most brilliant expropriators of modern East European History, one was Josip Vissarionovich Dzugashvili (later known as Stalin), whose daring hold-up of the Tiflis stage-coach brought a hoard of tsarist gold and the infant Bolshevik Party's biggest ever injection of cash; and the other was Józef Piłsudski, whose great mail-train robbery at Bezdany near Wilno provided the funds for his embryonic Polish Legions. Both these events took place in the same year, 1908, when, among other acts of terrorism, the Governor of Galicia was assassinated. In our century, political assassination has hardly been neglected, and much of it has come out of Eastern Europe. The Archduke Francis Ferdinand in 1914, President Narutowicz in 1922, Voykov, the Soviet Ambassador in Warsaw in 1927, King Alexander of Yugoslavia in 1934, Tadeusz Hołówko, the Polish socialist leader in 1931, Colonel Pieracki, Polish Minister of the Interior in 1934, were all victims of political terrorism. During the Second World War, the communist People's Guard aroused the anger of the main Resistance leaders for conducting a campaign of random terrorism which clearly contradicted the Home Army's orders for limiting action to military targets, and to the elimination of selected Nazi criminals. The GL's bombing of the *Wehrmacht*'s 'Café Club' in Warsaw in October 1942, for example, led to ferocious reprisals by the SS, and to the deaths of hundreds of innocent Polish hostages, without bringing any obvious political benefit.

With these skeletons in their own cupboard, it is not to be wondered that the Polish Military leaders should have been nervous about terrorism. They showed great unease about the nonacentenary of St. Stanisław (see p. 289), and prevented the Pope from attending the celebrations at Częstochowa in August 1982. With the same thoughts in mind, they closed down Warsaw's Dramatic Theatre for mounting a production of T.S. Eliot's play *Murder in the Cathedral*, which, in view of alleged Soviet involvement in the recent attempt to murder the Pope, was acutely topical. Yet knowing their adversarial mentality, they must have been pleasantly surprised that in 1980–1 SOLIDARITY's ten million members, with abundant access to industrial dynamite and technical expertise, never once resorted to bombings or sabotage, and that in 1982 the incidence of terrorism was limited to a small number of bloodless hijackings. In the eyes of the communist commissars the non-violence of the underground resistance might have been taken as a sign of weakness; in the eyes of the population at large, if they stay true to the teachings of the Church, it must be taken as a sign of responsibility and moral superiority.

6 *The Intellectuals' Dilemma*

The Polish *inteligencja*, which has always provided the cerebral and vocal power of the opposition movements (though not always its spine and muscle), was largely won over to the SOLIDARITY camp during 1980–1. Of course, in the strictest Polish tradition it is impossible to be both an *inteligent* and a supporter of the ruling regime; but in the course of the

last thirty years the distinction between the *inteligencja* proper
and the educated 'intellectuals' in general had become
blurred. The spread of higher education had created an
entirely new scientific and technical stratum of professional
people, who were all state employees but whose work did not
involve them in the same moral and political conflicts
encountered by writers, artists, or teachers. (A trained
mathematician, for example, is incontestably a highly educated person; but it is hard to say whether or not he is
inteligentny, unless he happens to have prefaced his dissertation
with a timely quotation from the great mathematician, Y.V.
Andropov.) Furthermore, since the communist state takes
special care to control and organize all aspects of cultural life,
including the fees, salaries, and pensions of cultural workers,
the proportion of the educated class which can afford to
maintain an independent livelihood in the stule of the leisured
inteligencja of former days, has shrunk significantly. Large
numbers of educated Poles who regarded themselves as the
cream of the *inteligencja* were none the less obliged to seek state
employment, or to join the Party-sponsored unions.

Yet the emergence of SOLIDARITY revealed how tenuous
the Party's hold on the educated class was, let alone on the
inteligencja. Most sections of the cultural and scientific world
switched their loyalties to the new movement as soon as they
were free to do so. The ideals of SOLIDARITY proved
attractive not only to the traditional Catholic intellectuals,
centred on the journals of *Więź*, and *Tygodnik Powszechny* in
Kraków, but also to the more open-minded circles of the
communist camp such as the 'Experience and Future' group
(DiP). SOLIDARITY branches in research institutes and
university departments attracted the same high level of
membership as in industrial enterprises. The Polish Journalists' Union under the outspoken Stefan Bratkowski, since
demoted and expelled from the Party, championed the cause
of *Odnowa* (Renewal) from the start. The Polish PEN-Club did
not need to be reformed; but the official Writers' Union held
its first turbulent and truly democratic conference in decades.
The Independent Student Union (NZS) supplied one of the
largest and most enthusiastic cohorts of SOLIDARITY
activists. Even the Schoolteachers Union, the vanguard of

official communist ideological education, was obliged by its own members to abandon central control and to create a semblance of independence. There was no greater proof of the power of SOLIDARITY's ideals than to see how many communist-run organizations had to feign conversion to democratic procedures simply to stay in business. By and large, despite the three decades of the communist monopoly in education, it was demonstrated without serious reservations that the new and very numerous educated class had the ideals of the old *inteligencja* very much at heart.

As a result of the December Coup, therefore, the battle lines between the dissident *inteligencja* and the collaborationist intellectuals were redrawn more clearly than at any time since the Stalinist era. SOLIDARITY's underground press regularly published a 'List of Collaborators' bearing the names of writers, actors, and artists who continued working as normal under the Military Regime. From this it would be easy to conclude that the division of the Polish educated class was a simple one, with the alienated patriots on one side and the official careerists on the other. Certainly, it made poignant reading at this time to turn to Mrożek's *Emigranci* (The Emigrants) with its ironic scenes of an intellectual in a monkey-cage, or of Herbert's *Pan Cogito* with its description of the 'Lowest circle of hell', the refuge of Beelzebub's official artists.

Yet the divisions were not quite so simple; for in that wide area between total alienation and total conformism there was an important category of honourable and intelligent people who were neither alienated beyond recall nor conformist to a fault. To their enemies on both sides, these 'conciliators' or compromisers were two-faced trimmers of the worst sort. In their own minds, they were realists, the shield of the nation's culture against all forms of extremism. Their viewpoint was best expressed in February 1982 in a remarkable article that appeared in the weekly *Polityka* under the title 'To Quit or not to quit'. At that juncture, *Polityka,* still the organ of the Deputy-Prime Minister Rakowski, had just been deserted by half its journalists whose consciences could not bear the disgrace of further service. Having joined *Polityka,* presumably in admiration of Rakowski's record as a flexible and open-minded editor, they resigned in disgust when Rakowski emerged as General Jaruzelski's right-hand man. The article, describing the journalists' dilemma, was written by Daniel Passent, a columnist who stayed on with Rakowski and who expounded his personal philosophy with candour and vigour:

Until and unless the present pattern of international relations, and the political division of the world into East and West, is altered, no good is done by emigrating, internally or externally, or by washing one's hands. The only thing that makes sense is to get on with the job. . . . Work is what . . . our readers expect of us. . . . Doubtless there will be those who . . . would prefer the paper not to appear at all; but others will go on reading it in the hope that it will remain true to itself, that it will preserve a judicious moderation and a commitment to organic work and communication with society. . . .

Since the end of the eighteenth century, or at any rate since the Great Emigration, the Polish educated class has been confronted more or less with the same dilemma which we now have. The thirteenth of December marks neither the birthday nor the demise of Poland. If all our writers had broken their pens for fear of being accused of collaboration, we would now live in a cultural desert, and our sole oasis of liberty would lie beyond our borders. We cannot all be buried in Père Lachaise.

'For over a hundred years', Stefan Kieniewicz wrote in his history of the January Insurrection, 'these two attitudes have been fighting a running battle. . . . In one corner, there have always been angry diehards who kept their scythes honed and were capable of spending over forty years in exile. One such, Walery Wróblewski wrote after the defeat of the Rising: "I cannot understand so-called Organic Work with its implication of legality and compromise" . . .'. A similar view was taken by Jarosław Dąbrowski, later one of the leaders of the Paris Commune. . . . Yet it was none other than an eminent and humane scholar, Julian Klaczko who commented of men like Dąbrowski that 'only recently they had been clawing their own mother's womb and taking soul-baths in their brothers' blood.' . . . 'Let the heedless authors of these woes,' wrote another author, 'answer before God, Poland, and posterity. Let their consciences groan beneath the blood of the noblest Polish youth, the tears of so many mothers and fathers; . . . for it would be vain to lay the responsibility on the enemy alone. It rests on those who at the inspiration of others and partly for their own ends precipitated an unequal battle without preparations, arms, leaders, and allies. . . .'

In short, it is not in the public interest for the press to cease publication or for its variety to be further restricted. We must work for a return of the Army to the barracks. . . . Someone has to argue the case for releasing our fellow-writers, and not only them. It would be wrong to kow-tow, but equally wrong to sit back with arms folded . . . All that is practicable and worth salvaging from the post-August period must be salvaged. . . . It would not do if our voice were missing from any chorus of prospective advocates of continued change . . . or from the defenders of writers and academics of genuine merit against the *chutzpah* of political shuksters and arrivistes. . . . who will do that if we slink away?

In a country lacerated by wars, insurrections, and invasions, continually laid waste and rebuilt anew, there is a need for some kind of continuity. Institutions, schools, papers, publishing houses that have survived longer than a generation are thin on the ground. The fact that *Polityka* has kept going as long as it has, is an argument for keeping it going. . . . Certainly, it would be more comfortable to wait for normalisation,—but who is to put our life on a normal footing if we all fold our arms?. . . .

In the foreseeable future, Poland can only be a socialist country forming an integral part of the Warsaw Treaty; but what remains of her within this framework depends just a bit on us: unless we choose to flounce off in a huff, and bide our time till a more propitious hour strikes. Only who will then be the bell-ringer, and for whom will it toll?[12]

Passent was a sympathizer, if not a member of SOLIDAR-ITY. He was also a Party member. Only a few weeks before the State of War, he had participated in a radio programme for the BBC in London where he confidently predicted the imminent revival of political parties in Poland. He did not dissemble about the identity of 'the enemy'. In spite of that, he stayed at his post under General Jaruzelski. He was perfectly aware of his predecessors, one hundred and two hundred years ago. He was a 'conciliator' of the purest type, besmirched by his own admission in the moral mire, but still clinging to his belief in the virtue of Polish positivism long after most of his positivist colleagues had quit. He earned himself the label of 'collaborator' from people who opposed his stand; and from a grateful regime, no doubt, the reputation of a trusty Comrade. Over the previous twenty years, these conciliators, these realists, probably formed a majority among intellectuals connected with official circles; in 1982 they were voices crying in the wilderness. But they have as much a part in the Polish intellectual tradition as the Romantics, the insurrectionaries, the dissidents, and the loyalists.

For even among the loyalists, there are those who pride themselves on their intelligence. The regime, too, has its tame intellectuals. Some of these, who are prepared to propagate the official ideology, can make fine careers as professors in the higher Party schools, or in such shadowy groves of academe as the Institute of Marxism–Leninism or the Centre for Research into the History of Soviet–Polish Relations. They are perhaps the most despised element of all, since, whatever they say, for professing views so completely at odds with those of Polish society as a whole, they cannot plead ignorance. Others sell their brains quite consciously and cynically in order to reap the comforts of the privileged élite. Within this select company, the employees of the Censorship form an inner cerebral guard, the cream of the sour cream, whose function in life is to outwit the rest of society. In those rare moments, when a censor has talked openly about his trade, it was obvious not only that the game has its fascinations for a nimble mind but also that the censors felt immensely superior to their political 'lords and masters' and to the average citizens alike:

... In my time on Mysia Street [the Main Censorship Office in Warsaw], the principle was that if a censor did not understand what he was reading, the article might be let through, because the average reader would not understand it either. We think that we are more intelligent than the average reader ... Fools are not employed. ... And quite frequently, the higher up you go the more liberal it gets. A censor crosses something out, and the Chief Censor restores it. ...[13]

These were the frank opinions of a young man who had taken part in the student protests of 1968 and who still tried to maintain contacts with his former class-mates. He described himself as 'basically a good and honest guy' who 'was doing something that was pretty nasty'.

Intelligence, therefore, is no guarantee of integrity. On the contrary, it sharpens the pain of moral choices. Polish intellectuals, although they may rationalize their attitudes more convincingly, show no more virtue than anyone else. Like every other social group, they have their resisters, their positivists, and their servile loyalists. But for them, since they tend to articulate what they are doing, the moral dilemma is particularly acute.

7 Historical Roles

Such is the burden of History in Polish consciousness, that any full appreciation of the Polish crisis requires a full examination of the way in which the chief actors on the political scene perceive their present roles in relation to the nation's traditions. Almost everyone in Poland lays claims to patriotism; so the fact that so many self-proclaimed patriots can disagree so profoundly with each other proves the existence not only of a large body of pseudo-patriotic impostors, but also to serious disparities in genuine patriots' views of themselves and their opponents. One need not probe too deeply to reveal profound differences in the self-perceptions of the communist Establishment, of the non-communist opposition, and of the Church. All of these native actors differ in their outlook from that of the chief impresario and self-appointed prompter of the Polish political theatre—the USSR.

As for the communist Establishment, it is doubtful after the events of 1980–1 whether it retained any unified view of its place in the nation's history or of its role in the nation's future. It knew full well that it was Poland's last line of defence against a Soviet invasion—hence its persistent 'Patriotic' illusions (see p. 92); and it knew from long practice that the outward forms of servility to Moscow and of 'total fraternal accord' must be maintained. At the same time, no one, not even the blindest *bumaga*-blotters buried in the bowels of the bureaucracy, can believe what they were told in the Party School, namely that they were the finest representatives of the Polish proletariat. That is one myth which SOLIDARITY exploded once and for all. The Polish communist movement was brought back to the Square One of 1945—it was a small, vulnerable band of careerists and devotees, kept in power by military force, ashamed of its poor reputation with the people, and fearful of its masters' wrath. The majority of careerists within it can have had no clear thoughts about the past or the future, but could only hope for a further stay of execution. Their careers nearly came to an end in 1981, and may not be reprieved at the next round of the crisis. All they could do was to pray—since most of them remember their Catholic mothers' advice in matters of life and death—that God would grant them to sit at their desks until retirement age. The minority of devotees, like Gomułka and his comrades at the end of the War, must have taken to beavering away once more, planning and dreaming in the true pioneer spirit to rebuild the foundations of a socialist society within their lifetime. In their view—as in the view of the communists' founding fathers in Poland at the beginning of the century, or of the Stalinists in Russia in 1929—what a hostile society needs is *more* Socialism, not less. The fervour and scientific knowledge of the chosen Party must compensate for the apathy and ignorance of a wretched population. If the *kulaks*, the *panowie* (the squires), and the reactionary clergy stand in their path, they must be swept away by the irresistible force of the revolutionary machine. . . .

By now, the point was whether the communist experiments in the Poland of 1945 (or in the Russia of 1929) could even be attempted in the new circumstances of the 1980s. In 1945, the Polish communists had a tide running strongly in their favour. They could set to work on a society already radicalized by the miseries of pre-war conditions and by the agonies of a brutal War, but as yet largely unindustrialized, unurbanized, uneducated; they had a Soviet patron basking in the glory of the Red Army's recent victory over the hated Nazi occupation; and they had an attractive theory, a message of optimism and progress, which had never been tried in practice. Above all, they had a ready supply of eager young recruits, the sons and daughters of the uprooted peasants and refugees of the post-war years who desperately needed education, employment, and encouragement. In the 1980s, none of these advantages applied. The tide had turned. Polish society was no longer the primitive, half-educated, peasant society of the 1940s. A new generation had come to the fore, which was more impressed by the peacetime catastrophes of communist policies than by the wartime successes of the Red Army, and which knew what 'building Socialism' meant in practice. Any attempt to relaunch the communist experiment in Poland would have to rely on Polish youth—to replenish a shattered Party, to fill the ranks of the People's Army, to revitalize the sluggish bureaucracy. Yet it was Polish youth, more than any other

402 — *Echoes: The Past in Poland's Present*

sector of Polish society, which had flocked to SOLIDARITY in its millions. It was an appalling thought for the communists—but Polish youth looks neither to Lenin nor to Leftism, but to Piłsudski, Poniatowski, and the Pope. Polish Communism never had much of a past; and its future looks distinctly empty.

Yet the 'Renewal' movement within the Party was not abandoned by the December Coup. 'ODNOWA' was one of those few slogans of 1980–1 shared both by the Party and by SOLIDARITY; and it has been used on several occasions since by General Jaruzelski himself. In the West, it was habitually interpreted as a positive sign that the Party was capable of reforming itself, and that the 'doves' and 'liberals' in the Party leadership might reach a genuine compromise with the people. This charmingly naïve view, which grossly over-simplified the Renewal movement, could only be held by people unfamiliar with the language of Leninism. In accordance with the Leninist precept of the primacy of the Party, *Renewal* means 'the renewal of the Party's dictatorship'; *reform* means 'any change which strengthens the Party apparatus'; *compromise* means 'a temporary concession made to help the Party recover its supremacy at a later date'. (Any change which does not strengthen the Party is called a *revision*.) Most Western observers have short memories. They forget—or they never knew—that the most radical reformer in the history of Communism was Joseph Stalin. Starting in 1929 with the Five Year Plans and the Collectivization of Agriculture and moving in 1934 into the Purges, Stalin implemented perhaps the most gigantic programme of reform ever seen in world history; and he was acting within the traditional Russian framework of autocratic reform, of innovation imposed by force 'from the top'. This tradition, which is the exact opposite of the Western, liberal concept of Reform by consent and by mutual concession, is as old as Russia, and it is the natural philosophy of the most illiberal, repressive, and actively dictatorial elements of a Soviet-style system. In Tsarist Russia, it was practised by Peter the Great and favoured by the *Okhrana*. In the modern USSR it inspires the most 'forward-looking' tendencies of the radical élite. Its best practitioner in recent years has been Y.V. Andropov, Soviet Ambassador in

Hungary, Secretary of the CPSU's department for relations with fraternal countries, and until May 1981, head of the KGB. As illustrated by Andropov's brilliant master-minding of Kadarism in Hungary, or by Honecker's regime in East Germany, it is extremely flexible, and relies on a combination of political terror (in the first phase) and economic moderniza-tion (in the second). Its aim in the short term is simply to destroy opposition: in the mid-term, by consumerism and relative prosperity to block the possibility of dissent; and in the long term to make totalitarianism strong, modern, and efficient. In the Polish communist movement, it has not been in fashion since the 1950s, and was discredited to some extent by Gierek's ham-fisted *(sic)* attempt to go for the consumerism without the Terror. But under present pressures, it is bound to be revived. Its most likely Polish advocate is Stefan Olszowski. Not surprisingly, its first patron in the present crisis was Stanisław Kania, who stepped into Party Secretaryship straight from the Party's Administrative Department (in charge of police, security, and military affairs), and who launched the slogan of 'Renewal' in September 1980.

It would appear, therefore, that the main division in the communist Establishment in Poland was not between the hard-line 'hawks' and the moderate 'doves' in the sense understood in the West; but rather between the hard-line, radical reformers of the Soviet School on the one hand and the moderate 'fudging' reformers of the incurable Polish School on the other. Since the Party apparatus in Poland had virtually collapsed, no one in the PZPR could possibly oppose change of some sort. The only question was; what sort of Reform should be adopted? The Comrades who had favoured democratization in the Western sense, and who had attracted great support in the Party at grass-roots level for their experiment in 'horizontal structures', were swiftly ruled out of order as counter-revolutionary and anti-Leninist. (This ele-ment, which had backed the Party's link with SOLIDARITY by belonging to both organizations, either left the Party in disgust, or was purged.) The radical Renewalists, too, were checked, partly because Kania turned out to be an unreliable fudger at heart, but mainly because the majority of the Comrades fear the people's wrath. If it ever occurred, the victory of neo-Stalinist Renewalism could cause an open revolt in the Party and a split in the Army; and it could be the trigger for uncontrollable demonstrations, for mass resistance backed by part of the Party and Army, and hence for Soviet intervention. In short, it could provide the most credible scenario for the next Polish Rising.

In which regard, it is not irrelevant to follow the war of symbols. It is known that in August 1981 'someone' entered the Powązki Cemetery in Warsaw and removed a new, seventon obelisk commemorating the victims of Katyn. It is known that the communist ZBoWiD organization has demanded a monument to its dead during the Civil War, of 1945–7; and if 'someone' were to decide to reinstate the full name of the Palace of Culture or to retouch the monuments of Feliks Dzierżyński, one would know which way the battle in the Party was running.

Within the broad front of the non-communist Opposition, special attention must be paid to the two pioneer oppositional organizations, the KPN and KOR, whose formation in the mid-1970s preceded, and in some degree anticipated the birth of SOLIDARITY itself. The Confederation of an Independent Poland (KPN), which came into the open in 1976, was the brain-child of Leszek Moczulski, and was the successor to earlier pioneer groups called 'RUCH' and 'ROPCiO'. It was a latter-day emanation of the old nationalist tradition, and the potential spiritual homeland of many clericalists and ex-National Democrats. The corner-stone of its programme, as expressed in Moczulski's *Rewolucja bez rewolucji* (Revolution without a revolution), was to be found in the nationalists' central idea of the mystical union of Church and Nation; though, interestingly enough, whilst adhering to the principle of non-violence, it also paid tribute to Piłsidski's concept of the 'moral imperative'. Its main theoretical difficulty lay in dissociating itself from the Party's view of Nationalism filched in large part from the National Democrats in 1945 (see p. 326); and in order to do so it was pushed into a categorical denunciation of the dependence of the People's Republic on the USSR. In this way, it was the first to meet with direct repression by the communist Militia. But it obviously gained considerable popularity, especially among Catholic youth, who know little of the nationalists' unsavoury reputation for intolerance and anti-semitism. In evoking the shades of both Dmowski *and* Piłsudski, it clearly tipped its cap at uniting the two main trends of pre-war opinion.

In contrast, the Committee for Workers' Defence (KOR), formed in 1976 in response to workers' distress at Radom and Ursus, was a latter-day emanation of the Polish social democratic tradition. Its leading members, like Jacek Kuroń and Adam Michnik, frequently possessed sound radical or *marxisant* credentials, and several were disillusioned ex-members the ruling Party. One strand of KOR, led by Michnik, author of a book entitled *Kościół-Lewica-Dialog* (Dialogue between the Church and the Left) enjoyed an open line to the Primate and to 'progressive circles' in the Hierarchy. This produced immediate compatibility with Wałęsa and with the mainstream of SOLIDARITY. Indeed, the drive for a merger with SOLIDARITY became so strong, that in September 1981 at SOLIDARITY's Gdańsk Congress, KOR's veteran chairman, Edward Lipiński, formally announced the termination of his Committee's separate existence. KOR's activities were immensely admired by the Western press, which probably overestimated its influence with the population at large. KOR's heroic initiative to champion workers' rights in an open manner, at a time when such things were not done openly, made it a worthy precursor of SOLIDARITY; but its wider impact was hindered by suspicions of its Marxist connections and by its internal rifts. Kuroń suffered from smears that he was 'a crypto-communist'; whilst Michnik had to bear charges from his own colleagues of 'hiding under the skirts of the clergy'.

All these complications point to the fact that the dissident Opposition of the 1970s needed to be viewed as a whole, and that both the KPN and KOR, with all their confusing splits, rivalries, and offshoots, played their part in reviving the broad panorama of Poland's native politics. The sentencing of Moczulski to hard labour in July 1981, and the promised treason trials of Kuroń and Michnik, bore eloquent witness to the gravity of their common challenge to the communists' artificial supremacy.

SOLIDARITY undoubtedly saw itself as heir to all the

nation's freedom fighters, the trustee of all their spiritual achievements. With almost ten million members, it obviously embraced a great variety of ideals and principles, some of them mutually contradictory; but within its ranks it included representatives of each of the main strands of the national tradition. As a trade union organization, it saw itself as the culmination of the century-old struggle for workers' rights and for socialism. It set special store on the memory of workers killed or persecuted in recent struggles with the communist state, and erected two great monuments—the first in Gdańsk to the victims of 1970, the second in Poznan to the victims of 1956; but it also had great regard for the workers' movements of the pre-war era, for the independent pre-war unions, for the pre-war Labour Party (SP), for the old PPS, even for the butchered KPP. Within its broad church of Polish socialism, it welcomed everyone from the majority group of Christian Socialists on one side to ex-Marxists, Marxists, and Marxist–Leninists on the other. SOLIDARITY's strong link with Christian Socialism and hence with the Catholic Church was manifest from the very start when icons of the *Matka Boska* decorated the gates of the Lenin Shipyard, and when the 17,000 strikers kneeled at Mass under the summer sun. Wałęsa, SOLIDARITY's Chairman, who ostentatiously signed the Gdańsk Agreement with a huge pen capped with a portrait of the Pope, was a devout Catholic, a daily church-goer, and a true son of Poland's traditionally Catholic proletariat. He sought the patronage in the first instance of Cardinal Wyszyński, whose pre-war clerical career had begun as a worker-priest in Silesia, and in due course of John Paul II, the ex-worker of the stone quarries and of a wartime chemical factory, and author, as Pope, of the encyclical on workers' rights *Laborem exercans* (1981). SOLIDARITY's ex-Marxists were strongest among the intellectual element, and included Wałęsa's advisers from KOR, like Kuroń or Tadeusz Mazow-iecki, editor of *Więź* (The Link), who had devoted a quarter of a century to building a bridge between Socialism and Catholicism, and who assumed the editorship of *Tygodnik Solidarność* (Solidarity Weekly). The Marxist–Leninists con-sisted almost exclusively of the one million Communist Party members—11 per cent of SOLIDARITY's membership and

30 per cent of the PZPR's—who contrived to belong to both rival organizations simultaneously. In the longer perspective, SOLIDARITY saw itself as a continuation of the wartime resistance movement in particular of the Home Army, whose anchor symbol and slogan—POLSKA WALCZY (Fighting Poland)—were used in many of the movement's publications and monuments. The red-and-white brassards worn by SOLIDARITY officials were taken over directly from Home Army practice during the Warsaw Rising. It also saw itself as a continuation of the Polish reformist tradition. It obliged the Party and Government to honour the Constitution of 3 May in the first official celebrations of their kind since 1939. It even saw itself as a continuation of the Polish nobles' struggle against Absolutism. *Nic o nas bez nas* (see p. 331) formed one of the favourite placards of 1980–1.

Indeed, SOLIDARITY took its role as guardian of the nation's History very seriously. Its leading activists numbered several prominent historians—Geremek, Jedlicki, J.J. Lipski, Modzelewski, Juzwenko, Kłoczowski—and it sponsored a vast series of lectures and discussions on all the taboo subjects. Under SOLIDARITY's sponsorship, in factory yards and football stadiums, tens of thousands of Polish workers would gather with eager anticipation to hear for the first time in their lives an honest presentation of the facts of the Battle of Warsaw, the Nazi–Soviet Pact, the Katyn Massacre, or the fate of the Home Army. In this, SOLIDARITY speakers were certainly expounding Polish History as they knew it; but they were making History as well.

Under SOLIDARITY's umbrella, a variety of political orientations emerged to revive the repressed traditions of Poland's earlier parties. RURAL SOLIDARITY, for instance, resuscitated the views of the old mainline Peasant Movement, the PSL (see p. 131), which had not been heard in public since 1947. There were socialists, Christian democrats, nationalists, peasant radicals, and not a few convinced communists. At the time of the declaration of the State of War in December 1981, the restoration of all the traditional political parties—the PPS, SP, SN, PSL, and possibly an independent communist party—was only a matter of weeks away.

Once SOLIDARITY had been suspended, and its leaders interned, the historical thoughts of its members were automatically deflected from memories of constructive political work to those deep folk memories of Poland's historical defeats and repressions. Since the Polish oppositionist was no longer permitted to operate openly, he was forced to choose between joining the collaborators or paying the consequences for refusing to do so. The test came with the notorious *weryfikacje* (The Declarations of Loyalty)—or more accurately, declarations of disloyalty to SOLIDARITY—with which all active oppositionists were faced in the first months of the State of War. Just as the former regime's supporters were faced with the dilemma 'to quit or not to quit' (see p. 396), so the regime's opponents were faced with the dilemma 'to sign or not to sign'. It was a predicament as old as Poland's modern history—an examination of conscience as organized by the UB of the 1950s, by the Gestapo and NKVD of the Second World War, by the *Okhrana* and German Military Police of the First War, by the security services of all the partitioning powers throughout the nineteenth century, by the agents of the Empress Catherine and of Peter the Great in the eighteenth. To sign or not to sign? The purest reflections on this theme were composed by a SOLIDARITY activist interned in Białołęka Prison, and published in the underground journal *Tygodnik Mazowsze* (Mazovia Weekly) in February 1982:

So freedom is a hand's reach away. A few strokes of the pen on the declaration of loyalty will suffice . . . It is as easy as that to exchange your barred window with its sharp outline of barbed wire for freedom. The iron gates of Białołęka will open before you . . . and you will see the streets of your native city, patrolled by police and tanks. You will see cars being stopped, and their boots searched. You will see the vigilant eye of the informer fishing out from the crowd people suspected of 'violating the regulations of the State of War.' You will hear the words which you had only heard from history books: *łapanka* (street raid), *Volksliste* (Declarations of Loyalty extracted from Polish Germans by the Nazis)—words torn from the stately patina of time but pulsating with today's ugly rhythm.

Sometimes they will try to scare you. My friend, a worker from a Warsaw factory, was promised 15 years in gaol. Another was threatened with a trial for espionage. A third was interrogated in

Russian. Still another was ordered out of his cell and told he was going to the depths of Russia—(they took him for an X-ray). But all this is bearable. Indeed, I think it is easier to bear than the morally and politically complicated situation on the other side of the barbed wire. . . . A young woman, the wife of a SOLIDARITY activist, was arrested and taken away from her sick baby, which they told her was to be placed in an orphanage. She signed the Declaration. My friend was torn away from a lonely mother dying of cancer and told 'there will not be so much as a lame dog to make your mother a cup of tea.' He signed the Declaration. The decision always lies with the individual's voice of reason and conscience. . . . Every declaration of loyalty is an evil, and a declaration coerced from you is an evil into which you have been coerced. . . . The act of signing deserves understanding, always sympathy, but never praise.

As yet you know little. . . . You do not know what this War means. You do not yet know how the factories, shipyards, steelworks, and mines will be stormed. . . . But one thing you do know: a declaration of loyalty would be a denial of yourself. It would wipe out your life's meaning. It would be a betrayal of the people who trusted you: the betrayal of your friends who are scattered in the prisons, sentenced and interned: the betrayal of all those who will defend you, in Kraków with a leaflet, in Paris and New York with a public statement. . . . You yourself, you can still choose; but you know instinctively that to abandon your dignity is not a price that should be paid for opening the prison gates. It is not a price worth paying.

It goes against common sense to make agreements with people who violate common agreements—with people for whom the Lie is their daily bread. You surely never met anyone who had anything to do with the secret police and did not feel cheated by them. . . . Your capitulation is not only their professional success. It is their *raison d'être*. You are arguing with them about the meaning of your own life, and how there is no meaning to theirs . . . You are continuing the argument of Giordano Bruno with the Inquisitioner, of the Decembrist with the Tsarist police superintendent, of Łukasiński with the exterminating angel, of Ossietzki with the blond man in the Gestapo uniform, of Mandelshtam with a Bolshevik wearing the blue lapels of the NKVD. You are taking part in an argument that will never end. . . . In other words, you win not when you gain power but when you remain faithful to yourself.

Common sense also tells you that if you sign the declaration of loyalty, you put the whip into the hands of the Functionaries. Later on, they will wave this whip around and threaten you . . . into making another declaration that you will co-operate. The declaration of loyalty transforms itself into a pact with the devil. . . . If you

do not wish to be afraid, do not make any agreements with the
functionaries. . . .

You remember the history of your nation. You remember that
within that history a declaration of loyalty made in prison was
always a disgrace. Remaining faithful to yourself and to the national
tradition was a virtue. You remember people tortured and
imprisoned for years who did not sign such a declaration. And there
are others in prison. . . . You think with horror of these human
shreds, of these people broken to bits by the police machine, and you
see your future is still an open state.

But you know that all this is nothing new. You will not want to
explain to those functionaries waving your release order under your
nose that it is they who are slaves, and that no order of release will
free them from their bondage. You will not explain to them
that . . . those worker-activists, professors and writers, students and
artists, friends and strangers . . . are the people who constitute
human and national freedom, and that it is for this that War has
been declared upon them. You will not want to explain to a sadistic
functionary, the meaning of Rozanov's essay describing the most
significant conflict in European culture as the antagonism between
the man who wields the whip and the man who bears the whipping.

It is over this that the battle is being waged. The functionaries
want to squeeze a declaration out of us that we have abandoned
hope. They realise that he who declares his loyalty to the system of
lies and coercion rejects hope for a Poland where lies and coercion
would be condemned. Their declarations are supposed to transform
us into base, servile creatures who will not revolt in the name of
freedom and dignity. But by refusing to co-operate . . . you are
preserving hope. . . .

You know how keen is the feeling of desolation. You feel that
you are helpless in the face of . . . this military machine which was
set in motion on a December's night. But you know as you stand
alone, bound in handcuffs and with tear-gas in your eyes . . .
thanks to your favourite poet, you know that *'the avalanche changes
course according to the stones over which it passes.'* And you want to be
the stone that will change the course of events.

Andrzej Zagozda (Białołęka)[14]

'Zagozda' was the pseudonym of Adam Michnik, the well-
known SOLIDARITY adviser. He had no intention of
compromising with the Military Regime. He was perfectly
aware of his predecessors over the centuries. He is a Polish
'idealist', a Romantic of the purest type—the type from which
the Polish Risings have always been made.

The Roman Catholic Church is not a political organization, but is condemned to play a political role. It has been interceding with the powers that be ever since the Partitions, and its present stature as the only national institution with genuine authority and legitimacy obliges the Hierarchy to hold the ring between Party and people. Yet the Hierarchy cannot necessarily be equated with the Church as a whole, and the Hierarchy's institutional interests do not necessarily coincide with those of its faithful subjects. The Primate and his Bishops cannot always perceive their role in the way that their flock might prefer. Strains in this relationship became apparent soon after Cardinal Wyszyński's replacement as Primate by Archbishop Józef Glemp. Many Catholics criticized the new Primate both for his initial, mooted response to Martial Law and for his failure during 1982 to restore the embryonic three-sided national dialogue. (See p. 25.) They realized that Archbishop Glemp could not force the regime to the negotiating table by himself; but they felt that a firmer stance was called for. In particular, they feared that the Primate might lose the respect of Poland's impatient youth. The Hierarchy, in fact, faced a challenge unprecedented in thirty years. It was sensing hostile pressures from the Party's hard-liners, encouraged from Moscow, who (rightly) saw the Church as the prime cause of the failure of 'Polish Socialism'. It had to foresee the possibility of the suspension of the Church–State agreements of 1956, and of an attack on the Church's privileges unparalleled since the Stalinist era. In that situation, it would either have to trim to the political winds and risk losing the support of the people—as in the early nineteenth century (see p. 340); or, on the example of Cardinal Wyszyński, who preferred imprisonment to indignity, it would steer into the gale, and risk a stormy passage. Fortunately—from the Catholic point of view—the Polish Church was stronger in 1982 than one hundred or two hundred years ago; and in John Paul II it possessed an admiral and helmsman of proven experience. It was unlikely that the Vatican under John Paul II would behave as it once did under Gregory XVI or Pius IX.

Which only leaves one actor on the Polish scene—the USSR. It is said that the Kremlin's role is scripted partly from

Marxist–Leninist ideology and partly from Russian imperialism. It acts partly from a perception of its duties as 'the first
socialist state', and partly from its pride as heir to the Tsars.
On either score, it must have looked with intense distaste on
People's Poland. From the Kremlin's viewpoint, a fraternal
regime which had lost control of its people and had lost faith
in Socialism, needed urgent assistance. A gangrenous member
of the Soviet Bloc, whose disease threatened to infect all the
other members, had to be judged in the interests of public
hygiene and required swift, surgical treatment. A Russian
ally, which showed no gratitude for Russia's immense
sacrifices, deserved to be punished. It was conceivable that
new leaders could be more flexible, and defy the precedents.
But only a daring break with the Russian and the Leninist
tradition, only a very imaginative appreciation of the consequences on all the Soviet Union's other interests, could
possibly have persuaded the Kremlin to leave Poland alone
indefinitely.

8 The Church Universal

Throughout the era of the Partitions, the Vatican's reserve in
its approach to Polish affairs was regarded by many Poles as a
scandal, a betrayal. (See p. 340.) From the purely Polish point
of view, it was incomprehensible why the Vicar of Christ in
Rome could not afford his faithful Polish subjects greater
comfort and support in their hour of need. Yet, viewed from
Rome, the issue was rather more complex. Quite apart from
the conservative philosophy of the Vatican's clerical administration and the indecisive temperament of successive ageing
Pontiffs, one has to realize that the Roman Catholic Church
possessed a wide range of interests in Eastern Euope, and that
the Vatican's order of priorities could rarely put Poland at the
top of the list. In the eighteenth century, for example, the
Vatican's strongest ties still lay with the imperial court at
Vienna; and the involvement of Maria Theresa and Joseph II
persuaded Rome that the Partitions in Poland, though
regrettable, would genuinely serve to strengthen Catholic
influence in the region. In the nineteenth century, the
Vatican's natural sympathy for Metternich, and its need to

maintain a working relationship with St. Petersburg, as evidenced by the interminable negotiations over the Concordats of 1847 and 1883, inevitably pushed Polish affairs into the background. Bismarck's *Kulturkampf* in Germany showed, if proof were needed, that the empires of Eastern Europe wielded immense power, and that conflict with the state could have dire consequences for the Catholic clergy, for Church property, for Church schools, and for the Church's standing in general. The Poles expected the Vatican to follow the way of valour, like themselves; but it is not surprising that Rome usually preferred the path of discretion. This is the background on which the Vatican's approach to contemporary Polish problems must be judged.

The Vatican of the 1980s is not the Vatican of the nineteenth century, and a Polish Pope on the throne of St. Peter has reinvigorated every aspect of Catholic affairs in eastern Europe. However, as in previous times, the Church's vision is long and wide, and many conflicting considerations have to be brought into focus. 'Papa Wojtyła' is not just the Pope of Poland.

The election of John Paul II must be attributed, above all, to his participation in the Second Vatican Council, and the reputation which he made in Rome at that time as a trusted lieutenant of Pope Paul VI. During the very first years of his pontificate, he showed that his mission was to bring the ideals of 'Vatican Two' to fruition. Thus, whilst upholding much traditional Catholic teaching on moral and ethical issues, he set out with no delay to open the Church to greater theological flexibility, to increased episcopal collegiality, to closer ties with other Christian denominations, and to an unprecedented, world-wide schedule of papal visits. At the outset, some uninformed voices were heard to wonder whether the Papacy had fallen into the hands of a dogmatic, provincial, Polish priest. They soon found that the Cardinal-Archbishop of Cracow was one of the most accomplished charismatic successors that St. Peter has ever had. As even his enemies were ruefully forced to admit, John Paul II—Karol Wojtyła of Wadowice, poet, playwright, philosopher, linguist, actor, skier, goalkeeper, worker, student, and priest —was a man of universal talents, a fitting leader for the

Universal church. Not everyone could believe that his attempted assassination on 13 May 1981 by a Turkish gunman, Mehmet Ali Agca, was the work of a lone fanatic. The Soviet empire was facing a challenge which it could not easily combat. It mattered little whether the arrest in Rome of Bulgarian agents suspected of complicity in the attempt to assassinate the Pope might eventually lead to a conviction or not. The fact remained that the Soviet Union had a definite interest in the removal of the Polish Pope. Rightly or wrongly, many people in Eastern Europe thought they had good reason to believe that the plot was masterminded by the KGB, whose proven record in such affairs was not exactly spotless.

Under its new management, the Vatican's *Ostpolitik*, underwent a subtle change of emphasis. There was no declaration of war on the Soviet Bloc, no ringing denunciations of atheism and communism in the spirit of the papal encyclical of 1937 'Divini Redemptoris' (inspired, incidentally, by Pius XI's earlier experience in Poland in 1919–20). As shown by the Pope's momentous visit to Poland in 1979, and his courteous dealings with the highest officials of the People's Republic, there was a proper readiness to 'render unto Caesar' whatever was thought properly to be Caesar's. But the spirit of resignation—some would say appeasement—which characterized the Vatican's initial contacts with the East under Paul VI evaporated fast. The Polish Pope, fortified by his own experiences as the citizen of a communist regime, breathed new energy and new confidence into Catholic activities throughout the Soviet Bloc. Faint-hearted Hierarchies, such as those in Hungary and Czechoslovakia, were urged to take heart. The persecuted Church in Catholic Lithuania, just over the border from Poland, received solid backing. Isolated Catholic communities elsewhere in the USSR, in Ukraine, Kazakhstan, and Siberia* were contacted and discreetly encouraged. In furtherance of the Pope's earlier policies in the archdiocese of Cracow, support was extended to the Catholic

*Largely of Polish origin, these Catholic communities derive from the exiles and deportees of both Tsarist and Soviet governments. Irkutsk has a Catholic cathedral. In Kazakhstan alone, an estimated 500,000 Catholics deported from the Ukraine in 1935–6, and deprived of clerical ministrations ever since, are still reported to maintain their separate religious and ethnic identity.

Uniates. The Vatican's offensive in the East was palpably based on peace and charity. The Vatican threw its weight for the first time into the ecumenical movement. British and American observers were probably most impressed on this score by John Paul's speeches in Ireland and America, and by that unforgettable scene on 29 May 1982 in Canterbury Cathedral. The Pope from a land often conceived of by Anglo-Americans as a den of papist fanaticism made a startling demonstration of the ease and grace with which Catholics and Protestants should settle their differences. Yet the main thrust of the Vatican's new-found Ecumenism lay less towards the Protestant Churches than towards the Orthodox, where the schism is much older. Here again, Eastern Europe, including Poland, where there is a small native Orthodox Church, was intimately involved.

Lastly, the Vatican finally shook itself free from its European preoccupations, and turned in earnest to the Third World. In the first four years of his reign John Paul II showed special concern for Asia, Africa, and above all for Latin America—visiting Japan, the Philippines, Pakistan, Guam, Zaïre, Kenya, Ghana, the Ivory Coast, Dominica, Mexico, the Bahamas, Brazil, and Argentina, as well as Ireland, the USA, France, West Germany, and Britain. What an experience for the boy from Wadowice to be greeted in Brazil by children dancing the *krakowiak,* and by choirs singing *Góralu czy ci nie żal* (the Polish equivalent of 'Will ye no come back again?')! But involvement in the Third World brought its complications. The Vatican establishment, whose stance towards the communist brand of totalitarianism had always been unambiguous, was now obliged to rethink its posture towards non-communist dictatorships, whose rulers had often been associated with the Catholic Hierarchy but whose methods were no more compassionate than those of the communists. In particular, it had to seek an understanding with the radical clergy of the Third World, whose 'liberation theology' made no secret of sympathy for violent, popular resistance movements. Here, the Polish Pope was presented with a delicate political teaser. If it was a mistake for the Vatican to have condemned the Risings of the Catholic Poles against tyranny in the nineteenth century, how then could it be in order to condemn the liberation struggles to the Catholic peoples of Latin America today?

From all this, it appeared that the Polish Crisis had been made relevant to the Church's problems in the most distant corners of the globe. Not merely on account of the Polish Pope himself, but more from the unprecedented publicity and interest in the Pope's homeland aroused throughout the World, Poland had become a test case both for Church–State relations in general and for the Vatican's policy towards political oppression in particular. Hence the Vatican's customary reticence was reinforced. John Paul II openly welcomed SOLIDARITY, and received Wałęsa like a son. But when SOLIDARITY was suppressed and Wałęsa arrested, there were no pontifical fireworks, no excommunications, no harsh language—only prayers, and consultations, and confidential letters. The Vatican held true to its original call for dialogue and for national reconciliation in Poland. It continued to press the view, when the Military Regime spurned all negotiations, that the Church could not be excluded from Polish affairs altogether. As the comical Polish saying had it, *Bez Glempu, nyet postępu* (It's a bad climate without the Primate). Towards the end of 1982, it even persuaded General Jaruzelski to meet with Archbishop Glemp, and to lay provisional plans for a papal visit in the summer of 1983. But on the essential political point, its position remained unchanged. In Poland—as in Ireland, in Indonesia, or in Argentina—the Universal Church of Christ does not condone violence. The words of the Church, like the literature of Poland's strongest tradition, preach the virtues not of political power but of spirituality.

9 Economic Regression

Despite all the quantitative and technological advances, economic regression has been a rather more common occurrence in Polish history than economic progress. Poland's economic decline began in earnest in the second quarter of the seventeenth century, and has continued, with only minor intervals, ever since. By the middle of the eighteenth century, the old Republic had sunk to the bottom of Europe's economic league; whilst in the nineteenth, Galicia vied with Sicily and southern Ireland as the most backward of Europe's poorest provinces. In the twentieth century, two World Wars wreaked devastation on a scale so colossal that economic recovery was retarded for decades. During the inter-war period, industrial production never regained 1913 levels, and in the People's Republic, after thirty years of reconstruction and socialist planning, the Polish economy has once more been crippled almost, it would seem, beyond repair. Economic failure has been the norm; the intervals of relative success have been the exception.

Yet, to any neutral observer, Poland's economic record defies any simple explanation. In rational, economic terms, it is impossible to explain why a country which is so rich in economic resources, which possesses great reserves of fertile farm land, industrial plant, energy potential, mineral deposits, and skilled labour, should be plunged into the pit of economic destitution. It is even stranger to see that majority of Western analysts attribute Poland's present distress to simple economic causes. 'Economism'—the contention that economic performance determines political events—is rampant in much prevailing comment, and is shared by Western and communist economists alike. Time and again, one reads that the emergence of SOLIDARITY in 1980, and the popular revolt against the Party, was caused and not just abetted by the grave mistakes in economic policy in the 1970s. Economic analysts, whose knowledge of Polish events spans all of ten or fifteen years, declare that the vital clue to the Polish crisis can be found in Gomułka's over-accumulation of investment capital, in Gierek's over-dependence on foreign loans, or on this, that, or the other economic deficiency. Opinions of that variety are *à la mode;* but they put the economic cart before the political horse. Economic analysis, of course, makes an essential contribution to the overall picture. But it describes the elements of the crisis, rather than explaining them. It is not sufficient to discover that the communist regime in Poland committed every conceivable blunder in the economic book. One has also to ask *why* the mistakes were committed. And there, the answer invariably lies in the dominant sphere of politics.

A full description of Poland's economic deformities would require a small encyclopaedia; but a summary of the dozen most spectacular items can serve to illustrate the scale of the catastrophe.

By 1980, Polish agriculture had ceased to supply sufficient food to feed the nation. After decades of official harassment and punitive procurement prices, the dominant private sector gradually reduced its sales of food products. The individual farmer, who could not buy suitable tools and equipment from his meagre cash income, lost the incentive to put surplus produce onto the market. The small but favoured collectivized state sector, which swallowed 80 per cent of public investment in agriculture, was so inefficient that it supplied less than a quarter of the country's food products.

The structure of prices and wages had developed grotesque imbalances. Owing to the Party's fear of popular protest, most food prices were frozen at 1969 levels for thirteen years. By 1980, food price subsidies were consuming between one-third and one-half of the state budget. At the same time, in a misguided effort to mollify the Polish consumer, wage levels were increased without any regard to the supply of the goods on which increased earnings could be spent. By 1980, 20 per cent of personal income was uncovered by unavailable goods, yet through pressure from SOLIDARITY wages were increased still further. The average public wage rose from 5,200 zlotys per month in 1980 to 7,250 zlotys per month in 1981. Poles were being paid in worthless currency. In conditions of acute shortage, they were driven into involuntary savings. Bank deposits soared. Inflation, both of the hidden and the open variety, was spiralling out of control.

Over-ambitious investment policies, absorbing over 30 per cent of national income in the early 1970s, were directed into abortive or unproductive projects. The lion's share went to the communist shibboleths—to heavy industry, to joint Soviet-Polish concerns (like the Huta Katowice Steelworks), to state farms, to ultra-modern but unnecessary show factories, and to armaments. By 1980, the investment programme of the Gierek regime was set to absorb the entire investment resources of the next decade, leaving no room for any new schemes.

Foreign loans, raised to finance the modernization of Polish industry, failed to produce the desired results. More and more loans were raised to facilitate repayment on the previous ones. By 1980, Poland's staggering foreign debt of $27 billion, owed both to Western banking consortia and to Western governments, exceeded the entire foreign debt of the USSR. By 1981, arrears on repayment equalled 160 per cent of Poland's hard currency revenue. Poland did not declare default; but she was technically bankrupt. Rescheduling of debt repayments was unavoidable.

Foreign Trade, closely linked to the foreign loan programme, lapsed into serious decline. With no cash to buy imported materials, spare parts, and technology, Polish industry could not produce the goods for export. Deliveries both to the West and to Comecon partners slumped. Foreign customers lost confidence. Poland's staple coal exports, the main hard currency earner, dropped from 41 million tonnes in 1979 to only 15 million tonnes in 1981. The Polish food trade, which had been a net exporter until 1973, was forced in 1976–81 to import 40 million tonnes of costly feed grain, mainly from the USA. With no further credits available to bridge the trade gap, Poland was forced to cancel orders on a wide variety of essential commodities.

Industrial productivity fell to an all-time low. Industrial plant stood idle through unrepaired machinery and severed supplies, or for the want of tiny components in the mass-production line. Half of the transport park dropped out of action. The bottle-necks and shortages multiplied. A country with billions of acres of prime forest could not produce household matches,* allegedly because there was no glue to stick the fire-heads to the matchsticks. Shoes could not be produced, because there was no adhesive to fix the soles to the uppers. Even the production of Silesian coal, the pride and joy of the Gierek regime, dropped from a peak of 201 million tonnes in 1979 to 163 million tonnes in 1981. The construction industry, with a vast backlog of housing projects, virtually

---

*At a rough estimate, Poland's 50,000 square miles of standing forest should provide enough timber for each of the country's 36 million inhabitants to keep striking a match once every second without interruption for the next thirty-nine years, 153 days, eleven hours and forty-six minutes—with 1,728 billion matches in reserve. Yet matches were in short supply.

ground to a halt. Overall national income saw negative growth for the first time since the War. 1980 saw a fall of 12 per cent, 1981 a projected 17–18 per cent. Official spokesmen, with their obligatory bent for optimism, did not foresee the level of output of 1978 being recovered before 1990.

Energy supplies dwindled. Despite the massive coal reserves, Poland could not meet its energy needs. Electric power cuts were a common occurrence in 1980–1, although reduced demands from stagnant industry obviated the necessity in 1982. Instead, domestic gas supplies were interrupted. Oil imports, largely dependent on Soviet charity, were under severe strain. Curtailment of electricity supplies on the international grid to Czechoslovakia and East Germany caused shortfalls in Comecon production.

Labour resources, always deployed in an inefficient manner, became hopelessly disorganized . A system which prided itself on the fiction of full employment had made little provision for labour mobility, and proved incapable of adjusting to the growing crisis. An inadequate work-force in key areas of the new industrial projects was matched by gross overmanning in the traditional sectors. For decades, the communist managers paid millions of workers for doing little or no work. They now faced the prospect of official unemployment levels unheard-of in the Western countries.

No details are published about the military sector of the economy (see pp. 366–74). But it is hard to imagine that this holy of holies of communist planning was spared the general suffering.

In human terms, the main casualty was the Polish standard of living. In the mid-1970s, the Polish consumer had been led to feel that long years of austerity were at last bringing their due reward. Rising wages; improved domestic goods, in the form of affordable washing machines and televisions; the arrival of the first family motor cars; adequate food and clothing supplies; slowly improving housing conditions; and for the first time, a small surplus for recreation and travel—created an illusion of well-being. The average Polish family, at over seventy kilos per caput per annum, was eating the same amount of meat as the British or the French. They were not to know that their short-lived prosperity had been bought by unsecured loans, and was not underpinned by matching productivity. So the eventual taste of disillusionment was all the sourer. A brief bout of sugar rationing in 1975 warned of worse things to come; but the main disaster was postponed until 1980. Since then all the staple consumer items—meat, butter, alcohol, tobacco, sanitary supplies, soap, petrol, shoes, and even underwear—were strictly rationed, at minimal levels. Those Poles who could remember, contrasted their present destitution to conditions during the Stalinist period or the Nazi Occupation.

Inevitably, the black market flourished as never before. Police action by the military regime against 'counter-revolutionary speculators', made no sense, so long as the official economy was incapable of meeting the people's basic needs.

In the wake of all these symptoms of economic catastrophe, communist Party spokesmen were finally forced to admit that the established economic system had actually ceased to function. The central organs of planning and management were going through their habitual motions, but agricultural, industrial, and service enterprises were no longer responding to the commands. Economic Reform was not merely desirable; it was unavoidable.

By 1980, however, the environment for economic reform in Poland could not have been worse. There was no prospect for an upturn in World Trade or in the Western Recession. There was no general consensus about the direction which reform should take, either in the ruling Party or in a disorientated society. There was no clear way of reconciling Poland's native economic particularities with the doctrinaire demands of Poland's fraternal allies. There was not even a reliable statistical basis on which to work, since in January 1981 the former president of the Central Statistical Office admitted that official statistics were still being systematically falsified.[15] What is more, the long-term trends in Eastern Europe revealed a gradual slow-down throughout the Soviet Bloc. Poland's existing difficultues were reducing the ability of its socialist allies to render effective assistance. The USSR, itself in a critical economic condition, could only contemplate increased aid to Poland at the cost of decreased aid to its other needy allies. Poland's reduced deliveries to Comecon impaired Comecon deliveries to Poland. Poland's virtual bankruptcy had ruined the credit rating of the entire Soviet Bloc in relation to Western creditors. The so-called 'Soviet Umbrella' of loan security was shown to be barely shower-proof. Most seriously, time was working against Reform. All experts agree that a time-lag invariably occurs between the implementation of reform and the onset of improved performance. The initial phase, during which the system is being changed, invarably involves disruption, improvization, 'teething troubles', and reduced efficiency. In other words, a Polish reform pro-gramme initiated in 1982 (when production was down by 15 per cent) would cause further hardships in 1983, 1984, and 1985, and would not begin to show results until the second half of the decade. By that time, however, new demographic pressures would be coming into play and would tend to undermine the benefits gained. Owing to the extreme peaks and troughs of Poland's population structure, caused by high wartime mortality and the astonishing compensatory birth-rate of the 1950s, the balance between people of working age and non-working age has been condemned to severe fluctua-tions. As bad luck would have it, the decade from 1980 to 1990 was scheduled to witness a sharp rise in the number of children—as the offspring of the 1950s baby boom began to produce their own offspring—and a sharp fall in the intake of young energetic workers into the labour force—as the products of the 1960s baby dearth reached maturity. The reproductive patterns of the Polish nation have already determined that the 1980s must witness the maximum discrepancy between the number of mouths to be fed and the economy's capacity to feed them. Economic Reform must go ahead, but with no clear prospect of success.

The debate on economic reform raged to no great effect throughout 1980 and 1981. SOLIDARITY produced a plethora of proposals, some sensible and some dotty, whose very profusion masked the consistency of its fundamental position. SOLIDARITY contended that social consent was the essential pre-condition for the success of any programme of economic reform. No reforms could be made to work in practice unless 'society' was allowed to participate in the process of their formulation and implementation. Reforms imposed from above, however brilliant, were condemned to failure, simply because the nation had lost all confidence in the Party's ability to govern. For all its good sense, this contention offended the hard-line element of the Party, which was able to block its acceptance; but it attracted much sympathy from Party members belonging to SOLIDARITY, who fought for it hard and long in the various reform commissions and in discussion in the Sejm. As a result, the draft bills on Economic Reform were endlessly amended and delayed, and the interim reform programme could not be put forward until after the declaration of the State of War.

On the whole, in an atmosphere greatly modified by SOLIDARITY's liberal approach, the communists did not have the nerve to argue strongly on the basis of the economic traditions of their own movement. The occasional article recalled the slogans of War Communism, which had brought the Bolsheviks through the Russian Civil War (and which General Jaruzelski's commissars were destined to practise in 1982). Sporadic mention was made of Lenin's NEP of 1921-9, whereby concessions to capitalist methods enabled the Bolsheviks to restore prosperity until the radical transformation of the economy could be thoroughly prepared. Few speakers mentioned Stalin by name—since that had lost respectability even in Party circles; but as the crisis deepened, it was more and more usual to hear criticism of the Party's failed policies on the grounds that there had been 'too little Socialism, not too much'. In plain men's language, this was a call to revive the Stalinist experiments of the 1950s.

Yet the most frequent talk was of 'Kadarism'. Many Comrades in Poland, and many commentators in the West, seriously wondered whether Poland's road to recovery might not lie along the route so successfully followed by Kadar in Hungary after 1956. The Hungarian model offered a variety of ideas which were very attractive to people who confined their thoughts to the economic sphere. The decentralization of management; the creation of labour incentives; the reduction of antiquated heavy industry which wasted vast quantities of energy; the 'reindustrialization' of the economy with emphasis on light industry, modern technology, and food-processing;

and the revitalization of agriculture through autonomous co-
operatives—all these items and some besides, were mixed into
the debate. But little action could be taken in a period when
the decision-making organs of the Party were rapidly approaching total paralysis.

Finally on 1 January 1982, under cover of the State of War,
a package of economic reform was put into effect, and some
fifteen related Statutes were passed by the Sejm in the course
of 1981–2. Those parts of the blueprint which contradicted
Martial Law regulations—such as the autonomous status of
enterprises controlled by military commissars—had to be left
in abeyance; but some progress was made in stemming the
reigning chaos and in laying the foundations of recovery. The
salesmen of the package—such as Professors Bobrowski and
Sadowski—explained that it was based on three principles: on
the central planning of economic input; on the independence
of self-managing and self-financing economic enterprises; and
on due observance of commercial rules and market mechanisms in the conduct of economic policy.[16] The central
element, the Enterprise Act, had already been passed in the
autumn of 1981 as soon as General Jaruzelski took power. It
envisaged a great variety of enterprise types, from large-scale,
vertically integrated combines in heavy industry to small,
diversified mixed enterprises in the light-industrial and service
sectors; and it included a scheme for self-management,
involving Employees' Councils, General Meetings of Employees, and, subject to future approval, 'workers' self-management'. The freedom of enterprises to run their own budgets, to
dispose of their profits, to borrow money, and to redistribute
workers' remuneration was intended to give management a
sense of genuine responsibility and, as a by-product, to
reactivate the moribund banking system. The Socio-Economic Planning Act of 1982 outlined the procedures whereby
central planning might be co-ordinated with the autonomous
enterprises through contracting and market controls. The
State held reserve powers where defence needs, emergency
supplies, or international commitments were involved. The
Price Act defined three new categories of prices—*fixed prices* for
consumer goods on the basic cost-of-living index; *controlled
prices* for industrial products, based on production costs plus

approved project margins; and *contractual prices* based on agreements between commercial partners. Most interestingly perhaps, Government Commissioners' Offices were created to replace the old 'branch associations' linking the central ministries with industrial enterprises. The number of economic ministries was sharply reduced, and the GCOs were allocated only one-fifth of the bureaucratic staff employed by the former associations. In the first flush of its difficult birth, the Economic Reform Package looked like a serious attack on the traditional communist Command Economy.

At the same time, the Military Regime showed no hestitation in introducing authoritarian measures designed to mitigate the worst effects of the reigning economic disequilibria. Military commissars were appointed in all sectors of the economy to break supply bottle-necks by peremptory orders, and to restore labour discipline. Recalcitrant workers could be arbitrarily dismissed. All the strongholds of SOLIDARITY membership—in the Silesian mines, the steelworks of Nowa Huta, Huta Katowice, and Huta Warszawa, in the shipyards of Gdańsk and Szczecin, and the armament factories of Radom and Stalowa Wola,—were formally militarized, making disobedient workers liable to the same penalties as mutineers and deserters. Economic crimes, such as sabotage, absenteeism, or incitement to strike were handed over to Courts Martial. A month-long propaganda campaign forewarned the public of the massive price rises introduced on 1 February 1982, together with compensatory wage adjustments. The price rises, which by common consent were a dozen years overdue, averaged 300 per cent across the board. Sugar went up from 11 to 46 zlotys per kilo; butter from 68 to 240; ham from 120 to 360. Wage compensations followed a sliding scale from 700 zlotys per month for low earners to 300 for highly paid workers. Generous special allowances of 1,400 zlotys per month were to be paid to every miner and 1,000 zlotys for every child. These changes, ten times more drastic than the price rise of 1976, which had caused serious rioting, were accepted without smiles but without a murmur of protest. Also on 1 February, an amended Miners' Charter came into force. Apart from the special wage allowances, this made provision for pension rights after only twenty-five years' underground service, for special housing assistance to young married couples, and for confirmation of the miners' traditional grades, titles, uniforms, and festivals. Some might say it was poor exchange against the loss of the five-day week, gained under SOLIDARITY, and the reintroduction of the hated four-shift brigade system. At least in the short run, the immediate aims were achieved. The miners went back to work, and the 1982 target of 190 million tonnes began to look attainable.

Official spokesmen were obliged to express cautious optimism; but to the outsider, the partial and improvised Reform of 1981–2 looked like a makeshift repair job—more than cosmetic tinkering, but less than a thorough overhaul. There was no sign of fundamental changes. Poland was still in the grip of economic regression with no early prospect of radical improvement.

10 *International Attitudes*

Ever since Poland's distress became the object of international comment in the mid-eighteenth century, both the critics and the sympathizers have produced a fascinating corpus of *bons mots*. Frederick the Great boasted of 'partaking eucharistically of Poland's body'; Voltaire made his famous quip—*un polonais un charmeur: deux polonais, une bagarre: trois polonais, c'est la Question Polonaise;* and Burke wrote solemnly that 'Poland must be regarded as situate on the Moon'. Richard Cobden announced after the November Rising that Poland's fate could only befall a 'neglected, decayed, disorganised, ignorant, and irreligious' society; Lamartine admitted more honestly, 'We love Poland . . . but most of all we love France.' In our own century, Vyacheslav Molotov called Poland 'the monstrous bastard of the Peace of Versailles'; J.M. Keynes called it 'an economic impossibility whose only industry is Jew-baiting'; and David Lloyd George was reported to say he would no more give it Upper Silesia 'than he would give a clock to a monkey'. In 1939 Adolf Hitler called Poland 'a ridiculous state where sadistic beasts give vent to their perverse instincts', 'the pet lap-dog of the Western democracies which cannot be considered a cultured nation at all', 'a so-called state lacking every national, historical, cultural, and moral foundation'. At that same juncture, a deputy in French Assembly enquired somewhat wearily whether Frenchmen were going to be ordered once again 'to die for Danzig'.

In this colourful collection of quotations, the Polonophobes clearly have the edge over the Polonophiles. Yet, if one may discount the animosities of the Germans and Russians on the grounds of normal bad neighbourliness, it is harder to explain why the likes of Keynes and Lloyd George should have agreed so closely with the likes of Hitler or Molotov. What is even more curious, is that in our own day, many of the old attitudes to Poland can still be encountered in the columns of *The Economist,* the *Guardian,* or the *New York Times.* Few people in the West have been prepared to say outright that SOLIDAR-ITY was a disruptive organization of fanatical trouble-makers who deserved their fate; but there were many who expressed the view that SOLIDARITY 'fell into the hands of extremists' or 'failed to steer clear of politics'. There are millions who wish that Poland—together with Northern Ireland, Lebanon, and El Salvador—would simply sink into the sea. On the Polish issue at least, the disciples of Voltaire's scepticism certainly outnumber the followers of Rousseau's enthusiasm.

The first category of Western sceptics belongs to the commercial interest. They are impressed by the fact that the Western banks have poured $80 billion into the Soviet Bloc in the last ten years—eight times more than the sum total of Marshall Aid to western Europe in the post-war era—and that so far the returns have been meagre. Fearful that these huge Western loans may never be repaid, they cling first and foremost to the hope of stability, and instinctively distrust any change in Eastern Europe which threatens further to destabil-ize a region already unstable. They are the natural allies of the communist governments, in whom they placed such unblinking confidence, and by extension the automatic critics of all the communists' opponents. In this, they are moved by pure business instincts. Since the communist governments of the Soviet Bloc are their contracted clients, the discrepancy between their own principles of free commercial enterprise and the communists' sworn hostility to capitalism is best forgotten. Their ingrained commercialism is highly characteristic of the great Western democracies which are also the world's great trading nations. The democracies live by trade and, if democratic scruples were allowed to interfere with trade, the democrats would lose their profits. If the democracies' trading partners happen to be tyrants, then it is regrettable; but the fate of the inmates of the tyrants' gaols is no immediate concern of theirs. In any case, the tyrants' opponents have probably broken the Law, and as disturbers of the peace have probably deserved their fate. Most significantly, the archetypal proponent of this line of reasoning was Richard Cobden, the 'Apostle of Free Trade' and pioneer of British Liberalism, whose derogatory remarks about Poland are to be found in a pamphlet advocating extended relations with Tsarist Russia. The arch-Liberal was an eager partner of the arch-Autocrat. Business was business. One can guess what Cobden's views on the present Polish crisis would have been from the remarks of Cobden's latter-day disciples. They would have pressed the Polish Government to release Wałęsa at a convenient date, and would have urged a word with the Church to calm popular feelings. But their first priority would be to return to business as usual. They may have a soft spot for Poland and for Poland's Romantic trouble-makers; but they would not lift a finger to help them. 'We love Poland', they might say with Lamartine, 'but most of all we love our pipeline.'

The second category of Western sceptics towards Poland, is allied to the bankers, and has a prime concern to uphold established authority. They usually come from the right wing of Western opinion, and as pillars of law and order at home see no reason to abet the disturbers of the peace abroad. So long as SOLIDARITY was non-violent (as it always was), and so long as the right to strike was sanctioned by the Polish authorities, then they were content to approve 'an interesting experiment'; but the minute that the State of War was declared, and support for SOLIDARITY in Poland was made illegal, they felt that all opposition to the Polish Government should cease. Henceforth, all resistance in Poland was judged 'counter-productive' and all comment in the West which continued to criticize the Polish Government was dubbed 'irresponsible'. In their view, people who dared to pressurize the Polish Government with protests were guilty of needlessly inflaming passions; whilst those who continued to warn of the danger of Soviet intervention obviously did so because they relished the prospect of thousands of young Poles slaughtered amidst scenes of rioting and bloodshed. Often enough, commentators of this persuasion, who abound in the conservative circles of the West and especially in ultra-authoritarian Japan, are the selfsame people who are constantly warning of the Soviet threat and urging the West to strengthen its defences against the evils of Communism.

The third category of Western sceptics is motivated by left-wing, socialist sympathies. Despite much evidence to the contrary, they are still convinced that the regimes of the Soviet Bloc are basically socialist in character, and that all open opposition to those regimes must somehow be 'anti-socialist'. Of course, they see that Soviet-style government has many blemishes, and that it treats its opponents more roughly than decadent capitalist regimes happen to do. But that, in their view, is all the more reason for keeping in touch with their fellow left-wingers in Eastern Europe and persuading them to soften their methods. It was on these grounds that the British TUC insisted on maintaining its link with the official Polish CZZZ until the latter was disbanded, and declined to establish formal contact with SOLIDARITY until official recognition had been granted. Democratic socialists of this persuasion, who are common in the British Labour Party or the West German SPD, are keen to organize strikes and days of action against the evils of their own (capitalist) society; but they were slow to voice support for action of the same sort in Poland. Western Communists suffered similar qualms of conscience. They wanted to solidarize with the Polish workers; yet they recognized the right of the dictatorship of the Polish proletariat to crush dissent by force. They ended up by supporting both the Polish Party and SOLIDARITY simultaneously. Happiest of all were the Western Trotskyists. Equally contemptuous of the USSR's Polish puppet as of the 'priest-ridden SOLIDARITY', they were delighted to pour ridicule on both sides of the Polish contest at once. In their view, it seemed that the entire crisis was cooked up by a conspiracy of Western capitalists dedicated to financing the oppression of

Eastern Europe by the Soviet Union. For this reason, they composed that resounding demo-chant slogan: 'WESTERN BANKS—RUSSIAN TANKS—OUT!'

To the suffering Poles, the spectacle of these intellectual contortions in the West would be comical if only they were not so insulting. To the simple mind, they are incomprehensible. The Poles watch Western bankers, the mandarins of Capitalism, hand in glove with the bosses of Communism. They see Western democrats, outspoken advocates of freedom and justice, taking sides in Poland with the self-confessed practitioners of totalitarian dictatorship and military rule; and they see Western socialists, the champions of the working people of their own countries, hesitate to help the Polish working people to those same rights which in Western Europe or the USA are taken for granted. They wonder why this is, and why it has always been so.

One must be careful not to over-simplify Western opinion, and one must accept, alas, that incoherence is one of the side-effects of free expression. There are certainly Western bankers who sincerely regret their policies in Eastern Europe, and not merely on practical grounds. There are Western parliamentarians, both of the Right and the Left, who have consistently encouraged the Polish cause; and there are Western labour leaders in the USA, European socialists, and Euro-communists in France and Italy, who gave unstinting support to SOLIDARITY. Even so, there was much to explain. Much of the pusillanimity about Poland does not come from entrenched politicians or from government agencies, but from intellectuals, academics, broadcasters, and independent journalists, who have no need to exercise caution. Yet they persist in seeing 'normalization in Eastern Europe' in terms which would gratify a lecturer in the Higher Party School in Prague or East Berlin, and 'stability' as synonymous with monopoly Party rule. What they seem to lack is any feeling for the moral element in politics. They imply, since the communist system in Eastern Europe commands overwhelming force, that is somehow *wrong* to challenge it. They imply, since the Polish challenge to Soviet rule has been repeatedly beaten, that it is guilty for being beaten, that the Poles, instead of resisting their tormentors, should rather have submitted themselves to their beating in an orderly fashion. They imply that Poland's troubles have no right to disturb their own welfare. Above all, they fail to notice any connection between Poland's fate and that of their own country. (Those Social Democrats in West Germany, who have suggested that Polish freedom should be sacrificed in the interests of European peace, at least have the virtue of honesty.) But usually, as Stanisław Barańczak has pointed out, 'They flatly deny any community of interest between the already-beaten and the not-yet-beaten. . . . Let us hope that the bully will be satisfied with just one thrashing, and meanwhile we can send the victim some food parcels.'[17]

It is a curious phenomenon. But after two hundred years of 'tragic repetitions' the Poles have not yet learned how to lie down flat and avoid their periodic thrashings; and Western opinion in general has still not learned to give them the credit for standing up to resist.

As for the attitudes of Poland's immediate neighbours, in the USSR, East Germany, and Czechoslovakia, it is difficult to disentangle any genuine opinion from the automated outpourings of their censored media. Much has to be divined by informational osmosis. Certainly, Prague and East Berlin, which are most immediately threatened with contagion, have kept up a chorus of anti-Polish denunciations worthy of Beneš in 1939 or Bismarck in 1863. To the disinterested, it must appear that the Czechs and the neo-Prussians have learned little, and have no intention of learning. They closed their frontiers to Polish tourists and visitors in the autumn of 1980, and have kept them closed.

Soviet attitudes have been rather more ambiguous. Of course, at critical moments, as in the late autumn of 1980 or in June 1981 when the Central Committee of the CPSU treated the Polish Comrades to a blunt summary of its views, Soviet officialdom blasted off with a public display of threats and innuendoes. Western journalists in the Soviet Union, probing the authoritative views of the proverbial Russian taxi-driver or hairdresser, report that traditional Russian prejudices against Poland have not changed. In the eyes of many ordinary Russians, the Poles are incurably hostile to Russia, and if left to themselves would set up a government of anti-Soviet, clerical fanatics. A Soviet invasion of Poland would

not fill the gutters of Moscow's streets with rivers of tears. The
Soviet Party, too, must have been strengthened in the
traditional Russian view about Polish 'incurable unreliability'. From their point of view, there has never been any
alternative to a communist-led Government in Warsaw; yet
the Polish communists seem for ever to be playing a game of
hide-and-seek with their Soviet superiors. For some reason,
Polish Communism has always to be completely different
from everyone else's, and in Poland a so-called socialist society
has still to be swarming with kulaks, priests, and dissidents.
Without fail, Polish communist leaders turn out to be half-
hearted cheats or incompetents. The leaders of the pre-war
KPP had to be shot for Trotskyism; Gomułka had to be
removed ¹for nationalist deviations, and deserved to be
removed again. Bierut gave himself a heart attack at a most
inconsiderate moment; whilst Gierek, Brezhnev's best Polish
friend, promptly put his country into pawn with the Western
capitalists. Kania, the right-hand man of the KGB, lacked
every inclination to follow in the steps of the glorious
Dzierżyński, and Jaruzelski, whose original promotion in 1960
was approved in order to strengthen Party control over the
Army, turned out to be a 'Bonapartist'. There can be little
doubt that the average Soviet Comrade regards the whole
Polish nation from top to bottom as incorrigible. Yet there
were no signs in the first years of the Polish Crisis after August
1980 that the Kremlin had yet developed any consistent
policy. There were long periods when the Soviet press,
preoccupied with other urgent crises at home and abroad,
relegated Polish news to the inside pages. The impression was
given that the Kremlin saw the Polish crisis as a storm in a
glass of *herbata*, a minor provincial mess, like the disturbances
of Estonia or the scandals of Azerbaijan, which could be
cleared up when convenient. When the December Coup took
place, and the Soviet Comrades learned that the Polish
Communist Party had finally collapsed, there were few
expressions of regret or open alarm. Marshal Kulikov came to
Warsaw to supervize final preparations in person, and must
have been well satisfied with Jaruzelski's performance. Jaruzelski quickly obtained the Kremlin's open approbation. Soviet
comment was far more concerned with reactions in the West,

and with American sanctions, than with the details of events in Poland itself. In short, Soviet feelings about Poland may be depressingly uniform; but Soviet views about practical action have appeared less cohesive, and some margin for flexible response has remained.

11 World-wide Repercussions

In each of the major crises of modern Europe, the Polish issue has proved a bone of contention between the great powers. In 1814–15 at the Congress of Vienna, it almost drove the partners of the Allied Coalition to resort to war against each other. (See p. 163.) In 1919–20, at the Peace Conference of Paris, where the Poles, Germans, and Russians took no part in the decisive negotiations, it none the less aroused much bad feeling between Britain and France. (See p. 116.) In 1943–5, at the Conferences of the Grand Alliance, it is generally considered to have been one of the prime causes of the developing 'Cold War'. Aristide Briand called Poland 'Europe's rheumatism'; President Roosevelt called it 'the world's headache'. Once again, after a decent interval of forty years, the lastest Polish crisis has become a focal point of East–West tensions, and the subject of a rhetorical marathon between the world's two superpowers. One is tempted to ask why a country of only medium size, which produced only two minor independent initiatives in foreign affairs in the last forty years,* should attract such attention. The answer lies in the fact that the ramifications of the Polish crisis reach into all the current problems of the USSR. Not just the USA, but the Kremlin itself, has reason to suspect that Poland may prove to be the Achilles' heel of the entire Soviet Bloc.

The Military Take-over in Poland undoubtedly strengthened the military interest in every country of the Warsaw Pact, and sent shudders down the spine of every fraternal Party. If it had happened in Poland, against all the rules of Leninism, then it was conceivable that it could happen in Romania, in East Germany, or most ominously in the USSR

---

*The Rapacki Plan for a Nuclear-Free Zone in Europe in 1957, and an act of abstention in the United Nations General Assembly on 21 November 1956 on a motion condemning Soviet intervention in Hungary.

itself. Wherever the Party apparatus is weak and corrupt,
wherever the Military has to compete for shrinking economic
resources, wherever the communist Establishment faces popular unrest, the Marshals and Generals now knew that they had
a chance of assuming power. Military ambitions in the Soviet
Bloc, which have traditionally been viciously excised, received
a definite boost. In the Soviet Union, the Marshals well
remember how the Party treated the Red Army's two greatest
leaders, Tukhachevsky and Zhukov, and they can hardly plan
the same fate for themselves. But now they have a hope.

It is no secret that the economy of the Soviet Bloc has been
moving inexorably into a period of declining growth. Indeed,
some Western experts hold that as from 1980 the GNP of the
USSR entered a phase of absolute regression. In this regard,
the Polish crisis must look especially dangerous. In the short
term, Poland was set to extract a constant drain on Soviet
financial and hard-currency reserves. Whether it liked it or
not, the USSR had to provide Poland with sufficient loans to
ensure Polish deliveries to Comecon and the Warsaw Pact,
and it had to supply sufficient hard currency to prevent
Poland declaring default on its Western debt. In both cases,
the Soviet Government faced the painful choice between
supporting Poland at a level which it could not afford or of
accepting a cut-back in inter-Comecon trade and in the Soviet
Bloc's Western credit. In the longer term, Poland presented
the Soviet Union with a still more disturbing prospect. If for
any reason the USSR were to be forced to intervene in Poland,
the colossal burden of Poland's debts, production shortfalls,
and organizational chaos would be piled on top of the USSR's
own existing burdens. In that event, any prospect of the Soviet
Union's economic recovery within the foreseeable future
would be effectively dispelled.

Within the overall economic crisis of the Soviet Bloc, the
issue of military expenditure was absolutely central. The
USSR desperately wishes to enjoy military parity with the
USA, but in order to do so must spend between two and three
times the proportion of its GNP. At the same time, Soviet
leaders wish to give their long-suffering citizens a greater
reward for their labours. In the 1970s, the Soviet people were
introduced to the joys of the television, the private car, and

the unshared bathroom. Yet, in a contracting economy, the competing demands of the military and the civilian sectors are plainly incompatible. In one of Brezhnev's last major speeches, in November 1982, he made a special point of publicly assuring the Marshals that they would be given everything they needed. It was a backhanded way of admitting that the Marshals feared a cut in their procurements. From the Marshals' point of view, they could take one of several courses. They could meekly accept a cut in their budget, which some Western experts have said is unavoidable; or they could sit back and trust that Brezhnev's dying promise would be respected by his successors. They might even accept a cut in strategic missile spending in the hope that funds could be diverted into conventional rearmament. More realistically, however, they might try to make themselves and their military budget indispensable, perhaps by pushing the Kremlin into some expensive military adventure. Given the ingrained Soviet mania for national security and military prestige, they might well view the outbreak of a modest and manageable conflict as the best safeguard for their threatened procurements. After all, the Party leadership could hardly refuse their requests once the Soviet Army's invincible record was at stake. And where else but in Eastern Europe could the Soviet Army conduct a short, popular, and victorious campaign without serious risk of American retaliation? If all else fails, the Soviet Marshals may be driven, in the event of prolonged cuts in their budget, to follow General Jaruzelski's example and teach their miserly political leaders a long overdue lesson. In this light, one might wonder whether General Jaruzelski's *démarche* in Poland should not be seen as a dummy run, backed by his military colleagues in the Warsaw Pact, and designed for future contingencies of the same sort in their own countries. It goes without saying that the position of the CPSU in the Soviet Union was incomparably stronger than that of the PZPR in Poland. In 1980, and despite the uncertainties of Brezhnev's succession, there was no sign of the Marshals' direct involvement. But the accumulating problems of the 1980s must inevitably take their toll. Every successive agricultural catastrophe, every failed investment in industry, every outburst of the national minorities, every crisis in

Eastern Europe, every confrontation with the USA, must inexorably strengthen the Military's hand. One may only muse; but it is not beyond the bounds of probability that within a decade of General Jaruzelski's take-over in Warsaw, a Soviet Marshal could be inspired to follow suit in the Kremlin.

More immediately, the Polish crisis threatened to affect the Soviet Union's main plans for strategic deployment. Unlike Hungary in 1956, which was overrun by Soviet divisions from the neighbouring Ukrainian Military Region, and unlike Czechoslovakia in 1968, where popular resistance was not expected, Soviet intervention in Poland would seriously disrupt the disposition of the USSR's standing forces and reserves. Military experts differ in their views; but if the occupation of an unresisting Czechoslovakia required a Warsaw Pact force approaching half a million men, it follows that the occupation of a truculent Poland, with twice the territory and almost twice the population, would necessitate a force of even greater dimensions. Even if the Polish Army were to remain neutral, replacements would have to be found for the fifteen Polish divisions allocated to the front line of the Warsaw Pact, whilst a further forty-five or fifty divisions would be needed to occupy and garrison Poland. The Soviet Army would be forced to withdraw an important contingent from its garrison on the Chinese frontier, and to mobilize a part of its reserves. It would be committing itself to an operation far larger than anything it has undertaken since the Second World War. What is more, by concentrating this massive effort on its western borders, it would significantly lower its guard in the East. Everyone who is familiar with Soviet writing on strategic problems knows how sensitive the Soviet leaders are to simultaneous commitments on two fronts. In practical terms, this means that the Soviet Military would be reluctant to involve itself in Poland unless it already had covered its rear in the East by some previous agreement with China. As always (see p. 345), Sino–Soviet tensions work to Poland's advantage. As always, a definite agreement between the USSR and China over mutual troop reductions in Asia would make anxious reading in Warsaw. But there is one final consideration. Poland is the strategic linchpin of Eastern Europe—the Soviet Army's main bridge to the

Warsaw Pact front line in Germany. If the situation in Poland were to deteriorate to the point where Soviet intervention were judged necessary, the problem could not be contained by one swift operation. A large Soviet garrison would be tied down in Poland for years, if not for decades. The demoralized remnants of the Polish Army—like the Czechoslovak Army after 1968—would be judged unsuitable for front-line action, and the Warsaw Pact's assault force would lose one-third of its battle strength overnight. Despite the huge transfer of Soviet resources to the West, the Soviet military establishment in the European theatre would be significantly weakened. The Soviet Army's capacity for a flexible response to emergencies elsewhere would be proportionately impaired. The Soviet Union could not afford to let its Polish linchpin drop out of place; but it could not afford to occupy Poland indefinitely either.

Thus, if the immediate outcome of a Polish–Soviet conflict would not be in doubt in military terms, the repercussions on the Soviet position in Eastern Europe would be incalculable. A Soviet military victory could quickly turn into a political disaster. The workings of Comecon would be no less disrupted than those of the Warsaw Pact; and the reputation of the Soviet Union as a friendly, peaceable ally would be shattered beyond repair. The invasion of Hungary in 1956 greatly diminished the world communist movement; the invasion of Czechoslovakia in 1968 produced 'Euro-communism' and the defection of many foreign parties from direct Soviet tutelage; the invasion of Poland, the third in the series, could deal a final blow to the whole Soviet alliance. The fraternal parties would live in fear and trembling of their deviant policies; and they would deeply resent the increased military contributions. The Soviet dream of a loyal, grateful, and prosperous Eastern Europe, cheerfully supplying the USSR with all the goods, services, and soldiers it requires, would be shattered for ever.

Most crucially, the fate of Poland in 1980–2 was closely tied to the most vital issue of our age—nuclear disarmament. The whole of Humanity needs nuclear disarmament in order to ensure our survival. The USA needed to pursue it to avoid wasteful expenditure, and to keep the trust of its democratic allies; and the USSR needed it most urgently of all, because of fears that its decelerating economy and ailing technology could not keep pace with a reinvigorated American arms programme. The Soviet Union's main effort in Rearmament was made under Brezhnev's guidance in the twenty years following the Cuban Missile Crisis of 1961; but it was questionable whether that effort could be matched by Brezhnev's successors. As the Polish Crisis edged ever closer to disaster, Soviet and American negotiators showed few signs of real progress. The INF and START talks over nuclear arms reduction at Geneva were as slow as the older MBFR talks over conventional arms at Vienna. Moscow was as suspicious of President Reagan's 'Zero Option' plan, as Washington was suspicious of Soviet attempts to divide the NATO alliance and to exploit the unilateral Peace Movement. But time was running out; and with American Pershing 2 and Cruise Missiles due to be deployed in Western Europe, failing an agreement, by the end of 1983, Soviet disarmament negotiators would be pressed to reach a compromise. In which context, Soviet intervention in Poland could prove ruinous for the most vital issue of the USSR's strategic and economic interests. The appearance of Soviet tanks in Warsaw would do the Peace Campaign no good at all. The unilateral disarmers would be disarmed overnight. American negotiators could hardly continue the disarmament talks with their Soviet counterparts. The Soviet Union would have destroyed its last cherished hope of lasting strategic parity. Human life on Earth would be one step nearer to its End.

In 1977, several years before the emergence of SOLIDARITY, a retired British General wrote a piece of futurist fiction about the 'Third World War'.[18] He chose to start the chain of events in Poland, where workers' riots led to a Soviet invasion; the westward advance of a large Soviet force aroused anxieties in NATO; and incidents on the front line in Germany provoked the general conflagration. One need not accept the good General's speculations in detail to recognize that Poland is not an insignificant Ruritania beyond our concerns. Burke was wrong. Poland is not quite on the Moon. As Castlereagh, Lloyd George, Chamberlain, and Churchill all had to learn, Poland lies at the nub of European affairs. More than most countries, it is a piece of the Continent, a 'part of the Main'; and its troubles are capable of troubling the whole world.

12 Baleful Precedents

In 1983, Poles looking back into their history were reminded
of many anniversaries and precedents. Wartime veterans
marked the fortieth anniversary of General Sikorski's death.
The literati marked the centenary of Cyprian Norwid. The
nation at large celebrated Sobieski's relief of the Siege of
Vienna. The communists, whilst marking the hundred years
of their movement since the 1883 trial of Waryński's
'Proletariat', remembered in private that it is only thirty years
since Stalin died, and only forty years since Stalin's break with
the Polish Government in London put them into business. In
public, they preferred to join in the Sobieski festivities, which
every organ of the official media was duty-bound to promote
to the point of tedium. As usual, the dissident activists plotted
to outwit the police in their hopes of celebrating the National
Day of 3 May, the anniversary of SOLIDARITY on 31
August, the anniversary of the Red Army's invasion on 17
September, or Independence Day on 11 November. Unless
exceptional circumstances intervened, they watched in dismay
as official parades marked the 1st of May (International
Workers' Day), the 22 July (the communist-sponsored National Day), and 7 November (the second Russian Revolution
of 1917). Whatever happened, one could be sure that on All
Saints' day, 1 November, Poland's cemeteries would be
thronged with people and flickering candles, mourning the
nation's dead.

In 1984, too, unless exceptional circumstances intervene,
this same historical competition takes place between the
regime and the people. The whole Soviet Bloc is looking over
its shoulder to see whether Orwell and Amalrik will have been
proved correct (or have already been vindicated). Apart from
that, the communists concentrate on the 40th Anniversary of
the PKWN; whilst the public at large prefers the Battle of
Monte Cassino; the first edition of *Ogniem i Mieczem;* or the
quatercentenary of the death of Jan Kochanowski.

As always, the long memories of the Poles search their
history for precedents which might illuminate their present,
agonizing condition. There are proponents of 1926, of 1830
and 1863, and 1791—and probably of 1772 and 1733, as well.

The events of 1926 are evoked by those who wish to tar the Military Regime with the brush of the pre-war Sanacja. (See p. 123.) The comparison of Jaruzelski's Military take-over in December 1981 with Piłsudski's May Coup of 1926 may be attractive for a minority of traditional nationalists—the 'post-Endeks'—to whose way of thinking Piłsudski and Jaruzelski are equally obnoxious; but it has little general appeal. Whilst Piłsudski in 1926 had significant public support—including that of the communists—Jaruzelski in 1981 had very little. Piłsudski acted to overthrow a corrupt political Establishment; Jaruzelski acted to preserve and renew it. Piłsudski, for all his faults, is now a national hero. Jaruzelski, whatever his motives, is generally regarded as a national disgrace. Piłsudski was the symbol of national independence from Russia. Jaruzelski is seen as the incarnation of Poland's subservience.

The events of 1830 are pondered by those who see a strong likeness between the position of the People's Republic and that of the Congress Kingdom. Both states were created at the end of a great European War, because Russian diplomacy did not feel strong enough to reassert the terms of an earlier Partition. Both must be seen as client states of Russia; but both were granted a separate Polish administration and a separate Polish Army. Both disappointed their subjects through the suppression of civil liberties in spite of a model constitution; but both ran into disrepute with their Russian masters for what, by Russian standards, was an excess of liberalism. In this context, the suppression of SOLIDARITY in 1981–2 and the imposition of the State of War might be compared to the suppression of the Patriotic Society and of the associated treason trials of 1827–8. In other words, it was an event which did not fire a Rising in itelf, but rather, by dashing the nation's hopes, set an atmosphere in which mutiny and insurrection could be conceived. Inexorably, one would suppose, the conservative Establishment was torn between the need to keep order and the refusal of the Russians to approve necessary concessions. General Jaruzelski faced a similar dilemma to that of General Chłopicki, the first dictator of 1830. After years of rumbling dissent, the Polish opposition movement was threatening to overthrow the Establishment completely. SOLIDARITY's alleged talk of potential rebellion on the December tapes might possibly be seen as the equivalent of Wysocki's abortive plot on the 'November Night'. Both outbursts were contained by the forces of order; but they led to a long period of uncertainty where the loyalty of the Polish Army was strained to the utmost, and where after due deliberation the Russian overlord decided to teach the Poles a lesson. Historians will recall that the point of no return in the tragedy of 1830–1 was not provided by the 'November Night'—Wysocki's conspiracy was crushed within a couple of days, by the *Polish* authorities—but by the demonstration in Warsaw on 25 January in favour of the Russian Decembrists, which inspired the Sejm, in a fit of enthusiasm, to vote for the dethronement of the Tsar. The Military Regime has had good reason to fear patriotic demonstrations. If the communists' historical advisers have done their homework, they must know that no great reliance can be put on the Army's indefinite loyalty, or on the Russians' indefinite tolerance. In any historical comparison, many details will always stay out of place; but the precedent of the November Rising, which suggests that minor conspiracies were less dangerous than the ruling Establishment's blockage of reform, is sure to win many adherents; and in this instance, the implications of Poland's separate military complex are particularly relevant.

The events of 1863–4, or rather of 1861–4, carry still greater conviction. Here, if the separate Polish military element was missing, one did have both a patriotic reform movement of massive proportions and a ruling Establishment which had committed itself to a version of Reform. The January Rising was a classic illustration of the adage that an absolute system is never so vulnerable as when it tries to catch up with the times. Strong parallels can be drawn on the one hand between the SOLIDARITY years of 1980–1 and the 'patriotic' years of 1861–2, and on the other hand between the leaders of the *Odnowa* (Renewal) movement in the PZPR and the reformist inclinations of the Polish ministers of Alexander II. Just as SOLIDARITY was rocked by the disputes of its moderates and its radicals, so the patriotic movement of the 1860s was torn by the feud of the 'Whites' with the 'Reds'; and just as General Jaruzelski stepped in to keep reforms within limits acceptable to Moscow, so the Marquis Wielopolski, a loyal admirer of a reforming Tsar, stepped in to keep reforms within limits acceptable to St. Petersburg. Jaruzelski and Wielopolski have both aroused the same fierce debates over the nature and extent of their patriotism. They both undertook to walk the knife-edge between the desires of the Polish people and the demands of their Russian masters. Wielopolski lost control, not when he introduced martial law and banned the open demonstrations of the patriotic movement, but when he tried to use force against the underground plotting of his opponents. One might point out that where Wielopolski's *Branka* failed, Jaruzelski's 'coup' was surprisingly successful. In the factual sense, this is undoubtedly true. But in psychological terms, the effect of the *Branka* in 1863 and of the 'State of War' in 1981–2, is more comparable. Even if Wielopolski's policing had been as effective as Jaruzelski's, he would have still been faced, after some delay, with a furious and frustrated people. When the Tsar's chief minister in Poland, albeit a reformer of sorts, 'declared war on his own people', he drove a largely peaceable opposition movement into the hands of the advocates of active resistance. The irresponsible use of violence by the authorities provoked a correspondingly violent response from a desperate and humiliated people.[19]

As for the 1790s, the comparisons with the present crisis in Poland are so striking that they hardly require comment:

Imagine a large country in the middle of Europe. Formerly prosperous and independent, now it is only a shabby Russian protectorate. Its economy is in a shambles, its culture decaying; it is ruled by a corrupt oligarchy that takes money and instructions from foreign ambassadors. It seems that nothing can stop the country's drive toward self-destruction.

But all of a sudden a miracle occurs. The people wake up. They want the right to decide their country's future. Represented by a new generation of activists and thinkers, they demand essential democratic and libertarian reforms. And, what is even more miraculous, they succeed in implementing some of them. Progressive Western circles applaud, but the governments are slightly upset by the prospect of a disturbance in Europe's balance of power. The Russian protectors threaten the country with open invasion; the domestic oligarchy is humiliated and furious. Backed by their foreign sponsors, they finally find the only 'solution' left to them:

they cook up a plot and declare a war against their own people. All previous reforms and democratic laws are abolished; the country is placed under occupation. European governments utter a furtive sigh of relief: order has been restored, the balance of power is intact.

Now the reader . . . may ask: . . . but what's the use of recounting yet again the well-known story of Solidarity? The reader is wrong. I have not summed up the story of 1980–1981 but that of 1791–1793: the story of democratic reforms embodied in the Constitution of the Third of May and their annihilation by a confederacy of Polish magnates backed and financed by Empress Catherine the Great, which in turn led to the Second Partition of Poland.[10]

Needless to say, the logical conclusion to this allegory is that the Polish People's Republic stands on the verge of extinction. After one or two heroic but futile insurrections against overwhelming Russian arms, the Polish state is due to be destroyed. By analogy with the Partitions, the greater part of Poland will end up as the seventeenth republic of the USSR; whilst East Germany is suitably compensated with Szczecin, and Czechoslovakia with Cieszyn.

In all probability, political leaders pay little attention to historical precedents. They always feel that their own predicament is unique; and today's leaders in Warsaw and Moscow are unlikely to be guided by any awareness of the Polish tradition. Yet even supposing, somewhere in the dim marble recesses of the Party House or the Kremlin, that there are some vague recollections of the Russo–Polish conflicts of the past, there could be no guarantee that the leaders of the Soviet world would heed them. After all, the Polish tradition was already old in 1791; and at the Court of St. Petersburg there were undoubtedly people who could remember the events of 1768–72 and of 1733–4. And such memories, if considered, did not prevent the Empress Catherine from ordering the destruction of Poland, or the Confederates of Targowica from putting her order into execution.

But then, one hears one's Polish friends surmise, the mere destruction of a rotten Polish state was not really the *end* of the story, was it?

* * * * *

Even the briefest of surveys of the Polish crisis of the 1980s reveals connections with a bewildering range of contingent problems—the place of the Military and of Workers' Control in communist systems; the fate of the intellectuals and the underground opposition; the intractable economic catastrophe: the rival self-perceptions of the Communist élite, the Opposition, and the Church; the repercussions on the countries of Comecon, on the internal politics of the USSR, on developments in distant China, Japan, and Afghanistan; on East–West Relations and on the vital world issue of Nuclear Disarmament.[21] From the historian's perspective, however, the most revealing items concern the coincidence of views between people in such widely separated periods—between Richard Cobden writing in 1835 and the views of European 'liberals' 150 years later; between Lamartine, the French Minister of 1848 and the spokesmen of Western governments in 1982; and above all between the Poles of 1780 or 1880 and their successors of 1980. The Western participants of the Polish drama seem to be largely ignorant of the antiquity of the poses which they strike; whereas the majority of Poles are acutely aware of the continuities of their predicament. In preceding pages, three figures of no particular prominence were given special attention, and their opinions quoted at length. Colonel Wiślicki, the military commissar (pp. 389–91), Daniel Passent, the compromising journalist (pp. 396–8), and Adam Michnik, the political prisoner (pp. 408–10) were brought by circumstance into three quite different spheres of the crisis. The commissar was the agent of official repression; the prisoner was one of the resisters; the journalist, who approved neither of the repression nor of the resistance, was determined to stay at his post, to play his part in 'saving that which could be saved'. Wiślicki, Passent, Michnik were real people in 1982. They were not the dramatis personae of some underground cabaret, or the stereotypes of some imaginary, schematized model of Polish behaviour. Their views were openly expressed for public consumption, and were recorded in papers which anyone could read. Yet it takes no great effort of the imagination to see that all three of them are archetypal representatives of Polish political traditions of extraordinary vintage dictated by Poland's subordination to foreign power

—the threefold traditions of Collaboration, Conciliation, and Resistance: or, to use the different terminologies of different periods, the traditions of Loyalism, Positivism, and Romanticism. The force of these historical continuities tempts one to describe them as something rather more tangible than mere echoes.

CHAPTER VII

BEYOND HISTORY

Specialists, one often suspects, exist for the purpose of making simple things complicated, and on an issue such as the present crisis in Poland, anyone who tries to take the broader view, and reduce the multiplicity of events to simple intelligible propositions, is in danger of being charged with the mortal offences of 'over-simplification', 'unwarranted generalizations', or worst of all 'schematization'. Anyone who dares to warn that in certain circumstances History *could* repeat itself in Poland, is easily misquoted as saying that History *will* repeat itself, and is even said to be relishing the prospect of another Polish blood-bath. Anything which smacks of a clear opinion, or which enters the uncertain world of predictions and probabilities, is generally thought in academic circles to lack the necessary degree of equivocation.

Of course, no one could deny that the ramifications of the Polish Crisis are extremely complex, and that they extend far beyond the immediate concerns of the Soviet Bloc. Economists, sociologists, anthropologists, historians, lawyers, political analysts, students of religion, literature, the arts, diplomacy, and military affairs all have a valuable contribution to make; and no one could reasonably maintain that any one discipline possessed a monopoly of understanding. No one would be justified in claiming that the outcome of the Polish Crisis is either obvious or predetermined. Poland's fate hangs precariously in the balance, and it would be an act of rashness, to predict which way the scales will eventually tip. On the other

446

hand, by dwelling interminably on the finer points, one is easily led into the view that nothing is intelligible, that nothing can be stated for certain. The specialists are so fond of their fine shades of grey, that they can sometimes deny the existence of black and white.

The simple fact of political oppression, for example, which millions of Polish people can recognize instinctively for what it is, proves far too elusive for many academic commentators, and for any number of strange reasons—because meat rations in the USSR are lower than in Poland (which they are); because open violence in Central America or in southern Africa is more acute than in eastern Europe (which it is); or because Russian policies towards Poland in the 1980s have so far been less harsh than those of the 1950s, the 1940s, the 1880s or the 1790s, or whenever (which they have been). What is more, the consequences of protracted political oppression are widely ignored. Whereas most observers seem to accept that economic deprivation can lead to social despair and eventually to political revolt, few of them consider that the indefinite denial of political expectations can produce similar results, especially in a society whose cultural traditions have always idealized individualism and liberty of conscience. For this reason, the most usual cure for Poland's ills is thought to lie in economic recovery. On this point, Western bankers and communist apologists share a large measure of agreement. They are presumably unfamiliar with de Tocqueville, or with the idea that economic improvements, pursued in disregard or in place of political reform, can actually precipitate social conflict, not divert it. People do not necessarily rebel when conditions are at their worst, and when every ounce of their energy is preoccupied with keeping their families alive. They are just as likely to rebel at a later date when material conditions are improving and immediate anxieties are reduced; but when an obtuse and discredited *ancien régime* persists in its offensive, autocratic ways. In other words, the correlation between economic distress and political explosion is not a direct one. Political forecasters need to keep their eye on the principles of social psychology and of elementary human nature, as well as on the graphs and statistics of the economic analysts. An unreformed communist regime in

Poland will probably run the greatest risk of a popular explosion two or three years after the economic nadir has been passed. In which case, it would be perfectly logical to argue that in the interests of self-preservation the Polish leadership should postpone the dawn of the economic upturn for as long as possible.

In the last resort, however, all calculations based exclusively on the internal dynamics of Polish events miss the main point of the exercise—namely, that ever since 1944–5 ultimate control of Poland's affairs has lain not in Warsaw but in Moscow. The old Polish motto about the primacy of external relations still holds. Questions regarding the policies of the Polish leadership, the performance or under-performance of the Polish economy, or the resistance or non-resistance of the Polish people, important though they are, cannot be judged of more than secondary importance. The key issues concern the fluctuating limits of Soviet tolerance towards Poland, and the reactions of the Kremlin to any new shifts on the Polish scene. Ultimate responsibility for Poland's fate has been bequeathed to Stalin's heirs in the Soviet Politburo, and it is their decisions, or lack of them, which will prove decisive in every new round of the crisis. The Soviet leaders are not omnipotent, and cannot impose an infallible cure-all on Poland's ills; but their negative powers of veto and coercion are immense. They can decide to back, or to remove a Polish leader; to ignore the failings of the Polish economy or to demand changes; to accept the possibility of popular unrest in Poland or to crush it; to leave the Poles to stew in their own juice or to intervene with overwhelming military force. They could come out with a clear-cut package of political and economic measures; or they could continue, in deference to Brezhnev's memory, to rely on threats, inertia, and on muddling through. Unless and until the existing structures of the Soviet Bloc are transformed or dismantled, Poland cannot escape from Soviet tutelage. Warsaw will continue to be dependent on the whims of its political masters; and Moscow will continue to be vulnerable to the unreliability of its wayward Polish client.

Much has been written to draw attention to features of the present crisis which can be observed in most of the unhappy Russo–Polish conflicts of the last 300 years. An unbending

Russian overlord, a subservient Polish government, a disaffected society, an economic collapse, a rising generation with shattered hopes, a bottomless gulf between Russian and Polish attitudes—all might be taken to imply that Polish History is sure to repeat itself and that a further violent conflict is inevitable. If so, this implication is mistaken; but equally it cannot be dismissed as pure fantasy. No contemporary problem can ever be an exact reconstruction of similar problems in the past. New factors must always come into play, and the outcome must always differ in certain respects from earlier precedents. Yet the burden of History in Poland is heavy indeed; and, despite the best of intentions on the part of individual leaders, the weight of Soviet oppression as enshrined in the ruling system is capable of dragging down its victims into the slough of violent despair. All is not yet lost. But it behoves the optimists to explain why History might *not* be repeated no less than the pessimists to justify their fears that it will.

The Polish Crisis, which came to the surface in 1980, unfolds in an ideological and international environment which bears little resemblance to that of the last Rising, in 1944, let alone that of 1920, 1905, 1863, 1830, 1794, 1791, 1768, or 1733. The chief hope of the optimists must lie in the belief that the new factors will prove stronger than the old, and will act more as a deterrent to conflict than a spur.

For one thing, the technological advances of recent years have ensured that all international conflicts take place in a blaze of publicity and a flood of instant information. Satellite reconnaissance and communication networks ensure that the progress of any major unrest or fighting could be immediately followed by unseen watchers and could conceivably be beamed, if the watchers so desired, on to the television screens of the whole world. Given the immense logistical tasks involved, the Soviet Army could not invade Poland with the same element of surprise that it achieved in Czechoslovakia in 1968, and the cost in terms of propaganda and prestige would be correspondingly high.

More importantly perhaps, the Soviet Union would be acting in a Polish Crisis where the German factor would be absent for the first time in more than two centuries. In 1944, the Warsaw Rising was directed against both the Germans and the Russians, and in all the insurrections of the eighteenth and nineteenth centuries, the support of the Prussian Government formed a vital pre-condition for Russian action. Nowadays, neither Prussia nor a united Germany exists any longer. The old Russian pretext of invading Poland in order to save her from the Germans can no longer be invoked. Since 1970, when West Germany renounced all claims to the land beyond the Oder–Neisse Line, Poland has little to fear from German revanchism, and still less from the prospect of German support for Soviet intervention. The Soviet Union would be operating without its flank on the German side fully secured, and with every chance of tensions between the Warsaw Pact and NATO being stretched to breaking-point. Without doubt, Russian uncertainties about Germany, which weigh heavily on Soviet leaders still haunted by the memories of 1941–3, must certainly act as a brake on Soviet plans for Poland.

The internal condition of the USSR places serious limitations on the conduct of Soviet policy. Most foreign observers agree that the USSR entered the 1980s facing a complex of interrelated failures which must be attributed more to the nature of the system than to specific schemes and blunders. In November 1982, the new Soviet Party Secretary, Yuri Andropov, dropped the comfortable self-congratulations of the Brezhnev era, and made no secret of the extent and intractability of accumulated problems. Although the Western world is suffering from a rash of maladies of its own, the causes of the West's unease are as varied as the free societies which produce them. The Soviet Union, in contrast, appears to be gripped by an accelerating systemic disease that cannot be arrested without prolonged and fundamental innovations. With the possible exception of military expenditure, all the targets which Krushchev set in 1961 for the USSR to overtake the USA within twenty years, have proved far beyond the wildest dereams of the most sanguine Soviet planners. The Eleventh Five-Year Plan for 1981–5 posited an annual NMP growth rate of only 3.4 per cent (compared with 13.1 per cent in 1951–5 and 8.6 per cent in 1961–5); but the Plans have ceased to be fulfilled long since. A declining, even a negative, rate of economic growth; a sharp fall in the size of the labour force; serious demographic imbalances; huge regional inequalities; recurrent agricultural disasters; uneven technological advances; an antiquated industrial base; poor communications; inaccessible power sources; productivity patterns whose quantitative success no longer compensates for traditional failings in quality; *and* a wide range of accompanying social problems, from alcoholism, crime, and juvenile disaffection—all indicate the onset of a general Soviet malaise. In particular, it seems impossible that the USSR, an underdeveloped country with the political and military ambitions of a superpower, can indefinitely sustain both its overblown military budget (c15 per cent of GNP) and its modest investments in an improved standard of civilian living. The old menu of the Brezhnev era, 'Many guns and a pat of butter', can no longer be served. To make matters worse, the post-Brezhnev leadership must change its priorities on behalf of a Soviet population which is more educated, more urbanized, more conditioned to consumerism, more conscious of nationality and minority issues, and less terrorized than any previous generation in modern Russian History. By Soviet standards, the people have never had it so good; but it would seem that the good times have already begun to come to an end. Of course, the coincidence of the Polish Crisis with a wider, generalized crisis in the Soviet system as a whole would hardly improve the prospects for Soviet magnanimity towards Poland. It could well have quite the opposite effect, and drive an embattled and over-anxious Kremlin to punitive measures. All one can say is that Soviet–Polish relations entered the storms of the 1980s in a sea of problems on both sides, and that the Kremlin's initial caution has undoubtedly been strongly influenced by domestic considerations.

On the external front, the Soviet leadership has had to weigh the pros and cons of its Polish policy in the light of its immense global commitments. Unlike 1944–5, when a war-torn and exhausted Soviet Union was incomparably weaker than the USA, or during earlier Polish crises of the eighteenth and nineteenth centuries, when Russia was merely one amongst several major powers in Europe, the USSR is involved in a world-wide strategy without precedent. Its forty-

year occupation of eastern Europe is without parallel.
Although some aspects of the Polish Crisis recall earlier stages
of Russian policy towards its 'buffer against Europe', other
elements, including the USSR's association with the member
countries of Comecon and the Warsaw Pact and its confrontation with the United States, are entirely new. As Henry
Kissinger once remarked only half in jest, the Soviet Union is
the only country in the world to be encircled by hostile
communist states; and its conduct to any one of them is bound
to affect its relations with all the others. Soviet relations with
the United States, after a brief flirtation with Brezhnev's
concept of *Détente* in the 1970s, have moved beyond the stage
where the rhetoric of peace can be accepted in place of
responsible conduct. The Soviet invasion of Afghanistan in
1979 cut short the period of probation for *Détente*, and Poland
has clearly been raised by Washington as a test case of further
Soviet intentions. No doubt, the Soviet leaders feel an acute
sense of injustice, when they are made to pay more heavily for
their strategic adventures than the Americans pay for theirs;
but as the current challengers for American supremacy, and as
desperate claimants for military parity and political respectability, they have no choice but to choke their rage. In all
spheres except that of armaments, the dice are loaded against
them. In earlier times, the Tsars could deal with Poland as
part of their purely regional, European, policies; and in
1944–5, Stalin, with masterly finesse, could exploit the special
circumstances at the close of the Second World War, in the
last months of the pre-Hiroshima age. In 1956 or 1968, the
Soviet Union could discipline Hungary and Czechoslovakia in
isolation, partly on account of Western diversions in Suez and
Vietnam, but largely because no immediate repercussions on
Western interests need have been contemplated. In the 1980s,
when the accumulated stack of Soviet–American disputes has
grown to greater proportions, the stakes surrounding the fate
of Poland are correspondingly higher. In a way without
parallel in previous Polish History, Poland finds itself not
merely as the linchpin of Soviet strategy in Europe but
equally as a focus for global tensions.

Finally, in a world which survives precariously beneath the
shadow of the Nuclear Bomb, all international crises have

assumed dangerous propensities unheard of in previous times. Nobody can take pleasure in raising the nuclear spectre, but the Poles, for all their non-violent methods, have been riling an adversary which is armed with nuclear weapons and which has never been famed for its squeamishness. Certain sobering propositions need at least to be mentioned. If Stalin could order the Red Army to stand by in 1944, whilst more people were killed in the Warsaw Rising than were killed by the first atomic bomb in Hiroshima; and if Harry S. Truman, at a time when the United States was no longer directly threatened by Japan, could decide to sacrifice some 350,000 Japanese civilians in order to save the lives of a greater number of young American soldiers; then it is not totally inconceivable that a hard-pressed Soviet leadership might consider the selective use of nuclear weapons to prop up its crumbling empire in Eastern Europe. It is said on credible authority that the leaders of the fraternal Parties have been invited in the past to witness Soviet nuclear tests in person, and such a lesson could hardly be lost on anyone. From the viewpoint of the Soviet marshals, whose young soldiers would be given the unenviable task of suppressing a full-scale revolt in Poland, the order of priorities might appear rather differently from those of kind-hearted spectators in the West. Which only makes the current drive for Nuclear Disarmament all the more urgent. For beyond the relatively slight prospect of the local use of so-called tactical nuclear weapons in eastern Europe looms the far more terrible prospect of a full-scale intercontinental nuclear exchange. One does not have to follow Sir John Hackett's scenario in detail (see p. 438), to accept that the possibility of nuclear conflict, precipitated by a local war in Europe, does exist. The world has been well warned by the tragedies of Sarajevo in 1914 and of Danzig in 1939; but one cannot complacently assume that the restiveness of eastern Europe has been cured by three decades of Soviet oppression. Both in the dispositions of the Soviet camp, and in the relations between the nuclear powers, a courageous and nerve-racking operation of defusion is urgently required, if an eventual explosion is to be avoided. In the Nuclear Age, political leaders, like their generals and marshals, must realize that political ambitions of all sorts involve risks out of all proportion to the potential gains. For they are playing not just with fire, but with fission.

In this context, therefore, it is inappropriate to place the chief responsibility for containing the Polish Crisis and for avoiding an incalculable disaster on the shoulders of the Poles alone. Ultimate responsibility lies with Poland's political masters, and success depends in large measure on their willingness to enter in good faith into a dialogue with the genuine representatives of Polish society. Further attempts of a corrupt and discredited Party to cling to power at all costs can only provoke further conflict, and some modification of the bankrupt political order and its irrelevant ideology is a necessary pre-condition to progress. No political regime, however discredited, can lightly resign even a part of its power, and in the Soviet Bloc the exercise is particularly dangerous and unfamiliar. Yet to rely indefinitely on brute force is simply to postpone the evil day; whilst to hold the population of a large country in penury and distress is to invite retaliation. It is the greatest accusation against the Polish regime that in 1981, with the approval of the USSR, it was the first to resort to political violence. Any further repetition of this approach, except as a temporary steadier prior to political concessions, must be regarded as a recipe for certain tragedy.

The options on Poland facing the post-Brezhnev leadership in Moscow are somewhat limited, therefore. It is not difficult to understand why Brezhnev exercised such restraint during the sixteen months of SOLIDARITY's existence, and why Brezhnev's successors will think twice before launching a more active policy. The sting of the Polish nettle, one of the most dangerous that the Kremlin has had to grasp in recent years, is rightly treated with caution.

The first option, always the most attractive to anxious politicians, is to do nothing—to leave the military regime in place in Poland, and to hope for a gradual improvement. Jaruzelski certainly earned his spurs in December 1981 in the eyes of the Kremlin, and his connections with the Soviet Military should not be easily discounted. Yet it is unlikely that the military regime could hold the line in Poland indefinitely, or, in face of a sullen and resentful population, restore even a modicum of prosperity. Sooner or later, the Kremlin will be obliged to demand more radical measures.

The second option, much discussed in recent years, is a Polish variant of 'Kadarization'—a combination of orthodox communist politics with a flexible, and relatively decentralized economy, containing elements of labour incentives and market mechanisms. In agriculture, it favours peasant co-operatives rather than state collectives, and in industry gives preference to the consumer and service sectors rather than to the old communist shibboleths of iron and steel. With the emergence of Yuri Andropov as Secretary of the CPSU, the advocates of Kadarization may well take heart once again. Andropov, as the Soviet Ambassador in Budapest during the decade following 1956, has widely been regarded as the master-mind of Kadar's success in Hungary. Yet there must be serious doubts whether Kadarization could be easily transplanted to Poland. Western analysts often forget that Kadar's economic reforms were only introduced in Hungary after the extended period of political purges which raged for five or six years after the suppression of the Rising of 1956. The formula was one of Political Terror plus Economic Liberalization; and the latter could not have been pursued without the former. In Hungary, Kadar's reforms were welcomed because they were seen as a move away from the preceding repressions. In Poland, in contrast, in the aftermath of SOLIDARITY, they would be seen as a move towards the intensification of repression, and as such might well be resisted. Hungarian peasants were happy to adopt co-operative farming as an improvement on the hated collectivized system. But Polish peasants, who own 76 per cent of the farming land, would inevitably regard compulsory co-operative schemes as a first step towards expropriation. In short, the political and social conditions for Kadarization simply do not exist in Poland. It is doubtful whether any such policy could be contemplated without direct Soviet intervention, and Soviet intervention would destroy all hopes of peaceful reform for years to come.

The third option would be to press the Polish comrades to move in the direction of Neo-Stalinism on the Soviet model. There has been much comment in the Soviet press, and in the

Stalinist circles of the Polish Party, that Poland's troubles are
the result of 'too little Socialism, not too much'. Following the
suppression of SOLIDARITY, it would be only natural for
the old dogmatists to resurface and to call for a return of the
good old days of the 1950s. A programme which called for an
attack on the Church, for the abolition of private farming, and
for a drive against corruption and political toleration, would
strike a sympathetic chord in the corridors of the Kremlin; but
would be anathema to the majority of Polish communists as
well as to the population at large. Re-Stalinization in Poland
would be the obvious adjunct to Soviet intervention; but as a
policy to solve the Polish Crisis by political means, it would be
even more dangerous than Kadarization. It would involve a
direct assault on the position of the Military regime, and
would be the surest means of driving the Polish people from
their present apathy into a mood of united and open rebellion.

The last option, therefore, is for the USSR to stage an
ideological retreat in Poland in return for a guarantee of its
strategic and military interests—in other words, to pursue a
limited version of 'semi-Finlandization'. If the Military
Regime were to be judged merely a stopgap measure; if
Kadarization and Re-Stalinization were both ruled out as
impractical; and if the price of direct Soviet intervention were
judged too high, then, in the logic of the Polish situation, the
Kremlin would have no choice but to write off the communist
experiment in Poland altogether, and to let the Poles run their
internal affairs in accordance with some new scheme of their
own invention. An absolute pre-condition would be Poland's
continued membership of Comecon and the Warsaw Pact,
together with the safeguarding of Soviet lines of communication to East Germany. Poland is not Finland, and could
never aspire to the same degree of autonomy that the Finns
enjoy; but a half-way house on the road to a Finnish solution
would seem to offer the least risks and the best chance of a
working compromise between Polish and Soviet interests.
This, after all, is what the most responsible, forward-looking
elements of SOLIDARITY were demanding.

Needless to say, a solution of the Polish Crisis whose main
feature would be political concessions from the Soviet side,
runs counter to everyting in the Russian political tradition.

Western analysts usually overlook the fact that Reform in its Russian version has exactly the opposite connotation from Reform in the Western liberal sense. Reform in Russia has traditionally been undertaken by the Autocrat, whether Tsar or Party, with the main purpose of revitalizing the Autocracy. It is imposed from above, if necessary by coercive methods, and is necessarily confined to the social and economic sphere. It is designed to strengthen dictatorship, not to relax it, and to obviate political concessions, not to promote them. It is no accident that the greatest reformers and innovators in Russian History, from Peter the Great to Joseph Stalin, have also been the greatest tyrants. To Western minds, a reformist despot is a contradiction in terms; to the Russian way of thinking, it is entirely normal.

Official Soviet sources offered few clues to the real views of the Kremlin leadership. Authorized Soviet commentaries on the situation in Poland, published for general consumption, were quite literally incredible. They contradicted many of the statements even of the Polish communist press. They might have been expected to argue, for example, that the SOLIDARITY movement had acted contrary to the best interests of the Polish working class. Instead, they denied that it bore any relation to the genuine aspirations of the Polish masses. They did not call it misguided; they pretended that it did not exist except as some sort of international capitalist conspiracy. They usually attributed the problems in Poland to unnamed 'anti-socialist forces' and, as in Afghanistan, to alleged Western interference in the internal affairs of a sovereign socialist state. By reiterating their determination to uphold 'the unshakable fraternal alliance of the Polish and Soviet peoples', they implied that the communist regime in Poland must be preserved at all costs, irrespective of the desires and feelings of the Polish people. There was no indication of their views on the implications of the Polish crisis for the wider policy and strategy of the Soviet Bloc as a whole, no indication that any important new tack might even have been considered.[1]

Yet it stands to reason that Soviet policy-makers must view the future with concern, and that somewhere under the layers of secrecy and silence someone in the Soviet bureaucracy must be laying contingency plans for prospective developments. The two key questions involve first, a judgement on the chances of the innovators in their battle against bureaucratic inertia within the Kremlin itself, and second, whether the innovators might opt for repression or for retreat. Certainly, on the Polish side, the advocates of *rapprochement* with Russia have always had to ask themselves these same two questions. Whilst seeking to put Russo-Polish relations on to a more stable and equitable basis, and whilst recognizing the primacy of Russian strategic interests, they could rarely be sure whether their fellow conciliators in Russia would be able to overcome internal opposition to an agreement, and secondly, if the old order broke down, whether the Russian bear would lurch forwards or backwards. Would-be conciliators have been mauled so often, that they are bound to take a sceptical stance on the chances of any easy settlement. What is more, since at the last real confrontation with Poland in 1956, the Russians did actually pull back, they may fear on the next occasion that the Kremlin might decide to move to the attack and recoup its earlier losses.

In this regard, the reflections of a Polish leader who knew Russia intimately and who set great store on a Russo–Polish agreement, are well worth remembering. Having surveyed the accumulation of social and economic problems, notably the recurrent crises in agriculture, and the growing incapacity of the Bureaucracy, he addressed himself to the central issue of *'Russia's Future'* and Poland's place within it. He concluded that the obstacles to fundamental improvement were all but insurmountable. Although a satisfactory resolution of the Russians' own problems depended to a large extent on Russian policy towards their European 'borderlands', and in particular towards Poland, the nature of the political system and the burden of traditional Russian attitudes stood in the path of a sensible compromise:

Russia's future was never more in question than it is today . . . and it is difficult to see any way out from an impasse that is a natural consequence of historical development. For Russia's development has always been projected outwards, not inwards.

Although the [Russian] state has grown with unparalleled rapidity, until in the course of a mere half-millennium the little principality of Muscovy became an immense empire covering one sixth of the globe, it has never developed social institutions, or economic performance at the same pace. Its entire energies have been directed to perfecting a state machine which is designed for external, not for internal expansion . . . and as a result, the needs of the State were bound to outpace the means of satisfying them. . . . The State was condemned from the outset to be the proverbial giant with feet of clay'. . . . This state machine, which has not rested on any institutions of social consent, has not been obliged to respond to society's aspirations, and has proved incapable of improving itself sufficiently to meet the growing demands made upon it. It is obvious that such a pattern of development must lead sooner or later to a dead end . . .

The question of the 'borderlands' is no less menacing than [that of the economy, and of agriculture] . . . Yet it is hard to suppose that Russia on that score should enter any new path of genuine reform from above. There are simply too many obstacles, among which Poland is perhaps the most serious. . . . A change of heart towards Poland is no easier to imagine in the wider spheres of Russian society than in the Bureaucracy itself. For it is their rooted conviction, that everything which their State conquered is 'the property of the Russian people, sealed with their blood.' . . . What they do not realise, however, is that Russia has grown so vast, not by the creative efforts and native genius of the Russian people, but by virtue of a specific form of political organisation, which has always treated the Russians themselves, like everyone else, as conquered subjects. . . . That organisation has not been primarily concerned with the welfare of the Russian homeland . . . but rather with forging the instruments of territorial expansion and control, at the Russians' own expense. Like all such predatory organisms, it has long been destined to collapse . . . . Step by step, it has lost its former resilience . . . . [and] in its present, overextended condition, it has only one possible source of salvation—to change its fundamental character. But will a weakened Russia be able to effect the changes which it could not achieve when it still felt itself to be strong?

Russia's standing in Poland today . . . is that of a mere military occupation. To grant the Poles genuine autonomy would involve nothing more than the organisation of a proper government, and the creation of conditions for normal life in place of primitive coercion. . . . Yet for many Russians . . . the prospect of a radical change affects their national pride. Brought up to believe in illusions about the indivisibility of Russia, they would see it as an act of national shame. Such sick megalomania has always been a trait of nations approaching disaster, and it is a trait which we can observe in the views of chauvinist circles in Russia concerning Poland today. In the meantime, Russia's own future depends to no small degree on her relations with Poland.[2]

One might feel that the emphasis on the Polish aspect of Russian problems, understandable enough in a Polish commentator, is somewhat exaggerated; and if that is a pro-Russian Polish view, one must shudder to think what an anti-Russian Pole would say. But the causal link between an expansive strategic policy and the over-extension of political and economic commitments would be recognized by most independent analysts of Soviet affairs. What is really interesting, though, is that Roman Dmowski was writing over seventy years ago about the impending collapse of the Russian Empire, not in 1981 or 1982 about the impending crisis of the Soviet Bloc.

Unfortunately, therefore—and this is a tack in the direction of pessimism—everything points to the fact that the emergence of Yuri V. Andropov after eighteen years of Brezhnevian inertia portends a determined effort to revitalize the existing system rather than a relaxed reappraisal of fundamental Soviet priorities. Andropov, if indeed he succeeds in consolidating his position, is more likely to be a radical innovator, Russian-style, than a liberal reformer Western-style. As head of the KGB until May 1982, Andropov has certainly better sources of reliable information than any previous Soviet leader, and far wider experience in foreign affairs. He appears to have a flexible mind, a business-like manner, and a willingness to experiment. His knowledge of Hungary, his Finno-Karelian connections, and his service as chief of the CPSU's department for relations with fraternal parties, must have given him an appreciation of the strong nationalisms and rich variety of the East European scene. To that extent, he is well equipped to approach the Polish problem with informed intelligence and imagination. On the other hand, the whole tenor of Andropov's career, first as an enterprising *apparatchik* of the Stalinist era and latterly as the ruthless and ingenious destroyer of the Soviet dissident movement, must have conditioned him to every form of ruse and cunning, but not to magnanimous political gestures. One cannot seriously expect the former chief of the KGB, the successor of Beria, Yezhov, and Dzierżyński, to turn out as a crypto-liberal. At the most, one can expect him to be restrained. At a moment when Andropov may not yet have consolidated his grip on the Soviet Establishment, and when no definitive statement about Poland has been made, it is impossible to make any sensible prediction. All one can say is that concessions to Poland of a political nature would run counter to the general direction of likely Reform within the Soviet Union itself, and that it would take a leap of unprecedented imagination for a Soviet leader to give Poland much preferential treatment. The tragic legacy of Russo–Polish relations is as strong in Moscow as it is in Warsaw. One can be sure that any proposal to abandon the formal structures of the communist system in Poland, and to cut the Polish galley loose, would meet with the instinctive disapproval of conservative Comrades in the Kremlin. With the multiplication of the USSR's domestic troubles, and the steady rise of the Soviet Military and the KGB, there would be a strong temptation at the first hint of further unrest in Poland, for the Soviet leadership to cast caution aside and to resort to force. Andropov or no Andropov, there must be many men in the higher reaches of the Soviet élite in full agreement with the late Marshal Zhukov, who in an unguarded moment in a reception at the British Embassy once volunteered the opinion that Poland was a perennial nuisance 'which we should swat like a fly'.

Poland's exact place in the Soviet Crisis is difficult to define. Divided Europe is but one of several major areas of tension, where unresolved problems are growing more acute; and it is impossible to say for certain whether the Kremlin leadership would continue to give priority to its interests in Europe over those at risk in an unstable Middle East, in a volatile Muslim world, and in face of the inexorable rise of China and Japan. All one can say is that Europe will come into the reckoning one way or another, and that Poland is at once the Soviets' most vital strategic link in Europe, and their most vulnerable point.

In the mean time, Poland's moral dilemma remains much as it was in the nineteenth century (see pp. 274–77). None of the elements of the equation are quite the same as they were, of course. The Government is as disreputable as ever; but it has much greater technical, logistical, and organizational support, and it can calibrate its response to popular resistance with far greater precision. It is no longer in the position where it must surrender to its opponents or call in the Cossacks to massacre them. The Church has grown in stature, and its influence over the masses has increased. As a result, the Hierarchy has so far enjoyed much greater success than its erstwhile predecessors in holding the people on the path of restraint and non-violence. For its own part, the patriotic opposition is torn between its contempt for the State, and its respect for the Church. In 1980–1, it was in the early stages of the Romantic, idealist upturn; and it was stunned by the December Coup. But it is inconceivable that it will lie low indefinitely. Every day without genuine Dialogue between the three contestants of the Polish scene hastens the day of an eventual explosion. If the younger generation is convinced that the peaceful methods advocated by the Church do not persuade the regime to treat their aspirations seriously, then sooner or later they will turn to Poland's insurrectionary tradition waiting in the wings. The Poles, as always, face a moral choice of agonizing proportions.

It is in this respect that Poland stands as a symbol of moral purpose in European life, and a warning of the dangers which beset the whole world. Poland is back in its usual condition of political defeat and economic chaos; but for all its troubles it is something more than an object of curiosity and pity. Once again, during the brief interlude of SOLIDARITY, it showed that it is a repository of moral ideas and ancient values that can outlast any number of military or political catastrophes. In the long run, the fate of the Polish People's Republic is of little significance; it is rotten to the core. But the fate of the Poles themselves must be of the geatest concern to everyone. Poland's destiny, in the cockpit of European conflict, is one of the few indicators of the destiny which lies in store for the rest of the continent. It is very tempting for each nation in Europe to pretend that it is entire of itself, that if Poland is washed away one's own manor might still be safe. But that is the greatest illusion. Poland's agony threatens to undermine the

Main. The bell on the Vistula tolls for us all. For Poland is the point where the rival cultures and philosophies of our continent confront each other in the most acute form, where the tensions of the European drama are played out on the flesh and nerves of a large nation. Poland is not just a clod, or even a distant promontory; it is the *heart* of Europe.

NOTES

Preface

1. Norman Davies, *God's Playground: a History of Poland*, Clarendon Press, Oxford, 1981; Columbia University Press, New York, 1982, 2 volumes. Oxford Paperback, January 1983.
2. Ibid., vol. II, p. 630.
3. Adam Mickiewicz, 'Romantyczność' (1822), in *Dzieła poetyckie*, Warsaw, 1963, I, pp. 105–6.
4. J. Słowacki, 'Podróż na Wschód' ('A Journey to the East', 1836), lines 85–90.
5. In particular,
    Timothy Garton Ash in the *Sunday Times*, 10 Jan. 1982;
    Alexander Lieven in the *Catholic Herald*, 22 Jan. 1982;
    Robert McLaughlan in the *Glasgow Herald*, 30 Jan. 1982;
    Eric Christiansen in the *Spectator*, 6 Feb. 1982;
    Neal Ascherson in the *Observer*, 7 Feb. 1982;
    Richard Davy in *The Times*, 11 Feb. 1982;
    Jonathan Steele in the *Guardian*, 11 Feb. 1982;
    Jędrzej Giertych in the *Tablet*, 13 Feb. 1982;
    Stephen Constant in the *Sunday Telegraph*, 14 Feb. 1982;
    D.C. Watt in the *Daily Telegraph*, 4 Mar. 1982;
    Hubert Zawadzki in *The Economist*, 6 Mar. 1982;
    Hugh Seton-Watson in the *Times Literary Supplement*, 19 Mar. 1982;
    Esmond Wright in the *Contemporary Review*, April 1982;
    Sheila Horko in *Tydzień Polski* (London), 8 May 1982;
    Gustaw Moszcz in the *New Statesman*, 21 May 1982;
    Emanuel Halicz in *Kultura* (Paris), May;
    R.F. Leslie in the *London Review of Books*, vol. 4, no. 9, 2 June 1982;
    George Błażyński in *The Month*, July 1982;
    Leszek Kołakowski in the *New York Times—Book Review*, 15 Aug. 1982;
    Czesław Jesman in *Dziennik Polski* (London), 11 Sept. 1982;
    Zbigniew Pełczyński in the *Times Higher Educational Supplement*, October 1982;
    Stanisław Barańczak in the *New Republic*, 15 Nov. 1982;
    Piotr Wandycz in *Zeszyty Historyczne* (Paris), No. 62, December 1982, pp. 3–25;
    W. Jędrzejewicz, A. Cienciała in *Niepodległość* (London), vol. 16, December 1982;
    Piotr Wandycz, in the *American Historical Review*, vol. 88, April 1983, p. 436;
    Anthony Polonsky, in *Soviet Jewish Affairs*, vol. 13, no. 2, 1983, pp. 79–86.

Chapter I

1. See J.B. de Weydenthal, *The Communists of Poland—an Historical Outline*, Stanford, Ca., 1978, the latest of several surveys.
2. See Neal Ascherson, *The Polish August—What happened in Poland?* London, 1981.
3. Thomas Lowit, 'Y a-t-il des États en Europe de l'Est?', *Revue française de sociologie*, vol. 20, 1974, pp. 431–66. This stimulating essay is accompanied by a valuable appendix listing the main offices and appointments of the Polish central *nomenklatura*.
4. *Czarna Księga Cenzury PRL—1* (The Black Book of the Censorship of People's Poland—Part 1), ed. T. Strzyżewski (Aneks), London, 1977.
5. Maria Hirszowicz, *The Bureaucratic Leviathan—A Study in the Sociology of Communism*, Oxford, 1980.
6. See Takayuki Ito, 'Controversy over Nomenklatura in Poland: twilight of a monopolistic instrument for social control', Slavic Research Centre, Sapporo, Japan. Typescript (1981), 50pp. Paper presented at The Western Slavic Association Conference, University of Hawaii, Honolulu, March 1982; to be published in *Acta Slavica Iaponica*, vol. 1, 1983 (Sapporo), pp. 57–103.
7. 'Nomenklator' in *Wielka Encyklopedia Powszechna*, Warsaw, 1966, vol. VII, p. 822: quoted by Ito, op. cit., 50. Both the *WEP* (above) and the *Encyklopedia Powszechna PWN*, Warsaw, 1975, 4 vols., have omitted entries under 'Nomenklatura', even in its scientific sense relating to the classification of biological species. See *Wielka Ilustrowana Encyklopedia Powszechna* (Gutenberg), Kraków, 1892–1914, vol. XI, under *nomenklatura*; also *Słownik Języka Polskiego*, ed. J. Karłowicz *et al.*, Warsaw, 1904, vol. III, p. 405.

Chapter II

1. *Nazi-Soviet Relations, 1939–41: Documents from the Archives of the German Foreign Office*, ed. R.J. Sonntag, J.S. Beddie, Washington, 1948, p. 38. The omission of this and other related documents from the series of *Dokumenty i Materiały z Historii Stosunków Polsko-Radzieckich*, vol. VII, published simultaneously in Moscow and Warsaw, is one of the scandals of recent historiography.
2. German–Soviet Boundary and Friendship Treaty, Moscow, 28 Sept. 1939, with additional protocols. See *Documents Relating to Polish–Soviet Relations, 1939–45*, London (Sikorski Institute), 1961, vol. I, Nos. 52, 53, 54, 55; also in *Documents on German Foreign Policy, VIII*, Nos. 157–60.
3. Memoirs of the Polish deportations of 1939–40 in English include: Anon, *The Dark Side of the Moon*, (Foreword by T.S. Eliot), New York, 1947; Maria Hadow, *Paying Guest in Siberia*, London, 1959; and most movingly, *War through Children's Eyes: the Soviet Occupation of Poland and Deportations, 1939–1941*, ed. I. and J.T. Gross, Stanford, 1981. See also S. Skrzypek, *Rosja jaką widziałem, 1939–42*, Newton, Mon., 1949; and Maria Januszkiewicz, *Kazachstan*, Paris, 1981.
4. Of all the documents about Katyń, none is more telling than the stark *Spis Katyński* (Katyn List), and the associated *Zbrodnia katyńska w świetl e dokumentów*, foreword by General W. Anders, 9th Edition, London, 1982.
5. See Jan Tomasz Gross, *Polish Society under German Occupation, 1939–44*, Princeton, 1979; and J. Gumkowski, J. Leszczyński, *Poland under Nazi Occupation*, Warsaw, 1961.
6. See Yehudah Bauer, *The Holocaust in Historical Perspective*, London, 1978.
7. The most revealing source about life in the Warsaw Ghetto is provided by *The Warsaw Diary of Adam Czerniaków, 1939–42*, ed. R. Hilberg, S. Staroń, J. Kermisz,

New York, 1979; for the Ghetto Rising itself, see L. Tushnet, *To Die with Honour: the Uprising of the Jews of the Warsaw Rising*, New York, 1965.

8. W. Bartoszewski, Z. Lewin, eds., *Righteous among Nations: how Poles helped the Jews 1939–45*, London, 1959; *idem, Warsaw Death Ring, 1939–44*, Warsaw, 1968; K. Iranek-Osmecki, *He Who Saves One Life*, New York, 1971.

9. J. Garliński, *Fighting Auschwitz: the Resistance Movement in the Concentration Camp*, London, 1970.

10. See Carlos Thompson, *The Assassination of Winston Churchill*, Gerrards Cross, 1969, for a review of attempts to cast doubts on the accidental nature of Sikorski's death. See also D. Irving, *Accident*, London, 1967, and R. Hochhuth, *The Soldiers, an Obituary for Geneva*, New York, 1968.

11. See Takayuki Ito, 'The Genesis of the Cold War: Confrontation over Poland, 1941–4', in *The Origins of The Cold War in Asia*, ed. N. Yonosuke, I. Akira, Tokyo, 1977, pp. 147–202.

12. See Vojtech Mastny, *Russia's Road to the Cold War: Diplomacy, Warfare, and the Politics of Communism, 1941–45*, New York, 1979, the authoritative work,—especially pp. 167–82, 'The Poles that one could talk to'. See also a recent study, George Kacewicz, *Great Britain, the Soviet Union, and the Polish Government in Exile, 1939–45*, The Hague, 1979.

13. See Z.S. Siemaszko, 'Powstanie Warszawskie—kontakty PKWN z ZSSR', *Zeszyty Historyczne* (Paris), XVI (1969), and Jan Nowak, 'Sprawa generała Berlinga', ibid., XXXVII (1976); also E. Puacz, 'Powstanie Warszawskie w protokołach PKWN', ibid., X (1966).

14. Andrzej Korboński, 'The Warsaw Rising revisited', *Survey* (London) no. 76, 1970, summarizes the polemics up to that point. Jan M. Ciechanowski, *The Warsaw Rising*, Cambridge, 1974, provides the fullest view of the Rising's genesis and international context. The most recent study is J.K. Zawodny, *Nothing but Honour*, New York, 1977.

15. See J. Kaps, *Die Tragödie Schlesiens, 1945–6*, Munich, 1953.

16. NB, owing to the dispute over Polish representation, Poland did not take part in the UN's founding Conference in San Francisco (24 Apr.–26 June 1945). Poland signed the UN Charter on 16 Oct. 1945, following general international recognition of the TRJN Government.

17. Zbigniew S. Siemaszko, *Narodowe Siły Zbrojne* (Odnowa), London, 1982.

18. Stanisław Kluz, *W potrzasku dziejowym: WIN na szlaku AK; Rozważania i dokumentacja*, London, 1978.

19. The basic source remains *Polskie Siły Zbrojne w Drugiej Wojnie Światowej* (Sikorski Museum), London 1959–75, 3 vols. For a recent survey, see M.A. Peszke, 'The Polish Armed Forces in Exile: Part I, September 1939 to July 1941', *Polish Review* XXVI (1981), no. I, pp. 67–114. See also, a pictorial history, S.J. Zaloga, *The Polish Army, 1939–45* (Osprey, Men-at-Arms Series), London, 1982.

20. Menahem Begin, *White Nights: the Story of a Prisoner in Russia, 1939–41*, London, 1957.

21. W. Anders, *An Army in Exile: the Story of the Second Polish Corps*, reprinted Nashville, Tenn., 1981.

22. Józef Garliński, *Hitler's Last Weapons: the Underground War against the V1 and V2*, London, 1978, also *idem, Poland, SOE and the Allies*, London, 1969. See also J. Nowak, *Kurjer z Warszawy* (Odnowa), London, 1976.

23. Piotr S. Wandycz, *Czechoslovak–Polish Confederation and the Great Powers*, Bloomington, Indiana, 1956; reprinted 1979. See also Edward Taborsky, 'A Polish–Czechoslovak Confederation; the story of the first Soviet veto', *Journal of Central European Affairs*, vol. 9, 1950, no. 2.

24. See Mastny's damning assessment of Beneš, Mastny, op. cit., pp. 132–44.

25. K. Morawski, ed., *Polska w pamiętnikach gen-de Gaulle'a, 1944–46,* Paris, 1960.
26. J.B. Weydenthal, *The Communists of Poland—an historical outline,* Stanford, 1978; quotes membership statistics of 6,310 in 1919, 875 in 1921 after the Soviet War, 9,327 (the maximum) in 1933, and 3,927 in 1937. See also K. Dziewanowski, *The Communist Party of Poland: an Outline History,* (2nd edn.), Cambridge, Mass., 1976.
27. J. Margules, ed., *Z zagadnień rozwoju Ludowego Wojska Polskiego,* Warsaw, 1964.
28. *Trial of the Organisers, Leaders and Members of the Polish Diversionist Organisation,* 1945 June 18–21, Moscow, Verbatim Report, London, 1945. See also Z. Stypułkowski, *Invitation to Moscow,* New York, 1962. General Okulicki's speech in his own defence is quoted by Garlinski; *Poland, SOE, and the Allies,* op. cit.; see note 22 above.
29. K. Moczarski, *Rozmowy z katem,* Warsaw, 1974.
30. See J. Zubrzycki, *Polish Immigrants in Britain,* The Hague, 1956, and Sheila Patterson, 'The Poles: an exile community in Britain', in *Between Two Cultures,* ed. J.L. Watson, Oxford, 1977. This subject is now ripe for academic study.
31. See Anthony Polonsky ed., *The Great Powers and the Polish Question, 1941–5,* London, 1976, pp. 197–9, cited by Mastny, op. cit., p. 174. The only unqualified support for the Soviet claim on Lwów and for the extreme interpretation of Poland's 'Recovered Territories' in the West, came from the non-communists of the Soviet camp, like Osóbka-Morawski.
32. During the heated discussion at Tehran over the Curzon Line, the draft report of the British Delegation noted 'The President seemed to be sleeping profoundly.' (FO 800/4033, p. 2) This and other comprising details were omitted from the printed record. (I am indebted to Dr Yutaka Akino of Hokkaido University for this information and for copies of the relevant documents.)
33. A.B. Lane, *I Saw Freedom Betrayed,* London, 1949, written by the former US Ambassador in Warsaw, among many others.
34. An excellent discussion of Allied Diplomacy on the Polish issue, and of its wider implications for the Western Powers, can be found in Richard Lucas, *The Strange Allies: the United States and Poland, 1941–45,* Knoxville, 1978. This same author's sequel study, *Bitter Legacy: Polish-American Relations in the Wake of World War Two,* Lexington, Kentucky, 1982, provides a very lucid survey of events in Poland in 1945–7 in addition to an analysis of American reactions.

Chapter III

1. On the Polish–Soviet War, see Norman Davies, *White Eagle–Red Star, the Polish–Soviet War 1919–20,* Foreword by A.J.P. Taylor (Macdonald), London, 1972; to be reprinted 1983 by Orbis Books, London; also Adam Zamoyski, *The Battle for the Marchlands,* Boulder, Colorado, 1981.
2. On Dmowski, there is little of worth in English, apart from the obituary note: S. Kozicki, 'Roman Dmowski, 1864–1939', *Slavonic and East European Review,* vol. 18, 1939, 118–28. See Andrzej Micewski, *Roman Dmowski,* Warsaw, 1971. The numerous works of the nationalist polemicist, J. Giertych,—e.g. *In Defence of My Country,* London, 1980,—convey much of the flavour of Dmowski's ideology.
3. See Wacław Jędrzejewicz, *Kronika życia Józefa Piłsudskiego 1867–1935* (Polish Cultural Foundation), London, 1977, 2 vols.; also the same author's *Piłsudski: a Life for Poland,* Preface by Wanda Piłsudska, Introduction by Zbigniew Brzeziński, New York, 1982.
4. An interesting paper on 'Roman Dmowski and Italian Fascism' by Anthony

Polonsky (to be published) suggests that Dmowski's Fascist leanings were even more pronounced than is generally supposed. Quoting Dmowski's series of articles on Nationalism and Fascism in the *Gazeta Warszawska Poranna* of June and July 1926, Polonsky documents Dmowski's high opinion of Fascism as 'the greatest revolution of our times', reveals Dmowski's explanation of the May Coup in Poland as part of the general decline of liberal democracy in Europe, and argues that the foundation of the Camp of Great Poland in 1926 was designed to prepare the politics of the Polish Right for some unspecified radical action on the Fascist model in the future.

5. See Zbigniew Wójcik, *Rola Józefa Piłsudskiego w Odzyskaniu Niepodległości* Polski (NSZZ-Solidarność, Ogólnopolski Zespół Historyczny Oświaty: Zeszyty Historyczne, 1), Warsaw, 1981.
6. J.M. Keynes in *The Economic Consequences of the Peace*, London, 1919.
7. Lloyd George in Parliament, November 1939. See Norman Davies, 'Lloyd George and Poland 1919–20', *Journal of Contemporary History*, vol. 6 (1971), 132–54.

Chapter IV

1. The standard introduction to the period remains Piotr Wandycz, *The Lands of Partitioned Poland, 1795–1918* (University of Washington Press), Seattle, 1975.
2. Although this point is anathema to official ideologists, some Polish historians are beginning to accept it. '... The Fact that each sector [of the Polish lands] had been integrated into the economy of its respective partitioning power prevented the creation of a national economic system embracing all Poiish lands.' Jerzy Skowronek, 'The direction of political change in the era of national insurrection, 1795–1864', in J.K. Fedorowicz, ed., *A Republic of Nobles: Studies in Polish History to 1864*, Cambridge, 1982, p. 262.
3. For a recent and wide-ranging collection of studies on the November Rising, see the proceedings of a commemorative symposium held in the University of Lille in May 1981: *Pologne: L'Insurrection de 1830–1: Sa Réception en Europe*, ed. Daniel Beauvois, Lille, 1982.
4. See Norman Davies, 'The January Rising in Poland in the light of British Consular Reports, 1863–4', in *War and Society in East Europe Central*, vol. XIV, ed. Bela Kiraly (Brooklyn College Studies on Society in Change), New York, 1983.
5. Indispensable to this subject is M. Janion, M. Żmigrodzka, *Romantyzm a historia*, Warsaw, 1978, illustrated, 638 pp.
6. On Krasiński, father and son, see M. Janion's long introduction to Z. Krasiński, *Nieboska komedia* ('The Undivine Comedy'), Wrocław (Ossolineum), 1965, pp. iii–cxxxii.
7. A contrary view holds that Mickiewicz wrote the *Księgi pielgrzymstwa* not only in emigration, but with the *émigré* community exclusively in mind. This would suggest that the concept of 'internal emigration', though widespread in contemporary Poland, was not very common in the nineteenth century.
8. Hans Hennig Hahn, *Aussenpolitik in der Emigration: die Exildiplomatie Adam Jerzy Czartoryskis, 1830–40*, Munchen-Wien, 1978.
9. This outline of the debates and differences of the Polish Romantics and Positivists is greatly indebted to the comments and published works of Adam Bromke (who prefers the labels 'Idealists' and 'Realists'), author of the fundamental work, *Poland's Politics: Idealism versus Realism*, Cambridge, Mass., 1967. See also Bromke's *Romantyzm czy realizm? Polska w latach 80-tych*, Hamilton, Ontario, 1982, which brings the discussion right up to date.
10. See Andrzej Walicki, *Philosophy and Romantic Nationalism*, Oxford, 1982.

11. On Lelewel, see Joan S. Skiernowicz, *Romantic Nationalism and Liberalism: Joachim Lelewel and the Polish National Idea* (Columbia University Press, East European Monographs, LXXXIII), New York, 1981.

12. Maria Konopnicka, 'Wąwóz Somosierra' ('The Defile of Somosierra'), lines 13–20.

13. See Roy Daniells, 'Sienkiewicz Revisited', in W. Stankiewicz, ed., *The Tradition of Polish Ideals* (Orbis Books), London, 1981, pp. 166–87.

14. The saying is sometimes attributed to Leon Chodźko (1800–71), historian of the Polish Legions, and one of the principal Polish publicists of the Great Emigration in France.

15. Maria Korzeniewicz, *Od ludowości ironicznej do ludowości mistycznej: przemiany postaw estetycznych Słowackiego* (PAN—Rozprawy Literackie, No. 34), Wrocław, 1981, a real gem.

16. See F. Ziejka, 'Upiór Grobów', in *W kręgu mitów polskich*, Kraków, 1977, pp. 141–79, which presents a full account of the Wernyhora legend.

17. Nałkowski, apart from his radical literary and political activities, was the founder of modern Polish Geography. See *Polski Słownik Biograficzny*, vol. XXIV, Kraków, 1977, pp. 500–2.

18. Ziejka, op. cit. (note 16) is a comprehensive study of the historical elements of Wyspiański's *Wesele*.

19. See Janion and Żmigrodzka, op. cit., Chapter V, *Powsłanie*.

20. Ibid., pp. 539 ff.

21. E.g. Andrzej Kijowski, *Listopadowy wieczór*, Warsaw, 1972. Poland's special place in the European revolutionary tradition is most convincing with reference to the events of 1830–1, less so with reference to the Romantic period as a whole.

22. Several reviewers of *God's Playground* have taken issue with the argument concerning the 'Impotence of Diplomacy' in modern Polish history, notably Wandycz in *Zeszyty Historyczne*, No. 62, p. 19. Yet the criticism appears to be based on a misapprehension. No one could fairly deny that the Polish Question has played a very prominent part in international relations, both in the nineteenth and in the twentieth centuries. Poland's central position in the disputes of the Powers and in the development of contemporary Diplomacy has been rightly emphasized by a number of distinguished studies, among them Wandycz's own works. That point is not contested. One merely doubts whether diplomatic action ever changed the course of Polish history as decisively as the diplomats and diplomatic historians might imply by the sheer quantity of their material.

23. The lines are from Słowacki's *Beniowski*. Piłsudski's tomb in the Crypt of Wawel Cathedral in Cracow, if one can see it beneath the permanent covering of flowers and offerings, is merely inscribed with his name and dates.

24. *Pamiętnik Filipka*, ed. W. Zambrzycki, Warsaw, 1957, pp. 115–17.

25. See Jacob Kipp, 'Policing Paskievich's Poland: The Corps of Gendarmes and Polish Society', a paper read at the CUNY conference on 'War and Society in East Central Europe, 1775–1856', New York, March 1981, to be published in Brooklyn College Studies on Society in Change, No. 13, Vol. IV, New York, 1983.

26. Neal Ascherson, in the *Observer*, 7 Feb. 1982, p. 28.

27. Wacław Jędrzejewicz, *Piłsudski: a Life for Poland*, New York, 1982, p. 143.

28. Jan Słomka, *From Serfdom to Self-Government*, translation by W.J. Rose, London, 1941.

29. I am indebted to Dr Keith Sword of the M.B. Grabowski Polish Migration Project at SSEES, University of London, for comments and materials concerning Polish economic migration.

30. See I.T. Sanders, E.T. Morawska, *Polish–American Community Life: a Survey of Research*, New York, 1975, with an extensive bibliography.

31. The early history of Poles in Siberia from the sixteenth century to 1917 is comprehensively summarized in M. Janik, *Dzieje Polaków na Syberji*, Kraków, 1928. The continuation of the story into the Soviet period, which witnessed mass deportations and official crimes on a scale far exceeding those of Tsarist times, still awaits systematic academic attention.

32. John Paul II, Speech at the Crystal Palace Stadium, London, 30 May 1982, personal recollection.

33. See Daniel Beauvois, *Lumières et société en Europe de l'Est: l'Université de Vilna et les écoles polonaises de l'Empire Russe*, Paris, 1977. This work of incomparable scholarship is by no means restricted to narrow educational matters, but explores an immense range of social and cultural problems of the Polish community in Russia in the first quarter of the nineteenth century.

34. Brigadier-General Zygmunt Podhorski (1891–1960), 'Wspomnienia' (unpublished), in private, family possession in London.

35. See J. Maternicki, Ed., *Edukacja historyczna społeczeństwa polskiego w XIX wieku: Zbiór studiów*, Warsaw, 1981, which contains a summary of church and secular influences: 'Rola Kościoła', pp. 28–33.

36. John K.J. Kulczycki, *The School Strikes in Prussian Poland, 1901–7: the struggle over bilingual education* (Columbia University Press, East European Monographs, LXXXII), New York, 1981.

37. See Bohdan Cywiński, *Rodowody niepokornych*, Warsaw, 1971, a penetrating study of the intelligentsia in late-nineteenth-century Poland, written from a position sympathetic to the Romantic viewpoint.

38. Aleksandra Piłsudska, née Szczerbińska, *Wspomnienia*, London, 1960, pp. 55–7: also published in English as *The Memoirs of Mme Pilsudski*, New York, 1940. Piłsudski's own reflections of Patriotism are contained in his article 'O patriotyzmie' (1902), in which he clearly gives priority to patriotic, national goals over socialist ideology: *Pisma*, vol. 2.

39. Adam Mickiewicz, *Dziady III*, Prologue, lines 144–7, 54–5; ed. S. Pigoń, Warsaw, 1974, p. 20.

40. From Konrad's 'Great Improvisation', *Dziady III*, Act I, scene ii, lines 170–8. Ibid., p. 55.

41. Adam Mickiewicz, *Księgi narodu i pielgrzymstwa polskiego*, VII, lines 291–8.

42. Baykowski's Memoirs, quoted by Janion and Żmigrodzka, op. cit., p. 373.

Chapter V

1. See M. Serejski, *Europe a rozbiory Polski*, Warsaw, 1970 (with French summary).

2. If the official Polish version is open to question, the enquiring reader is even worse served by many Western forays into East European prehistory. For example, *The Times Atlas of World History*, ed. G. Barraclough, London, 1978, contains a series of maps bearing a mass of self-contradictory information. In this version, the lands between the Oder and Vistula lay to the east of Slav settlement *c.*1000 BC (pp. 60–1); were inhabited by certain 'proto-Slavs' *c.*800 BC; were vacated by the aforementioned in the Roman period in favour of 'Germania' (p. 89); only to be invaded by Slavs emerging fresh from the 'Pripet Marshes' at two different dates, on p. 98 and p. 99. See Andrzej Piskozub, 'Idiotom dla nauki, melancholikom dla rozrywki', *Polityka* No. 13, 3 Mar. 1979. The two standard introductions to Polish prehistory in

English—K. Jazdzewski, *Poland* (1965) and M. Gimbutas, *The Slavs* (1971)—
both in the 'Ancient Peoples and Places' series, also present mutually
contradictory versions.
3. See J.K. Fedorowicz, ed., *A Republic of Nobles: Studies in Polish History to 1864*,
Cambridge, 1982, which is the best attempt to summarize contemporary writing
in Poland on the pre-Partition period.
4. See Georges Luciani, 'Les origines polonaises de l'idéologie des slaves unis', in *La
Société des Slaves Unis 1823-5*, Bordeaux, 1963, pp. 77-154. On Duchiński, see
Ivan L. Rudnytsky, 'F. Duchinski and his impact on Ukrainian Political
Thought', *Harvard Ukrainian Studies*, III/IV (1979-80), 690-705.
5. For a discussion of Wysłouch's contribution to the Piast Concept, see F. Ziejka,
W kręgu mitów polskich, Krakow, 1977, pp. 171 ff. Curiously enough, Wysłouch's
position was supported by Ukrainian nationalists, including Ivan Franko,
presumably because it promised to solve the Polish–Ukranian dispute over
national territory; ibid., p. 260, note 82.
6. Comprehensive surveys of Polish Literature in English include M. Kridl, *Survey
of Polish Literature and Culture*, The Hague, 1956; C. Milosz, *A History of Polish
Literature*, London, 1969; J. Krzyżanowski, *A History of Polish Literature*, Warsaw,
1978 (in English).
7. For a convenient summary of Polish political thought, see Eugenuisz Jarra,
Historia Polskiej Filozofii Politycznej, 966-1795, London, 1968, which contains
systematic introductions to each of the principal writers and thinkers.
8. On the modern history of the Catholic Church in Poland, see W. Urban, *Ostatni
etap dziejów Kościoła w Polsce przed nowym tysiącleciem, 1815-1965*, Rome, 1966.
9. See A. Lewak, *Dzieje emigracji polskiej w Turcji*, Warsaw, 1935; J/Skowronek,
Polityka bałkańska Hotelu Lambert, 1833-56, Warsaw, 1876; also Makoto Haya-
saka, 'La politique orientale de l'émigration polonaise—la tendance turco-slave
à la mi-XIX siècle, *SHi Hō* (Historical Alliance), Sapporo, No. 15 (1982), pp.
13-41.

Chapter VI

1. See A. Polonsky, B. Drukier, eds., *The Beginnings of Communist Rule in Poland,
1943-5*, London, 1980.
2. See A. Ross Johnson, 'The Polish Military', *East European Military Establishments:
the Warsaw Pact Northern Tier* (Rand Corporation, R-2417/1-AF/FF), Santa
Monica, Ca., 1980, pp. 19-73, which is by far the most accessible and
authoritative summary of this subject. Official Polish sources are naturally
reticent about key problems and deficiencies, but much can be gleaned from
the numerous publications of the Ministry of National Defence (MON)
—e.g. *Ludowe Wojsko Polskie, 1943-73*, Warsaw, 1975; *Mała Kronika Ludowego
Wojska Polskiego, 1943-73*, Warsaw, 1975; *Mała encyklopedia wojskowa*, Warsaw,
1970, etc.
3. Particularly valuable on the subject of the military economy are the works of
Michał Chęciński; 'Ludowe Wojsko Polskie', *Zeszyty Historyczne* (Paris), No. 44,
1978, pp. 14-31, with references.
4. Maria Janion, 'Nigdy przed mocą nie ugniemy szyi', *Pismo*, Warsaw, 1981,
Postscriptum, pp. 16-17.
5. Ibid.

6. Ibid.
7. *Rota* (The Oath) Words by M. Konopnicka (1908), melody by F. Nowowiejski (1908):

See Norman Davies, *God's Playground*, vol. II, p. 136.
8. Czesław Miłosz, 'Który skrzywdziłeś' in *Światło dzienne* ('Daylight'), Paris, 1953. An English version was read by the author on the USIS TV programme 'Let Poland be Poland', 13 Feb. 1982. Another, by M. Mikoś, appeared in *Polish Review*, vol. 26, 1981, no. 2, p. 3.
9. Marion Janion, op. cit. See also: J. Maciejewski, 'Literatura barska', in *Przemiany tradycji barskiej: studia*, Cracow, 1972.
10. Jacek Kuroń, 'Tezy o wyjściu z sytuacji bez wyjścia'; Zbigniew Bujak, 'Walka pozycyjna'; Wiktor Kulerski, 'Trzecia możliwość'. The full Polish texts appeared in *Informacja-Solidarność*, (Montreal), No. 3, 21 May 1982, English translations in *Committee in Support of Solidarity—Reports*, New York, No. 1.
11. 'The Commissar's Counsel', *Committee in Support of Solidarity—Reports*, New York, No. 3, 7 June 1982, pp. 7–12.
12. Daniel Passent, *Polityka*, Warsaw, 20 Feb. 1982.
13. 'Inside a Censor's Mind—an interview with K–62: on the practice of thought control', *Encounter*, London, vol. 57, no. 6, December 1981, pp. 8–15.
14. Andrzej Zagozda, 'Why are you not singing?' *Committee in Support of Solidarity —Reports*, New York, No. 3, 7 June 1982, pp. 12–15.
15. M. Ellmann, B. Simatupang, 'Odnowa in Statistics', *Soviet Studies* (Glasgow), vol. 34, no. 1, 1982, pp. 111–17.
16. See *Current Problems of the Polish Economic Reform*: text of speeches by Professors C. Bobrowski and Z. Sadowski at a meeting with Ambassadors; Ministry of Foreign Affairs, Warsaw, June 1982.
17. Stanisław Barańczak, 'Tragic Repetitions', *The New Republic* (Washington DC), 15 Nov. 1982.
18. General Sir John Hackett, *The Third World War*, London, 1977.
19. See Henryk Wereszycki, 'Spór o powstanie styczniowe', *Odra*, May 1963, Vol. III, no. 5, pp. 33–40.
20. Barańczak, op. cit.
21. For the fullest survey of current problems, see Jean Woodall, ed., *Policy and Politics in Contemporary Poland: Reform, Failures, Crisis*, London, 1982.

Chapter VII

1. e.g. A. Sergeyev, 'The hypocritical intrigues around Poland', *Mezhdunarodnaya Zhizn'* ('International Affairs'), Moscow, 1982, no. 4, pp. 67f.; Y. Nikolayev, V. Belyshev, 'The unshakeable alliance of two fraternal peoples', Ibid., no. 5, pp. 92f.
2. Extracts in translation from Roman Dmowski, 'Przyszłość Rosji' ('The Future of Russia, 1909), *Pisma*, vol. XI (1938), reprinted as *Przyszłość Rosji—Zagadnienie rządu*, Orbis Books, London, n.d., pp. 5–6, 31–6.

Appendix I   The Polish Armed Services
(1982)

*Poland**

Population: 35,900,000.
Military service: Army, internal security forces, Air Force 2 years; Navy, special services 3 years.
Total regular forces: 317,000 (187,000 conscripts).
Estimated NWP 1980: Zl 1,936.2 bn.
Estimated 1981 GNP range: $88.1–133.8 bn.
Defence expenditure 1981: Zl 75.18 bn ($5.41 bn). $1 = 3.35 zloty (1981 official), 13.9 (adjusted).

Army: 207,000 (154,000 conscripts).
3 Military Districts:
    5 armd divs.
    8 mech divs.
    1 AB div.
    1 amph assault div.
    3 arty bdes, 1 arty regt, 5 AA arty regts.

---

*Extract from *The Strategic Balance, 1982–3,* Institute of Strategic Studies, London, 1982, pp. 22–3

AAM	Air to Air Missiles	LCM	Landing Craft—Motorized
AB	Airborne	LCT	Landing Craft—Tanks
AD	Air Defence	MBT	Main Battle Tank
AFV	Armoured Fighting Vehicle	MCM	Mine Counter Measures
APC	Armoured Personnel Carrier	MRL	Motorized Rocket Launchers
AIK	Anti-tank	NMP	Net Material Product
FAC	Fast Attack Craft	SAM	Surface to Air Missile
FGA	Fighter Ground Attack	SP	Self-propelled
GNP	Gross National Product	SSB	Surface to surface Missile
LCA	Landing Craft—Assault		

3 ATK regts.
1 AD bde with SA-4 SAM.
4 SSM bdes with *Scud.*
3,000 T-54/-55, 60 T-72 MBT, 130 PT-76 lt tks; 2,800 OT-65/FUG
and BRDM-1/-2 scout cars; 5,500 BMP-1, SKOT/SKOT-2AP,
MT-LB, TOPAS APC; 400 100mm, 122mm guns; 200 122mm incl
SP, 250 152mm guns/how; 250 BM-21 122mm, 130mm, 140mm,
240mm MRL; 51*FROG*-3/-7, 36 *Scud* SSM; 650 82mm, 120mm
mor; 450 85mm, 100mm towed ATK guns; 73mm, 82mm, 107mm
RCL; *Snapper,* AT-4 *Spigot, Sagger* ATGW; 730 23mm, 37mm, 57mm,
85mm and 100mm towed, 75 ZSU-23-4 SP AA guns; SA-4/-6/-7/-
9 SAM.

Navy: 22,000 (6,000 conscripts).
4 W-class submarines.
1 *Kotlin* destroyer with 1×2 *Goa* SAM.
13 *Osa* FAC(M) with 4 *Styx* SSM.
15 FAC(T): 5 *Pilica.* 10 *Wisła*<.
23 large patrol craft: 13 *Obluze,* 1 *Oksywie,* 9 *Gdańsk.*
49 MCM: 12 *Krogulec,* 11 T-43 ocean, 1 *Noteć* coastal minesweepers;
25 K-8 boats.
23 *Północny* LTC, 4 *Marabut* LCM, 15 *Eichstaden* LCA.
4 intelligence vessels (AGI): 1 B-10, 2 *Moma,* 1 T-43 radar picket.
1 Naval Aviation Div (52 combat aircraft):
1 attack regt: 3 sqns with 42 MiG-17.
1 recce sqn with 10 Il-28.
1 hel regt: 2 sqns with 25 Mi-2/-4/-8.

Bases: Gdynia, Hel, Swinoujście, Kołobrzeg, Ustka.

Air Force: 88,000 (27,000 conscripts): 705 combat ac, 5 armed hel.
4 air divs:
6 FGA regts: 18 sqns: 3 with 35 Su-7/-7U; 3 with 35 Su-20; 12 with
150 MiG-17.
10 AD regts: 33 sqns with some 430 MiG-17/-21/-21U.
6 recce sqns: 35 MiG-21 RF, 5 Il-28, 15 LIM-6.
2 tpt regts: 9 An-2, An-12, 12 An-26, 12 Il-14.
1 comms/liaison sqn with 2 Tu-134A, 5 Yak-40 Il-18 ac; 4 Mi-8
hel.
3 hel regts with 165 Mi-1/-2, 5 Mi-4, 22 Mi-8, 5 Mi-24.
300 trg ac: TS-8/-11, MiG-15/-21UT1, Su-7U.
AAM: AA-1 *Alkali,* AA-2 *Atoll.*
3 AD divs: 9 SAM regts: some 50 sites: 425 SA-2/-3.

RESERVES: (all services): 605,000.

Forces Abroad: Syria (UNDOF): 129.

Para-Military Forces: 85,000. Ministry of Interior border troops 20,000L 12 bdes, some 34 coastguard patrol craft incl 5 *Obluze,* 9 *Gdańsk* above. Internal defence troops 65,000: tks, AFV, ATK guns. Citizen's Militia 350,000. 'League for National Defence' (some 200,000 active).

Appendix II Poland's Rulers

Polish People's Republic, since 1944

since
Sept. 1981 General Wojciech Jaruzelski (First Secretary PZPR; also Prime Minister, Minister of Defence, Chairman of WRON, etc.)

1980–1 Stanisław Kania (First Secretary PZPR)

since 1972 Henryk Jabłonski (Chairman of Council of State = President)

1970–80 Edward Gierek (First Secretary PZPR)

1970–2 Józef Cyrankiewicz (President)

1956–70 Władysław Gomułka (First Secretary PZPR)

1968–70 Marian Spychalski (President)

1964–8 Edward Ochab (President)

1952–64 Aleksander Zawadzki (President)

1944–56 Bolesław Bierut (Party Chairman and First Secretary PZPR, 1948–56; Prime Minister, 1954–6; President of the Polish Republic, 1947–52; President of the KRN, 1944–7)

Władysław Gomułka (First Secretary PZPR, 1943–8; Deputy Prime Minister, 1947–51)

1954–70, 1947–52 J. Cyrankiewicz (Prime Minister)

1945–7 Edward Osóbka-Morawski (Prime Minister)

1944–5 Edward Osóbka-Morawski (Chairman of PKWN, RTRP)

Rzeczpospolita Polska, The Polish Republic, since 1918

Presidents		Prime Ministers	
since 1945 Presidents of the Government-in-Exile	since 1979 Edward Raczyński 1972-79 Stanisław Ostrowski 1947-72 August Zaleski 1939-47 Władysław Raczkiewicz		
		1944-5	Tomasz Arciszewski
		1943-4	Stanisław Mikołajczyk
		1939-43	General Władysław Sikorski, also C in C
1926-39	Ignacy Mościcki	1936-9	General F. Sławój-Składkowski
		1935-6	M. Kościałkowski-Zyndram
		1935	Colonel Walery Sławek
		1934-5	Leon Kozłowski
		1933-4	Janusz Jędrzejewicz
		1931-3	Colonel A. Prystor
		1930-1	Colonel W. Sławek
		1930-1	J. Piłsudski
		1930	Colonel W. Sławek
		1929-30	Kazimierz Bartel
		1929	Kazimierz Świtalski
		1928-9	Kazimierz Bartel
		1926-8	J. Piłsudski
		1926	Kazimierz Bartel
1922-6	Stanisław Wojciechowski	1926	Wincenty Witos
		1925-6	Aleksander Skrzyński
		1923-5	Władsław Grabski
		1923	Wincenty Witos
		1922-3	General Władysław Sikorski
Gabriel Narutowicz (Dec. 1922)		1922	J. I. Nowak
		1922	Artur Śliwiński
Józef Piłsudski (Head of State 14 Nov. 1918-9 Dec. 1922)		1921-2	Antoni Ponikowski
		1920-1	Wincenty Witos
		1920	Wł. Grabski
		1919-20	Leopold Skulski
		1919	I. J. Paderewski
		1918-19	Jędrzej Moraczewski

1918, 8-14 Nov. I. Daszynski
(Premier of the Provisional Government of the People's Republic of Poland, Lublin)

478   *Appendix II   Poland's Rulers*

The Period of Partition, 1795–1918

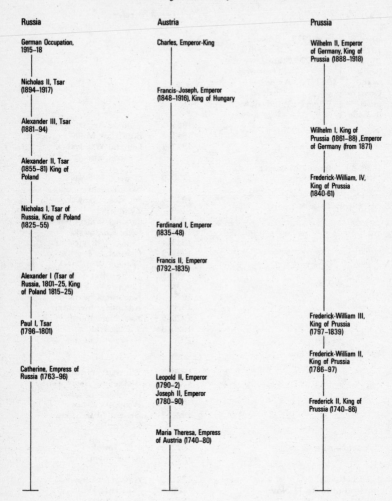

Russia	Austria	Prussia
German Occupation, 1915–18	Charles, Emperor-King	Wilhelm II, Emperor of Germany, King of Prussia (1888–1918)
Nicholas II, Tsar (1894–1917)	Francis-Joseph, Emperor (1848–1916), King of Hungary	
Alexander III, Tsar (1881–94)		Wilhelm I, King of Prussia (1861–88), Emperor of Germany (from 1871)
Alexander II, Tsar (1855–81) King of Poland		Frederick-William, IV, King of Prussia (1840-61)
Nicholas I, Tsar of Russia, King of Poland (1825–55)	Ferdinand I, Emperor (1835–48)	
	Francis II, Emperor (1792–1835)	
Alexander I (Tsar of Russia, 1801–25, King of Poland 1815–25)		Frederick-William III, King of Prussia (1797–1839)
Paul I, Tsar (1796–1801)		Frederick-William II, King of Prussia (1786–97)
Catherine, Empress of Russia (1763–96)	Leopold II, Emperor (1790–2) Joseph II, Emperor (1780–90)	Frederick II, King of Prussia (1740–86)
	Maria Theresa, Empress of Austria (1740–80)	

*Rzeczpospolita, United Republic of Poland–Lithuania, 1569–1795
(Elected Kings)*

1764–95	Stanisław-August Poniatowski
1733–63	Augustus III Wettin, Elector of Saxony
1733,	Stanisław Leszczyński
1704–10	

1697–1704	Augustus II Wettin, Elector of Saxony
1710–33	

1674–96	Jan III Sobieski
1669–73	Michał Korybut Wiśniowiecki
1648–68	Jan Kazimierz Waza (John Casimir)
1632–48	Władysław IV Waza (Ladislas IV)
1587–1632	Zygmunt III Waza, King of Sweden, 1593–1604
1576–86	Stefan Bathory, Prince of Transylvania
1573–4	Henry Valois, King of France, 1574–89

Poland and Lithuania, 1386–1572

1548–72	Zygmunt August (Sigismund Augustus), King of Poland, Grand Duke of Lithuania
1506–48	Zygmunt I Stary (Sigismund I), King of Poland, Grand Duke of Lithuania
1501–6	Aleksander (Alexander), King of Poland, Grand Duke (1492–1506)
1492–1501	Jan Olbracht (John Albert), King of Poland
1444–92	Kazimierz IV Jagiellończyk (Casimir Jagiellon), King of Poland (1446–92), Grand Duke of Lithuania (1440–92)
1434–44	Władysław III Warneńczyk (Ladislas of Varna), King of Poland (1434–44), King of Hungary (1440–4)
1386–1444	Władysław Jagiełło (Ladislas-Jagiello), Grand Duke of Lithuania (1377–1401), King of Poland (1386–1444)

Zygmunt, Grand Duke 1432–40

Swidrygiełło, Grand Duke 1430–2

Witold, Grand Duke 1401–20

Kingdom of Poland, up to 1386

1384–6	Jadwiga *Rex* (Hedwig of Anjou), King of Poland, 1385–99. married Jagiełło, Grand Duke of Lithuania, 1386
1370–82	Ludwik I (Louis of Anjou), King of Hungary, 1342–82; King of Poland from 1370
1333–70	Kazimierz III (Casimir the Great) King of Poland
1306–33	Władysław I Łokietek (Ladislas I), King of Poland, 1320
1305–6	Wacław III (Vaclav), King of Bohemia and Poland
1300–5	Wacław II (Vaclav), King of Bohemia; from 1283, King of Poland
1290–1300	Przemysł I, of Wielkopolska
1288–90	Henryk IV Probus (Henry the Righteous, of Silesia)
1279–88	Leszek Czarny (Leszek the Black)
1243–79	Bolesław V Wstydliwy (Boleslaus the Chaste, of Sandomierz)
1241–3	Konrad I, Mazowiecki (Conrad of Mazovia)
1238–41	Henryk II Pobożny (Henry the Pious of Silesia)
1231–8	Henryk I Brodaty (Henry the Bearded of Silesia)
1228–31	Władysław III Laskonogi (Ladislas Spindleshanks of Wielkopolska)
1202–27	Leszek Biały (Leszek the White of Sandomierz)
1194–1202	Mieszko III (Mieszko the Elder of Wielkopolska), restored
1177–94	Kazimierz II (Casimir the Just of Sandomierz)
1173–7	Mieszko III, dethroned
1146–77	Bolesław IV (Boleslaus the Curly of Mazovia)
1138–46	Władysław II (Ladislas the Exile)
1102–38	Bolesław III Krzywousty (Boleslaus the Wry-mouthed)
1079–1102	Władysław I Herman (Ladislas Herman)
1058–79	Bolesław II Szczodry (Boleslaus the Generous), King
1038–58	Kazimierz I Odnowiciel (Casimir the Restorer)
1025–37	Mieszko II, King
992–1025	Bolesław I Chrobry (Boleslaus the Brave), King
died 992	Mieszko I

Appendix III

Genealogical Tables

THE PIASTS

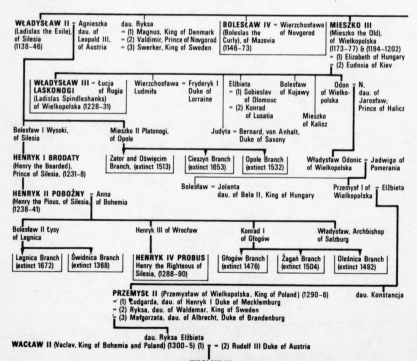

CAPITALS indicate names of Kings/senior Princes providing the line of succession
Dates are regnal dates

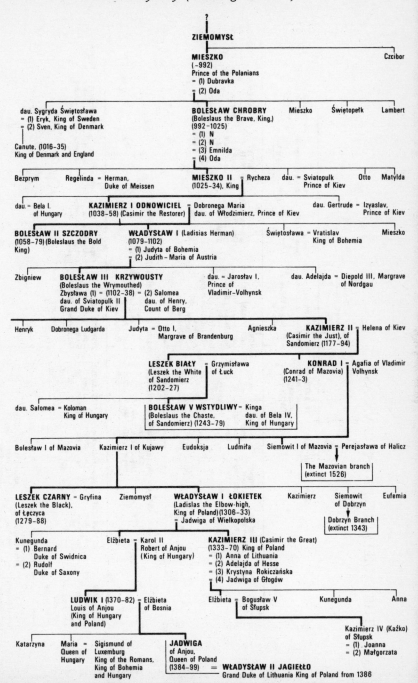

THE JAGIELLONS AND THE VASAS

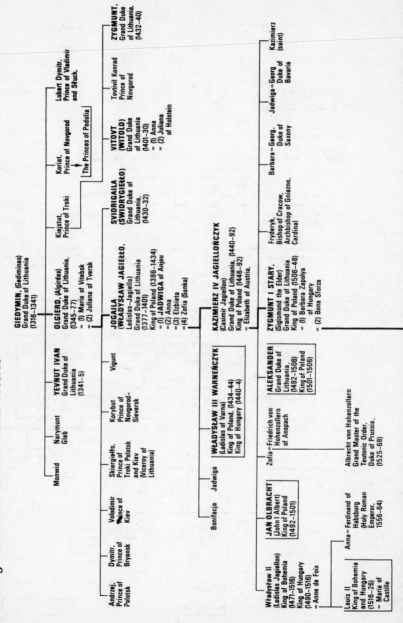

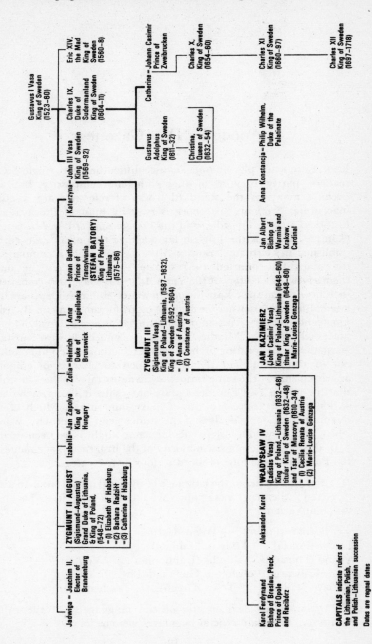

Appendix IV   Gazetteer

East European place-names cause difficulties for Anglo-Saxon readers, partly because of their inherent complexity, but also because many of the standard works of reference are woefully inaccurate. Students are poorly served by most of the available historical atlases. The editors of the *Penguin Atlas of World History,* for example, which is the English language edition of an atlas earlier published in Germany, translated the German text accompanying the maps but omitted to translate the names on the maps themselves. The editors of the *Times Atlas of World History* committed such howlers on their East European material that students are best advised to look elsewhere, except perhaps for amusement. By using nineteenth-century Russian or German names on medieval maps for places which in the Middle Ages had no connection with Russia or Germany, or by locating prehistoric sites on maps over a millennium out of true, they laid themselves open to charges of culpable anachronism. At the same time, they demonstrate by their mistakes that the key to East European place-names lies in fixing each name in its relevant context of time, space, and usage. Much of the reigning confusion dissolves if the student can reflect why, where, when, and by whom any particular name might have been used.

In this regard, the great majority of the historical place-names of the Polish lands can be reduced to four or five categories:

(1) *Local place-names* in the language of the local inhabitants. In areas of mixed settlement, these names would often come in two or three different variants:

e.g. Poznań (Polish)   Posen (German)
Lwów (Polish)   L'viv (Ukrainian)
Wilno (Polish),   Vilnius (Lithuanian),   Vil'na (*Ruski*)
Góra Kalwaria (Polish)   Gur (Yiddish)
Cieszyn (Polish),   Tešin (Czech),   Teschen (German)

(2) *Official place-names* in the official language(s) of the ruling authority. The main official languages were as follows:

486

Kingdom of Poland	—Latin, Polish
Grand Duchy of Lithuania	—*Ruski,* Latin, Polish
Certain royal cities	—German, Latin, Polish
Austrian Galicia	—German, Latin: Polish from 1867
Kingdom of Prussia	—German
Tsarist Empire to 1917	—Russian
USSR, from 1922	—Russian (USSR and RSFSR): Ukrainian, Latvian, Lithuanian, Byelorussian, etc. in the union republics.

As the ruling authorities changed, so official names changed with them:

e.g. Varsovia (Latin), Warszawa (Polish) to 1795; Warschau (German), 1795–1807; Warszawa, 1807–64; Varshava (Russian), 1864–1915; Warszawa, 1916–39; Warschau, 1939–45; Warszawa, since 1945.

Wholesale renaming campaigns were undertaken in Prussia and Russia in the late nineteenth century: in the USSR, 1939–41, and 1945; and by the Polish authorities 1918–21, and 1945–6. The renaming of the place-names of Poland's 'Recovered Territories' after the Second World War was accompanied by a transfer of populations, and the new Polish names did not necessarily coincide with historic or former local names:

e.g. Wrocław from 1945; Breslau (German, 1526 to 1945, under Austria and Prussia) Vraclav (Czech, under Bohemian rule 1335 to 1526; Vratislavia (Latin), Wratislaw (medieval West Slav) before 1335.

(3) *Political place-names.* The practice of giving cities the names of prominent political figures or of political slogans is as old as politics itself. In Poland, it goes back at least to Casimir the Great, who named his model satellite city near Kraków—Kazimierz. Curiously enough, the city of Augustów, founded by Sigismund-August, was also known at one period as Zygmuntowo. Private benefactors, whether noble magnates or industrial tycoons, ensured a place in history by giving their names to their foundations. Frampol (1702) was founded by Franciszek Butler; Żyradów (1833) by the French textile entrepreneur, Phillippe Girard.

From the early nineteenth century, government politics came more into evidence:

e.g. Koenigshutte (1797–1921)   now Chorzów
Novogeorgievsk (1833–1915)   now Modlin
Ivangorod (1842–1915)   now Dęblin
Alexandrovo (1855–1915)   now Aleksandrów Kujawski
Hindenburg (1915–45)   now Zabrze
Legionowo (1934)   formerly Jabłonna
Gotenhafen (1939–45)   now   Gdynia;   pre-1920 Gdingen
(in USSR) Ivanofrankovsk (1945)   formerly Stanisławów
Stalinogród (1953–5)   now Katowice

(4) *Names in the Polish language.* Like most languages, Polish possesses its own forms and spellings for familiar places. These names are used in Polish texts and on Polish atlases without implying that the particular places may have Polish connections in the ethnic or political sense.
e.g. Londyn (London), Waszyngton (Washington), Rzym (Rome), Paryż (Paris), Lipsk (Leipzig), Drezna (Dresden), Kijów (Kiev), Wiedeń (Vienna), Władywostok (Vladivostok).

(5) *Foreign versions of Polish names.* All the main European languages possess their own versions of the most common Polish placenames. English usually adapted German forms:
Warsaw←Warschau; Cracow←Krakau; Dantsick (obsolete)←Danzig;
whereas Latin forms provided the basis for French, Italian, or Spanish derivatives.
e.g. Varsovia→Varsovie (French), Varsovia (Italian), Varsavia (Spanish)
Cracovia→Cracovie (French), Cracovia (Italian, Spanish)
but Vistula→Vistule (French), Weichsel (German), Vistula (English)
Put together, all the possible variants for the name of each place became rather numerous:
Lwów—Lviv—Lemberg—Lvov—Leopolis—Léopol
Polska—Polen—Polin—Pol'sha—Polonia—Pologne—Poland.
Due warning should be given that place-names are subject to strict censorship in all the countries of the Soviet Bloc. In Poland, all former German names are suppressed in popular works of reference, just as, in the USSR, all former Polish names are suppressed. According to official practice, present-day place-names are the only 'correct' forms, even for previous periods of history.

Index

OXFORD

MORE OXFORD PAPERBACKS

This book is just one of nearly 1000 Oxford Paper-
backs currently in print. If you would like details of
other Oxford Paperbacks, including titles in the
World's Classics, Oxford Reference, Oxford
Books, OPUS, Past Masters, Oxford Authors, and
Oxford Shakespeare series, please write to:

UK and Europe: Oxford Paperbacks Publicity Man-
ager, Arts and Reference Publicity Department,
Oxford University Press, Walton Street, Oxford
OX2 6DP.

Customers in UK and Europe will find Oxford
Paperbacks available in all good bookshops. But in
case of difficulty please send orders to the Cash-
with-Order Department, Oxford University Press
Distribution Services, Saxon Way West, Corby,
Northants NN18 9ES. Tel: 01536 741519; Fax:
01536 746337. Please send a cheque for the total cost
of the books, plus £1.75 postage and packing for
orders under £20; £2.75 for orders over £20. Customers outside the UK should add 10% of the cost
of the books for postage and packing.

USA: Oxford Paperbacks Marketing Manager,
Oxford University Press, Inc., 200 Madison Av-
enue, New York, N.Y. 10016.

Canada: Trade Department, Oxford University
Press, 70 Wynford Drive, Don Mills, Ontario M3C
1J9.

Australia: Trade Marketing Manager, Oxford University Press, G.P.O. Box 2784Y, Melbourne 3001,
Victoria.

South Africa: Oxford University Press, P.O. Box
1141, Cape Town 8000.

HISTORY IN OXFORD PAPERBACKS
TUDOR ENGLAND
John Guy

Tudor England is a compelling account of political and religious developments from the advent of the Tudors in the 1460s to the death of Elizabeth I in 1603.

Following Henry VII's capture of the Crown at Bosworth in 1485, Tudor England witnessed far-reaching changes in government and the Reformation of the Church under Henry VIII, Edward VI, Mary, and Elizabeth; that story is enriched here with character studies of the monarchs and politicians that bring to life their personalities as well as their policies.

Authoritative, clearly argued, and crisply written, this comprehensive book will be indispensable to anyone interested in the Tudor Age.

'lucid, scholarly, remarkably accomplished . . . an excellent overview' *Sunday Times*

'the first comprehensive history of Tudor England for more than thirty years' Patrick Collinson, *Observer*

HISTORY IN OXFORD PAPERBACKS
THE STRUGGLE FOR THE MASTERY OF EUROPE 1848–1918
A. J. P. Taylor

The fall of Metternich in the revolutions of 1848 heralded an era of unprecedented nationalism in Europe, culminating in the collapse of the Hapsburg, Romanov, and Hohenzollern dynasties at the end of the First World War. In the intervening seventy years the boundaries of Europe changed dramatically from those established at Vienna in 1815. Cavour championed the cause of *Risorgimento* in Italy; Bismarck's three wars brought about the unification of Germany; Serbia and Bulgaria gained their independence courtesy of the decline of Turkey—'the sick man of Europe'; while the great powers scrambled for places in the sun in Africa. However, with America's entry into the war and President Wilson's adherence to idealistic internationalist principles, Europe ceased to be the centre of the world, although its problems, still primarily revolving around nationalist aspirations, were to smash the Treaty of Versailles and plunge the world into war once more.

A. J. P. Taylor has drawn the material for his account of this turbulent period from the many volumes of diplomatic documents which have been published in the five major European languages. By using vivid language and forceful characterization, he has produced a book that is as much a work of literature as a contribution to scientific history.

'One of the glories of twentieth-century writing.'
Observer

A Very Short Introduction

CLASSICS

Mary Beard and John Henderson

This *Very Short Introduction* to Classics links a haunting temple on a lonely mountainside to the glory of ancient Greece and the grandeur of Rome, and to Classics within modern culture—from Jefferson and Byron to Asterix and Ben-Hur.

'This little book should be in the hands of every student, and every tourist to the lands of the ancient world . . . a splendid piece of work'
Peter Wiseman
Author of *Talking to Virgil*

'an eminently readable and useful guide to many of the modern debates enlivening the field . . . the most up-to-date and accessible introduction available'
Edith Hall
Author of *Inventing the Barbarian*

'lively and up-to-date . . . it shows classics as a living enterprise, not a warehouse of relics'
New Statesman and Society

'nobody could fail to be informed and entertained—the accent of the book is provocative and stimulating'
Times Literary Supplement

POLITICS

Kenneth Minogue

Since politics is both complex and controversial it is easy to miss the wood for the trees. In this Very Short Introduction Kenneth Minogue has brought the many dimensions of politics into a single focus: he discusses both the everyday grind of democracy and the attraction of grand ideals such as freedom and justice.

'Kenneth Minogue is a very lively stylist who does not distort difficult ideas.'
Maurice Cranston

'a dazzling but unpretentious display of great scholarship and humane reflection'
Professor Neil O'Sullivan, University of Hull

'Minogue is an admirable choice for showing us the nuts and bolts of the subject.'
Nicholas Lezard, *Guardian*

'This is a fascinating book which sketches, in a very short space, one view of the nature of politics . . . the reader is challenged, provoked and stimulated by Minogue's trenchant views.'
Talking Politics

A Very Short Introduction

ARCHAEOLOGY

Paul Bahn

'Archaeology starts, really, at the point when the first recognizable 'artefacts' appear—on current evidence, that was in East Africa about 2.5 million years ago—and stretches right up to the present day. What you threw in the garbage yesterday, no matter how useless, disgusting, or potentially embarrassing, has now become part of the recent archaeological record.'

This Very Short Introduction reflects the enduring popularity of archaeology—a subject which appeals as a pastime, career, and academic discipline, encompasses the whole globe, and surveys 2.5 million years. From deserts to jungles, from deep caves to mountain-tops, from pebble tools to satellite photographs, from excavation to abstract theory, archaeology interacts with nearly every other discipline in its attempts to reconstruct the past.

'very lively indeed and remarkably perceptive . . . a quite brilliant and level-headed look at the curious world of archaeology'
Professor Barry Cunliffe,
University of Oxford